Exploring Corporate Strategy

FOURTH EDITION

Exploring Corporate Strategy

FOURTH EDITION

GERRY JOHNSON

Cranfield School of Management

KEVAN SCHOLES

Sheffield Business School

PRENTICE HALL

LONDON   NEW YORK   TORONTO   SYDNEY   TOKYO   SINGAPORE
MADRID   MEXICO CITY   MUNICH   PARIS

First published 1997 by
Prentice Hall Europe
Campus 400, Maylands Avenue
Hemel Hempstead
Hertfordshire, HP2 7EZ
A division of
Simon & Schuster International Group

Typeset in 10½/12½pt Century Schoolbook
by MHL Typesetting Ltd, Coventry

Library of Congress Cataloging-in-Publication Data

Johnson, Gerry,
    Exploring corporate strategy / Gerry Johnson, Kevan Scholes. —
4th ed.
        p.   cm.
    Includes bibliographical references and index.
    ISBN 0-13-525619-4 (pbk.)
    ISBN 0-13-525635-6 (pbk.)
    1.Business planning.   2. Strategic planning.   I. Scholes, Kevan.
    II. Title.
    HD30.28.J648   1997
    658.4′012–DC20   96-41425
    658.4′012–DC21   96-47881
                                                                CIP

British Library Cataloguing in Publication Data

A catalogue record for this book is available from
the British Library

ISBN 0-13-525619-4 (text only)
ISBN 0-13-525635-6 (text & cases)

---

    2   3   4   5   01   00   99   98   97

Figure 3.5 (p. 102) reprinted with the permission of The Free Press, a division of Simon & Schuster. Copyright ©
1990 Michael E. Porter. Figure 3.6 (p. 107) adapted with the permission of The Free Press, a division of Simon &
Schuster. Copyright © 1980 The Free Press. Figure 4.4 (p. 147) and Figure 4.5 (p. 148) reprinted/adapted with the
permission of The Free Press, a division of Simon & Schuster. Copyright © 1985 Michael E. Porter. Figure 4.11d (p.
171) reprinted by permission of John Wiley & Sons, Ltd. Figure 6.7 (p.271) reprinted by permission of John Wiley &
Sons, Ltd. (John Wiley and Sons, Inc. in USA). Illustration 6.7 (p. 261) reprinted by permission of Sage
Publications Ltd., 6 Bonhill Street, London EC2A 4PU. Illustration 11.1 (p. 454) reproduced with permission of
The McGraw-Hill Companies. Illustration 11.2 (p. 460) reprinted with kind permission from Elsevier Science
Ltd., The Boulevard, Langford Lane, Kidlington OX5 1GB, UK.

Contents

Illustrations

Figures

Preface

It is now four years since our third edition was published and thirteen since the first edition. There have been many interesting and important developments in the subject of corporate strategy during that time. Equally important has been the vastly increased recognition of the importance of the subject to practising managers in both the public and private sectors. This has been reflected in the widespread inclusion of corporate strategy in educational programmes at undergraduate, postgraduate and professional levels, as well as its adoption in short courses and consultancy assignments. It is now widely accepted that an understanding of the principles and practice of strategic issues is not just the concern of top managers, but is essential for most levels of management — though clearly the detailed requirements will vary. We have consistently argued the importance of this wider 'uptake', so these are changes which we welcome.

The combined sales of our first three editions exceeded 280,000. In revising the book for this fourth edition, we have therefore tried to ensure that we reflect the changing views, attitudes and approaches to corporate strategy, but that we do this within the framework and style of the previous editions, which many readers have kindly complimented us on. We hope we have achieved this and that readers continue to find *Exploring Corporate Strategy* a useful and stimulating text. Some of its content has changed — and this is explained more fully below — but the purpose of the book remains the same: to develop a greater capability for strategic thinking among managers and potential managers.

We began the first edition by quoting the group corporate planner of one UK company explaining that the main problem he faced was to get managers to understand that it was their responsibility to formulate strategy:

> This is my biggest difficulty. First, because they seem to think it's someone else's responsibility and, second, because they think there is some set of techniques which is going to create strategy for the company. I try to get them to understand that if the managers of the business aren't responsible for strategy, then no one is

and that they already have — or can easily get — any techniques that are necessary. The problem is the inability of managers to think strategically.

Thirteen years on, we would still regard this as the core issue which this book aims to address, through providing readers with an understanding of the following:

- What corporate strategy is.
- Why strategic decisions are important.
- Approaches to formulating and implementing strategy.
- The role of managers, at all levels, in the strategic management process.

It is not a book of corporate planning techniques, but rather builds on the practice of good strategic management, as researchers and practitioners in the area understand it. It is a book primarily intended for students of strategy on undergraduate, diploma and master's courses in universities and colleges; students on courses with titles such as Corporate Strategy, Business Policy, Strategic Management, Organisational Policy and Corporate Policy. However, we know that many such students are already managers who are undertaking part-time study: so this book is written with the manager and the potential manager in mind.

Traditionally, the study of corporate strategy in organisations had been taught using intensive case study programmes. There remain teachers who argue that there can be no substitute for such an intensive case programme. At the other extreme, there is a growing school of thought which argues that the only reason cases were used was that there was an insufficient research base to the problems of strategy, resulting in a lack of theoretical underpinning. They argue that since the 1960s the strides made in research and the development of theory make such intensive case programmes redundant. It seems to us that this is a fruitless division of opinion probably rooted in the academic traditions of those involved, rather than a considered view of the needs of students.

The position taken here is that case work, or appropriate experiential learning, is of great benefit in the study of strategy, for it allows students both to apply concepts and theories, and — just as important — to build their own. However, it is also the case that the growing body of research and theory can be of great help in stimulating a deep understanding of strategic problems and strategic management. Our approach builds in substantial parts of such research and theory, and encourages readers to refer to more; but we also assume that readers will have the opportunity to deal with strategic problems through such means as case study work or projects, or, if they are practising managers, through their involvement in their own organisations. Our view in this respect is exactly the same as the writers of a medical or engineering text, and we encourage readers to take the same view. It is that good theory helps good practice, but that an understanding of the theory without an understanding of the practice is very dangerous — particularly if you are dealing with a patient, a bridge or, as with this book, organisations.

For this reason the book is again available in two versions — text only or text and cases. The 24 case studies consist of 14 entirely new cases and 10 which have been completely updated and rewritten from the last edition. We have been reluctant to extend the size of the text or text and case version, but are conscious of the continuing demand for more material — whether it be further depth in topics, more coverage of particular sectors or simply more examples and tasks for students. We are now responding to this through additional publications. Two of these will be released at the same time as this book:

- A comprehensive and extended instructor's manual.
- A video for instructors which includes some further material on key themes in the text and selected case studies.

A book of analytical techniques for strategy analysis and formulation is also in preparation (due 1998). This will provide more depth on selected techniques across many of the themes in the text.

Each chapter is concluded with a set of work assignments. These take the main issues from each chapter and suggest ways in which readers can consolidate their understanding by applying these concepts to appropriate case studies, illustrations and organisations of their own choice. These assignments are provided at three levels of difficulty, in order to give maximum flexibility in their use:

- Level 1 (normal script) are straightforward applications of concepts or techniques to specific situations.
- **Level 2 (bold script) require the comparison of concepts and/or of different situations.**
- *Level 3 (italic script) require a more comprehensive analysis usually linking two or more concepts and/or situations and requiring 'reading round' the issues.*

In preparing this fourth edition, we have tried to bear in mind the needs of the manager in understanding strategic problems in many different organisations. In so doing, we have developed further some of the themes running through the previous editions.

The text more explicitly develops the theme that strategy and the management of strategy can be thought of in at least two rather different ways. First, it can be seen as a matter of essentially *analysis and planning.* Second, it can be seen as a matter of *organisational decision making* within a *political and cultural context.* Both these aspects of strategic management are relevant to the study of strategy, and the text incorporates both. For example, one of the themes running through the book is the importance of a clear analysis of the strategic situation facing the organisation and a rational assessment of the future options available to it. In considering such issues, the book includes, for example, discussion of the value of environmental audits, structural and strategic group analysis of competitive environments, the relevance of experience curve concepts, value chain analysis, life cycle models of strategic analysis and choice, and the findings of those researchers who have tried to understand the relationship between strategic positioning of organisations and financial performance. The recent interest in resource-led strategies and the core competences of organisations is now given a much fuller treatment. In short, one of the themes is that the employment of rational models of analysis and choice in organisations is important to strategic management.

There is also a growing expectation that managers will be able to take decisions about change and implement change with more assurance and skill than hitherto. Yet the evidence is that managers are not good at handling change, particularly of the magnitude involved with strategic change. Strategic management cannot be developed by providing a 'bag of management techniques'; it is also to do with developing in managers a sensitivity to an increasing turbulent environment, together with an understanding of the culture of the organisation in which they work and the means whereby they can manage change within that culture. Herein lies one of the fundamental problems of strategic management. The environment that organisations face is increasingly complex and turbulent, so the need for management sensitivity to change is growing. Yet the values, expectations and assumptions of members of an organisation working within a particular culture can be a very constraining and conservative influence on the understanding of strategic problems and the development of solutions.

This fourth edition develops this theme much further. It draws on the growing amount of research and literature on decision-making processes within a political and cultural context, and considers explicitly how such influences can be analysed and what mechanisms exist for managing strategic change within such systems. In particular, readers familiar with previous editions will note the important changes made to the content of Chapters 2, 5 and 11. There is, therefore, an expectation that readers will seek to reconcile 'analytical management' about the complex issues of strategy with an understanding of the human and social side of management. While this is a demanding task, it is the key to the effective management of strategy and a fundamental task of managers in today's organisations. The discussion of the cultural and political context has been extended by giving a much fuller treatment to issues of *corporate governance*, including international comparisons. Chapter 5 is now centred around the issue of whom organisations are there to serve and how strategic management should address this issue.

As in the previous editions, the book also recognises that strategic management is as relevant to the public sector and to not-for-profit organisations as it is to the private sector of industry and commerce. Indeed, the period since the second edition was published has seen unprecedented changes in the recognition of strategic management in the public sector against the background of significant changes in their role and method of operation. This 'new era' is reflected in discussions and examples throughout the book. We also have a good many references, examples and illustrations of the application of strategic management concepts to the public sector. Many of these changes in the public sector are also mirrored in the larger private sector organisations, and our coverage of the importance of organisation design and processes of resource allocation and control has been substantially revised to reflect these changes. For example, concepts of networks, virtual organisations, internal market mechanisms, benchmarking, and performance indicators and business process re-engineering are now discussed within a common framework as to how an organisation can best create the circumstances for success. This includes the recognition that managers contribute to successful strategy not only through their own direct efforts, but also through *shaping the context* in which other people work.

Another issue of major importance to many more organisations over the past few years has been the need to think of corporate strategy and an organisation's performance much more in an *international context*. In Europe this has clearly been pushed along by the impetus of the single European market — indeed, the third edition of the book was published on the very first day of the market. But this issue of internationalisation has spread much wider than those narrowly and immediately affected by the single market. It is now expected in many industries and public services that an aspiration to perform well — by *international standards* — is important. The rapidly growing communications of all types are making managers — and those who judge their performance — much more familiar with what *best international practice* means in their context. The third edition of this book made major changes in recognising the importance of this international dimension through additional concepts and analytical methods — but more importantly through the tone of the discussion, and particularly the choice of illustrations and (in the text and cases edition) a much wider international choice of case studies. This trend has been continued in this fourth edition.

The book, while using up-to-date theory and research, is not primarily an academic treatise, but a book for managers and those who intend to be managers: so a few words about its style are in order. The reader will find that throughout the book there are 'illustrations' which enlarge upon or give case material related to a point in the text. These illustrations are all taken from actual incidents reported in the press or in journals, from case studies, or from the authors' personal experience, and wherever possible the organisation or individuals involved are named. Many teachers, students and managers have told us how useful they find these examples.

As far as terminology is concerned, we have tried to avoid some of the pitfalls of jargon that management writers often fall into; if we have failed to do so on occasions, it is not for the want of trying. The word 'organisation' has been used most frequently, but there are times when 'company', 'enterprise' or 'firm' is used: these tend to be where commercial operations are being discussed, but it does not mean that the discussion relates only to the private sector. We have also chosen not to make dogmatic distinctions between descriptions of the subject, such as 'corporate strategy', 'strategic management' and so on.

The structure of the book is explained in some detail in Chapter 1. However, it might be useful to give a brief outline and some of the changes from the third edition. The book is in four parts.

Part I comprises an introduction to corporate strategy, first in terms of its characteristics and the elements of strategic management (Chapter 1), and then in terms of how strategic decisions actually come about in organisations (Chapter 2), and also examines the relationship between organisational strategy and culture.

Part II of the book is concerned with strategic analysis. The chapter structure remains the same, but a number of key themes have been expanded. For example, Chapter 3 has much more on the analysis of an organisation's competitive position. Chapter 4 devotes more time to the analysis of the factors underpinning strategic capability — particularly issues of analysing and understanding core competences. Chapter 5 remains concerned with analysing and understanding organisational purposes. It is centred around the question of whom the organisation is there to serve. There is now a much fuller treatment of corporate governance — including international comparisons.

Part III deals with strategic choice, and the division of material between Chapters 6, 7 and 8 has changed. Chapter 6 is concerned with analysing and establishing the broad bases of strategic choices and extends beyond the issue of positioning and generic product/market strategies in the third edition. It includes other bases of strategic choice, such as strategic intent, ownership, scope of activities and corporate parenting. Chapter 7 deals with choices of both strategic direction and method, and provides a new discussion of how core competences might provide directions for development and a fuller treatment of strategic alliances. Chapter 8 is devoted to strategy evaluation and selection.

The final part of the book — Part IV — is about strategy implementation. It picks up strongly the recent literature on strategic architecture, and Chapters 9 and 10 have been reversed and reshaped to achieve this. Chapter 9 is about organisation design through three levels of detail: structures; centralisation/devolution; and organisational configurations.

Chapter 10 now combines resource allocation and control in a way which reflects important new themes and changes: the importance of information technology, business process re-engineering, internal market mechanisms and the importance of shaping the context as well as the content of strategy. Chapter 11 considers approaches to and methods of managing change and provides important links back to Chapters 2 and 5.

Many people have helped us with the development of this new edition. First and foremost have been the adopters of the current edition — many of whom we have had the pleasure of meeting at our annual seminars, which are now into their ninth year in England and their third in Scotland. Many of you have provided us with constructive criticism and thoughts for the new edition — we hope you are happy with the results! Also, our students and clients at Sheffield and Cranfield are a constant source of ideas and challenge. It would be impossible to write a book of this type without this direct feedback. Our own work and contacts have expanded considerably as a result of our book and we now both have important links across the world who have been a source of stimulation to us. Our contacts in Australia, New Zealand, Denmark, Sweden, France and Singapore are especially valued.

We would like to thank those who have contributed directly to the book by providing case studies, and those organisations which have been brave enough to be written up as case studies. The growing popularity of *Exploring Corporate Strategy* has often presented these case study companies with practical problems in coping with direct enquiries from tutors and students. We hope that those using the book will respect the wishes of the case study companies and not contact them directly for further information. **Sheffield Theatres Trust has made this a proviso of releasing the case study for inclusion**. Raje Jagden and Tony Clayton of PIMS Associates have been helpful in commenting on Chapters 7 and 8, as have Tony Grundy and David Pitt-Watson on Chapters 5 and 8 and Phyl Hughes on Chapters 2 and 3. Special thanks are due to Sara Martin and Tony Jacobs who have been centrally involved in preparing many of the illustrations, and to Steve Lawson who has also assisted in the process. Many colleagues from our own universities and other institutions have provided us with illustrations, and their assistance is acknowledged at the foot of those illustrations — thank you to all these contributors. Special thanks are due to the library staff at Cranfield and Sheffield for their valuable assistance with references. Our thanks are also due to those who have had a part in preparing the manuscript for the book, particularly Claire Larkin at Sheffield and Alison Southgate at Cranfield.

Gerry Johnson
Kevan Scholes
January 1997

The authors

Gerry Johnson BA PhD is Professor of Strategic Management at Cranfield School of Management. He is author of numerous books and papers on Strategic Management, is a member of the editorial board of the Strategic Management Journal and referees for many European and US academic journals. His research work is primarily concerned with processes of strategy development and change in organisations. He is a regular visitor to universities throughout Europe, the USA, Australasia and South Africa; and he works extensively as a consultant at a senior level on issues of strategy formulation and strategic change with many UK and international firms.

Kevan Scholes MA, PhD, DMS, CIMgt, FRSA is Professor of Strategic Management and Director of Sheffield Business School, UK. He has extensive consultancy experience in both private and public sector organisations and has a wide range of on-going international work including regular commitments with Business Schools in Australia, New Zealand and Singapore. He has a special interest in the strategic management of Professional Service Organisations — in both the public and private sectors.

Introduction

CHAPTER 1

Corporate strategy: an introduction

By 1996 Ingvar Kamprad had seen IKEA transformed from the mail-order furniture business he set up in Sweden in 1949 into a £3 billion retail furnishing empire with over 120 stores in 26 countries. Retail commentators and business analysts saw the firm as a major success story; success based on its customer focus, its clear long-term strategy and its skill in implementing that strategy. The issue that faced Ingvar Kamprad and Anders Moberg, the chief executive of IKEA, was whether the strategy pursued so successfully in the past could be maintained. Illustration 1.1 gives an overview of the developments of IKEA.

The approach IKEA had taken to meeting customer needs and developing its business had followed a consistent pattern over many years. However, the changes that had taken place, albeit in an evolutionary way, had substantially changed the direction of the business in that time: they were changes which were long-term in nature and had far-ranging implications for organisational structure and control, and the logistics of the operation. They also raised challenges for the future. In short, they were major *strategic* developments.

All organisations are faced with the need to manage strategies: some developing from a position of strength, like IKEA; some needing to overcome significant problems. This book deals with why reviews of strategic direction take place in organisations, why they are important, how such decisions are taken, and some of the tools and techniques that managers can use to take such decisions. This chapter is an introduction and explanation of this theme, and deals with the questions of what is meant by 'corporate strategy' and 'strategic management', why they are so important and what distinguishes them from other organisational tasks and decisions. In discussing these it will become clearer how the book deals with the subject area as a whole. The chapter draws on the IKEA illustration for the purposes of discussion; and as the book progresses, other such illustrations are used to help develop discussion.

One other point should be made before proceeding. The term 'corporate strategy' is used here for two main reasons: first, because the book is concerned with strategy and strategic decisions in all types of organisation — small and large commercial enterprises as well as public services — and the word 'corporate' embraces them all; and second, because, as the term is used in this book (discussed more fully in section 1.1.2), 'corporate strategy' denotes the most general level of strategy in an organisation and in this sense embraces other levels of strategy. Readers will undoubtedly come across other terms, such as 'strategic management', 'business policy', 'management policy' and 'organisational strategy', all of which deal with the same general area.

1.1   The nature of strategy and strategic decisions

Why are the issues facing IKEA described as 'strategic'? What type of decisions are strategic decisions, and what distinguishes these from other decisions that were no doubt being taken in the company?

1.1.1 The characteristics of strategic decisions

The characteristics usually associated with the words 'strategy' and 'strategic decisions' are these.

1. Strategic decisions are likely to be concerned with or affect the *long-term direction* of an organisation. IKEA set out along a path which was difficult to reverse. In the 1950s and 1960s the company could have been defined, essentially, as a Scandinavian furnishing retailer. The whole thrust of its strategy had moved to being a multinational retailer; and the resource and managerial commitments of this were such that it was difficult to envisage how it could be reversed.

2. Strategic decisions are normally about trying to achieve some *advantage* for the organisation: for example, over competition. IKEA has been successful not because it is the same as all other furniture retailers, but because it is different and offers particular benefits which distinguish it from other retailers. Similarly, strategic advantage could be thought of as providing higher-quality, value for money services than other providers in the public sector, thus attracting support and funding from government. Strategic decisions are sometimes conceived of, therefore, as the search for effective *positioning* to give such advantage in a market or in relation to suppliers.

3. Strategic decisions are likely to be concerned with the *scope of an organ-*

isation's activities: does (and should) the organisation concentrate on one area of activity, or should it have many? For example, IKEA had clearly defined the *boundaries* of its business in terms of the type of product ('furnishing items of good design and function') and mode of service (large retail outlets and mail order). While not owning its manufacturing, it also had an in-house design capability which specified and controlled what manufacturers supplied to the company. It had also decided to widen its geographic scope substantially in the 1980s and 1990s.

The issue of scope of activity is fundamental to strategic decisions because it concerns the way in which those responsible for managing the organisation conceive its boundaries. It is to do with what they want the organisation to be like and to be about.

4. Strategy can be seen as the *matching of the activities of an organisation to the environment* in which it operates. This is sometimes known as the search for *strategic fit*.[1] While the market for furnishings was mature with little prospect of overall growth, the management of IKEA had seen that the retail provision of furnishing in most countries did not meet the expectations of customers. Customers frequently had to wait for delivery for items which were highly priced. The market provided another opportunity. Customer tastes were relatively common in different countries except in specialised segments of the market: buyers wanted everyday furniture which was well designed and looked good, but was reasonably priced.

However, IKEA also knew that it faced significant differences in its markets. By the 1990s the number of countries in which IKEA was represented was a great deal larger than in the company's early days. This meant that IKEA had to understand buying habits and preferences from a much wider base, from markets close to its Swedish home, to the USA, and even to the Far East and eastern Europe. IKEA could no longer assume that its knowledge of earlier markets would necessarily apply: for example, it had found that shopping habits in the USA differed substantially from those in Europe, and this had required a change in the way it serviced the market. Therefore, while the principles of IKEA's business idea were adhered to around the world to produce a consistent product quality and shopping experience, store management had been given a greater degree of freedom to adapt to local market needs.

IKEA's management had, however, decided that there were some markets, attractive though they were, where it did not make sense to try to control IKEA's operations directly. In the Far East and Australia, IKEA stores operated under a franchise arrangement. Here the company recognised that local knowledge in fine tuning the business to local needs was vital; or the problems of long-distance control were too great to manage the operation effectively on this basis.

Illustration 1.1   IKEA

We shall offer a wide range of furnishing items of good design and function, at prices so low that the majority of people can afford to buy them.

Ingvar Kamprad

Since its beginnings in 1953, IKEA has created a global network of over 120 stores in 26 countries, generating revenues in excess of US $5,082 million in 1995. While impressive, this growth has been gradual. Initially, stores were only opened in Scandinavia, but as greater success was experienced, stores were built further afield where rewards, but also risks, were higher. In all these countries the retailing concept of Ingvar Kamprad remained the same.

The 1980s were boom years with rapid growth fuelled by changing customer attitudes, from status and designer labels to functionality, encouraged by an economic recession. Yet IKEA remained frugal in its spending, relocating to Denmark to escape Swedish taxation. Anders Moberg became the chief executive, although Ingvar Kamprad's influence could still be found. Indeed, echoes of his philosophy and style could be seen in Anders Moberg. He dressed informally, arrived at the office in the company Nissan Primera, clocked in just as other employees did, when abroad travelled on economy-class air tickets, stayed in modest hotels and expected his executives to do likewise. Such carefulness was extended to the company, the shares of which were held in trust by a Dutch charitable foundation. Furthermore, IKEA's expansion plans envisaged only internal funding, with 15 per cent of turnover being reinvested.

There were a number of unique elements to IKEA's winning business formula; simple high-quality Scandinavian design, global sourcing of components, furniture kits that customers transported and assembled themselves, huge suburban stores with plenty of parking and cafés, restaurants, wheelchairs and supervised child care facilities. A key feature of IKEA's concept was universal customer appeal crossing national boundaries, with both the products and shopping experience designed to support this appeal. Customers came from different lifestyles: from new homeowners to business executives needing more office capacity. They all expected well-styled, good-quality furnishings, reasonably priced and readily available. IKEA met these expectations by encouraging customers to create value for themselves by taking on certain tasks traditionally done by the manufacturer and retailer: for example, the assembly and delivery of products to their homes.

IKEA made sure every aspect of its business system was designed to make it easy for customers to adapt to their new role. Information to assist customers make their purchase decisions was provided in a glossy catalogue, and during their visit to the store, customers were supplied with tape measures, pens and note paper to reduce the number of sales staff required; furniture was displayed in 100 model rooms and sales staff were required to participate only when asked.

To deliver low-cost yet high-quality products consistently, IKEA also redefined its relationship with its suppliers by establishing 30 buying offices around the world, whose prime purpose was to vet potential suppliers. Designers at headquarters then reviewed these to decide which would provide what for each of the products, their overall aim being to design for low cost and ease of manufacture. The most economical suppliers were chosen over traditional suppliers, so a shirt manufacturer might be employed to produce seat covers. Although the process through which acceptance to become an IKEA supplier was not easy, it was coveted, for once they were part of the IKEA system, suppliers gained access to global markets and received technical assistance, leased equipment and advice on how to bring production up to world-quality standards. IKEA and its customers benefited from this combination of a caring philosophy and a rigid supplier assessment process. It was able to offer a core range of 12,000 items from 1,800 suppliers in 45 countries at prices 20 to 40 per cent lower than for comparable goods.

Having to cope with widely dispersed sources of components and high-volume orders made it imperative for IKEA to have an efficient logistics system for ordering parts, integrating them into products and delivering them to the stores, while minimising the costs of inventory. This was achieved through a world network of 14 warehouses. These provided storage facilities, acted as logistical control points, consolidation centres and transit hubs, and aided the integration of supply and demand, reducing the need to store production runs for long periods, holding unit costs down and helping stores to anticipate needs and eliminate shortages.

IKEA blossomed into the world's largest retailer of home furnishings, and succeeded in creating greater total profit than all but a handful of other companies in the consumer industry. By 1996 it had turned its attention to eastern Europe and the one time Soviet republics, believing they represented great potential, though posing challenges, particularly over how to support and modernise local suppliers and the value of local currency.

In January 1996, Ingvar Kamprad announced that the IKEA group would be split into three, comprising the retailing operations, an organisation holding the franchise and trademarks, and a third business mainly in finance and banking. While the first two, which formed the core of the group, would be controlled at arm's length by trust-like organisations, the shares of the third would be jointly owned by Kamprad's three sons. The new structure meant that the family would not have access to the capital of the IKEA businesses, or the right to inherit it; however, it would continue to have 'influence-rich roles' in the governance of IKEA, a structure devised to ensure that the privately held organisation would not be broken up or sold off in a succession battle. He wanted to be sure IKEA would survive him, preserving both its profitability and egalitarian culture.

Sources: R. Norman and R. Ramirez, 'From value chain to value constellation: designing interactive strategy', *Harvard Business Review*, vol. 71, no. 4 (1993) pp. 65–77. Company data. Prepared by Sara Martin, Cranfield School of Management.

There were wider environmental issues with which IKEA had to be concerned, and which affected its strategic development: for example, IKEA realised in the first two decades of its trading that it was less susceptible to economic downturn than many of its competitors. This may have been because its prices were often lower; but it was also because, when someone took a purchasing decision at IKEA, they walked away with the goods. In other stores, since delivery was often delayed, purchase decisions were also often delayed. However, economic conditions in the different countries in which it operated affected its success: for example, the growth in car ownership, particularly in less highly developed countries, determined the percentage of the population which could shop at an IKEA store.

This notion of strategic fit is the traditional way of conceiving how strategies should develop. The task of the strategist is seen as planning or designing the future direction of the organisation in terms of the opportunities and threats which exist in the environment of the organisation.

5.   However, strategy can also be seen as *building on or 'stretching' an organisation's resources and competences* to create opportunities or capitalise on them.[2] This does not mean just trying to ensure that resources are available, or can be made available, to take advantage of some new opportunity in the market place. Rather, it means identifying existing resources and competences which might be a basis for creating new opportunities in the market place. IKEA illustrates this well.

The product range IKEA had designed and developed was not only low cost but unique in its style and its image of the product, and therefore distinguished it from other ranges of furnishings. Moreover, IKEA benefited from years of design experience dedicated to its operation and markets. Product range was further enhanced by the design of the stores, even down to the food served in them. The logistics of the operation, from sourcing of products to control of stock, had been learned over many years and provided not only a quite distinct way of operating, but a service greatly appreciated by customers. The policy to finance development internally had also led to a concentration on strong and secure financing, and careful evaluation of projects to ensure adequate cash flow. In short, both the physical aspects of resources and the experience built up over the years had been consciously developed to service the opportunity afforded in the market place. However, all of this experience had been employed, in effect 'stretched', to redefine the nature of its market for furniture. IKEA's approach had been described as follows:

> IKEA set out systematically to reinvent value and the business system that delivers it for an entire cast of economic actors. The work-sharing, co-productive arrangements the company offers to customers and suppliers alike force both to

think about value in a new way — one in which customers are also suppliers. Suppliers are also customers and IKEA itself is not so much a retailer as the central star in a constellation of services, goods, design, management, support and even entertainment.[3]

6. Strategies may require *major resource* changes for an organisation. For example, the decision that IKEA took to develop its operations internationally had significant implications in terms of its need to obtain properties for development and access to funds by which to do this, sometimes for projects which might be seen as high risk — for example, entering new markets in times of recession. The size of the operation in terms of numbers of people working in it, managerial levels and sheer physical stock held had to rise significantly. The need to control a multinational enterprise, as opposed to a national operation, also began to require skills and control systems of a different sort. It was a problem which many retailers had found difficulty coping with. Many retailers have found overseas development difficult; and one of the major reasons has been that they underestimate the extent to which their resource commitments rise and how the need to control them takes on quite different proportions. Strategies, then, need to be considered not only in terms of the extent to which the existing resource capability of the organisation is suited to opportunities; but also in terms of the extent to which resources can be obtained and controlled to develop a strategy for the future.

7. Strategic decisions are therefore likely to *affect operational decisions*: for example, the internationalisation of IKEA required a whole series of decisions at operational level. Management and control structures to deal with the geographical spread of the firm had to change. The methods of developing and distributing stock required revision to deal with the extended distribution logistics. Marketing and advertising policies needed to be reviewed by country to ensure their suitability to different customer behaviours and tastes. Personnel policies and practices had to be reviewed. Store operations needed to change too: for example, in the USA, IKEA saw the need to add to the core product range from local suppliers, install serviced loading bays, and erect bollards to stop the shopping trolleys being taken to all parts of the car parks, which were bigger in the USA.

This link between overall strategy and operational aspects of the organisation is important for two other reasons. First, if the operational aspects of the organisation are not in line with the strategy, then, no matter how well considered the strategy is, it will not succeed. Second, it is at the operational level that real strategic advantage can be achieved. IKEA has been successful not only because of a good strategic concept, but also because the detail of how it is put into effect — the *strategic architecture* — in terms of its logistics of buying and servicing, shop layout and merchandising to supplier and customer relations, all developed over many years, would be difficult to imitate.[4]

8. The strategy of an organisation will be affected not only by environmental forces and resource availability, but also by the *values and expectations* of those who have *power* in and around the organisation. In some respects, strategy can be thought of as a reflection of the attitudes and beliefs of those who have most influence on the organisation. Whether a company is expansionist or more concerned with consolidation, and where the boundaries are drawn for a company's activities, may say much about the values and attitudes of those who influence strategy — the *stakeholders* of the organisation. In IKEA the insistence on internal financing influenced long-term development and direction of the company; and Anders Moberg's emphasis on frugality and simplicity affected the way the company operated. The powerful influences of the founder and the chief executive remained pronounced.

There are, of course, other stakeholders who have influence: in many companies, shareholders or financial institutions; certainly management and the workforce, buyers and perhaps suppliers; and the local community. The beliefs and values of these stakeholders will have a more or less direct influence on the strategy development of an organisation.

Overall, if a *definition* of a strategy is required, these characteristics can provide a basis for one.

> Strategy is the *direction* and *scope* of an organisation over the *long term*: which achieves *advantage* for the organisation through its configuration of *resources* within a changing *environment*, to meet the needs of *markets* and to fulfil *stakeholder* expectations.

A consequence of these characteristics of strategic decisions is that they are likely to be *complex in nature*. This is especially so in organisations with wide geographic scope, such as multinational firms, or wide ranges of products or services. However, there are other significant problems in developing effective strategies. Strategic decisions can involve a *high degree of uncertainty*: they may involve taking decisions on views of the future which it is impossible for managers to be sure about. Strategic decisions are also likely to demand an *integrated* approach to managing the organisation. Unlike functional problems, there is no one area of expertise, or one perspective, that can define or resolve the problems. Managers, therefore, have to cross functional and operational boundaries to deal with strategic problems and come to agreements with other managers who, inevitably, have different interests and perhaps different priorities. They also have to manage and perhaps change relationships and networks outside the organisation: for example, with suppliers, distributors and customers.[5]

Strategic decisions may also involve *major change* in organisations. Not only is it problematic to decide upon and plan those changes, it is even more problematic to implement them if the organisation has been used to operating in ways, perhaps developed over years, which are not in line with future strategy.

1.1.2 Levels of strategy

Strategies exist at a number of levels in an organisation. Individuals may say they have a strategy — to do with their career, for example. This may be relevant when considering influences on strategies adopted by organisations, but it is not the subject of this book. Taking IKEA as an example, it is possible to distinguish at least three different levels of organisational strategy. First, there is the *corporate* level: for IKEA as for many corporate headquarters, the main issues here are about overall purpose and scope of the organisation; this may involve consideration of diversification and acquisition, but also how the organisation is to be run in structural and financial terms; and how resources are to be allocated to the different IKEA operations across the world. All of these are likely to be influenced by the overall mission of the organisation. Being clear about this level of strategy can be very important: it is a key *basis* of other strategic decisions. IKEA's mission was to provide good-value home furnishings around the world at prices that the majority of people were able to afford. This is based on ideas of egalitarianism and Swedish social values as much as on good business through the creation of a large market. IKEA truly believed it had something of value to offer the world.

The second level can be thought of in terms of *competitive or business unit strategy*. Here strategy is about how to compete successfully in a particular market: the concerns are therefore about how advantage over competitors can be achieved; what new opportunities can be identified or created in markets; which products or services should be developed in which markets; and the extent to which these meet customer needs in such a way as to achieve the objectives of the organisation — perhaps long-term profitability, market growth or measures of efficiency. So, whereas corporate strategy involves decisions about the organisation as a whole, strategic decisions here need to be related to a *strategic business unit* (SBU).[6] An SBU is a unit within the overall organisation for which there is an external market for goods or services distinct from another SBU. (In public sector organisations a corresponding definition of an SBU might be a part of the organisation or service for which there is a distinct client group.) At this level of strategy, the basis of strategic decisions is how customer or client needs can best be met, usually to achieve some sort of competitive advantage for the organisation. It is therefore very important that there is a clarity about the needs of customers (or clients) and who competitors are for a particular SBU. Confusion can often arise here because an SBU may not be defined in terms of an organisational structure. Divisions of a large company are not synonymous with SBUs for example. A company which markets paint is likely to have a number of SBUs because it may sell paint to different industrial market segments, some of which may have different characteristics from each other, and for home use through retailers. Since such retailers may include huge multiple chain stores which buy direct and smaller retailers which buy through distributors, these also need to be conceived as separate SBUs for strategic purposes, even though within the organisational structure they may be part of the same division.

A question for IKEA is at what level business unit strategy should be defined. At the corporate level, IKEA wishes to ensure that its image, ranges and style of operation are consistent throughout the world. Management must decide to what extent corporate-level strategy should be amended according to different markets. Notionally, at least, each store is a separate SBU; but realistically it may be that specific competitive strategies need to differ, perhaps by national geographic markets. This matching of competitive-level SBU strategy with corporate-level strategy is an issue which exists for all organisations and certainly for most multinational corporations. For IKEA, it is largely resolved by the overall corporate mission and strategy guiding the choice of markets in which it operates, and the sorts of product and service it provides. Other organisations might choose to compete differently in different markets, in which case the corporate influence may be much less and SBU strategies may need to be more diverse.

The third level of strategy is at the operating end of the organisation. Here there are *operational strategies* which are concerned with how the component parts of the organisation in terms of resources, processes, people and their skills are pulled together to form a *strategic architecture* which will effectively deliver the overall strategic direction. For example, in IKEA it was of crucial importance that design, store operations and sourcing operations dovetailed into higher-level decisions about product range and market entry. Indeed, in most businesses, successful business strategies depend to a large extent on decisions which are taken, or activities which occur, at the operational level. The integration of operations and strategy is therefore of great importance.

1.1.3 The vocabulary of strategy

At the end of section 1.1.1, a definition of strategy was given. It can be dangerous to offer a definition, because lengthy semantic discussions can follow about whether or not it is precise enough, and whether everyone

TERM	DEFINITION	A PERSONAL EXAMPLE
Mission	Overriding purpose in line with the values or expectations of stakeholders	Be healthy and fit
Vision or strategic intent	Desired future state: the aspiration of the organisation	To run the London marathon
Goal	General statement of aim or purpose	Lose weight and strengthen muscles
Objective	Quantification (if possible) or more precise statement of the goal	Lose 10 pounds by 1 September and run the marathon in 1998
Core competences	Resources, processes or skills which provide 'competitive advantage'	Proximity to a fitness centre, supportive family and friends and past experience of successful diet
Strategies	Long-term direction	Associate with a collaborative network (e.g. join running club), exercise regularly, compete in marathons locally, stick to appropriate diet
Strategic architecture	Combination of resources, processes and competences to put strategy into effect	Specific exercise and diet regime, appropriate training facilities, etc.
Control	The monitoring of action steps to: • assess effectiveness of strategies and actions • modify strategies and/or actions as necessary	Monitor weight, miles run and measure times: if satisfactory progress, do nothing; if not, consider other strategies and actions.

Figure 1.1 The vocabulary of strategy

would agree with it. In fact, there are different definitions according to different authors.[7] There are also a variety of terms used in relation to strategy, so it is worth devoting a little space to clarifying some of these.

Figure 1.1 and Illustration 1.2 employ some of the terms that readers will come across in this and other books on strategy. Figure 1.1 explains these in relation to a personal strategy we may have followed ourselves — becoming fit. Illustration 1.2 shows how these relate to an organisation — in this case, British Airways. Not all these terms are always used in organisations, or in strategy books: indeed, in this book the word 'goal' is rarely used. Moreover,

Illustration 1.2　British Airways and the vocabulary of strategy

The annual reports and public statements of companies often contain elements of the vocabulary of strategy used in this book. The following examples are taken from British Airways' annual reports for 1993/4 and 1994/5.

Mission
'To be the best and most successful company in the airline business.'

'To build profitably the world's premier global alliance, with a presence in all major world markets.'

Vision/strategic intent
'To ensure that British Airways is the customer's first choice through the delivery of an unbeatable travel experience.'

Goals*
'To be a good neighbour, concerned for the community and the environment.'

'To provide overall superior service and good value for money in every market segment in which we compete.'

'To excel in anticipating and quickly responding to customer needs and competitor activity.'

Core competence
'Anyone can fly airplanes, but few organisations can excel in serving people. Because it's a competence that's hard to build, it's also hard for competitors to copy or match.'

it may or may not be that mission, goals, objectives, strategies and so on are written down precisely. In some organisations this is done very formally. In others it is not. As will be shown in Chapter 2, a mission or strategy especially might sometimes more sensibly be conceived as that which is implicit or can be deduced about an organisation from what it is doing. However, as a general guideline the following terms are often used.

A *mission* is a general expression of the overriding purpose of the organisation, which, ideally, is in line with the values and expectations of major stakeholders and concerned with the scope and boundaries of the organisation. It is sometimes referred to in terms of the apparently simple, but actually challenging question: '*What business are we in?*'

Strategies
'To maintain our position in the forefront of the globalisation of the airline industry.' 'By the turn of the century almost eighty per cent of the world air travel will be based on 6 major markets in the world . . . British Airways' strategy is geared to securing a significant presence in these markets.'

'Continuing emphasis on consistent quality of customer service and the delivery to the marketplace of value for money.'

Strategic architecture
'Franchising is proving to be a successful way of expanding the British Airways network, benefiting from British Airways' infrastructure support and the franchisees' low operating costs, at minimal financial risk to British Airways.'

'Arranging all the elements of our service so that they collectively generate a particular experience: to orchestrate the service.'

Controls
'The marketplace performance unit tracks some 350 measures of performance, including aircraft cleanliness, punctuality, technical defects on aircraft, customers' opinions on check-in performance and the time it takes for a customer to get through when telephoning a reservations agent.'

'The Board has established a system of internal financial control which includes manuals of policies and procedures and a Code of Business Conduct to provide guidance and assistance to all employees in their dealing with customers and suppliers.'

*Many organisations make public broad goals rather than specific objectives, as the latter can give competitors valuable insights into the company's strategy.

Source: Company Annual Reports.
Prepared by Sara Martin and Tony Jacobs, Cranfield School of Management.

A *vision* or *strategic intent* is the desired future state of the organisation. It is an aspiration around which a strategist, perhaps a chief executive, might seek to focus the energies of members of the organisation.

If the word *goal* is used, it usually means a general statement of direction in line with the mission. It may well be qualitative in nature. On the other hand, an *objective* is more likely to be quantified, or at least to be a more precise statement in line with the goal. However, in this book the word 'objective' is used whether or not there is quantification.

Core *competences* are the bases upon which an organisation achieves strategic advantage in terms of activities, skills or know-how which distinguish it from competitors and provide value to customers or clients.

The concept of *strategy* has already been defined. It is the long-term direction envisaged for the organisation. It is likely to take form in fairly broad statements of the direction that the organisation should be taking and the types of action required to achieve objectives: for example, in terms of market entry, new products or services, or ways of operating.

Strategic architecture, as used in this book, means the combination of resources, activities and competences needed to put the strategy into effect. This in turn will need to be translated into specific *actions* and *tasks* which link broad direction to specific operational issues and individuals.

It is then important to exercise some degree of *control* so as to monitor the extent to which the action is achieving the objectives and goals.

1.2   Strategic management

What, then, is 'strategic management'? It is not enough to say that it is the management of the process of strategic decision making. This fails to take into account a number of points important both in the management of an organisation and in the area of study with which this book is concerned.

The nature of strategic management is different from other aspects of management; Figure 1.2 summarises some of these differences. An individual manager is most often required to deal with problems of operational control, such as the efficient production of goods, the management of a sales force, the monitoring of financial performance or the design of some new system that will improve the efficiency of the operation. These are all very important tasks, but they are essentially concerned with effectively managing resources already deployed often in a limited part of the organisation within the context and guidance of an existing strategy. Operational control is what managers are involved in for most of their time. It is vital to the effective implementation of strategy, but it is not the same as strategic management.

Strategic management	Operational management
■ Ambiguous ■ Complex	■ Routinised
■ Organisation-wide ■ Fundamental	■ Operationally specific

■ Long-term
  implications
	■ Short-term
	  implications

Figure 1.2   Characteristics of strategic management and operational management

Nor is strategic management concerned only with taking decisions about major issues facing the organisation. It is also concerned with ensuring that the strategy is put into effect. It can be thought of as having three main elements within it, and it is these that provide the framework for the book. There is *strategic analysis*, in which the strategist seeks to understand the strategic position of the organisation. There is *strategic choice*, which is to do with the formulation of possible courses of action, their evaluation and the choice between them. And there is *strategy implementation*, which is concerned with both planning how the choice of strategy can be put into effect, and managing the changes required.

Before discussing these elements it is useful to make clear how they relate to each other and, therefore, why Figure 1.3 is shown in the form it is. The figure could have been shown in a linear form — strategic analysis preceding strategic choice, which in turn precedes strategy implementation. Indeed, many texts on the subject do just this. However, in practice, the stages do not take this linear form. It is very likely that the elements are interlinked: one way of evaluating a strategy would be to begin to implement it, so strategic choice and strategy implementation may overlap. Since strategic analysis should be an on-going activity, it will overlap with the implementation of strategy. It is for structural convenience only that the process has been divided into sections in this book; it is not meant to suggest that the process of strategic management must follow a neat and tidy path.

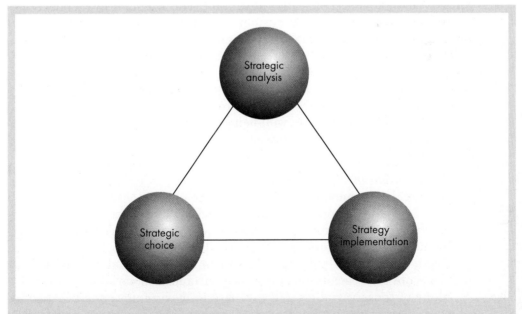

Figure 1.3   A basic model of the strategic management process

Evidence for how strategic management occurs in practice is given in Chapter 2 so as to provide readers with a better 'feel' for the realities.

1.2.1 Strategic analysis

Strategic analysis is concerned with understanding the strategic position of the organisation. What changes are going on in the environment, and how will they affect the organisation and its activities? What are resources and competences of the organisation and can these provide special advantages or yield new opportunities? What is it that those people and groups associated with the organisation — managers, shareholders or owners, unions and others who are stakeholders in the organisation — aspire to, and how do these affect what is expected for the future development of the organisation?

The history of IKEA suggests that a great deal of care was taken by those planning the development of the business in analysing different strategic moves. Decisions to enter new geographic markets required careful consideration about the economy in those countries, current and future demand in the market for furnishings, the historical and likely future activities of competitors, the most attractive locations in terms of demographic profiles of potential customers, and so on. An equally important issue was how the particular and special competences of the firm might be configured to provide competitive advantage. This was done by reconceiving how value might be provided to customers. 'Upstream' value was provided by careful design and sourcing of a wide range of merchandise. However, uniquely, the added value of IKEA was also provided by the management's design of the operation 'downstream' so that customers could add value themselves in their selection, transportation and assembly of the furniture.

The aim of *strategic analysis* is, then, to form a view of the key influences on the present and future well-being of the organisation, and what opportunities are afforded by the environment and the competences of the organisation. These are discussed briefly below.

1. The *environment*. The organisation exists in the context of a complex commercial, economic, political, technological, cultural and social world. This environment changes and is more complex for some organisations than for others: how this affects the organisation could include an understanding of historical and environmental effects, as well as expected or potential changes in environmental variables. This is a major task because the range of environmental variables is so great. Many of those variables will give rise to *opportunities* and others will exert *threats* on the organisation. A problem that has to be faced is that the range of variables is likely to be so great that it may not be possible

or realistic to identify and analyse each one; and therefore there is a need to distil out of this complexity a view of the main or overall environmental impacts on the organisation. Chapter 3 examines how it might be possible.

2. The *resources and competences* of the organisation which make up its *strategic capability*. Just as there are outside influences on the organisation and its choice of strategies, so there are internal influences. One way of thinking about the strategic capability of an organisation is to consider its *strengths* and *weaknesses* (what it is good or not so good at doing, or where it is at a competitive advantage or disadvantage, for example). These strengths and weaknesses might be identified by considering the resource areas of a business, such as its physical plant, its management, its financial structure and its products. Here, then, the aim is to form a view of the internal influences — and constraints — on strategic choice.

   However, it is also important to consider the particular competences of the organisation and the way in which they may yield opportunities. On occasions, specific resources — for example, the particular location of an organisation — could provide it with competitive advantage. But competences which provide real advantage — in this book we refer to them as 'core competences' — are more likely to be activities, know-how and skills which *in combination* provide advantages for that organisation which others find difficult to imitate. An understanding of what these are may lead to the identification of new opportunities for the organisation. Here, then, resources and competences are seen as aspects of the organisation not so much to be 'fitted' into environmental opportunities or demands; but rather to be 'stretched' to create new opportunities. Chapter 4 examines resource and competence analysis in detail.

3. The mission of an organisation tries to encapsulate its *purpose*. There are a number of influences on and manifestations of such purpose, and Chapter 5 explores these. Formally, the issue of *corporate governance* is important. Here the question is: which stakeholder group *should* the organisation primarily serve and how should managers be held responsible for this? The *expectations* of different *stakeholders* affect purpose and what will be seen as acceptable in terms of strategies advocated by management. Which views prevail will depend on which group has the greatest *power*, and understanding this can be of great importance in recognising why an organisation follows the strategy it does. *Cultural influences* from within the organisation and from the world around it also influence the strategy an organisation follows, not least because the environmental and resource influences on the organisation are likely to be interpreted in terms of the assumptions

inherent in that culture. Chapter 5 builds on the discussion in Chapter 2 to show how cultural influences on strategy can be examined. All of this raises *ethical* issues about what managers and organisations do and why. This array of influences also takes form in statements of *objectives*. These are also discussed in Chapter 5.

Together, a consideration of the *environment, strategic capability*, the *expectations* and the *purposes* within the *cultural* and *political* framework of the organisation provides a basis for the strategic analysis of an organisation. Such an understanding must take the future into account. Is the current strategy capable of dealing with the changes taking place in the organisation's environment? Is it likely to deliver the results expected by influential stakeholders? If so, in what respects, and if not, why not? It is unlikely that there will be a complete match between current strategy and the picture which emerges from the strategic analysis. The extent to which there is a mismatch here is the extent of the strategic problem facing the strategist. It may be that the adjustment that is required is marginal, or it may be that there is a need for a fundamental realignment of strategy. Assessing the magnitude of strategic change required and the ability of the organisation to effect such changes is another important aspect of strategic analysis. Chapter 2 provides an understanding of problems of strategic change.

1.2.2 Strategic choice

Strategic analysis provides a basis for strategic choice. This aspect of strategic management can be conceived of in the following ways.

1. *Identifying bases of strategic choice*. There are a number of fundamental issues which need to be addressed in generating and considering strategic options open to the organisation. Some of these *bases of strategic choice* arise from an understanding of stakeholder expectations and influence; and it may be important to reflect these in statements of *strategic mission* and *intent* which provide overall guidance about the nature or aspirations of the organisation: for example, in terms of *product*, market and geographical *scope* or matters as fundamental as *ownership* of the organisation. There are also bases of strategic choice in terms of how the organisation seeks to compete, at SBU level. This requires an identification of *bases of competitive advantage* arising from an understanding of both markets and customers, and special competences that the organisation has to offer which contribute to its *generic* strategy. IKEA had achieved a basis of retailing which was quite unique — or *differentiated* from other furniture retailers — and sought to build future strategy on that distinctive generic strategy. A corporate

body with many business units also faces challenges to do with the balancing of its *portfolio* of SBUs, its overall *financial strategy* and the extent to which it can reconcile the bases of strategy at the corporate level with those at the business unit level. This is an issue of *parenting*. It is less of a problem for an organisation like IKEA which seeks to offer a similar service throughout the world; but for the organisation that comprises different types of business, finding ways in which the centre adds value, rather than diminishing value, for the businesses is a significant parenting challenge.

2. *Generation of strategic options.* There may be several possible courses of action that an organisation could follow. In the 1970s and 1980s, IKEA had faced a decision about the extent to which it was to become a truly multinational firm. By the 1990s the international scope of its operations posed the organisation other choices of *strategic direction*. Which areas of the world were now most important to concentrate on? Could the existing experience and competences of IKEA be used as bases for entering new markets or providing new services or products? Within these, what *methods* of strategic development direction were most appropriate? Should the company attempt to follow these strategies by internal development, or was increasing joint venture activity — for example, through franchising — more sensible?

All of these considerations are important and need careful consideration: indeed, in developing strategies, a potential danger is that managers do not consider any but the most obvious course of action — and the most obvious is not necessarily the best. A helpful step in *strategic choice* can therefore be to generate *strategic options*.

3. *Evaluation and selection of strategic options.* Strategic options can be examined in the context of the strategic analysis to assess their relative merits. In deciding between options open to them, IKEA management might have asked a series of questions. First, which of these options built upon strengths, overcame weaknesses and took advantage of opportunities, while minimising or circumventing the threats that the business faced? This is an assessment of the *suitability* of the strategy. It can be thought of as evaluating if there is a 'fit' between the resource capability of the organisation and its environment; or if resource capability can be developed, or 'stretched', to yield new opportunities. However, a second set of questions is important. To what extent could a strategic option be put into effect? Could required finance be raised, sufficient stock be made available at the right time and in the right place, staff be recruited and trained to reflect the sort of image IKEA was trying to project? These are questions of *feasibility*. Even if these criteria could be met, would the choice be *acceptable* to the stakeholders?

For example, suppose, in reviewing strategic options, IKEA management could see logic in substantial variation by country in product range and store design. Would this be acceptable to the corporate centre, and perhaps ultimately to the heritage established by Ingvar Kamprad? It might also be regarded as too risky because it could dilute the overall image of IKEA worldwide: acceptable risk is an important criterion.

Useful though such criteria of evaluation are, there is unlikely to be a clear-cut 'right' or 'wrong' choice because any strategy must inevitably have some dangers or disadvantages. So in the end, choice is likely to be a matter of management judgement. The *selection* process cannot always be viewed or understood as a purely objective, logical act. It is strongly influenced by the values of managers and other groups with interest in the organisation, and ultimately may very much reflect the power structure in the organisation.

Strategic choice is dealt with in Part III of the book. Chapter 6 deals with questions concerning the identification of bases of strategy both in terms of overall corporate mission and parenting, and in terms of competitive advantage at the business unit level, especially in terms of how it positions itself with regard to competition. Chapter 7 discusses strategic options in more detail, particularly in terms of the direction that an organisation might take in terms of product or market development; how resources and competences can be stretched to achieve this; and what methods of strategy development, such as internal development, joint ventures or acquisition, might be appropriate. Chapter 8 goes on to consider criteria of evaluation and the bases of choice of strategies.

1.2.3 Strategy implementation

Strategy implementation is concerned with the translation of strategy into action. The ways in which this is done can be thought of as the *strategic architecture* of the organisation, and successful implementation of strategy is likely to be dependent on the extent to which these various components work together to provide, in themselves, competences which other organisations find it difficult to match. The sorts of question that are likely to be important in planning strategy implementation can include the following.

Who is to be responsible for carrying through the strategy? What changes in *organisational structure* and design are needed to carry through the strategy? There may also be a need to adapt the *systems* used to manage the organisation. What will different departments be held responsible for? What sort of information systems are needed to monitor progress? Implementation will also involve *resource planning*, including the logistics of implementation. What are the key tasks needing to be carried out? What changes need to be made in the resource mix of the organisation? Is there a need for new people or the retraining of the workforce?

The implementation of strategy also requires the managing of *strategic change*; and this requires action on the part of managers in terms of the way they manage change processes, and the mechanisms they use for it. These mechanisms are likely to be concerned not only with organisational redesign, but also with changing day-to-day routines and cultural aspects of the organisation, and overcoming political blockages to change.

Part IV of the book deals with strategy implementation. Issues of organisation structure and design are dealt with in Chapter 9, resource allocation and control are discussed in Chapter 10, and issues of managing strategic change are discussed in Chapter 11.

1.2.4 Strategic management processes

The influences on, and elements of, strategic management discussed above are summarised in Figure 1.4 and form the structure of the remainder of the book. However, there is a danger of thinking of the process of strategic management as an orderly sequence of steps not least because readers might not find the elements described here existing in practice, and might therefore argue that strategic management in their organisation does not take place. It is important to stress that the model used in this book, and summarised in this chapter, is a useful device for the structuring of the book and a means by which managers and students of strategy can *think through* strategic issues and explore the domain of 'corporate strategy' — it is not, however, an attempt to describe how the processes of strategic management necessarily take place in the social, political and cultural arenas of organisations. It is sufficient here to point out that there are two broadly different ways in which the process of strategic management can be explained.

One view of strategic management is, indeed, that strategy can and should be managed through planning processes in the form of a sequence of steps involving objective setting, the analysis of environmental trends and resource capabilities, continuing through the evaluation of different options, and ending with the careful planning of the strategy's implementation. Here, then, the underlying principle is that strategies are the outcome of careful objective analyses and planning.[8] Many organisations do have formal planning systems, and find that they contribute usefully to the development of the strategy of their organisation. However, not all organisations have them, and even when they do, it would be a mistake to assume that the strategies of organisations necessarily come about through them.

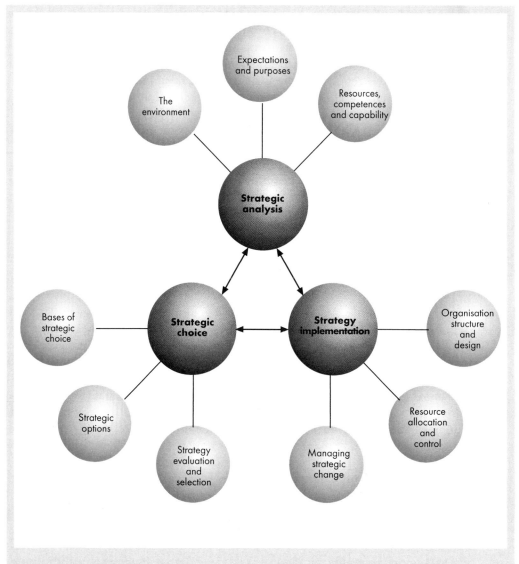

Figure 1.4 A summary model of the elements of strategic management

The management of the strategy can also be thought of as a process of *crafting*.[9] Here strategic management is seen not as a formal planning process, but rather in terms of processes by which strategies develop in organisations on the basis of managers' experience, their sensitivity to changes in their environments and what they learn from operating in their markets. This means not that managers are not thinking about the strategic position of their organisation, or the choices it faces; but that it may not be taking place in a highly formalised way. These and other views about the management of strategy and how strategies develop in organisations are discussed in Chapter 2.

However strategy is developed, there is another overarching issue which needs to be borne in mind. Strategies typically develop by organisations adapting or building on existing strategies — an *incremental* approach. However, either through the necessity of the inadequacy of existing strategy, or because management see the need to change fundamentally the direction of the organisation, this approach may not be appropriate. There is a need for *transformational* strategic change. Here it may be especially important for there to exist a clear and compelling *vision* or *strategic intent* so that strategy development is based not on where the organisation has come from, but on its new horizon. These different approaches are discussed more fully in Chapters 2 and 11.

1.2.5 Strategic management as 'fit' or 'stretch'[10]

These discussions of processes of strategy development raise a second issue which concerns the extent to which the emphasis is on developing strategy on the basis of 'fit' with the environment as management understand it; or 'stretching' the organisation on the basis of resources and competences which can create opportunities for strategy development.

The notion of *fit* sees managers trying to develop strategy by identifying or being sensitive to the organisation's environmental forces and developing the organisation's resources to address these. Here it would be seen as important to achieve the correct *positioning* of the organisation: for example, in terms of the extent to which it meets clearly identified market needs. This might take the form of a small business trying to find a particular niche in a market; or a multinational corporation seeking to place most of its investments in businesses which have found successful market positions or have identified attractive markets. Traditionally, the emphasis in books on strategy has tended to be on developing strategies in this way.

However, this emphasis has been questioned because there is little evidence to suggest that firms competing in markets which appear to offer attractive opportunities perform better than organisations that compete in markets which seem less attractive.[11] Success may result from creating strategies not so much on existing market opportunities, but on the basis of views of the future in which competences unique to the organisation provide advantages over competition or create new opportunities, even new markets. This *stretch* view of strategy development emphasises the need to be acutely aware of the special competences of the organisation, how these might be developed to give competitive advantage and the need to search for opportunities on the basis of these. The small business might try to change the 'rules of the game' in its market to suit its own competences, for example; or the large multinational corporation be

Aspect of strategy	Environment-led 'fit'	Resource-led 'stretch'
Underlying basis of strategy	Strategic fit between market opportunities and organisation's resources	Leverage of resources to improve value for money
Competitive advantage through ...	'Correct' positioning Differentiation directed by market need	Differentiation based on competences suited to or creating market need
How small players survive ...	Find and defend a niche	Change the 'rules of the game'
Risk reduction through ...	Portfolio of products/businesses	Portfolio of competences
Corporate centre invests in ...	Strategies of divisions or subsidiaries	Core competences

Source: Adapted from G. Hamel and C.K. Prahalad, *Competing for the Future*, Harvard Business School Press, 1994.

Figure 1.5 The lead edge of strategy: fit or stretch

concerned less with trying to identify businesses which have achieved historic success in terms of market position, than with trying to identify businesses with particular competences which it can help develop to give competitive advantage or create new opportunities. These differences are summarised in Figure 1.5.

Chapter 2 examines different patterns of strategy development. It will be seen that some organisations adopt a more incremental path of development than others, building on current strategy rather than trying to transform it. Arguably, IKEA, having originally created a strategy based on competences unique to itself which created a new approach in the market, has subsequently developed in an incremental way, building and developing on its original strategy. Indeed, it will be shown in Chapter 2 that incremental strategy development is common and more transformational strategic development rarer. A challenge which managers face is to identify when it is appropriate to build strategies in this incremental way and when more substantial change is required. This in turn may be linked to the culture of the organisation.

1.3 Strategic management in different contexts

The retail development of IKEA has been used in this chapter to illustrate different aspects of strategic management. To a greater or lesser extent, all these aspects are relevant for most organisations. However, it is likely that different aspects will be more important in some contexts, and some organisations, than in others. For example, IKEA is a retail business, and in retailing the need to understand customer needs and values and to consider these in relation to product and customer service is crucially important; more so than it would be in a firm supplying commodity raw materials in an industrial setting, for example. However, in IKEA itself, the strategic emphases have changed over time. Its multinational scope meant that structural and control issues became much more important in the 1980s and 1990s than they had been when it was more geographically limited in the 1960s. It would, then, be wrong to assume that all aspects of strategic management are equally important in all circumstances: this section reviews some of the ways in which aspects differ in different contexts. Differences are also shown in Illustration 1.3.

1.3.1 The small business context[12]

Small businesses are likely to be operating in a single market or a limited number of markets, probably with a limited range of products or services. The scope of the operation is therefore likely to be less of a strategic issue than it is in larger organisations. It is unlikely that small businesses will have central service departments to undertake complex analysis and market research; rather, it may be senior managers themselves, perhaps even the founder of the firm, who has direct contact with the market place and whose experience is therefore very influential. Indeed, in small firms the values and expectations of senior executives who may be in an ownership position are likely to be very important, and even when current management are not owners, it may be that the values and expectations of the founders still linger on. It is also likely that, unless the firm is specialising in some particular market segment — and identifying a market niche of some sort may make a lot of sense — it will be subject to significant competitive pressures: so issues of competitive strategy are likely to be especially important for the small firm. However, decisions on competitive strategies are likely to be strongly influenced by the experience of those running the business, so the questions and challenges posed on the nature of competition in Chapter 3 and bases of competitive strategy in Chapter 6 are likely to be especially relevant.

Small firms are also likely to be private companies. This significantly affects their ability to raise capital. Combined with the legacy of the founder's influence on choice of product and market, this may mean that choices of strategy are limited. The firm may see its role as consolidating its position within a particular market. If it does not, and is seeking growth, then the raising of finance for the development of strategic relationships

---

Illustration 1.3 Strategic issues in different contexts

Strategic issues faced by managers in different organisations depend on their business context.

Multinational corporation

'Any big multinational corporation is intrinsically complex. It has multiple layers of managers, and in most cases, multiple businesses — it develops products, manufactures and sells them, and services them in multiple countries ... A choice [of strategy] in principle ... has to be embedded in a complex industrial and managerial structure so that the myriad choices made daily within the organisation fall in line with the chosen strategic orientation.'

Y. Doz, *Introduction to Strategic Management in Multinational Companies*, Pergamon, 1986, pp. 6–7.

Small business

'Every small business has only got one commodity to sell and that's themselves. It doesn't matter if you're a window cleaner or whether you're an accountant, at the end of the day when the person comes to you, all you've got to offer is yourself. They can get the same quality of product and the same price somewhere else. The only thing you've got is your own personal commitment.'

A UK greengrocer

Professional partnership

'In recent years, "professional partnerships" like accountants have become huge organisations with sales in excess of $5 billion. Yet they still tend to be organised to serve national or regional markets, with partners being responsible for all aspects of service delivery to clients, with which they may personally identify. You also need to remember that partnerships are not hierarchies: you can't easily tell partners what to do. However, clients are beginning to require international service delivery. This cuts across the traditional structure and culture of partnerships: for example, in the way it requires team working across national boundaries, and therefore planned

---

with funding bodies such as banks becomes a key strategic issue.

1.3.2 The multinational corporation[13]

The key strategic issues facing multinationals are substantially different from those facing the small business. Here the firm is likely to be diverse in terms of both products and geographic markets. It may be that the firm is in integration of resources. It is not always easy to get partners to go along with this. As one of my colleagues said: a great deal of management of a professional service organisation has to do with "keeping the fleas in the bucket".'

David Pitt-Watson, director of Braxton Associates.

Charity sector

'If your mission is, say, to eliminate poverty or save the planet, then almost anything you do can be justified. If management is weak and without legitimacy (which is too often the case), this means staff often set their own personal agendas. To a greater extent than most private organisations, there are also multiple stakeholders. This is at its most extreme in membership organisations. Senior managers can find themselves buffeted by warring factions both outside and inside the organisation. Commitment is also a two-edge sword. Young staff in particular often join with a view that they are going to change the world and find out that many jobs are pretty routine. There is a great danger that they then invest their energy in trying to create their vision of the world within the organisation. Many not-for-profit organisations have had terrible problems with in-fighting. Some become unmanageable and implode.'

Sheila McKechnie, Chief Executive, Consumers' Association; director of Shelter until 1995.

Public sector

'In highly developed societies such as ours, the consumer/the citizen increasingly demands greater choice in the services and goods provided. Such choice can only be developed and enhanced in an environment of competition and so far no other mechanism for guaranteeing this choice has been found to exist. It is inevitable that public services, such as local government, will be subject to even greater competition, in the broadest sense, and the way in which its services are both funded and provided will therefore radically change. Even if free market models of provision are found wanting, competition in the provision of public services is here to stay because consumers demand it.'

Rob Hughes, President of the Society of Local Authority Chief Executives. Public Lecture at Sheffield Business School in May 1995 entitled 'The power of choice'.

a range of different types of business in the form of subsidiary companies within a holding company structure, or divisions within a multidivisional structure. Therefore, issues of structure and control at the corporate level (see Chapter 9), and relationships between businesses and the corporate centre, are usually a major strategic issue for multinational firms. Indeed, a central concern is the extent to which the centre adds to or detracts from the value of its businesses (see Chapters 6 and 9). At the business unit level, many of the competitive strategic issues will, perhaps, be similar to those faced by smaller firms — though the strength of the multinational within a given geographical area may be greater than for any small firm. However, for the multinational parent company a significant issue will be how corporate business units should be allocated resources given their different, and often competing, demands for them; and how this is to be co-ordinated. Indeed, the co-ordination of operational logistics across different business units and different countries may become especially important. For example, a multinational manufacturing company such as Toyota or General Motors has to decide upon the most sensible configuration of plants for the manufacture of cars. Most have moved from manufacturing a particular car at a particular location, and now manufacture different parts of cars in different locations, bringing together such components for the assembly of a given car in a given location. The logistics problems of co-ordinating such operations are immense, requiring sophisticated control systems and management skills far removed from those in the smaller firm. An important choice that a major multinational has to make is the extent to which it controls such logistics centrally, or devolves autonomy to operating units. It is, again, an issue of structure and control, the subject of Chapters 9 and 10 of this book.

1.3.3 Manufacturing and service organisations[14]

While differences exist between organisations providing services and those providing products, there is also an increasing awareness of similarities. Competitive strategy for a service firm is concerned less with a product itself and more with wider aspects of the organisations that make up that service, whereas Ford's ability to compete effectively with Japanese manufacturers depends to a greater extent on the physical product which gives it advantages over Japanese producers at a price which is also competitive — factors which are likely to be linked back into the production process. For a firm which competes on the basis of the services it provides — for example, insurance, management consultancy and professional services — there is no physical product. Here competitive advantage is likely to be much more related to the extent to which customers value less tangible aspects of the firm. This could be, for example, the soundness of advice given, the attitude of staff, the ambience of offices, the swiftness of service and so on. Senior management in manufacturing organisations may therefore believe they exercise more direct control over competitive strategy than can be exercised in a service firm. However, most have come to understand that, since physical products are often perceived by customers as very similar, other features such as service or brand image are just as important in achieving competitive advantage. Bases of competitive advantage related to physical products, resources, organisational competences and value to customers are discussed in Chapters 4, 6 and 10 in particular.

1.3.4 Strategy in the public sector[15]

The concepts of strategy and strategic management are just as important in the public sector as in commercial firms. However, like the private sector, the public sector is diverse, as some examples show.

- *Nationalised companies* may be similar in many respects to commercial organisations; the differences are associated with the nature of ownership and control. There is likely to be a good deal of direct or indirect control or influence exercised from outside the organisation, by government in particular. A commercial enterprise that is state controlled may find planning horizons determined more by political than market conditions; and constraints on investment capital and therefore bases of financing, and on the latitude managers have to change strategies. The latter may be influenced by a requirement for top management to control their organisation more centrally for reporting purposes — for example, to government ministers. Understanding the power of different stakeholders (see Chapter 5) and constraints on change (see Chapter 2) may be especially important here.
- A *government agency* has a labour market, and a money market of sorts; it also has suppliers and users or customers. However, at its heart lies a political market which approves budgets, and provides subsidies. It is the explicit nature of this political dimension which managers — or officers — have to cope with which particularly distinguishes government bodies, be they national or local, from commercial enterprises. This may in turn change the horizons of decisions, since they may be heavily influenced by political considerations, and may mean that analysis of strategies requires the norms of political dogma to be considered explicitly. However, although the magnitude of the political dimension is greater, the model of strategic management discussed here still holds. What is different is that certain aspects of strategic analysis and choice, notably those to do with political influences (see Chapter 5), are more important.
- *Public service* organisations — for example, health services and many of the amenities run by local government — face difficulties from a strategic point of view because they may not be allowed to specialise, and may not be able to generate surpluses from their services to invest in development. This can lead to a mediocrity of service where strategic decisions mainly take the form of striving for more and more efficiency so

as to retain or improve services on limited budgets. Careful analyses of resources (see Chapter 4) and allocation of those resources become very important (see Chapter 10).

- In the public sector, the notion of competition is usually concerned with competition for *resource inputs*, typically within a political arena. The need to demonstrate *value for money* in outputs has become increasingly important. Many of the developments in management practices in the public sector, such as changes to internal markets, performance indicators, competitive tendering and so on, are attempts to introduce elements of competition in order to encourage improvements in value for money.

- Overall, the role of ideology in the development of strategy in the public sector is probably greater than that in commercial organisations. Putting it in the terminology of this book, the criterion of *acceptability to stakeholders* in strategic choice is probably of greater significance in the public sector than in the commercial sector.

1.3.5 Privatised utilities

Increasingly, organisations that were once within the public sector have been privatised. This change in status has typically been made because government sees benefits in requiring such organisations to become more sharply focused on markets; and specifically, on customer requirements and competitive pressures. Managers in such organisations therefore find themselves more explicitly having to face an understanding of the dynamics of competition (see Chapter 3) and the formulation of clear competitive strategies (see Chapter 6). This is important internally for the clarification of strategy, but also because these organisations may also be answerable to government regulators, acting as a surrogate for a real competitive market, or there to create a competitive market (as in the electricity supply industry in the UK) by progressive deregulation. Indeed, it may be that formalised planning systems (see Chapter 2) are important not only for internal purposes, but also as a way of ensuring visible public accountability.

1.3.6 The voluntary and not-for-profit sectors[16]

In the voluntary sector it is likely that underlying values and ideology will be of central strategic significance. The values and expectations of different stakeholder groups in organisations play an important part in the development of strategy; and this is particularly the case where the *raison d'étre* of the organisation is rooted in such values, as is the case with organisations providing services traditionally not for profit, such as charities.

CHARACTERISTICS	LIKELY EFFECTS
Objectives and expectations • May be multiple service objectives and expectations • May be multiple influences on policy • Expectations of funding bodies very influential	• Complicates strategic planning • High incidence of political lobbying • Difficulties in delegating/decentralising responsibilities and decision making
Market and users • Beneficiaries of service not necessarily contributors of revenue/resources	• Service satisfaction not measured readily in financial terms
Resources • High proportion from government, or sponsors • Received in advance of services • May be multiple sources of funding	• Influence from funding bodies may be high • May be emphasis on financial or resource efficiency rather than service effectiveness • Strategies may be addressed to sponsors as much as clients

Figure 1.6 Some characteristics of strategic management in not-for-profit organisations

In not-for-profit organisations such as charities, churches, private schools, foundations and so on, the sources of funds may be diverse and are quite likely not to be direct beneficiaries of the services offered. Moreover, they may provide funds in advance of the services being offered — in the form of grants, for example. There are several implications. Influence from funding bodies may be high in terms of the formulation of organisational strategies. Competition is likely to be for funds from such bodies; but the principles of competitive strategy (see Chapter 6) nonetheless still hold. However, since such organisations might be dependent on funds which emanate not from users but from sponsors, there is a danger that they may become concerned more with resource efficiency than with service effectiveness (see Chapter 4). The multiple sources of funding likely to exist, linked to the different objectives and expectations of the funding bodies, might also lead to a high incidence of political lobbying, difficulties in clear strategic planning, and a requirement to hold decision making and responsibility at the centre, where it is answerable to external influences, rather than delegate it within the organisation. The characteristics and difficulties of strategic management in not-for-profit organisations are summarised in Figure 1.6.

1.3.7 Professional service organisations

Traditionally based values are often of particular importance in professional service organisations where professional advice has traditionally been seen as more important than revenue-earning capability. To a large extent this was the case in medicine, accountancy, law and other professions.

Private sector professional firms may also have a partnership structure. Partners may be owners and perhaps bear legal responsibility for advice and opinion offered by the firm; they may therefore carry considerable power; and there may be many of them — each of the top four accountancy firms now aspires to global strategies, but each may have thousands of partners. Traditionally, although interacting with clients and exercising actual or potential control over resources, these partners may not have regarded themselves as managers at all. As a partner in a major accountancy firm put it: 'We see ourselves as the largest network of sole traders in the world.' The problems of developing and implementing strategy within such a context are, therefore, heavily linked to the management of internal political influences (see Chapter 5) and the ability to take account of, and where necessary to change, organisational culture (see Chapters 2 and 11). Another factor is the pressure those in the professions find themselves under to be more 'commercial' in their approach. Such pressure may come from government, as in the case of doctors; or it may be a function of size, as has been found in the growing accountancy firms. This has meant that such organisations have had to be concerned with competitive strategy (see Chapter 6).

1.4 Summary: the challenge of strategic management

In a study examining the rejuvenation of businesses in mature markets, Baden-Fuller and Stopford[17] concluded that the success of such businesses could not be explained by the conditions in their markets or the general state of the industry. Success was the result of the strategies pursued by the firms and the effective development of those strategies by management. They concluded that the success they observed arose from managers' abilities in identifying strategies for growth, typically on an international scale, 'stretching' organisational capabilities and embedding strategic thinking throughout the organisation, not just at the top. These key elements of strategic management are all central themes of this book.

The rest of the book expands on these and other issues, but it is worthwhile emphasising some key implications for the effective strategic manager at this stage.

1. It should be clear that the scope of strategic management is much greater than that of any one area of operational management. This was seen in Figure 1.2. To a much greater extent, strategic management is concerned with complexity arising out of ambiguous and non-routine situations with organisation-wide rather than operational-specific implications. This is a major challenge for managers who are used to managing the resources they control on a day-to-day basis. It can be a particular problem because of the background of managers who may have been trained, perhaps over many years, to undertake operational tasks and to take operational responsibility. Accountants find that they still tend to see problems in financial terms, marketing managers in marketing terms and so on. Each aspect in itself is important, of course, but none is adequate alone. The manager who aspires to manage, or influence, strategy needs to develop a capability to take an overview, to conceive of the whole rather than just the parts of the situation facing an organisation.

2. To develop an ability as a strategist therefore requires that the manager is able to conceptualise key strategic issues. Most aspects of management involve:

    ▪ *Analysis and planning* required to gather and organise *information* about the situation or issue faced.
    ▪ *Action* to undertake tasks: this may vary from action in the form of arranging for analysis to take place, to action in terms of ensuring that change takes place.
    ▪ *Conceptualisation* of problems and choices: this is not simply a matter of analysis, but has to do with *making sense* of the situation.

Because strategic management is characterised by its complexity, it is necessary to make decisions and judgements based on the conceptualisation of difficult issues. Yet the early training of managers is often about taking action, or about detailed planning or analysis. This book discusses analytical approaches to strategy, and it is also concerned with action related to the management of strategy; but the emphasis is on developing concepts of relevance to the complexity of strategy which informs this analysis and action.

3. A major challenge for the strategic manager is to help develop an organisation which is able simultaneously to meet stakeholder expectations while building capabilities and competences which provide bases of internal efficiency, as well as meeting the needs of customers better than competitors within a changing environment. It is a demanding challenge which cannot be done by the intellectual understanding or the sheer energy of the lone strategist. The need is to

build organisational capability in strategic response and action. This book should be regarded less as a guide for the individual manager than as a guide for building this organisation-wide capability.

4. It is also worth repeating the points made earlier about the distinction between 'fit' and 'stretch'. A challenge to management is the extent to which they see their strategy developing essentially on the basis of a finely tuned responsiveness to changes in their business environments; or the extent to which they see themselves leading change on the basis of their particular competences. These are, of course, not mutually exclusive: indeed, a challenging understanding of environmental changes which might take place could galvanise new insights into ways in which organisational competences could be developed. Conversely, imaginative ways of developing such competences might lead to the identification of environmental opportunities from which the organisation might prosper.

5. Managing strategic change is a particular problem for managers. To cope with the vast variety and range of environmental outputs in the strategic decision process, managers have to operate within some simplified model of that environment. Essentially, managers reduce the 'infinite' to a personally manageable frame of reference. More precisely, there is evidence to show that to some extent these frames of reference are inherited by the manager in terms of managerial experience which relates to key factors for business success in a particular business environment. However, this experience can be a significant restraint on change. It is not always easy for senior executives with long experience in their organisation to envisage, or implement, a significant shift in the strategy of that organisation. The ability to understand strategic issues outside such constraining frames of reference is of particular importance, and this is discussed more fully in Chapter 2.

References

1. In the 1980s much of the writing and practice of strategic management was influenced by the writings of industrial organisations economists. One of the most influential books was Michael Porter, *Competitive Strategy*, Free Press, first published 1980. In essence, the book describes means of analysing the competitive nature of industries so that managers might be able to select between attractive and less attractive industries and choose strategies most suited to the organisation in terms of these forces. This approach, which assumes the dominant influence of industry forces and the overriding need to tailor strategies to address those forces, has become known as a 'fit' view of strategy.

2. The notion of strategy as 'stretch' is perhaps best explained in G. Hamel and C.K. Prahalad, *Competing for the Future*, Harvard Business School Press, 1994.

3. R. Norman and R. Ramirez, 'From value chain to value constellation: designing interactive strategy', *Harvard Business Review*, vol. 71, no. 4 (1993) pp. 65--77.

4. Strategic architecture is discussed by various

authors in different ways. Hamel and Prahalad (see 2 above) devote a chapter to it and John Kay uses the term extensively in *Foundations of Corporate Success*, Oxford University Press, 1993.

5. There are many books and papers which discuss the concept of networks and relationships in and between organisations. For example, see J.C. Jarillo, *Strategic Networks: Creating the borderless organisation*, Butterworth-Heinemann, 1993, for networks between organisations; and M.S. Granovetter, 'The strength of weak ties', *American Journal of Sociology*, vol. 78, no. 6 (1993), pp. 1360–-80, for networks within organisations.

6. The term 'SBU' can be traced back to the development of corporate-level strategic planning in General Electric in the USA in the early 1970s. For an early account of its uses, see W.K. Hall, 'SBUs: hot, new topic in the management of diversification', *Business Horizons*, vol. 21, no. 1 (1978), pp. 17–-25.

7. For a discussion of alternative definitions, see C.W. Hofer and D. Schendel, *Strategy Formulation: Analytical concepts*, West, 1978, pp. 16–20.

8. There were many books that took a formalised strategic 'planning approach' in the 1970s. These are less common now, but there remain texts which take a similar approach (e.g. G. Greenley, *Strategic Management*, Prentice Hall, 1989) and others which take an explicitly analytical approach, largely excluding social, political and cultural aspects of strategic management (e.g. R.

Grant, *Contemporary Strategy Analysis*, 2nd edition, Blackwell, 1995).

9. See H. Mintzberg, 'Crafting strategy', *Harvard Business Review*, vol. 65, no. 4 (1987), pp. 66–75.

10. See reference 2 above.

11. Richard Rumelt has shown that firm strategy had a greater impact on performance than the nature of the industry in which the firm was operating ('How much does industry matter?', *Strategic Management Journal*, vol. 12, no. 3 (1991), pp. 167–85).

12. For strategy development in small businesses, see C. Barrow, R. Brown and L. Clarke, *The Business Growth Handbook*, Kogan Page, 1995.

13. There are now many books on managing strategy in multinationals. In this book we will refer often to C. Bartlett and S. Ghoshall, *Managing Across Borders: The transnational solution*, Harvard Business School Press, 1989; and G. Yip, *Total Global Strategy*, Prentice Hall, 1995.

14. There are several papers on the particular issues facing the management of strategic development in service industries in C. Armistead (ed.), *Future of Services Management*, Kogan Page, 1994.

15. D. McKevitt and A. Lawton, *Public Sector Management: Theory, critique and practice*, Sage, 1994.

16. See J.M. Bryson, *Strategic Planning for Public and Nonprofit Organizations*, Prentice Hall, 1995.

17. See C. Baden-Fuller and J.M. Stopford, *Rejuvenating the Mature Business: The competitive challenge*, Routledge, 1992.

Recommended key readings

It is useful to read about how strategies are managed in practice and some of the lessons which can be drawn from this which inform key themes in this book. For example:

- For readings on the concepts of strategy in organisations, John Kay's book, *Foundations for Corporate Success: How business strategies add value*, Oxford University Press, 1993, is a helpful explanation from an economic point of view. For a wider perspective, see R. Whittington, *What is Strategy and Does it Matter?*, Routledge, 1993.

- It is also useful to read some accounts of where the management of strategy in organisations has made an impact on organisational performance. For example, C. Baden-Fuller and J.M. Stopford, *Rejuvenating the Mature Business: The competitive challenge*, Routledge, 1992, shows how the strategies of some firms in relatively unattractive industries gave competitive edge to those firms. Reference is also often made in this book to G. Hamel and C.K. Prahalad, *Competing for the Future*, Harvard Business School Press, 1994, which draws extensively on examples of successful strategies in organisations. For a discussion of strategy in different types of organisations, see H. Mentzberg and J. Quinn, *The Strategy Process: Concepts, contexts and cases*, 3rd edn, Prentice Hall, 1995.

Work assignments

1.1   Using the characteristics discussed in section 1.1.1, write out a statement of strategy for IKEA, British Steel or an organisation with which you are familiar.

1.2   Using Figure 1.1 and Illustration 1.2 as a guide, identify, note down and explain examples of the vocabulary of strategy used in the annual report of a company.

1.3   *Using annual reports and press articles, write a brief case study (similar to the IKEA illustration or the British Steel* case) which shows the strategic development and current strategic position of an organisation.*

1.4   Using Figure 1.4 as a guide, note down the elements of strategic management discernible in the British Steel* case or an organisation of your choice.

1.5   *With particular reference to section 1.2.5, note down the characteristics of strategy development in IKEA which would be explained by the notion of (a) strategic management as 'environmental fit', and (b) strategic management as the 'stretching' of capabilities.*

1.6   **Using Figure 1.4 as a guide, show how the different elements of strategic management differ in:**
      (a) a multinational business (e.g. ISS* or Burmah Castrol*)
      (b) a professional services firm (e.g. KPMG*)
      (c) a public sector organisation (e.g. Royal Alexandra hospital*)
      (d) a small business.

*This refers to a case study in the Text and Cases version of this book.

CHAPTER 2

Strategic management in practice

2.1 Introduction

In Chapter 1 the idea of corporate strategy was introduced, as were the elements of strategic management — strategic analysis, strategic choice and strategy implementation. These elements make up a model, the purpose of which is to help readers *think* about strategic problems and formulate strategy. It is important to understand, however, that the model does not describe how organisational strategies *actually* come about. So before going on to examine the elements of the model in more detail in Parts II, III and IV, it is useful to have a clearer understanding of how strategies come about in practice. This chapter provides a basis for that understanding.

The chapter has three parts (see Figure 2.1). The first part looks at *patterns of strategy development*: that is, the ways in which strategies are observed to develop over time in organisations. The conclusion reached is that strategic changes may take different forms, but they do not usually occur as major, one-off changes in direction; rather, they are more gradual, incremental developments, with only occasional, more 'transformational' change.

The second and main part of the chapter discusses three general *explanations of strategy development* in organisations: first, that strategies develop as a result of deliberate *managerial intent*; second, that strategies can be better explained as the *outcome of cultural and political processes* in and around organisations; and third, that strategy development is *imposed* on organisations. These three explanations are discussed in some detail not only because they provide different insights into how strategies come about, but also because they are important when it comes to considering how, in practice, managers might influence strategic decisions and implement strategic change. However, it is rare to find organisations in which singular explanations are adequate to explain the complexity of strategic decision making and strategy development. There is evidence that different types of

Figure 2.1   A framework for understanding strategic management in practice

organisation tend to have different *configurations of strategy processes* in which the different explanations provided in this part of the chapter are more or less in evidence. Some typical configurations are reviewed and examples given.

The final part of the chapter builds on this review of processes to raise some *challenges in strategy development*. Since cultural and political processes of strategy development help explain strategic drift, the first section describes a framework — the *cultural web* — by which such influences can be explored. It is a framework which is subsequently used throughout the book. There is then a discussion as to why there is a tendency in organisations for *strategic drift*, in which strategies fail to change and organisational performance declines. Third, given an increasingly turbulent and unpredictable world, managers need to find ways of challenging their own and others' experience; the notion of a *learning organisation* is therefore discussed. Here organisations are seen as being reliant less on analysis and formalised processes of planning, and more on debate, experimentation and challenge.

In the *summary* at the end of the chapter, lessons are drawn from the practice of strategic decision making in terms of *implications for the study of strategy* and the content of this book. It is, however, important to sound a warning: because managers behave in particular ways does not mean that these are the right ways or the most sensible ways. The approach taken in this book is that readers will be able to assess a good deal better for themselves the importance and relevance of different approaches, concepts and techniques covered in the rest of the book if they understand the management of strategy as it happens in practice, and that is the role of this chapter.

2.2   Patterns of strategy development

Since strategy is about the long-term direction of an organisation, it is typically thought of in terms of major decisions about the future. However, it is a mistake to conceive of organisational strategy as necessarily developing through one-off major changes. The strategic development of organisations is better described and understood typically in terms of continuity. There is a tendency towards 'momentum' of strategy:[1] once an organisation has adopted a particular strategy, it tends to develop from and within that strategy, rather than fundamentally changing direction.

2.2.1 Punctuated equilibrium

Historical studies of organisations have shown that typically there are long periods of relative *continuity* during which established strategy remains unchanged or changes *incrementally*; and there are also periods of *flux* in which strategies change but in no very clear direction. *Transformational* change, in which there is a fundamental change in strategic direction, does

Figure 2.2   Patterns of strategy development

Illustration 2.1   Punctuated equilibrium: The Burton Group

Organisations undergo transformational change on an infrequent basis. In the main, organisations experience longer periods of stability during which established strategies change gradually.

The family era, 1901–70: 'consistent momentum'
Prior to 1970, Burton saw itself as a manufacturer of men's made-to-measure suits sold through its retail outlets. The company was family controlled with a paternalistic and centralised view of management. By the late 1960s, the rise in demand for ready-to-wear suits by younger, fashion-conscious men and increased competition from fashion boutiques led the family to appoint Ladislas Rice as CEO to realign the company's strategy.

The Rice era, 1970–76: 'attempted transformation and flux'
Rice attempted the radical reorganisation of changing focus from manufacturing to retailing, with an emphasis on ready-to-wear fashion clothes, and embarked on a strategy of diversification into different types of retailing to utilise Burton's strong capital base and extensive property portfolio. The retail businesses were organised as divisions and encouraged to make annual plans for profitable development.

The Spencer era, 1977–81: 'consolidation'
Continued poor performance led to a strategy of consolidation of existing units rather than continued broadening of Burton's retail base. A boardroom struggle was resolved with Rice resigning as Chief Executive. His successor, Spencer, stated that his aim was 'to eliminate loss-making business' and modernise retail outlets.

The Halpern era, 1981–90: 'successful transformation and flux'
Ralph Halpern sought to refocus the business on fashion retailing. He rapidly closed down manufacturing, disposed of non-fashion retail chains and invested heavily in 'lifestyle' retailing: different fashion retail concepts for different market segments. This transformed not only Burton's retail presence, but also its performance. However, following the takeover of Debenhams in 1985, there was concern that the company, and the attention of Halpern and his board, had lost the clear direction and success of the early 1980s. Ralph Halpern resigned in 1990.

Burton in the 1990s: 'back to basics'
The appointment of John Hoerner as CEO in 1992 saw the company enter a period of consolidation. The initial concentration on cost reduction was followed by shortening the lines of communication, reducing bureaucracy and eliminating 2,000 full-time jobs to be replaced by cheaper, more flexible part-timers.

Prepared by Tony Jacobs, Cranfield School of Management.

take place but is infrequent. This pattern has become known as *punctuated equilibrium*[2] and is illustrated in Figure 2.2 and Illustration 2.1.

A specific strategic move — perhaps a product launch, or a significant investment decision — establishes a strategic direction which, itself, guides decisions on the next strategic move — an acquisition perhaps. This in turn helps consolidate the strategic direction, and over time the overall strategic approach of the organisation becomes more established. As time goes on, each decision taken is by this *emerging* strategy and, in turn, reinforces it. Figure 2.3 shows this. This process could, of course, lead to a quite significant shift in strategy, but incrementally.

In many respects, such gradual change makes a lot of sense. No organisation could function effectively if it were to undergo major revisions of strategy frequently; and, in any case, it is unlikely that the environment will change so rapidly that this would be necessary. Incremental change might therefore be seen as an adaptive process to a continually changing environment; and in this sense it corresponds to what was referred to in Chapter 1 as the classical or 'fit' concept of strategic management. There are, however, dangers. Environmental change may not always be gradual

Figure 2.3   Strategic evolution and consolidation

enough for incremental change to keep pace: if such incremental strategic change lags behind environmental change, the organisation may get out of line with its environment and, in time, need more fundamental, or transformational, change. Indeed, transformational change tends to occur at times when performance has declined significantly. There is another danger: that organisations become merely reactive to their environments and fail to question or challenge what is happening around them; in short, become complacent. Some of these dangers can be seen as inherent in the descriptions of strategic management which follow.

Such dangers are also the concern of those who advocate a *stretch* view of strategic management, who argue that it is not sufficient just to be responsive to the environment; that the strategist should be more proactively trying to *create* new markets, or new opportunities. For example, companies that develop entirely new products or services may be creating customer needs and expectations that did not previously exist, and in this way be creating new markets. It can, of course, be risky to do so because the innovations may not be accepted in the market (see section 2.8.2); but if they are, this is another way in which transformational change can occur.

2.2.2 Intended and realised strategies

Conceiving of organisations' strategies in terms of such patterns of change means that it is important to be careful about just what is meant by 'strategy' and how it comes about. This can be explained in different ways.

1. Typically, strategy has been written about as though it is developed by managers in an *intended*, planned fashion. Strategy is conceived of as being formulated, perhaps through some planning process, resulting in a clear expression of strategic direction, the implementation of which is also planned in terms of resource allocation, structure and so on. The strategy then comes about, or is *realised* in practice. Strategy is here conceived of as a deliberate, systematic process of development and implementation (see route 1 in Figure 2.4).[3] As explained in Chapter 1, it is broadly the framework adopted in this book because it is a convenient way of thinking through the issues relating to strategy. However, it does not necessarily explain how strategies are actually realised.

2. In many organisations which attempt to formulate strategies in such systematic ways, the intended strategies do not become realised; or only part of what is intended comes about. Much of what is intended follows route 2 in Figure 2.4 and is *unrealised*; it does not come about in practice. There may be all sorts of reasons for this, and the rest of the chapter helps explain some of these. It may also be the case, of course, that

managers decided that a strategy, as planned, should not be put into effect: for example, if circumstances facing the organisation change.

3. Strategy could also be *imposed* on an organisation (route 3 in Figure 2.4) in a number of ways. It could be imposed by an external agency such as government, as has occurred in the deregulation of industries in many countries; or by a parent company on an SBU. It could be that environmental conditions limit the choices that managers can make or the strategies they can follow. For example, retrenchment, with divestments and the cutting of costs, may be forced by recession or conditions in a commodity market, and may mean there is little opportunity to follow strategies substantially different from other companies in that market.

4. If strategy is regarded as the long-term direction of the organisation, which develops over time, then it can also be conceived of as the *outcome of cultural and political processes* (route 4 in Figure 2.4).[4] The management of organisations depends a great deal on the knowledge and experience of those involved. This experience and ways of doing things are built up over years, often taken for granted (or tacit) and applied in managing the strategy of organisations. This is often evident in small businesses in which the experience of an owner/manager is

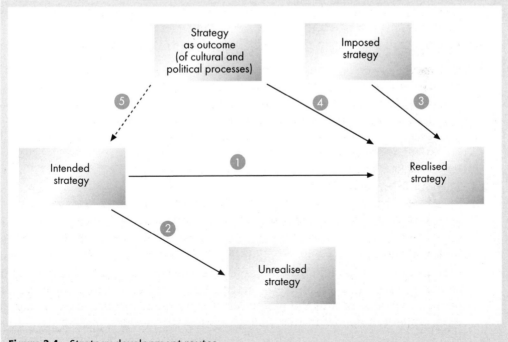

Figure 2.4   Strategy development routes

accepted within the culture as the driving force of the strategy. In organisations, managers typically reconcile different views, based on experience, through *negotiation* or the exercise of *power*; and this occurs within established ways of doing things that make up the culture of the organisation. In these ways, strategy can be seen as the outcome of political and cultural processes. If plans exist, they may perform the role of monitoring the progress or efficiency of a strategy which emerges as the outcome of such experience and ways of doing things. Or they may do little more than pull together the views and 'wisdom' which has built up over time in the organisation. Indeed, it is often a complaint of chief executives that the planning systems in their organisation have degenerated into little more than routinised elaborations of where the organisation has come from, and the received wisdom which has been built up in it. This is route 5 in Figure 2.4. It can be dangerous because the organisation appears to be taking a proactive, systematic approach to strategy development when it is not.

These different explanations of how strategies and their implications are developed are now explored in more depth. However, it is important to stress that it is most unlikely that any one of the explanations given here accounts entirely for the processes at work in an organisation: strategy development needs to be understood in terms of a mix of processes; and this is demonstrated in section 2.7.

2.3 Strategy development as managerial intent

The idea that strategy comes about in organisations through deliberate managerial intent can, itself, be explained in different ways. Here the *planning* view, a *command* view and the notion of *logical incrementalism* are discussed.

2.3.1 The planning view[5]

In the 1960s and 1970s, books were written about strategy which took the view not only that strategy could, but that it should come about through highly systematised forms of planning. They advocated the setting up of corporate planning departments and prescribed tools and techniques that should be used. These include the setting of objectives or goals; the analysis of the environment and the resources of the organisations, so as to match environmental opportunities and threats with resource-based strengths and weaknesses; the generation of strategic options and their evaluation; and the planning of implementation through resource allocation processes, the structuring of the organisation and the design of control systems. An example of such a system is given as Illustration 2.2.

While many of the steps described in such a planning system are similar to those adopted in this book, the difference is that proponents of such a planning view tend to argue that a highly systematic approach is *the* rational approach to strategy formulation. The evidence of the extent to which the formalised pursuit of such a systemised approach results in organisations performing better than others is, however, equivocal[6] — not least because it is difficult to isolate planning as the dominant or determining effect on performance. Formalised planning can, however, be useful in various ways:

- It can provide a structured means of *analysis and thinking* about complex strategic problems, requiring managers to *question and challenge* what they take for granted.
- It can be used as a way of involving people in strategy development, therefore helping to create *ownership* of the strategy and contributing to the *co-ordination* of resources to put it into effect.
- Strategic planning may also help to *communicate* intended strategy.
- It can be used as a means of *control* by regularly reviewing performance and progress against agreed objectives or previously agreed strategic direction.

There may, however, be dangers in the formalisation of strategic planning: they include the following.[7]

- Strategies are more or less successfully implemented through people. Their behaviour will not be determined by plans. So the *cultural and political dimensions* of organisations have to be taken into account. Planning processes are not typically designed to do this.
- The strategy resulting from deliberations of a corporate planning department, or a senior management team, may not be *owned* more widely in the organisation. In one extreme instance, a colleague was discussing the strategy of a company with its planning director. He was told that a strategic plan existed, but found that it was locked in the drawer of the executive's desk. Only the planner, and a few other senior executives, were permitted to see it!
- The managers responsible for the implementation of strategies, usually line managers, may be so busy with the day-to-day operations of the business that they cede responsibility for strategic issues to specialists. However, the specialists do not have power in the organisation to make things happen. The result can be that strategic planning becomes an *intellectual exercise* removed from the reality of operation. As General William Sherman said in 1869 in the context of the American Civil War: 'I know there exist many good men who honestly believe that one may, by

Illustration 2.2   National Health Service (NHS) business planning cycle 1995/6

NHS Trusts in England formulate annual strategic plans to meet the specific health needs of their local populations in line with national health policy, baseline requirements and medium-term (3–5-year) objectives. They have to meet set deadlines for business plans.

Organisation	September	October	November	December	January	March
NHS Executive	• Issue availability of revenue		• Issue common information requirements	• Issue revenue allocation to Health Authorities • Review plans • Announce initial capital allocations		
NHS Executive Regional Offices		• Review Trust draft strategic direction of service providers			• Review Trust draft business plans and notify External Finance Limits (EFL)	• Arbitrate • Sign off corporate contracts with RHA/DHAs
Regional Health Authorities (RHA)		• Review contracting intentions of purchasers of services		• Joint agreement on capital investment (by 23/12)	• Notify Health Authorities of capital cash limits	
District Health Authorities (DHA) (purchasers of services)	• Publish initial purchasing plans and contracting intentions (by 15/9)		• Submit draft outline of corporate contract to Regional Office		• Issue finalised contracting intentions (by 20/01) • Submit final local corporate contract to Regional Office	• Agree and sign all contracts (by 15/03) • Make purchasing plans public
NHS Trusts (service providers)	• Submit draft strategic direction (if appropriate) • Inform purchasers of major changes to pricing structure	• Submit business plans for capital investment	• Publish initial first cut prices • Submit draft business plans based on analysis of needs		• Provide finalised prices to purchasers of services	• Agree and sign all contracts (by 15/03) • Publish strategic direction

Vertical group labels: NATIONAL (NHS Executive); REGIONAL (NHS Executive Regional Offices, Regional Health Authorities); LOCAL (District Health Authorities, NHS Trusts)

Source: Philip Davies, Cranfield School of Management.

Notes:
1. A similar process is followed in Wales and Scotland.
2. General practitioners (GPs), who deliver primary care, also use a formal planning cycle.

the aid of modern science, sit in comfort and ease in his office chair, and, with figures and algebraic symbols, master the great game of war. I think this is an insidious and most dangerous mistake.'[8]

- The process of strategic planning may be so cumbersome that individuals or groups in the firm might contribute to only part of it and *not understand the whole*. This is particularly problematic in very large firms. One executive, on taking over as marketing manager in a large multinational consumer goods firm, was told by his superior: 'we do corporate planning in the first two weeks of April: then we get back to our jobs'.

- There is a danger that strategy becomes thought of as *the plan*. Managers may see themselves as managing strategy because they are going through the processes of planning. Strategy is, of course, not the same as 'the plan': strategy is the long-term direction that the organisation is following, not a written document on an executive's shelf. Here we get back to the difference between *intended* and *realised* strategies.

- Strategic planning can become over detailed in its approach, concentrating on extensive analysis which, while sound in itself, may miss the major strategic issues facing the organisation. For example, it is not unusual to find companies with huge amounts of information on their markets, but with little clarity about the strategic importance of that information. The result can be *information overload* with no clear outcome.

- Planning can become obsessed with the search for absolute determinants of performance — a set of economic indicators, for example — or a definitively *right strategy*. In the first place, it is unlikely that a 'right' strategy will somehow naturally fall out of the planning process. It might be more important to establish a more generalised strategic direction within which there is flexibility. As Mintzberg puts it: 'If you have no vision, but only formal plans, then every unpredicted change in the environment makes you feel your sky is falling in.'[9]

2.3.2 The command view

If planning has to do with managerial intent, so too does the second explanation of how strategies develop in organisations: a command view. Here strategy is seen as the outcome of the influence of an individual or small group, but not necessarily through formal plans.

At the extreme, strategy could be seen as the product of an *autocratic leader* who brooks no argument and sees other managers as there to implement his or her decisions. Less extreme, but more common perhaps, is the situation where a dominant leader has become personally associated with strategy development of the organisation. It could be that this individual turned round the business in times of difficulty and, as such, personifies the success of the organisation. *Charismatic leaders* are also often seen as central to the strategy of their organisation:[10] their personality or reputation may be seen as a positive force, and other managers may willingly defer to such an individual and see strategy as their province. In some organisations an individual is central because he or she is its *owner* or *founder*: this is often the case in small businesses. Others in the organisation may see strategic direction of the organisation as inevitably and properly associated with that individual.

In public sector organisations, officials or civil servants are meant to work to the direction of their political masters, which at least in theory is the command or 'will of the people', perhaps through a process of mandate and elections. Indeed, political leaders often call upon such mandated authority to justify their assertion of an overall economic or social strategy.

2.3.3 The logical incremental view

Given the complexity of organisations and the environments in which they operate, managers cannot consider all possible strategic options in terms of all possible futures and evaluate these against preset, unambiguous objectives, especially in an organisational context in which there are conflicting views, values and power bases. So the idea that strategies can be managed through neat, logical, sequential planning mechanisms is unrealistic. Rather, it has been argued that strategic choice takes place by comparing options against each other and considering which would give the best outcome and be possible to implement; that strategy building takes place through 'successive limited comparisons', in the everyday world of managing.[11]

In a study of major multinational businesses, Quinn[12] concluded that the management process could best be described as *logical incrementalism*. Managers have a view of where they want the organisation to be in years to come and try to move towards this position in an evolutionary way. They do this by attempting to ensure the success and development of a strong, secure, but flexible core business, building on the experience gained in that business and perhaps experimenting with 'side bet' ventures. There is a recognition that such experiments cannot be expected to be the sole responsibility of top management — that they should be encouraged to emerge from lower levels, or 'subsystems' in the organisation. Effective managers accept the uncertainty of their environment because they realise that they cannot do away with this uncertainty by trying to 'know' about how the environment will change. Rather, they try to be sensitive to environmental signals through constant scanning and by testing changes in strategy in small-scale steps. Commitment to strategic options may therefore be tentative in the early stages of strategy development. There is also a reluctance to specify precise objectives too early, as this might stifle ideas and prevent experimentation. Objectives may therefore be fairly general in nature.

Such a process is seen by managers to have benefits. Continual testing and gradual strategy implementation provides improved quality of information for decision making, and enables the better sequencing of the elements of major decisions. Since change will be gradual, the possibility of creating and developing a commitment to change throughout the organisation is increased. Because the different parts, or 'subsystems', of the organisation are in a continual state of interplay, the managers of each can learn from each other about the feasibility of a course of action. Such processes also take account of the political nature of organisational life, since smaller changes are less likely to face the same degree of resistance as major changes. Moreover, the formulation of strategy in this way means that the implications of the strategy are continually being tested out. This continual readjustment makes sense if the environment is considered as a continually changing influence on the organisation. It is a process through which the organisation keeps itself in line with such change, as shown diagrammatically in Figure 2.5.

Logical incrementalism does not, then, see strategic management in terms of a neat sequential model. The idea that the implementation of strategy somehow follows a choice, which in turn has followed analysis, does not hold. Rather, strategy is seen to be worked through in action.

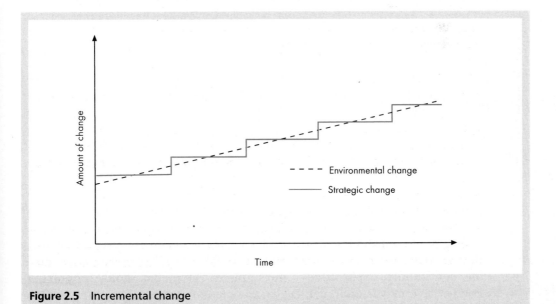

Figure 2.5   Incremental change

Illustration 2.3 An incrementalist view of strategic management

Managers often see their jobs as managing adaptively; continually changing strategy to keep in line with the environment, while maintaining efficiency and keeping stakeholders happy.

- 'You know there is a simple analogy you can make. To move forward when you walk, you create an imbalance, you lean forward and you don't know what is going to happen. Fortunately, you put a foot ahead of you and you recover your balance. Well, that's what we're doing all the time, so it is never comfortable.'[1]
- 'The environment is very fast changing. You can set a strategic direction one day and something is almost certain to happen the next. We do not have a planning process which occurs every two years because the environment is stable, but a very dynamic process which needs to respond to the unexpected.'[1]
- 'I begin wide-ranging discussions with people inside and outside the corporation. From these a pattern eventually emerges. It's like fitting together a jigsaw puzzle. At first the vague outline of an approach appears like the sail of a ship in a puzzle. Then suddenly the rest of the puzzle becomes quite clear. You wonder why you didn't see it all along.'[2]
- 'The real strength of the company is to be able to follow these peripheral excursions into whatever . . . one has to keep thrusting in these directions; they are little tentacles going out, testing the water.'[3]
- 'We haven't stood still in the past and I can't see with our present set-up that we shall stand still in the future; but what I really mean is that it is a path of evolution rather than revolution. Some companies get a successful formula and stick to that rigidly because that is what they know — for example, [Company X] did not really adapt to change, so they had to take what was a revolution. We hopefully have changed gradually and that's what I think we should do. We are always looking for fresh openings without going off at a tangent.'[3]

Sources:
[1] Quotes from interviews conducted by A. Bailey as part of a research project sponsored by the Economic and Social Research Council (Grant No.: R000235100).
[2] Extract from J.B. Quinn, *Strategies for Change*, Irwin, 1980.
[3] Extracts from G. Johnson, *Strategic Change and the Management Process*, Blackwell, 1987.

This view of strategy making is similar to the descriptions that managers themselves often give of how strategies come about in their organisations. Illustration 2.3 provides some examples of managers explaining the strategy development process in their organisation. They see their job as 'strategists' as continually, proactively pursuing a strategic goal, countering competitive moves and adapting to their environment, while not 'rocking the boat' too much, so as to maintain efficiency and performance. Quinn himself argues that 'properly managed, it is a conscious, purposeful, pro-active, executive practice'.[13]

There is, however, another explanation of incremental strategy development. Quinn and others suggest that the incremental way in which managers develop strategy is intentional: that they consciously seek to experiment and make small-scale changes. A further explanation[14] is that it is an inevitable outcome of the cultural and political processes of organisations: that problems are dealt with by applying taken-for-granted experience and ways of doing things, and by negotiation to make decisions. Strategy develops as an accumulation of such decisions over time. This is a view which is now discussed in more detail.

2.4 Strategy development as the outcome of cultural and political processes

This part of the chapter explains how the development of strategies can be explained in cultural terms (section 2.4.1) and as a political or networking process (section 2.4.2). It then brings these explanations together and shows their relevance in the context of how strategic decisions are made in organisations (section 2.4.3).

2.4.1 The cultural view

Organisational culture is the 'deeper level of basic *assumptions and beliefs* that are shared by members of an organisation, that operate unconsciously and define in a basic taken-for-granted fashion an organisation's view of itself and its environment'.[15] Management cannot be conceived of just in terms of the manipulation of techniques or tools of analysis; it is also about the application of experience built up over years often within the same organisation or industry. This is rooted not only in individual experience, but also in group and organisational experience accumulated over time. It is therefore important to recognise the significance of cultural aspects of management.

This taken-for-grantedness is likely to be handed down over time within a group. That group might be, for example, a managerial function such as marketing or finance; a professional grouping, such as accountants; an organisation as a whole; and more widely an industry sector, or even a national culture. There are, then, many cultural frames of reference which influence managers: Figure 2.6 shows this graphically and Illustration 2.4 gives examples of 'taken-for-grantedness' at the regional and industry levels (sometimes called an *industry recipe*).[16] Such taken-for-granted assumptions

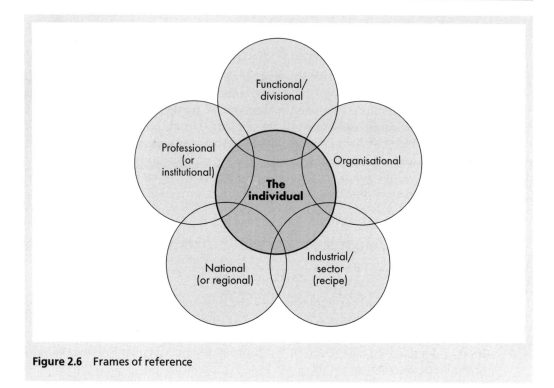

Figure 2.6 Frames of reference

are also likely to exist at the organisational level — the organisational *paradigm*[17] — and can be especially important as an influence on the development of organisational strategy.

An organisation's paradigm can be traced to different influences:

- An organisation with a relatively stable management, and a long-term *momentum of strategy*, is likely to have a more homogeneous paradigm than one in which there has been rapid turnover of management and significant change forced upon it.
- Organisations with a dominant *professional influence*, perhaps an accountancy firm, are likely to demonstrate a homogeneous paradigm.
- *Industry influences* may be particularly strong if the transfer of staff between firms tends to be limited to that industry, as it often is in engineering, banking and many parts of the public sector, for example.

The paradigm includes the sort of *assumptions* which are rarely talked about, which are not considered problematic, and about which managers are unlikely to be explicit. It is likely to evolve gradually rather than change rapidly. For an organisation to operate effectively there has to be such a generally accepted set of assumptions; in effect, it represents *collective experience* without which people would have to 'reinvent their world' for different circumstances that they face. The paradigm allows the experience

Illustration 2.4   A cultural perspective: taken-for-grantedness at regional and industry levels

Shared assumptions help explain the way business is done and strategy develops.

At regional level: the overseas Chinese in East Asia[1]

■ The Chinese work hard not only because they have been brought up to value hard work, associated material rewards and social esteem, but also because they believe financial success brings honour to their ancestors.

■ A high value is placed on human relations and trust, built on social obligation. If an overseas Chinese fails to demonstrate trustworthiness to members of the business community, credits and financial help will not be extended and exclusion from the overseas Chinese network locally and internationally is likely.

■ Harmony and reciprocity are emphasised, with an avoidance of confrontation and business relationships dictated by legality. To initiate business relationships, Chinese entrepreneurs never approach one another directly, but rather use a mutual acquaintance, who acts as the matchmaker. Relationships begin with minor transactions with little risk involved and little trust required. Gradually, larger exchanges involving more risks and greater mutual trust are transacted.

■ Mythological influences affect business: for example, that the Japanese race had its origins in China, explaining why so much business is done with the Japanese.

At industry sector level: producers in the Scottish knitwear industry[2]
Managers in the industry assume:

■ Scottish firms are not good at designing high-fashion garments.

■ The competitive boundaries of the industry are defined to include only Scottish producers. Other knitwear producers, even elsewhere in the UK, are in a different industry.

■ Only gentlemanly competition is permitted on the basis of design, service and quality. Price competition is frowned upon.

■ Retailer satisfaction, achieved through producing small lots of customised garments, is the key to success.

■ Scottish producers only ever buy dyed yarn from local suppliers which are considered to be the best. Machinery will never fully replace the labour-intensive, highly skilled methods of hand finishing.

■ Design, service and quality are more important than price to the consumer.

■ Consumers are from the top 5 per cent of wage earners, so demand will be price inelastic.

Sources:
[1] D.C.L. Ch'ng, *The Overseas Chinese Entrepreneurs in East Asia*, Committee for Economic Development of Australia, December 1993.
[2] J.F. Porac, H. Thomas and C. Baden-Fuller, 'Competitive groups as cognitive communities: the case of Scottish knitwear manufacturers', *Journal of Management Studies*, vol. 26, no. 4 (1989) pp. 397–416.

Prepared by Sara Martin, Cranfield School of Management.

Figure 2.7 The role of the paradigm in strategy formulation

gathered over years to be applied to a given situation to make sense of it, to conceive of a likely course of action and the likelihood of success of that course of action. The paradigm is not, then, the same as the explicit *values* of an organisation, though these may be informed by the paradigm; nor is it the same as the *strategy* of an organisation, though that, too, will be informed by the paradigm.

The relationship between the paradigm and organisational strategy needs to be made clear. Figure 2.7 helps to do this. Environmental forces and organisational capabilities do not in themselves create organisational strategy; people create strategy. The forces at work in the environment, and the organisation's capabilities in coping with these, are made sense of in terms of the individual experience[18] of managers and the collective assumptions within the paradigm. However, environmental forces and organisational capabilities, while having this indirect influence on strategy formulation, nonetheless impact on organisational performance more directly. For example, many consumer goods companies which were very powerful in the 1970s lost significant market share as grocery retail chains became bigger and buying power became more centralised. Initially, many failed to recognise the impact such changes would have on them. Their view about market structure assumed direct influence by them over consumer buying behaviour; the retailer was seen just as a distributor. It took many years for some to come to terms with the fact that the retailers had become of major strategic importance as customers in their own right. The consumer goods companies' strategies continued to be driven by their long-established paradigms, while the behaviour of the retailers — for example, in moving to other suppliers — directly affected their performance, for many resulting in loss of market share and profits, and for some eventual takeover. The potential difference between the actual influences and managerial perceptions of the influences on the organisation can give rise to significant problems — and is an issue returned to later.

The taken-for-grantedness in organisations or industries may, then, have very conservative influence on strategy. This is the more so since, at the organisational level at least, it is likely to be linked to other aspects of organisational culture, such as organisational *rituals*, *stories* and the everyday *routines* of organisational life. Section 2.8.1 of this chapter considers further how these wider cultural aspects of organisations are linked to other aspects of strategic management.

2.4.2 Organisational politics and networks

Strategy development can also be explained in political terms.[19] Powerful internal and external interest groups in organisations can influence the different inputs into decisions.

- Different interest groups (or *stakeholders*) may have different expectations and may even be in conflict; there may be differences between groups of managers, between managers and shareholders, or between powerful individuals. These differences are resolved through processes of *bargaining*, *negotiation* or perhaps *edict*.
- Powerful individuals or groups may also influence the sort of *information* that is seen to be important. Information is not politically neutral, but rather can be a source of power for those who control what is seen to be important; so the withholding of information, or the influences of one manager over another because that manager controls sources of information, can be important.
- Powerful individuals and groups may also strongly influence the *identification of key issues*, the *objectives* of the organisation and even the strategies eventually selected. Differing views may be pursued not only on the basis of the extent to which they reflect environmental or competitive pressures, for example, but also because they have implications for the status or influence of different stakeholders.

Even if an organisation is not overtly political in such ways, it is important to understand the extent to which the relationships between individuals, perhaps built up over many years, may be important. There are those who explain organisational working on the basis of *social networks*.[20] Here organisations are not depicted as hierarchies or power groupings, so much as different interest groups or operations which need to co-operate with each other, negotiate what should be done and find ways of accommodating different views. For example, in professional services firms such as accountants or lawyers, partners may not be organised hierarchically, but will have co-operated and found ways of working with each other over many years. Those managers who work for them may, similarly, have worked for many years in the firm and have become trusted by the partners. In such circumstances, it is likely that decisions will come about as a result of the discussions and, again, bargaining that goes on within the social interaction and networks that exist between such individuals. Such patterns also exist in more conventional commercial organisations. A multinational firm working on a global scale is unlikely to be solely reliant on formal structural processes to make things happen. It is likely that it will be dependent on the network of contacts that builds up over time between different parts of the organisation.

Such a perspective on decision making, whether seen as explicitly political or more to do with networks, therefore suggests that strategies may emerge through processes of bargaining and negotiation (see Illustration 2.5). Understanding the influence of such processes is important; Chapter 5 returns to this in more detail.

2.4.3 Cultural and political processes in strategic decision making

Studies which have traced how particular strategic decisions are made in organisations[21] show how cultural and political processes play a part in strategy development. These processes are represented in Figure 2.8.

The *awareness* of strategic issues in organisations is not necessarily an analytical process; rather, people get a 'gut feeling' based on their previous experience. These people may not be managers; they may be those in most direct contact with whatever stimulates this awareness, such as sales staff dealing with customers. This awareness 'incubates' as various stimuli help build up a picture of the extent to which circumstances deviate from what is normally to be expected, perhaps in terms of internal performance measures such as turnover or profit performance; or perhaps customer reaction to the quality and price of service or products. This accumulation of stimuli eventually reaches a point where the presence of a problem cannot be ignored. Typically, a *triggering point* is reached when the formal information systems of the organisation highlight the problem; a variance against budget may become undeniable or a number of sales areas may consistently report dropping sales. At this stage, however, issues may still be ill-defined.

Issue formulation involves a number of processes. Information gathering

Illustration 2.5   Negotiation, networking and political activity

Managers explain how strategies may come about through processes of negotiation, networking or political activity.

Bargaining and negotiation
'There is negotiation in the sense that strategy is generated by the management team trying to work out amongst themselves who gets what in what way. Then it is a political process, the top management team negotiating amongst themselves where they should be.'

'There is always some sort of jockeying for position, but it is a fairly equal balance in terms of power, I suppose. We tend to be reasonably open about bidding for power in terms of developing strategy and bidding for resources for those strategies.'

Networking
'It's very, very baronial: it's very much strategy development on the informal network, which, as an outsider, is difficult. I found this one of the hardest companies to get into because of the informal networks. Things are done through a "my mates will sort it out for me" approach.'

'If you get some partners, partners who are perhaps less influential, but bring other partners along with them, then clearly they will have a certain amount of success because they will have backing. And if you have got a clear strategic thinker, but he doesn't have the backing of the partnership, then clearly that is going to be a barrier to making progress.'

Political activity
'The politics of what he [the leader] wants and the senior executives want will pervade strategy as, at the lower level, will the individual strategies of individual managers . . . I wouldn't view it negatively; I would say in terms of our organisation that whilst people have agendas, those agendas are up front, rather than hidden — although common sense and experience tells me that this isn't always the case.'

'It's partly to do with the fact that we are structured in directorates and the directorates tend to try and fight their own corner, and there are times when one directorate will quite clearly be more powerful than another one. It's partly been based on the individuals concerned; powerful individuals who have been around for a long time.'

Source: Quotes from interviews conducted by A. Bailey as part of a research project sponsored by the Economic and Social Research Council (Grant No.: R000235100).

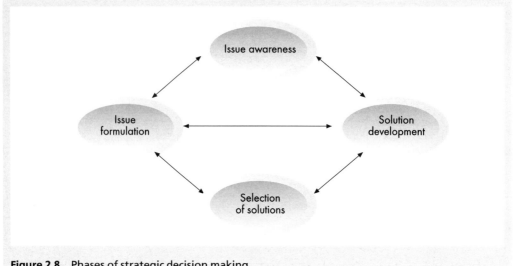

Figure 2.8   Phases of strategic decision making

takes place, but not always in a highly structured, objective manner. Information is likely to be sought and gathered on a verbal and informal basis, though this may be supplemented through more formal analysis. However, the rationalisation of information so as to clarify the situation draws heavily on *managerial experience*. The role of information generated from more formalised analysis is often to post-rationalise or legitimise managers' emerging views of the situation.

Through *debate and discussion*, there may be an attempt to reach an organisational view on the problem to be tackled. The emerging view therefore takes shape in terms of both individual and collective experience, with different views resolved through political processes or by drawing on social networks. It may also be that these processes of issue formulation trigger a different problem; or it may be that no consensus is reached and the issue may re-enter an information-gathering phase. So the process tends to be interactive.

It is worth noting that there is an underlying assumption in much management literature that *consensus* is a 'good thing' because it facilitates collective action and a clear understanding about strategy. However, the evidence on this is equivocal.[22] It can be argued that a lack of consensus encourages challenge, questioning and experimentation. It may be that consensus is beneficial in some circumstances, perhaps when the organisation is facing crisis or needs to make changes quickly; but that in circumstances where the organisation has time to develop strategies and to 'play with ideas' a lack of consensus may be of benefit given the sorts of iterative process described here.

In *developing solutions*, managers typically 'search' for known, existing or tried solutions; or wait for possible solutions to emerge. It is likely that there will be a number of these searches in which managers draw on experience before design of a solution custom-built to address the problem is attempted. Managers begin with a rather vague idea of a possible solution and refine it by recycling it through selection routines (see below) back into problem identification or through further search routines. The process is based on debate and discussion within the organisation and collective management wisdom and experience.

The process of developing solutions may, then, overlap with processes of *selecting solutions*. They might be regarded as part of the same process, in which a limited number of potential solutions get reduced until one or more emerges. It is not so much formal analysis which plays the major role here, but managerial judgement, negotiation and bargaining. It should also be remembered that the process might well be taking place below the most senior levels of management, so referring possible solutions to a higher hierarchical level may be required, and another way of selecting between possibilities may be to seek this authorisation.

Studies of how strategic decisions are made therefore suggest that they emerge as the *outcome* of managerial experience within a social, political and cultural context, even if formal planning procedures exist.

In some respects, this is reflected in the different ways in which many organisations now set about the development of strategy. For example, in the last decade there has been a substantial growth of *strategy workshops*. These may be for senior groups of managers, perhaps the board of an organisation. Other organisations have recognised that such workshops might beneficially involve a wider community, including managers from different levels and, for example, operatives experienced in dealing with customers, suppliers and so on. The participants remove themselves from day-to-day responsibilities to tackle strategic issues facing their organisation. Such events may well use the sorts of techniques of analysis and planning employed in this book. However, rather than just relying on such tools and techniques to throw up strategic solutions, a successful workshop process is likely to work through issues in face-to-face debate and discussion, drawing on and surfacing different experiences, interests and views.

2.5   Imposed strategy development

2.5.1 Enforced choice

There may be situations in which managers face enforced choice of strategy. Government may dictate a particular strategic course of direction — for example, in the public sector, or where it exercises extensive regulation over an industry — or choose to deregulate or privatise an organisation previously in the public sector. In the 1980s and early 1990s in many countries, governments decided to privatise public utilities and deregulate state-controlled enterprises. In the privatisation plans for British Rail in the 1990s, it was the government which laid down the overall industry structure. This included setting up Railtrack as a free-standing business controlling tracks and many of the stations, such that newly established rail-operating businesses running the trains would be required to become customers of Railtrack. This was not a choice of the managers, it was the intent of government. Businesses in the private sector may also be subject to such enforced direction, or significant constraints. The multinational corporation seeking to develop businesses in some parts of the world may be subject to governmental requirements to do this in certain ways, perhaps through joint ventures or local alliances. An operating business within a multidivisional organisation may regard the overall corporate strategic direction of its parent as akin to enforced choice; or a subsidiary may have strategies imposed on it from corporate head office.

2.5.2 The environment as constraint

In some organisations, managers see their scope of strategic choice as severely limited. For example, in the oil industry, senior executives argue that they have to manage strategy for a commodity in a market dominated by raw material prices and availability, and that all they can do is to keep costs down, learn to be as good as possible at forecasting changes in that environment and respond as rapidly as possible to such changes.

Some writers argue that the strategic choice available to an organisation is severely limited;[23] that the environment is such a dominant influence that most organisations, perhaps other than those that are very large, are unable to influence their operating environments — they merely buffer themselves from, or respond to, changes in that environment. Such strategy development as exists occurs through a process similar to that of *natural selection*. Variations occur within the sort of organisational processes, structures and systems described in section 2.4 above. These variations may be more or less relevant to the environmental pressures that the organisation faces, and therefore may result in one organisation performing better, or worse, than another. Those organisations that perform better may then be able to retain, duplicate or reduce such positive variations, and so improve their standing in relation to other organisations.

There are, then, different ways in which the world external to an organisation, in the form of its environment, the government or its parent body, may exercise significant influence such that degrees of managerial latitude are severely reduced. It is the view in this book that, while this may be so for managers in some organisations, it is not so for all; and that, even where such pressures are severe, it is the job of managers to develop the skills and strategies to cope with the situation. This is the point made by Baden-Fuller and Stopford[24] in their study of businesses in mature, often unattractive, industry environments. It was the firms with managers who could develop strategies to overcome such apparently constraining environments which performed well.

2.6   A note on strategic vision

The idea of strategic *vision* was introduced in Chapter 1. How such a vision might emerge demonstrates that no one explanation given above is likely to provide a complete explanation of how strategies develop. For example, a strategic vision might be deliberately formulated as part of the planning process in an organisation. Or it might be associated more personally with the founder of a business and perhaps have become embedded in the history and culture of the organisation. This seems to be the case for IKEA, where the original vision of Ingvar Kamprad to provide good-value furniture at a price all could afford has become part of the paradigm.

Vision might also be associated with an external agency's imposition of strategy. Those public sector organisations subject to the privatisation and deregulation of the UK government of Mrs Thatcher in the 1980s, or the rapid movement towards the free market in the Czech Republic after 1989, have been affected by the 'vision' of governments.

Vision could also be thought of as related to intuition. Some writers suggest that strategic management has so consistently emphasised the importance of analysis — as in the planning view — that the role of intuition has been neglected.[25] They argue that setting up new businesses, new ventures, turnaround and new strategies are the product of creative management rather than detailed planning. This may be associated with executives of especially high intuitive capacity, who see what other managers do not see and espouse new ways of working. However, the extent to which such intuition has an effect on strategy is likely to depend on the power or influence of the intuitive manager. So the outcome of the intuition may be seen as a 'vision' associated with the 'command' of a leader, or a political process of influence if the manager is in a more junior position.

2.7   Configurations of strategy development processes[26]

What has been provided in sections 2.3 to 2.6 are different explanations of how strategies develop. However, it is likely that elements of these will be found in

Profile	Dominant dimensions	Characteristics
(a) Logical incremental	Planning Incrementalism	Standardised planning procedures Systematic data collection and analyses Constant environmental scanning On-going adjustment of strategy Tentative commitment to strategy Step-by-step, small-scale change
(b) Rational command	Planning Command	Senior figure determines and directs strategy Strong vision or mission Definite and precise objectives Analysis and evaluation of environments Clear plans
(c) Muddling through	Cultural Political Incremental	Bargaining, negotiation and compromise accommodate conflicting interests of groups Powerful groups with control over critical resources more likely to influence strategy Standardised 'way of doing things' Routines and procedures embedded in organisational history Deeply rooted beliefs and assumptions Strong resistance to change Gradual adjustments to strategy
(d) Externally dependent	Enforced choice Political	Strategy is imposed by external forces (e.g. legislation, parent organisation) Freedom of choice severely restricted Groups dealing with the environment have greater influence over strategy Political activity within organisation and between environment likely Externally driven strategy

Key: PL = Planning; I = Incrementalism; CU = Cultural; PO = Political; CO = Command; EC = Enforced choice.

Figure 2.9   Configurations of strategy development processes

Rather than	Organisational type and context
Intrusive external environment Dominant individuals Political processes Power groups	Manufacturing and service sector organisations Stable or growing markets Mature Benign environment
Pronounced political influences Traditional 'way of doing things' External forces determine strategy	Large manufacturing and financial services businesses Growing and stable markets Competitive environment
Analytic, evaluative 'rationality' Deliberate, intentional process Managers in control of organisation's destiny Well-defined procedures Analytic evaluation and planning Externally driven strategy Deliberate managerial intent	Professional service firms (e.g. consultancy or law firms) Unstable, turbulent environment New and growing markets
Strategy determined within the organisation Planning systems impact on strategy development Managers influence strategic direction	Public sector organisations and larger manufacturing and financial service subsidiaries Threatening, declining, unstable and hostile environments Low sales growth and market share increase

Illustration 2.6 Configurations of strategy development processes

The characteristics of two of the strategy development configurations are evident in how managers in a law firm and in local government explain how strategy comes about in their organisations.

Muddling through
'Muddling Through' characterises a strategy development process in which the political and cultural dimensions are dominant resulting in an incremental process of strategy development. Such a configuration is often a feature of professional service firms. Strategy evolves over time in tune with well established 'ways of doing things', guided by a strong professional ethos and influenced by bargaining and negotiating behaviour between influential groups or individuals. The following quotes from partners of a law firm illustrate this:

'... clearly there are different groups of partners some of whom have greater influence than others. In developing strategy there will be a greater chance of them being successful if they have performed well in the past and are seen to be a core part of the firm'.

'There will be partners who are persuasive because they have ideas and usually because their fee-earning is spectacularly good. Anybody who earns a lot of money for the firm tends to have more credence than anybody who doesn't, however good their ideas are.'

'Sometimes we have to make concessions to partners if we favour a certain direction or option, in order to encourage them to accept the idea.'

'I think it comes back to the structure of the partnership; that to have successful strategy you have to take the vast majority of the partners along with you.'

Externally dependent
This configuration is often found within public sector organisations. The strategy development process is characterised by external enforced choice with strategy developed in response to forces such as legislation. Political influences also impinge as groups or individuals dominate the process, bargaining for limited resources between departments or because it is they who are negotiating with the external authority. The following quotes from members of a local government council illustrate this:

'We feel severely constrained by the policies of central government and the community influence is also quite strong — sometimes vociferously articulated by interest groups who lobby members'.

'Whatever the Government says, in terms of how it approaches local authorities, has a massive effect on where we go'.

'There is obviously the overlay of the party political situation and that has a lot of impact in terms of whether we can, or how we can, go forward in particular ways'.

'I think it's intensely political, we are structured in directorates, directorates tend to try and fight their own corner and it's partly based on the actual individuals concerned. There are the big directorates — housing and environment — which will always have an awful lot of power in the sense of getting things done and not getting things done'

Prepared by Clare Avery, Cranfield School of Management.

all organisations to a greater or lesser extent. Different processes account for the development of strategy; and the mix of such processes is likely to differ by organisation or organisational context, forming *configurations of strategy development*. Figure 2.9 shows some of these configurations graphically and summarises the dominant characteristics of each as managers see them, as well as the organisational contexts of each. Although it is not suggested that these configurations define precisely how strategy develops across all organisations, they represent typical general tendencies of strategy development according to a number of organisational contexts. Illustration 2.6 also gives fuller examples of two of the configurations.

A number of observations can be made about these configurations which help our understanding of strategy development processes.

1. Unidimensional processes of strategy development are not common in practice. For example, elements of planning are commonly evident but in conjunction with other processes of strategy development.

2. There seem to be two overarching explanations given by the managers about strategy development. Figure 2.9(a) and (b) represent views of strategy development which are essentially proactive, planning, rational views of the process. Figure 2. 9(c) and (d) emphasise more cultural and political processes in organisations. If the command dimension is considered too, it further emphasises the importance of managerial experience, since individuals who take a lead in strategy development are likely to do so on the basis of their experience not just analytical procedures.

3. There is evidence that these two overall views may arise because of the experience of how strategies develop at different levels in the organisation. The more rational, planning view of strategy tends to be seen most by senior executives, particularly chief executives. The cultural and political processes tend to be seen most by managers below the level of the board. This is, perhaps, not surprising, since it may be the chief executives who have put into place planning procedures, whereas the managers are operating on an everyday basis within the culture of the organisation.

    The notion of incrementalism, for example, can therefore be explained in two ways: first, as represented by Figure 2.9(a), which describes it as an essentially logical incremental process; and second, as represented by Figure 2.9(c), which acknowledges that strategy changes incrementally, but sees this as the outcome of cultural and political processes. It could be that in the same organisation it is evident that strategies do change incrementally; but different explanations of this might be forthcoming from the chief executive, for example, than from managers in the organisation.

4. There is some evidence that different configurations are associated with different contexts. The *logical incremental* (Figure 2.9(a)) account of strategy development is most commonly to be found among managers in organisations in relatively stable or benign environments. The *rational command* (Figure 2.9(b)) dimension, on the other hand, tends to be most evident in hostile or competitive organisational environments. *Muddling through* (Figure 2.9(c)) is commonly found in professional service type businesses, where there may be many influential partners and long-established traditions. Not surprisingly, the *externally dependent* (Figure 2.9(d)) account is found in public sector organisations or subsidiaries of conglomerates where there is a likelihood of strategy being imposed from outside the organisation.

5. It is difficult to relate these configurations to organisational performance. The suggestion that one particular configuration is better than another is problematic because what might be best for a small independent manufacturing company might be inappropriate for accountancy or a law partnership. Such evidence as does exist suggests that organisations which change incrementally seem to perform better than those that do not. However, this could be because incremental change tends to take place in environments which are relatively benign or stable; so it may not be the processes of incrementalism which account for the success, but the nature of the environment they are in.

The overall lesson is that there is no one way in which strategies develop. It matters that those who are seeking to influence strategy development in organisations are aware of, and can take account of, the processes actually at work in the organisations. For example, in an organisation strongly dominated by a commanding figure, or by the cultural and political processes of the organisation, it may be a mistake to assume that the introduction of formal planning procedures will necessarily lead to more effective strategy formulation. Quite possibly, such procedures will be seen as peripheral or bureaucratic.

2.8   Challenges in strategy development

So far this chapter has concentrated on explaining how strategies develop in organisations. In this section, implications arising from these explanations are raised which form some of the challenges in trying to manage the process. There are two key issues underlying these challenges. The first is the evident influence of managerial experience within a political and cultural organisational context. A clear understanding of how such influences come about and their impact is important. A framework — the *cultural web* — which provides this understanding is introduced; the implications are then discussed in terms of the risk of *strategic drift* in organisations.

The second key issue is the difficulty that organisations face in developing strategies in complex, changing environments; and the possibility that traditional mechanistic ways of doing so are inadequate. The notion of the *learning organisation* is therefore discussed.

2.8.1 The cultural web[27]

Trying to understand the culture of an organisation is clearly important, but it is not straightforward. A strategy and the values of an organisation may be written down, but the underlying assumptions which make up the paradigm are usually evident only in the day-to-day conversation or discussions of people; or may be so taken-for-granted that they can be observed only in what people actually do. To understand the taken-for-grantedness may, then, mean being very sensitive to signals from the wider culture of an organisation. Indeed, it is especially important to understand these wider aspects because not only do they give clues about the paradigm, but they are also likely to reinforce the assumptions within that paradigm. In effect, they are the representation in organisational action of what is

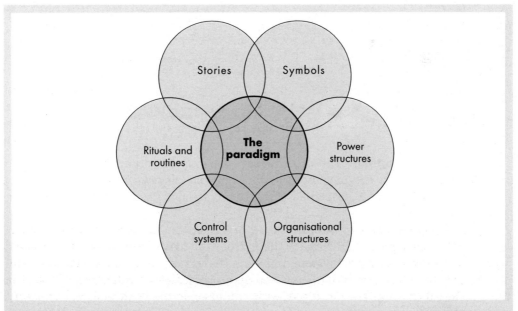

Figure 2.10   The cultural web of an organisation

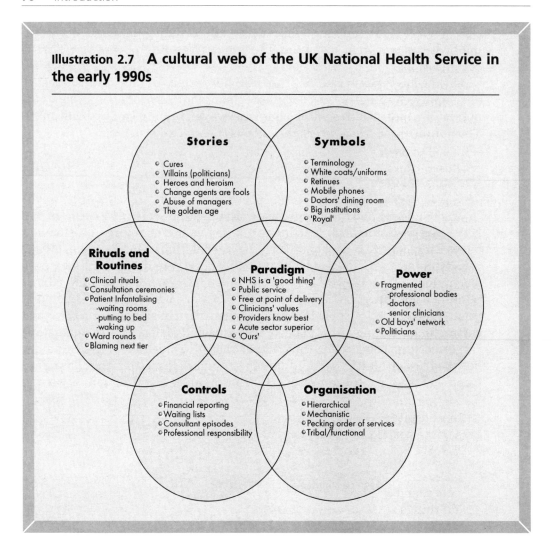

Illustration 2.7 A cultural web of the UK National Health Service in the early 1990s

Stories
- Cures
- Villains (politicians)
- Heroes and heroism
- Change agents are fools
- Abuse of managers
- The golden age

Symbols
- Terminology
- White coats/uniforms
- Retinues
- Mobile phones
- Doctors' dining room
- Big institutions
- 'Royal'

Rituals and Routines
- Clinical rituals
- Consultation ceremonies
- Patient Infantalising
  - waiting rooms
  - putting to bed
  - waking up
- Ward rounds
- Blaming next tier

Paradigm
- NHS is a 'good thing'
- Public service
- Free at point of delivery
- Clinicians' values
- Providers know best
- Acute sector superior
- 'Ours'

Power
- Fragmented
  - professional bodies
  - doctors
  - senior clinicians
- Old boys' network
- Politicians

Controls
- Financial reporting
- Waiting lists
- Consultant episodes
- Professional responsibility

Organisation
- Hierarchical
- Mechanistic
- Pecking order of services
- Tribal/functional

taken-for-granted. These different aspects of organisational culture, together with the paradigm itself, comprise the *cultural web* (see Figure 2.10) and are now described using Illustration 2.7 as a basis for discussing its relevance.

It is important to stress that all organisations must develop a degree of coherence in their culture for them to be able to function effectively. Indeed, at its best a cultural system, in which the various parts of the organisation are all working to a common end, can provide great advantage. It will be shown in Chapters 4 and 10 that it can provide the very basis of *competitive advantage* in markets because it may prove so difficult to imitate. However, it may also be very difficult to change. There are those who argue[28] that organisations are captured by their own cultures, which are the product of history, or the product of institutional forces that exist across organisations: that professional service firms all tend to behave in the same way; that organisations in the public sector have common cultures; that engineering firms tend to be similar and so on. Certainly, the evidence is that organisational cultures are not easy to change, and that therefore they can impair the development of organisational strategies. This is an issue returned to particularly in Chapter 11.

Illustration 2.7 shows a cultural web drawn up by trust managers in the National Health Service in the UK in 1994, shortly after trusts were established. It is now used as a basis for explaining the cultural web. (It should, however, be borne in mind that this is the view of managers; clinicians might well have quite different views.)

The assumptions within the *paradigm* reflect the common public perception in the UK that the NHS is 'a good thing'; a public service which should be provided equally, free of charge. However, it is medical values that are central and, in general, those providing them who know best. This is an organisation about the provision of medical care for those who are ill, subtly different from an organisation to serve the needs of those who are ill, and quite different from serving the needs of those who are not ill — for example, pregnancy is not an illness, but pregnant women often argue that hospitals treat them as though they have one. Overall, the NHS is seen as 'belonging' to those who provide the services; and it is the acute sector within hospitals which is central to the service rather than, for example, care in the community.

The other elements of the cultural web include the following.

1. The *routine* ways that members of the organisation behave towards each other, and towards those outside the organisation, make up 'the way we do things around here'. At its best, this lubricates the working of the organisation, and may provide a distinctive and beneficial organisational competency.[29] However, it can also represent a taken-for-grantedness about how things should happen which is extremely difficult to change and protective of core assumptions in the paradigm. For most of its history, doctors and nurses in the NHS, indeed patients too, took for granted that the doctor or nurse knew best. This took form, for example, in routines of consultation and of prescribing drugs. A hospital might espouse 'patient care', but staff would find it unusual, even uncomfortable, if patients exercised this in terms of questioning and challenging the wisdom of a doctor or a course of medication.

2. The *rituals* of organisational life are the special events through which the organisation emphasises what is particularly important and reinforces 'the way we do things around here'. Examples of ritual can include relatively formal organisational processes — training

programmes, interview panels, promotion and assessment procedures, sales conferences and so on. An extreme example, of course, is the ritualistic training of army recruits to prepare them for the discipline required in conflict. However, rituals can also be thought of as relatively informal processes such as drinks in the pub after work or gossiping round photocopying machines. A checklist of rituals is provided in Chapter 11 (see Figure 11.7).

In the NHS, rituals had to do with what the managers termed 'infantilising', which 'put patients in their place' — making them wait, putting them to bed, waking them up and so on. The subservience of patients was further emphasised by the elevation of clinicians with ritual consultation ceremonies and ward rounds. These are routines and rituals which emphasise that it is the professionals who are in control. Overall, the rituals and routines are about ensuring that everyone 'knows their place'. They also had the effect, at least for the clinicians, of formalising relationships and thus distancing them from patients.

3. The *stories*[30] told by members of the organisation to each other, to outsiders, to new recruits and so on, embed the present in its organisational history and also flag up important events and personalities. They typically have to do with successes, disasters, heroes, villains and mavericks who deviate from the norm. They distil the essence of an organisation's past, legitimise types of behaviour and are devices for telling people what is important in the organisation.

   For example, it can be argued that the dominant culture of the health service in many countries is one of curing sickness rather than promoting health; and most of the stories within health services concern developments in curing — particularly terminal illnesses. The heroes of the health service are in curing, not so much in caring. By 1994, many in the NHS regarded the system as under attack by government changes, so it is perhaps not surprising that there were also stories about villainous politicians trying to change the system, the failure of those who try to make changes, and tales about their mistakes and of heroic acts by those defending the system (often well-known medical figures).

4. *Symbols*,[31] such as logos, offices, cars and titles, or the type of language and terminology commonly used, become a short-hand representation of the nature of the organisation. For example, in long-established or conservative organisations it is likely that there will be many symbols of hierarchy or deference to do with formal office layout, differences in privileges between levels of management, the way in which people address each other and so on. In turn this formalisation may reflect difficulties in changing strategies within a hierarchical or deferential system. The form of language used in an organisation can also be

particularly revealing, especially with regard to customers or clients. For example, the chief executive of a retail chain described customers as 'the b.....s with our money in their pockets'; and the head of a consumer protection agency in Australia described his clients as 'complainers'. In a major teaching hospital in the UK, consultants described patients as 'clinical material'. While such examples might be amusing, they reveal an underlying assumption about customers (or patients) which might play a significant role in influencing the realised strategy of an organisation. The sort of distancing from the emotional side of patient care in a hospital inherent in such terminology is likely to be reflected in behaviour and therefore in realised strategy.

Other symbols in the NHS reflected the various institutions within the organisation, with uniforms for clinical and nursing staff, distinct symbols for clinicians, such as their staff retinues, and status symbols such as mobile phones and dining rooms. The importance of the size and status of physical buildings was reflected, not least, in the designation of 'Royal' in the name of a hospital, seen as a key means of ensuring that it might withstand the threat of closure.

Although symbols are shown separately in the cultural web, it should be remembered that many elements of the web are symbolic, in the sense that they convey messages beyond their functional purpose. Routines, control and reward systems and structures are symbolic in so far as they signal the type of behaviour valued in an organisation.

5. *Power structures* are also likely to be associated with the key constructs of the paradigm. The paradigm is, in some respects, the 'formula for success', which is taken for granted and likely to have grown up over years. The most powerful managerial groupings within the organisation are likely to be closely associated with this set of core assumptions and beliefs.[32]

For example, accountancy firms may now offer a whole range of services, but typically the most powerful individuals or groups have been qualified accountants with a set of assumptions about the business and its market rooted in the audit practice. It could, of course, be that power is not just based on seniority. In some organisations, power could be lodged within other levels or functions: for example, with technical experts in a hi-tech firm. In the NHS, the power structure was fragmented between, for example, clinicians, nursing and management in the organisation, each of which had its own symbolic distinctions. However, historically senior clinicians were the most powerful and managers had hitherto been seen as 'administration'. As with many other organisations, there was a strong informal network of individuals and groups which coalesced around specific issues to promote or resist a particular view.

6. The *control systems*, measurements and reward systems emphasise what it is important to monitor in the organisation, and to focus attention and activity upon. For example, public service organisations have often been accused of being concerned more with stewardship of funds than with quality of service; and in their procedures, more with accounting for spending than with regard for outputs. This was reflected in the NHS with an emphasis on financial controls and reporting. Reward systems are important influences on behaviours, but can also prove to be a barrier to success of new strategies. For example, an organisation with individually based bonus schemes related to volume could find it difficult to promote strategies requiring teamwork and an emphasis on quality rather than volume.

7. *Organisational structure* is likely to reflect power structures and, again, delineate important relationships and emphasise what is important in the organisation. Both structural and control aspects of the NHS were formal: formal hierarchical, mechanistic structures with a lot of reporting of a financial nature, but also monitoring of waiting lists and the time taken by consultants to see patients, reflecting assumptions about what patient care involved. However, underlying formal structures and controls were the less formal systems, described as 'tribal', relating to the professional constraints and norms that exercised control over individuals; and the 'old boys network', which allowed the organisation to come together, particularly under threat. Moreover, participants pointed out that, when it came to organisation and control, the formal systems had been largely imposed on them: 'it is not what the NHS is all about; they are just the measures placed upon people'.

The overall picture of the NHS was of a system fundamentally about medical practice, fragmented in its power bases historically, with a division between clinical aspects of the organisation and its management; indeed, a system in which management had traditionally been seen as relatively trivial. As one executive put it: 'there is an arrogance of clinicians, but it is a justifiable arrogance; after all, it is they who deliver on the shopfloor, not management'. The managers were not finding strategy development and strategic change easy to manage.

The cultural web is, then, a useful conceptual tool for understanding the underlying assumptions, linked to political, symbolic and structural aspects, of an organisation. How the web can be used analytically is discussed in section 5.5.6 of Chapter 5.

2.8.2 The risk of strategic drift[33]

The influence of the paradigm and 'the way we do things around here' is likely to have important implications for the development of strategy in organisations.

Faced with pressures for change, managers typically try to minimise the extent to which they are faced with ambiguity and uncertainty, by looking for that which is familiar. This raises difficulties when managing strategic change because it may be that the action required is outside the scope of the paradigm and the constraints of the cultural web, and that members of the organisation would therefore be required to change substantially their core assumptions and routines. Desirable as this may be, the evidence is that it does not occur easily. Managers are more likely to attempt to deal with the situation by searching for what they can understand and cope with in terms of the existing paradigm. Figure 2.11 illustrates how this might occur.[34] Faced with a stimulus for action — in this case, declining performance — managers first seek means of improving the implementation of existing strategy. This could be through tightening controls and improving the accepted way of operating. If this is not effective, a change of strategy may occur, but a change which is in line with the existing paradigm. For example, managers may seek to extend the market for their business, but assume that it will be similar to their existing market, and therefore set

Source: Adapted from P. Grinyer and J.-C. Spender, *Turnaround: Managerial recipes for strategic success*, Associated Business Press, 1979, p. 203

Figure 2.11 The dynamics of paradigm change

Figure 2.12   The risk of strategic drift

about managing the new venture in much the same way as they have been used to. There has been no change to the paradigm, and there is not likely to be until this attempt to reconstruct strategy in the image of the existing paradigm also fails. What is occurring is the predominant application of the familiar and the attempt to avoid or reduce uncertainty or ambiguity.

This is, of course, an alternative explanation of incremental strategy development. Indeed, it may be that changing the strategy within the paradigm makes sense: after all, it does encapsulate the experience of those in the organisation, and permits change to take place within what is familiar and understood. However, the outcome of processes of this kind may not be an adaptive approach which keeps strategy in line with environmental change, as shown in Figure 2.5. Rather, it may be adaptation in line with the experience enshrined in the paradigm. Nonetheless, the forces in the environment will have an effect on performance. Over time this may well give rise to the sort of *strategic drift* shown in Figure 2.12 (phase 1) in which the organisation's strategy gradually, if imperceptibly, moves away from addressing the forces at work in its environment. Illustration 2.8 shows how even the most successful companies may drift in this way. Indeed, they may become victims of the very success of their past.[35]

This pattern of drift is made more difficult to detect and reverse because not only are changes being made in strategy (albeit within the parameters of the paradigm), but, since such changes are the application of the familiar, they may achieve some short-term improvement in performance, thus tending to legitimise the action taken.

However, in time either the drift becomes apparent or environmental change increases, and performance is affected (phase 2 in Figure 2.12). Strategy development is then likely to go into a state of flux, with no clear direction (phase 3), further damaging performance. Eventually, more transformational change is likely, if the demise of the organisation is to be avoided (phase 4).

The paradigm is, therefore, an inevitable feature of organisational life which, in positive terms, can be thought of as encapsulating the distinctive competences of the organisation; or, more dangerously, as a conservative influence likely to prevent change and result in a momentum of strategy which can lead to strategic drift. Identifying when an organisation is at risk of, or in a state of, strategic drift is a challenge to the manager of strategy. Arguably, there is a fine dividing line between the organisation which is running smoothly and effectively, building on competences embedded in its culture, and an organisation which is at risk of drift. Some guidelines on symptoms of strategic drift are given as part of the discussion of the management of strategic change in Chapter 11 (see section 11.3.1).

This description of strategic drift conforms to the notion of a *lack of fit* with the environment. However, it is worth noting a different problem that organisations can face. Those organisations that seek to *stretch* what they regard as their core competences to create new opportunities could also find problems. In section 2.2.1, it was noted that transformational change might be attempted through the development of entirely new products or services which seek to create new customer needs and expectations not previously in existence. This could succeed and in so doing create a shift in the market in line with the intended strategy. However, there is the risk that such an organisation could find itself 'ahead' of its environment (represented by phase 5 in Figure 2.12). In the figure, the strategy and the environment eventually realign, but in reality this might not happen and the lag in time before such realignment could in any case cause significant problems, not least in performance.

All this goes to emphasise the delicate balance that an organisation faces in developing its strategy. It has internal cultural pressures which tend to constrain strategy development, and environmental forces, not least in terms of its markets, which it must cope with. How it might do so is the central theme of this book.

2.8.3 Uncertainty and the learning organisation

The speed of electronic communications across the world in the late 1990s could not have been conceived of by managers 20 or 30 years ago; major

Illustration 2.8   The Icarus Paradox

In The Icarus Paradox, Danny Miller draws a parallel between Icarus, who persisted in flying towards the sun and melted his wings, and exceptional companies which persist in pursuing previously successful strategies until they too become unstuck.

Miller identifies four 'trajectories' by which outstanding companies amplify their strengths to the point where 'one goal, one strategic vision, one department and one skill overwhelms all others': excesses and deficiencies very much related to their once successful strategies.

Craftsmen (the focusing trajectory) becoming Tinkerers

Founder Ken Olsen of Digital Equipment Corporation and his team of design engineers invented the minicomputer, a cheaper, more flexible alternative to its mainframe cousins. Digital honed their minis until they could not be beaten for quality and durability. Their VAX series proved highly reliable and the profits poured in.

But Digital turned into an engineering monoculture. Technological fine tuning became such an obsession that customers' needs for smaller machines, more economical products and more user-friendly systems were ignored. By focusing too closely on product refinement, customer needs and new markets were forgotten.

Builders (the venturing trajectory) becoming Imperialists

Harold S. Geneen, an entrepreneurial accountant, examined ITT's diverse operations and through divestment and consolidation forged a cohesive corporate entity. He installed state-of-the-art management information systems and built a head office corps of young executives to help him control his growing empire and identify opportunities for creative diversification.

changes in global political structures, such as the breaking up of the Soviet bloc in 1989, surprised even informed commentators; the extent to which scientific innovations will achieve medical breakthroughs, and when, is difficult to predict.

Chaos theorists[36] who write about management argue that the organisational world appears to be so turbulent and chaotic that it is not possible to predict what will happen or when, so traditional approaches to strategic management are simply not relevant. There is no point in formalised planning approaches with predetermined fixed objectives and analysis that may take weeks or months to work through. The idea that top managers can formulate strategies implemented by others becomes redundant because top managers are less in touch with such a complex and

Unfortunately, ITT's success at diversification and controlled decentralisation led to managers' overconfidence, resulting in 'too much of the same'. Consequently, diversification went from a selective tactic, to an engrained strategy, to a fanatical religion. ITT expanded and diversified too aggressively and indiscriminately.

Pioneers (the inventing trajectory) becoming Escapists

Rolls Royce was a most progressive, state-of-the-art aircraft engine manufacturer, with an impressive history of innovation — the first air-cooled turbine blades, turbo-fan engines and vertical take-off engine.

However, Rolls' unequalled history of design innovation was to be its downfall. Its senior executives were virtually all engineers concerned with engineering excellence; and when competing for the engine contract for Lockheed's Tristar, the design proved far too costly to develop and impossible to implement. Time delays, manufacturing problems and costs far exceeding budgets all plagued the project. The downfall was caused by dedicated engineers getting carried away by invention.

Salesmen (the decoupling trajectory) becoming Drifters

In his five years as CEO, Lynn Townsend doubled Chrysler's US market share and tripled its international share — a success due to aggressive marketing, involving forceful selling and promotion, and to sporty styling of the cars.

However, the company's concern with style and image led to a proliferation of product lines, the 'triumph of packaging over content' and a consequent lack of focus, which raised costs, reduced quality, confused the customer and heightened political tension in the organisation.

Source: Danny Miller, *The Icarus Paradox*, Harper Business, 1990.
Prepared by Roger Lazenby, Cranfield School of Management.

turbulent world than those in the organisation. The notion that there needs to be agreement and consensus around the issues facing the organisation is also questionable: the environment is too complex and rapidly changing for this to be likely or even desirable.

This means that strategy needs to be managed in a different way. The need is to build on a recognition of the innate ability of managers to draw on their experience, but to develop the capacity for this to be used more flexibly and in a *questioning, learning organisation*.[37] Rather than regarding experience as something which is fixed and a constraint on development, managers need to develop organisations in which they continually *challenge* such experience from the world around them and from the different experiences of their colleagues. To do this they need to develop organisations which are *pluralistic*, in which different, even conflicting ideas and views are welcomed; in which such differences are surfaced and become the basis of debate; in which experimentation is the norm. The job of top management is to create this sort of organisation by building teams that can work in such ways; by allowing enough *organisational slack* to allow time for debate and challenge. This may be done in a number of ways: for example, through the development of different types of organisational structure (see Chapter 9) and through the development of the everyday behaviour and culture of the organisation (see Chapters 10 and 11).

It is the view in this book that, while intuition and experience are of great importance, there is a fine dividing line between their positive contribution and the risk of false certainty based on such experience. In this book it is argued that the tools of analysis and planning can be used as bases for challenge and questioning, which are vital in a changing and unpredictable world.

2.9   Summary and implications for the study of strategy

This chapter has dealt with the processes of strategic management as they are to be found in organisations: it has therefore been descriptive rather than prescriptive. There is no suggestion here that, because such processes exist, this is how strategy *should* be managed. However, it is important to understand the reality of strategy development in organisations, not least because those who seek to influence the strategy of organisations must do so within that reality. Moreover, it is this book's intention that the subject should be approached in such a way that it builds upon this understanding of that reality.

Some of the lessons of this chapter are now summarised and related to what follows in the rest of the book.

- It is important to distinguish between the *intended* strategy of managers — that which they say the organisation should follow — and the *realised* strategy of an organisation — that which it is actually following. This is particularly important when considering how relevant current strategy is to a changing environment: it is likely to be more useful to consider the relevance of realised strategy than that of intended strategy.

- Strategy usually evolves *incrementally*: strategic change tends to occur as a continual process of relatively small adjustments to existing strategy, through activity within the subsystems of an organisation. However, there is likely to be an overall strategic direction, a strategic *momentum*, which is persistent over time.

- There are different explanations of how strategies develop in different ways in organisations.

- Formal *planning* (e.g. corporate planning systems or the techniques associated with this) may be important as an aid to analysing strategic positions and thinking through options, but it is not necessarily the vehicle by which strategies are developed.
- The incremental change in organisations can also be explained in terms of *cultural and political processes*, or by managers experimenting and *learning by doing*.
- Managers are likely to assess the need for strategic change through an essentially *qualitative assessment of signals* which accumulate from inside and outside the organisation.
- The definition of strategic issues and the choice of strategies by managers are sometimes based not on a dispassionate analysis of data, but (a) on perceptions of what powerful individuals in the organisation see as the problem, and (b) on the manager's reconciliation of the circumstances of the situation with past experience and the received wisdom encapsulated in the core assumptions and beliefs of the organisation, termed here the *paradigm*.
- The *cultural web* of an organisation — its political structures, routines, and rituals and symbols — is likely to exert a preserving and legitimising influence on the core beliefs and assumptions that comprise the paradigm, hence making strategic change more difficult to achieve.
- Over time the organisation may become out of line with a changing environment (*strategic drift*), eventually reaching a point of crisis. At this time, more fundamental or transformational change may occur.
- As environments become more unpredictable, however, the reliance on managerial experience, but within more flexible, *learning organisations*, becomes especially important. In such organisations, the surfacing of assumptions, explicit debate about them and a diversity of views are encouraged.

The approach taken in this book has been influenced by this understanding of how strategies develop in organisations. First, as has been said in Chapter 1, the idea of a purely sequential model of strategic management has been rejected. The headings of strategic analysis, choice and implementation are a useful structure for the book, and for thinking about the problems of strategy, but readers are urged to regard these aspects of strategic management as interdependent and an influence on one another.

This chapter has also highlighted the substantial influences of the beliefs and assumptions of the managers within a cultural setting. For this reason, emphasis is also placed in this book on the importance of understanding the nature of core assumptions (the paradigm) in an organisation, and the cultural and political context in which they exist. This chapter has provided a framework (the cultural web) by which such influences can be understood, and this framework is used elsewhere in the book. In Chapter 4 it is related to an analysis of core competences of organisations; and these are in turn considered in the development of competitive strategy, discussed in Chapters 6 and 10. In Chapter 5 the cultural web is used as a tool or checklist for analysing the relationship between strategy and culture. In Chapter 11 it is recognised that such aspects of the organisation provide a major stumbling block to the implementation of strategic change. The chapter therefore returns to the processes of strategic management with a view to examining how strategy and strategic change can be managed.

While the reality of judgement and the prevalence of bargaining processes in organisations are accepted, the book also contains examples of, and references to, many techniques of quantitative and qualitative analysis. The value of such analytical approaches is not to be diminished. Not only do they provide an essential tool for managers to think through strategic problems and analyse possible solutions, but they also provide means whereby the 'taken-for-granted' wisdom of the organisation and assumed courses of action can be questioned and challenged.

The overall aim is, then, to provide a framework for strategy and strategic management which usefully combines the rigour of analysis with the reality of the processes of management.

References

1. The idea of strategy 'momentum' is explained more fully in D. Miller and P. Friesen, 'Momentum and revolution in organisational adaptation', *Academy of Management Journal*, vol. 23, no. 4 (1980), pp. 591–614.

2. The concept of punctuated equilibrium is explained in E. Romanelli and M.L. Tushman, 'Organisational transformation as punctuated equilibrium: an empirical test', *Academy of Management Journal*, vol. 37, no. 5 (1994), pp. 1141–61.

3. The framework used here is, in part, derived from the discussion by H. Mintzberg and J.A. Waters, 'Of strategies, deliberate and emergent', *Strategic Management Journal*, vol. 6, no. 3 (1985), pp. 257–72.

4. There are now numerous books and papers which show the significance of cultural and political processes: for example, the books published by researchers at the Centre for Corporate Strategy and Change at Warwick Business School, including A. Pettigrew, *The Awakening Giant*, Blackwell, 1985; and A. Pettigrew, E. Ferlie and L. McKee, *Shaping Strategic Change*, Sage, 1992. See also G. Johnson, *Strategic Change and the Management Process*, Blackwell, 1987.

5. For books with an avowedly planning approach to strategy, see the books by John Argenti, especially *Practical Corporate Planning*, George Allen and Unwin, 1980. For a text based on a similar approach, see A.J. Rowe, K.E. Dickel, R.O. Mason and N.H. Snyder, *Strategic Management: A methodological approach*, 4th edition, Addison-Wesley, 1994.

6. L.C. Rhyne, 'The relationship of strategic planning to financial performance', *Strategic Management Journal*, vol. 7, no. 5 (1986) pp. 423–36, indicates that, while most research on the subject does show some benefits from financial planning, other studies give contrary or non-conclusive findings on the relationship between formal planning and performance. P. McKiernan

and C. Morris, 'Strategic planning and financial performance in the UK SMEs: does formality matter?', *Journal of Management*, vol. 5, (1994), pp. S31–S42, also conclude that there is little evidence of direct links between formal planning and performance.

7. These conclusions are drawn from H. Mintzberg, *The Rise and Fall of Strategic Planning*, Prentice Hall, 1994.

8. Sherman's quote is taken from B.G. James, *Business Wargames*, Penguin, 1985, p. 190.

9. Also from *The Rise and Fall of Strategic Planning* (see reference 7).

10. Much of what writers such as Tom Peters set out to show is the central role of corporate leaders in the formulation and change of strategy: for example, see T. Peters and R.H. Waterman, *In Search of Excellence*, Harper and Row, 1982; and T. Peters and N.K. Austin, *A Passion for Excellence: The leadership difference*, Random House, 1988.

11. Lindblom's paper, 'The science of muddling through', *Public Administration Review*, vol. 19 (spring 1959), pp. 79–88, is one of the earliest which criticises an overrational view of strategy formation and argues for an incremental perspective within a social and political context.

12. J.B. Quinn's research involved the examination of strategic change in companies and was published in *Strategies for Change*, Irwin, 1980. See also J.B. Quinn, 'Strategic change: logical incrementalism', in H. Mintzberg, J.B. Quinn and S. Ghoshal (eds.), *The Strategy Process* (European edition), Prentice Hall, 1995.

13. See *Strategies for Change* (reference 12), p. 58.

14. This alternative explanation is given in G. Johnson, 'Rethinking incrementalism', *Strategic Management Journal*, vol. 9, no. 1 (1988), pp. 75–91.

15. This definition is taken from E. Schein, *Organisational Culture and Leadership*, Jossey-Bass, 1985, p. 6.

16. The term 'industry recipes' originates in the work of J.-C. Spender: see P. Grinyer and J.-C. Spender, *Turnaround: Managerial recipes for strategic success*, Associated Business Press, 1979, and *Industry Recipes: The nature and sources of management judgement*, Blackwell, 1989.

17. 'Paradigm' is a term used by a number of writers: see, for example, J. Pfeffer, 'Management as symbolic action: the creation and maintenance of organisational paradigms', in L.L. Cummings and B.M. Staw (eds.), *Research in Organisational Behaviour*, JAI Press, 1981, Vol. 3, pp. 1–15, and G. Johnson, *Strategic Change and the Management Process*, Blackwell, 1987.

18. Here the term 'experience' is used. Studies which have examined this at the individual level are often referred to as research in managerial cognition. For an explanation and examples of such work, see A. Huff, *Mapping Strategic Thought*, Wiley, 1990; and for a summary of work in the field, see J.P. Walsh, 'Managerial and organisational cognition: notes from a trip down memory lane', *Organization Science*, vol. 6, no. 3 (1995), pp. 280–321.

19. There has been relatively little published which has examined strategic management explicitly from a political perspective, but it is a central theme of D. Buchanan and D. Boddy, *The Expertise of the Change Agent: Public performance and backstage activity*, Prentice Hall, 1992, as it is of the books cited in reference 4.

20. The concept of the organisation as a set of social networks is discussed by, for example, M.S. Granovetter, 'The strength of weak ties', *American Journal of Sociology*, vol. 78, no. 6 (1973), pp. 1360–80, and G.R. Carroll and A.C. Teo, 'On the social networks of managers', *Academy of Management Journal*, vol. 39, no. 2 (1996), pp. 421–40.

21. This section brings together the work of a number of researchers. For a thorough discussion of the problem of awareness and diagnosis stages of the decision-making process, see M.A. Lyles, 'Formulating strategic problems: empirical analysis and model development', *Strategic Management Journal*, vol. 2, no. 1 (1981), pp. 61–75; H. Mintzberg, O. Raisinghani and A. Theoret, 'The structure of unstructured decision processes', *Administrative Science Quarterly*, vol. 21, no. 2 (1976), pp. 246–75; and L.M. Fahey, 'On strategic management decision processes', *Strategic Management Journal*, vol. 2, no. 1 (1981), pp. 43–60.

22. Evidence on the importance of consensus in organisations can be found in G. Dess and N. Origer, 'Environment, structure and consensus in strategy formulation: a conceptual integration', *Academy of Management Review*, vol. 12,

no. 2 (1987), pp. 313–30, and G. Dess and R. Priem, 'Consensus–performance research: theoretical and empirical extensions', *Journal of Management Studies*, vol. 32, no. 4 (1995), pp. 401–17.

23. For example, see H.E. Aldrich, *Organisations and Environments*, Prentice Hall, 1979, and B. McKelvey and H. Aldrich, 'Populations, natural selection and applied organisational science', *Administrative Science Quarterly*, vol. 28, no. 1 (1983), pp. 101–28.

24. See C. Baden-Fuller and J.M. Stopford, *Rejuvenating the Mature Business: The competitive challenge*, Routledge, 1992.

25. For a discussion of the intuitive role of strategic management, see D.K. Hurst, J.C. Rush and R.E. White, 'Top management teams and organisational renewal', *Strategic Management Journal*, vol. 10, (1989), pp. 87–105. This is also a theme developed by R. Stacey, *Managing Chaos: Dynamic business strategies in an unpredictable world*, Kogan Page, 1992.

26. At the time of writing this book, the research on which these configurations is based is not published. However, interested readers can find a more detailed account of the work in the Cranfield School of Management Working Paper series.

27. A fuller explanation of the cultural web can be found in G. Johnson, 'Managing strategic change: strategy, culture and action', *Long Range Planning*, vol. 25, no. 1 (1992), pp. 28–36.

28. The 'population ecologist' researchers (see reference 23) argue that there is little evidence of managers' ability to change organisations' cultures proactively.

29. The organisational benefits of routines are discussed by economists such as R.R. Nelson and S.G. Winter, *An Evolutionary Theory of Economic Change*, Harvard University Press, 1982. In Chapter 4 of this book, the importance of routines is also shown as potentially underlying the core competences of organisations. In this sense, routines at their most valuable can be thought of as what G. Hamel and C.K. Prahalad refer to as 'bundles' of skills and 'the integration of a variety of individual skills': *Competing for the Future*, Harvard Business School Press, 1994.

30. The significance of organisational stories is explained in A.L. Wilkins, 'Organisational stories as symbols which control the organisation', in L.R. Pondy, P.J. Frost, G. Morgan and T.C. Dandridge (eds.), *Organisational Symbolism*, JAI Press, 1983, and in J. Martin, M. Feldman, M. Hatch and S. Sitkin, 'The uniqueness paradox in organisational stories', *Administrative Science Quarterly*, vol. 28, no. 3 (1983), pp. 438–53.

31. The significance of organisational symbolism is explained in G. Johnson, 'Managing strategic change: the role of symbolic action', *British Journal of Management*, vol. 1, no. 4 (1990), pp. 183–200.

32. A number of writers and researchers have pointed to the links between the locus of power in organisations and the perceived ability of such powerful individuals or groups to 'reduce uncertainty': see D.J. Hickson *et al.*, 'A strategic contingencies theory of intra-organisational power', *Administrative Science Quarterly*, vol. 16, no. 2 (1971), pp. 216–29; D.C. Hambrick, 'Environment, strategy and power within top management teams', *Administrative Science Quarterly*, vol. 26, no. 2 (1981), pp. 253–76. Since the paradigm is, in effect, the 'perceived wisdom' of how to operate successfully, it is likely that those most associated with it will be the most powerful in the organisation.

33. For a fuller discussion of strategic drift, see G. Johnson, 'Rethinking incrementalism', *Strategic Management Journal*, vol. 9, no. 1 (1988), pp. 75–91.

34. This figure is based on that shown in P. Grinyer and J.-C. Spender, *Turnaround*, p. 203 (see reference 16).

35. See D. Miller, *The Icarus Paradox*, Harper Business, 1990.

36. The reference of chaos theory to management is explained by R. Stacey in *Managing Chaos* (see reference 25 above) and a summary paper, 'Strategy as order emerging from chaos', *Long Range Planning*, vol. 26, no. 1 (1993) pp. 10–17.

37. See P. Senge, *The Fifth Discipline: The art and practice of the learning organisation*, Doubleday/Century, 1990.

Recommended key readings

- For an explanation and examples of the patterns of strategy development over time, see E. Romanelli and M.L. Tushman, 'Organisational transformation as punctuated equilibrium: an empirical test', *Academy of Management Journal*, vol. 37, no. 5 (1994), pp. 1141–61.

- On incremental strategic change, see J.B. Quinn, *Strategies for Change: Logical incrementalism*, Irwin, 1980; also summarised in H. Mintzberg, J.B. Quinn and S. Ghoshal (eds.), *The Strategy Process*, Prentice Hall, 1995. Compare this with G. Johnson, 'Rethinking incrementalism', *Strategic Management Journal*, vol. 9, no. 1 (1988), pp. 75–91, and D. Miller, *The Icarus Paradox*, Harper Business, 1990.

- A debate between Henry Mintzberg and Igor Ansoff on the merits of different approaches to strategic management appeared in the *Strategic Management Journal* in 1990 and 1991. These papers were 'The design school: reconsidering the basic processes of strategic management' by H. Mintzberg (vol. 11, no. 3, 1990), a critique of this by I. Ansoff (vol. 12, no. 6, 1991) and a riposte by Mintzberg entitled 'Learning 1, Planning 0' in the same volume.

- For explanations of organisational culture, see E. Schein, *Organisational Culture and Leadership*, Jossey-Bass, 1992; and for a discussion of the importance of organisational culture on strategy developments, see G. Johnson, 'Managing strategic change: strategy, culture and action', *Long Range Planning*, vol. 25, no. 1 (1992), pp. 28–36.

- Good discussions of the relevance of chaos theory to strategic management are in R. Stacey, *Dynamic Business Strategies in an Unpredictable World*, Kogan Page, 1992, and 'Strategy as order emerging from chaos', *Long Range Planning*, vol. 26, no. 1 (1993) pp. 10–17.

- The concept of the learning organisation is explained in P. Senge, *The Fifth Discipline: The art and practice of the learning organisation*, Doubleday/Century, 1990.

Work assignments

2.1 Read the annual report of a company with which you are familiar as a customer (e.g. a retailer or transport company). Identify the main characteristics of the *intended* strategy as explained in the annual report; and the characteristics of the *realised* strategy as you perceive it as a customer.

2.2 Using the categories explained in sections 2.3 to 2.6, characterise how strategies have developed in different organisations (e.g. Strategy Development in Newtown* and Strategy Development in Castle Press,* IONA,* KPMG,* ISS*).

2.3 Planning systems exist in many different organisations. What role should planning play in the National Health Service (see Illustration 2.2), a multinational corporation such as IKEA (see Illustration 1.1) or ISS*.

2.4 With reference to the explanations of incremental strategy development in Illustration 2.3, what are the main advantages and disadvantages in trying to develop strategies incrementally?

2.5 What is the difference between 'logical incrementalism', 'muddling through' and 'intuitive management'? (References 11, 12, 14 and 25 will be helpful here.)

2.6 *Incremental patterns of strategy development are common in organisations, and managers see advantages in this. However, there are also risks of strategic drift. How might such drift be avoided while retaining the benefits of incremental strategy development? (Reference to the recommended readings by Quinn, Miller and Senge could be useful here.)*

* This refers to a case study in the Text and Cases version of this book.

PART II

Strategic analysis

In Chapters 1 and 2 it was explained that there are different explanations of how strategies develop in organisations. There are those who argue that managers have little choice about the strategies they follow because the impact of their environment is so great as to force strategies upon them or constrain them with regard to strategic choice. Others argue that for commercial organisations the forces at work in an industry are the most important influence on performance: for example, that industries in more attractive environments will perform better that those in less attractive environments.[1] This is disputed by others,[2] who provide evidence that the resources, competences and strategies of particular organisations explain differences in performance. There is, then, a debate between those who argue that it is the environment and environmental influences that are most important to consider; and those who argue that it is organisation-specific resources and competences that are most important to consider when analysing the strategic position of an organisation.

This in turn relates to the difference between a 'fit' view of strategic management and a 'stretch' view of strategic management, as explained in Chapter 1. A 'fit' approach is about identifying opportunities in the environment and building strategy by matching resource capabilities to those opportunities. A 'stretch' view[3] argues that strategies should be built on the unique competences and resources of an organisation; by seeking out markets in which such competences have special value; or trying to create new markets on the basis of such competences.

There are other considerations too. Cultural similarities across industries or within, for example, professions may give rise to organisations having similar purposes and strategies and responding to environmental forces in similar ways.[4] There is, however, evidence that different organisations have different cultures which are associated with their being more or less proactive in their markets, with more or less aggressive strategies. The implication is that culture will affect strategy and performance.

Strategic analysis is concerned with understanding the relationship between the different forces affecting the organisation and its choice of strategies. It may be that the environment exercises severe constraints or yields potential opportunities, and this needs to be understood. It may be that the firm has particular competences on which it can build, or that it needs to develop these. It may be that the expectations and objectives of stakeholders who influence the organisation or the culture of the organisation play an important role in determining the strategy.

- Chapter 3 is concerned with the environment of an organisation in terms of macro influences, future scenarios and specific forces affecting competition. The challenge is to make sense of this so as to understand the key variables affecting the performance of the organisation and how the organisation is positioned in terms of such influences.
- Chapter 4 is concerned with analysing and understanding an organisation's strategic capability and how it underpins the competitive advantage of the organisation or sustains excellence in providing value-for-money products or services. This is done in relation to three issues: the resource base of the organisation; how these resources are deployed and controlled to create organisational competences; and how activities are linked together, both inside the organisation and in the 'supply' and 'distribution' chains, to provide more generic competences. Core competences are also explained as those which underpin the competitive edge of the organisation and are difficult to imitate.
- Chapter 5 looks at the organisational purposes and how they arise. It is concerned with understanding whom the organisation is there to serve. This is divided into four themes: corporate governance; stakeholder analysis; business ethics; and cultural analysis. Together they provide an assessment of the cultural and political context in which strategies are developed and pursued.

Although this part of the book is divided into three chapters, it should be stressed that there are strong links between these different influences on strategy. Environmental pressures for change will be constrained by the resources available to make changes, or by an organisational culture which may lead to resistance to change; and capabilities yielding apparent opportunities will be valuable only if opportunities in the environment can be found. The relative importance of the various influences will change over time and may show marked differences from one organisation to another.

References

1. R. Schmalensee, 'Do markets differ much?', *American Economic Review*, vol. 75 (1985), pp. 341–51.

2. G.S. Hansen and B. Wernerfelt, 'Determinants of firm performance', *Strategic Management Journal*, vol. 10 (1989), pp. 399–411; R. Rumelt, 'How much does industry matter?', *Strategic Management Journal*, vol. 12 (1991), pp. 167–85.

3. G. Hamel and C.K. Prahalad, *Competing for the Future*, Harvard Business School Press, 1994.

4. P. DiMaggio and W. Powell, 'The iron cage revisited: institutional isomorphism and collective rationality in organizational fields', *American Sociological Review*, vol. 48 (1983), pp. 147–60.

CHAPTER 3

Analysing the environment

3.1 Introduction

In trying to understand the environment, managers face difficult problems. First, 'the environment' encapsulates many different influences; the difficulty is making sense of this diversity in a way which can contribute to strategic decision making. Listing all conceivable environmental influences may be possible, but it may not be much use because no overall picture emerges of really important influences on the organisation.

The second difficulty is that of uncertainty. Managers typically claim that the pace of technological change and the speed of global communications mean more and faster change now than ever before. Whether or not change is in fact faster now than hitherto,[1] and whether or not the changes are more unpredictable, it remains the case that, while it is important to try to understand future external influences on an organisation, it is very difficult to do so.

Third, it must be realised that managers are no different from other individuals in the way they cope with complexity. They tend to simplify such complexity by focusing on aspects of the environment which, perhaps, have been historically important, or confirm prior views (see section 3.6).[2] These are not perverse managerial behaviours; they are the natural behaviour of everyone faced with complexity. Arguably, one of the tasks of the strategic manager is to find ways in which he or she and their colleagues can break out of oversimplification or bias in the understanding of their environment, while still achieving a useful and usable level of analysis.

In this chapter, frameworks for understanding the environment of organisations are provided with the aim of trying to identify key issues, find ways of coping with complexity and also challenging managerial thinking. These frameworks are provided in a series of steps briefly introduced here and summarised in Figure 3.1.

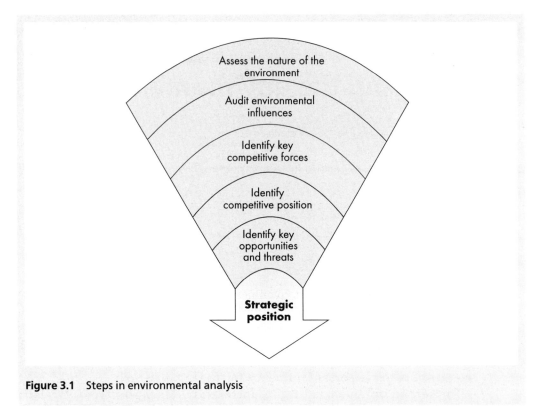

Figure 3.1   Steps in environmental analysis

1. It is useful to take an initial view of the *nature of the organisation's environment* in terms of how uncertain it is. Is it relatively static or does it show signs of change, and in what ways? Is it simple or complex to comprehend? This helps in deciding what focus the rest of the analysis is to take.

2. A second step might be the *auditing of environmental influences*. Here the aim is to identify which of the many different macro environmental influences are likely to affect the organisation's development or performance. This is done by considering the way in which *political, economic, social and technological* influences impinge on organisations. It is increasingly useful to relate such influences to growing trends towards *globalisation* of industries. It may also be helpful to construct pictures — or *scenarios* — of possible futures, to consider the extent to which strategies might need to change.

3. The third step moves the focus more towards an explicit consideration of the immediate environment of the organisation — for example, the competitive arena in which the organisation operates. *Five forces analysis* aims to identify the key forces at work in the immediate or competitive environment and why they are significant.

From these steps should emerge a view of the really important developments taking place around the organisation. It may be that there are relatively few of outstanding significance; or it could be that there are many interconnected developments. What matters is that there should be an attempt to understand why these are of strategic significance.

4.   The fourth step is to analyse the organisation's *competitive position*: that is, how it stands in relation to those other organisations competing for the same resources, or customers, as itself. This may be done in a number of ways, but this chapter concentrates on: (a) *strategic group analysis*, which maps organisations in terms of similarities and dissimilarities in the strategies they follow; (b) the analysis of *market segments*, which seeks to establish the segments of markets which might be most attractive; (c) *competitor analysis*; and (d) *attractiveness analysis*, which maps the organisation's competitive position in relation to the attractiveness of the market(s) in which it operates.

The aim of such analyses is to develop an understanding of *opportunities* which can be built upon and *threats* which have to be overcome or circumvented: an understanding which needs to be considered in terms of the resource base and competences of the organisation (Chapter 4) and which will contribute to strategic choice (Part III).

3.2 Understanding the nature of the environment

Since one of the main problems of strategic management is coping with uncertainty, it is useful to begin by considering how uncertain the environment is and why.

Environmental uncertainty increases the more environmental conditions are dynamic or the more they are complex;[3] and the approach to making sense of this may differ both by the extent to which the environment is stable or dynamic, and also by the extent to which it is simple or complex, as shown in Figure 3.2.

1.   In *simple/static* conditions, the environment is relatively straight-forward to understand and not undergoing significant change. Raw material suppliers and some mass manufacturing companies are examples. Technical processes may be fairly simple, and competition and markets fixed over time, and there may be few of them. In such circumstances, if change does occur, it is likely to be predictable, so it could make sense to analyse the environment extensively on an historical basis, perhaps as a means of trying to forecast likely future conditions.

In situations of relatively low complexity, it may also be possible to

Figure 3.2   Approaches to making sense of the environment

identify some predictors of environmental influences. For example, in public services, demographic data such as birth rates might be used as lead indicators to determine the required provision of schooling, health care or social services.

2. In *dynamic* conditions, managers need to consider the environment of the future, not just of the past. They may do this intuitively, or employ more structured ways of making sense of the future, such as *scenario planning*, which is discussed later in the chapter (see section 3.3.3).

3. Organisations in *complex* situations face an environment difficult to comprehend. They may, of course, face dynamic conditions too. With more and more sophisticated technology, there is an increasing move towards this condition of greatest uncertainty. The electronics industry is in this situation. A multinational firm, or a major public service such as a local government authority with many services, may also be in a complex condition because of its diversity, while different operating companies within it face varying degrees of complexity and dynamism.

    It is difficult to handle complexity by analysis. Complexity as a result of diversity might be dealt with by ensuring that different parts of the organisation responsible for different aspects of diversity are separate, and given the resources and authority to handle their own part of the environment. So organisational *structure* is important (see Chapter 9).

Or it may be that an organisation has *learned* to cope with complexity especially well, and this strategic competence based on *experience* may provide competitive advantage (see Chapter 4).

3.3   Auditing environmental influences

Illustration 3.1 shows some of the macro environmental influences important to organisations. It is not intended to provide an exhaustive list, but it does give examples of ways in which strategies are affected by such influences and some of the ways in which organisations seek to handle aspects of their environment.[4]

Environmental forces which are especially important for one organisation may not be the same for another; and, over time, their importance may change. A multinational corporation might be especially concerned with government relations and understanding the policies of local governments, since it may be operating plants or subsidiaries within many different countries with different political systems. It is also likely to be concerned with labour costs and exchange rates, which will affect its ability to compete with multinational rivals. A retailer, on the other hand, may be primarily concerned with local customer tastes and behaviour. A computer manufacturer is likely to be concerned with the technical environment which leads to innovation and perhaps obsolescence of equipment. Public sector managers and civil servants are likely to be especially concerned with public policy issues, public funding levels and demographic changes. However, none of these forces will remain constant, and managers need to be aware of their changing impact.

3.3.1 PEST analysis

As a starting point, it is useful to consider what environmental influences have been particularly important in the past, and the extent to which there are changes occurring which may make any of these more or less significant in the future for the organisation and its competitors. Figure 3.3 is designed to help by providing a summary of some of the questions to ask about key forces at work in the macro environment. It is sometimes known as a PEST analysis, indicating the importance of political, economic, social and technological influences on organisations.

The headings in Figure 3.3 can be used as a *checklist* to consider and prompt analysis of the different influences. However, although a great deal of information can be generated in this way, it will be of limited value if it remains a listing of influences, however detailed. It is, therefore, important

Illustration 3.1   **Examples of environmental influences**

Government action and restructuring
- By the mid-1990s, pressures for cost containment from governments had become a priority issue within public health services around the world. This pressure required pharmaceutical companies to ensure that new drugs were safe, efficient and cost-effective in order to obtain a licence.
- The introduction of market-based economies in eastern Europe had led to a new imperative for profit. This and the transfer of western technology and work practices led to great productivity gains, but also higher unemployment and job insecurity.

Capital markets
During 1996, Eurotunnel, the operator of the Channel Tunnel, was negotiating to restructure its debt, having suspended interest payments in autumn 1995. The bank consortium — not wishing to see Eurotunnel declared bankrupt — considered a debt-for-equity swap as part of the deal to keep the company in business. However, other shareholders did not wish to see their equity further diluted. Eurotunnel was caught in the middle, needing to placate shareholders with very different interests.

Demographics
By the mid-1990s, the trend of an ageing population was well established in the western economies. This provided many companies with an easily identifiable target market for their goods/services.

Other markets, such as Asia, however, were experiencing a population explosion and a resulting reduction in the average age of their population, giving these markets their own particular needs and opportunities.

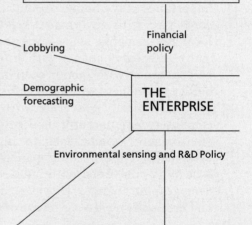

Sociocultural
Growing health consciousness, sophisticated and social pressures on smokers in western countries has affected the sales of tobacco products in these markets. This situation led to controversial advertising campaigns by tobacco companies such as Philip Morris, which attempted to play down the risks of passive smoking in an attempt to protect their market, and a switch by the tobacco companies into concentrating their efforts on the developing world.

Technology
- The high costs of R & D, the long lead times and the critical need for new products to treat *antibiotic-resistant drugs* led Glaxo Wellcome and SmithKline Beecham to announce their first scientific collaboration in 1996.
- The development of 3D graphic accelerator chips has enabled computer games companies to create PC-based games which match those found in arcades in terms of graphics quality and realistic 3D effects, leading to increased sales of computer games.

Labour markets
High levels of unemployment combined with continued 'downsizing' of workforces and the automation of many processes changed the face of the UK labour market.

The labour force had to become more flexible as there was an increasingly high demand for labour on short-term contracts and for part-time working — especially in the service sector.

Competition
Deregulation of the UK financial services sector led to intense competition in the industry. Building societies began to compete directly with domestic banks in the early 1980s. By the mid-1990s, many had shed their mutual ownership status and converted into public companies.

In response, many banks merged or acquired other financial service providers to obtain the critical mass required to be successful in an increasingly competitive industry.

Labour policy and industrial relations

Marketing policy

Economic conditions
By 1996, Japan had witnessed four years of economic stagnation, exchange rate pressure, financial crisis and political upheaval. This forced many Japanese companies to restructure, shifting production overseas and reducing their workforce in Japan.

The change in corporate fortunes enabled Ford to take management control of Mazda, and News Corporation to buy a stake in a Japanese television station — both unprecedented investments which would have been unthinkable before the recession.

Economic forecasting

THE ENTERPRISE

Purchasing

Environmental sensing andR &D policy

Ecology
Widespread concern and anger caused by the failure of UK water companies to plug water leaks — in some cases as high as 30 per cent — while introducing bans on the use of water helped companies which produce hazard detection and measurement equipment to increase their sales as the water companies were forced by Ofwat, the industry's regulator, to address the problem and reduce leakage rates.

Suppliers
■ Brazil is the world's largest coffee producer. In 1994, severe frosts cut the yield of the 1995 coffee bean harvest to less than half that predicted. This disruption to supplies forced Brazil's coffee-roasting industry to import coffee for domestic consumption for the first time ever.
■ In mid-1996 the price of platinum surged on the world's markets as threatened strike action led to concerns over the metal's availability.

Prepared by Tony Jacobs, Cranfield School of Management

---

1.   **What environmental factors are affecting the organisation?**
2.   **Which of these are the most important at the present time?**
     In the next few years?

Political/legal
- Monopolies legislation
- Environmental protection laws
- Taxation policy
- Foreign trade regulations
- Employment law
- Government stability

Economic factors
- Business cycles
- GNP trends
- Interest rates
- Money supply
- Inflation
- Unemployment
- Disposable income
- Energy availability and cost

Sociocultural factors
- Population demographics
- Income distribution
- Social mobility
- Lifestyle changes
- Attitudes to work and leisure
- Consumerism
- Levels of education

Technological
- Government spending on research
- Government and industry focus of technological effort
- New discoveries/development
- Speed of technology transfer
- Rates of obsolescence

Figure 3.3   A PEST analysis of environmental influences

that the sort of models discussed in the rest of the chapter are used to inform and guide analysis. It is useful to begin by considering two important questions.

What are key influences and drivers of change?

It may be possible to identify a number of *key environmental influences* which are, in effect, *drivers of change*. A good example is the forces which are increasing the globalisation of some markets (see Figure 3.4).[5]

1.   There is an increasing *convergence of markets* worldwide for a variety of reasons. In some markets, customer needs and preferences are becoming more similar: for example, there is increasing homogeneity of consumer tastes in goods such as soft drinks, jeans, electrical items (e.g. audio equipment) and personal computers. The opening of McDonald's in Moscow signalled similar tendencies in fast food. As some markets globalise, those operating in such markets become *global customers* and may search for suppliers who can operate on a global basis. For example, some of the global clients of the major accountancy firms now expect the accountancy firms to provide global services. In turn this may provide opportunities for *transference of marketing* across countries. Marketing

policies, brand names and identities, and advertising may all be developed globally. This further generates global demand and expectations from customers, and it may also provide marketing cost advantages for global operators.

2. There may, then, be *cost advantages* of global operations. This is especially the case in industries in which large-volume standardised production is required for optimum *economies of scale*, as in some components to the electronics industry. Other cost advantages might be achieved by central *sourcing efficiencies* from lowest-cost suppliers across the world. *Country-specific costs*, such as differentials in labour or exchange rates encourage businesses to search globally for low cost in these respects as ways of achieving cost parity with competitors which inherit such advantages by their location. For example, given increased reliability of communication and cost differentials of labour, some software companies base their customer service departments in India, where there is highly skilled but low-cost staff. A telephone enquiry from Holland could well be routed to Bombay. Other businesses face high *costs of product development* and may see advantages in operating globally with fewer products rather than incurring the costs of wide ranges of products on a more limited geographic scale.

3. The activities and policies of *government* have also tended to drive the globalisation of industry. Political changes in the 1990s have meant that almost all trading nations function with market-based economies, and their *trade policies* have tended to help develop free markets between nations. This has been further encouraged by *technical standardisation* between countries of many products, such as in the airline industry. However, it is worth noting here that in many industries country-specific regulations still persist and reduce the extent to which global strategies are possible. It may also be that particular *host governments* actively seek to encourage global operators to base themselves in their countries. The Conservative government in the UK in the 1980s and 1990s regarded the country's move to a lower-wage economy as a benefit in attracting investment from such companies.

4. *Global competition* is therefore becoming increasingly evident, and as it does, it in turn encourages further globalisation. This is likely to be encouraged if the levels of *exports and imports* between countries are high because it increases interaction between competitors. If a business is competing globally, it also tends to place globalisation pressures on competitors, especially if customers are also operating on a global basis. It may also be that the *interdependence* of a company's operations across the world encourages the globalisation of its competitors. For example,

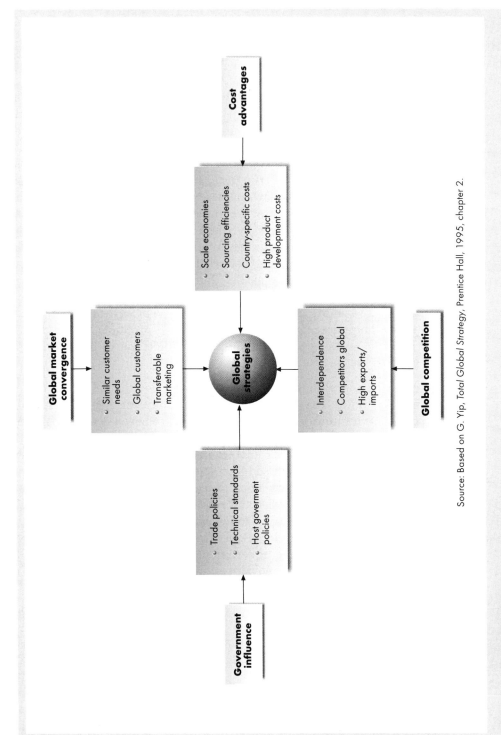

Source: Based on G. Yip, *Total Global Strategy*, Prentice Hall, 1995, chapter 2.

Figure 3.4   Drivers of globalisation

if a company has sought out low-cost production sites in different countries, these low costs may be used to subsidise competitive activity in high-cost areas against local competitors, thus encouraging them to follow similar strategies.

What are the differential impacts of key environmental influences?

PEST analysis may also help examine the *differential impact* of external influences on organisations, either historically or in terms of likely future impact. This approach builds on the identification of key drivers, and asks to what extent such influences will affect different organisations or industries differently. As Illustration 3.2 shows, the automobile industry has more potential for global development than over-the-counter (OTC) pharmaceuticals; ethical pharmaceuticals, however, show increasing signs of globalisation.

Here the illustration focuses on industry drivers for globalisation. However, the same sort of exercise can be undertaken by managers in a particular organisation to consider the differential impact of key drivers in the environment on competitors or the strategic options they are considering.

3.3.2 Porter's diamond

An example of one set of key environmental influences particularly relevant in the context of global competition is provided by Michael Porter in his book, *The Competitive Advantage of Nations*.[6] He argues that there are inherent reasons why some nations are more competitive than others; and why some industries within nations more competitive than others. The framework he uses for this has become known as 'Porter's diamond' (see Figure 3.5).

Porter suggests that the national home base of an organisation plays an important role in shaping the extent to which it is likely to achieve advantage on a global scale. This home base provides basic factors which organisations are able to build on and extend to provide such advantage.

1. There may be specific *factor conditions* which help explain the basis of advantage on a national level. These provide initial advantages which are subsequently built upon to yield more advanced factors of competition. For example, in countries such as Sweden and Japan, in which either legislation or custom means that it is difficult to lay off labour, there has been a greater impetus towards automation of industries; and the linguistic ability of the Swiss has provided a significant advantage to its banking industry.

Illustration 3.2   Industry globalisation drivers

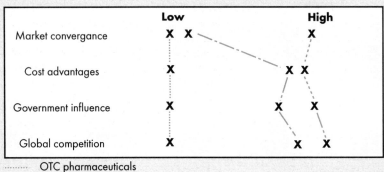

	Low	High
Market convergance	X X	X
Cost advantages	X	X X
Government influence	X	X X
Global competition	X	X X

.... OTC pharmaceuticals
·—— Ethical pharmaceuticals
- - - - Automobiles

Market convergence

Higher. Japanese automobile companies were successful at exploiting common customer needs when they first entered markets. Focusing on fundamental needs common to all countries, such as reliability and economy, their standardised products became acceptable in most countries. Subsequently, other car companies followed this approach.

Lower. Over-the-counter (OTC) pharmaceuticals are different in most major markets: for example, in the brand names used for products. Differences also remain between markets for ethical (prescription) pharmaceuticals because medical treatment differs in regions of the world.

2. Home *demand conditions* provide the basis upon which the characteristics of the advantage of an organisation are shaped. For example, Japanese customers' high expectations of electrical and electronic equipment have provided an impetus for those industries in Japan. The remoteness of Sweden's power plants from centres of population and the existence of energy-intensive paper and steel industries have placed extensive home demand on high-voltage electrical distribution equipment suppliers, and historically helped to

Cost advantages

Higher. Ford's 'centres of excellence' aim to reduce the duplication of R & D efforts and exploit the differing expertise around the world. One example was the Ford Mondeo, introduced in 1993 as Ford's first global car. In the case of ethical pharmaceuticals, the high cost of R&D provides an incentive for globalisation to achieve economies of scale.

Lower. The marketing budgets of OTC pharmaceuticals are geared up for national brand names, leaving little scope for global economies of scale.

Government influence

Higher. US government action and threats of tariffs, quotas and protectionist measures have encouraged Japanese automobile companies to open manufacturing plants in the USA and to use production facilities in the UK and other countries as a springboard into mainland Europe.

In the case of ethical pharmaceuticals, governments are adopting policies of cost containment in health care. This and the harmonisation of clinical standards are facilitating more globalised approaches to markets.

Lower. There are legislative standards on OTC pharmaceuticals, such as maximum allowed dosage, but these vary from country to country. This incompatibility means that there is little scope for globalisation.

Global competition

High. Automotive companies trade across countries and across continents. Companies with largely regional bases (e.g. BMW, Peugeot) face competitive pressures to develop globally. Similarly, the advent of global companies in ethical pharmaceuticals is itself a spur to globalisation in the industry.

Low. Because of the different legislation governing the use of OTC pharmaceuticals, competition is only at the local level rather than global.

Source: Adapted from G. Yip, *Total Global Strategy*, business school edition, Prentice Hall, 1995, chapter 2.

Prepared by Tony Jacobs, Cranfield School of Management.

create advantage for that industry.

3. One successful industry may lead to advantage in *related and supporting industries*. In Italy, for example, the leather footwear industry, the leather working machinery industry and the design services which underpin them benefit from one another. In Denmark, the successes in dairy products, brewing and industrial enzymes industries are interrelated; and in Singapore, port services and ship repair industries are mutually advantageous.

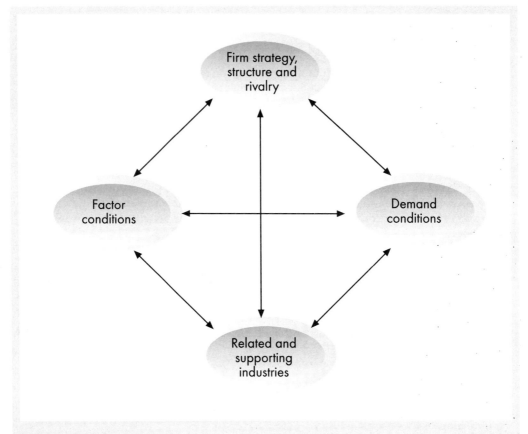

Figure 3.5   The determinants of national advantage (Porter's diamond)

4.   The context of characteristics of *firm strategy, structure and rivalry* in
different countries also helps explain bases of advantage. In Germany,
the propensity for systematic, often hierarchical processes of
management has been particularly successful in providing reliability
and technical excellence in engineering industries. Further, domestic
rivalry and the search for competitive advantages within a nation can
help provide organisations with bases for achieving such advantage on
a more global basis. Japanese electrical and automobile industries are
good examples of this. Especially important is the extent of domestic
rivalry within a nation. Porter argues that one of the main reasons for
success in Japan is the extent of domestic rivalry within many of its
industries. Germany is successful in the chemical industry in part
because of the competition between its domestic chemicals companies;
and pharmaceuticals in Switzerland are successful because of
competition between local competitors in that industry.

Porter's diamond has been used in various ways. At a national level it has been employed by governments to consider the policies that they should follow to encourage the competitive advantage of their industry. Since Porter's arguments are, in essence, that domestic characteristics of competition should yield advantages on a wider basis, the implication is that competition should be encouraged at home, rather than industries being protected from overseas competition. However, governments can also act to foster such advantage by, for example, ensuring high expectations of product performance, safety or environmental standards; or encouraging vertical co-operation between suppliers and buyers on a domestic level, which could lead to innovation.

Organisations have also used Porter's diamond as a way of trying to identify the extent to which they can build on home-based advantages to build competitive advantage in relation to others on a global front. For example, British Steel and British Telecom in the UK might argue that their experience of privatisation before similar businesses in other countries might provide a basis for their achieving advantage in global competition. Benetton, the Italian clothing company, has achieved global success by using its experience of working through a network of largely independent, often family owned manufacturers to build its network of franchised retailers using advanced information systems.

3.3.3 The use of scenarios[7]

The identification of major influences and drivers can also usefully be built into the construction of scenarios as a way of considering environmental influences. Scenario planning is especially useful in circumstances where it is important to take a *long-term view* of strategy, probably a minimum of five years; where there are a *limited number of key factors* influencing the success of that strategy; but where there is a *high level of uncertainty* about such influences. For example, in the oil industry there is a need for views of the business environment of up to 25 years; and while a whole host of environmental issues are of relevance, a number of these, such as raw material availability, price and demand, are of crucial importance. Obviously, it is not possible to forecast precisely such factors over a 25-year time horizon, but it can be valuable to have different views of possible futures.

Scenario building is not just based on a hunch, but tries to build plausible views of different possible futures for the organisation based on groupings of key environmental influences and drivers of change which have been identified. The result is a limited number of logically consistent, but different scenarios which can be considered alongside each other. There are two main benefits of such an exercise. The first is that managers can

Illustration 3.3(a)   Building scenarios from configurations of factors: the book publishing industry

Step 1. Identify high-impact, high-uncertainty factors in the environment.

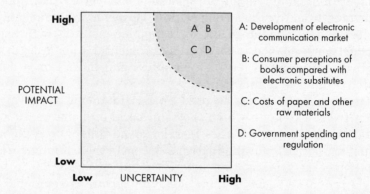

A: Development of electronic communication market

B: Consumer perceptions of books compared with electronic substitutes

C: Costs of paper and other raw materials

D: Government spending and regulation

Step 2. Identify different possible futures by factor:

A: (i) Rapid change   (ii) Measured change
B: (i) Favourable   (ii) Unfavourable
C: (i) High and increasing   (ii) Stabilising
D: (i) In support of books   (ii) In support of electronic media

Step 3. Build scenarios of plausible configurations of factors.

Scenario 1: no great change
Favourable consumer perceptions of books compared with electronic substitutes (B(i)) is supported by government spending and regulation (D(i)). There is measured change in the development of electronic communications markets (A(ii)) and stable costs of paper and other raw materials (C(ii)).

Scenario 2: electronic chaos
Rapid change in the development of the electronic communications market (A(i)) is encouraged by government spending and regulation in support of electronic media (D(ii)). Furthermore, an unfavourable consumer perception of books compared with electronic substitutes (B(ii)) is combined with high and increasing costs of paper and other raw materials (C(i)).

Scenario 3: information society
Stable consumer perceptions of books compared with electronic substitutes (B(ii)), measured change in the development of electronic communications markets (A(ii)) and government spending and regulation in support of books are favourable (D(i)). However, there is concern over the high and rising cost of paper and other raw materials (C(i)).

Prepared by Sara Martin and Tony Jacobs, Cranfield School of Management.

Illustration 3.3(b)   Thematic scenarios at Shell

The oil industry faces an ever-changing environment which is hard to predict on the basis of past experience.

In an attempt to develop strategies for the 25 years between 1995 and 2020, the companies of the Royal Dutch/Shell Group have developed two global scenarios. While at an initial reading these scenarios might appear as 'favourable' and 'unfavourable', they can be seen as more complex in their implications.

New frontiers
In this scenario, economic and political liberalisation increase wealth creation in the societies which adopt them. However, enormous upheavals are also experienced as long-standing barriers are dismantled and poor countries assert themselves, claiming a larger role on the world's economic and political stage. While rapid economic growth of 5–6 per cent is sustained in these developing countries, there is slow erosion of the comparative wealth of the developed world, which produces problems as new priorities and lifestyles are gradually established. Big companies find themselves increasingly challenged, as cheaper capital and fewer international barriers lead to an environment of relentless competition and innovation. This creates a high level of energy demand, and substantial new resource development and improvements in efficiency are required to fuel this growth and prevent demand outstripping supply.

Barricades
In this scenario, liberalisation is resisted and restricted because people fear they might lose what they value most — jobs, power, autonomy, religious traditions, cultural identity. This creates a world of regional, economic, cultural and religious division, and conflict in which international business cannot operate easily. Markets are constricted and difficult for outsiders to enter, as reforms are structured to help insiders. Oil prices are depressed because of instability, followed by a huge rise as trouble flares in the Middle East. There is increasing divergence between rich and poor economies as many poor countries become marginalised, partly due to a lack of foreign investment. In the developed world, coalitions of 'green' and other political interests increasingly cause energy to be regarded as something bad, other than for its tax raising potential. The unfavourable investment climate which this produces is reinforced by the deep divides around the world. Widespread poverty and environmental problems are experienced in poorer countries, while in richer nations, a shrinking labour force and ageing population are causes for concern.

Sources: *Long Range Planning*, vol. 28, no. 6 (1995), pp. 38–47; *Accountancy*, March 1995, pp. 54–5.
Prepared by Sara Martin, Cranfield School of Management.

examine strategic options against the scenarios and ask: 'what should we do if . . .?'; or 'what would be the effect of . . .?' In effect, the scenarios can be used for sensitivity testing of possible strategies (see Chapter 8). The second benefit is that the implications of scenarios can be used to challenge the taken-for-granted assumptions about the environment in which managers operate. This may be particularly important where change is unpredictable and the future uncertain, or where there are long time horizons, because operating managers may be so concerned with the short term that they neglect to consider the long term. Two examples of scenarios are shown in Illustration 3.3.

The main steps in drawing up scenarios are as follows.

1.   First it is necessary to identify the key assumptions, or forces, that are to be included. This may build on the sort of PEST analysis described above. These assumptions should be restricted to environmental forces, rather than including the strategic action of the organisation, or of competitors. It is also important that the number of assumptions is kept relatively low, since the complexity in drawing up scenarios rises dramatically according to the number of assumptions included. This can be done in two ways:

     ▪   By using the forces which historically have had the greatest impact on the organisation, although the danger here is that this does not take into account the uncertainty of future change.
     ▪   By focusing on the factors which (a) have high potential impact, perhaps as drivers of change, as identified in the PEST analysis, and (b) are uncertain, as with the factors identified in step 1 in Illustration 3.3(a) on the book publishing industry.

2.   Scenarios may be built in two ways:

     ▪   The first is to build up scenarios from the factors. This is a sensible approach if the number of factors is very low, such as the four in Illustration 3.3(a). Different, but consistent configurations of these factors might be systematically examined to build three, or perhaps four, scenarios, as shown in steps 2 and 3 of Illustration 3.3(a).
     ▪   If the number of factors being considered is larger, it may not be feasible to undertake this 'building up' process. Instead, the 'tone' of scenarios is set — for example, (a) an optimistic future and a pessimistic future, or (b) according to dominant themes, as in Shell (Illustration 3.3(b)). In either case, in using the factors to build scenarios the allocation of probabilities to factors should be avoided; it endows the scenarios with spurious accuracy, which can be unhelpful given the purpose of the scenarios.

3. If factors with both high impact and high uncertainty have been used then the scenarios must represent possible futures worthy of building into the process of strategic choice: section 8.2.2 in Chapter 8 discusses this.

3.4   The competitive environment: 'five forces' analysis

So far the concern has been with understanding broad aspects of the environment. However, inherent within the notion of strategy is the search for the opportunity to identify bases of advantage. In business, this might be advantage over competitors; in the public sector, advantage in the procurement of resources. There is then a need to identify if there are factors in the environment which influence the capability of an organisation to position itself to such advantage.

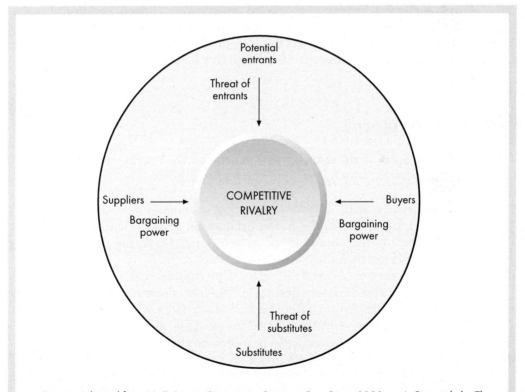

Source: Adapted from M. E. Porter, *Competitive Strategy*, Free Press, 1980, p. 4. Copyright by The Free Press, a division of Macmillan Publishing Co., Inc. Reproduced with permission.

Figure 3.6   Five forces analysis

There has already been some discussion of this in terms of factors at the national and supranational level which are likely to effect an organisation's — or indeed a nation's — ability to compete effectively (section 3.3.2 above). This section draws on the 'five forces' approach that Porter[8] proposes as a means of examining the competitive environment at the level of the strategic business unit or SBU (see Chapter 1, section 1.1.2), so as to provide an understanding of what forces influence degrees of competition and opportunities for building competitive advantage. Although designed primarily with commercial organisations in mind, it is of value to most organisations. The section concludes by using the framework to consider when *collaboration*, rather than head-on competition, is likely to provide a basis for advantage.

It is important to emphasise that, to be of most value, a five forces analysis needs to be carried out by examining the influences on the immediate, or competitive, environment of individual SBUs. If the analysis is attempted at a more generalised level, the variety of influences in the environment will be so great as to reduce the value of the analysis. Indeed, one useful test of whether different SBUs exist within an organisation is to consider the extent to which the five forces differ by product markets. If they do, it points to the existence of different SBUs. The five forces will now be discussed in detail.

3.4.1 The threat of entry

Threat of entry to an industry will depend on the extent to which there are *barriers to entry*, which most typically are as follows:

- *Economies of scale.* In some industries, economies of scale are extremely important: for example, in the production of electrical components, in distribution (e.g. brewing) or in sales and marketing (e.g. fast-moving consumer goods industries).
- *The capital requirement of entry.* The capital cost of entry will vary according to technology and scale. The cost of setting up a retail clothing business with leased premises and stock from wholesalers is minimal when compared with the cost of, for example, entering capital-intensive industries such as chemicals, power or mining.
- *Access to distribution channels.* For decades brewing companies, in Germany, the UK and France, have invested in the financing of bars and pubs, which has guaranteed the distribution of their products and made it difficult for competitors to break into their markets.
- *Cost advantages independent of size.* To a large extent these are to do with early entries into the market and the experience so gained. It is difficult for a competitor to break into a market if there is an

established operator which knows that market well, has good relationships with the key buyers and suppliers, and knows how to overcome market and operating problems. However, the increasing globalisation of markets is facilitating market entry to one part of the world from another. A company may have gained experience and built a reputation in its home market which it can transfer to another. This phenomenon is related to the 'experience curve' and is dealt with in more detail in Chapter 4.

- *Expected retaliation.* If a competitor considering entering a market believes that the retaliation of an existing firm will be so great as to prevent entry, or mean that entry would be too costly, this is also a barrier. Entering the breakfast cereal market to compete with Kellogg's would be unwise unless very careful attention was paid to a strategy to avoid retaliation.

- *Legislation or government action.* Legal restraints on competition vary from patent protection, to regulation to control markets (e.g. over-the-counter pharmaceuticals and insurance), through to direct government action. In 1995, the US government threatened the Japanese government with trade sanctions because, it argued, the Japanese government promoted restrictions to the access of foreign competition. Of course, managers in hitherto protected environments might face the pressures of competition for the first time if governments remove such protection. For example, in the late 1980s and 1990s many public services such as health services or rail systems, traditionally operated as state monopolies, increasingly faced deregulation and privatisation.

- *Differentiation.* By differentiation is meant the provision of a product or service regarded by the user as different from and of higher value than the competition; its importance will be discussed more fully in Chapter 6. However, here it is important to point out that organisations able to achieve strategies of differentiation provide for themselves real barriers to competitive entry. For example, Marks and Spencer in the UK has an image for reliability and quality underpinned by staff training, product and quality specification and control at supplier level, and strong corporate values supportive of the quality image. Nor is the idea of differentiation peculiar to the private sector. For example, in universities and hospitals, research excellence may serve to differentiate the services offered; and symphony orchestras might achieve this through their repertoire and style of performance.

Barriers to entry differ by industry and by product/market, so it is impossible to generalise about which are more important than others (see Illustration 3.4). What is important to establish are: (a) which barriers, if

Illustration 3.4   Barriers to market entry

Entry barriers vary from industry to industry and by product/market.

The European Union telecoms industry

On 1 January 1998, all remaining restrictions on telecoms companies operating in the EU will be abolished. However, in 1996 there was concern that national governments could erect barriers to entry by creating a regulatory framework that protected their national operators. Concerns included rights of access to national networks in other countries and the setting of high charges for connecting newcomers' customers through existing networks.

Within the lucrative new telecoms market of providing entertainment and other multimedia services, there was also concern that national operators would freeze out new entrants by exploiting their telephone links to homes to dominate the market.

The pharmaceutical industry

The pharmaceutical industry's barriers to entry were historically high R&D costs and long lead times which required access to large amounts of capital. Other barriers included varying clinical standards and regulations across different markets, which increased development costs by duplicating the regulatory approval process.

More recently, governments have sought cost containment. As a result, drugs companies have to show that the benefits of new branded drugs are clinically desirable and quantifiable, and that they perform better than existing drugs, to ensure that they appear on 'approved prescribing' lists.

The UK supermarket grocery retail industry

Within this industry, the main barrier has been planning restrictions on out-of-town developments. New site availability has been limited, pushing up land and building costs. There is also a high initial investment cost in the technology required for POS scanning and stock control systems.

There are economies of scale to be gained in purchasing and distribution which a new entrant would not have immediate access to. The profitable area of selling own brand goods would also not be available to a new entrant until it could buy in a volume that would interest manufacturers.

Competition among existing retailers is intense, with the top five retailers having over 50 per cent of the market, making entry more difficult and requiring a disproportionate amount to be spent on marketing to gain market presence.

Prepared by Tony Jacobs, Cranfield School of Management.

any, exist; (b) to what extent they are likely to prevent entry in the particular environment concerned; and (c) the organisation's position in all this — is it trying to prevent the competition of entrants, or is it attempting to gain entry, and how?

3.4.2 The power of buyers and suppliers

The next two forces can be considered together because they are linked. All organisations have to obtain resources and provide goods or services; this is what has become known as the supply chain, value chain or value system of an organisation (see Chapter 4, section 4.3.1). Moreover, the relationship of buyers and sellers can have similar effects in constraining the strategic freedom of an organisation and in influencing the margins of that organisation.

Buyer power is likely to be high when:

- There is a concentration of buyers, particularly if the volume purchases of the buyers are high. This is the case in grocery retailing in France and the UK, where just a few retailers dominate the market.

This power will be further increased when:

- The supplying industry comprises a large number of small operators.
- There are alternative sources of supply, perhaps because the product required is undifferentiated between suppliers or, as for many public sector operations in the 1980s, when the deregulation of markets spawned new competitors.
- The component or material cost is a high percentage of total cost, since buyers will be likely to 'shop around' to get the best price and therefore 'squeeze' suppliers.
- The cost of switching a supplier is low or involves little risk.
- There is a threat of backward integration by the buyer (e.g. by acquiring a supplier) if satisfactory prices or quality from suppliers cannot be obtained.

Supplier power is likely to be high when:

- There is a concentration of suppliers rather than a fragmented source of supply. This is usually the case, of course, in the provision of finance by central government to public corporations such as the NHS or the BBC in the UK.
- The 'switching costs' from one supplier to another are high, perhaps because a manufacturer's processes are dependent on the specialist products of a supplier, as in the aerospace industry, or a product is clearly differentiated. (Switching costs may be the actual cost of

changing suppliers — for example, because machines or systems would have to be changed; or an unacceptably high risk of change — for example, if a low-cost component is nonetheless of critical importance in a manufacturing process.)

- If the brand of the supplier is powerful. This links to switching costs because, as might be the case for some consumer goods, a retailer might not be able to do without a particular brand.
- There is the possibility of the supplier integrating forward if it does not obtain the prices, and hence the margins, it seeks.
- The supplier's customers are highly fragmented, so their bargaining power is low.

Some organisations may rely on supplies other than tangible goods. For example, for professional services, such as management consultancy, corporate tax advice or teaching, the availability of skilled staff is crucial. However, while this may be a significant constraint, the suppliers may not be organised to exert power. In other cases, most obviously if trade union power is strong, labour supply may not only be important, but also exercise power.

A significant problem in constructing strategies is therefore the extent to which power can be enhanced, or mutual interest accommodated, in the supplier–buyer channel. For example, local government authorities in the UK, having realised that their historically fragmented mode of buying reduced buying power, sought to increase this by forming buying groups in the 1980s. Many manufacturers, faced with competitive demands for higher productivity at lower cost, have reduced suppliers of components significantly. The suppliers remaining gained in volume orders, but have had to prove themselves against strict criteria of quality and delivery. Of course, it might be possible for a supplier to seek out market segments with less powerful buyers, or to differentiate products so that buyers become more dependent on that product. It might also be possible to build mutually advantageous links with suppliers and buyers: a point discussed below and also in Chapter 4 in the context of an organisation's value chain.

3.4.3 The threat of substitutes

The threat of substitution may take different forms:

- There could be *product-for-product substitution* — the fax for the postal service and then e-mail for the fax are examples.
- There may be *substitution of need* by a new product or service rendering an existing product or service superfluous: for example, if more precise casting means that engine blocks are cast to a finer specification, it may reduce demand for cutting tools.

▦ *Generic substitution* occurs where products or services compete for need: for example, furniture manufacturers and retailers compete for available household expenditure with suppliers of televisions, videos, cookers, cars and holidays.

▦ *Doing without* can also be thought of as a substitute; certainly for the tobacco industry this is so.

The availability of substitutes can place a ceiling on prices for a company's products; or make inroads into the market and so reduce its attractiveness. The key questions that need to be addressed are: (a) whether or not a substitute poses the threat of obsolescence of a firm's product or service, or provides a higher perceived benefit or value; (b) the ease with which buyers can switch to substitutes, usually determined by the one-time costs facing the buyer making such a change; and (c) to what extent the risk of substitution can be reduced by building in switching costs, perhaps through added product or service benefits meeting buyer needs.

3.4.4 Competitive rivalry

Organisations need to be concerned with the extent of direct rivalry between themselves and competitors. What is it based upon? Is it likely to increase or decrease in intensity? How can it be influenced?

In strategic terms, the most competitive conditions will be those in which *entry* is likely, *substitutes* threaten and *buyers* or *suppliers* exercise control; previously discussed forces are relevant here.

However, there are likely to be other forces which affect competitive rivalry:

▦ The extent to which competitors are *in balance*: where competitors are of roughly equal size, there is the danger of intense competition as one competitor attempts to gain dominance over another. Conversely, the most stable markets tend to be those with dominant organisations within them.

▦ Market *growth rates* may affect rivalry. The idea of the life cycle[9] suggests that conditions in markets, primarily between growth stages and maturity, are important, not least in terms of competitive behaviour. For example, in situations of market growth, an organisation might expect to achieve its own growth through the growth in the market place; whereas when markets are mature, this has to be achieved by taking market share from competitors. Figure 3.7 summarises some of the conditions that can be expected at different stages in the life cycle.

▦ The existence or development of *global customers* may increase competition among suppliers as they try to win their business on a global scale.

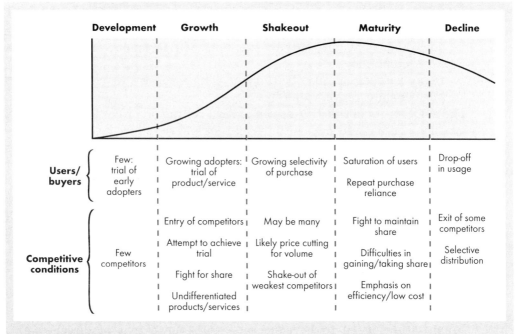

Figure 3.7 The life cycle model

- *High fixed costs* in an industry, perhaps through high capital intensity or high costs of storage, are likely to result in competitors cutting prices to obtain the turnover required. This can result in price wars and very low-margin operations.

- If the addition of *extra capacity is in large increments*, the competitor making such an addition is likely to create at least short-term overcapacity and increased competition.

- Again, *differentiation* is important. In a commodity market, where products or services are not differentiated, there is little to stop customers switching between competitors.

- If the *acquisition of weaker companies* by stronger companies results in the provision of funds to improve the competitive standing of such firms, their ability to compete more effectively may be enhanced.

- Where there are *high exit barriers* to an industry, there is again likely to be the persistence of excess capacity and consequently increased competition. Exit barriers might be high for a variety of reasons: they may vary from a high investment in non-transferable fixed assets such as specialist plant, to the cost of redundancy, to the reliance on one product in order to be credible within a market sector even if the product itself makes losses.

Illustration 3.5   The UK mobile phone industry

Five forces analysis provides an understanding of the competitive nature of an industry.

Competitive rivalry
By 1996 the level of competitive rivalry was increasing as operators sought to differentiate themselves to attract new subscribers. With the executive market approaching saturation, emphasis was placed on attracting domestic consumers. This led to price reductions, customer incentives and higher advertising costs. Operators recognised the need to retain business and reduce customer switching between networks.

Buying power
Buying power varied. With *dealers* it was low. As operators paid bonuses for new subscribers, dealers could give away handsets and still make a profit on each sale. The power of the *service providers* was greater. Although their statutory monopoly position was removed in 1993, a small number of businesses were responsible for 80 per cent of the mobile phone subscriber base by 1994. Unlike Vodafone and Cellnet, both Mercury one2one and Orange had largely avoided the service provider route, preferring to develop their own direct dealer relationships and customer support structures. Although fragmented, the power of the *consumer* was high, with operators vying for their business.

Power of suppliers
The power of suppliers was dependent on the supplier. The design and price of a handset could play a significant part in attracting new subscribers to a network operator, particularly where service features and tariffs were similar. However, there were at least seven *equipment manufacturers* competing for market share. Manufacturers with a considerable presence, such as Motorola and Ericsson, posed a threat of forward integration into network operations. The *government* played a prominent role in the growth of the mobile phone market by issuing operators' licences to increase competition. The government maintained an active interest in the industry and intervened when it felt justified.

Threat of substitutes
The threat of substitutes existed as high tariffs could drive consumers back to cheaper *fixed line* alternatives or discourage them from entering the mobile phone market. The *internet, pagers and fax* communication systems were increasing in popularity, but did not pose a major threat to mobile phones. Cheaper pricing of these substitutes, however, reduced the use and revenue potential of the mobile phone operators.

Threat of entrants
The threat of entrants was low. Obtaining an operators' licence was the principal barrier to entry, although the high cost of entry was a deterrent to many potential entrants. This position could, however, change as the long-term profitability of the mobile phone industry becomes more fully established.

Prepared by Sara Martin and Tony Jacobs, Cranfield School of Management.

Illustration 3.5 shows an analysis of the forces faced in the competitive environment of the UK mobile phone industry.

3.4.5 Competition and collaboration[10]

Much of the discussion so far has emphasised the notion of competition and the competitive nature of an industry or market. However, this section began by explaining that organisations need to seek a basis of achieving advantage, and this may not always be achieved through direct competition. It is possible that collaboration between organisations may be a more sensible route to achieving advantage; that organisations may seek to compete in some markets and collaborate in others, or in other markets be competing and collaborating simultaneously. However, identifying opportunities for collaboration also requires an understanding of the structure of industries, and the frameworks explained above can be used for this purpose too.

Collaboration between potential competitors or between buyers and sellers is likely to be advantageous when the combined costs of buying and transactions (such as negotiating and contracting) are less through collaboration than the internal cost that would be incurred by the organisation operating alone: for example,

- When the result of collaboration gives greater added value to an organisation than operating singly.
- When the collaboration allows the organisation to concentrate on its own core competences (see Chapter 4) and avoid peripheral, wasteful activities.

Some examples of this can be seen by using the five forces framework.

1. *Buyer–seller collaboration.* A manufacturer of automobile components faces daunting competition to secure orders from one of the major car manufacturers if the basis of competition is the product alone. However, a number of component manufacturers have sought to build close links with car manufacturers so as to reduce lead times for delivery, to help in research and development activities, to build joint information systems and reduce stock, and even to take part in planning teams to design new models. The collaborative relationships which are then built up have the effect of raising switching costs for the manufacturers.

2. *Collaboration to increase buying power.* In setting up the structure of the National Health Service in the UK, the government may have been trying to foster a spirit of healthy competition between hospitals. However, doctors may place much less emphasis on competition

Illustration 3.6   Collaboration in the Danish textile industry

A network of co-operation between firms and local government helped textile firms in Jutland buck the trend in the European textile industry.

Slow growth in demand, technological improvements and intensified competition from low-wage countries led to a decrease of 50 per cent in employment from 1970 to 1990 in the textile industry in Europe.

The Danish textile and clothing industry was hit as hard as any other. In 1965 there were 53,000 employees; in 1989 just over 24,000. However, even in a small nation like Denmark, the response to intensified competition had been different by area. The Danish textile industry has always had a strong basis in the Ringkobing county in Jutland. In 1965, 14 per cent of total employment in the industry was located in this county, inhabited by only 5 per cent of the Danish population; by 1992 it was more than 40 per cent. This was due to an *increase* in employment there of 30 per cent, while in the same period two out of three jobs were lost in the rest of Denmark. The concentration of employment was extremely high around Herning and Ikast. With just 78,000 inhabitants, it had 25 per cent of total employment in the industry. It accounted for almost 85 per cent of total turnover in the knitwear sector and 55 per cent of total turnover in the whole clothing industry. Textile firms in that area showed higher sales growth and profitability than the rest of Denmark. Yet it was an area traditionally dominated by small firms.

In the Herning–Ikast area, there had always been strong co-operation between local authorities and the private sector, and the combined forces had created institutions such as the largest trade fair centre in Scandinavia and a number of textile schools. These specialised institutions of education, not found anywhere else in Denmark, had helped create a highly skilled labour force. The concentration of activity served as a magnet: external suppliers of yarn, fabric and machinery could concentrate their selling efforts; and specialised operations such as sewing, dyeing and marketing could be carried out by the growing number of independent firms concentrated in the area.

In a small society where everyone seemed to know everybody else, a kind of collective learning developed among the firms. Due to a fairly free flow of information, it was possible to learn from the successes of other firms as well as from their failures. The firms saw each other as competitors; however, in periods of excess demand for the products of one firm, it would place its orders with another firm which had idle capacity.

Prepared by Kent Nielsen, University of Aarhus, Denmark.

between hospitals and much more on competition for resources from government. They may seek to collaborate within professional bodies to try and exert influence on the government, as a supplier, for increases in resources.

3. *Collaboration to build barriers to entry or avoid substitution.* Faced with threatened entry or substitute products, organisations in an industry may collaborate to invest in research and development or marketing: for example, marketing boards in agriculture have been set up to promote the joint interests of producers; trade bodies have been established to promote the generic features, such as safety standards or technical specifications, inherent in an industry. In effect, both are collaborative means of promoting differentiation.

4. *Collaboration to gain entry and competitive power.* An organisation that seeks to develop its operations on a global scale is likely to find that collaboration is needed through either informal networking or formal alliances (see Chapter 7) for a variety of reasons. Illustration 3.6 shows how collaboration between competitors and suppliers helped overcome market threats in the Danish textile industry. The only way of gaining local market knowledge may be to collaborate with local operators. Indeed, in some parts of the world, governments require entrants to collaborate in such ways. Collaboration may also be advantageous for purposes of developing required infrastructure such as distribution channels, information systems or research and development activities. It may also be needed for cultural reasons: buyers may prefer to do business with local rather than expatriate managers.

3.4.6 Key questions arising from five forces analysis

Five forces analysis can be used to gain insights into the forces at work in the industry environment of an SBU which need particular attention in the development of strategy. The following questions help focus the analysis.

1. What are the *key forces* at work in the competitive environment? These will differ by type of industry. For example, for grocery manufacturers the power of retail buyers is likely to be of extreme importance, whereas for computer manufacturers the growing power of chip manufacturers and the growth in competitive intensity might be regarded as most crucial. For a deregulated public service, new entrants with more commercial experience might be the central issue.

2. Are there *underlying forces* — perhaps identified from the PEST analysis or from an analysis of global forces — which are driving competitive

forces? For example, the competitive strength of lower-cost, high-technology manufacturers in the Asia Pacific region is an underlying and persistent threat to European and US automobile producers.

3. Is it likely that the forces will *change*, and if so, how? For example, pharmaceutical businesses built strong market positions on their expertise in marketing branded drugs to a highly fragmented set of buyers — the doctors. However, government action in many countries, such as the promotion of generic drugs and the introduction of new treatment protocols, buying procedures and price regulation, has had the effect of significantly increasing competitive pressures on such firms and forcing them to reconsider their competitive strategies.

4. How do particular competitors stand in relation to these competitive forces? What are their strengths and weaknesses in relation to the key forces at work? The issues of *competitive standing* and *competitive positioning* are therefore important and are dealt with next.

5. What can be done to *influence* the competitive forces affecting an SBU? Can barriers to entry be built, power over suppliers or buyers increased, or ways found to diminish competitive rivalry? These are the fundamental questions relating to *competitive strategy* and will be a major concern of Chapter 6.

6. Are some industries more *attractive* than others? It can be argued that some industries are intrinsically more profitable than others because, for example, entry is more difficult, or buyers and suppliers are less powerful. In theory, then, the corporate strategist might use industry analysis as a means of identifying which industries are more or less attractive than others (see section 3.5.4). However, it is dangerous to assume that the forces identified in such an analysis are deterministic of business success. For example, why would the Koreans wish to enter what appear to be highly unattractive markets such as chemicals, tanker building or automobiles? The answer may be that they believe that they can achieve competitive advantage which others cannot achieve: that competitive success depends more on their particular competences, which give them competitive advantage, than on the characteristics of the industry. This theme is returned to in Chapters 4 and 6.

3.5   Identifying the organisation's competitive position

Arguably, all organisations — public or private — are in a competitive position in relation to each other, in so far as they are competing either for customers or, notably in the public services, for resources. It is therefore important that they understand their relative positioning and its implications in strategic terms. The auditing of environmental influences outlined in section 3.3 and the structural analysis in section 3.4 provide indications of key factors which will affect positioning, but there are some useful ways of pulling these together to help analysis. This section reviews different ways of doing this.

3.5.1 Strategic group analysis[11]

One problem in analysing competition is that the idea of the 'industry' is not always helpful because its boundaries can be unclear and are not likely to provide a sufficiently precise delineation of competition. For example, Guinness and Albani, the Danish brewer, are presumably in the same industry — brewing — but are they competitors? The former is a publicly quoted multinational drinks business; the latter is owned by a foundation and concentrates on a local market in Denmark. In a given industry there may be many companies each of which has different interests and which compete on different bases. There is a need for some intermediate basis of

It is useful to consider the extent to which organisations *differ* in terms of **characteristics** such as:

- Extent of **product (or service) diversity**
- Extent of **geographic coverage**
- Number of **market segments served**
- **Distribution channels** used
- Extent (number) of **branding**
- **Marketing effort** (e.g. advertising spread, size of salesforce)
- Extent of **vertical integration**
- Product or service **quality**
- **Technological leadership** (a leader or follower)
- **R&D capability** (extent of innovation in product or process)
- **Cost position** (e.g. extent of investment in cost reduction)
- **Utilisation of capacity**
- **Pricing policy**
- Level of **gearing**
- **Ownership structure** (separate company or relationship with parent)
- Relationship to **influence groups** (e.g. government, the City)
- **Size** of organisation

Source: Adapted from M.E. Porter, *Competitive Strategy*, Free Press, 1980; and J. McGee and H. Thomas, 'Strategic groups: theory, research and taxonomy', *Strategic Management Journal*, vol. 7, no. 2 (1986), pp. 141–60.

Figure 3.8 Some characteristics for identifying strategic groups

Illustration 3.7   Strategic groups and strategic space

Mapping of strategic groups in the food industry can provide insights into the competitive structures of industries, and the opportunities and constraints for development.

(a) Strategic groups: food industry in the 1980's

(b) Summary of mobility barriers

(c) Strategic space analysis

Source: Adapted from J. McGee and S. Segal-Horn, 'Strategic space and industry dynamics', *Journal of Marketing Management*, vol. 6, no. 3 (1990).

understanding the relative position of organisations between the level of the individual firm and the industry. One such level is the market segment, and this is taken up in section 3.5.2 below; another is the strategic group.

Strategic group analysis aims to identify finely defined groupings so that each represents organisations with similar strategic characteristics, following similar strategies or competing on similar bases. Such groups can usually be identified using two, or perhaps three, sets of key characteristics as a basis of competition. The sort of characteristics which distinguish between organisations and help identify strategic groupings are summarised in Figure 3.8.[12] Which of these characteristics are especially relevant in terms of a given organisation or industry needs to be understood in terms of the history and development of that industry, the identification of the forces at work in the environment, the strategies of the organisations being considered and so on. The analyst is seeking to establish which characteristics most differentiate organisations or groupings of organisations from one another.

For example, in Illustration 3.7, diagram (a) shows a strategic group map of the European food manufacturing industry in the 1980s.[13] Here the key characteristics of geographic coverage of the European Community and marketing intensity are used, showing clear distinctions between four groupings at the time. A1 are multinational companies operating across the world with strong brands. A3 are national companies with major brands and high levels of marketing support, although for a more limited range than A1 companies. B2 companies operate nationally, but are typically not market leaders. C3 are companies specialising in own-label supplies and focusing on low-cost production.

This sort of analysis is useful in several ways:

- It helps identify who the most direct competitors are, on what basis competitive rivalry is likely to take place within strategic groups, and how this is different from that within other groups. For example, the multinationals were competing in terms of marketing (and especially branding) and the control of manufacturing resources across countries. The own-label suppliers were especially concerned with keeping down costs.
- It raises the question of how likely or possible it is for an organisation to move from one strategic group to another. Mobility between groups is, of course, a matter of considering the extent to which there are barriers to entry between one group and another. In Illustration 3.7, diagram (b) shows the sort of mobility barriers for the groupings identified in the industry. These may be substantial, particularly for the multinational group, but probably also for the own-label producers: the minor national brands are, perhaps, less secure in their position, being susceptible to both major brand and low-price competition.

- Strategic group mapping might also be used to identify strategic opportunities. For example, in Illustration 3.7, diagram (c) suggests there were vacant 'spaces' in the European food industry at the end of the 1980s which could provide opportunities for new strategies and new strategic groups. It is interesting to see that by the mid-1990s some of these spaces were, indeed, becoming occupied. For example, B1 (pan-European branders) was an attractive space, since it offered economies of scale across a market which was developing its logistics network, harmonising legislation and showing signs of converging consumer tastes in some product areas. In the 1990s it became clear that Unilever, Nestlé and Mars were beginning to focus on just such a strategy.
- Strategic group mapping can also help identify significant strategic problems. As suggested above, minor national brands were identified as occupying an insecure position, without marketing support or manufacturing economies. It was not surprising when Colmans, one of the firms identified in diagram (a), was acquired by Unilever in 1995. Unilever then began to use its own marketing resources to build the Colman's brand.

3.5.2 Market segmentation

Strategic group analysis is about analysing differences between organisations which are potential or actual competitors. Market segmentation is about analysing similarities and differences between customers or users. This is important because not all users are the same: they have different characteristics and needs, behave differently, and so on. Markets are therefore most usefully thought of in terms of market segments, and identifying which organisations are competing in which market segments is, in itself, a useful and important exercise.[14]

In undertaking a market segmentation analysis, the following should be considered.

1. There are many bases of market segmentation: Figure 3.9 summarises some of these. It is important to consider which bases of segmentation are most important. For example, in industrial markets, segmentation is often thought of in terms of industrial classification of buyers — 'we sell to the car industry', for example. However, it may be that this is not the most useful basis of segmentation when thinking of strategic development. Segmentation by buyer behaviour (for example, direct buying versus those users who buy through third parties such as contractors) or purchase value (for example, high-value bulk purchasers versus frequent low-value purchasers) might be more appropriate in some markets. Indeed, it is often useful to consider

Type of factor	Consumer markets	Industrial/organisational markets
Characteristics of people/organisations	Age, sex, race Income Family size Life cycle stage Location Lifestyle	Industry Location Size Technology Profitability Management
Purchase/use situation	Size of purchase Brand loyalty Purpose of use Purchasing behaviour Importance of purchase Choice criteria	Application Importance of purchase Volume Frequency of purchase Purchasing procedure Choice criteria Distribution channel
Users' needs and preferences for product characteristics	Product similarity Price preference Brand preferences Desired features Quality	Performance requirements Assistance from suppliers Brand preferences Desired features Quality Service requirements

Figure 3.9   Some criteria for market segmentation

different bases of segmentation in the same market to help explain the dynamics of that market and suggest strategic opportunities for development.

2. It is also important to assess the attractiveness of different market segments. This can be done by applying the five forces analysis described in section 3.4 by market segment.

3. Relative market share (i.e. share in relation to competitors) within market segments is important to consider. There is an important relationship between market power and performance in commercial organisations.[15] This is not just because of scale benefits of size, but also because of 'experience curve' effects which are discussed more fully in the next chapter (see section 4.3.3). The firm which has built up most experience in servicing a particular market segment not only should have lower costs in so doing, but should also have built relationships which may be difficult to break down. The previous discussion on life cycles of markets (see page 113) suggests that it might be useful, for example, to distinguish segments which are growing and where there is no dominant share competitor, from mature segments, with little growth and a competitor with a dominant

share. The opportunities, competitive dynamics and required strategies will be different in each.

4. In the introduction to this part of the book and in the next chapter, the importance of identifying the strategic competences of the organisation is discussed (see section 4.3). The key point is that organisations are most likely to achieve competitive advantage by developing and building strategies upon their own unique competences. It may therefore be important to try to identify market segments which are especially suited to particular competences. Illustration 3.8 provides an example

---

Illustration 3.8   Foseco's match of core competences and market segments

---

The ability to identify market segments especially suited to core competences can provide defensible bases of competitive advantage.

Foseco, part of Burmah Castrol's Chemicals Group, has long supplied chemical refractories (materials capable of withstanding very high temperatures) to steel mills, with which to line the 5–10 metre tundishes into which molten steel is poured. However, Foseco realised that, for a steel mill involved in the continuous casting of steel, it is its ability in steel metallurgy which is of most importance, not refractory technology. Although the lining of tundishes is vitally important to the steel mill because of the financial and health and safety consequences of anything going wrong, and the need to ensure the longevity of the tundishes themselves, the process is peripheral to the competences involved in steel production. 'The cost of tundish lining is modest to a steel mill unless anything goes wrong; then the consequences are extremely costly.'

Foseco management identified a market opportunity not just for the supply of refractories, but also for the management of their application in tundish lining. In so doing, they allowed the management of the steel mills to focus on their competences of production and to subcontract to Foseco the potentially high risk of the peripheral operation of tundish lining.

In searching for competitive advantage in markets, Foseco has learned that it is more likely to achieve this by spotting market segment opportunities in which it can utilise its particular competences, than by manufacturing and selling mixes of chemicals. In the case of steel mills, these competences include Foseco's metallurgical expertise, combined with its understanding of its customers' processes and its willingness to deploy sales, technical and commercial expertise to solve customers' problems. However, as one group executive explained: 'These are generalisable competences across several of our businesses in the group as a whole; what we are doing is seeking out markets and customer-specific processes in which we can apply them.'

of the way in which Foseco, one of the businesses within the Chemicals Group of Burmah Castrol, has developed its steel mills business by recognising that the competences on which they can build competitive advantage have to do with their ability to identify and service peripheral operations in their customers' operations. This theme is further developed in the discussion in Chapter 7 of different strategic directions open to organisations.

5.   It may therefore be beneficial to concentrate on a narrow, specialist focus in one or more segments, rather than to take a broad approach to a market. This issue of *focus* is a key issue relating to strategic choice and forms an important part of the discussion in Chapter 6 (see section 6.3.4).

3.5.3 Analysing perceived value by customers

Chapter 6 shows that the development of competitive strategy needs to be based on a clear understanding of dimensions of strategy valued most by customers. Faulkner and Bowman[16] suggest a number of steps for doing this:

▨   The first is to identify relevant market segments within which customers and competitors can be identified. This could be the luxury car market, which is used as an example in Figure 3.10.

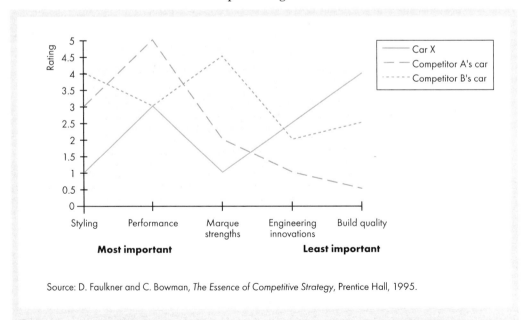

Source: D. Faulkner and C. Bowman, *The Essence of Competitive Strategy*, Prentice Hall, 1995.

Figure 3.10   **Perceived value by customers: the luxury car market**

- The second step is to ask what characteristics of the product or service customers value most. This may be done by market research, for example. In the luxury car market, these characteristics could be styling, performance and the strength of the marque.
- The third step is to rate how important these dimensions are to customers.
- Different competitors can then be profiled against the dimensions which have been identified to consider the relative strengths of competitors. For example, in Figure 3.10 it is clear that the strengths which car X has are not the dimensions most valued by customers.
- This in turn raises important questions about the basis of an organisation's competitive strategy. The manufacturer of car X will need to consider if it should attempt to switch its resources to improve the styling, performance and brand strength of its cars; try to shift customers' perceptions of its performance and styling; attempt to persuade customers that, for example, build quality is of greater importance in luxury cars; or focus on a market niche in which customers already believe this to be so.

3.5.4 Market attractiveness and business strength (or the directional policy matrix)

One way to consider the competitive position of an SBU is by means of what has become known as the *directional policy matrix*,[17] which is a form of *portfolio analysis* used by some organisations. This maps SBUs according to: (a) how attractive the industry (or market) is in which they are operating; and (b) the competitive strength of the SBU. Each business unit is positioned within the matrix according to a series of indicators of attractiveness and strength. The factors typically considered are set out in Figure 3.11. However, these should not be thought of as preordained. The factors should be those most relevant to the organisation and its market: for example, as identified by PEST or five forces analysis for industry attractiveness and through competitor analysis to identify SBU strength. The resulting matrix positions the different SBUs of the organisation according to both attractiveness and strength. Some analysts also choose to show graphically how large the market is for a given business unit's activity, and even the market share of that SBU. So the resulting output might look something like Figure 3.12.

This matrix provides a useful way of directing managers' attention to key forces in the environment, and raises questions about appropriate strategies for different business units and the portfolio as a whole. For example, managers in a firm with the portfolio shown in Figure 3.12 may be concerned

Indicators of SBU strength compared with competition	Indicators of market attractiveness
▨ Market share ▨ Salesforce ▨ Marketing ▨ R&D ▨ Manufacturing ▨ Distribution ▨ Financial resources ▨ Managerial competence ▨ Competitive position in terms of, e.g., image, breadth of product line, quality/reliability, customer service	▨ Market size ▨ Market growth rate ▨ Cyclicality ▨ Competitive structure ▨ Barriers to entry ▨ Industry profitability ▨ Technology ▨ Inflation ▨ Regulation ▨ Workforce availability ▨ Social issues ▨ Environmental issues ▨ Political issues ▨ Legal issues

Figure 3.11   Indicators of SBU strength and market attractiveness

Figure 3.12   Market attractiveness/SBU strength matrix

that they have relatively low shares in the largest and most attractive market, whereas their greatest strength is in markets with little long-term attractiveness.

It should be borne in mind that the value of this approach depends on information of a comparative nature between competitors being available; and obtaining the depth of information required is not always straightforward (see section 3.5.5 below).

There are other portfolio approaches. Chapters 4 (section 4.5) and 6 (section 6.4.1) refer to such portfolios in considering the balance of an organisation's activities in terms of its SBUs; and in Chapter 8 a life cycle mapping approach is used as a basis for strategy evaluation (see section 8.2.1).

3.5.5 Competitor analysis

In order to establish a view on the organisation's competitive position, it is necessary to obtain and consider information about competitors. This book provides many frameworks by which this can be done. Figure 3.13 identifies many of these and references where in the book explanations of them can be found.

3.6 Environmental analysis in practice

There is evidence that organisations which are good at sensing the environment perform better than those that are not.[18] However, a major problem is the difficulties that managers have in understanding the complexity of the environment of a modern organisation and relating signals in the environment to likely influences on the organisation. Research which has looked at how managers make sense of their environment emphasises a number of key points:[19]

- Managers have to simplify the complexity of the environment they face. It is not possible for them to operate in terms of 'perfect knowledge'. Understanding the effect of the *simplification processes* is important, not least because it shows how analysis using some of the frameworks in this chapter can be helpful.
- Given the complexity of the environment and its influences on organisations, even if a manager has a very rich understanding of that environment, it is unlikely that he or she will bring that complex understanding to bear for all situations and all decisions. Rather, and necessarily, the manager will access part of that knowledge. This is

All the following bases of analysing competitors are discussed in the sections of this book shown:

2.4.1	The core assumptions (paradigms) of competitors
2.8.1, 5.5	The culture of competitors
3.3.1, 3.3.2	Differential impacts of environmental influences/drivers
3.3.3	Impact of different scenarios or competitors
3.4	Differential impact of competitive forces on competitors
3.5.1	Identification of bases of competitive rivalry (strategic group analysis)
3.5.2	Which market segments are targeted by which competitors
3.5.3	How competitors rate against what customers most value
3.5.4	Relative strengths of competitors and market attractiveness
4.3.1	Value chain comparisons among competitors
4.3.2	Core competences of competitors
4.3.3	Relative cost efficiencies of competitors
4.3.4	Relative cost effectiveness of competitors
4.4	Comparative analysis and benchmarking against competitors
4.5	Comparative analysis of portfolios of competitors
4.6.1	SWOT analysis to identify relative strengths and weaknesses of competitors
4.6.2, 10.3.1	Critical success factors (CSF) to outperform competitors
5.3	Influence of competitors' stakeholders on their strategies
5.6.1, 6.2.2	The different missions of competitors
5.6.2, 5.6.3	The objectives of competitors
7.3.2	Mergers and acquisitions — could be *of* a competitor or between competitors
7.3.3	Strategic alliances — could be with competitors
8.3.3	Analysing acceptability — reaction of stakeholders of competitors to their strategies
10.2.5	How resource configuration influences competitive advantage
6.2.1	The different ownership structures of competitors and their implications
6.2.3, 6.4.1	The bases of relatedness of portfolios of competitors
6.2.3	Different bases of global competition between competitors
6.3	Bases of competitive advantage of competitors*
6.3.2	Different bases of differentiation of competitors* (* and the extent to which these are defensible)
6.4.2	The suitability of competitors' financial strategy to their portfolios
6.4.3	The extent to which corporate parents have suitable parenting skills for their portfolio
7.2	The strategic directions being followed by competitors
7.3	The methods of strategic development being followed by competitors

Figure 3.13 Bases of competitor analysis

called *selective attention*: the manager selects from a part of his or her total understanding the parts of knowledge which seem most relevant.

■ Managers also use *exemplars* and *prototypes* as a way of making sense of, for example, competition. It is not unusual for managers to refer to a dominant competitor rather than a list of competitive characteristics.

'We compete against the Japanese ...' or 'The service on Singapore Airlines ...' are ways of encapsulating quite complex sets of characteristics.

- Over time, the partial representations of reality become very fixed. The Japanese become a generic competitor; Singapore Airlines *is* competition. The risk is that the 'chunk' of information most often used becomes the only information used. The danger is then that stimuli from the environment are selected out to fit these *dominant representations of reality*. Information which squares with Singapore Airlines being the main competitor is absorbed, while information counter to this is not. Sometimes this distortion can lead to severe errors as managers miss crucial indicators because they are, in effect, scanning the environment for issues and events that are familiar or at least recognisable.[20]

- Over time, managers' experience can build up and contribute to a collective know-how, which is taken for granted in the organisation and in Chapter 2 is referred to as a *paradigm*. As explained in Chapter 2, this can lead to both a filtering of information and, consequently, significant strategic inertia in organisations.

- There is also evidence that, overall, managers tend to be biased towards seeing *threats rather than opportunities*,[21] largely because forces which are perceived to have a potentially high impact on the organisation but to be outside its control are seen as threatening. Managers then become sensitive to information which confirms or reinforces such a bias, rather than to other information which counters it. There is therefore a need to find ways of challenging such confirmation of bias.

- Theoretically, at least, the various functions or parts of an organisation scan the environment for signals which can be fed into strategic decision making. However, the evidence is that middle-level management tend to have a very parochial outlook. Finance managers scan for financial changes in the environment; marketing managers for changes in the market and so on. So there may be difficulties in building up an overall strategic view of the environment on the basis of such partial outlooks.

The overall picture which emerges is that it is difficult for managers to cope with the level of complexity they face. They must simplify this in order to get on with the job of managing. However, if strategies are to be developed effectively, there have to be means of questioning and challenging that which is taken for granted by managers. The major role of the frameworks of analysis described in this chapter is to do just this. In themselves they do not provide answers or even categoric conclusions; their primary purpose is to question and challenge.

3.7   Summary

The ability to sense changes in the environment is important because perceived changes in environmental influences signal the possible need for changes in strategy: they throw up opportunities and warn of threats. These can be built into a SWOT (strengths, weaknesses, opportunities and threats) analysis, outlined at the end of Chapter 4. This chapter has discussed some analytical ways in which this sensing can be done. It began by warning against the analysis degenerating into a trivial listing of the ways in which different forces affect an organisation. The approach here is a structured way of avoiding this, so as to move towards an interpretation, or synthesis, of such forces. The proposed sequence of analysis is as follows:

- Clarifying the *nature of the environment* in terms of its level of uncertainty, so as to take an initial view on appropriate ways of undertaking analysis.
- Carrying out an initial *audit of environmental influences*, beginning at the macro level in order to gain an overall view of the variety of forces at work, but also to identify key influences and *drivers of changes* and, where useful, to build *scenarios* for considering future conditions.
- Focusing more specifically on the forces which determine the nature of the competitive environment through *five forces analysis*.
- Considering the *positioning* of the organisation in relation to others with which it competes for customers or resources, in order to establish its relative strengths in its market by means of *strategic group analysis*, *market segmentation* and *attractiveness analysis*.

All this should encourage managers to focus on the wider world in which the organisation exists, rather than on the operational detail of running the organisation on a day-to-day basis. In so doing, it both challenges current thinking and helps identify the threats and opportunities that the organisation faces. However, as was argued in the introduction to this part of the book, driving the development of strategy from an entirely external perspective is not adequate. It is also important to consider the resource capabilities and especially the strategic competences of the organisation, and this is the subject of the next chapter.

References

1. Henry Mintzberg argues that environmental change is not now faster than it was: see *The Rise and Fall of Strategic Planning*, Prentice Hall, 1994, chapter 4.
2. References concerned with bias in managerial perception are given below (see reference 19), but readers should also refer back to the discussion in Chapter 2 on the influence of cultural aspects of organisations on environmental scanning (see section 2.4.1).

3. R. Duncan's research, on which this classification is based, can be found in 'Characteristics of organisational environments and perceived environmental uncertainty', *Administrative Science Quarterly*, vol. 17, no. 3 (1972), pp. 313–27.

4. Of the books which review environmental influences on organisations, L. Fahey and V.K. Narayanan, *Macroenvironmental Analyses for Strategic Management*, West, 1986, remains one of the best.

5. See G. Yip, *Total Global Strategy*, Prentice Hall, 1995, chapter 2.

6. See M.E. Porter, *Competitive Advantage of Nations*, Macmillan, 1990.

7. See P. Schwartz, *The Art of the Long View*, Century Business, 1991 and G. Price's chapter, 'The why and how of scenario planning' in V. Ambrosini with G. Johnson and K. Scholes (eds) *Exploring Techniques of Analysis and Evaluation in Strategic Management*, Prentice Hall (1998).

8. See M.E. Porter, *Competitive Strategy: Techniques for analysing industries and competitors*, Free Press, 1980.

9. For a discussion of the value of life cycle models, see P. McKiernan, *Strategies of Growth*, Routledge, 1992.

10. The benefits and problems of collaborative strategies between organisations are discussed in F.J. Contractor and P. Lorange, 'Cooperative strategies in international business', and J.C. Jarillo and H.H. Stevenson, 'Cooperative strategies: the payoffs and pitfalls', *Long Range Planning*, vol. 24, no. 1 (1991), pp. 64–70.

11. For examples of different uses of strategic group analysis, see P. Lewes and H. Thomas, 'The linkage between strategy, strategic groups and performance in the UK retail grocery industry', *Strategic Management Journal*, vol. 11, no. 5 (1990), pp. 385–97; R. Reger and A. Huff, 'Strategic groups: a cognitive perspective', *Strategic Management Journal*, vol. 14, no. 2 (1993), pp. 103–24; and the paper by J. McGee and S. Segal-Horn in reference 13 below.

12. The characteristics listed in Figure 3.8 are based on those discussed by Porter (reference 6) and by J. McGee and H. Thomas, 'Strategic groups: theory, research and taxonomy', *Strategic Management Journal*, vol. 7, no. 2 (1986), pp. 141–

60. This paper also provides a useful background to strategic group analysis.

13. This discussion on strategic group mapping and strategic space is based on the paper by J. McGee and S. Segal-Horn, 'Strategic space and industry dynamics', *Journal of Marketing Management*, vol. 6, no. 3 (Winter 1990) p. 175–193.

14. A useful discussion of segmentation in relation to competitive strategy is provided in M.E. Porter, *Competitive Advantage*, Free Press, 1985, chapter 7. See also the discussion on market segmentation in P. Kotler, *Marketing Management*, 8th edition, Prentice Hall, 1994.

15. A useful discussion of the relationship between market share and business performance is to be found in R.D. Buzzell and B.T. Gale, *The PIMS Principles: Linking strategy to performance*, Free Press, 1987, especially chapter 5.

16. See D. Faulkner and C. Bowman, *The Essence of Competitive Strategy*, Prentice Hall, 1995, pp. 11–21.

17. See A. Hax and N. Majluf, 'The use of the industry attractiveness–business strength matrix in strategic planning', in R. Dyson (ed.), *Strategic Planning: Models and analytical techniques*, Wiley, 1990.

18. D. Norburn's work supports this and is summarised in 'Directors without direction', *Journal of General Management*, vol. 1, no. 2 (1974) pp. 37–49. See also D. Miller and P. Friesen, 'Strategy making in context: ten empirical archetypes', *Journal of Management Studies*, vol. 14, no. 3 (1977) pp. 253–280, and A. Pettigrew and R. Whipp, *Managing Change for Competitive Success*, Blackwell, 1991.

19. For a review of many of these points, see the introduction to J. Dutton, E. Walton and E. Abrahamson, 'Important dimensions of strategic issues: separating the wheat from the chaff', *Journal of Management Studies*, vol. 26, no. 4 (1989), pp. 380–95.

20. See A. Tversky and D. Kahnemann, 'Judgements under uncertainty: heuristics and biases', *Science*, vol. 185 (1995), pp. 1124–31.

21. See J.E. Dutton and S.E. Jackson, 'Categorizing strategic issues: links to organizational action', *Academy of Management Review*, vol. 12, no. 1 (1987), pp. 76–90.

Recommended key readings

- L. Fahey and V.K. Narayanan, *Macro-environmental Analyses for Strategic Management*, West, 1986, is a structured approach to analysing the strategic effects of environmental influences on organisations.
- G. Yip, *Total Global Strategy*, Prentice Hall, 1995, chapter 2, explains in more detail the forces for globalisation in industries.
- M.E. Porter, *Competitive Strategy: Techniques for analysing industries and competitors*, Free Press, 1980, is essential reading for those who are faced with an analysis of an organisation's competitive environment.
- V. Ambrosini with G. Johnson and K. Scholes (eds.), *Exploring Techniques of Analysis and Evaluation in Strategic Management*, Prentice Hall, 1998, contains papers on 'Scenario planning' (by G. Price) and 'Analysing competitors' (by C. Bowman and D. Faulkner).

Work assignments

In the assignments which follow, the analysis of an industry is normally required. For this purpose, the European Brewing Industry,* the World Automobile Industry,* the Pharmaceutical Industry* or an industry of your choice could be useful.

3.1 Identify characteristics of stable, dynamic and complex industry environments. Using these characteristics, identify organisations which you think face stable, dynamic or complex environments.

3.2 Using Illustration 3.1 and Figure 3.3 as a guide, undertake an audit of an industry environment. What are the key environmental influences on firms in that industry? What are the main drivers of change?

3.3 Drawing on section 3.4, carry out a five forces analysis of an industry. What are the key competitive forces at work in that industry? Are there any changes that might occur which would significantly affect bases of competition in the industry?

3.4 **Compare two industries in terms of the key environmental influences and competitive forces in them. Assess and compare the entry barriers, and the extent of competitive rivalry in the two industries.**

3.5 **Building on assignments 3.3 and 3.4, identify the main changes likely in an industry. Following the guidelines in section 3.3.3 and Illustration 3.3, construct scenarios for the industry for an appropriate time period.**

3.6   Building on section 3.5.1 and Illustration 3.7:
   (a) Identify the strategic characteristics which most distinguish organisations in an industry. Construct one or more strategic group maps on these bases.
   (b) Assess the extent to which mobility between strategic groups is possible. (If you have constructed more than one map for the industry, do the mobility barriers you identify differ between them? What does this signify?)
   (c) Identify any vacant strategic spaces in the maps. Do any represent viable strategic positions? What would be the characteristics of an organisation competing in such a space?

3.7   Assume you have just become personal assistant to the chief executive of a major pharmaceutical company. He knows you have recently undertaken a business management degree and asks if you would prepare a brief report summarising how scenario planning might be useful to a company in the pharmaceutical industry.

3.8   **To what extent are the models discussed in this chapter appropriate in the analysis of the environment of a public sector or not-for-profit organisation?**

3.9   *Using the tools of analysis in this chapter, write a report for an organisation (e.g. Peugeot Citroën*, BMW* or Kronenbourg*) which assesses their industry environment and their competitive position within it.*

3.10 *Using Figures 3.10, 3.11 and 3.12 as a basis for your work, undertake a competitor analysis of an industry of your choice.*

*This refers to a case in the Text and Cases version of this book.

CHAPTER 4

Resources, competences and strategic capability

4.1 Introduction

Chapter 3 has underlined the importance of analysing and understanding the external environment in which an organisation is operating. This environment creates both opportunities for and threats to the organisation's strategic development. But successful strategies are also dependent on the organisation having the *strategic capability* to perform at the level which is required for success. This chapter is concerned with analysing the strategic capability of an organisation. It will be seen that strategic capability can be related to three main factors: the *resources* available to the organisation; the *competence* with which the activities of the organisation are undertaken; and the *balance* of resources, activities and business units in the organisation.

Analysing the strategic capability of an organisation is clearly important in terms of understanding whether the resources and competences *fit* the environment in which the organisation is operating, and the opportunities and threats which exist. Many of the issues of strategic development are concerned with changing strategic capability to fit a changing environment better. The major upheavals in many manufacturing industries during the 1980s were examples of such adjustments in strategic capability, involving major gains in labour productivity and the adoption of new technologies. However, understanding strategic capability is also important from another perspective. The organisation's capability may be the lead-edge of strategic developments, in the sense that new opportunities may exist by *stretching* and exploiting the organisation's unique resources and competences in ways which competitors find difficult to match and/or in genuinely new directions.[1]

This chapter will be concerned with analysing and understanding strategic capability with both the 'fit' and 'stretch' perspectives in mind. This will require an assessment of the resources and competences which have been built up through the delivery of the organisation's current and previous strategies. Herein lies a danger. It is possible that managers will favour new strategies which exploit these resources and competences, and may not see many of the opportunities and threats discussed in Chapter 3. This could lead to *strategic drift*, as discussed in Chapter 2. The resource management systems of the organisation will reinforce this tendency, since they are geared to the management of resources and processes to support current strategies. For example, plants are located in particular places, and communication systems have been set up in certain ways. In other words, strategy formulation is not occurring in a greenfield site situation. This may not encourage managers to think about how resources and competences can be stretched to create new opportunities.

In order to understand strategic capability, it is necessary to consider organisations at various levels of detail. There are broad issues of capability which are relevant to the organisation as a whole. These are largely concerned with the *overall balance* of resources and *mix* of activities. At the detailed level there are assessments to be made of the quantity and quality of each *key resource area*, such as buildings, machines and people. However, a major theme of this chapter is that the central issue in understanding the strategic capability of an organisation is an assessment of the *competences* which exist to undertake the various separate activities of the business, such as design, production, marketing, delivery, and customer liaison and support. It is an understanding of the competence in performing these various *value activities* and managing the *linkages* between activities which is crucial when assessing strategic capability.

Before reviewing the range of analytical methods which can contribute to understanding an organisation's strategic capability, it is necessary to see how the various analyses will contribute to the overall assessment of this capability. Figure 4.1 provides a systematic way to move from an audit of resources to a deeper understanding of strategic capability.

1. The *resource audit* identifies the resources 'available' to an organisation in supporting its strategies both from within and outside the organisation. Some of these resources may be unique in the sense that they are difficult to imitate — for example, patented products, low-cost source of supply or the location of a facility.

2. *Assessing competence* requires an analysis of how resources are being *deployed* to create competences in separate activities, and the processes through which these activities are linked together. Usually, the key to good or poor performance is found here rather than in the resources *per se*. Value chain analysis can be useful in understanding and describing these activities and linkages.

3. Although an organisation will need to reach a *threshold level* of competence in all the activities which it undertakes, it is only some of

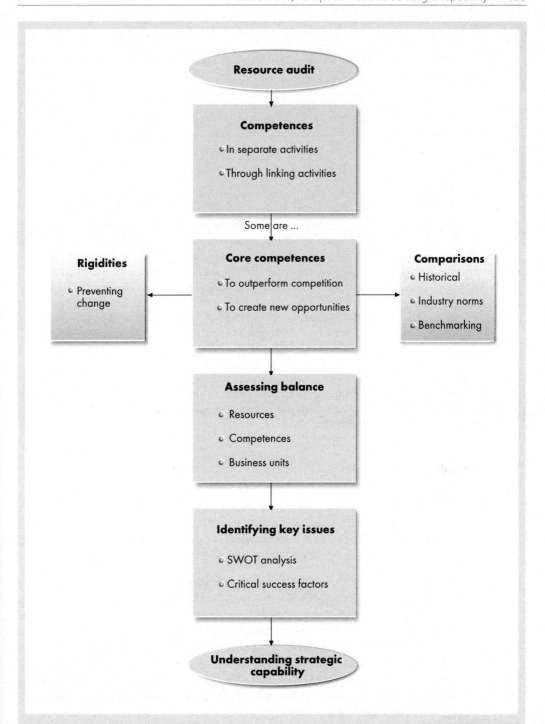

Figure 4.1   Analysing strategic capability

Illustration 4.1 Competitive advantage through resources and competences

---

The examples below demonstrate how a variety of resources and competences have formed the bases of competitive advantage for their organisations. What is common to all is that the resources and competences in question are difficult to imitate.

Caterpillar

In the early 1940s, Caterpillar was one of several medium-sized firms in the heavy construction equipment industry struggling to survive intense competition. Just before the outbreak of the Second World War, the US Department of War announced that, in order to pursue a global war, it would need one worldwide supplier of heavy construction equipment to build roads, air ships and army bases. After brief competition, Caterpillar was awarded the contract and, with the support of the Allies, was able to develop a worldwide service and supply network for heavy construction equipment at very low cost. By continuing to own and operate this network after the war had ended, Caterpillar was able to become the dominant firm in the heavy construction equipment industry. Furthermore, this valuable capability enables Caterpillar management still to advertise their ability to deliver any part, for any Caterpillar equipment, to any place in the world, in under two days. In fulfilling this promise, Caterpillar remains the market share leader in most categories of heavy construction equipment, despite economic recessions and labour strife. The high costs associated with duplicating its worldwide network prevent many firms from competing with Caterpillar even in the 1990s.

these activities which are *core competences*. These are the competences which underpin the organisation's ability to outperform competition (or demonstrably provide better value for money). They may also provide the basis on which new opportunities can be created.

4. Competences are difficult to assess in absolute terms, so some basis of *comparison* is needed. The two most frequently used comparisons are *historical* (improvement or decline over time) and *industry norms* (comparison with the performance of similar organisations, often competitors). A third basis of comparison, *benchmarking*, is now in common use and involves comparison of competences with *best practice*, including comparisons beyond the 'industry'. Figure 4.2 shows that the strategic importance of resources and competences is strongly linked to an assessment of how easy they are to *imitate*. So to compete in an industry or to be a public service provider requires a necessary set of resources and competences to a threshold level. However, competitive

Mailbox Inc.

Mailbox Inc. is a very successful firm in the bulk mailing business in the Dallas–Fort Worth market, enjoying an enormous market share. However, just like other firms in the industry, Mailbox gathers mail from customers, sorts it by postal code, and then takes it to the post office to be mailed. Rather than its competitive advantage having been generated from any 'big decisions', its success depends on doing lots of little things right. For example, the way it manages accounting, finance, human resources and production separately is not exceptional. However, to manage all these functions so well, and so consistently over time, is exceptional. Thus, firms seeking to compete against Mailbox will not have to imitate just a few internal attributes, but thousands of such attributes — a seemingly daunting task.

Hewlett Packard

The powerful and enabling culture of Hewlett Packard is an organisation phenomenon which, like reputation, trust, friendship and teamwork, is not patentable, but is very difficult to imitate. One of the most important components of Hewlett Packard's culture is that it supports and encourages teamwork and co-operation even across divisional boundaries. Using this capability, Hewlett Packard has been able to enhance the compatibility of its numerous products, including printers, plotters, personal computers, mini computers and electronic instruments. By co-operating across these product categories, Hewlett Packard has been able almost to double its market value, without introducing any radical new products or technologies.

Source: J.B. Barney, 'Looking inside for competitive advantage', *Academy of Management Executive*, vol. 9, no. 4 (1995), pp. 49–61.

Prepared by Sara Martin, Cranfield School of Management.

advantage is built on the uniqueness of resources and/or (more often) the core competences described above. Illustration 4.1 shows some examples.

As discussed in Chapter 2, many of an organisation's competences are likely to be 'taken for granted'. They are part of the tacit knowledge[2] about 'how you run an organisation like this', and are embedded in the organisation's routines and rituals, as seen in Illustration 4.2. This is a two-edged sword: it is often a strength in relation to the delivery of current strategies, since this tacit knowledge is not easy to imitate; but it is potentially a major weakness too, since it may prevent managers recognising the need for change and ensuring that the tacit knowledge in the organisation is challenged and that learning of new competences occurs. So the organisation needs the ability to change and adapt over time.

5.   These various analyses concerning resources and competences usually

Illustration 4.2   Knowledge creation in Japanese firms

Tacit knowledge is of key importance in achieving competitive advantage in organisations.

Organisations need to acknowledge the importance of tacit knowledge in achieving and sustaining competitive advantage. In their book, *The Knowledge Creating Company*, Ikujiro Nonaka and Hirotaka Takeuchi explain that with a Zen philosophy Japanese managers do not see the same division between body and mind as is common in the West. At a presentation in 1996 on knowledge creation, Takeuchi explained that tacit knowledge is felt through the senses as well as the intellect. Understanding occurs and action takes place through both — driving a car is a good example. He went on to explain that tacit knowledge may be developed and utilised in different ways. For example:

- By the sharing of tacit knowledge through *socialisation*.
  In Japanese firms, social events are common; different levels of managers mix, often drink a good deal and 'let it all out'; social events also include Karaoke evenings in which they 'grab a mike and make fools of themselves'. In such events there is no hierarchy, no formality and junior managers often 'say what they think' about more senior staff.
- Other events not only build on such informality, but emphasise visual informality and touch; hot tub bathing and massage are common — again breaking down formalities and allowing ready communication of ideas.
- By converting tacit knowledge to explicit knowledge through *externalisation*; the use of metaphor and analogy are important.
  When Canon developed its mini copier, the major barrier to lowering costs was the internal drum. In the end, a disposable drum was used. The origins of that idea came from Hiroshi Tanaka, leader of the task force to solve the problem. At a task force meeting he sent out for cans of beer. When these were consumed he used the empty cans to ask why drums could not be produced at an equivalent cost to them. The task force explored how processes of manufacturing beer cans might be relevant to the production of the drums for the copiers.

Source: I. Nonaka and H. Takeuchi, *The Knowledge Creating Company*,
Oxford University Press, 1995.

relate to separate *strategic business units* in the way which was defined and discussed in Chapter 1. An organisation's overall strategic capability will also be influenced by the extent to which its resources, competences and strategic business units are *balanced* as a whole. *Portfolio analyses* can be helpful in addressing issues of balance and will be important considerations at the corporate centre of an organisation.

6. Resource analysis can often prove difficult or fruitless if attempts are made to list the key issues (such as *strengths and weaknesses*) before some of these other analyses have been undertaken. This *identification of key issues* is critical and is best undertaken as a means of summarising the key strategic insights which have emerged from other analyses.

4.2   Resource audit[3]

A resource audit can be a useful starting point in understanding strategic capability. It attempts to assess the inherent strength of the resource base — the quantity of resources available, the nature of those resources, and the extent to which the resources are unique and difficult to imitate. Typically, resources can be grouped under the following four headings:

▪ *Physical resources*. An assessment of an organisation's physical resources should stretch beyond a mere listing of the number of machines or the production capacity. It should ask questions about the nature of these resources, such as the age, condition, capability and location of each resource, since these factors will determine the usefulness of the resources in gaining competitive advantage.

▪ *Human resources*. The analysis of human resources should examine a number of questions. An assessment of the number and types of different skills within an organisation is clearly important, but other factors, such as the adaptability of human resources, must not be overlooked.

▪ *Financial resources*. These include the sources and uses of money, such as obtaining capital, managing cash, the control of debtors and creditors, and the management of relationships with suppliers of money (shareholders, bankers, etc.).

▪ *Intangibles.*[4] A mistake which can be made in a resource analysis is to overlook the importance of intangible resources. There should be no doubt that these intangibles have a value, since when businesses are sold part of their value is 'goodwill'. In some businesses, such as professional services, retailing or the catering industry, goodwill could represent the major asset of the company and may result from brand names, good contacts or corporate company image.

If the resource audit is to be useful as a basis for further analyses, two important points need to be borne in mind:

▪ The audit should include all resources which the organisation can *access* to support its strategies, and should not be narrowly confined to the resources which it owns in a legal sense. Some strategically important resources may be outside the organisation's ownership, such as its network of contacts or customers.

LINK TO COMPETITIVE ADVANTAGE

	Same as competitors or Easy to imitate	**Better than competitors* and Difficult to imitate**
RESOURCES	Necessary resources	Unique resources
COMPETENCES	Threshold competences	Core competences

* Provides the basis to outperform competitors or
demonstratably provide better value for money.

Figure 4.2   Resources, competences and competitive advantage

⬚ Although the audit needs to be comprehensive, it is important to identify the resources which are critical in underpinning the organisation's strategies — in contrast to those which are necessary, but which are not the means through which the organisation's advantage is built. This also relates to how easy it is for competitors to acquire or imitate these unique resources, as summarised in Figure 4.2.

4.3   Analysing competences and core competences

The difference in performance of different organisations in the same 'industry' is rarely fully explainable by differences in their resource base *per se*. Superior performance will also be determined by the way in which resources are *deployed* to create competences in the organisation's separate activities, and the processes of linking these activities together to sustain excellent performance. Although the organisation will need to achieve a threshold level of competence in all of its activities, only some will be core competences. These are the competences which underpin the organisation's ability to outperform competition — or demonstrably to provide better value for money. Core competences need to be difficult to imitate, otherwise they will not provide long-term advantage. They may also be the basis on which new opportunities are created (as discussed in Chapter 7).

This section of the chapter will consider how an organisation's competences can be understood and analysed in two 'steps' (see Figure 4.3):

* *Value chain analysis* will be used to describe the various activities which are necessary to undertake a particular business or public service, and how these separate activities link together (section 4.3.1). It will also be used to describe which of these many activities underpin the competitive advantage of the organisation — the core competences as discussed above (section 4.3.2).
* The latter part of the section will be concerned with analysing the *bases* on which an organisation's core competences can be built. The discussion will look at *cost efficiency* (section 4.3.3), *value added* (section 4.3.4), the management of *linkages* between activities (section 4.3.5) and the issue of the *robustness* of competences to imitation or competitive threat (section 4.3.6).

Together these discussions are designed to help readers understand the importance of analysing organisational competences and how these

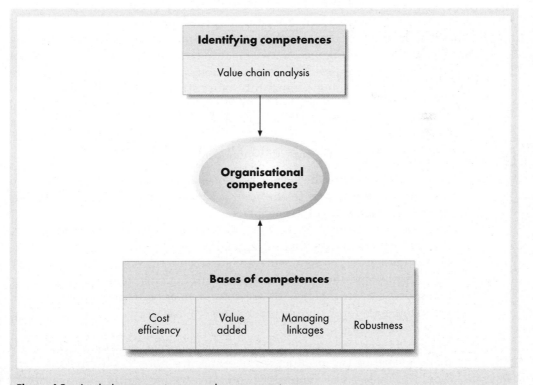

Figure 4.3   Analysing competences and core competences

determine the overall strategic strength or weakness of the organisation (its strategic capability).

4.3.1 Value chain analysis[5]

Value chain analysis has been widely used as a means of describing the activities within and around an organisation, and relating them to an assessment of the competitive strength of an organisation (or its ability to provide value-for-money products or services). Value analysis[6] was originally introduced as an accounting analysis to shed light on the 'value added' of separate steps in complex manufacturing processes, in order to determine where cost improvements could be made and/or value creation improved. These two basic steps of identifying *separate activities* and assessing the *value added* from each were linked to an analysis of an organisation's competitive advantage by Michael Porter.

One of the key aspects of value chain analysis is the recognition that organisations are much more than a random collection of machines, money and people. These resources are of no value unless deployed into activities and organised into routines and systems which ensure that products or services are produced which are valued by the final consumer/user. In other words, it is these competences to perform particular activities and the ability to manage linkages between activities which are the source of competitive advantage for organisations. Porter argued that an understanding of strategic capability must start with an identification of these separate *value activities*. Figure 4.4 is a schematic representation of the value chain within an organisation. The *primary activities* of the organisation are grouped into five main areas: inbound logistics, operations, outbound logistics, marketing and sales, and service.

- *Inbound logistics* are the activities concerned with receiving, storing and distributing the inputs to the product/service. This includes materials handling, stock control, transport, etc.
- *Operations* transform these various inputs into the final product or service: machining, packaging, assembly, testing, etc.
- *Outbound logistics* collect, store and distribute the product to customers. For tangible products this would be warehousing, materials handling, transport, etc. In the case of services, it may be more concerned with arrangements for bringing customers to the service if it is a fixed location (e.g. sports events).
- *Marketing and sales* provide the means whereby consumers/users are made aware of the product/service and are able to purchase it. This would include sales administration, advertising, selling and so on. In public services, communication networks which help users access a

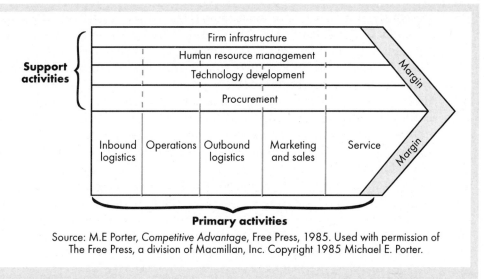

Source: M.E Porter, *Competitive Advantage*, Free Press, 1985. Used with permission of The Free Press, a division of Macmillan, Inc. Copyright 1985 Michael E. Porter.

Figure 4.4   The value chain

particular service are often important. For example, this became one key role for Passenger Transport Executive bodies following the deregulation of buses in the UK in the late 1980s.

■ *Service* — all those activities which enhance or maintain the value of a product/service, such as installation, repair, training and spares.

Each of these groups of primary activities are linked to support activities. These can be divided into four areas:

■ *Procurement*. This refers to the *processes* for acquiring the various resource inputs to the primary activities (not to the resources themselves). As such, it occurs in many parts of the organisation.

■ *Technology development*. All value activities have a 'technology', even if it is simply know-how. The key technologies may be concerned directly with the product (e.g. R&D product design) or with processes (e.g. process development) or with a particular resource (e.g. raw materials improvements).

■ *Human resource management*. This is a particularly important area which transcends all primary activities. It is concerned with those activities involved in recruiting, managing, training, developing and rewarding people within the organisation.

■ *Infrastructure*. The systems of planning, finance, quality control, information management, etc. are crucially important to an organisation's performance in its primary activities. Infrastructure also consists of the structures and routines of the organisation which sustain its culture.

One of the key features of most industries is that very rarely does a single organisation undertake all of the value activities from the product design through to the delivery of the final product or service to the final consumer. There is usually specialisation of role and any one organisation is part of the wider *value system* which creates a product or service (see Figure 4.5). In understanding the basis of an organisation's strategic capability, it is not sufficient to look at the organisation's internal position alone. Much of the value creation will occur in the supply and distribution chains, and this *whole process* needs to be analysed and understood. For example, the quality of an automobile when it reaches the final purchaser is not only influenced by the activities which are undertaken within the manufacturing company itself. It is also determined by the quality of components and the performance of the distributors. The ability of an organisation to influence the performance of other organisations in the value chain may be a crucially important competence and a source of competitive advantage.

Source: Adapted from M. E. Porter, *Competitive Advantage*, Free Press, 1985.
Used with permission of The Free Press, a division of Macmillan, Inc
Copyright 1985 Michael E. Porter

Figure 4.5   The value system

4.3.2 Identifying core competences[7]

Value chain analysis is useful in describing the separate activities which are necessary to underpin an organisation's strategies and how they link together both inside and outside the organisation.

Although a threshold competence in all of these activities is necessary to the organisation's successful operation, it is important to identify those competences which critically underpin the organisation's competitive advantage. These are known as the *core competences* and will differ from one organisation to another depending on how the company is positioned and the strategies it is pursuing. For example, consider how small shops compete with supermarkets in grocery retailing. All shops need to have a threshold competence in the basic activities of purchasing, stocking, display, etc. However, the major supermarkets are pursuing strategies which provide lower prices to consumers through their core competences in merchandising, securing lower cost supplies and managing in-store activities more efficiently. This gives a supermarket competitive advantage over smaller shops: it is difficult for smaller shops to imitate these competences, since they are underpinned by key resources such as computerised stock/ordering systems and own brand labels. So the typical 'corner shop' grocery store gains competitive advantage over supermarkets by concentrating more on convenience and service through *different* core competences — the personal service to customers, extended opening hours, informal credit, home deliveries, etc. The key resources for the successful corner shop are the style of the owner and the choice of location. These aspects of service are valued by some consumers and are difficult for the supermarkets to imitate without substantially increasing their costs.

It is also important to understand that those unique resources and core competences which allow supermarkets to gain competitive advantage over corner shops are not unique resources or core competences in the competitive rivalry between supermarkets. They are necessary resources and threshold competences to survive as a supermarket (i.e. within this particular strategic group, as discussed in Chapter 3). The competitive rivalry between supermarkets is therefore achieved through other unique resources (perhaps a key site) or core competences (perhaps in the management of 'own brand' supply). In this industry, experience shows that these tend to be easily imitated. So long-term competitive advantage needs to be secured by continually shifting the ground of competition.

It is crucially important for managers in this industry to recognise this reality. However, because an organisation's competences are often 'taken for granted', as discussed in Chapter 2, it may not be easy for managers to identify which competences are core or when core competences may need to change.

The development of global competition in the automobile industry[8] over

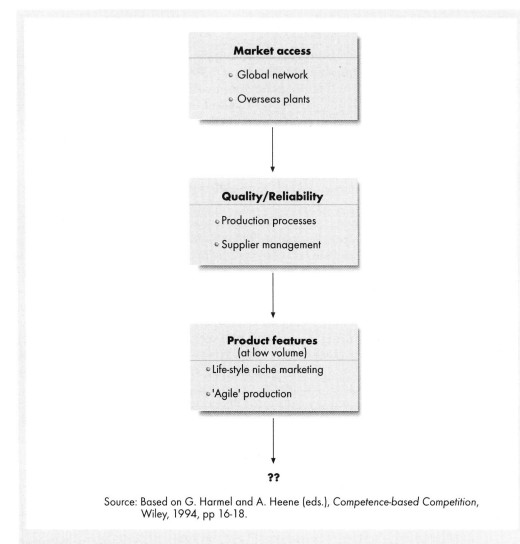

Source: Based on G. Harmel and A. Heene (eds.), *Competence-based Competition*, Wiley, 1994, pp 16-18.

Figure 4.6 How core competences change over time: the world automobile industry

recent decades also illustrates this issue well (see Figure 4.6). During the 1950s and 1960s, the US giants such as Ford and GM dominated the global market through their *market access* core competences of establishing dealer networks and later overseas production plants. Meanwhile, Japanese manufacturers were developing competences in defect-free manufacture. By the mid-1970s they were significantly outperforming Ford on *quality and reliability* — which became critical success factors (see section 4.6.2 below) in allowing them to achieve global sales. By the mid-1980s, both Ford and the major Japanese companies had achieved similar competence in these two areas of global networks and quality. Although maintaining a global network was a critical success factor which continued to distinguish Ford and the Japanese from many European companies such as Peugeot, the production and supplier management activities underpinning quality (reliability) were becoming threshold competences. The competitive arena then switched to competences which would create some uniqueness of product in an increasingly 'commodity-like' industry. The new core competences became the ability to provide unique product designs/features at low volumes of manufacture — the so-called 'lifestyle niche' was produced by companies like Mazda. This agility in design and manufacturing techniques became a new and important core competence in the global competition.

It should be remembered from earlier discussions that it is important to identify an organisation's core competences not only for reasons of ensuring or continuing good 'fit' between these core competences and the changing nature of the markets or environment, as illustrated in this example. Core competences may also be the basis on which the organisation stretches into new opportunities. So, in deciding which competences are core, this is another criterion which should be used — the ability to exploit the competence in more than one market or arena. The development of 'added-value' services and/or geographical spread of markets are two typical ways in which core competences can be exploited to maintain progress once traditional markets are mature or saturated. These issues will be discussed more fully in Chapter 7 when looking at how strategic choices relate to an organisation's core competences.

Value chain analysis is a reminder that the long-term competitive position of an organisation is concerned with its ability to sustain value-for-money products or services, and it can be helpful in *identifying* those activities which the organisation must undertake at a threshold level of competence and those which represent the core competences of the organisation. However, in order to do this, it is necessary to identify the *basis* on which an organisation has gained competitive advantage and hence which are the core competences in sustaining this advantage. The subsections which follow look at how different bases of organisational competences can be analysed and understood.

4.3.3 Analysing cost efficiency[9]

One contributor to the provision of value-for-money products or services is the efficiency with which the organisation undertakes its activities. Cost efficiency is determined by a number of factors (often called *cost drivers*) (see Figure 4.7), and it is important to understand the competences associated with each of these factors and whether or not they are core competences (i.e. provide competitive advantage).

1. *Economies of scale* are traditionally an important source of cost advantage in manufacturing organisations, since the high capital costs of plant need to be recovered over a high volume of output. In other industries, similar economies are sought in distribution or marketing costs. So organisations may sustain their competitive advantage through core competences in activities which maintain these scale advantages. This could include the ability to secure funding for large-scale investments, competence in mass-consumer advertising (to maintain volume) or the ability to develop and sustain global networks of partners or distributors.

2. *Supply costs* clearly influence an organisation's overall cost position, and they are of particular importance to organisations which act as intermediaries where the value added through their own activities is low and the need to identify and manage input costs is critically important to success. Trading organisations sustain their competitive advantage in this way. The way in which supplier relationships are controlled is of major importance in sustaining this position and will be discussed in section 4.3.5 below. In commodity or currency trading,

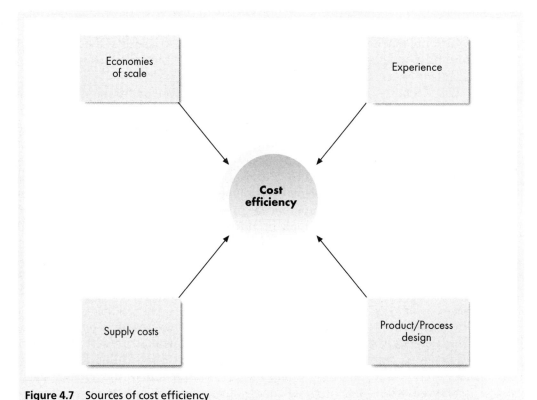

Figure 4.7 Sources of cost efficiency

the key resource is information and hence competitive advantage can be gained through core competences which maintain higher-quality information than competitors. Traditionally, this was concerned with personal contacts and networks, but now the information technology capability of traders is critical to their success.

3. *Product/process design* also influences the cost position. Assessments of efficiency in production processes have been undertaken by many organisations over a number of years through the monitoring of *capacity fill, labour productivity, yield* (from materials) or *working capital* utilisation. The important issue is to analyse which of these are the cost drivers that underpin the core competences of the organisation. For example, managing capacity fill has become a major competitive issue in many service industries, involving marketing special offers (while protecting the core business) and having the IT capability to analyse and optimise revenue. The highly complex pricing regimes in the airline industry are manifestations of this competitive activity. Illustration 4.3 shows that in some industries the processes of product development may also be critical areas to improve efficiency.

   In contrast, much less attention has been paid to how product *design* may contribute to the overall cost competitiveness of the company. Where it has been undertaken, it has tended to be limited to the production processes (e.g. ease of manufacture). However, product design will also influence costs in other parts of the value system — for example, in distribution or after-sales service. The ability to conceive of the design/cost relationship in this more holistic way and to gain the information needed for such an analysis requires successful organisations to have good contacts and relationships throughout their value chain (as discussed in section 4.3.5 below).

4. *Experience*[10] is a key source of cost advantage and there have been many studies concerning the important relationship between the cumulative experience gained by an organisation and its unit costs — described as the *experience curve*. The premise of these findings is that, in any market segment of an industry, price levels tend to be very similar for similar products. Therefore, what makes one company more profitable than the next must be the level of its costs. The *experience curve* suggests that an organisation undertaking any activity learns to do it more efficiently over time, and hence develops core competences in this activity based on the cost advantage arising from its experience. Since companies with higher market share have more cumulative experience than others, it is clearly important to gain and hold market share, as discussed in Chapter 3. It is important to remember that it is the *relative market share* in definable market segments which matters. In highly fragmented industries it is quite possible to operate profitably without dominating

Illustration 4.3 Drivers of cost efficiency: the drug-testing process

The larger pharmaceutical companies are now acknowledging that, since the lifespan of a drug is limited to 20 years of patent protection, each day they can cut from clinical trials will create an extra day of patent-protected sales. If the drug is ultimately successful, the rewards for doing so are high, with eventual revenues of £600,000 a day being assured.

Until recently, pharmaceutical companies have tended to operate inefficiently, largely because their success and ability to make money have not provided any incentive to become more efficient. However, a number of changes in the industry are now forcing companies to review their operations.

According to the UK Centre for Medicines Research, it takes $11\frac{1}{2}$ years for a typical drug to pass through basic research, clinical testing and regulatory approval. But the time taken up by both basic research and regulatory approval is reducing. This is due to a better understanding of the structure and functions of drug molecules at the basic research end of the continuum, and to pressure being applied by patient lobby groups forcing regulatory bodies to work more quickly. The net effect has been to increase the proportion of pre-product launch time taken up by clinical trials from 46 per cent in the 1970s to 55 per cent in the early 1990s. However, in an attempt to increase revenues, the larger pharmaceutical companies are now aiming to cut the time a drug spends in clinical trials from almost seven years to five. So competitive advantage is being sought through redesigning this trials process.

At the core of these efforts is information technology. It has been estimated that by collecting data electronically at hospitals and transferring it to a central location, analysis will be more rapid, such that the period between the end of a trial and the completion of statistical analysis can be cut from months to weeks. Pharmaceutical companies have also looked to reduce the number of different trials conducted, a factor encouraged by the increasing willingness of national regulators to accept results from trials held in foreign countries. Also, some companies have chosen to use contract research organisations (CROs) which specialise in running trials, to reduce the time taken up by this activity. While using CROs is not cheaper than in-house drug development, it is faster because the company does not need to recruit staff to run the trials.

Elsewhere, the basics of trial design are being questioned. For example, at the moment only responses to one size of dose are recorded. While it may be more difficult mechanically and statistically to test a range of doses, so taking account of differences in metabolism between individuals, it is argued that it may be more economical.

Source: *Financial Times*, 11 January 1996.
Prepared by Sara Martin, Cranfield School of Management.

a market. The objective is to have more experience than anyone else in that segment.

There are two important implications of the experience curve work which should influence organisations' thinking about their strategic position:

- Growth is not optional in many markets. If an organisation chooses to grow more slowly than the competition, it should expect the competitors to gain cost advantage in the longer term — through experience. The Japanese car manufacturers are an example of this phenomenon occurring on an international scale from the 1970s onwards. The core competences which helped an organisation establish itself in a market will be of little long-term competitive value in growing markets. They will be displaced by the need for new core competences — for example, in marketing and distribution to mass markets.
- Organisations should expect their real unit costs to decline year on year. In high-growth industries this will happen quickly, but even in mature industries this decline in costs should occur. Organisations which fail to recognise and respond to this are likely to suffer fierce competition. These cost reductions may relate to any of the activities of the organisation, including the management of linkages with the supply and distribution chain (section 4.3.5). Historically, one of the criticisms of public services was that their quasi-monopoly status had tended to shield them from the pressures to push down unit costs and provide better value for money.

4.3.4 Analysing value added (effectiveness)[11]

The assessment of effectiveness is essentially related to how well the organisation is matching its products/services to the identified needs of its chosen customers and the competences which underpin this effectiveness (or vice versa). Unlike cost analysis, the potential sources of value added or effectiveness are likely to be many and varied. Figure 4.8 summarises the kind of value-added features which may need to be provided to perform effectively. The key question is: what are the critically important features and the core competences which underpin these features? For example:

- How well matched are the product or service features to the requirements of customers? More importantly, is the added cost of providing unique features more than recovered through the value which customers place on this uniqueness (through better prices or improved budget allocation)? Are these features easy to imitate by competitors? In organisations employing doctors, lawyers or teachers, the personal

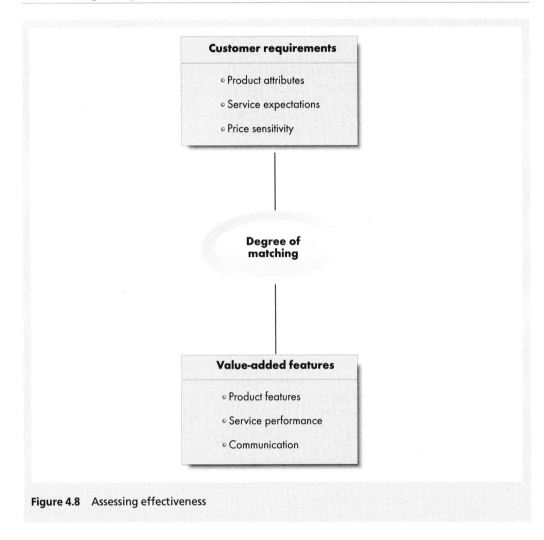

Figure 4.8   Assessing effectiveness

competence of individual professionals may be the key feature of the service from the customer viewpoint.

▪ Are the services which support the product matched with client expectations and, again, do these represent perceived value? For example, this could apply to systems of delivery or technical back-up.

▪ Are the systems for communicating with customers before, during and after purchase adding value to the relationship? For example, this could apply to the processes through which brand names or corporate image are built and communicated through the marketing literature or sales information. Any one of these could be a core competence.

If organisations are to compete on a value-added basis, it is important to remember that the detailed assessment of value added must be done from the viewpoint of the customer or user of the product or service. Although this may seem a self-evident statement, it may not be done by organisations for several reasons:

- Many manufacturers may be distanced from the final users by several intermediaries — other manufacturers and distributors. Although it is important to recognise the strategic role of intermediaries (as direct customers), there is a danger that an understanding of value to the final customer is filtered through or interpreted by these other parties rather than assessed directly. In other words, many manufacturers are out of touch with the realities of their markets. In the extreme, this could result in their product or component being substituted, for any of the reasons discussed in Chapter 3 (section 3.4.3).

- Value of the product or service is often conceived of by groups of professionals (such as designers, engineers, teachers or lawyers) and not tested out with customers or clients. This is an important criticism of many public service organisations. It can result in a false view of what the core competences of the organisation are or need to be, as discussed in section 4.3.2 above.

- Customers' concept of value changes over time — either because they become more experienced (through repeat purchase) or because competitive offerings become available which offer better value for money. So value is a relative rather than an absolute measure. The automobile industry example in section 4.3.2 illustrated this point. In order to avoid some of these pitfalls it may be necessary to undertake research on customer perceived use value,[12] as discussed in Chapter 3 (see Illustration 3.8). This identifies customer perception of product features first in terms of their relative importance, and second in terms of how they 'rate' the attractiveness of competitive products on each feature (such as styling, performance and after-sales service). This will be important in assessing the suitability of these strategies and how easy they are to imitate (see Chapter 8, Figure 8.4).

4.3.5 Managing linkages

Core competences in separate activities may provide competitive advantage for an organisation, but nevertheless over time may be imitated by competitors. Core competences are likely to be more robust and difficult to imitate if they relate to the management of *linkages* within the organisation's value chain and linkages into the supply and distribution chains. It is the management of these linkages which provides 'leverage' and levels of performance which are difficult to match (see Figure 4.9). For example:

Type of linkage	Type of activity	Example
Internal linkage	Primary–primary	Interdepartmental co-ordination
	Primary–support	Computer-based operational systems
	Support–support	Human resource development for new technologies
External linkage	Vertical integration	Extend ownership of activities in supply/distribution chain
	Specification and checking	... of supplier/distributor performance
	Total quality management Merchandising activities	Working with suppliers/distributors to improve their performance
	Reconfigure value chain	... by deleting activities
	Strategic alliances	(See Chapter 7.)

Figure 4.9   Core competences through managing linkages

1. The ability to *co-ordinate* the activities of specialist teams or departments may create competitive advantage through improving value for money in the product or service. Specialisation of roles and responsibilities is common in most organisations and is one way in which high levels of competence in separate activities is achieved. However, it often results in a set of activities which are incompatible — different departments pulling in different directions — adding overall cost and/or diminishing value in the product or service.

   This management of internal linkages in the value chain could create competitive advantage in a number of ways:

   - There may be important linkages between the *primary activities*. For example, a decision to hold high levels of finished stock might ease production scheduling problems and provide for a faster response time to the customer. However, it will probably add to the overall cost of operations. An assessment needs to be made of whether the value added to the customer by this faster response through holding stocks is greater than the added cost.
   - It is easy to miss this issue of managing linkages between primary activities in an analysis if, for example, the organisation's competences in marketing activities and operations are assessed separately. The operations may look good because they are geared to high-volume, low-variety, low-unit-cost production. However, at the same time, the marketing team may be selling speed, flexibility

and variety to the customers. So high levels of competence in separate activities are not enough if, as here, the competences are incompatible: that is, they are not related to the same view of what value for money means to the customer.

- The management of the linkages between a *primary activity* and a *support activity* may be the basis of a core competence. It may be key *investments in systems or infrastructure* which provide the basis on which the company outperforms competition. Computer-based systems have been exploited in many different types of service organisation and have fundamentally transformed the customer experience. Travel bookings and hotel reservation systems are examples which other services would do well to emulate. They have created within these organisations the competence to provide both a better service and a service at reduced cost. They have allowed the organisations to create genuinely new services from these core competences or to expand rapidly into new markets.

- Linkages between different *support activities* may also be the basis of core competences. For example, the extent to which human resource development is in tune with new technologies has been a key feature in the implementation of new production and office technologies. Many companies have failed to become competent in managing this linkage properly and have lost out competitively.

2. In addition to the management of internal linkage, competitive advantage may also be gained by the ability to *complement/co-ordinate* the organisation's own activities with those of suppliers, channels or customers.[13] Again, this could occur in a number of different ways:

- *Vertical integration* attempts to improve performance through ownership of more parts of the value system, making more linkages internal to the organisation. However, the practical difficulties and costs of co-ordinating a wider range of internal activities can outweigh the theoretical benefits.

- Within manufacturing industry the competence in *closely specifying* requirements and controlling the performance of suppliers (sometimes linked to quality checking and/or penalties for poor performance) can be critical to both quality enhancement and cost reduction.

- A more recent philosophy has been *total quality management*,[14] which seeks to improve performance through closer working relationships between the various specialists within the value system. For example, many manufacturers will now involve their suppliers and distributors at the design stage of a product or project.

- The *merchandising* activities which manufacturers undertake with their distributors are now much improved and are an important

---

Illustration 4.4   Human resources and the value chain at Levi Strauss

Levi Strauss believe that being viewed as a 'good company' leads to favourable relationships with stakeholders, which in turn result in important competitive advantages for the firm. With such rewards on offer, Levi Strauss has developed a means by which advantages are systematically achieved. In essence, each link in the value chain is seen to present opportunities for managers to affect the development of reputation, and it is managed as such.

External linkages
In response to dramatic price competition from countries with lower labour costs, Levi Strauss has sought to develop relationships with manufacturers in low-wage countries in such areas as Latin America and South East Asia. In the process of doing so, the company recognised that explicit and strict global sourcing guidelines, covering ethical policies to environmental requirements, would enable them to avoid relationships with firms whose practices could threaten their reputation. Application of the guidelines has led Levi to make some difficult decisions: for example, withdrawing from partnerships in the People's Republic of China due to human rights problems.

However, it is much more common for the organisation to work with suppliers to help them comply. An example is a supplier factory in Bangladesh which was found to employ children under the age of 14. Rather than refusing to work with the organisation, Levi Strauss decided to pay for 25 under-age employees to go to school, while the contractors continued to pay them as if they were working and agreed to hire them back once they achieved legal working age. This example shows a strong commitment to the reputational effects of supplier relations within the value chain segment of inbound logistics.

---

means of increasing their control over distributor performance through training, incentives, joint promotions, in-store displays and so on.

■ Performance may sometimes be improved by *reconfiguring* the value chain to reduce costs or increase effectiveness. This could mean deleting activities altogether. New entrants to industries might achieve entry in this way, since the incumbent organisations have 'taken for granted' that the value chain *must* be configured in the traditional way. For example, in the UK, Direct Line Insurance revolutionised the household and motor insurance markets in the 1990s by cutting out the need for insurance brokers and going direct to individual householders. Many of the changes in the public services during the 1980s and 1990s (such as competitive tendering

Internal linkages

Opportunities are seen to exist which enhance reputation through the way in which Levi Strauss utilises both human and physical resources in the manufacturing process. Given the labour intensity of production in the garment industry, the human resource management support function plays an especially important role. A reputation for fairness and progressive employee practices results in an exceptional labour pool and the foundation for an above average company workforce. Several human resource initiatives within Levi Strauss have contributed to its overall firm reputation. The broadest example is its aspirations statement, which addresses issues like employee opportunities and empowerment, ethics, communication and the need to have fun in all endeavours.

Specifically, the operations benefit from this reputation as this aspirations statement is translated into everyday practice on the shop floor. For example, Levi Strauss pursues empowerment by encouraging employees actively to develop their own abilities through company-sponsored training and development, and to accept as much authority and responsibility as is within their capabilities. Further millions of dollars have been invested to convert assembly lines into team manufacturing processes. As well as enhancing the quality of life — including improving health and safety conditions, and reducing tedium — greater efficiencies have been achieved, such as a 70 per cent reduction in time taken to produce each item, reduced need for resewing, lower absenteeism, lower turnover and fewer days lost to injury.

Source: S. Preece, C. Fleisher and J. Toccacelli, 'Building a reputation along the value chain at Levi Strauss', *Long Range Planning*, vol. 28, no. 6 (1995), pp. 88–98.
Prepared by Sara Martin, Cranfield School of Management.

and internal markets) were attempts to improve performance through reconfiguring the value chain.

- There are often circumstances where the overall cost can be reduced (or value increased) by formal *collaborative arrangements* between different organisations in the value system. It will be seen in Chapter 7 that this is often the rationale behind joint ventures, such as the technology sharing in the international aerospace or telecommunications industries.

3. Most of these examples of improving performance through managing linkages emphasise the benefits which can arise through developing competences in various types of *co-ordination*. However, it needs to be remembered that in the best organisations these competences are

not only concerned with systems and procedures, but found in the routines of the organisation and, as such, are embedded in the culture. So co-ordination occurs 'naturally' because people know their place in the wider picture or it is simply 'taken for granted' that activities are done in particular ways. Competences which are embedded within the culture are difficult to imitate and therefore are usually core competences.[15] The implication of this is that a critically important issue in sustaining value-for-money products and services is how the tacit knowledge and routines[16] within the organisation are maintained and developed in ways which match the intended strategies. This is discussed in the later sections of the book — particularly Chapter 10. The downside of culturally sustained core competences is that they can become *key rigidities*[17] and difficult to change. Illustration 4.4 shows how Levi Strauss attempted to improve its management of both internal and external linkages as a source of competitive advantage.

4.3.6 Robustness

It has already been noted that the strategic importance of an organisation's competences relates to how easy or difficult they are to imitate. This is why competences in managing linkages between activities tend to be more robust than simply competences in separate activities. But robustness also relates to the specific nature and 'ownership' of the organisation's competences.

1. It depends on who *owns* the competence and whether it is easily transferable. For example, in professional service organisations, some services are built around the competence of specific *individuals* — such as the surgeon in 'lead-edge' medicine. Clearly, the organisation is vulnerable to the loss of this individual's services. Other (routine) services are sustained through a *corporate* competence to organise and deliver the service — for example, in orthopaedic clinics. These are more robust competences as they are less dependent on one individual.

2. Most organisations have difficult decisions to make about which activities (in the value chain) they should undertake themselves and which should be subcontracted and/or undertaken by others. Usually, it is advisable to ensure that core competences reside within the organisation, since they fundamentally underpin current strategies and/ or may be the basis for new avenues of strategic development. The problem is that organisations may not have adequately analysed which of their competences are core and which are threshold, as mentioned above. Or, perhaps more frequently, they may not regard 'new'

competences as core and hence may continue to access them from external sources, inhibiting the organisation's ability to learn and to develop these competences and increasing their vulnerability to these 'suppliers'.[18] IT developments in organisations have been blighted by this problem, in the sense that managers in the organisation have failed properly to comprehend how IT investments can transform the way in which activities are performed. In turn, the external suppliers, or consultants, do not understand the business well enough to tailor their advice and ensure that it becomes properly embedded in the organisation.

4.4   Comparative analysis and benchmarking

An organisation's strategic capability is ultimately assessed in *relative* terms. This section will look at a number of different *bases* for this comparative analysis or benchmarking of an organisation's capability.

The preceding sections have considered how analysing the resources and competences of an organisation can build up an understanding of the competitive position of the organisation in its industry. It is also valuable to assess how these resources and competences have changed and developed historically, since this gives insights into why the organisation has chosen, or been forced, to change.

This section discusses these two different bases of comparison, the *historical* and the *industry norm*, as valuable means of improving the understanding of an organisation's strategic capability. It will also be suggested that more valuable insights can be developed by comparing *best practice* beyond the industry in which the organisation currently operates. The role of financial analyses in assessing organisational competence will also be discussed (section 4.4.4).

4.4.1 Historical analysis

An historical analysis looks at the deployment of the resources and performance measures of an organisation by comparison with previous years in order to identify any significant changes. Typically, financial ratios such as sales/capital and sales/employees will be used, and any significant variations in the proportions of resources devoted to different activities will be identified. This can reveal trends which might not otherwise be apparent.

It is important that historical comparisons are made against a realistic set of expectations. For example, an expectation of *continuous improvement* means that historical performance is something to be improved upon not simply matched. This has been the subject of heated debate in many public

Illustration 4.5   Comparative analyses using local authority league tables

Council taxpayers can judge the value for money provided by their council using annually produced league tables to compare authorities across England and Wales. The tables disclose figures for everything from recycling rubbish to rent collection and care of the elderly. Such indicators make it possible to see if councils are improving their performance year on year.

According to the Audit Commission, the league tables for 1994/5 (excerpts of which are set out below) illustrate that 'local authorities are remarkably complacent about the efficient delivery of basic services. While those councils which performed worst in 1993/4 improved, the overwhelming majority made little progress. Most councils provide a majority of services to a high average level, but there are still wide variations between the best and worst performances for similar services provided by comparable authorities. The figures further show that neither political control nor prosperity guarantees good performance.'

(a) Average council tax bills (£)

	Councils	1996/7	1995/6	% increase
England		**541.51**	**511.60**	**5.80**
Conservative	19	525.48	525.65	−0.03
Independent	13	528.97	505.38	4.67
Labour	165	521.90	490.70	6.36
Lib Dem	52	569.60	561.27	1.48
Hung	109	562.07	521.61	7.76

services as performance indicators have been developed and continuous year-on-year efficiency gains have been demanded.

4.4.2 Comparison with industry norms

An historical analysis can be improved significantly by the additional comparison with similar factors analysed for the industry as a whole[19] or between similar public service providers. Illustration 4.5 shows that these comparisons (particularly in the public services) are often in the form of

(b) Total expenditure per head of population

Borough Council	£ per head
London Boroughs: average	911.00
Tower Hamlets	1,452.92
Richmond	584.88
County Councils: average	629.00
Powys	795.35
Dorset	547.81
Metropolitan Councils: average	761.00
Manchester	1,005.50
Solihull	606.20

(c) Averages for 15 worst-performing councils

	1993/4	1994/5	Improvement
Average time taken to relet council homes	14 wks	10 wks	29%
% of tenants in arrears of 13 weeks or more	20%	14%	30%
Rent collected as % of rent due	93%	96%	3%
% householder planning applications processed in 8 weeks	45%	60%	33%
% council tax benefit claims processed in 14 days	29%	61%	110%
% of council tax collected compared to amount budgeted to collect	84%	89%	6%
Average length of stay of homeless families in B&B accommodation	46 wks	26 wks	43%
% housing benefit claims processed in 14 days	35%	68%	94%
% student grants paid on time	54%	88%	63%
% pupils with special needs assessed in 6 months	2%	18%	Improved by a factor of 9

Sources: *Independent, The Times, Financial Times*, 21 March 1996.
Prepared by Sara Martin, Cranfield School of Management.

'league tables'. Again, this helps to put the organisation's resources and performance into perspective and reflects the fact that it is the *relative* position of a company which matters in assessing its strategic capability. This analysis needs to be undertaken in relation to the organisation's separate activities and not just its overall product or market position.

One danger of industry norm analysis (whether it be in the private or public sector) is that the whole industry may be performing badly and losing out competitively to other industries that can satisfy customers' needs in different ways, or to different countries.

Illustration 4.6　Benchmarking: comparing property performance

Benchmarking can start in simple ways — often revealing some startling differences. This can then be developed into a much more comprehensive set of comparisons.

Property typically accounts for about 40 per cent of company assets and 10 per cent of operating costs. Through benchmarking, managers can know whether they are using their properties more or less efficiently than their peers, and so whether or not they have a competitive edge.

In 1994, Hillier Parker set up a benchmarking club to collect and analyse information on office properties from nine members. The first batch of data produced some telling comparisons. Members of the club paid on average £26.91 to £34.98 per square metre in rates, yet one of the members had an average bill of £69.96 per square metre. A spokesperson for Hillier Parker commented that: 'Looking at the location of their properties, there is no reason for such a large difference. This is clearly an area for potential savings.'

While, like Hillier Parker, most benchmarking clubs are relatively small, there are plans for a new Occupational Property Databank collecting data on thousands of properties from dozens of occupiers. If successful, benchmarks based on a much wider spread of data would be possible. Fourteen companies including Barclays, National Westminster, Eagle Star, Sears, BT and British Gas have already agreed to supply information on 25,000 properties. The plan is to evolve benchmarks covering four main areas:

- Property costs, including space and detailed information on rents and rates.
- Utilisation of property: space per employee and broad measures of efficiency such as transactions per square metre.
- Estate management costs: how much it costs companies to manage their property.
- Asset performance: the rate of return companies achieve on property investment and the capital value of occupational properties over time.

It is intended that the databank will stimulate debate and discussion, helping companies to arrive at the best way of organising their property management.

Source: *Financial Times*, 7 April 1995.
Prepared by Sara Martin, Cranfield School of Management.

Therefore, if an industry comparison is performed, it is wise to make some assessment of how resources and competences compare not only with direct competitors, but also with those in other countries and industries. This can be done by looking at a few of the more important measures of resource utilisation, such as stock turnover and yield from raw materials.

The shortcomings of industry norm analysis have encouraged organisations to develop different approaches to inter-company comparisons. Rather than attempting to establish the 'norm', there is a search for *best practice* and the establishment of *benchmarks of performance* related to that best practice. For example, *competitor profiles*[20] are detailed dossiers about the resources and competences of competitors and their relative performance activity by activity and not just overall. The greatest value of this type of best-practice analysis is to be gained if comparisons are also made *beyond* the industry, as will now be discussed.

4.4.3 Benchmarking[21]

Ideally, benchmarking should seek to assess the competences of the organisation against 'best-in-class', wherever that is to be found. For example, the activities involved in patient care in a hospital may be compared not only with other hospitals, but also with those similar activities in the hotel industry; similarly, the exploitation of IT systems to create organisational competences is not unique to a particular industry. In large organisations, internal benchmarking (e.g. between departments or sites) may prove valuable as a means of raising overall organisational competence.

Illustration 4.6 shows that benchmarking can often be started in simple ways and then later developed into a more comprehensive set of comparisons.

Level of benchmarking	Through	Examples of measures
Resources	Resource audit	Quantity of resources, e.g. • revenue/employee • capital intensity Quality of resources, e.g. • qualifications of employees • age of machinery • uniqueness (e.g. patents)
Competences in separate activities	Analysing activities	Sales calls/sales person Output/employee Materials wastage
Competences through managing linkages	Analysing overall performance	Market share Profitability Productivity

Figure 4.10 Benchmarking — at three levels

It has been argued in this chapter that the competitive advantage of an organisation is likely to be underpinned by a combination of (some) unique resources, core competences in the performance of separate activities, and core competences concerned with the management of linkages between activities. Benchmarking can be undertaken at each of these 'levels', as shown in Figure 4.10.

Base budget reviews[22] have been used to build benchmarking into a wider strategic review by some organisations in which historically the idea of external comparison has been ignored or even resisted. Such reviews are most effective where they are applied to strategic business units or service areas and four fundamental questions are asked: first, *why* are these products/services provided at all; second, why are they provided in *that particular way*; third, what are the examples of *best practice* elsewhere; fourth, how should the activities be *reshaped* in the light of these comparisons? Although this process is at least partially subjective, there are many examples of its successful application.

4.4.4 Financial analyses[23]

Financial information and analyses may be one way in which assessments of competence can be made. Many of the measures listed in Figure 4.10 would be expressed in financial terms. Inevitably, those inside the organisation (particularly managers) are likely to have access to considerably more information than other stakeholders. The first important issue to recognise is that there will not be a single agreed view on how to assess the financial performance of a company, since different stakeholders will have different expectations of the company. This concept of stakeholder expectations is covered more fully in Chapter 5, but for the current purpose it is important to distinguish between three different types of financial expectation which will influence the view taken on an organisation's competences and performance, and the type of financial information needed or used in such an assessment:

- *Shareholders* are essentially concerned with assessing the quality of their *investment* and the payoffs they can expect both in dividends and in capital growth (reflected in share price). Therefore, they will be mainly concerned with measures such as earnings per share, P/E ratio and dividend yield. Comparisons across companies are a key measure of attractiveness to investors and a basis of their judgement on the overall competence of the organisation. Shareholder value analysis is discussed in more detail in Chapter 8 (section 8.3.1).
- *Bankers* and other providers of interest-bearing loans are concerned about the *risk* attached to their loans and the competence with which this is managed. A consistently good track record could be regarded (in

itself) as a core competence by bankers and a reason to invest further with some companies and not others. This might be assessed through looking at the capital structure of the company — particularly the gearing ratio (of debt to equity), which indicates how sensitive the solvency of the company is to changes in its profit position. Interest cover is a similar measure which relates interest payments to profit.

- *Suppliers* and *employees* are likely to be concerned with the *liquidity* of the company, which is a measure of its ability to meet short-term commitments to creditors and wages. Bankers will share this concern because a deteriorating liquidity position may require correction through loans and the increased risk profile discussed above. Again, a track record in this area could be a core competence — for example, in improving supplier relationships, resulting in discounts or improved credit.

The following issues need to be borne in mind when using financial analyses to assess organisational competences:

- Financial ratios (stock turnover, sales margin, etc.) are of no importance in themselves. It is the implications of these ratios which are important, and these may not emerge until some sensible basis of comparison is established (see above). Even then a word of warning is necessary. It may be that an organisation is successfully differentiating itself from its competitors by extra spending in selected areas (e.g. advertising). Provided this results in added value (possibly through price or market share), this may well be a defensible spending pattern.
- Financial analyses which relate to those activities which are core competences of the organisation will be particularly useful. For example, rate of stock turnover may be important to a high street store, unit profit margins to a market stallholder, and sales volume to a capital-intensive manufacturer. It is important to be selective in the use of ratios.
- It should be remembered that core competences may change over time and so should the key financial measures to monitor. For example, during the introduction of a new product, the key factor may be establishing *sales volume*; once established, *profit/unit* might be most important; while during decline, *cash flow* may be essential to support the introduction of the next generation of products.

A major concern about traditional financial analysis from a strategic perspective is that it has tended to exclude two key stakeholder groups:

- *Community* — who are concerned with the *social cost* of an organisation's activities, such as pollution or marketing. This is rarely accounted for in traditional financial analyses, but it is an issue of growing concern. Matters of business ethics will be discussed more fully in Chapter 5 (section 5.4). Failure to pay proper attention to these issues could be a source of strategic weakness.

- *Customers* — who are concerned about value for money in products or services. This assessment is rarely made in traditional financial analyses, the implication being that companies which survive profitably in a competitive environment *must* be providing value for money. Where competitive pressures have not existed, such as among many public services, there are now serious attempts to develop performance measures more related to value for money. Financial analysis can assist this process only if information is collected for that purpose. Many management information systems are not geared to such a detailed analysis of separate value activities, making this process difficult. In the UK in the early 1990s, political weight was put behind this process by the development of a *citizens' charter* for many public services. This defined what was expected of each public service in terms of client expectations and value-for-money performance standards.

4.5   Assessing the balance of the organisation

The previous sections have been concerned with analysing the competences of an organisation through looking in detail at the separate activities which are undertaken and also the way that linkages are managed between these separate activities and within the wider value system. Such an analysis should provide a useful analysis of an organisation's competences within its separate strategic business units. However, in many organisations the strategic capability of the organisation will also be determined by the extent to which the organisation's business units are *balanced as a whole*.

Portfolio analyses[24] can be useful in assessing this balance, and it is a key aspect of strategic capability to ensure that the portfolio is strong. Portfolio analysis can be used to describe the current range of SBUs and to assess the 'strength' of the mix both historically and against future scenarios. The Boston Consultancy Group (BCG) proposed one of the first ways of classifying business units — in relation to market growth and company relative market share. Figure 4.11 shows this original matrix together with a number of other matrices.

The growth/share matrix permits SBUs to be examined in relation to (a) market (segment) share and (b) the growth rate of that market. Market growth rate is important for an SBU seeking to dominate a market because it may be easier to gain dominance when a market is in its growth state. In a state of maturity, a market is likely to be stable with customer loyalties fairly fixed, so it is more difficult to gain share. But if all competitors in the growth stage are trying to gain market share, competition will be very fierce: so it will be necessary to invest in that SBU in order to gain share and market dominance. Moreover, it is likely that such an SBU will need to price low

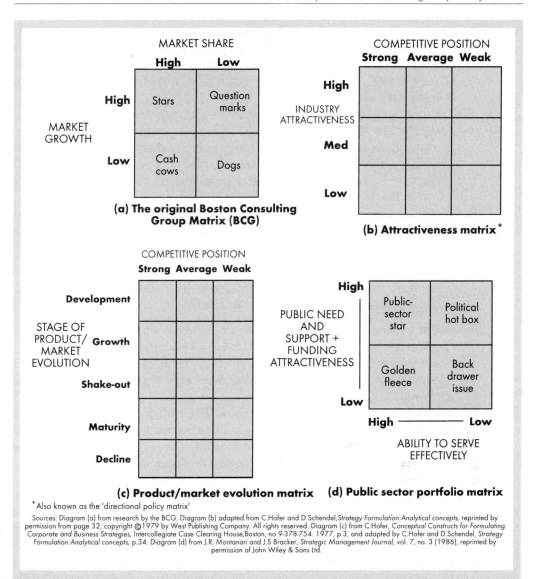

Figure 4.11   Product portfolio matrices

The following labels appear within the figure:

MARKET SHARE

High   Low

MARKET GROWTH

High — Stars / Question marks

Low — Cash cows / Dogs

(a) The original Boston Consulting Group Matrix (BCG)

COMPETITIVE POSITION

Strong Average Weak

INDUSTRY ATTRACTIVENESS

High / Med / Low

(b) Attractiveness matrix*

COMPETITIVE POSITION

Strong Average Weak

STAGE OF PRODUCT/ MARKET EVOLUTION

Development / Growth / Shake-out / Maturity / Decline

(c) Product/market evolution matrix

PUBLIC NEED AND SUPPORT + FUNDING ATTRACTIVENESS

High / Low

Public-sector star / Political hot box

Golden fleece / Back drawer issue

High ——————— Low

ABILITY TO SERVE EFFECTIVELY

(d) Public sector portfolio matrix

*Also known as the 'directional policy matrix'

Sources: Diagram (a) from research by the BCG. Diagram (b) adapted from C.Hofer and D.Schendel,*Strategy Formulation:Analytical concepts*, reprinted by permission from page 32; copyright ©1979 by West Publishing Company. All rights reserved. Diagram (c) from C.Hofer, *Conceptual Constructs for Formulating Corporate and Business Strategies*, Intercollegiate Case Clearing House,Boston, no 9-378-754. 1977, p.3, and adapted by C.Hofer and D.Schendel, *Strategy Formulation:Analytical concepts*, p.34. Diagram (d) from J.R. Montanari and J.S Bracker, *Strategic Management Journal*, vol. 7, no. 3 (1986), reprinted by permission of John Wiley & Sons Ltd.

and/or spend high amounts on advertising and selling. This strategy is one of high risk unless this low-margin activity is financed by products earning higher profit levels. This leads to the idea of a balanced mix of SBUs.

■ A *star* is an SBU which has a high market share in a growing market. It may be spending heavily to gain that share, but experience curve benefits (see section 4.3.3) should mean that costs are reducing over time and hopefully at a rate faster than that of the competition.

- The *question mark* (or problem child) is also in a growing market, but does not have a high market share. It may be necessary to spend heavily to increase market share, but if so, it is unlikely that the SBU is achieving sufficient cost reduction benefits to offset such investments.
- The *cash cow* has a high market share in a mature market. Because growth is low and market conditions are more stable, the need for heavy marketing investment is less. But high relative market share means that the SBU should be able to maintain unit cost levels below those of competitors. The cash cow should then be a cash provider (e.g. to finance question marks).
- *Dogs* have low share in static or declining markets and are thus the worst of all combinations. They may be a cash drain and use up a disproportionate amount of company time and resources.

Although portfolio analyses can be useful in assessing how strategic business units contribute to the strategic capability of the organisation, some caution needs to be exercised in their use:

- There can be practical difficulties in deciding what exactly 'high' and 'low' (growth and share) can mean in a particular situation.
- The analysis should be applied to *strategic business units* (i.e. a *bundle* of products/services and the associated market *segments*) not to whole markets.
- Corporate management must develop the ability and devote time to reviewing the role of each strategic business unit in the overall mix of company activities. This is an important 'parenting' responsibility of the corporate centre in divisionalised organisations, and will be discussed in Chapters 6 and 9.
- Some authors are somewhat sceptical of whether the corporate headquarters really do add value to the company through these processes of buying, selling, developing or running down individual units to keep the portfolio balanced. They suggest that the free market might well allocate resources more effectively if the activities were separated and the corporate centre closed down. This issue will be discussed more fully in Chapter 10.
- The original BCG analysis concentrated on the needs of a business to plan its cash flow requirements across its portfolio. So *cash cows* will be used to fund the development of *question marks* and *stars*. However, little is said about the behavioural implications of such a strategy. How does central management motivate the managers of *cash cows*, who see all their hard-earned surpluses being invested in other businesses? Indeed, perhaps the single factor which makes the creation and management of a balanced portfolio difficult in practice is the jealousy which can arise between the various strategic business units.

- In many organisations the critical resource to be planned and balanced will not be cash, but the time and creative energy of the organisation's managers, designers, engineers, etc. *Question marks* and *stars* are very demanding on these types of resource.

- The portfolio approach has also been used in the public sector,[25] as seen in Figure 4.11(d). Here the key judgements are concerned with the organisation's ability to provide perceived value for money with the resources which are likely to be available, and the political requirement to offer services. This latter point is often forgotten by public sector managers when reviewing their portfolio of activities for the future. A provider of public services will often need to keep a wider portfolio of services in order to satisfy the political objectives within which it operates.

- The position of *dogs* is often misunderstood. Certainly, there may be some products which need immediate deletion — but even then there may be political difficulties if they are the brain-child of people with power within the organisation. However, other dogs may have a useful place in the portfolio. They may be necessary to complete the product range and provide a credible presence in the market. They may be held for defensive reasons — to keep competitors out. They may be capable of revitalisation.

Despite these concerns, however, portfolio analysis remains an important method of assessing the balance of an organisation and identifying strategic choices (see Chapter 6, section 6.4.1).

4.6   Identification of key issues

The last major aspect of resource analysis is the identification of the key issues arising from previous analyses. It is only at this stage of the analysis that a sensible assessment can be made of the major strengths and weaknesses of an organisation and their strategic importance. The analysis then starts to be useful as a basis against which to judge future courses of action.

4.6.1 SWOT analysis[26]

SWOT analysis can be a very useful way of summarising many of the previous analyses and combining them with the key issues from environmental analysis. So it brings together the main issues raised in this chapter and the previous one. The aim is to identify the extent to which the current strategy of an organisation and its more specific strengths and

Illustration 4.7 SWOT analysis

A SWOT analysis can be a useful way to summarise the relationship between key environmental influences, the strategic capability of the organisation and hence the agenda for developing new strategies.

The table below is from a SWOT analysis undertaken by a District Health Authority in the UK in 1996. The role of the Health Authorities at that time was to 'purchase' health care on behalf of their communities both directly from hospitals and indirectly through health care practitioners (GP fundholders). The organisation concluded that the most important areas of strength were the links with GPs and the capacity for innovation — and that these were core competences. Other areas needed development, such as information systems and performance assessments of different medical treatments.

Strengths and weaknesses	Key issues in the environment							
	Politics/ legislation	Link between deprivation and health	New technologies (medical)	Rising public expectation	Demographic trends	Competitive market	+	−
Main strengths								
Capacity for innovation	+	+	+	++	+	++	8	0
Good GP links	+	++	+	+	+	+	7	0
Committed employees	+	+	+	+	0	+	5	0
Good joint working with Social Services	+	++	0	+	+	−	5	1
Main weaknesses								
Lack of outcome measures	−	−−	−	−	−	−	0	7
Information measurement systems	−	0	−	−−	−	−−	0	7
Provider dominated agenda	0	0	−−	−−	−−	++	2	6
Health Authority is still defining its role and its membership	−	−	0	0	0	−−	0	4
No financial growth	+	−	−	−	−	+	2	4
+	5	6	3	5	3	7		
−	3	4	5	6	5	6		

Source: Debbie Sloan, MBA student. Reproduced with permission.

weaknesses are relevant to, and capable of, dealing with the changes taking place in the business environment. It can also be used to assess whether there are opportunities to exploit further the unique resources or core competences of the organisation. SWOT stands for strengths, weaknesses, opportunities and threats, but rather than just listing these in terms of managers' perceptions, the idea is to undertake a more structured analysis so as to yield findings which can contribute to the formulation of strategy. The procedure can be undertaken as follows:

■ Identify the key changes in the organisation's environment following the analyses outlined in Chapter 3. While there is no fixed number which should be agreed upon, it is helpful if the list does not exceed seven or eight key points.

■ The same process should then be undertaken in terms of the resource profile and competences of the organisation, following the analysis outlined in this chapter to identify the organisation's strengths and weaknesses. It is useful to keep the total list to no more than eight points. It is important to avoid overgeneralising this analysis and to keep to quite specific points: a statement such as 'poor management' means very little and could be interpreted in any number of ways. If it really means that senior managers have, historically, not been good at managing change in the organisation, that is a more specific and more useful point.

When this procedure is completed, the analysis should look something like the completed Illustration 4.7. This should provide some useful strategic insights. For example, Illustration 4.7 shows that the organisation already has many of the competences needed to meet the rising public expectations of health care. It also reveals that its good links with GPs were of particular benefit in meeting many of the key issues in the environment. Some issues (such as demographic trends — the ageing population) could be either opportunities or threats, depending on the extent to which the organisation can capitalise on its strengths in innovation and links with social services while coping with the redistribution of financial resources and the attitudes of providers (e.g. hospitals) to these changes. An analysis of perceived weaknesses should also recognise that their importance varies depending on the types of strategy the organisation is likely to pursue. For example, the concerns about the providers dominating the agenda would diminish if the health care provision became more market driven — an extreme example would be by providing citizens with vouchers to purchase their own health care from GPs and hospitals. In these circumstances, the Health Authority would be the key driver of demand for specific health care services by the way in which it chose to allocate vouchers to reflect (for example) the demographic characteristics of individuals (age, social deprivation or whatever). Providers would have to respond to this market demand.

4.6.2 Critical success factors (CSFs)[27]

Many organisations are now taking on board one of the key messages from this chapter: namely, that there is not a 'best' and 'worst' set of resources and competences. 'Strength' and 'weakness' can be assessed only in relation to the types of strategy the organisation is pursuing and/or wishes to pursue.

This is also a reminder that the separation of strategic analysis from strategic choice is somewhat artificial.

In Chapter 10 the idea of critical success factors (CSFs) will be used to map out the core competences needed to support specific strategies. Given this natural connection between analysis and choice, many organisations find the idea of CSFs a useful way of reflecting on the strategic messages which should come out of resource analysis. Critical success factors are those aspects of strategy in which an organisation must excel to outperform competition, and they are underpinned by core competences in specific activities or in managing linkages between activities. For example, if 'speed to market' with new product launch is a CSF, it may be underpinned by core competences in the logistics of physical distribution and negotiating skills with key account retail outlets. The example in Figure 4.6, the world automobile industry, illustrates how the critical success factors changed over time from market access to quality/reliability to product features. This required the different core competences to gain competitive advantage as illustrated and previously discussed in section 4.3.2. CSF analysis underlines this important relationship between resources, competences and choice of strategies, which is also central to the idea of balanced scorecards for assessing performance. These will be discussed in Chapter 10 (section 10.4.3).

4.7 Summary

There are some important implications for managers of a resources and competence perspective on the strategic development of organisations, and how they accommodate the 'issues' from the environment and the stakeholder expectations discussed in Chapters 3 and 5.

- The choice of 'good' strategies by an organisation can only be partly guided by general principles of 'strategic fit' between the business environment and the resource base of organisations. Many competitors may achieve similar degrees of fit, yet some outperform others. This difference in performance results from the way in which resources are deployed to create competences in separate activities, how these are matched to the requirements for particular types of strategy and, crucially, the competence with which these activities are linked together to improve value for money in products or services. Value chain analysis can be a useful way of describing and analysing these important relationships between an organisation's resources, competences and strategies. An analysis also needs to identify which competences are *core* to the success of strategy and how these core competences can provide the basis of new opportunities.

- There can be a mismatch between the changing requirements from the business environment and the core competences of the organisation. This can be addressed in two broad ways: first, to acknowledge that new core competences need to be developed; and second, to find new opportunities where traditional core competences will provide competitive advantage. These issues will be discussed more fully in Chapter 7.

- The competences of an organisation are likely to be 'taken for granted' as part of the tacit knowledge and routines within the organisation. This can give the organisation real competitive advantage if this tacit knowledge is valuable, rare (in the sense that competitors do not have it) and difficult to imitate. However, because this knowledge is tacit, managers often find it difficult to identify explicitly which are their core competences, to acknowledge the need for change and/or to develop new competences to address a changing situation. Therefore, there must be processes through which the tacit knowledge is surfaced and challenged, and new competences are learnt. Otherwise, the core competences become *rigidities* preventing change.

- The analysis of competences is useful for understanding an organisation at the level of the *strategic business unit*. In addition, a judgement needs to be made on the strength or weakness of the *portfolio* of strategic business units.

- Organisation performance can only really be judged in *relative* terms, either against *history* or in the context of the *norm* for the industry (i.e. against competition). Ideally, it should be judged against *best practice* wherever that may be found. *Benchmarking* analysis can provide such comparisons of the resources, competences in separate activities and overall competence of the organisation.

- Specific techniques for analysing resources and competences may provide only a partial picture. There a need to pull these together to give an overall assessment of strategic capability. This may be done through a SWOT analysis or by assessing the extent to which the resources and competences relate to the critical success factors.

References

1. The concept of resource-based strategies was discussed by B. Wernerfelt, 'A resource-based view of the firm', *Strategic Management Journal*, vol. 5, no. 2 (1984) pp. 171–180. The idea of driving strategy development from the resources and competences of an organisation is discussed in G. Hamel and C.K. Prahalad, 'Strategic intent', *Harvard Business Review*, vol. 67, no. 3 (1989), pp. 63–76; G. Hamel and C.K. Prahalad, 'Strategy as stretch and leverage', *Harvard Business Review*, vol. 71, no. 2 (1993), pp. 75–84; G. Stalk, P. Evans and L.E. Shulman, 'Competing on capabilities: the new rules of corporate strategy', *Harvard Business Review*, vol. 70, no. 2 (1992), pp. 57–69; D. Collis and C. Montgomery, 'Competing on resources: strategy in the 1990s', *Harvard Business Review*, vol. 73, no. 4 (1995), pp. 118–28; and D.J. Teece, G. Pisano and A. Shuen, 'Dynamic capabilities and strategic management', *Harvard Business School Working Paper*, 1992.

2. The importance of analysing and understanding tacit knowledge is discussed in I. Nonaka and H. Takeuchi, *The Knowledge Creating Company*, Oxford University Press, 1995.

3. Resource audits are covered in V. Ambrosini with G. Johnson and K. Scholes (eds.), *Exploring Techniques of Analysis and Evaluation in Strategic Management*, Prentice Hall, 1998. There are also a number of papers and standard texts which include traditional resource audits: for example, G.A. Steiner, *Strategic Planning: What every manager must know*, Free Press, 1979, chapter 8; R.M. Grant, *Contemporary Strategy Analysis*, 2nd edition, Blackwell, 1995, p. 122; and R.B. Buchelle, 'How to evaluate a firm', *California Management Review* (Fall 1962). The latter provides extensive checklists under functional areas. Readers who are unfamiliar with resource analysis in any functional area may wish to consult one of the following standard texts: P. Kotler, *Marketing Management: Analysis, planning, implementation and control*, 8th edition, Prentice Hall, 1993; N. Slack and S. Chambers, *Operations Management*, Pitman, 1995; R. Wild, *Production and Operations Management*, 5th edition, Nelson, 1995; M.W.E.

Glautier and B. Underdown, *Accounting Theory and Practice*, 5th edition, Pitman, 1994; D. Torrington and L. Hall, *Personnel Management: A new approach*, 3rd edition, Prentice Hall, 1995; C. Fombrun, N. Tichy and M. Devanna, *Strategic Human Resource Management*, Wiley, 1990.

4. Intangible resources have become increasingly recognised as being of strategic importance: see R. Hall, 'The strategic analysis of intangible resources', *Strategic Management Journal*, vol. 13, no. 2 (1992) pp. 135–144 and 'A framework linking intangible resources and capabilities to sustainable competitive advantage', *Strategic Management Journal*, vol. 14, no. 8 (1993) pp. 607–18. J. Smythe, C. Dorwood and J. Reback, *Corporate Reputation: The new strategic asset*, Century Business, 1992, and J. Kay, *Foundations of Corporate Success*, Oxford University Press, 1993, chapter 6, look at one particular intangible asset — reputation.

5. An extensive discussion of the value chain concept and its application can be found in M.E. Porter, *Competitive Advantage*, Free Press, 1985. See also A. Shepherd's chapter, 'Understanding and using value chain analysis' in V. Ambrosini with G. Johnson and K. Scholes (see ref. 3).

6. Value analysis was developed in the post-war period by Lawrence Miles. See, for example, L.D. Miles, *Techniques of Value Analysis and Engineering*, McGraw-Hill, 1961.

7. There are a number of recent books and articles about the importance of analysing and understanding core competences: G. Hamel and A. Heene (eds.), *Competence-Based Competition*, Wiley, 1994; M. Tampoe's chapter, 'Getting to know your organisation's core competences' in V. Ambrosini with G. Johnson and K. Scholes (see ref. 3). G. Hamel and C.K. Prahalad, 'The core competence of the corporation', *Harvard Business Review*, vol. 68, no. 3 (1990), pp. 79–91; R.H. Hayes and G.P. Pisano, 'Beyond world class: the new manufacturing strategy', *Harvard Business Review*, vol. 72, no. 1 (1994), pp. 77–86; K. Gronhaug and O. Nordhaug, 'Strategy and competence in firms', *European Management*

Journal, vol. 10, no. 4 (1992), pp. 438–44.

8. This example is from Hamel and Heene (reference 7 above), pp. 16–18.

9. Cost advantage is discussed by Grant (reference 3 above), chapter 7, and B. Karlof, *Strategic Precision*, Wiley, 1993, chapter 3.

10. P. Conley, *Experience Curves as a Planning Tool*, available as a pamphlet from the Boston Consulting Group. See also A.C. Hax and N.S. Majluf, in R.G. Dyson (ed.), *Strategic Planning: Models and analytical techniques*, Wiley, 1990.

11. A useful reference on adding value is Kay (reference 4 above), chapter 2.

12. Customer perceived use value analysis is discussed in D. Faulkner and C. Bowman, *The Essence of Competitive Strategy*, Prentice Hall, 1995, pp. 11–12.

13. The importance of managing vertical relationships has been stressed by Porter (reference 5 above) and Kay (reference 4 above), chapter 17.

14. See T. Powell, 'Total quality management as competitive advantage: a review and empirical study', *Strategic Management Journal*, vol. 16, no. 1 (1995), pp. 15–37; J.S. Oakland, *Total Quality Management*, 2nd edition, Butterworth-Heinemann, 1995.

15. J.B. Barney, 'Organisational culture: can it be a source of competitive advantage?', *Academy of Management Review*, vol. 11, no. 3 (1986), pp. 656–65.

16. See Nonaka and Takeuchi (reference 2 above) for a discussion of tacit knowledge.

17. D. Leonard-Barton, 'Core capabilities and core rigidities: a paradox in managing new product development', *Strategic Management Journal*, vol. 13, (summer 1992), pp. 111–25.

18. The dangers of over-subcontracting are discussed in J.C. Jarillo, *Strategic Networks: Creating the borderless organisation*, Butterworth-Heinemann, 1993, chapter 4.

19. Inter-company comparisons are discussed in J. Ellis and D. Williams, *Corporate Strategy and Financial Analysis*, Pitman, 1993, chapter 7.

20. Competitor profiles are discussed in M.E. Porter, *Competitive Strategy*, Free Press, 1980, p. 49.

21. G.H. Watson, *Strategic Benchmarking*, Wiley, 1993, is a practical guide to benchmarking. See also G. Tomlinson's chapter, 'Comparative analysis: benchmarking' in V. Ambrosini with G. Johnson and K. Scholes (see ref. 3). T. Clayton and B. Luchs, 'Strategic benchmarking at ICI Fibres', *Long Range Planning*, vol. 27, no. 3 (1994), pp. 54–63, is a useful case example. See also L.S. Pryor and S.J. Katz, 'How benchmarking goes wrong (and how to do it right)', *Planning Review (USA)*, vol. 21, no. 1 (1993), pp. 7–11; G.H. Watson, 'How process benchmarking supports corporate strategy', *Planning Review (USA)*, vol. 21, no. 1 (1993), pp. 12–15; D.L. Ransley, 'Training managers to benchmark', *Planning Review*, vol. 21, no. 1 (1993), pp. 32–6.

22. Base budget reviews have been used by a number of public sector organisations in an attempt to take on board the philosophy of zero-based budgets in a way that could be worked in practice (see G. Roberts and K. Scholes, 'Policy and base budget reviews at Cheshire County Council', *Waves of Change Conference Proceedings*, Sheffield Business School, 1993).

23. A.N. Grundy with G. Johnson and K. Scholes, *Exploring Strategic Financial Management*, Prentice Hall (1998), shows how a range of financial analyses can contribute to a strategic analysis. Also useful are J. Ellis and D. Williams, *Corporate Strategy and Financial Analysis*, Pitman, 1993; K. Ward, *Corporate Financial Strategy*, Butterworth-Heinemann, 1993.

24. A review of a range of portfolio analyses can be found in D. Faulkner's chapter, 'Portfolio matrices', in V. Ambrosini with G. Johnson and K. Scholes (see ref. 3). The use of growth/share matrices is discussed by Hax and Majluf (reference 10 above). See also Karlof (reference 9 above), chapter 2. Some authors have warned of the need to use portfolio matrices with care: for example, S.P. Slatter, 'Common pitfalls in using the BCG portfolio matrix', *London Business School Journal* (Winter 1980).

25. J.R. Montanari and J.S. Bracker, 'The strategic management process at the public planning unit level', *Strategic Management Journal*, vol. 7, no. 3 (1986) pp. 251–265.

26. The idea of SWOT as a commonsense checklist has been used for many years: for example, S. Tilles, 'Making strategy explicit', in I. Ansoff (ed.), *Business Strategy*, Penguin, 1968. See also

J. Verity and G. Johnson's chapter on SWOT analysis in V. Ambrosini with G. Johnson and K. Scholes (see ref. 3).

27. See M. Hardaker and B.K. Ward, 'Getting things done', *Harvard Business Review*, vol. 65, no. 6 (1987), pp. 112–20.

Recommended key readings

- A number of the chapters in V. Ambrosini with G. Johnson and K. Scholes (eds) *Exploring Techniques of Analysis and Evaluation in Strategic Management*, Prentice Hall 1998, provide further discussion of approaches to analyses introduced in this chapter. Specifically: Shepherd on value chain analysis; Tampoe on core competences; Tomlinson on benchmarking; Faulkner on portfolio matrices; Verity and Johnson on SWOT analysis.
- A.N. Grundy with G. Johnson and K. Scholes, *Exploring Strategic Financial Management*, Prentice Hall, 1998, shows how a range of financial analyses can contribute to a strategic analysis.
- An extensive discussion of the value chain concept and its application can be found in M.E. Porter, *Competitive Advantage*, Free Press, 1985.
- J. Kay, *Foundations of Corporate Success*, Oxford University Press, 1993, discusses many aspects of the links between strategic capability and competitive success.
- The use of growth/share matrices is discussed by A.C. Hax and N.S. Majluf, in R.G. Dyson (ed.), *Strategic Planning: Models and analytical techniques*, Wiley, 1990.

Work assignments

4.1 Undertake a resource audit of an organisation with which you are familiar. Then identify which resources, if any, are unique in the sense that they are difficult to imitate (see Figure 4.2). Has the organisation gained competitive advantage as a result of this uniqueness? Why/why not? You can answer this in relation to Laura Ashley* if you so wish.

4.2 Use Figures 4.4 and 4.5 to map out the key value activities for Laura Ashley* or an organisation of your choice, both within the company and in the wider value system in which it operates.

4.3 **By referring to Figure 4.3, explain how the organisation you have analysed in assignment 4.2 does or does not gain competitive advantage from:**
   (a) competence in the separate value activities
   (b) managing linkages within the value chain.

4.4 *Use Figures 4.7, 4.8 and 4.9 to explain how the control of relationships within the value chain could be changed to improve the efficiency and/or effectiveness of an organisation. Illustrate your answer by reference to an organisation of your choice, Laura Ashley,* Illustration 4.3 or Illustration 4.4.*

4.5 **Choose two organisations in the same industry and compare the configurations of their value chain. Explain how these relate to the organisation's competitive positioning.**

4.6 Take any industry and public service and sketch out a map of how core competences have changed over time (use Figure 4.6 as an example). Why have these changes occurred? How did the relative strengths of different companies or service providers change over this period? Why?

4.7 **Identify the strategic business units in an organisation of your choice. Use one of the portfolio matrices shown in Figure 4.11 to assess the extent to which these represent a well-balanced portfolio. How would you strengthen this portfolio?**

4.8 *It has been said that the power of benchmarking is in understanding how value for money is created or lost in the separate activities of the organisation against the 'best in class' organisations for each activity. To what extent do you feel this is a universal prescription for improving competitive performance? Are there any dangers/pitfalls in this approach? Discuss.*

4.9 Prepare a SWOT analysis for an organisation of your choice (see Illustration 4.7). Explain carefully why you have chosen each of the key items in your shortlists.

*This refers to a case in the Text and Cases version of this book.

CHAPTER 5

Stakeholder expectations and organisational purposes

5.1 Introduction

There is a temptation to look for a neat and tidy way of formulating strategy. Such a method might, apparently, be achieved through the analysis of the organisation's environment (Chapter 3) and the extent to which the company's resources, or strategic capability (Chapter 4), are matched with or fit the environment, or vice versa. However, this strategic logic can fail to recognise the complex role which people play in the evolution of strategy, as introduced in Chapter 2. Strategy formulation is also about the *purposes* of the organisation and what people want the organisation to be like. This chapter is concerned with examining how the *political* and *cultural context* of an organisation can be analysed and understood as part of a strategic analysis. There has been a growing awareness of the central importance of these issues since the early 1980s.

Figure 5.1 summarises how the theme will be progressed through the chapter by identifying four broad influences on an organisation's purposes. Although these will be discussed separately, it should be remembered that, in reality, they form part of a connected web of influences which *together* shape the purposes of an organisation at any given time:

■ The fundamental questions are *whom should* the organisation be there to serve and *how* the direction and purposes of an organisation *should be* determined. This is the province of *corporate governance*. This relates not only to the power to influence purposes, but also the processes of supervising executive decisions/actions and the issues of *accountability* and the *regulatory framework* within which organisations operate. There are significant differences in the approach to corporate governance in different countries and this will be reflected in the discussion.

■ *Whom* the organisation *does actually* serve in practice is the second important issue. This will be addressed through the concept of

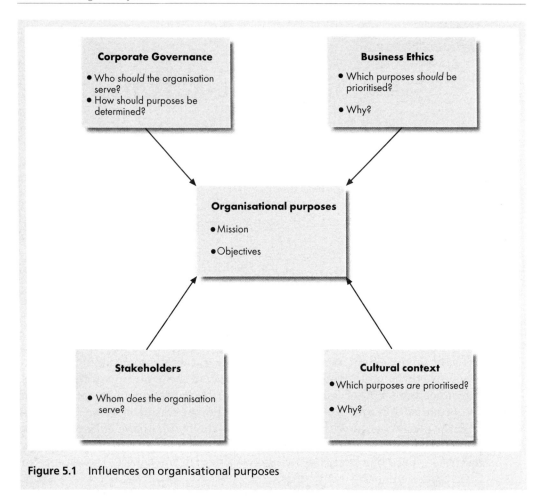

Figure 5.1   Influences on organisational purposes

organisational stakeholders and the extent to which they are interested in and/or able to influence the organisation's purposes. Stakeholders are those individuals or groups who depend on the organisation to fulfil their own goals, and on whom, in turn, the organisation depends. Typically, they include shareholders, customers, suppliers, banks employees and the community at large. Understanding this requires an analysis or assessment of both the *power* and *interest* of different stakeholder groups.

■   *Which purposes* an organisation *should* fulfil is influenced by *ethical* considerations. At the broadest level, these issues impinge on corporate governance — particularly in relation to the accountability of organisations. The ethical agenda is also strongly culturally driven and is concerned with *corporate social responsibility* to the various stakeholders — particularly those with little formal power (such as the community at large). It is also concerned with the ethical standards and behaviour of *individuals*.

▪ *Which purposes are actually* prioritised above others is also related to a variety of factors in the *cultural context* in which the organisation is operating. This relates back to the concept of the *cultural web*, introduced in Chapter 2 as a means of analysing an organisation's culture. This same approach can be used to understand how culture at several 'levels' might influence organisational purposes. This will include the broader issues of *national cultures* through important *reference groups* — such as professional groups/bodies — to the *subcultures* within an organisation — perhaps at the business function level.

The chapter concludes with a discussion of the formal ways in which organisational purposes are expressed and communicated — particularly the role of *mission statements* and *objectives*.

Overall, this chapter is concerned with exploring how this set of influences can be analysed and understood as part of a strategic analysis. Managers may enter this analysis through any of the four main 'strands' in Figure 5.1, but it is important to understand the connections between these broad influences on an organisation's purposes.

5.2   Corporate governance[1]

The starting point in discussing an organisation's purposes will be the corporate governance framework within which the organisation is operating. This determines whom the organisation is there to serve and how the purposes and priorities of the organisation should be decided. It is concerned with both the functioning of the organisation and the distribution of power between different stakeholders. It will be seen that this is strongly culturally bound, resulting in different traditions and frameworks in different countries.[2]

The corporate governance agenda in most countries tends to be more implicit than explicit. This means that the legal and regulatory measures form only a part of the corporate governance.

5.2.1 The governance chain

The complexity of corporate governance has arisen for two main reasons. First, the practical need to separate *ownership* and *management control* of organisations is now the norm — except with very small businesses. The result has been that most organisations operate within a hierarchy or chain of governance. Although the details of the chain will vary from one organisation to another, Figure 5.2 illustrates a typical chain of governance for a publicly quoted company in the UK. Second, there has been an

Reports received

Limited reports

Limited investment
performance reports

Accounts
Analysts' reports
Company briefings

Budgets/qualitative reporting

Budgets/qualitative reporting

Budgets/other
operating reports

Source: David Pitt-Watson, Braxton Associates with permission

Figure 5.2   The chain of corporate governance: typical reporting structure

Illustration 5.1   Sir Rocco Forte, Granada and the 'Ice Maiden'

Pension fund managers have become increasingly powerful players in determining the future of companies — sometimes shown dramatically during takeover bids.

The UK tabloid newspapers have dubbed Carol Galley the 'Ice Maiden' and described her as the most powerful woman in the UK. This will certainly strike a chord with Sir Rocco Forte, who lost his celebrated hotel chain partly because Galley and her associates no longer considered him the right man for the job. In 1996, Carol Galley was Vice-Chairman and Fund Manager of Mercury Asset Management (MAM), controlling over 900 pension funds throughout Britain. Even though Rocco Forte had a high profile in the business world, sentiment meant little to Galley who told him coolly that she had examined the £3.8 billion bid for Forte by Granada and considered it to be good. MAM voted its 14.6 per cent shareholding in Forte in favour of Granada. This action was seen as decisive by other shareholders.

Sir Rocco was devastated, but Galley had no regrets. She had done what she was paid to do — she was responsible to pension fund holders for the value of their stake in Forte.

Although, traditionally, pension fund managers had been discreet, barely visible players in the financial world, all this changed after the 'Big Bang' in the City of London in the 1980s. The pension fund plutocrats emerged from the shadows and became regarded as the key power players in the 'governance chain' and the most deadly beasts in the corporate jungle.

Source: *Sunday Times*, 21 April 1996.

increasing tendency to make organisations more visibly accountable not only to owners (e.g. shareholders), but also to other stakeholder groups. The rights of these various stakeholders will be discussed later.

Even in the simplified example (Figure 5.2) it can be seen that the managers who are driving strategy in the organisation may be very remote from the ultimate beneficiaries of the company's performance. The figure also highlights the information typically available to each 'player' in the chain to judge the performance of others. In the example, it is likely that many beneficiaries are either ignorant of or indifferent to the details of companies in which their money is invested. Many beneficiaries will have their interests 'guarded' by intermediaries — for example, asset managers for pension funds. Illustration 5.1 shows how powerful these intermediaries may be in determining the future of companies.

Given this degree of complexity in corporate governance, there are likely to be several *conflicts of interest* both between different stakeholder groups and for individual managers or directors as they try to balance these various interests. This is a particular issue for boards of directors and has resulted in important developments in both the role of the board and the disclosure of information. A very important question in large publicly quoted corporations is whether corporate managers should regard themselves as solely responsible to shareholders, or whether they have a wider responsibility as 'trustees of the assets of the corporation' on behalf of a wider range of stakeholders.[3]

5.2.2 Shareholders and the role of the governing bodies

The primary statutory responsibility of the governing body of an organisation is to ensure that the organisation actually fulfils the wishes and purposes of the 'owners'. In the private sector, this would be the board of directors working on behalf of shareholders. In the public sector, the governing body would be accountable to the political arm of government — possibly through some intermediate 'agency'. There are important differences between countries regarding the role, composition and *modus operandi* of the board of directors.[4] In the UK, the USA and Australia, the wide spread of shareholdings tends to limit the power of the individual shareholders and heighten that of intermediaries (such as pension fund managers). In most other European countries (e.g. Belgium, the Netherlands and France), shareholding is more closely held and often minority led — perhaps by the founding family, financial institutions or other interests either acting together or using protective mechanisms such as preference shares. The board is strongly controlled by these particular shareholder interests. In Japan, the board tends to be viewed as just one part of a multilayered corporate decision-making process, and hence is usually dominated by corporate executives. Japanese banks tend to have shareholdings in organisations, as against simply providing loan capital. There is also likely to be a complex web of cross-shareholdings between companies. These latter two factors tend to reduce the pressure for short-term results[5] as against longer-term performance, in marked contrast to US/UK companies. In turn, this influences the approach to important aspects of strategy, such as investment.

These different traditions naturally bring with them different structures and compositions of the board. In the UK and USA, there is a single-tier board usually incorporating both executive and non-executive directors. The board essentially supervises the activities/performance of managers to a greater or lesser extent. Many organisations have adopted a subcommittee structure which allows for a more detailed involvement of the board with the work of the managers of the organisation. Non-executive directors sometimes represent the interests of key stakeholders (e.g. institutional investors).

In many other European countries (notably Germany, the Netherlands and France), the *two-tier board* is either mandatory or prevalent. For example, in Germany, the 'upper-tier' or supervisory board oversees the work of the 'lower-tier' board, which is entrusted with the day-to-day management of the organisation. Importantly, the composition of this supervisory board is built around the principles of *co-determination* — half of the members being elected by shareholders, the other half by employees. However, the shareholders maintain the final say through the chairperson's casting vote.

The main potential benefit of the two-tier form of governance is the counterbalancing of the power of managers, which is often a feature of management-dominated unitary boards in the UK and USA — particularly where non-executive directors are weak or ineffective. There has been particular concern that managerial interests have dominated strategic decisions on issues such as diversification and acquisitions — decisions which have proved unsuccessful and not in the best interests of shareholders.[6] There has been much debate as to whether a legally prescribed balance of power is or is not beneficial. Proposals for industrial democracy were put forward in the UK in 1977 by the *Bullock Committee*,[7] but these were not acted on by government. In France, the two-tier system is optional.

In Japan, the composition of the board is heavily weighted towards executive members. However, as membership of the board is seen as a tier in the management hierarchy, the entry of executives on to the board is controlled by the chairperson, who will often take external advice (for example, from bankers) before a manager is promoted to director. In Japanese corporate culture, a prerequisite of a good director is someone who is able to continue to promote the interests of employees. So, in contrast to Germany, employees in Japan have power through cultural norms (trust and the implicit 'duties' of directors) rather than through the legal framework of governance.

The role of the board in nationalised industries is — in theory — very similar to the private sector, except that capital expenditure and borrowings are directly controlled by the responsible minister. In reality, the power of boards is often curtailed by political priorities and the involvement of ministers in management decisions (for example, prices, wages and plant closures). The desire to remove this conflict between political expediency and the need for longer-term strategic direction was an important reason behind the major privatisation programmes in many countries during the 1980s and 1990s.

The public services have a wide variety of arrangements for governing bodies, but there are some commonalities. There has been a move in many countries to increase the proportion of (so-called) independent members on governing bodies. These independent members are the nearest equivalent of

Illustration 5.2   The Patient's Charter

There has been an increasing concern that the rights and voice of individual consumers should be enhanced. The public services have been attempting to do this.

In the early 1990s, many public services, in the UK and elsewhere, were keen to redress the balance of attention they were paying to their various stakeholders. In particular, the voice of the client was encouraged through various means, including, in the UK, what became known as the *Citizen's Charter*. This was prompted by the government, and major public services adopted their own charter.

In the case of the National Health Service, this was known as the *Patient's Charter* and was launched in 1992. The charter contained three main elements: a reaffirmation of seven existing rights of patients; the introduction of three new rights; and the publication of performance standards (both national and local). Standards were not rights, but helped clarify the expectations which government had of management in the health service in terms of quality of service.

Seven existing rights
- Health care on the basis of clinical need not ability to pay.
- Registration with a family doctor (GP).
- Emergency care at any time.
- Referral to a hospital consultant (through GP).
- Clarification of proposed treatment, including risks and alternatives.
- Access to health records.
- Freedom of whether to take part in medical research/training.

the non-executive director in the private sector. Governing bodies are often factional/representational in practice even if not by regulation. This particularly applies to the place of employees and/or unions on governing bodies.

5.2.3 Rights of creditors/lenders

One of the reasons why the corporate governance situation varies so much from one country to another is the differing arrangements for corporate finance. There are the different 'traditions' regarding *equity/debt ratios* and the extent to which the *relationship* with bankers is regarded as one of partnership or simply 'contractual'. At one extreme, particularly in the USA and UK, equity is the dominant form of long-term finance and

Three new rights
- Detailed information on local health services, including quality standards and maximum waiting time.
- Guaranteed admission for treatment by a specific date no longer than two years after being placed on a waiting list.
- Any complaints to be fully and promptly investigated and a written reply sent by the chief executive or general manager.

Nine national standards
- Respect for privacy, dignity, and religious and cultural beliefs.
- All people — including those with special needs — to be able to use services.
- Information to relatives and friends.
- Waiting time for ambulance (14 minutes maximum in urban areas).
- Waiting time for assessment in emergency (immediate assessment).
- Waiting time in outpatients (within 30 minutes of appointment time).
- Cancellation of operations (no cancellations on the day).
- A *named* nurse — or other professional — responsible for each patient.
- Discharge arrangements (follow-up needs).

In addition, local health authorities were required to develop a series of more detailed local standards for the guidance of patients.

Source: *Patient's Charter*, Department of Health, 1991.

commercial banks provide debt capital; relationships with bankers are towards the contractual end of the spectrum. In contrast, in Japan (and to a lesser extent Germany), banks often have significant equity stakes and may be part of the same parent company, and the lead banks may organise the activities of other banks. The power of lenders in these two extremes is very different and exercised in different ways. UK and US banks may exercise their power through *exit* (i.e. withdrawing funds) even if this liquidates the company. Japanese banks are more concerned to steer the longer-term strategy of the organisation and to use their power to have their voice heard.

The trade creditor is the least protected stakeholder in the trading process and there is little in the corporate governance framework to redress this. So creditors need to mitigate their risk through prudence in their dealings.

5.2.4 Relationships with customers and clients

The legal framework of many countries enshrines the principle of *caveat emptor*, placing the burden of risk on the customer and giving the balance of power to the company. However, there have been some significant moves to temper this apparently harsh situation. Legislation to protect consumers' interests grew substantially from the 1960s onwards. In situations of natural monopolies, many governments created 'watch dog' bodies to represent the customers' interests. In the case of the privatised utilities in the UK and elsewhere, this has become enshrined in the office of the regulator (OFTEL, OFWAT, etc.), whose powers of regulation set them up as a surrogate for the market (see Chapter 10, section 10.4.3) and who exert control over prices and services through a set of performance targets. This has important implications for how the companies construct their competitive strategies.

Even without the use of a legally binding framework, there have been other attempts to give more rights and voice to individual consumers. The *Citizens' Charter Initiative* in the UK public services was one such attempt. Each public service had to develop and publish a charter which stated the rights of clients and the performance standards which they could expect from the organisation (see Illustration 5.2). These performance standards raised the visibility to users of the organisation's performance, creating some measure of 'market pressure'.

5.2.5 Changes of ownership: mergers and takeovers

The impact of corporate governance systems on strategy, and the differences between the USA and UK, and continental European countries such as Germany, is shown most clearly in the area of takeovers (particularly hostile takeovers). In the USA and UK, the exposure of managers to the threat of takeover (i.e. a market-pressure-based system) is regarded as a primary means of ensuring the good performance of organisations. In contrast, in Germany the performance of companies is seen as being primarily controlled through institutional mechanisms such as equity ownership by banks, two-tier boards and co-determination. Therefore, the corporate governance issues around (hostile) takeovers are largely confined to those countries which have adopted the Anglo-Saxon market-based approach to governance. The specific issue has been the extent to which a free market in buying and selling shares and companies — over the head of the board of directors — should be constrained in law and/or codes of conduct, to produce a semi-regulated framework for takeovers. Equally important has been a concern with the *conflict of interest* which directors face in defending against a hostile bid, and the extent to which *defensive measures* should be regulated. Often, bids are regarded as hostile by boards of directors because they might

Illustration 5.3   The Greenbury Report on directors' pay in the UK

The Greenbury Report set down a number of proposals aimed at dealing with public and shareholder concerns about directors' remuneration. In the light of controversy over pay awards for directors, the report recommended that a number of changes were necessary if company accountability was to be strengthened.

In July 1995 the Greenbury Committee published the following proposed framework for executive pay. It recommended that all listed companies should comply with the code 'to the fullest extent practicable'.

- In determining directors' salaries, remuneration committees (RCs) should be sensitive to the wider scene — in particular, pay and employment conditions elsewhere in the company — so that their decisions are consistent and fair and are seen as such. Bonuses should not be allowed to become another guaranteed element of pay, and should normally be subject to an upper limit, such as a specified percentage of basic pay.
- RCs should be made up of non-executive directors who have no personal financial interest in the decisions taken. There should be no cross-directorships with executive directors, which could offer scope for 'mutual agreements to bid up each other's remuneration'. Non-executives should have a good knowledge and understanding of the company.
- Companies should detail all elements of remuneration for every individual director by name, including basic salary, the nature and value of benefits in kind, annual bonuses, pension entitlements and long-term incentive schemes, including share options.
- Grants of share options should be phased over time rather than issued as a block, and should never be offered at a discount. Full details of share options for each director should be disclosed.
- There is a strong case for setting directors' notice periods at, or reducing them to, one year or less.
- Directors of the recently privatised public utilities (gas, water, electricity) should command a greater pay premium where there is substantial competition and risk, where there is a wide diversity of activities or an international spread of operations, or where significant technological or structural change is under way.

The Greenbury Report also recommended that the government bring forward legal changes to tax share option gains as income rather than capital, and secondary legislation on small changes in company and pensions law on disclosure. The Stock Exchange should introduce continuing obligations for listed companies to enact the new code on executive pay. Investor institutions should use their power and influence to ensure the implementation of best practice on pay.

Source: *The Times*, 18 July 1995.
Prepared by Sara Martin, Cranfield School of Management.

jeopardise their *personal* position (as executives), whereas a takeover may actually be in the longer-term interests of the shareholders and positively beneficial to other stakeholders, such as employees or customers.

In the public services, similar questions have been asked about the role of managers and board members faced with privatisation and/or 'de-merger' of the organisation — as in the case of British Rail in the mid-1990s. Executive board members may well diminish their personal career prospects through the privatisation and de-merger. This raises difficult ethical issues for managers, as will be discussed below (section 5.4.3).

5.2.6 Disclosure of information

In understanding the political context within which organisations operate, it needs to be acknowledged that information is a key source of power. Therefore, it is an important aspect of corporate governance to establish a framework about *disclosure of information* to various stakeholder groups. This clearly has to be balanced with the commercial prerogative for confidentiality on certain aspects of an organisation's operation.

In the early 1990s in the UK, there was mounting criticism of the quality of financial reporting and the effectiveness of the independent auditing. This led to the establishment of the Cadbury Committee, which reported in late 1992 and again in 1996. The first report, which had the backing of the Bank of England, the London Stock Exchange and the Accounting Bodies, sought to establish a Code of Best Practice on disclosure and audit arrangements. Companies listed on the Stock Exchange were required to make a statement in their annual report that they complied with the Code of Best Practice. So this aspect of corporate governance was exercised not through statute but in a 'voluntary' way — albeit with severe penalties (de-listing) for non-compliance.

It is interesting to note that the single issue which attracted most attention was the disclosure of *directors' pay*. This was the subject of a separate report in the UK — the Greenbury Report (see Illustration 5.3). Again, this indicated the need for corporate governance arrangements to address issues where there is potentially a conflict of interest. Of course, disclosure can be a costly and time-consuming business and is an important consideration for privately owned businesses when considering public flotation.

5.2.7 Conflicts of expectations

The differing forms of corporate governance outlined above are intended to provide a framework within which the interests of different stakeholder

- In order to grow, short-term profitability, cash flow and pay levels may need to be sacrificed.
- 'Short-termism' may suit managerial career aspirations but preclude investment in long-term projects.
- When family businesses grow, the owners may lose control if they need to appoint professional managers.
- New developments may require additional funding through share issue or loans. In either case, financial independence may be sacrificed.
- Public ownership of shares will require more openness and accountability from the management.
- Cost efficiency through capital investment can mean job losses.
- Extending into mass markets may require a decline in quality standards.
- In public services, a common conflict is between mass provision and specialist services (e.g. preventive dentistry or heart transplants).
- In public services, savings in one area (e.g. social security benefits) may result in increases elsewhere (e.g. school meals, medical care).

Figure 5.3   Some common conflicts of expectations

groups are given formal power of decision within organisations. Although this may prove useful in smoothing the strategic decision-making process, it will not remove conflict of interests. Since the expectations of stakeholder groups will differ, it is quite normal for conflict to exist within organisations regarding the importance and/or desirability of many aspects of strategy. In most situations, a compromise will need to be reached between expectations which cannot all be achieved simultaneously.

Figure 5.3 shows some of the typical stakeholder expectations that exist and how they might conflict. They include the conflicts between growth and profitability; growth and control/independence; cost efficiency and jobs; volume/mass provision and quality/specialisation; and the problems of suboptimisation, where the development of one part of an organisation may be at the expense of another. 'Short-termism' is often driven by the career aspirations of managers at the expense of the long-term health of the organisation. The different corporate governance traditions and frameworks tend to result in a different prioritisation of many of these items, as can be seen in the critique given in Figure 5.4.

5.3 Stakeholder expectations[8]

The corporate governance framework of an organisation needs to be understood when analysing whom the organisation should be serving and how the purposes of the organisation should be determined. However, in reality this tends to provide no more than a broad framework for

ANGLO-SAXON MODEL (US AND UK)

Strengths	Weaknesses
• Dynamic market orientation	• Volatile instability
• Fluid capital	• Short-termism
• Internationalisation possible	• Inadequate governance structures

EUROPEAN MODEL (GERMANY)

Strengths	Weaknesses
• Long-term industrial strategy	• Internationalisation difficult
• Very stable capital	• Vulnerable to global market for companies
• Strong governance procedures	

ASIAN MODEL (JAPAN)

Strengths	Weaknesses
• Long-term industrial strategy	• Growth of merger activity
• Stable capital	• Growth of institutional investor activism
• Overseas investments	• Growth of financial speculation
	• Secretive, sometimes corrupt, procedures

Source: T. Clarke and E. Monkhouse (eds), *Re-thinking the Company*, Financial Times/Pitman, 1994. Reproduced with permission.

Figure 5.4 A critique of some different corporate governance systems

understanding the actual *political context* in which strategies are formulated and implemented within organisations. It is helpful to analyse and understand the expectations of different stakeholders in much more detail, and in particular to consider the extent to which they are likely to show an active interest in the strategic development of the organisation and/or seek to exercise an influence over its purpose and strategies. *Stakeholders are those individuals or groups who depend on the organisation to fulfil their own goals and on whom, in turn, the organisation depends.*

Few individuals have sufficient power to determine unilaterally the strategy of an organisation. Influence is likely to occur only because individuals share expectations with others by being a part of a stakeholder group. Individuals need to identify themselves with the aims and ideals of these stakeholder groups, which may occur within departments, geographical locations, different levels in the hierarchy, etc. Also important are the external stakeholders of the organisation, who would typically include bankers, customers, suppliers, shareholders and unions. They may seek to influence company strategy through their links with internal stakeholders. For example, customers may pressurise sales managers to represent their interests within the company. Even if external stakeholders are passive, they may represent real constraints on the development of new strategies.

5.3.1 Identifying stakeholders

When identifying stakeholders there is a danger of concentrating too heavily on the formal structure of an organisation as a basis for identification, since this can be the easiest place to look for the divisions in expectations mentioned previously. However, it is necessary to unearth the 'informal' stakeholder groups and assess their importance. Other problems in analysis are that individuals tend to belong to more than one group and also stakeholder groups will 'line up' differently depending on the issue or strategy in hand. For example, marketing and production departments could well be united in the face of proposals to drop certain product lines, while being in fierce opposition regarding plans to buy in new items to the product range. It is *specific events* which trigger off the formation of stakeholder groups. For these reasons, stakeholder analysis is most useful when related to an assessment of specific strategic developments, such as the introduction of a new product or extension into a new geographical area. In this sense it is also a tool for evaluating strategies, as will be seen in Chapter 8.

5.3.2 Stakeholder mapping[9]

Stakeholder mapping can be useful both for identifying stakeholders and for establishing political priorities in terms of managing stakeholder relationships. It consists of making judgements on two issues:

- How *interested* each stakeholder group is to impress its expectations on the organisation's choice of strategies.
- Whether they have the means to do so. This is concerned with the *power* of stakeholder groups (see section 5.3.3).

Power/interest matrix

The power/interest matrix can be seen in Figure 5.5. This classifies stakeholders in relation to the power they hold and the extent to which they are likely to show interest in the organisation's strategies. The matrix indicates the type of relationship which the organisation needs to establish with each stakeholder group. As such, it is a useful analytical tool both in assessing the political ease or difficulty of particular strategies and also in planning the political dimension of strategic changes. Clearly, the acceptability of strategies to the *key players* (segment D) should be a major consideration during the formulation and evaluation of new strategies (see Chapter 8, section 8.3.3). Often the most difficult relationship to plan is with stakeholders in segment C (institutional shareholders often fall into this

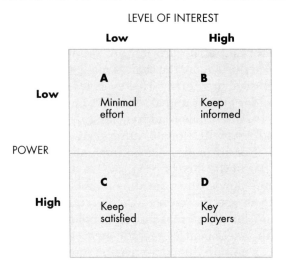

LEVEL OF INTEREST

Source: Adapted from A. Mendelow, *Proceedings of 2nd International Conference on Information Systems*, Cambridge, MA, 1991.

Figure 5.5 Stakeholder mapping: the power/interest matrix

category). Although these stakeholders might, in general, be relatively passive, a disastrous situation can arise if their level of interest is underrated and they suddenly *reposition* to segment D and frustrate the adoption of a new strategy. A view might also be taken that it is a *responsibility* of strategists or managers to raise the level of interest of powerful stakeholders (such as institutional shareholders), so that they can better fulfil their expected role within the corporate governance framework. This could also be concerned with how non-executive directors are assisted in fulfilling their role, say, through good information and briefing.

Similarly, the needs of stakeholders in segment B need to be properly addressed — largely through information. They can be crucially important 'allies' in influencing the attitudes of more powerful stakeholders: for example, through *lobbying*. Again, it may be a key responsibility of managers to undertake this informing process with, for instance, representatives of community interests. The value of stakeholder mapping is in assessing the following:

■ Whether the levels of interest and power of stakeholders properly reflect the corporate governance framework within which the organisation is operating, as in the examples above (non-executive directors, community groups).

▧ Whether strategies need to be pursued to *reposition* certain stakeholders. This could be to lessen the influence of a key player or, in certain instances, to ensure that there are more key players who will champion the strategy (this is often critical in the public sector context).

▧ Who are the key *blockers* and *facilitators* of change and how this will be responded to — for example, in terms of education/persuasion.

▧ The extent to which stakeholders will need to be assisted or encouraged to *maintain* their level of interest and/or power to ensure successful implementation of strategies. For example, public 'endorsement' by powerful suppliers or customers may be critical to the success of a strategy. Equally, it may be necessary to discourage some stakeholders from repositioning themselves. This is what is meant by *keep satisfied* in relation to stakeholders in segment C, and to a lesser extent *keep informed* for those in segment B. The use of *side payments*[10] to stakeholders as a means of securing their acceptance of new strategies has traditionally been regarded as a key maintenance activity.

These questions, of course, raise some difficult ethical issues for managers in deciding the role they should play in the political activity surrounding strategic change. For example, are managers really the honest brokers who weigh the conflicting expectations of stakeholder groups? Or are they answerable to one stakeholder — such as shareholders — and hence is their role to ensure the acceptability of their strategies to other stakeholders? Or are they, as many authors suggest, the real power behind the throne, constructing strategies to suit their own purposes and managing stakeholder expectations to ensure acceptance of these strategies?

These are important issues for managers and other stakeholders to consider.[11] The corporate governance arrangements for the organisation will answer these questions only at the most general level. Against that backdrop, the balancing of the conflicting interests of different stakeholders is strongly determined by the ethical stance of the organisation and the individual managers. This will be discussed fully in section 5.4 below.

Illustration 5.4(a) shows how a stakeholder mapping exercise can assist in determining the political priorities involved in pursuing a new strategy, and some of the practical issues often encountered when undertaking such an analysis. The analysis relates to a manufacturing company based in Frankfurt and with production facilities in both Frankfurt (D) and Toulouse (F). It is considering the closure of its Toulouse production facility. The analysis needs to address several issues.

1. It may be necessary to *subdivide* a stakeholder group into more than one group because there are important differences in expectations or power within that group. In the illustration, *customers* have been divided into those who are largely supportive of the strategy (customer X), those who are actively hostile (customer Y) and those who are indifferent

Illustration 5.4(a)   Stakeholder mapping at Tallman plc

Due to falling sales, Tallman plc is having to rationalise its operations. It is proposing to close down its poorly performing operations in Toulouse, and increase production capabilities at its more efficient Frankfurt plant.

Two power/interest maps have been drawn up by company officials to establish likely stakeholder reactions to the proposed closure of the Toulouse plant. While Map A represents the most likely situation, Map B represents the company's most preferred situation, where support for the proposal is regarded as sufficient to ensure success.

Low	INTEREST	High		Low	INTEREST	High
	Shareholder M(−)		**Low**	French minister	Shareholder M (−)	
	Toulouse plant (−)				Toulouse plant (−)	
	Customer X (+)				Production (−)	
	French minister (−)					
A	Production (−)	B	**POWER**	A		B
Customer Z	Customer Y (−)			Customer Z	Customer X (+)	
Supplier A	Marketing (+)		**High**	Supplier A	Customer Y (+)	
German minister	Frankfurt plant (+)			German minister	Marketing (+)	
					Frankfurt plant (+)	
C		D		C		D

Map A: The likely situation   **Map B: The preferred situation**

Referring to Map A, it can be seen that with the exception of customer X the stakeholders in quadrant B will currently contest the closure of the Toulouse plant. If Tallman plc is to have any chance of convincing these stakeholders to change their stance

(customer Z). In using stakeholder mapping, there is clearly a balance to be struck between describing stakeholders too generically — hence hiding important issues of diversity — and too much subdivision making the map confusing and difficult to interpret.

2. Most stakeholder groups consist of large numbers of individuals (such as customers or shareholders), and hence can be thought of largely independently of the expectations of individuals within that group. With some stakeholder groups this is not the case: they consist of a small number of individuals or even single individuals (e.g. the chairperson of the company or the minister of a government department). It is useful that the analysis properly acknowledges the extent to which the

to a more supportive one, the company must address their questions and where possible alleviate their fears. If such fears are overcome, these people may become important allies in influencing the more powerful stakeholders in quadrants C and D. The supportive attitude of customer X could be usefully harnessed in this quest.

The relationships Tallman plc has with the stakeholders in quadrant C are the most difficult to manage, since while they are considered to be relatively passive, largely due to their indifference to the proposed strategy, a disastrous situation could arise if their level of interest was underrated. For example, if the German minister were replaced, his successor might be opposed to the strategy and actively seek to stop the plant closure. In this case he would shift to quadrant D.

The acceptability of the proposed strategy to the current players in quadrant D is a key consideration. Of particular concern is customer Y, who is considered to be opposed to the closure of the Toulouse plant, and may have the power to prevent it from happening. The company clearly needs to have open discussions with this stakeholder.

Comparing the position of stakeholders in Map A and Map B, and identifying any changes/mismatches, Tallman plc establishes a number of strategies that may be pursued to change the stance of certain stakeholders to a more positive one and to increase the power of certain stakeholders. For example, customer X could be encouraged to champion the proposed strategy and assist Tallman plc by providing media access.

Tallman plc could also seek to dissuade or prevent powerful stakeholders from changing their stance to a negative one. For example, unless direct action is taken, the German minister's level of interest may well be raised by lobbying from his French counterpart. This has implications for how the company handles the situation in France. Thus, time would be effectively spent talking the strategy through with the French minister and also customer Y, so as to try and shift them away from opposition at least to indifference, if not support.

Prepared by Sara Martin, Cranfield School of Management.

mapping of the *role* (e.g. chairperson) is concerned with that particular *individual*. It is useful to know if a new individual in that role would shift the positioning. Serious misjudgements can be made if proper care is not paid to this point.

In the example, it has been concluded that the German minister has been plotted in segment C on the grounds that he is largely indifferent to the new development — it is very low in his priorities. However, a change of minister might shift this situation overnight. Although it will be impossible to remove such uncertainties entirely, there are implications for the political priorities. For example, those permanent officials who are advising the minister need to be kept satisfied, since they will outlive individual ministers and provide a continuity which

Illustration 5.4(b)   Assessment of power

Internal stakeholders

Indicators of power	Marketing dept	Production	Frankfurt plant	Toulouse plant
Status				
Position in hierarchy (closeness to board)	H	L	H	M
Salary of top manager	H	L	H	L
Average grade of staff	H	M	H	L
Claim on resources				
Number of staff	M	H	M	M
Size of similar company	H	L	H	L
Budget as % of total	H	M	H	L
Representation				
Number of directors	H	None	M	None
Most influential directors	H	None	M	None
Symbols				
Quality of accommodation	H	L	M	M
Support services	H	L	H	L

External stakeholders

Indicators of power	Supplier A	Customer Y	Shareholder M
Status	H	H	L
Resource dependence	L	H	H
Negotiating arrangements	M	H	L
Symbols	H	H	L

H = high   M = medium   L = low

The marketing department is seen as powerful by all measures, and the production department universally weak. Equally, the Frankfurt plant is particularly powerful in relation to the Toulouse plant. This analysis provides important data in the process of stakeholder mapping, since the strategic importance of power is also related to whether individuals or groups are likely to exercise their power. This assessment thus helped in deciding where to locate the stakeholders on the power/interest maps.

Combining the results of this analysis with the stakeholder mapping exercise, it can be seen that Toulouse's only real hope is to encourage supplier A to reposition by raising its level of interest in opposition to the closure. Perhaps shareholder M could be helpful in this process through lobbying the supplier.

Prepared by Sara Martin, Cranfield School of Management.

can diminish uncertainty. It is also possible, of course, that the German minister's level of interest may well be raised by lobbying from his French counterpart. This has implications for how the company handles the situation in France.

3. Illustration 5.4(a) shows how the political priorities can be established from stakeholder mapping:

    ▪ Plot a map showing how stakeholders would *line up* in relation to a new strategy (geographical expansion in the illustration).
    ▪ Plot a second map showing how you would *like stakeholders to line up* if the strategy is to have the best chance of success.
    ▪ By comparing these two maps and looking for the *mismatches*, the political priorities can be established. In the illustration, these are changing the interest of the French minister and customer Y away from opposition; and enfranchising customer X (to champion the strategy), perhaps by assisting with media access.
    ▪ It needs to be remembered that political priorities may also be concerned with *maintaining* stakeholders in their current positioning. In the illustration, this involves keeping the issue low in the priorities of the German minister (through efforts in France to discourage lobbying).

5.3.3 Assessing power[12]

The previous section was concerned with analysing stakeholder expectations and highlighted the need to assess the power of the various stakeholders. Power is the mechanism by which expectations are able to influence strategies. It has been seen that in most organisations power will be unequally shared between the various stakeholders.

Before proceeding, it is necessary to understand what is meant here by 'power'. In particular, a distinction needs to be drawn between, on the one hand, the power that people or groups derive from their position within the organisation and through the formal corporate governance arrangements, and on the other, the power that they possess by other means. For the purposes of strategic analysis, power is best understood as the extent to which individuals or groups are able to persuade, induce or coerce others into following certain courses of action. This is the mechanism by which one set of expectations will dominate strategic development or seek compromise with others. Analysis of power must, therefore, begin with an assessment of the sources of power.

Figure 5.6 summarises the various sources of power for both internal and external stakeholders, and can be used as a checklist against which to make an assessment of how powerful each stakeholder is in influencing the

SOURCES OF POWER

(a) Within organisations
- Hierarchy (formal power),
  e.g. autocratic decision making
- Influence (informal power),
  e.g. charismatic leadership
- Control of strategic resources,
  e.g. strategic products.
- Possession of knowledge/skills,
  e.g. computer specialists
- Control of the environment,
  e.g. negotiating skills
- Involvement in strategy implementation,
  e.g. by exercising discretion

(b) For external stakeholders
- Control of strategic resources,
  e.g. materials, labour, money
- Involvement in strategy implementation,
  e.g. distribution outlets, agents
- Possession of knowledge (skills),
  e.g. subcontractors
- Through internal links,
  e.g. informal influence

INDICATORS OF POWER

(a) Within organisations
- Status
- Claim on resources
- Representation
- Symbols

(b) For external stakeholders
- Status
- Resource dependence
- Negotiating arrangements
- Symbols

Figure 5.6   Sources and indicators of power

strategic development under consideration. Since there are a variety of different sources of power, it is often useful to look for *indicators of power*, which are the visible signs that stakeholders have been able to exploit one or more of the sources of power listed in Figure 5.6. There are four useful indicators of power:

- The *status* of the individual or group. One measure of status might be position within the hierarchy, but others are equally important: for example, an individual's salary, or job grades of groups. Equally, the reputation that a group or individual holds with others will be very relevant.
- The *claim on resources* as measured by the size of a department's budget, or the number of employees within that group. In particular, trends in the proportion of resources claimed by that group may be a useful indicator of the extent to which their power is waxing or waning. A useful comparison can be made with similar groups in comparable organisations.
- *Representation* in powerful positions. This needs to be judged in relation to the corporate governance arrangements for the organisation. A good

example of this is the composition of the board of directors and their particular specialisms. The weakness of the production function may result from lack of representation at board level. Within other organisations, representation on important committees could be a measure of power, although a simple head count would overlook the extent to which the individuals are influential. Here individual status should be taken into consideration.

- *Symbols of power.* Internal division of power may be indicated in a variety of ways. Such physical symbols as the size and location of people's offices, and whether they have a secretary, carpets, or newspapers delivered each morning, are all important clues. Whether individuals are addressed by their first or second names, even the way they dress, may be symbols of power. In more bureaucratic organisations, the existence of 'distribution lists' for internal memoranda and other information can give useful clues to the power structure. These lists do not always neatly reflect the formal hierarchical structure and may provide pointers as to who is viewed as powerful within the organisation.

No single indicator is likely to uncover the structure of power within a company. However, by looking at all four indicators, it may be possible to identify which people or groups appear to have power by a number of these measures. More importantly, this assessment of power needs to be made *in relation to the particular strategy under consideration.* For example, the corporate finance function is likely to be more powerful in relation to developments requiring new capital or revenue commitments than in relation to ones which are largely self-financing and/or within the financial authority of separate divisions or subsidiaries. Illustration 5.4(b) shows how such an analysis was performed to assess the relative power of the marketing and production departments and the plants of the two-site manufacturing company previously discussed. The marketing department was seen as powerful by all measures and the production department as universally weak. Equally, the Frankfurt plant was particularly powerful in relation to Toulouse.

Alongside this internal assessment of power, a similar analysis of the power held by external stakeholders needs to be carried out. The indicators of power here are slightly different:

- The *status* of an external party such as a supplier is usually indicated by the way that it is discussed among company employees, and whether the company responds quickly to the supplier's demands.
- *Resource dependence* can often be measured directly. For example, the relative size of shareholdings or loans, the proportion of a company's business tied up with any one customer, or a similar dependence on suppliers, can normally be easily measured. Perhaps the key indicator

is the ease with which that supplier, financier or customer could switch or *be switched* at short notice. It might also be useful to examine the routines of the organisation — particularly the external linkages. These should indicate how dependency has been 'built in' to the organisational culture. This can be a problem for small businesses which are very dependent as tied suppliers on large manufacturers such as Ford, or large retailers such as Marks and Spencer.

▨ *Negotiating arrangements* include whether external parties are treated at arm's length or are actively involved in negotiations with the company. For example, a customer which is invited to negotiate over the price of a contract is in a more powerful position than a similar company which is given a fixed price on a take-it-or-leave-it basis.

▨ *Symbols* are also valuable clues: for example, whether the management team wines and dines a customer or supplier, or the level of person in the company who deals with a particular supplier. The care and attention paid to correspondence with outsiders will tend to differ from one party to another.

Again, no single measure will give a full understanding of the extent of the power held by external stakeholders, but the combined analysis will be very useful. Illustration 5.4(b) shows how an analysis of the power of external stakeholders can be performed. This analysis was used in the process of *stakeholder mapping* to make a political assessment of the strategy of closing down the Toulouse plant. It can be seen that Toulouse's only real hope of survival is to encourage supplier A to reposition by raising its level of interest in opposition to the closure. Perhaps shareholder M could be helpful in this process through lobbying the supplier.

5.4   Business ethics[13]

The discussion in the previous sections has viewed organisational purposes as being concerned with the expectations of stakeholders — but particularly those who have formal 'rights' through the corporate governance framework and/or those stakeholders who are most interested and powerful in other ways.

However, there has been little discussion so far about the nature of stakeholder expectations: which purposes are regarded as more important than others and why? The answer to this question is concerned with two issues: first, the *ethical context* of the organisation; and second, the *cultural context* within which the organisation is operating. These issues are clearly related — for example, the very different attitudes to practices such as bribery in different countries. This and the subsequent section will discuss these two related issues, commencing with business ethics.

Ethical issues concerning business and public sector organisations exist at three levels:

▨ At the *macro* level, there are issues about the role of business in the national and international organisation of society. This is largely concerned with assessing the relative virtues of different political/social systems, such as free enterprise and centrally planned economies, and the purposes which business enterprises are expected to fulfil. There are also important issues of international relationships and the role of business on an international scale. As mentioned in section 5.2, the differing corporate governance arrangements from country to country reflect differing emphases on these macro issues. So the first issue for individual organisations is the broad *ethical stance* which it takes in relation to the corporate governance framework within which it is operating.

▨ Within this macro framework, *corporate social responsibility* is concerned with the ethical issues facing corporate entities (private and public sector) when formulating and implementing strategies. This concerns the extent to which the organisation should move beyond the minimum obligations provided through corporate governance, and how the conflicting demands of different stakeholders can be reconciled.

▨ At the *individual* level, it concerns the behaviour and actions of individuals within organisations. This is clearly an important issue for the management of organisations, but it is discussed here only in so far as it affects strategy, and in particular the role of managers in the strategic management process.

5.4.1 The ethical stance

The corporate governance arrangements for an organisation determine the minimum obligations of an organisation towards its various stakeholders. Therefore, a key strategic issue within organisations is the *ethical stance* which is taken regarding the extent to which the organisation should exceed these minimum obligations in relation to any specific stakeholder group.

The key issue for managers is to understand and influence the ethical stance which the organisation is taking. Figure 5.7 outlines four *stereotypes* to illustrate the range of difference stances found in organisations:

1. At one extreme there are organisations which have taken the view that the only responsibility of business is the short-term interests of shareholders.[14] Their ethical stance is that it is the domain of government to prescribe, through legislation, the constraints which society chooses to impose on businesses in their pursuit of economic efficiency (i.e. the arrangements for corporate governance). The

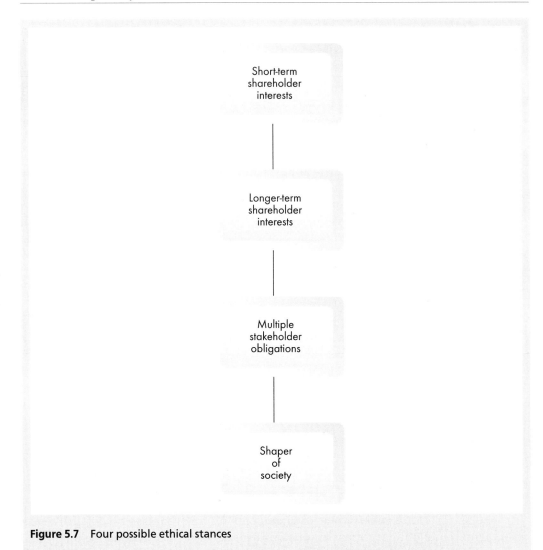

Figure 5.7 Four possible ethical stances

organisation will meet these minimum obligations, but no more. Expecting companies to exercise other social duties can, in extreme cases, undermine the authority of government and give business organisations even more power: for example, multinationals operating in developing countries are often accused of usurping the legitimate roles of government.

2. The ethical stance of category 2 is similar to the previous group, but it is tempered with a recognition of the *long-term benefit to the shareholder* of well-managed relationships with other stakeholders. Many of the issues are therefore managed proactively and carefully as a matter of long-term

Illustration 5.5   Body Shop and corporate responsibility: good works not just good words

Operating over 1,000 stores in 45 countries, by 1996 Body Shop had become a symbol of how business success can be achieved while maintaining responsible — even missionary — attitudes to care for the environment and the rights of people in developing countries.

Body Shop, which manufactures and sells skin and hair care products and cosmetics, was created and developed by Anita Roddick from her first shop in Brighton, UK, in 1976. The following are extracts from the second in a series of lectures which she gave in 1994, providing an insight into Body Shop's ethical stance and its practical approach to corporate social responsibility:

'I am no loony do-gooder, traipsing the world hugging trees and staring into crystals . . . I am also not one of those people who is opposed to trade or change . . . But I am concerned about *quality* in trade not just quantity.'

'We need trade that respects and supports communities and families . . . safeguards the environment . . . [and] encourages countries to educate their children, heal their sick, value the work of women and respect human rights. We need to measure progress by human development not gross product.'

'Business must not only avoid hideous evil, it must actively do good.'

'Our political postures must change — we have to stop endlessly whining for easier rules, lower costs and fewer restrictions . . . we have to take longer-term views, invest in the communities and build long-lasting markets.'

'Inside Body Shop we are arguing whether we should follow Levi Strauss' example [and stop purchasing from China] . . . many, including my husband Gordon, argue that we can make a positive difference [by trading with China].'

'Investing in Easterhouse, Glasgow, one of the worst examples of unemployment and housing in western Europe, was a moral choice. I would rather employ the unemployable than the already employed. The [products] are up to 30% more expensive and we are putting [25%] of the net profits back into the community. But it is better for the company. It is an example of what keeps the soul of the company alive.'

'We . . . could not wait for the European Union to ratify environmental auditing; we did it ourselves.'

'I would rather be measured by how I treat weaker and frailer communities I trade with than by how great are my profits.'

Source: 'Anita Roddick speaks out on corporate responsibility', Body Shop, 1994.

self-interest. For example, external sponsorships or welfare provision might be regarded as sensible expenditures akin to any other form of investment or promotion expenditure. The avoidance of 'shady' marketing practices is necessary to prevent the need for yet more legislation in that area. It is argued that, if managers wish to maintain discretion in the long run over issues such as marketing practices, then they are wise to operate responsibly in the short term.

3. The third category takes a different ethical stance. Their view is that stakeholder interests and expectations (wider than just shareholders) should be more *explicitly incorporated in the organisation's purposes* and strategies, and they will often go beyond the minimum obligations of corporate governance.[15] They also argue that the performance of the organisation should be measured in a much more pluralistic way than just through its bottom line. The Quaker companies of the nineteenth century are a good example: to a considerable extent, the attitudes of these companies have remained more socially progressive than others during the twentieth century. Companies in this category might argue that they would retain uneconomic units to preserve jobs, would avoid manufacturing or selling 'anti-social' products (see Illustration 5.5) and would be prepared to bear reductions in profitability for the social good. However, there are clearly important issues of balance. Many public sector organisations are, rightly, positioned within this group. They are subject to a wide diversity of expectations from their stakeholder groups, and unitary measures of performance are often inadequate in reflecting this diversity.

4. The final group represents the *ideological* end of the spectrum. They have purposes which are concerned with *shaping society*, and the financial considerations are regarded as of secondary importance or a constraint. The extent to which this is a viable ethical stance clearly depends upon issues of corporate governance and accountability. Arguably, it is easier for a private, family owned organisation to operate in this way, since it is not accountable to external shareholders. Some would argue that the achievements in public services have been largely because they have been mission driven in this way, and supported by the political framework in which they have operated. In many countries since the mid-1980s, there has been a major challenge to the legitimacy of this mission-driven stance within public services and a reassertion of the rights of citizens (as taxpayers) to expect demonstrable value for money from its public services. This has severely curtailed the ability of public services — particularly at the local level — to be proactive shapers of society.

    Charitable organisations face similar dilemmas — it is often fundamental to their existence that they have a zeal to protect/improve the interests of particular groups in society. But this has to be achieved within the corporate governance framework within which they operate. This can prove difficult given the inevitable political dimension to their work. They also need to remain financially viable, which can bring problems with their image — sometimes seen as being overcommercial and spending too much on administration or promotional activities.

Whichever ethical stance an organisation takes, this stance should become an integral element of corporate strategy. Strategically, it helps a company to decide what kind of company it wishes to be — an important element in defining its organisational *purposes*. There is likely to be a strong relationship between the ethical stance and the character of the company. The ethical stance also helps to determine *how* the organisation will try to reach its goals and how it will relate to its various stakeholders.

5.4.2 Corporate social responsibility[16]

The previous section has identified the overall 'stance' which an organisation may take concerning its role in society, and the extent to which it will operate within or beyond its framework of corporate governance. This still leaves the need to identify the more detailed 'agenda' of issues which an organisation may be taking into account when developing strategies, and the way in which the organisation will manage the agenda. Figure 5.8 outlines a number of these issues, both internal and external to the organisation, and provides a checklist against which an organisation's actions on corporate social responsibility can be assessed.

One survey[17] showed several issues of concern in how organisations were addressing the various items listed in Figure 5.8. Although a large number of companies had produced guidelines on some or all of the issues, a significant number had no programme by which to put them into effect: 'the picture which emerges is one of good intentions often unfulfilled'. The authors concluded that companies in Britain had generally increased their awareness of and level of activity in some aspects of social responsibility, but they seemed to limit their involvement to a relatively narrow range of issues. They also indicated that most organisations failed to seek out best practice elsewhere, and this, they suggested, indicated that social responsibility considerations were not pursued as keenly as commercial activities.

5.4.3 The role of individuals/managers

It should be clear from the preceding discussion that business ethics — as part of strategic management — raises some difficult issues for individuals and managers within organisations:

Should organisations be responsible for . . .

Employee welfare
. . . providing medical care, assistance with mortgages, extended sickness leave, assistance for dependants, etc.?

Working conditions
. . . enhancing working surroundings, social and sporting clubs, above minimum safety standards, etc.?

Job design
. . . designing jobs to the increases satisfaction of workers rather than economic efficiency?

Internal aspects

Green issues
. . . reducing pollution below legal standards if competitors are not doing so?
. . . energy conservation?

Products
. . . danger arising from the careless use of product by consumers?

Markets and marketing
. . . deciding not to sell in some markets?
. . . advertising standards?

Suppliers
. . . 'fair' terms of trade?
. . . blacklisting suppliers?

Employment
. . . positive discrimination in favour of minorities?
. . . maintaining jobs?

Community activity
. . . sponsoring local events and supporting local good works?

External aspects

Figure 5.8 Some questions of corporate social responsibility

1. What is the responsibility of an individual who believes that the strategy of his or her organisation — for example, its trading practices — is unethical or is not adequately representing the legitimate interests of one or more stakeholder groups? Should the individual report the organisation; or should he or she leave the company on the grounds of a mismatch of values? This has often been called *whistleblowing*.[18]

2. Managers are usually in a powerful position within organisations to influence the expectations of other stakeholders. They have access to information and channels of influence which are not available to many other stakeholders. With this power comes an ethical responsibility to behave with *integrity*.

Given that strategy development can be an intensely political process, managers can often find real difficulties establishing and maintaining this position of integrity. As we have seen, there is a potential conflict for managers between what strategies are best for their own career and what strategies are in the longer-term interests of their organisation. Integrity is particularly threatened by the potential for insider-trading prior to acquisitions. The international business community was beset by a series of such cases in the 1980s.

Integrity is a key ingredient of professional management and is included in the code of conduct of professional bodies such as the Institute of Management.[19] Best practice is shared through the international links between these professional bodies.

5.5 The cultural context

Chapter 2 introduced the concept of culture and its importance to strategic management, and provided an approach to analysing culture: the *cultural*

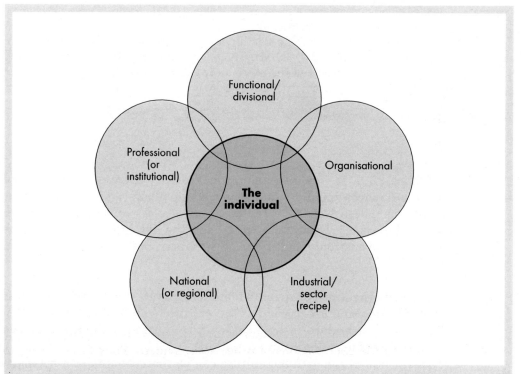

Figure 5.9   Frames of reference

Illustration 5.6   Eurotunnel

The different national traditions and cultures are reflected in the legal and governance frameworks too. This can cause difficulties for stakeholders, such as banks, when dealing with cross-country clients, such as Eurotunnel.

By the end of the summer season 1995, Eurotunnel, the Anglo-French operator of the Channel Tunnel, faced severe financial problems. Opening 18 months later than planned had cost it two summer seasons' revenue, which, together with a doubling of the £4.8 billion construction and development costs, meant that £7.8 billion of debt owed to 225 banks incurred a £700 million p.a. interest bill that dwarfed half-year turnover of £107 million or net cash inflow of £28 million (before interest).

Thus, on 14 September 1995, Eurotunnel simply announced that it would stop payment of interest for up to 18 months, allowed in the credit agreements, in order to review operations and the financing of the tunnel.

The banks had little option but to negotiate, but they were conscious that the management had grown traffic to 34 per cent of car cross-Channel traffic, 50 per cent of lorry cross-Channel traffic and 40 per cent of London to Paris/Brussels rail passengers. Therefore, replacing the management was unlikely to boost receipts. Also, the tunnel 'asset', while valued in the balance sheet at £9.4 billion, would realise a low sale value as a 'hole in the ground plus infrastructure'.

But the greatest problem (for the banks) was that Eurotunnel was actually two companies, Eurotunnel plc (UK) and Eurotunnel SA (France), co-chaired by the combative Sir Alastair Morton and the conciliatory Patrick Ponselle respectively, and subject to two contrasting commercial law systems. Under UK insolvency procedures,

---

web (Figure 2.10). It was also acknowledged that there are a variety of cultural influences on individuals and stakeholders which shape their expectations. These were referred to as the *frames of reference* and are reproduced here as Figure 5.9. It is not the intention to repeat the introductory discussion of culture in this chapter, but to build on it in two ways:

- To identify the kinds of specific factors and issues which the strategist should be looking for in each of the cultural *frames of reference*, when building up a picture of how the cultural context will influence the prioritising of purposes by organisations.
- To show how organisational culture can be *characterised*, as a means of understanding the influences of culture on both current and future organisational purposes.

banks stand above most creditors. Thus, while most able to determine a company's behaviour and future, the banks also bear least risk via their 'secured creditor' status. French legal procedures are at the other end of the spectrum. Under *redressment judiciarie*, the interests of the enterprise and the employees rank above banks. French shareholders, who were 80 per cent of Eurotunnel's 721,000 shareholders, also had recourse under French law if a financial restructuring treated them unfairly as stakeholders.

In November 1995, Eurotunnel set up French and UK shareholders' committees with Mr Maurice le Maire appointed to the group board, novel in France and unique in the UK. On 12 February 1996, at the request of the group's auditors, the Paris commercial court appointed two mediators *mandataire ad hoc*, Lord Wakeham and Robert Badinter, to facilitate negotiations between Eurotunnel and its creditors over the restructuring of the debt, including unpaid interest since September 1995. The banks still had the power to terminate the interest standstill 'agreement' with Eurotunnel prior to March 1997, if 65 per cent by loan value voted to do so; nor did they need to co-operate in negotiation. But the prospect of at best the conflict progressing to the Paris commercial court, and at worst the precipitation of Eurotunnel into 'redressment' in France *and* administration in the UK, was likely to concentrate the banks' attention on achieving a negotiated restructuring that at least satisfied shareholders, employees and the company in addition to themselves. By 1996, the only completely satisfied stakeholder was the customer, enjoying a price war over cross-Channel travel provision and the price of duty-frees.

Sources: Eurotunnel Prospectus, Reports and Accounts; *Financial Times.*
Prepared by Geoff Goddin, Thames Valley University, London.

5.5.1 National and/or regional culture[20]

It has already been noted that there are significant differences in the corporate governance frameworks between countries, and that the ethical stance and corporate social responsibility agenda will also differ. But the cultural context also influences the expectations of stakeholders directly.[21] For example, attitudes to work, authority, equality and a number of other important factors differ from one location to another.[22]

From the point of view of understanding organisational purposes, it is important to understand these influences for two reasons. First, values of society change and adjust over time, and therefore strategies which were acceptable and successful 20 years ago may not be so today. There has been an increasing trend within many countries for the activities of companies to be constrained by legislation, public opinion and the media. Second, companies which operate *internationally* have the added problem of coping with the very different standards and expectations of the various countries in which they operate. Illustration 5.6 shows how this can create issues and difficulties for stakeholders too in the case of Eurotunnel — a joint venture between the UK and France.

Although it is not shown separately in Figure 5.9 (for reasons of simplification), it may often be necessary to identify important *subnational* (usually regional) cultures. For example, attitudes to some aspects of employment, supplier relationships and, certainly, consumer preferences would differ significantly at a regional level even in a relatively small and cohesive country like the UK, and quite markedly elsewhere in Europe (e.g. between northern and southern Italy). In some respects there are also developing aspects of *supranational* culture beyond a single nation. For example, judgements on whether there is likely to be a move towards a 'Euro-consumer' with converging tastes and preferences are of crucial strategic importance to many organisations in planning their product and distribution strategies. Illustration 2.4 (Chapter 2) also showed an example of this issue in relation to Chinese culture.

5.5.2 Professional/institutional culture

Many individuals are members of a professional or institutional group whose values and beliefs are a powerful influence on that individual's expectations of the organisation and its purposes.[23] These allegiances may be highly institutionalised and directly related to the work situation, such as membership of a trade union or professional association. They may also be more informal and unrelated, such as membership of churches or political groups, but still very influential. An important trend in the 'post-industrial' economies has been the declining power of organised trade unions and the growing importance of professional groups as the number of 'knowledge workers' increases. Many organisations are now employing large numbers of professional staff from a number of different professions with very different professional values. So in health care the medical doctors, paramedics, nurses and finance/managerial professionals may agree on purposes at one level (improving health), but there are key differences in expectations when purposes become specific through debates about priorities and resource allocation.

5.5.3 Industry recipes[24]

Within an industry or public service there tends to develop a common view about organisational purposes and a 'shared wisdom' on how you develop and manage organisations (see, for example, Scottish Knitwear in Illustration 2.4 of Chapter 2). It may prove difficult for individual firms to step out of line from this industry recipe without being dubbed as mavericks or cowboys. There is clearly an advantage to such cultural influences, in terms of maintaining standards and consistency between individual providers. Many industries have trade associations which also reinforce these norms, such as the Association of British Travel Agents (ABTA). Sometimes this occurs on an international scale, as with OPEC (the Organisation of Petroleum Exporting Countries).

The danger is, of course, that managers may not look beyond their industry in thinking through strategies for the future. They become victims of industry 'groupthink' and do not see the lessons which can be learnt from outside their own industry. One of the advantages of *benchmarking*, as discussed in Chapter 4, is to challenge these taken-for-granted 'industry' assumptions by looking at best practice wherever it is found.

Because the dominant culture varies from one industry to another, the transition of managers between sectors can prove quite difficult. A number of private sector managers were encouraged to join public services during the 1980s in an attempt to inject new cultures and outlooks into the public sector. Many were surprised at the difficulties they experienced in adjusting their management style to the different tradition and expectations of their new organisation — for example, in issues like consensus building as part of the decision-making process.

5.5.4 Organisational culture

It has been suggested that it is useful to conceive of the culture of an organisation as consisting of three layers[25] (see Figure 5.10):

- *Values* may be easy to identify in an organisation, and are often written down as statements about the organisation's mission, objectives or strategies. However, they tend to be vague, such as 'service to the community' or 'equal employment opportunities'.
- *Beliefs* are more specific, but again they are issues which people in the organisation can surface and talk about. They might include a belief that the company should not trade with Iraq, or that professional staff should not have their professional actions appraised by managers.
- *Taken-for-granted assumptions* are the real core of an organisation's culture. They are the aspects of organisational life which people find difficult to identify and explain, and are known as the organisational *paradigm*.

The existence of these three layers of culture presents an analytical dilemma. As organisations increasingly make visible their carefully

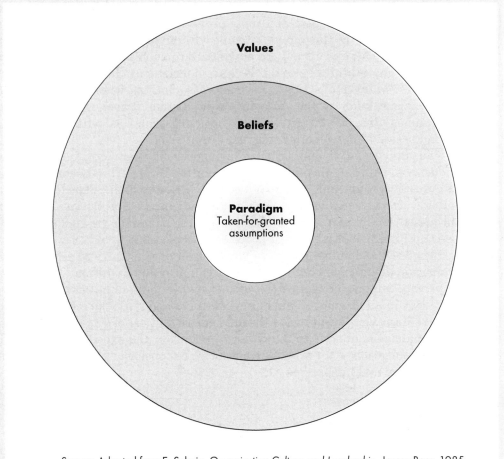

Source: Adapted from E. Schein, *Organisation Culture and Leadership*, Jossey-Bass, 1985.

Figure 5.10   Culture in three layers

considered public statements of their values, beliefs and purposes — for example, in annual reports, mission statements and business plans — there is a danger that these are seen as useful and accurate descriptions of the organisational paradigm. But they are likely to be at best only partially accurate, and at worst misleading, descriptions of the *real* organisational culture. This is not to suggest that there is any organised deception. It is simply that the statements of values and beliefs are often statements of aspiration or strategic intent of a particular stakeholder (such as the CEO) rather than accurate descriptions of the culture as it exists in the minds and hearts of people within and around the organisation. This 'real' culture is evidenced by the way the organisation actually operates: it is the taken-for-granted assumptions about 'how you run an organisation like this' and 'what really matters around here', as discussed in Chapter 2, and it may be a source of real competitive advantage.[26] For example, an outside observer of a police force might conclude from its public statements of purpose and priorities that it had a balanced approach to the various aspects of police work — catching criminals, crime prevention, community relations, etc. *However*, a deeper probing might quickly reveal that (in cultural terms) there is the 'real' police work (catching criminals) and the 'lesser work'.

5.5.5 Functional/divisional culture

In seeking to describe, analyse and understand the relationship between culture and an organisation's strategies, it is not usually possible to characterise the whole organisation as one particular type of culture. There are usually important *subcultures* within organisations. These subcultures may arise in a number of ways — some of which are concerned with one or more of the external frames of reference already mentioned, such as unions or professions. The subcultures may also relate directly to the structure of the organisation. For example, the differences between geographical divisions in a multinational company, or between functional groups such as finance, marketing and operations, can be very powerful to the extent that they can be self-perpetuating (see section 5.5.6) and exclusive. In a divisional structure, different divisions may be *positioned* in different ways and pursue different generic strategies, as discussed in Chapter 3. These different positionings require and/or foster different cultures. Indeed, it will be seen later (Chapters 10 and 11) that matching strategic positioning and organisational culture is a critical feature of successful organisations.

5.5.6 Analysing the cultural web[27]

The *cultural web* can be used to describe and analyse culture at any of the levels discussed above. This can be done by observing the way in which the organisation (or industry or nation) actually operates — the cultural artefacts (the routines, rituals, stories, structures, systems, etc.). Out of these will also come the *clues* about the taken-for-granted assumptions. To use an analogy, it is like trying to describe an iceberg (which is mainly submerged). This is done by observing the parts of the iceberg which show and also (from these clues) inferring what the submerged part of the iceberg must look like.

Figure 5.11 outlines some of the questions which might be asked when analysing the cultural web. For example, a simple and effective way of gathering clues through organisational stories is to ask people to describe 'the most significant things that have happened to the company in the last

Stories
- What core beliefs do stories reflect?
- How pervasive are these beliefs (through levels)?
- Do stories relate to:
    strengths or weaknesses?
    successes or failures?
    conformity or mavericks?
- Who are the heroes and villains?
- What norms do the mavericks deviate from?

Routines and rituals
- Which routines are emphasised?
- Which would look odd if changed?
- What behaviour do routines encourage?
- What are the key rituals?
- What core beliefs do they reflect?
- What do training programmes emphasise?
- How easy are rituals/routines to change?

Organisational structure
- How mechanistic/organic are the structures?
- How flat/hierarchical are the structures?
- How formal/informal are the structures?
- Do structures encourage collaboration or competition?
- What type of power structures do they support?

Control systems
- What is most closely monitored/controlled?
- Is emphasis on reward or punishment?
- Are controls related to history or current strategies?
- Are there many/few controls?

Power structures
- What are the core beliefs of the leadership?
- How strongly held are these beliefs (idealists or pragmatists)?
- How is power distributed in the organisation?
- Where are the main blockages to change?

Symbols
- What language and jargon is used?
- How internal or accessible is it?
- What aspects of strategy are highlighted in publicity?
- What status symbols are there?
- Are there particular symbols which denote the organisation?

Overall
- What is the dominant culture (defender, prospector, analyser)?
- How easy is this to change?

Figure 5.11   Analysing the cultural web: some useful questions two or three years'. Observing which stories people *select* is an important clue to the taken-for-granted assumptions. Training programmes in an organisation can also be useful pointers to the paradigm. It can also be useful to observe how hierarchical or informal are the structures and control systems. These are important clues to how new strategies might best be developed and implemented (as discussed in Chapters 9 and 10).

It must be remembered that it is not the separate answers and clues which matter, but the collective picture which they paint of the culture and subcultures. The important strategic issue is how these clues allow the strategist to characterise this culture, as discussed in the next section.

5.5.7 Characterising an organisation's culture

In understanding the influence of culture on organisational purposes, it is important to be able to characterise culture (at the various levels discussed above). In this section, the process of characterisation will be illustrated at the level of the organisation and its subcultures.

Miles and Snow[28] categorised organisations into three basic types in terms of how they behave strategically (Figure 5.12). When undertaking a strategic analysis, this provides a means of assessing the dominant culture of the organisation. By reviewing the clues from the cultural web analysis, it is possible to distinguish between a *defender* and a *prospector* organisation, and hence judge the extent to which new strategies might fit the current *paradigm*.

For example, defender cultures find change threatening and tend to favour strategies which provide continuity and 'security'. This is supported by a bureaucratic approach to management. In contrast, a prospector culture thrives on change, favouring strategies of product and/or market development supported by a more creative and flexible management style.

When characterising organisational cultures for the purposes of strategic analysis, it is important to remember several issues.

1. There is not a 'best' and 'worst' culture. The issue is how well the culture matches and supports the product/market positioning of the organisation (and vice versa). This needs to be linked to a parallel issue, which will be discussed in Chapter 10, about the match between positioning and organisational competences (see Figure 10.4).

   - A 'low-price' positioning — for example, a *commodity* product or service — is best supported by competences which emphasise cost improvement and perhaps a largely bureaucratic management regime. In turn, this is often well matched to a *defender* culture.
   - In contrast, a positioning of differentiation — perhaps through product features or service quality — requires more creative

Organisation type	Characteristics of strategic decision making		
	Dominant objectives	**Preferred strategies**	**Planning and control systems**
Defender	Desire for a secure and stable niche in market	Specialisation; cost-efficient production; marketing emphasises price and service to defend current business; tendency to vertical integration	Centralised, detailed control; emphasis on cost efficiency; extensive use of formal planning
Prospector	Location and exploitation of new product and market opportunities	Growth through product and market development (often in spurts); constant monitoring of environmental change; multiple technologies	Emphasis on flexibility, decentralised control, use of *ad hoc* measurements
Analyser	Desire to match new ventures to present shape of business	Steady growth through market penetration; exploitation of applied research; followers in the market	Very complicated; co-ordinating roles between functions (e.g. product managers); intensive planning

Source: Adapted from R.E. Miles and C.C. Snow, *Organizational Strategy, Structure and Process*, McGraw-Hill, 1978.

Figure 5.12 Characterising culture

competences and a more flexible management regime. This matches well with a *prospector* culture.

2. This matching of positioning, competences and dominant culture is likely to become embedded in successful organisations over a period of time. In other words, the key elements of the strategy become taken for granted and may represent core competences of the organisation, as mentioned in Chapter 4.

Indeed, the relationship between strategy and dominant culture is often *self-perpetuating*. So not only does a defender culture match well with a 'commodity' positioning, but it is likely to *seek out* those parts of the market which secure such a positioning. Moreover, the organisational routines — for example, *selection/recruitment* — are likely to perpetuate the dominant culture by not selecting individuals who will 'rock the boat'.

3. In many organisations, *cohesiveness* of culture is found at a level below the corporate entity, as discussed in section 5.5.5 above. Therefore, it is important to decide whether this collection of subcultures is a strength or a weakness to the organisation. For example:

    ▪ A cohesive corporate culture can be characterised as one of *corporate clones*. Established routines are not deviated from; powerful symbols and stories exist which encourage a commitment to the strategies which the organisation has pursued *historically*; there is little tolerance of questioning and challenge, and so on. These are the circumstances where *strategic drift* is likely to occur, as discussed in Chapter 2.

    ▪ The opposite situation is equally worrying and could be described as *open (or covert) warfare*. Cultural cohesion is found only at the level of the sub-unit, and the ability to act corporately is very limited. The real 'enemy' or competitors are internal to the organisation. It has already been mentioned in section 5.5.5 that organisational design and control (for example, divisionalisation) can often create this situation and accidentally lose all the benefits for which the structures were put in place.

    ▪ Perhaps the most healthy situation is one of *constructive friction* — where a strong corporate culture is maintained, but where the core beliefs and assumptions are continuously subjected to critique from within the organisation. Challenge and debate, although not comfortable, are regarded as legitimate and signs of strength.

5.6 Organisational purposes

The previous sections of this chapter have looked at the four main forces which will shape an organisation's purposes: *corporate governance*, *stakeholder expectations*, *business ethics* and the *cultural context*. This final section will look at ways in which organisations express and operationalise purposes at different levels of detail — through *mission*, *vision*, *intent* and *objectives*. Illustration 5.7 is an example for a Police Force.

5.6.1 Mission statements

The *mission statement* of an organisation is the most generalised statement of *organisational* purposes and can be thought of as an expression of its *raison d'être*. If there is substantial disagreement within the organisation or with

---

Illustration 5.7   Organisational purposes

Increasingly, organisations are finding it useful to 'publish' a statement of their purposes. This is usually done at several levels of detail, as the example of the Sussex Police shows.

The Sussex Police standard

1. Purposes
The aims of the Sussex Police are to work with the community to:
- preserve a peaceful society
- protect life and property
- prevent and detect offences
- assist those in need

2. Values
- services to the public
- openly and fairly
- delivered to the highest quality
- and with value for money

As individuals we shall carry out our duties:
- with honesty and integrity
- without fear or favour
- using the minimum necessary force
- courteously
- exercising responsible direction

3. Objectives
The strategic focus for 1995/6 is preserving a peaceful society. We will therefore concentrate our efforts on:
1.   The prevention and detection of crime.
2.   Answering and attending calls from the public within the stated targets.

Crime objectives
To increase the detection rate for violent crime to 70%.
To achieve an overall burglary dwelling detection rate of 20%.
To achieve a detection rate for total crime of 30%.

---

extreme stakeholders as to its mission, it may well give rise to real problems in resolving the strategic direction of the organisation. If there is a mission statement and it is to be useful, it should address the following issues:[29]

- It should be *visionary*[30] and likely to persist for a significant period of time. This is important as a backcloth against which more detailed objectives and strategies can be developed, delivered and changed over time. In Chapter 1, the distinction was made between a *vision* as a 'desired future state of the organisation'; and *mission* as the 'overriding purpose of the organisation . . . in line with the values and expectations of major stakeholders'. There is a great deal of difference between a mission

Administration of justice objectives
Of those offences suitable for formal cautioning to caution 50% by way of instant caution.
80% of Manual of Guidance files [paperwork completed following the arrest of crime offenders] to be without error on first submission.

Response to calls objectives
90% of 999 calls to the Sussex Police Control Room to be answered within 10 seconds.
90% of non-999 switchboard calls to be answered within 30 seconds.
90% of grade 1 calls to be responded to within the relevant target time (10 mins urban, 20 mins rural).
All letters from the public to be answered within 10 working days (or an acknowledgement will be sent).

Public order and reassurance objectives
To release 30 police officers for operational duty (by elimination of, or civilianisation of, non-operational police posts).
To maintain the level of one Special Constable for every five divisional police officers.
To reduce the number of working days lost through sickness by 5%.

Traffic objectives
To reduce road accident casualties by one-third of the average of the 1981–5 figures by the year 2000.

Source: *A Policing Plan for Sussex, 1995/6.*
Prepared by Sara Martin, Cranfield School of Management.

statement which makes it clear that long-term profit growth is required; and a vision which is challenging, even exciting.

▨ It should clarify the main *intentions and aspirations* of the organisation and the reasons why the organisation exists. Hamel and Prahalad[31] prefer the term *strategic intent* to that of vision or mission; they see it as an 'animating dream'. A powerful strategic intent is one that encapsulates both the logic of the strategic direction and the animating challenge — the sense of discovery and destiny — that motivates managers and employees alike throughout the organisation. The challenge for corporate executives is that they can achieve this; the implications for business unit executives is that it will, in turn, strongly influence the strategic choices they make.

- It should describe the organisation's main activities and the *position* it wishes to attain in its industry.
- There should be a statement of the key *values* of the organisation, particularly regarding attitudes towards stakeholder groups and the ethical agenda discussed above.
- The organisation should have the intention and capability to *live up to* the mission statement.

Although mission statements have become much more widely adopted in the 1980s and 1990s, many critics regard them as bland and wide ranging. However, this may be necessary given the political nature of strategic management, since it is essential *at that level* to have statements to which most if not all stakeholders can subscribe.

The extent to which a mission statement is developed by wide involvement of stakeholders and/or communicated widely will be determined by many of the issues discussed in the previous sections on corporate governance, the ethical stance of the organisation and the relative power of external stakeholders. Mission statements can play very different roles in different circumstances (see Figure 5.13):

- If strategy is driven by managers who see other stakeholders and the corporate governance requirements largely as constraints, they may be *secretive* about organisational purposes and see little value in mission statements. When they do exist, they are simply paid lip-service and are

ETHICAL STANCE

	Legal minimum	Ideological
Internal managers	Secretive	Evangelical
External stakeholders	Regulations and procedures	Political

DRIVERS OF STRATEGY

Figure 5.13 The role of mission statements

not powerful influences on the strategic development of the organisation.

- In contrast, managers who have a missionary zeal for the organisation are likely to use the mission statement in an *evangelical* way to 'sell' purposes to other stakeholders. The mission of the organisation is closely aligned to the *strategic intent* of these managers.
- Where strategy is dominated by powerful external stakeholders whose main concern is that the organisation *complies* with the corporate governance arrangements, the purposes are likely to become enshrined in the *regulations and procedures* of the organisation. The danger, of course, is that people lose sight of the mission and the *procedures become the purpose*, as with the classic faceless bureaucracy found in the centrally planned economies of eastern Europe prior to 1990.
- In contrast, if strategy is dominated by external stakeholder(s) with missionary zeal, the purposes of the organisation may become highly politicised. So the ability to produce a mission statement acceptable to all stakeholders can be difficult. This has remained one of the unresolved dilemmas of nationalised industries with government as a major stakeholder. The inability of national governments to sanction capacity reduction in basic industries such as steel (because of the social consequences) created major problems for the profitable management of steel companies in Europe throughout the 1970s, 1980s and early 1990s.

5.6.2 Corporate objectives

Corporate objectives and unit objectives are distinguished in this chapter because there are different 'levels' of objectives with different characteristics. Corporate objectives are often expressed in financial terms. They could be the expression of desired sales or profit levels, rates of growth, dividend levels or share valuations. Increasingly, organisations use corporate objectives of a non-financial nature, such as employee welfare or technological advance, but it is rare for these to be unaccompanied by financial objectives. They are frequently formal statements of how the organisation intends to address stakeholder expectations. It is becoming increasingly recognised that there should be formal statements of objectives to be met on behalf of a variety of stakeholders, including customers, suppliers, employees and the community at large.

5.6.3 Unit objectives

Unit objectives are here distinguished from corporate objectives in so far as they are likely to have the following characteristics:

■   They relate to the individual units of the organisation. For example, they may be the objectives of a division or of one company within a holding company. In the case of public sector organisations, the unit could be a department of a local authority or a hospital.

■   They may be financial objectives stated in much the same way as corporate objectives, but at a unit level. A corporate objective of a given growth in profit after tax might be translated into an objective for each business unit. They are likely to be more operational in nature than corporate objectives.

■   Multiple objectives might well be more common at the unit level than at the corporate level. This is likely to be the case if objectives are conceived of in operational terms, since the operations of a business are multifaceted.

5.6.4 The precision of mission and objectives

Many writers[32] have argued that objectives are not helpful unless they are capable of being measured and achieved — unless they are closed. This view is not taken here. Open statements may in fact be just as helpful as closed statements. For example, mission statements are very difficult to make in closed terms. Their role is to do with *focusing* strategy rather than deciding when it has been 'achieved'. In addition, there may be some objectives which are important, but which are difficult to quantify or express in measurable terms. An objective such as 'to be a leader in technology' may be highly relevant in today's technological environment, but it may become absurd if it has to be expressed in some measurable way. It is nonetheless valid as a statement of purpose and is an example of the importance of *flag-waving* in steering an organisation's strategy. So the aim of being a leader in technology is handed down not as a detailed blueprint or plan from the corporate centre, but as an indication of broad direction and focus, which then becomes a detailed reality as groups and individuals respond to this signal and progress it through their own priorities.

However, there are times when specific objectives are required. These are likely to be when urgent action is needed, such as in a crisis or at times of major transition, and it becomes essential for management to focus attention on a limited number of priority requirements. An extreme example would be in a *turnaround* situation. If the choice is between going out of business and surviving, there is no room for latitude through vaguely stated requirements and control.

5.7   Summary

This chapter has been concerned with analysing and understanding what many managers might regard as the 'softer' factors which influence an organisation's strategies. This requires both a *political* and a *cultural* analysis of an organisation, and how these forces influence the organisation's purposes.

The *political* analysis starts with understanding the corporate governance framework within which the organisation is operating, since this determines whom the organisation should be there to serve (e.g. the shareholders) and the processes through which their interests become adapted as organisational purposes. In reality, the political situation is more complex than this. Organisations have multiple stakeholders with different expectations and different levels of interest in and power over the organisation's purposes. So a political analysis must address this situation — for example, through stakeholder mapping.

The *cultural* analysis also needs to be undertaken in two ways. First, the ethical stance of an organisation will influence the way in which purposes become prioritised. But there are many cultural factors in and around organisations which will influence not only this ethical stance, but also the detailed way in which organisations work and the priorities which actually emerge in practice.

This overall set of influences needs to be understood by managers when deciding how statements of purpose should be constructed and used — for example, statements of mission or objectives. These statements can play many different roles, from being broad indications of vision and strategic intent to providing detailed aims and targets for business units, departments or even individuals.

References

1. Useful general reference books on corporate governance are: D.D. Prentice and P.R.J. Holland, *Contemporary Issues in Governance*, Clarendon Press, 1993; T. Clarke and E. Monkhouse (eds.), *Rethinking the Company*, Pitman, 1994; J. Charkham, *Keeping Good Company: A study of corporate governance in five countries*, Oxford University Press, 1994 (a précis of the findings can be found in J. Charkham, 'Corporate governance: lessons from abroad', in W. Nicoll, D. Norburn and R. Schoenberg (eds.), *Perspectives on European Business*, Whurr Publishers, London, 1995); G. Mills, *Controlling Companies*, Unwin, 1988; and N. Bain and D. Band, *Winning Ways through Corporate Governance*, Macmillan, 1996. A special issue of *Human Relations*, vol. 48, no. 8 (1995) was also devoted to the topic.

2. These differences between countries are discussed in the general books (reference 1 above) and also in M. Yoshimori, 'Whose company is it? The concept of the corporation in Japan and the West', *Long Range Planning*, vol. 28, no. 4 (1995), pp. 33–44.

3. J. Kay and A. Silberston, 'Corporate governance', *National Institute Economic Review*, no. 153 (1995), pp. 84–96.

4. See T. Clarke and R. Bostock, 'International corporate governance', in Clarke and Monkhouse (reference 1 above).

5. Short-termism as an issue in the Anglo-American tradition is contrasted with the 'Rhine model' more typical of Germany, Switzerland, Benelux and northern European countries by M. Albert, 'The Rhine model of capitalism: an investigation', in Nicoll *et al.* (reference 1 above).

6. The influence of board composition on these issues of conflicts of interest is discussed in J. Goodstein, K. Gautam and W. Boeker, 'The effects of board size and diversity on strategic change', *Strategic Management Journal*, vol. 15, no. 3 (1994), pp. 241–50.

7. *Report of the Committee of Inquiry on Industrial Democracy*, Chairman: Lord Bullock, HMSO, 1977.

8. The early writing about stakeholders was concerned with 'coalitions' in organisations: for example, the seminal work by R.M. Cyert and J.G. March, *A Behavioural Theory of the Firm*, Prentice Hall, 1964. In recent years, stakeholder analysis has become central to strategic analysis: for example, I.I. Mitroff, *Stakeholder of the Organisational Mind*, Jossey-Bass, 1983; R.E. Freeman, *Strategic Management: A stakeholder approach*, Pitman, 1984; J. Harrison and H. Caron, *Strategic Management of Organisations and Stakeholders: Concepts*, West, 1993.

9. This approach to stakeholder mapping has been adapted from A. Mendelow, *Proceedings of 2nd International Conference on Information Systems*, Cambridge, MA, 1981. See also C. Cassel and P. Johnson's chapter, 'Stakeholder analysis' in V. Ambrosini with G. Johnson and K. Scholes (eds) *Exploring Techniques of Analysis and Evaluation in Strategic Management*, Prentice Hall, 1998.

10. See Cyert and March (reference 8 above).

11. See Kay and Silberston (reference 3 above).

12. J. Pfeffer, *Managing with Power: Power and influence in organisations*, McGraw-Hill, 1994, and I.C. Macmillan and P.E. Jones, *Strategy Formulation: Power and politics*, 2nd edition, West, 1986, both provide a useful analysis of the relationship between power and strategy. C. Hardy (ed.), *Power and Politics in Organisations*, Ashgate, 1995, is also on this general theme.

13. There is a prolific flow of literature on business ethics. Readers can gain some useful insights into the field by reading the following: G. Chryssides and J. Kaler, *Business Ethics*, Chapman and Hall, 1993; J. Mahoney, 'An international look at business ethics: Britain', *Journal of Business Ethics*, vol. 9, no. 7 (1990) pp. 545–550; R. Johns, *Company Community Involvement in the UK*, R. Johns Associates, 1991; S. Hamilton, 'Cashing in on good works', *Business*, July 1991, p. 99; K. Smith and P. Johnson (eds.), *Business Ethics and Business Behaviour*, Thomson Business, 1996.

14. This position was argued strongly in the 1970s by M. Friedman, 'The social responsibility of business is to increase its profits', *New York Times Magazine*, 13 September 1970. He and others were concerned that business managers had been 'diverted' from their main role.

15. This is similar to what Kay and Silberston (reference 3 above) refer to as corporate managers being the 'trustees of the assets of the corporation'.

16. Useful books on corporate social responsibility are: W. Frederick, J. Post and K. Davis, *Business and Society: Management, public policy, ethics*, 7th edition, McGraw-Hill, 1992; and T. Cannon, *Corporate Social Responsibility*, Pitman, 1992.

17. D. Clutterbuck and D. Snow, *Working with the Community*, Weidenfeld and Nicolson, 1991.

18. R. Larmer, 'Whistleblowing and employee loyalty', *Journal of Business Ethics*, vol. 11, no. 2 (1992), pp. 125–8; M. Miceli and J. Near, *Blowing the Whistle: The organisational and legal implications for companies and employees*, Lexington Books, 1992.

19. S. Evers, *The Manager as a Professional*, Institute of Management, 1993. This is a document which checklists and expands upon the Code of Conduct and Guides to Professional Management Practice of the Institute of Management.

20. One of the earlier works on the influence of national culture was G. Hofstede, *Culture's Consequences*, Sage, 1980. A comprehensive coverage of this topic can be found in R. Mead, *International Management: Cross-cultural dimensions*, Blackwell, 1994.

21. See also C. Hampden-Turner and F. Trompenaars, *The Seven Cultures of Capitalism: Value systems for creating wealth in the United States, Britain, Japan, Germany, France, Sweden and the Netherlands*, Piatkus Business, 1994.

22. See S. Schneider, 'Strategy formulation: the

impact of national culture', *Organization Studies*, vol. 10, no. 2 (1989) pp. 149–168; S. Schneider and A. Meyer, 'Interpreting and responding to strategic issues: the impact of national culture', *Strategic Management Journal*, vol. 12, no. 4 (1991) pp. 307–320; C. Randlesome *et al.*, *Business Cultures in Europe*, Heinemann, 1990; R.M. Kanter, 'In search of a single culture', *Business*, June 1991, pp. 58–66.

23. For a discussion of strategy in professional service organisations, see H. Mintzberg and J. Quinn, *The Strategy Process: Concepts, contexts and cases*, 3rd edition, Prentice Hall, 1995; K. Scholes, 'Strategic management in professional service organisations', Professorial Lecture, Sheffield Business School, 1994.

24. The term 'recipe' is used by J. Spender, *Industry Recipes: The nature and sources of management judgement*, Blackwell, 1989.

25. E. Schein, *Organisation Culture and Leadership*, Jossey-Bass, 1985.

26. J. Barney, 'Organisational culture: can it be a source of sustained competitive advantage?', *Academy of Management Review*, vol. 11, no. 3 (1986), pp. 656–65.

27. A detailed coverage of cultural web analysis can be found in G. Johnson, 'Mapping and re-mapping organisational culture', in V. Ambrosini with G. Johnson and K. Scholes (eds.), *Exploring Techniques of Analysis and Evaluation in Strategic Management*, Prentice Hall, 1998.

28. R.E. Miles and C.C. Snow, *Organisational Strategy: Structure and process*, McGraw-Hill, 1978.

29. See A. Campbell and K. Tawadey, *Mission and Business Philosophy*, Butterworth-Heinemann, 1993; A. Campbell, M. Devine and D. Young, *A Sense of Mission*, Financial Times/Pitman, 1990; J. Abrahams, *The Mission Statement Book*, Ten Speed Press, 1995.

30. The importance of vision is discussed in I. Wilson, 'Realising the power of vision', *Long Range Planning*, vol. 25, no. 5 (1992), pp. 18–28; and R. Whittington, *What is Strategy and Does it Matter?*, Routledge, 1993, chapter 3.

31. See G. Hamel and C. Prahalad, 'Strategic intent', *Harvard Business Review*, vol. 67, no. 3 (1989), pp. 63–76.

32. For example, I. Ansoff, *Corporate Strategy*, Penguin, 1968, p. 44, argued that objectives should be precise and measurable.

Recommended key readings

▓ Useful general reference books on corporate governance are: D.D. Prentice and P.R.J. Holland, *Contemporary Issues in Governance*, Clarendon Press, 1993; T. Clarke and E. Monkhouse (eds.), *Rethinking the Company*, Pitman, 1994.

▓ For more about the stakeholder concept, read either I.I. Mitroff, *Stakeholders of the Organisational Mind*, Jossey-Bass, 1983, or R.E. Freeman, *Strategic Management: A stakeholder approach*, Pitman, 1984.

▓ Readers should be familiar with the political context of strategic decision making by reading either J. Pfeffer, *Managing with Power: Power and influence in organisations*, McGraw-Hill, 1994, or I.C. Macmillan and P.E. Jones, *Strategy Formulation: Power and politics*, 2nd edition, West, 1986.

▓ Readers can gain some useful insights into business ethics by reading G. Chryssides and J. Kaler, *Business Ethics*, Chapman and Hall, 1993; K. Smith and P. Johnson (eds.), *Business Ethics and Business Behaviour*, Thomson Business, 1996.

▓ Useful books on corporate social responsibility are: W. Frederick, J. Post and K. Davis, *Business and Society: Management, public policy, ethics*, 7th edition, McGraw-Hill, 1992; T. Cannon, *Corporate Social Responsibility*, Pitman, 1992.

▓ E. Schein, *Organisation Culture and Leadership*, Jossey-Bass, 1985, is still useful in understanding the relationship between organisational culture and strategy.

A comprehensive coverage of the influence of national culture on strategy can be found in R. Mead, *International Management: Cross-*

cultural dimensions, Blackwell, 1994.

R.E. Miles and C.C. Snow, *Organisational Strategy: Structure and process*, McGraw-Hill, 1978, is useful in understanding strategy as a product of culture.

Work assignments

5.1   For an organisation of your choice, map out a governance chain which clearly identifies all the key players through to the beneficiaries of the organisation's good (or poor) performance. To what extent are managers:
(a) knowledgeable about the expectations of beneficiaries?
(b) actively pursuing their interests?
(c) keeping them informed?
How would you change any of these aspects of the organisation's operations? Why?

5.2   *Critique the different traditions of corporate governance in the UK/USA, Germany and Japan in terms of your own views of their strengths and weaknesses. Is there a better system than any of these? Why?*

5.3   Choose any organisation which does not operate a two-tier board (or the public sector equivalent).
(a) Would a two-tier board be a better form of governance? Why?
(b) What would you need to do to move to a two-tier system?
(c) Is this likely to be possible?

5.4   Discuss the reasons which led to the Greenbury Report on executive pay (Illustration 5.3). Do you agree with the proposals? (Why/why not?)

5.5   Using Illustration 5.4 as an example, identify and map out the stakeholders for Iona* or the Sheffield Theatres* or an organisation of your choice in relation to:
(a) current strategies
(b) a number of different future strategies of your choice.
What are the implications of your analysis for the management?

5.6   For The News Corporation* or an organisation of your choice, use Figure 5.7 to establish the *overall stance* of the organisation on ethical issues.

5.7   **Identify the key corporate social responsibility issues which are of major concern in an industry or public service of your choice (refer to Figure 5.8). Compare the approach of two or more organisations in that industry, and explain how this relates to their competitive standing.**

5.8   Use the questions in Figure 5.11 to plot out a tentative cultural web for Iona*
      or an organisation of your choice.

5.9   Use Figure 5.12 to identify organisations with which you are familiar which
      are close to the three Miles and Snow stereotypes. Justify your
      categorisation.

5.10 *By using a number of the examples from above, critically appraise the assertion
      that 'culture can only really be usefully analysed by the symptoms displayed in
      the way the organisation operates'. Refer to Schein's book in the recommended
      key readings to assist you with this task.*

5.11 Criticise the statements of purpose presented in Illustration 5.7 in terms of
      their usefulness to the strategic management of the organisation. Repeat the
      process for one or more organisations of your choice.

      *This refers to a case in the Text and Cases version of this book.

PART III

Strategic choice

In many ways strategic choice is the core of strategic management. It is concerned with decisions about an organisation's future and the way in which it needs to respond to the many pressures and influences identified in strategic analysis. In turn, the consideration of future strategies must be mindful of the realities of strategy implementation, which can be a significant constraint on strategic choice.

Chapter 2 showed that organisations are continually attempting to readjust to their environment, and one of the major criticisms which can be made of managers concerns their inability or unwillingness to consider the variety of strategic options open to the organisation. Rather, they tend to remain bound by their paradigm and resistant to change. It is for this reason that this part of the book presents a systematic way of looking at strategic choice. The steps outlined here help to promote a wider consideration of strategy and the appropriateness and consequences of options available to the organisation.

The discussion of strategic choice has been divided into three chapters to reflect the three elements of any development strategy. It is important that these elements are consistent with each other.

- Chapter 6 looks at some of the bases on which an organisation's strategies are built. These include issues which relate back to Chapter 5, such as the influence of organisational purposes or vision and the way in which ownership decisions affect strategic choice. The scope of the organisation in product/services and market terms is also considered, which also raises questions of international strategy. Bases of strategic choices at the SBU level are then considered by examining choices of generic competitive strategies (positioning). The chapter concludes by reviewing how corporate parents might or might not add value to the strategies of SBUs. This includes issues of portfolio management, financial strategy and corporate parenting.
- Chapter 7 deals with choices of both strategic direction and method. This includes considerations of how directions of strategic development can

be built around market opportunities; developments of product; development of competences; and the various combinations of these three parameters. Development methods range from internal development, through strategic alliances to acquisitions and mergers.

- Chapter 8 is concerned with strategy evaluation. This begins with a discussion of the evaluation criteria of suitability, feasibility and acceptability. Assessing the suitability of a strategy can be a useful means of 'screening' options before more detailed analyses. There are different techniques to undertake the screening, such as ranking options, decision trees and scenario planning. The assessment of acceptability is concerned with three things: the likely return should a strategy be adopted, the level of risk in a strategy and the attitudes/ reactions of stakeholders. Feasibility involves an assessment of whether the resources and competences are available to support a strategy. There are important links with discussions in Chapters 4 and 10. The chapter concludes with a brief review of how strategies are selected in organisations, with important links to the management of change (discussed in Chapter 11).

CHAPTER 6

Bases of strategic choice

6.1 Introduction

Bases of choice need to be considered both at the level of the SBU and at the level of the parent organisation. However, the questions to be asked at both of these levels are potentially mutually reinforcing. The strategic choices at SBU level can enhance the standing of the corporate level (for example, of a corporation with its investors) and the choices at the corporate level enhance those at the SBU level. This issue is addressed by considering *bases of strategic choice* at both the corporate and SBU levels, and links between these which can yield strategic advantage for an organisation. Figure 6.1 provides an outline of how this is discussed in the chapter.

1. The chapter begins with a discussion of *corporate-level* strategic issues in terms of *purposes and aspirations*. The issues raised here relate to some of the expectations which stakeholders have of the organisation (see Chapter 5).

    -   For some organisations there may be issues of *ownership* to be addressed.
    -   It is important for executives to make clear the overarching theme, *intent* or *mission* for the organisation: for example, in a commercial organisation in terms of type of business, levels of expected growth or dominance of markets.
    -   The *scope* of the organisation is important, in terms of the number of businesses or activities it chooses to be involved in, and the strategic logic behind this. This relates to the extent of *diversity* of the organisation. Decisions need to be made as to the extent of relatedness of the organisation's activities. If relatedness is important, this may facilitate the development of *synergies* between business activities or common *competences* at the corporate level.
    -   *Global dimensions* of such aspirations are considered specifically

Figure 6.1 Bases of strategic choice

because they are increasingly raising fundamental challenges for organisations.

2. The chapter then moves to a discussion of *generic competitive* strategies: the fundamental bases on which an SBU seeks to achieve a lasting advantageous position in its environment by meeting the expectations of buyers, users or other stakeholders. These bases are summarised in Figure 6.2. They should in turn inform considerations discussed in Chapter 7 about the *directions* which business units may follow, such as developing new products or new markets, and the different *methods* by which these might be achieved: for example, through internal development, acquisition or alliances. These options are also indicated in Figure 6.2.

3. The extent to which SBU strategies can be enhanced at the corporate level is then addressed. The issue here is how a parent body can add value to SBUs.

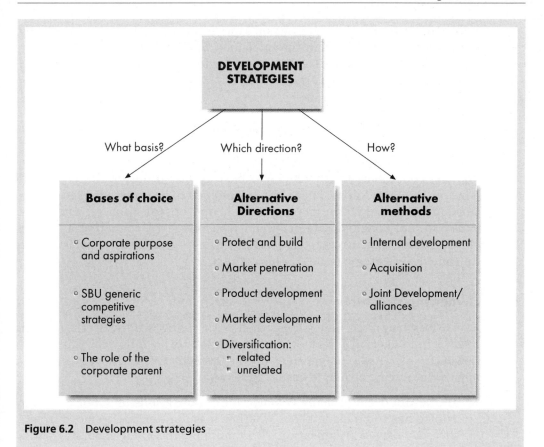

Figure 6.2   Development strategies

- *Portfolio management* approaches are discussed here and elsewhere in the book as ways of trying to gain an understanding of the extent to which multiple SBUs make strategic sense in corporate terms.
- There are implications here for the financial *strategy* of the corporate body.
- The notion of corporate parenting is then explored in more detail, both in terms of *roles of corporate parents* and in terms of a *parenting matrix*, which is a further way of considering the portfolio of SBUs in the organisation.

In considering all this, it needs to be remembered that decisions at the corporate level and decisions on SBU generic competitive strategy, direction and method are not independent of each other. An organisation pursuing a *competitive strategy* of differentiation may also be pursuing a strategic *direction* of product or service development. Both these levels of strategic choice are likely to be influenced by the overall thrust of strategy at the *corporate level*; as is the *method* by which new developments are best achieved—through the organisation's own efforts, jointly with others, or by acquisition. As explained in the introduction to this part of the book, the important point is that these various dimensions of strategic decisions need to be consistent with each other.

6.2 Corporate purpose and aspirations

As shown in Chapter 5 (section 5.3), whatever the size or structure of an organisation, it has stakeholders who have greater or lesser interest in and power over what it does. These influences need to be taken into account in developing strategy. The management of the organisation — whether a multinational conglomerate or a family business, the council of a charity or the senior executives of a public service — need to consider some fundamental strategic issues in this context.

6.2.1 Ownership structures

Executives may face issues concerned with changes in ownership which have a fundamental effect on the strategies to be followed. They may, however, also have to consider if the current ownership structure is appropriate to the strategic needs of the organisation.

1. In the life cycle of many commercial organisations, a major strategic choice has to be made about whether it is appropriate to move from a *privately owned* organisation — a family business, for example — to a *publicly quoted* corporation. Such a decision might be made because the owners decide that increased equity is required to finance the growth of the business (see section 6.4.2). The decision is of major importance not least because the family members who own the business need to recognise that their role will change. They become answerable to a much wider group of shareholders and to city institutions acting for such shareholders. It therefore changes the stakeholder basis of the organisation and thus the influences and constraints on the development of organisational strategy. Illustration 6.1 shows how organisations have felt it necessary to change ownership structures to pursue the strategies they wish to follow.[1]

2. The board of directors of a business has a responsibility to shareholders to provide them with a reasonable rate of return on their investment. It may be that the board arrives at the view that the sale to a *different corporate parent* may be to the advantage of a company or a business within the corporation. For example, a family controlled firm might consider selling out to a corporation as a way of realising its assets. Or it may be that the board of a firm decides that it is not able to compete as

Illustration 6.1   Changing ownership structures

Ownership structures can be changed to fit corporate strategy better.

Virgin Group: private–public–private[1]

Having built up the Virgin Group as a private company, Richard Branson took the music publishing and retailing side public in 1986. This allowed him to capitalise on the success of the company and raise capital to facilitate continued expansion. It also gave the Virgin Group easier access to finance at a lower cost, while attracting better management into the business.

Despite the benefits, Branson tired of the public listing obligations. Compliance with the rules governing public limited companies and reporting to shareholders were both expensive and time consuming, and he resented making presentations in the City to people who did not understand the business. The pressure to create short-term profit, especially as the share price began to fall, was the final straw: the decision was made to return to private ownership and the shares were bought back at the original offer price, which valued the company at £240 million. Less than four years later, the music division was sold to Thorn EMI for £510 million.

Woolwich Building Society: mutual building society–public quoted bank[2]

Against a backdrop of intense environmental change — most notably economic, demographic and technological developments creating greater competition, diversification and considerable regrouping among its competitors — the Woolwich Building Society announced, in January 1996, its desire to convert into a public limited company as a bank. It cited as its reason the need to have the most effective form of corporate structure to achieve its objective of remaining a significant player in the personal financial services market.

The Woolwich argued that the benefit of conversion was greater operational flexibility, arising from the move away from the laws governing building societies to those governing UK banks. This not only reduced the costs of borrowing money, but also made the process of raising additional capital easier. The conversion would also enable it to achieve critical mass within the industry, broaden its geographical coverage, expand its products and services beyond the traditional building society base, and generate economies of scale.

Sources: [1]M. Vander Weyer, 'Only fools and masochists', *Management Today*, January 1996.
[2]Company information.
Prepared by Tony Jacobs, Cranfield School of Management.

an independent unit as well as it might within a corporate body, perhaps because it is trading nationally within increasingly global markets. The sale of the business might therefore make sense.

Businesses also become the targets for acquisitions (see Chapter 7, section 7.3.2), and a board might decide that such an offer is more attractive to shareholders than the returns they can promise in the future. On occasions, businesses decide to merge, perhaps because the executives believe that the synergies resulting from coming together are greater than the businesses would achieve by operating independently. These decisions are, then, the outcome of considerations of strategy where a decision is reached that the business would be better off under other ownership.

3. Historically, most public sector bodies have been tightly controlled by the equivalent of their 'owners', the central or local government or government departments. However, latterly this has changed in a number of respects in many countries, notably by the *privatisation* of such public bodies.[2] In the UK, this process began in the 1980s with the government selling British Telecom and gas, water and electricity utilities. The effects were significant in terms of strategic choice. The government took such decisions in order to require organisations to face up to market forces, to become more aware of customer needs and competitive pressures. In turn, managers found more latitude in terms of strategic choice — what they could provide in terms of product or services; the ability to diversify, raise capital for expansion and so on.

4. In both publicly quoted and state-owned companies, another example of changing ownership is when all or part of the organisation is sold to management — a *management buyout*.[3] This has happened, for example, in commercial organisations when managers of a business have been faced with a corporate decision to close or dispose of that business. Those who work in the organisation may have sufficient faith in its future to raise capital to buy the business themselves. In the public sector, too, buyouts have occurred: for example, when a public corporation has chosen to withdraw from a particular market or when the government has sold off a utility.

Many of the executive teams running the operating subsidiaries of British Rail decided to bid for the businesses when privatised in the mid-1990s. Decisions on the sale of the businesses were based not only on the bid price for them, but also on the basis of the strategic plans for those businesses. The decision to sell off the subsidiaries was therefore made in the belief that it would enhance the competitive standing of the businesses; and the decision to go for a buyout was made by the management teams following their own appraisal of future strategy. Many of the management teams which made such bids also decided to enter into joint ventures or alliances with third parties to raise finance or to become part of a wider portfolio of businesses. Again, then, decisions on ownership influence other strategic decisions relating to the organisation.

5. Even when a change in ownership has not been made, public sector organisations have been required to face questions of corporate purpose by other means.[4]

    ▨ *Deregulation* has taken place in public sector monopolies such as broadcasting, public transport and airlines (especially in the USA), varying from completely opening access to private sector providers (creating a true market) to auctioning franchises to private sector bids (as with TV contracts in the UK and other countries). *Compulsory competitive tendering (CCT)* and *market-testing* have required the separation of the roles of the *client*, who specifies the detail of the services required on behalf of 'customers', and the *provider*, who may previously have been in-house but is required to bid alongside other bidders. In central government departments in the UK, the same process of splitting the client (policy-makers) and providers (government services) has occurred through granting *agency status* to the service providers. For example, the UK Employment Services Group (providers of services relating to unemployment benefits and job seeking) was separated from the Employment Department in this way.

    ▨ *Quasi-markets* have also been created, driven by the view that value for money is not delivered by the 'natural' public sector monopolies, since there are fewer pressures to improve performance than in open markets. One type of quasi-market has been the appointment of *regulatory offices* (as with telecom, gas, water and electricity) as a substitute for a real market. Another approach has been the introduction of customer–supplier relationships *internal* to the organisation — the (so-called) *internal markets* — health care in the UK and New Zealand are examples. (This is discussed further in Chapter 10, section 10.4, in terms of resource allocation and control.)

These devices to reshape the product/market strategies of (previously) public sector enterprises have usually resulted in the need to revisit fundamentally issues of *positioning* and *competitive strategies*, discussed in section 6.3.

  These, then, are examples of the relationship between ownership and strategic choice. In all cases, they make the point that choices of ownership are fundamental strategic decisions, which in turn require managers of those organisations to consider other bases of strategic choice and issues of direction and method. These are now considered.

6.2.2 Mission and strategic intent[5]

Managers need to be clear about what they see as the role of their organisation, and this is often expressed in terms of a statement of mission or strategic intent (see Chapter 5, section 5.6.1). This is important because both external stakeholders and other managers in the organisation, not least in subsidiary parts of it, need to be clear about what the organisation is seeking to achieve and, in broad terms, how it expects to do so. At this level, strategy is not concerned with the details of SBU competitive strategy or the directions and methods the businesses might take to achieve competitive advantage (these are discussed later in this chapter and in Chapter 7). Rather, the concern here is overall strategic direction.

The importance of this can be seen when there is an absence of clarity. For example, investors are often wary of investing in highly diversified firms because they are not clear about what the purpose of the organisation is. They are likely to question what is added by the corporation and could take the view that the different businesses would be more attractive for investment as independent entities. (Illustration 7.6 in the next chapter gives examples of businesses in which this has occurred.)

The managers of a subsidiary, charged with developing a strategy for that business, also need to be clear where they fit into the corporate whole. For example, is their business seen as central to corporate aspirations or peripheral? If they are not clear, it is unlikely that they will manage the business in ways to enhance the overall aspirations of the organisation. As Hamel and Prahalad[6] have highlighted, the importance of clear strategic intent can go much further: it can help galvanise motivation and enthusiasm throughout the organisation by providing what they call a sense of destiny and discovery. In the absence of this, there is a risk of the different parts of the organisation, different levels of management, indeed all members of the organisation, pulling in different directions.

Illustration 6.2 shows how mission or intent can encapsulate the basis of overall strategy for the benefit both of external stakeholders and, internally, of those who have to formulate and deliver SBU strategies. Some specific examples of this bridging role of mission and intent are now provided.

- Successful family businesses face difficult issues to do with family ownership. Part of the mission may be to retain ownership in the family. If this is so, not only does it potentially place constraints on the business, perhaps because of difficulties of financing the business for growth; it may also influence the strategies which are followed. For example, family businesses may seek to build on networks of family relationships, as is often the case in Chinese-controlled businesses in the Far East; or seek out market segments in which family heritage is seen as important, as is the case in some sections of merchant banking.

Illustration 6.2   Komatsu's mission to encircle Caterpillar

Clarity of strategic intent can motivate an organisation to achieve its goals.

Komatsu is the second largest producer of earth-moving equipment after its arch rival, Caterpillar. However, this was not always so. In the 1950s it produced a limited range of low-quality products and, with a protected home market, had little or no incentive to improve. This position changed when Japan opened this market to foreign competition in the early 1960s.

In 1964, Kawai succeeded his father as chairman of Komatsu and announced the goal of 'Maru C': to 'encircle Caterpillar'. This statement of strategic intent — to concentrate all its efforts on surpassing Caterpillar — was to be the driving force of the company for more than two decades.

Initially, Komatsu focused on improving product quality to limit the loss of sales in its home market. Komatsu then signed licensing agreements with Caterpillar's competitors to gain access to the latest American technology. This move also enabled it to expand its product range, which made it more attractive to dealer networks — crucial if Komatsu was to build up sales volume. The next stage towards its goal was to enter secondary export markets such as China and eastern Europe, which helped build the critical mass required to challenge Caterpillar in the main markets of Europe and America.

By the 1980s, Komatsu was very successful: its growth from a regional producer of low-quality products to the second largest producer was impressive and was widely attributed to its goal of encircling Caterpillar. Yet Katada, Komatsu's third president, was beginning to question this strategy.

The goal that had served the company so well for over two decades was beginning to be overtaken by the changing business environment. Komatsu's sales began to fall as demand for heavy earth-moving equipment decreased and competition intensified; Komatsu was less focused on its markets' needs and more concerned with outdoing Caterpillar.

Katada changed the company's emphasis from providing construction equipment to being a 'total technology enterprise', and the new goal of 'Growth, Global, Groupwide' was adopted. In the three years since the new goal was introduced, Komatsu has reversed its sales decline and seen a 40 per cent growth in its non-construction equipment business.

Sources: C.A. Bartlett and S. Ghoshal, 'Changing the role of top management', *Harvard Business Review*, vol. 73, no. 1 (1994) pp. 79–88; G. Hamel and C.K. Prahalad, *Competing for the Future*, Harvard Business School Press, 1994.
Prepared by Tony Jacobs, Cranfield School of Management.

▪ Decisions on overall mission in a major corporation will exercise constraints elsewhere. Does the corporation aspire to short-term profits or long-term growth; to a focused set of highly related businesses or a more diversified set of businesses; to global coverage or the focus on selected countries; to investment in internal innovation and new products, or the acquisition of other businesses? These are, of course, all matters of strategic choice, but they are unlikely to change regularly. The overall stance of the corporation with regard to such matters may develop over many years, but by being made explicit it can help direct strategic choice.

▪ Mission or intent may, of course, result from the arrival of a new leader; indeed, some would see this as the primary role of leaders.[7] Ingvar Kamprad's vision of the market opportunity and positioning of IKEA has played a fundamental role in guiding the successful strategy of that business over many decades. Margaret Thatcher's mission to reduce public expenditure and require public services to face competitive pressures resulted in the deregulation and privatisation of many such services in the UK in the 1980s and 1990s. In such cases, a clarity of mission or intent was important in providing a basis on which further strategic choice could be made.

6.2.3 What business are we in? The issue of scope and diversity

The deceptively simple question 'What business are we in?' needs to be considered because it puts boundaries around and gives guidance on the nature of the business. Indeed, many organisations try to address this, too, in their statements of mission or intent. When British Airways coined its stated intent to be 'the world's favourite airline' in the late 1980s, it was not just setting out an ambition; it was setting boundaries to the activities it would choose to get involved in and develop, and on what scale. When national and local governments started to describe themselves as 'enabling organisations' in the UK in the 1980s, it signalled a progressive withdrawal from the direct delivery of public services by government agencies, which had increased massively since 1945 in many countries.

Diversity or relatedness

Most organisations begin their existence focused on a particular product or service. Some retain a focused approach with, perhaps, highly related SBUs; others become much more diversified. Decisions about the extent of diversity are important not least because there is evidence of a relationship between decisions on the extent of relatedness of a corporation and financial performance at the corporate level.[8] In particular, there is a relationship between the extent of relatedness and the type of strategic management control exercised at the corporate level. A corporate body may be able to manage many unrelated businesses if it chooses to follow a 'hands-off' relationship with those businesses. However, if it chooses to become involved in helping to form the strategic direction of those SBUs, it is likely that a much lesser number and more related set of businesses is appropriate and will give rise to better performance.[9] This issue is dealt with in more detail in Chapters 9 and 10, where the structure and control systems of organisations are discussed.

The questions posed at the corporate level are, first, whether the corporate body wishes to have a related set of SBUs or not; and if so, on what basis. This issue of relatedness in turn has direct implications on decisions about diversification (see Chapter 7, section 7.2.4).

Relatedness might exist in different ways:

- SBUs might all build on similar *technologies* or all provide similar sorts of *products* or *services*.
- SBUs might be serving similar or different *markets*. Even if technology or products differ, it may be that the customers are similar. For example, the technologies underpinning frozen food, washing powders and margarine production may be very different; but all are sold through retail operations, and Unilever operates in all these product fields.
- Or it may be that other *competences* on which the competitive advantage of different SBUs are built have similarities. Unilever would argue that the marketing skills associated with the three product markets are similar, for example.

The global dimension

The increasing globalisation of products and services was discussed in Chapter 3. An increasingly important issue is what geographical boundaries managers envisage for an organisation. Some organisations have chosen to retain a strong *domestic focus*, in the belief that their future is best served by concentrating on a distinct understanding of local markets. For example, German brewers see themselves as serving a consumer whose taste for their products will persist within what was historically a regulated environment, and one in which competitive entry remains difficult. In the public sector, geographical scope may be prescribed — for example, in local government. Other corporations, such as some of the commodity companies in oil and other raw materials, have long operated on a worldwide basis with very narrow product ranges. Other types of business, once traditionally domestic, are following strategies of geographic expansion. For example, Aldi and Netto are becoming European-wide grocery retailers.

Many organisations now consider the pursuit of *global strategies* as offering distinct benefits of cost reduction, improved quality, better ability

Illustration 6.3 Focused global strategies

Strategic focus on a global scale has given Germany's Mittelstands — small to medium-sized companies — world leadership in terms of market share.

Mittelstands concentrate on a specific product/market and focus on areas that customers value most. By attempting to match their strengths with customers' needs, they are able to offer high-value products at premium prices, while globalisation increases sales to a level where R&D costs are covered. Examples include Hauni, with a 90 per cent market share in cigarette machines, SAP, producing business software, and Leybold, which focuses on coating and vacuum technology.

Mittelstands identify the following qualities as being most valued by customers; their competitive advantage comes from focusing on, and differentiation along, these lines.

Innovative, technological and quality products

Mittelstands focus on highly technical and innovative product/market niches and concentrate on perfecting products — 38 per cent cited quality as a source of competitive advantage. This focus on innovation and technological leadership creates differentiation and ensures self-reliance in R&D, which strengthens their product knowledge and prevents leaks of technical information. Mittelstands have a much higher level of patents per employee than larger companies.

Closeness to the customer

By being close to their customers, Mittelstands receive invaluable information about product performance. This can then be used to strengthen their overall capabilities and ensure that developments have practical applications. Facilities are sometimes located close to customers to ensure that they do not lose touch with their market's needs.

Mittelstands also prefer to take full control of overseas operations, viewing the customer relationship as too important to delegate. They have on average 9.6 foreign subsidiaries — a high number for companies of their size. This commitment has paid off in terms of market share.

Quality of employees

Continuity of staff ensures that long-term relationships with customers can develop, creating commitment on both sides to the business relationship. Contact between customers and technical staff ensures that new product developments have practical applications, tailored to customers' needs.

Service

By creating strong service networks and an emphasis on customer training in the handling and maintenance of products, Mittelstands have a method of ensuring customer satisfaction and differentiating their product from that of their competitors.

Sources: A. Fisher, 'Hidden champions', *Financial Times*, 30 January 1996; H. Simon, 'Lessons from Germany's midsize giants', *Harvard Business Review*, vol. 70, no. 2 (1992) pp. 115–123.
Prepared by Tony Jacobs, Cranfield School of Management.

Global strategy levers	Cost reduction	Improved quality	Benefits Enhanced customer preference	Competitive leverage	Major drawbacks All levels incur co-ordination costs, plus ...
Global market participation	Increases volume for economies of scale	Via exposure to demanding customers and innovative competitors	Via global availability, global serviceability and global recognition	Advantage of early entry Provides more sites for attack and counterattack, hostage for good behaviour	Earlier or greater commitment to a market than warranted on own merits
Global products	Reduces duplication of development efforts Reduces purchasing, production and inventory costs	Focuses development and management resources	Allows consumers to use familiar product while abroad Allows organisations to use same product across country units	Basis for low-cost invasion of markets Offsets disadvantage of low market share	Less responsive to local needs
Global location of activities	Reduces duplication of activities Helps exploit economies of scale Exploits differences in country factor costs Partial concentration allows flexibility versus currency changes and versus bargaining parties	Focuses effort Allows more consistent quality control		Allows maintenance of cost advantage independent of local conditions Provides flexibility on where to base competitive advantage	Distances activities from customer Increases current risk Increases risk of creating competitors More difficult to manage value chain
Others	Reduces design and production costs of marketing programmes	Focuses talent and resources Leverage scarce, good ideas	Reinforces marketing messages by exposing customer to the same mix in different countries	Magnifies resources available to any country Provides more options and leverage in competitive attack and defence	Reduces adaptation to local customer behaviour and marketing environment Local competitiveness may be sacrificed

Source: Based on G. Yip, *Total Global Strategy*, Prentice Hall, 1995, chapter 6.

Figure 6.3   How global strategy levers achieve globalisation benefits to meet customer needs and increased competitive leverage. These are not always large corporations, as Illustration 6.3 shows. Indeed, there are lessons to be learned about global operations from the successes and failures of smaller businesses which have sought to operate on a global scale. A study of such start-ups on a global scale revealed that the key characteristics of success included the presence of a global vision by the founders of the start-up, the involvement of internationally experienced managers with international business networks, and the existence of some clear advantage in product or service terms capable of being exploited and sustained.[10] Such findings illustrate well the way in which the success of the strategy integrates clarity of corporate purpose and the exploitation of competitive advantage at the business unit level.

The benefits of global strategies are shown in Figure 6.3.[11] On the other hand, there are drawbacks to such global strategies, such as the difficulty of penetrating certain markets, or the failure to meet local customer needs because of product standardisation or global marketing (also see Figure 6.3).

6.3   Bases of SBU competitive advantage: the 'strategy clock'

The previous section discussed some bases of strategic choice mainly at the corporate level. However, it also showed that there needs to be a compatibility between corporate-level strategy and the strategy of the SBUs. In some organisations, notably small businesses, these may be one and the same; but in most organisations there are a number of SBUs. In either event, it is important to be clear about the bases of strategic choice at this level.

Bases of strategic choice for organisations can usefully be considered in the context of the overall *generic competitive* strategy which an organisation might pursue. This section reviews these strategies, drawing on previous discussions concerning the competitive environment (Chapter 3) and competences and the value chain (Chapter 4); and looks forward to chapters which consider more specific strategic directions and methods (Chapter 7), the evaluation of strategies (Chapter 8) and the building of competences to sustain selected strategies (Chapter 10).

For commercial organisations, the discussions in this section are concerned with establishing the bases on which a company can build and sustain competitive advantage. For public service organisations, the section is concerned with an equivalent issue: the bases on which the organisation chooses to sustain the quality of its services within agreed budgets; how it provides 'value for money'.

In 1980, Michael Porter's book *Competitive Strategy*[12] highlighted the importance and relevance of generic competitive strategies. Managers were

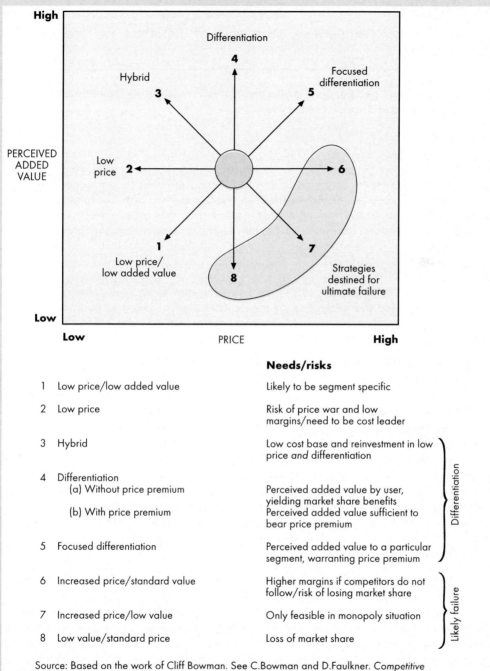

	Needs/risks
1 Low price/low added value	Likely to be segment specific
2 Low price	Risk of price war and low margins/need to be cost leader
3 Hybrid	Low cost base and reinvestment in low price *and* differentiation
4 Differentiation (a) Without price premium	Perceived added value by user, yielding market share benefits
(b) With price premium	Perceived added value sufficient to bear price premium
5 Focused differentiation	Perceived added value to a particular segment, warranting price premium
6 Increased price/standard value	Higher margins if competitors do not follow/risk of losing market share
7 Increased price/low value	Only feasible in monopoly situation
8 Low value/standard price	Loss of market share

Differentiation (braces for items 3–5)

Likely failure (braces for items 6–8)

Source: Based on the work of Cliff Bowman. See C.Bowman and D.Faulkner. *Competitive and Corporate Strategy*, Irwin, 1996.

Figure 6.4   The strategy clock: Bowman's competitive strategy options

Illustration 6.4 Competitive strategies of Japanese car firms in Europe

The strategy clock helps to explain how the strategies followed by Japanese car firms have developed in Europe since the 1960s.

Route 1
During the 1960s and early 1970s, the Japanese car manufacturers entered the European market by targeting the low-cost/low-added-value sector, which they believed would not be defended by European manufacturers. Their products were recognised as being 'cheap and cheerful', and were bought as such. The sales volume that this produced and the experience gained from this market entry strategy allowed them to form a bridgehead into Europe and develop other, more profitable, strategies.

Route 2
By the late 1970s and early 1980s, the improved quality and reliability of their products changed the perception of their cars to that of being as good as their European competitors. However, the Japanese cars continued to be sold at a cheaper price than their rivals, which allowed them to increase sales volume further.

Route 3
Following their earlier success, the late 1980s saw the Japanese further advance their position by producing competitively priced cars that were more reliable and of better quality than their rivals. Competitors followed the Japanese and attempted to maintain their position by improving the quality and reducing the relative prices of their own cars.

Route 4
By the mid-1990s, the main Japanese manufacturers, in common with other car firms, were seeking ways to differentiate their products on the basis of providing extra features such as air-bags, air conditioning and longer-term warranties. However, the Japanese lead times for such innovations were less than most of their competitors.

Route 5
Toyota's Lexus model — which stands alone from the rest of its range and does not use the Toyota name — is competing against manufacturers such as Jaguar and Mercedes in the luxury market segment. Because it is a new entrant, it does not have the 'pedigree' of its competitors; advertising campaigns aim to persuade buyers that they should be buying cars not on name, but on features.

Prepared by Tony Jacobs, Cranfield School of Management.

provided with a 'language' for considering the bases of competitive advantage. Here Porter's arguments are developed in the light of their subsequent critique by others.[13] The approach is based on the principle that organisations achieve competitive advantage by providing their customers with what they want, or need, better or more effectively than competitors; and in ways which their competitors find difficult to imitate.

Assuming that the products or services of different businesses are more or less equally available, customers may choose to purchase from one source rather than another either because (a) the price of the product or service is lower than another firm; or (b) the product or service is perceived by the customer to provide better 'added value' than that available elsewhere.[14] Though these are very broad generalisations, important implications which represent generic strategic options for achieving competitive advantage flow from them. These are shown in Figure 6.4 and portrayed in Illustration 6.4 in the context of Japanese car firms in the European car market. They are now discussed.

6.3.1 Price-based strategies (routes 1 and 2)

Route 1 may seem unattractive, but there are successful organisations which have followed it. It is the 'cheap and cheerful' option which entails reducing price and perceived added value and focusing on a price-sensitive market segment. It might be viable because there could exist a segment of the market which, while recognising that the quality of the product or service might be low, cannot or chooses not to afford to buy better-quality goods. For example, this is Lada's position in the car market, and in Europe the grocery retail chains Aldi and Netto follow this strategy. Their stores are basic, their merchandise range is relatively limited with few speciality or luxury products, and their prices are very low. As Illustration 6.4 shows, a business may also seek to achieve market entry through route 1 and use this as a bridgehead to build volume before moving on to other strategies.

Route 2 entails reduced price, while trying to maintain the quality of the product or service. The problem here is that this is likely to be imitated by competitors which can also reduce price. The result is a reduction in margins in the industry as a whole, and an inability to reinvest to develop the product or service for the long term. In the public sector, costs are, in effect, the 'price' of a service to government as the provider of funds. Here the expectation may, indeed, be that there will be year-on-year efficiency gains and that these will be achieved without loss of quality.

There are, however, ways in which a strategy of low price might be successful.

1.   The most ambitious is for the organisation to seek to sustain reduced prices over competition on the basis of having *the lowest* cost base such

that competitors cannot hope to emulate it — of being a *cost leader* — and being prepared to sustain and win a price battle if necessary. However, cost leadership is very difficult to achieve. It has been argued that it can be achieved by means of substantial *relative market share advantage* because this provides a firm with cost advantages through economies of scale, market power (for example, buying power) and experience curve effects (see Chapter 4, section 4.3.3). However, it is not clear what 'substantial relative market share advantage' means.[15] In developing strategy, it is in any case dangerous to assume a direct link between relative market share advantage and sustainable advantage in the market because there is little evidence of sustainability; dominant firms lose market share and others overtake them. Moreover, if the idea of cost leadership is to be taken seriously as an industry-wide strategy, it is problematic for all but a very few firms — indeed, arguably in a given industry, for all but one firm. In its literal form, it is therefore not a basis for an industry-wide strategy.

2.   Porter actually defines[16] *cost leadership* as '*the* low-cost producer in its industry ... a low-cost producer must find and exploit all sources of cost advantage'. So the notion here is concerned with cost advantages through organisationally specific competences driving down cost throughout the value chain (see Chapter 4, section 4.3.3 and Figure 4.7). Cost advantages may reside in what is produced — for example, in terms of how a product is designed or in terms of its quality. But here the danger is that the customer receives lower added value and an intended route 2 strategy slips to route 1 by default. Indeed, Porter observes that such 'low-cost producers typically sell a standard, or no-frills, product ... [Such a firm] will be an above-average performer in its industry provided it can command prices at or near the industry average'. It is therefore actually likely to be following a strategy which is somewhere between routes 1 and 2.

3.   Cost advantage might also be achieved in terms of how a product is produced, perhaps because a business is able to obtain raw materials at lower prices than competitors, or able to produce more efficiently or benefit from economies of scale; or because it is located in an area where labour cost is low; or again because its distribution costs provide advantages. However, while all of these are potential advantages, if low cost is the basis of a strategy of low price, managers need to be sure that competitors cannot easily imitate or catch up with their cost advantages. This is problematic not least because most businesses have very little accurate information about the cost base of their competitors.

4.   It may be feasible to follow a strategy of low price to achieve competitive advantage within a market segment in which (a) low price is important;

and (b) a business has cost advantage over competitors *operating in that segment*. An example here is the success of dedicated producers of own-brand grocery products for supermarkets. They are able to hold prices low because they can avoid the high overhead and marketing costs of major branded manufacturers. However, they can only do so provided they focus on that product/market segment.

It is important that the distinction between cost and price and therefore cost leadership and low price is clear. Competitive advantage is achieved in terms of customer needs through an organisation's output. Because a firm is trying to achieve cost leadership, or low cost, it does not necessarily mean that it will choose to price lower than competition. It may choose to invest surpluses from higher margins in research and development, or marketing — arguably, what Kellogg's or Mars do. In itself, low cost does not yield competitive advantage; it is how managers employ a low cost base that matters.

6.3.2 Added value, or differentiation strategies (route 4)

The next option is a broad differentiation strategy which seeks to be unique in terms of dimensions widely valued by buyers, and which is also *different* from competitors. The aim is to achieve higher market share than competitors (which in turn could yield cost benefits) by offering better products or services at the same price; or enhanced margins by pricing slightly higher. In public services, the equivalent is the achievement of a 'centre of excellence' status which could attract higher funding from government: for example, as universities try to show that they are better at research or teaching than other universities. This strategy might be achieved through the following:

- Uniqueness or improvements in products: for example, by investment in R&D or design expertise. This is often the basis upon which manufacturing firms such as those in the car industry seek to compete, by investing in technology or design to achieve greater reliability, product life or performance.
- Marketing-based approaches — in effect, demonstrating better than the competition how the product or service meets customer needs. Here the strategy is likely to be built on the power of the brand or by powerful promotional approaches — for example, Levis in clothing, or Heinz in food.

The extent to which these approaches will be successful is likely to depend on a number of factors, some of which are demonstrated in Illustration 6.5 in relation to British Airways.

1. It is necessary to consider whether the organisation has clearly identified *who the customer is*. This is not always straightforward. For example, for a newspaper business, is the customer the reader of the newspaper, the

Illustration 6.5   Customer service: a basis for differentiation

By providing a value-added, differentiated service that customers want, British Airways can charge premium prices.

The airline industry is highly competitive. Many airlines compete on price and reduce service quality to cut costs. BA's strategy, however, is one of differentiation. It believes that by providing a high-quality service it is able to charge premium prices for all its services.

Sir Colin Marshall, BA's chairman, believes that 'orchestrating service to fill customers' value-driven needs' is a basis of differentiation. BA's processes are driven by customer service considerations, as it tries to make the experience of flying as effortless and pleasant as possible. Its recruitment policy ensures that only the 'right' people are employed; staff attend customer service training programmes and are given the freedom to react to individual circumstances to ensure customer satisfaction.

Marshall says that BA should 'excel in listening to its most valuable customers'. This has led to the continuous use of focus groups to establish what customers value and need; research is even conducted into why customers 'defect' to other airlines, and where necessary procedures are changed to improve service quality.

This process of differentiation has led to many changes: for example, BA's airport lounges are included as part of the total package, with everything they contain — from drinks to telephones — free to premium passengers; and fast-track check-in channels have been installed to enable premium passengers to move through immigration and customs with the minimum of delay.

Inflight, BA ensures that cabin crews are highly visible throughout the flight; research has shown that this creates a high level of customer satisfaction. BA's 'well-being in the air' programme provides healthy food options and demonstrates exercises that customers can perform to reduce the discomfort of long flights.

A sleeper service was also introduced for first-class customers on long-distance routes. Customers eat before boarding the flight, sleep onboard and use the arrivals lounge to shower, change and prepare themselves for the day ahead, while waiting for public transport or an office to open.

Marshall believes that, by arranging 'all the elements of [its] service so that they collectively generate a particular experience', BA has a good basis of differentiation. It appears to have worked. In an industry that has lost billions in the last few years, BA remains profitable and strives to become the world's first integrated, global transport system.

Source: S.E. Prokesch, 'Competing on customer service', *Harvard Business Review*,
vol. 73, no. 6 (1995) pp. 100–116.
Prepared by Tony Jacobs, Cranfield School of Management.

advertiser, or both? They are likely to have different needs and values. If a strategy of differentiation is to be followed, which will it be based upon? Public sector organisations face a similar issue. It may be very important that they offer perceived added value; but to satisfy whom? There may be no market-based mechanisms for users to buy services. It may be that perceived added value is measured in terms of the extent to which pressure groups, institutions or politicians are satisfied.

2.   The extent to which the organisation understands *what is valued by the customer*, user or perhaps a stakeholder group (such as a provider of funds in the public sector) can be dangerously taken for granted by managers. As explained in Chapters 2 and 4, managers may pursue strategies either on the basis of traditional ways of operating and taken-for-granted assumptions rooted in experience, or on the basis of resources and skills the organisation has. Managers may therefore fail to address the most basic of questions, which is what the market values. A manager may conceive of a strategy of differentiation in technical terms: for example, as a better-engineered product. While the uniqueness may be real in technical terms, it is of no value in achieving competitive advantage unless it is of greater perceived value to the user than products or services of competitors. Indeed, a differentiating factor for an organisation may be the ability of the managers to be closer to the market than competitors, so that they can better sense and respond to customer needs.

3.   It is important to be clear *who the competitors are*. For example, does the SBU see itself competing with a wide competitor base or with a much narrower base, perhaps within a particular market segment? In the latter case, a strategy of focused differentiation may be appropriate (see section 6.3.4 below). In the case of broad-based differentiation, it is likely that the SBU will have to concentrate on bases of differentiation commonly accepted across the industry or a market. For example, it is unlikely that a car manufacturer trying to compete in the broadly based saloon car market could achieve competitive advantage without recognising the buyers' concern with quality and reliability, which have become threshold requirements. The emphasis must, then, be on how to achieve an advantage in other ways, requiring a much more sophisticated understanding of customer needs and how these can be met by building on core competences.

4.   Another problem in identifying relevant competitors occurs as markets globalise. For example, a company may find its bases of differentiation eroded by another company which it did not previously see as a competitor because it did not share common geographical markets. As the two competitors increase their geographic scope, they may become

competitors. Or it could be that a competitor develops a basis of differentiation in one market and then enters another on the basis of this, thus challenging an established operator's strategic position.

5. The extent to which the basis of differentiation is *difficult to imitate* also needs to be considered. For example, a firm of accountants which carries out a relatively standardised audit procedure will find it difficult to differentiate its services based on variations of those procedures. Even if it can develop such variations, they may be copied rapidly by others. It is more likely that differentiation can be achieved on the basis of the extent to which those involved in the firm understand the needs of their clients, build relationships with individuals within the client base, and can ensure that their own services are integrated to meet the clients' needs.

   To take another example, an industrial goods company selling to contractors needs to recognise that the ability to provide assured delivery on time, up-to-date information on the progress of orders and rapid after-sales service may be of critical importance. How this is done will depend on different parts of the manufacturer's operations or value chain. So differentiation is based on a mix of activities, relationships and competences. This is likely to be an important basis of the sustainability of a strategy of differentiation, and is taken up again in Chapter 10 (see section 10.2.5).

6. The idea that competitive advantage through differentiation can be achieved on a static basis is questionable. There are two reasons for this. In many markets customer needs change, and therefore *bases of differentiation may need to change*. However, even if relatively constant customer needs can be identified, over time competitors may be able to imitate bases of differentiation. The implication is that a business following a differentiation strategy may have to review continually bases of differentiation, and keep changing, as is the case for those car manufacturers following strategies of broad differentiation. This was also the strategy so successfully followed by Microsoft with the rapid introduction of improvements in software features and shortening product life cycles, which made it difficult for competitors to keep pace.

Some of the problems of identifying bases of differentiation are demonstrated in Illustration 6.6.

6.3.3 The hybrid strategy (route 3)

It is possible simultaneously to provide added value in customer terms, while seeking to price lower than competitors; arguably, this is the strategy

Illustration 6.6   Crinkly biscuits as competitive advantage?

In building a competitive strategy, executives need to be wary of spurious bases of competitive advantage.

Senior executives of an international food manufacturing company were taking part in a strategy workshop, discussing bases of competitive advantage for their strategic business units. The issues of competitive advantage based on perceived customer needs was raised, and one of the executives, the quality assurance manager for a biscuit business, commented as follows:

'I totally agree. In our business we know what customers want and we have invested to provide it. Our research shows that customers care a lot about the crinkles on the edges of their biscuits. They like neat regular crinkles. We have just invested in equipment that will deliver just that with very little wastage. We are the leader in this field.'

In the discussion which followed, it became clear that there were at least three flaws in what the manager had said. First, his point of reference for considering his strategy was the end user, the consumer. In fact, the company referred to grocery retailers as 'competitors' because such retailers sold own-brand goods. Yet if the major retailers, which controlled 50 per cent of the distribution of biscuits, did not stock the product, it never reached the consumer. The strategic customer was the retailer, but the business had no clear strategy for achieving competitive advantage with regard to the retailers.

Second, it became clear that the identification of customer need was based on a survey which had pre-specified certain characteristics of biscuits, one of which was 'regular crinkles'. His fellow managers were of the opinion that the fact that 'consumers had ticked a few boxes to do with ideas thought up by some guys in the R&D department' was a spurious basis upon which to build a strategy, let alone invest large amounts of capital.

Third, when challenged, the manager had to admit that there was nothing to stop a competitor buying similar equipment and achieving just the same quality of crinkles. If there was any competitive advantage — and this was dubious — it was easily imitable.

pursued by IKEA (see Illustration 1.1). Here the success of the strategy depends on the ability both to understand and to deliver enhanced value in terms of customer needs, while also having a cost base that permits low prices and is sufficient for reinvestment to maintain and develop bases of differentiation.[17] This should not be confused with just trying to keep costs down in general, while seeking to achieve differentiation; after all, presumably managers should always be trying to operate at the lowest cost commensurate with the strategy they are following.

It might be argued that, if differentiation can be achieved, there should be no need to have a lower price, since it should be possible to obtain prices at least equal to competition, if not higher. However, the hybrid strategy could be advantageous in the following circumstances:

- If much greater volumes than the competition can be achieved, and margins still kept attractive because of a low cost base. This is what some Japanese car manufactures might claim.
- If there is a market segment with particular needs which also facilitates a low-price approach. IKEA is a useful example. It offers good quality but to a market segment that is prepared to build and transport the furniture.
- As an entry strategy in a market with established competitors. This is a strategic approach to new market development that Japanese firms sometimes use on a global basis. They search for the 'loose brick'[18] in a competitor's portfolio of businesses — perhaps a poorly run operation in a geographical area of the world — then enter that market with a superior product and, if necessary, a lower price. The aim is to take share, divert the attention of the competitor, and establish a foothold from which they can move further. However, in following such a strategy it is important to ensure that (a) the overall cost base is such that low margins can be sustained; and (b) a clear follow-through strategy has been considered for when entry has been achieved.

6.3.4 Focused differentiation (route 5)

Here the aim is to offer higher value to the customer at a price premium. However, if this strategy is followed, it is likely to mean that the business is competing in a particular market segment, which may be a real advantage. In the market for saloon cars, Ford, Rover, Peugeot, Renault, Volkswagen and Japanese competitors are all competing within the one market, trying, often with some difficulty, to convince customers that their product is differentiated from their competitor. A Lexus is also a saloon car, but it is not seeking to compete directly with these other manufacturers. It is offering a product with higher perceived value at a substantially higher price than in the saloon car market. It is therefore trying to attract different sorts of customers; a different market segment. However, this strategy raises some important issues:

- The choice may have to be made between broad differentiation across a market or a more focused strategy. Indeed, this may take on global

Illustration 6.7   Breadth or focus in European businesses

European book publishers, banks and brewers recognise the need to consider carefully the breadth of their markets.

A study of European businesses showed that managers saw their strategies for the 1990s as increasingly dependent on the careful choice of breadth of markets, and on the linkage of market power and market segmentation.

'In the 1990s, for the big brewers, there will be more possibilities of up-scaling. I also strongly believe in the small niche breweries, either in a specific segment of the beer market, or in a specific area selling to bars. Medium-size breweries must make a choice. Either they must become big, or they must aim at some precise segment of the industry.'

Netherlands brewer

'I do not think that the universal bank, such as BNP, will be more successful than specialised banks such as La Compagnie Bancaire . . . I think there will be six to eight universal banks in Europe by the year 2000, three French banks, two British ones and a couple of German banks . . . The other ones will have to specialise.'

French retail bank

'You have to divide the market into several segments . . . Everybody knows that a high net worth individual in general is more profitable for a bank than just a blue collar worker in any factory. And the top of the market is an opportunity to become more international.'

Netherlands retail banker

'Our target is to get within the top six companies because we think there are going to be six major players, and then a lot of minnows swimming around the edge. We think that is the place to be successful; the time of the middle ground has been and gone. There will be no middle ground players any more. You have either got to be investing heavily in major schemes, production and marketing, or you have to go for little niche markets.'

British book publisher

'If there is to be a European market in book publishing, it will be in the domain of heavy products (art books, encyclopaedias, etc.) or products having a high profitability threshold. On the other hand, in general literature, groups do not have any European strategy; it is a more risky and fragmented business where small firms can be effective.'

French book publisher

Source: R. Calori and P. Lawrence (eds.), *The Business of Europe: Managing change*, Sage, 1991, pp. 140–7.

proportions, as managers have to decide between a broad approach in increasingly global markets, or much more selective focus strategies — as shown in Illustration 6.7.

- Because an organisation choosing to follow a focus strategy is likely to be targeting a particular market segment, it is important to realise that, within that segment itself, the strategy clock is just as relevant so managers face further choices. Lexus competes in the luxury car segment, but within that segment it is following a strategy quite distinct from other luxury car companies. Its competitors might be seen as top-of-the-range Mercedes and BMW. Against these competitors in this segment, Lexus is following a low-price or perhaps hybrid strategy. Its quality is just as good, but relative to those other models, its prices are lower.

- An organisation may choose to follow a multifocus strategy, choosing different market segments in which it can offer premium-price products. This is the case for perfumes, or where manufacturers may offer highly priced fashion brands targeted at tightly defined market segments. Retail chains such as Burtons in the UK also do this, with chains such as Top Shop and Top Man for the younger market and Principles for fashion buyers.

- It is again important to be clear about which market segment (or segments) is being targeted, defined in terms of a coherent set of customer needs; and this needs to be translated into action which satisfies those customers. This may be difficult to do, if the organisation is attempting to compete in different market segments, with different needs. For example, department stores attempt to sell wide ranges of product in one store. They may also attempt to appeal to different customer types in so doing. But they run into problems because the store itself, the fixtures and fittings, the décor and store ambience, and the staff, may not be differentiated according to the different market segment needs.

- Focus strategies may conflict with stakeholder expectations. For example, a public library service could undoubtedly be run more cost efficiently if it were to pull out of low demand market niches and put more resources into its popular branch libraries. It might also find that an extension of its services into audio and video tapes or new forms of public information service would prove popular. However, the extent to which these strategies would be regarded as within the library's remit might be hotly debated.

- New ventures often start in very focused ways — for example, new 'leading-edge' medical services in hospitals. It may, however, be difficult to find ways to grow such new ventures. Moving from route 5 to route 4 will mean a lowering of price and therefore cost, while maintaining differentiation features. On the other hand, maintaining a highly focused (route 5) approach may not be easy because users may not be prepared, or able, to pay the price; or, as in the public sector, provide funding support to subsidise such projects.

- The advantages of the focused approach have to be carefully monitored because the market situation may change. Differences between segments may be eroded, leaving the organisation open to much wider competition. This was a concern for the manufacturers of luxury cars, such as Jaguar, as the top end of the executive car range came closer and closer to the style of luxury cars. Or the market may be further segmented by even more differentiated offerings from competitors.

6.3.5 Failure strategies (routes 6, 7 and 8)

The strategies suggested by routes 6, 7 and 8 are probably destined for ultimate failure. Route 6 suggests increasing price without increasing value to the customer. This is, of course, the very strategy that monopoly organisations are accused of following. However, unless the organisation is protected by legislation, or high economic barriers to entry, competition is likely to erode market share. Route 7 is an even more disastrous extension of route 6, involving the reduction in value of a product or service, while increasing relative price.

Route 8, reduction in value while maintaining price, is also dangerous, though firms have tried to follow it. There is a high risk that competitors will increase their share substantially.

Porter argues that there is another basis of failure, which is for an SBU to be unclear as to its fundamental generic strategy: he argues that too many end up being 'stuck in the middle'. They are following no clear generic strategy — a recipe for failure.

The strategy clock is, then, a market-based model of generic strategy options rooted in the question 'What is of value in the product or service to the customer, user or provider of funding?' It does not deny that the cost base of an organisation is crucially important, but it sees this as a means of developing generic strategies, and not as a basis for competitive advantage in itself.

6.3.6 The management challenge of generic competitive strategies

The various arguments made in this first part of the chapter pose significant challenges to managers in the development of strategy. To achieve real bases of sustainable advantage, it is important to do the following:

- Be clear which customers (or users) are the target for the strategy to be followed.

- Clearly identify customer needs and bases of added value in the market place, defined either broadly or, more likely, by market segment.
- Build sufficient knowledge of competitors' competences and cost structures to take an informed view about bases of competitive advantage.
- Given this understanding, consider and establish which of the generic strategy routes is most appropriate for the organisation given its purpose and aspirations.
- Operationalise this strategy in such a way that customer needs are met by a mix of activities which is distinctly different from that of competitors and which is embedded in organisational competences (see Chapter 10, section 10.2).
- Ensure that the strategic directions and methods (see Chapter 7) of the organisation are in line with the generic strategy.

6.4 Enhancing SBU strategy: corporate parenting

This chapter began with a discussion of how corporate purpose and aspirations are important elements of strategic choice. It made it clear that a significant question at the corporate level is to what extent SBU strategies are enhanced, or how they are managed, at the corporate level.

The relationship which different corporate bodies or divisions have with their SBUs varies considerably. Some see their role as aiding SBUs in the development of their strategy, by enhancing the basis of their competitive advantage. This might take the form of creating linkages between businesses, facilitating the international development of those businesses, transferring knowledge between businesses and so on. Other corporate bodies see their role as primarily being answerable to external stakeholders — for example, financial institutions and shareholders — and letting the businesses get on with their own affairs. The form of this corporate control is discussed in Chapter 9 (section 9.4). What is discussed here are the ways in which corporate bodies might add value to SBU-level strategy.

6.4.1 Managing portfolios

A major issue is the extent to which a mix of SBUs mutually reinforce each other, are balanced, and are compatible with corporate aspirations. A technique which has long been used for considering these issues is portfolio analysis, which can help clarify the mix and scope of SBUs that an organisation chooses to be involved in, which should be grown and developed, which are likely to provide long-term earnings and which should be divested.

A number of such bases of analysis are covered in the book. The *attractiveness* or *directional policy matrix*, which looks at the extent to which different businesses are in more or less attractive markets, is discussed at the end of Chapter 3 (section 3.5.4). The *growth/share matrix* is discussed in section 4.5 of Chapter 4. A *parenting matrix* is discussed in section 6.4.4 of this chapter. The life cycle matrix is used in Chapter 8 (section 8.2.1) as a way of considering strategy evaluation, but it can also be used to consider the appropriateness of a portfolio of SBUs.

All these portfolio approaches can be useful in addressing issues of mix and scope of SBUs. For example, if the corporate aspiration is high growth in income and the business is prepared to invest to gain that growth, then it may be prepared to support more *stars* and *question marks* than a parent which is concerned with stable cash generation and which may concentrate on preserving or building its *cash cows*. Other corporate bodies take the view that a balanced portfolio is desirable, with reliable cash cows providing surpluses which can be channelled into investments in growing market shares of fast-growing new SBUs, to turn them into stars and eventually cash cows. Managers do need to exercise care here, however. They may neglect to think through the implications of decisions arising from such categorisation. For example, a *dog* could be written off without regard for the competitive consequences of pulling out of a market, and therefore handing a more dominant competitor even more market power and a stronger portfolio. Or, if cash cows are used to fund potential growth businesses, how will this affect the motivation of managers in the SBUs regarded as cash cows?

A different problem may arise for managers in public sector organisations. They may find it difficult to develop stars — services with real growth potential — or generate surpluses to be reinvested, because this may not be their brief from government. They may be expected to manage services which cannot make money, but which are public necessities. Further, if they seek to develop services which can grow and make money, these may be privatised or put out to private tender. It may be seen as legitimate for a local government leisure department to manage public parks and recreation grounds, but the development of indoor tennis and swimming pools with profit potential may be seen as an inappropriate activity. The definition of the appropriate portfolio of activities therefore requires a clarity of corporate purposes and aspirations.

6.4.2 Corporate financial strategy[19]

A basic issue which has to be faced is how an organisation is to be financed. Decisions on finance will be influenced by ownership — for example, whether the business is privately held or publicly quoted — and

STARS GROWTH PHASE Business risk high Financial risk low **Equity** (growth investors)	QUESTION MARKS LAUNCH PHASE Business risk very high Financial risk very low **Equity** (venture capital)
CASH COWS MATURITY PHASE Business risk medium Financial risk medium **Debt and equity** **(retained earnings)**	DOGS DECLINE PHASE Business risk low Financial risk high **Debt**

Source: Adapted from K.Ward, *Corporate Financial Strategy*, Butterworth-Heinemann, 1993, p.32.

Figure 6.5   Source of funding

by the overall corporate intent of the organisation. For example, there will be a different financial need if a business is seeking rapid growth by acquisition or development of new products than if it is seeking to consolidate its past performance. Executives also need to recognise that the financial strategy they choose to follow could be helpful or could hinder strategies at SBU level. So financial strategy decisions are also linked to the added value that can be provided to SBU strategies. This section explains how this is so using the growth/share matrix as a basis of explanation (see Figure 6.5).

The financial strategy of an organisation needs to take into account the relationship between financial risk and financial return. The greater the risk, the greater the return required to investors. The growth/share matrix is a convenient way of considering the risk/return relationship among the various businesses that could exist in a corporation (see also Chapter 8, section 8.3.1 on return and section 8.3.2 on risk). The relationship between financial strategy, SBU strategy and the overall strategy of a corporation with a portfolio of SBUs is important, then, not only for shareholders, but also for those who seek to manage a portfolio effectively.

Question marks (or *problem children*) are clearly high risk. They are at the beginning of their life cycle and are not yet established in their markets;

moreover, they are likely to require substantial investment. For those who wish to invest in them, therefore, there is a need to understand the nature of risk and a desire to seek high returns. A stand-alone business in this situation might, for example, seek to finance such growth from specialists in this kind of investment, such as venture capitalists who, themselves, seek to offset risk by having a portfolio of such investments.

The degree of risk remains high in high-growth situations even if relatively high market shares are being achieved — as is the case with *stars*. The market position here remains volatile and probably highly competitive. It could be that a business has been financed on the basis of venture capital initially, but as it grows and becomes established it needs to seek other financing. Since the main attractions to investors here are the product or business concept and the prospect of future earnings, equity capital is likely to be appropriate; a business might seek to raise equity by public flotation.

Businesses which operate in mature markets with high shares (*cash cows*) should be generating regular and substantial surpluses. Here the risk is lower and the opportunity for retained earnings is high, and in the case of a portfolio of businesses, the corporation may be seeking to recycle such a surplus into its growth businesses. In these circumstances, it may make sense to raise finance through debt capital as well as equity, since reliable returns can be used to service such debt and, in any case, the return expected by lenders is likely to be less than those providing equity. (Since interest on debt has to be repaid, the risk for the business itself is higher than equity finance; so it is also reasonable for the business to expect the cost of debt to be lower than equity.) Provided increased debt (sometimes called *gearing* or *leverage*) does not lead to an unacceptable level of risk, this cheaper debt funding will in fact increase the residual profits achieved by a company in these circumstances. The danger is that the corporation overstretches itself, takes on too much debt, increases its risk by so doing, suffers a downturn in its markets and is unable to service its interest payments.

If a business is in decline, in effect a *dog*, then equity finance will be difficult to attract. However, borrowing may be possible if secured against residual assets in the business. At this stage, it is likely that the emphasis in the business will be on cost cutting, and it could well be that the cash flows from such businesses are quite strong. These businesses may provide relatively low-risk investment.

Conglomerates face a problem if they seek to develop a financial strategy for a portfolio of businesses where there is a mix of businesses more or less growing and in high- or low-share positions. What is the appropriate financial strategy? This cannot be answered in isolation from a consideration of overall corporate strategy. The corporation needs to consider its overall risk/return position. For example, if a corporation is seeking to follow a high growth strategy by diversification and acquisition, then it may be perceived by the investing community as a high-risk business;

as such, it may have difficulty raising debt capital, and those who provide equity may expect high return. Corporations which have sought high growth through an acquisitive diversification strategy have suffered because they have not had appropriate financial strategies. They have been either unable to attract equity investment or unwilling to do so, and have sought to finance growth out of borrowings, in effect relying on ever growing cash growth to finance such borrowing. A decline in such growth means that debt cannot be serviced and could lead to bankruptcy.

The crucial point is that a corporation seeking to operate a portfolio must consider the links between its corporate strategy, SBU strategy and its financial strategy. For example:

- Should it seek a balanced portfolio with a mix of businesses and a mix of equity and debt capital?
- Should it focus more on one type of business? For example, historically Hanson focused on acquiring cash cow type businesses so, although it was acquisitive, it generated high cash flows through such businesses and through the divestment of some of its portfolio. In such circumstances, it might well be attractive for both equity and debt financing.
- A corporation seeking to develop new and innovative businesses on a regular basis might, in effect, be acting as its own venture capitalist, accepting high risk at the business level and seeking to offset such risk by encouraging new and innovative ideas. If it does so, it should consider if it has a role to play as those businesses mature; or if it needs to consider selling them on to other corporations, not least to raise capital for further investment.

6.4.3 Corporate parenting: the role of the parent

A corporate parent has to take a view on how it will relate to and seek to enhance the strategies of SBUs. There are different approaches to this,[20] as shown in Figure 6.6. There are parents who seek to operate in a *portfolio management* style, with slim corporate head office staff seeking to balance investments in businesses by reviewing acquisition targets, buying wisely and divesting poor performers. However, there is limited evidence for the success of such an approach on its own.

A second role is as a *restructurer* of businesses, the role taken by the Hanson Group until the mid 1990s. It focused on acquisitions of businesses, certainly, but built these around its corporate-level skills in identifying restructuring and transformation opportunities. Its skills lay not just in an ability to buy and sell companies, but also in an ability to move executives, experienced in such restructuring, into organisations rapidly to improve performance.

	Portfolio managers	Restructurers	Skill transferers	Activity sharers
Strategic requirements	• Identifying and acquiring undervalued assets • Divesting low-performing SBUs quickly and good performers at a premium	• Identifying restructuring opportunities • Intervention in SBUs to transform performance • Sale of SBUs when restructuring complete or unfeasible market conditions favourable	• Transferring skills to give competitive advantage in SBUs • On-going transfer of skills • Identification of appropriate skills to transfer	• Sharing activities to provide competitive advantage to SBUs • Identification of benefits of sharing which outweigh costs • Overcoming SBU resistance to sharing
Organisational requirements	• Autonomous SBUs • Small, low-cost corporate staff • Incentives based on SBU results	• Autonomous SBUs • Turnaround skills of corporate staff • Incentives based on acquired SBU results	• Autonomous but collaborative SBUs • Corporate staff as integrators • Cross-SBU taskforces • Incentives based partly on corporate results	• SBUs encouraged to share • Strategic planning at different levels • Corporate staff as integrators • Incentives based on corporate results

Source: Adapted from M. Porter, 'From competitive to corporate strategy', *Harvard Business Review*, May–June 1987.

Figure 6.6 Roles of corporate parents

A parent may also seek to add benefits to businesses by helping with the interrelationships between the businesses themselves. This is sometimes called *managing synergy* (see Chapter 8, section 8.2.1). The corporation may seek *to transfer skills and competences* from one business unit to another. These could be competences learned in the management of one value chain which are relevant to the value chain of another business. It could be that the marketing skills, highly developed in a consumer products business like Lever Brothers, part of Unilever, could be transferred into a less sophisticated business acquired by Unilever: for example, by moving experienced marketing executives. Unfortunately, in many cases this concept of synergy does not come to fruition. Skills are not always that easily identifiable or transferable because the businesses or their markets are dissimilar.

Another approach is the *sharing of activities*. Marriott sought to share activities across its hotels, restaurants and airport facilities. Such shared activities included the ability to provide and learn from standardised hotel procedures and to benefit from shared procurement and distribution. They were supported by an organisational structure that encourages integration and co-operation.

6.4.4 The parenting matrix[21]

The four roles of the parent shown in Figure 6.6 can be expanded to include a fuller set of parenting skills and capabilities. These are discussed more fully in Chapter 9 (section 9.4.1), where issues of corporate structure and design are considered. However, in deciding on the appropriateness of the role of the parent and the mix of SBUs for the parent, the *parenting matrix* can be useful. This is another way of looking at the portfolio of SBUs, but in relation to two key questions:

- To what extent is there a fit between the strategies and *strategic characteristics of the SBUs* and the *purpose* and *aspirations of the corporate parent*? For example, at the corporate level the emphasis may be on the need for global businesses with high growth potential: to what extent do the existing or future strategies of the SBUs fit with these aspirations?
- To what extent is there a fit between the *parenting needs or opportunities of the SBU* for its development and *corporate parenting skills and capabilities*? For example, an SBU might be aiming to develop internationally, but may lack the experience and infrastructure to do so. The corporate parent might be able to provide such infrastructure, in terms of offices, contacts, perhaps distribution; and it may also be able to provide managers with local knowledge and experience who have operated in similar SBUs.

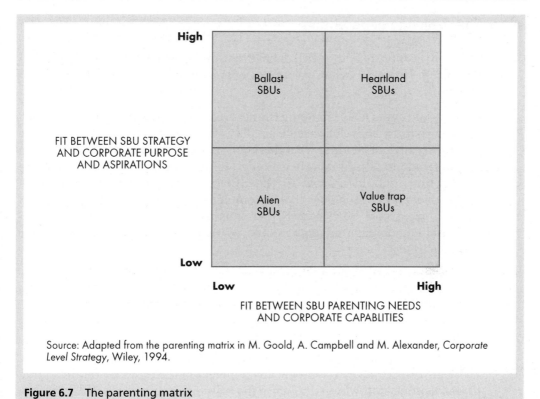

High

Low

Ballast
SBUs

Heartland
SBUs

Alien
SBUs

Value trap
SBUs

FIT BETWEEN SBU STRATEGY
AND CORPORATE PURPOSE
AND ASPIRATIONS

Low   High

FIT BETWEEN SBU PARENTING NEEDS
AND CORPORATE CAPABLITIES

Source: Adapted from the parenting matrix in M. Goold, A. Campbell and M. Alexander, *Corporate Level Strategy*, Wiley, 1994.

Figure 6.7   The parenting matrix

Figure 6.7 shows what a resulting portfolio might look like. The businesses with the greatest fit in both dimensions — the *heartland* businesses — are the ones which the parent can most usefully help to develop, and those with the greatest fit between corporate and SBU strategic aspirations. *Ballast* businesses have good strategic fit, but are not ones where the SBU can expect a great deal of help from the corporate parent for its development. So the corporate parent needs to ask what added value they are providing. It may decide that such a business is useful, but with a hands-off relationship, whereas there is a need for more involvement in heartland businesses.

Value trap businesses are dangerous. Here there is a fit between the SBU's needs and opportunities for parenting and corporate parenting skills, but little fit between the corporate strategy of the parent and the SBU strategy. The corporate parent should ask if it is likely to invest time and resources helping develop the businesses for no particular advantage to the corporate direction it wishes to take. With *alien* SBUs there is little strategic fit. They are not following strategies compatible with corporate aspirations and can benefit little from parenting skills. They may be candidates for disposal.

6.4.5 The challenge of parenting

Different corporate bodies will choose to exercise different roles in regard to parenting. However, whatever the role, it is important to ask a number of questions.

▣ If the parent is not enhancing the strategies of the SBUs, what is its role? A corporate body has a role to play with regard to purely corporate affairs, such as dealing with financial institutions and negotiating with governments. But if its role is limited to this, the cost of delivering these functions should be low to the SBU. A large and costly corporate headquarters which does little to enhance the strategies of its SBUs can be a great cost burden to SBUs, thus undermining potential market-based competitive advantage, and so reducing the overall returns for the parent.

▣ If the corporate body seeks to enhance the strategies of the SBUs, it must be very clear that there is a match between its skills in so doing and the competences which the SBUs require to achieve competitive advantage. It must avoid undertaking roles which do not enhance strategies at the SBU level. For example, the corporate parent may impose cumbersome strategic planning more to do with providing information to the centre than with aiding the strategic development of the units; or retain a large head office staff which duplicate the roles of executives in SBUs.

▣ If the corporate parent does, indeed, seek to enhance SBU strategies, it needs to consider the extent to which there is a fit between the SBUs and the parent (see section 6.4.3 above), and the number of SBUs for which it can sensibly do so (see Chapter 9, section 9.4.1).

▣ Where, then, is greatest value to be added? An overall pattern has emerged in the last decade or so which suggests that organisations throughout the world are attempting to drive responsibility for strategic decisions nearer and nearer to markets. There is an attempt to ensure that SBU-specific competences are directed at developing successful competitive strategies. For example, the UK-based chemicals conglomerate ICI[22] chose to demerge into two separate businesses, one based on its pharmaceutical operations, which it renamed Zeneca, and one based on its heavy chemicals business, for which the name ICI was retained (see Illustration 6.8). The strategic logic underlying this demerger reflects many of the strategic considerations at corporate level discussed so far; and shows the link between these issues and those of structure and control discussed in Chapters 9 and 10.

The trend towards deregulation and privatisation of public utilities and government authorities, increasing throughout the world, has a similar rationale underlying it. The aim is to give the responsibility for

Illustration 6.8   The challenge of parenting

If a parent no longer adds sufficient value to its SBUs, then what is its role?

In 1991 the Hanson Group acquired a 2.8 per cent stake in ICI. Although a full-scale takeover bid failed to materialise, the episode underlined the urgent need for ICI to raise shareholder value.

ICI had long assumed that its success was built on the synergies and mutual interdependence between its business units. External consultants concluded, however, that there was a technological fault line within ICI. Pharmaceuticals and other bioscience-related activities fell on one side and the traditional chemical businesses on the other. The realisation that synergy only existed within each business cluster and not across them argued for de-merging the two distinct parts of ICI.

The de-merger confirmed that the links between the businesses in the two new companies were closer than in the old ICI as a whole. An advantage of the new structure was that it aligned corporate objectives more closely with those of the individual businesses. The two successor companies faced different strategic priorities and managerial challenges. Zeneca's task was to manage high growth based on innovative new products in pharmaceuticals and biosciences, with an emphasis on strengthening its worldwide sales organisation and improving the productivity of R&D. ICI's chemical business was cyclical, mostly capital intensive and less dependent on research. Its goal was to achieve market leadership in areas in which it had technological advantage.

The case for de-merger was that it separated two distinct sets of problems and assigned them to corporate parents more focused on dealing with them. However, the de-merger also preserved the advantages of retaining, under a single ownership, businesses that shared technical competences, and benefited from common services and informed central direction. The parents could again add value to their SBUs as the narrower focus and greater homogeneity of the problems shortened and sharpened lines of communication between the new parents and their SBUs.

ICI could claim that the de-merger has been a financial success. In May 1996, the market capitalisation of the two companies combined stood at £19.3 billion, compared with the £7.6 billion valuation of the old ICI in July 1992.

Source: G. Owen and T. Harrison, 'Why ICI chose to demerge', *Harvard Business Review*, vol. 73, no. 2 (1995) pp. 133–142.
Prepared by Tony Jacobs, Cranfield School of Management.

developing strategic capability and achieving competitive advantage in markets to the business unit level — to managers who are most closely in touch with their markets. The role of the parent has therefore been increasingly seen as one of facilitation or of taking a hands-off approach as far as possible.

6.5 Summary

This chapter has looked at bases of strategic choice in terms of *corporate-level strategy, generic competitive strategies* of SBUs and *parenting*. It has done so by arguing that a clarity of purpose for the organisation is important in terms of issues such as the types of business it seeks to be involved in, how related these are and what geographical scope is envisaged. Such issues need to be compatible with SBU strategic decisions, the basis of which lies in questions to do with value for money as perceived by buyers — the foundation of competitive strategy. This compatibility of SBU and corporate-level strategy can in turn be considered in terms of the extent to which the corporate parent enhances the strategic position of its SBUs.

In considering these bases of strategy of organisations, it should be evident that questions are raised which are pivotal in strategy development.

- Bases of strategic choice need to take account of the *environment* in which the organisation operates: for example, corporate aspirations or SBU competitive advantages may be eroded as technology changes or as new competitors enter markets. Similarly, the links to Chapter 4 should be clear in relation to the central importance of *core competences*. These relate both to the bases on which competitive advantage may be built — for example, in achieving and maintaining differentiation — but also to the parenting skills exercised at the corporate level, which may, themselves, be core competences which can help achieve competitive advantage.
- Clearly, the expectations and influence of *stakeholders* also play a key role in determining the purpose and aspirations of an organisation, and these, in turn, can be seen to play an important role in determining the appropriate mix of SBUs in a portfolio.
- Little of the discussion so far has dealt with how the broad strategic choices discussed in this chapter might be put into effect. This raises questions about the *strategic direction* that an organisation might follow. Should it seek to develop new products or competences, enter new markets or diversify into different businesses, and by what *methods* should this be done? Should it be by internal development, alliances with other organisations or acquisitions? These issues are dealt with in Chapter 7.

⬚ Reference has also been made throughout the chapter to the important links between decisions about the relationship between corporate-level strategies and SBU strategies, and the *structure and control* of organisations. These are the central issues of Chapters 9 and 10.

⬚ Finally, in developing successful strategies, it is important to recognise that they need to be built not only on what already exists, but also on what needs to be developed in the organisation. So developing the *resources and competences* to deliver the crucial bases of strategic advantage needs to be thought about in detail, as should the extent to which such required *change* is possible and how this might be managed. These subjects are considered in Chapters 10 and 11.

References

1. A discussion and examples of changes in ownership can be found in M. Vander Weyer, 'Only fools and masochists', *Management Today*, January 1996, pp. 26–30.

2. The privatisation of public utilities is discussed in P. Jackson and C. Price, *Privatisation and Regulation: A review of the issues*, Longman, 1994, chapter 3.

3. A useful paper on management buyouts is by M. Wright, B. Chiplin and S. Thompson, 'The market for corporate control: divestments and buy-outs', in M. Bishop and J. Kay (eds.), *European Mergers and Merger Policy*, Oxford University Press, 1993.

4. See other chapters in *Privatisation and Regulation* (reference 2 above). M. Bishop, J. Kay and C. Mayer, *Privatisation and Economic Performance*, Oxford University Press, 1994, provides a number of in-depth case studies of deregulation.

5. For a discussion of the role of a clarity of mission, see A. Campbell, M. Devine and D. Young, *A Sense of Mission*, Hutchinson Business, 1990. However, G. Hamel and C.K. Prahalad argue in chapter 6 of their book, *Competing for the Future*, Harvard Business School Press, 1994, that mission statements have insufficient impact for the competence of a clarity of 'strategic intent'. This is more likely to be a brief but clear statement which focuses more on clarity of strategic direction (they use the word 'destiny') than on how that strategic direction will be achieved. See also Hamel and Prahalad on

strategic intent in the *Harvard Business Review*, vol. 67, no. 3 (1989), pp. 63–76.

6. See reference 5 above.

7. This is the view of leadership taken by Hamel and Prahalad (see reference 5 above).

8. There is a very extensive literature on this topic. Influential research evidence for the link between relatedness and performance was provided in R. Rumelt, *Strategy, Structure and Economic Performance*, Harvard University Press, 1974. A review of the topic is provided in V. Ramanujam and P. Varadarajan, 'Research on corporate diversification: a synthesis', *Strategic Management Journal*, vol. 10, no. 6 (1989), pp. 523–52.

9. See R.M. Grant, A.P. Jammine and H. Thomas, 'Diversity, diversification and profitability among British manufacturing companies, 1972–84', *Academy of Management Journal*, vol. 31, no. 4 (1988) pp. 771–801.

10. See B.M. Oviatt and P.P. McDougall, 'Global startups: entrepreneurs on a world-wide stage', *Academy of Management Executive*, vol. 9, no. 2 (1995), pp. 30–45.

11. Figure 6.3 is based on the discussion in G. Yip, *Total Global Strategy*, Prentice Hall, 1995, chapter 6. The book provides a helpful overall discussion of global dimensions of strategy.

12. See M.E. Porter, *Competitive Strategy*, Free Press, 1980.

13. There are a number of papers which provide useful critiques of Porter's generic strategies: M.

Cronshaw, E. Davis and J. Kay, 'On being stuck in the middle or Good food costs less at Sainsburys', working paper, Centre for Business Strategy, London School of Business, 1990; C.W.L. Hill, 'Differentiation versus low cost or differentiation and low cost: a contingency framework', *Academy of Management Review*, vol. 13, no. 3 (1988), pp. 401–12; A. Karnani, 'Generic competitive strategies: an analytical approach', *Strategic Management Journal*, vol. 5, no. 4 (1984), pp. 367–80; S.S. Mathur, 'How firms compete: a new classification of generic strategies', *Journal of General Management*, vol. 14, no. 1 (1988) pp. 30–57, 'Generic strategies and performance: an empirical examination with American data. Part 1: Testing Porter', *Organisation Studies*, vol. 7, no. 1 (1986), pp. 37–55; D. Miller and P.H. Friesen, 'Porter's (1980) generic strategies and performance: an empirical examination with American data. Part 2: Performance implications', *Organisation Studies*, vol. 7, no. 3 (1986), pp. 255–61; R.E. White, 'Generic business strategies, organisational context and performance: an empirical investigation', *Strategic Management Journal*, vol. 7, no. 3 (1986), pp. 217–31; and D. Faulkner and C. Bowman, *The Essence of Competitive Strategy*, Prentice Hall, 1995.

14. Figure 6.3 is similar to the arguments and figures which Philip Kotler employs in discussing marketing-mix alternatives in his book *Marketing Management*, 8th edition, Prentice Hall, 1994. Section 6.3 is, however, based more specifically on the work of D. Faulkner and C. Bowman, *The Essence of Competitive Strategy*, Prentice Hall, 1995. But it should be noted that they use the term 'perceived use value' rather than 'perceived added value'.

15. The debate on the benefits of relative market share are complicated. There are perhaps three key points: (a) a firm with a high absolute market share may not have a high relative share because there may be a competitor which also has a comparable share; (b) arguments differ as to whether relative market share should be measured in terms of the nearest individual competitor, or the nearest two or three competitors; and (c) estimates of the relative market share necessary to achieve sustainable market power advantage vary between about 40 and 70 per cent. For discussion on this debate, see, for example, R.D. Buzzell and B.T. Gale, *The PIMS Principles*, Free Press, 1987, chapter 5. See also R.D. Buzzell, 'Are there natural market structures?', *Journal of Marketing*, vol. 45, no. 1 (1981), pp. 42–51.

16. These quotes concerning Porter's three generic strategies are taken from his book *Competitive Advantage*, Free Press, 1985, pp. 12–15.

17. The researchers and writers who argue that cost-based strategies are not incompatible with differentiation include D. Miller, 'The generic strategy trap', *Journal of Business Strategy*, vol. 13, no. 1 (1992), pp. 37–42; and Hill (see reference 13 above). Their arguments are supported by the work of PIMS (see reference 15), who argue for the benefits of a 'virtuous circle' in strategy, by which they mean the search for low cost which provides surpluses to reinvest in differentiation and product advantages.

18. See G. Hamel and C.K. Prahalad, 'Do you really have a global strategy?', *Harvard Business Review*, vol. 63, no. 4 (1985), pp. 139–48.

19. For readers who wish to follow up the discussion in this section, see K. Ward, *Corporate Financial Strategy*, Butterworth-Heinemann, 1993, and T. Grundy and K. Ward (eds.), *Developing Financial Strategies: A comprehensive model in strategic business finance*, Kogan Page, 1996.

20. The approaches described here are based on Michael Porter's paper, 'From competitive to corporate strategy', *Harvard Business Review*, no. 65 (1987) pp. 43–59.

21. The discussion in this section draws on M. Goold, A. Campbell and M. Alexander, *Corporate Level Strategy*, Wiley, 1994, which provides an excellent basis for understanding issues of parenting.

22. See G. Owen and T. Harrison, 'Why ICI chose to demerge', *Harvard Business Review*, vol. 73 (1995) pp. 133–142.

Recommended key readings

- The importance of a clarity of purpose and aspirations for an organisation is argued in G. Hamel and C.K. Prahalad, *Competing for the Future*, Harvard Business School Press, 1994, chapter 6, and in their paper 'Strategic intent', *Harvard Business Review*, vol. 67, no. 3 (1989), pp. 63–76.

- The strategic logic and benefits underlying global strategy development is provided in G. Yip, *Total Global Strategy*, Prentice Hall, 1995, chapter 6.

- M.E. Porter, *Competitive Advantage*, Free Press, 1985, chapter 2, provides a succinct review of his arguments on generic strategies. For an extension of the discussion of the 'strategy clock' approach used here, see Cliff Bowman and David Faulkner's chapter, 'Competitive positioners', in V. Ambrosini with G. Johnson and K. Scholes (eds.), *Exploring Techniques of Analysis and Evaluation in Strategic Management*, Prentice Hall, 1998.

- A summary of different portfolio analyses, their benefits and limitations is provided in David Faulkner's chapter, 'Portfolio analysis', in V. Ambrosini with G. Johnson and K. Scholes (eds.), *Exploring Techniques of Analysis and Evaluation in Strategic Management*, Prentice Hall, 1998.

- The issue of parenting is discussed in detail in M. Goold, A. Campbell and M. Alexander, *Corporate Level Strategy*, Wiley, 1994.

Work assignments

6.1 **Consider and compare (a) what the main aspirations of key stakeholders are, (b) how these affect corporate purpose, and (c) the implications on strategy for IKEA (Illustration 1.1), the NHS (Illustration 2.7), the Body Shop (Illustration 5.5) and a global corporation such as the News Corporation.***

6.2 *Write a discussion paper explaining how privatisation of public services will or will not change the delivery of such services to the benefit of (a) taxpayers who finance the services and (b) the users of such services.*

6.3 Choose a company with a wide geographical scope in its products or services (e.g. ISS*). Using Figure 6.3 as a guideline, identify the benefits and drawbacks of such scope.

6.4 Using Figure 6.4, the strategy clock, identify examples of organisations following strategic routes 1 to 5. If you find it difficult to be clear about which route is being followed, note down the reasons for this, and consider if the organisations have a clear generic strategy.

6.5 Michael Porter argues that a business must have a clear competitive (or generic) strategy. Assess the extent to which any, or all, of the following have a clear generic strategy:
(a) Peugeot Citroën*
(b) Laura Ashley* (throughout its existence)
(c) an organisation of your choice.

6.6 You have been appointed as personal assistant to the chief executive of a major manufacturing firm, who has asked you to explain what is meant by 'differentiation' and why it is important. Write a brief report addressing these questions.

6.7 *Michael Porter argues that 'cost leadership' is a generic competitive strategy. Drawing on Porter's arguments, critiques cited in reference 13 and section 6.3 of this chapter, consider if this is appropriate.*

6.8 *How appropriate are bases of competitive advantage explained in section 6.3 for considering the strategies of public sector organisations? Illustrate your argument by reference to a public sector organisation of your choice.*

6.9 Choose a number of companies with portfolios of SBUs (e.g. ISS,* Burmah Castrol,* News Corporation*). Using Figure 6.6 as a guide, identify and explain the role of the corporate parent. Explain how, if at all, the parent enhances or could enhance SBU strategies.

* This refers to a case in the Text and Cases version of this book.

CHAPTER 7

Strategic options: directions and methods of development

7.1 Introduction

The previous chapter was concerned with the bases of strategic choice for organisations. Within this broad 'steer' for an organisation there are a number of specific options concerning both the *direction* and the *method* of developing the organisation's strategies, as previously indicated in Figure 6.2. This chapter will discuss these issues in the following way.

1. Figure 7.1 is an adaptation of the traditional product/market matrix[1] often used for generating *directions* for strategic development. It considers the development directions 'available' to an organisation in terms of the *market coverage, products* and *competence base* of the organisation. This last dimension is an important extension of the traditional approach. Indeed, the figure is meant to emphasise that in the long run development in any of the boxes is likely to require the development of competences to cope with a changing situation.

2. Figure 7.1 outlines the broad types of development direction in term of these three dimensions of markets, products and competences. These range from strategies concerned with protecting and building an organisation's position with its existing products and competences, through to major diversifications requiring development and change of both products and competences to enter or create new market opportunities. Each of the development directions shown in Figure 7.1 will be discussed in the next part of the chapter. Illustration 7.1 shows that, in reality, a combination of development directions is usually pursued.

3. The later parts of the chapter consider the issue of development *methods*, which are an additional consideration whichever generic strategies and specific directions an organisation might be pursuing.

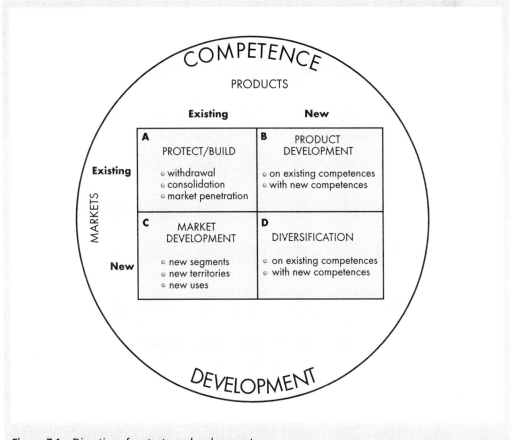

Figure 7.1   Directions for strategy development

For example, an organisation may be pursuing a broad strategy of growth, through positioning itself as the cheapest provider of 'regular' quality products (route 2 on the strategy clock in Figure 6.4). The development direction within this generic approach is one of *building* the organisation's competitive position by gaining market share (*market penetration*) through continued reduction of costs passed on to customers in price reductions. However, there are still choices as to the *method* by which this might be achieved. The cost improvements may be achieved *internally* by increasing the efficiency of current operations or through *strategic alliances* — perhaps to share distribution outlets with another (non-competitive) company; or it may be achieved by *acquisition* of a competitor to gain market share and to benefit from the associated economies of scale.

Illustration 7.1   Development directions at Rolls-Royce

Organisations usually adopt a combination of the 'pure' types of development direction discussed in this chapter.

Following major problems in the late 1960s, Rolls-Royce became a nationalised company until 1987 (except for the automobile division, which was sold to Vickers in 1971). By 1990, the company was again experiencing problems in its major markets (power generation equipment and aerospace), resulting from a combination of factors, including deregulation of power generation, the Gulf war (reducing airline passenger traffic) and the reduction of military budgets (the so-called 'peace dividend' after the ending of the Cold War in 1989). Notwithstanding these problems, both power generation and aerospace were forecast to have good medium/long-term growth prospects. The issue was how to survive and become a truly competitive player.

Rolls-Royce tried to achieve this in a number of ways:

- Radical and unpopular cost cutting.
- Broadening the product range through continued investment in R&D and finding the widest possible applications for its products.
- Reducing R&D lead times by the increasing use of computer programs and a reduction in engineering staff.
- Acquisition of the US Allison engine to increase its range of engines.
- This acquisition also eased market access into the USA.
- Backward integration into finance companies to allow Rolls-Royce to provide customers with the necessary finance.

Source: *Accountancy*, June 1995.

7.2   Alternative directions for strategy development

This section reviews the different directions available to organisations in their development of strategies. The section is structured around the broad categories of development direction represented by boxes in Figure 7.1 and introduced above.

7.2.1 Protect/build on current position

Many strategic developments within organisations are concerned with developing the organisation from where it is currently, rather than being 'greenfield site' developments. Box A in Figure 7.1 represents development options which are concerned with protecting or building on the organisation's current position. These are options built around both the current products and competences of the organisation and how they can be *stretched* to improve the competitive position of the organisation in its current markets. Within this broad category there are a number of specific options which organisations might consider.

Withdrawal

It was emphasised in Chapter 6 that an important 'generic' consideration is the way in which the *scope* of an organisation's activities might change. Although this may be achieved through new strategies, it is also likely to require withdrawal from some current activities, particularly where the organisation lacks the competences to compete. There are many circumstances where complete or partial withdrawal would be the most sensible course of action. For example:

- Perhaps the most compelling reason for withdrawal from particular markets is that the organisation is unable to secure the resources or achieve the competence levels of the leaders in the market overall and/ or the niches or segments of the market. The cost of repositioning or 'downsizing'[2] the organisation may be prohibitive, making withdrawal the most sensible course of action.
- In some markets, the *intrinsic value* of a company's products or assets is subject to changes over time, and a key issue may be the astute acquisition and disposal of these products, assets or businesses. This is particularly important for companies operating in markets which are subject to *speculation*, such as energy, metals, commodities, land or property.
- Since an organisation's unique resources and core competences are limited, there may need to be a review of the *priorities* for their deployment. So withdrawal from some activities releases resources and/ or competences for others. The shift in a local authority's range of services over time is a good example of such a policy, as was Richard Branson's decision in 1992 to sell his original business, Virgin Records, to concentrate on the airlines business. The key issue is which activities should be dropped and which should remain. This choice can be driven either by market opportunity or by a judgement on the degree to which particular strategies are likely to exploit the resources and core competences of the organisation.
- The expectations of dominant stakeholders may also be a reason for withdrawal. For example, the objective of a small entrepreneur may be to 'make a million' and then retire. So the expectations of the dominant stakeholder are largely short term, leading to a preference for strategies which make the company an attractive proposition to sell, rather than being guided by longer-term considerations of viability.

- It has already been mentioned in Chapters 5 and 6 that short-termism may also result from the expectations of the stock market putting pressure on managers to achieve short-term results or to divest activities (particularly in the USA and the UK). So large, diverse companies may view their subsidiary companies as assets to be bought and sold as part of an overall corporate portfolio of investments.[3] Indeed, in some conglomerate companies, these activities of acquisition and disposal are the core competences of the corporate centre of the organisation and a key part of their parenting role (as discussed in Chapters 6 and 9).

- This lack of corporate concern for the longer-term viability and prospects of subsidiaries is one of the reasons why managers of subsidiaries look seriously at the possibility of a *buy-out*[4] of the company from the parent. During the late 1980s and 1990s, buy-outs (either complete or partial) by management and/or employees became common in the UK and to a lesser extent in France. Sometimes buy-outs were triggered by the privatisation of companies in the public sector, where the management were able to bid for the company on sale (as with British Rail in 1995/96).

- Sometimes organisations will *partially* withdraw from a market by licensing the rights to other organisations. Whether this makes sense for the organisation is largely concerned with the relative competences of the organisation and the potential licensee in delivering value for money in that particular market. In turn, this will relate to the issues affecting the cost of operation and how the quality of product and service are maintained. Not surprisingly, the use of licence arrangements is common in overseas operations, as will be discussed below (section 7.3.3).

- Although hard-headed logic may point towards withdrawal as a sensible strategy, it is often culturally and politically difficult for organisations to swallow this pill. This is the reason why far too many organisations eventually have to withdraw from markets by voluntary or forced *liquidation*, where their position has become untenable.

Consolidation

Consolidation is concerned with protecting and strengthening the organisation's position in its current markets. Since this market situation is likely to be changing — for example, through improved performance of competitors or new entrants — consolidation does not mean standing still. It will require attention to the extent to which the organisation's resources and competences continue to fit the market need and/or how they should be adapted/developed to maintain the competitive position of the organisation.

Since consolidation is concerned with the maintenance of market share in existing markets, it is worth exploring *why* the maintenance of market share

Source: PIMS Associates Ltd. Reproduced with permission.

Figure 7.2   The PIMS framework for assessing strategic potential

might be an important consideration to organisations when reviewing their strategic choices. In this context, the continuing work of the Strategic Planning Institute (SPI) through its PIMS (Profit Impact of Market Strategy) database is useful[5] (see Figure 7.2). This database contains the experiences of over 3,000 businesses (both products and services). Some of the more important PIMS findings, together with other research, are used in the various subsections of section 7.2. The link between performance and relative market share, which is also emphasised by the experience curve work (see Chapter 4, section 4.3.3), is supported by the findings of the PIMS database as shown in Figures 7.3 and 7.4. Return on investment rises steadily in line with relative market share.

A number of reasons are suggested as to why relative market share and ROI should be linked:

▪ The major factor seems to be *asset turnover*, with low-share businesses showing substantially higher investment/sales ratios than high-share businesses (sometimes nearly 25 per cent poorer). This can be attributed to scale economies in the use of fixed assets.

▪ The purchase/sales ratio differences between high- and low-market-share

Source: PIMS Associates Ltd. Reproduced with permission.

Figure 7.3   Market share drives profitability

firms are also startling — high-market-share companies are able to buy more competitively or add more value to purchases. Economies of scale also show up in some other cost categories, such as marketing, but not in R&D. High-share businesses have higher R&D/sales ratios, largely because they are better placed to exploit innovation, as discussed below.

- A PIMS study of fast-moving consumer goods businesses[6] published in 1991 showed a strong interaction between *brand rank*, the *mix* of advertising and promotion activities, and profitability. The evidence showed that it is difficult to make profits unless the company has one of the leading three brands.

As well as underlining the importance of maintaining or improving market share, the PIMS database is useful in identifying those factors which help sustain a successful (profitable) strategy of consolidation:

- The indications are that high-market-share firms are more likely to develop strategies of higher price/higher quality than low-share competitors. Longer-term PIMS evidence shows that this phenomenon may be self-sustaining. High-share firms tend to be more profitable, providing extra resources for R&D to improve and differentiate products, enhancing their market position and also justifying higher prices, which in turn increase profits. However, it must be remembered that high market share and size are not always the same. There are large firms which do not dominate the markets in which they operate; and there are small firms which dominate market segments.

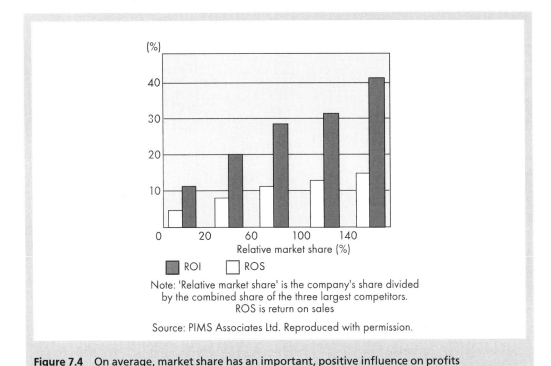

Figure 7.4   On average, market share has an important, positive influence on profits

- A PIMS study of competitiveness in Europe and North America[7] showed that key drivers of market share (whether maintenance of current share or share improvement, and value-added growth) were the organisation's competences to sustain *quality, innovation* and *intellectual property* (e.g. patents). All of these factors impact on the perceived value for money of the organisation's products or services, and can also act as barriers to entry for new competitors.

- The evidence shows that quality is important in the improvement of profit performance (Figure 7.5(a)). The best situation appears to be a combination of high share and high product/service quality, but even firms with low market shares demonstrate significantly higher profit performance if they have offerings of superior quality. (In this sense, quality can be a partial substitute for market share in sustaining advantage.)

- Sometimes organisations try to defend or consolidate their position through increasing marketing expenditure. Figure 7.5(b) suggests that in itself this is unlikely to be effective. Heavy marketing expenditure (as a percentage of sales) is likely to damage ROI for organisations with low market shares.

- The combined effect of marketing expenditure and product quality has also been studied. High marketing expenditure is not a substitute for

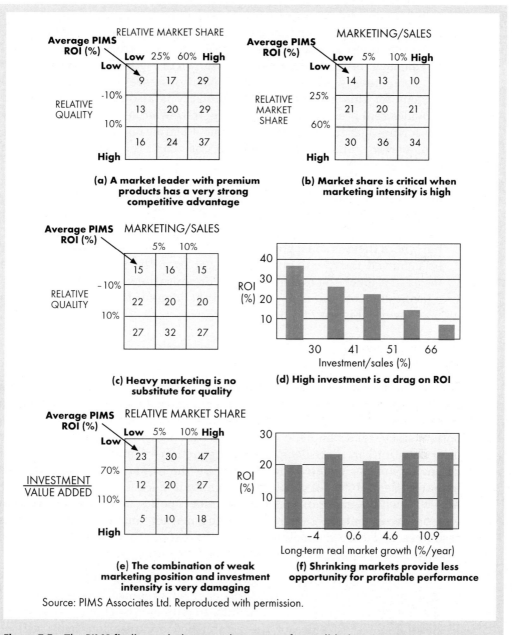

(a) **A market leader with premium products has a very strong competitive advantage**

(b) **Market share is critical when marketing intensity is high**

(c) **Heavy marketing is no substitute for quality**

(d) **High investment is a drag on ROI**

(e) **The combination of weak marketing position and investment intensity is very damaging**

(f) **Shrinking markets provide less opportunity for profitable performance**

Source: PIMS Associates Ltd. Reproduced with permission.

Figure 7.5   The PIMS findings relating to various types of consolidation strategy

quality: indeed, it appears that high marketing expenditure damages ROI most when quality is low (Figure 7.5(c)). It must be concluded that simply gearing up marketing expenditure as a means of consolidating a company's position is not sufficient.

▨   Another consolidation strategy is to seek improved productivity through *capital investment* — for example, by the mechanisation of routine tasks. However, there is evidence to suggest that increased capital intensity can damage return on investment, as shown in Figure 7.5(d), particularly for companies with weak market positions (see Figure 7.5(e)). The reasons for this are that capital intensity is also an exit barrier and provides real pressure to fill capacity. In this situation, firms are likely to sacrifice margins to increase volume. Flexible manufacturing systems can partly relieve this pressure, as can the strategic use of subcontracting.

▨   During the transition from a mature to a declining market, an organisation may follow a strategy of harvesting: that is, gaining maximum pay-off from its strong position. One of the most difficult strategic decisions is how long to remain in markets which are in decline, but where there is some hope of a market recovery. If turnaround cannot be achieved fairly quickly, withdrawal from the market may well be necessary, since the extent to which organisations are likely to sustain a profitable position is dependent on the long-term real market growth (as shown in Figure 7.5(f)).

Market penetration

Within the broad category of protecting and building the organisation's position, there may be opportunities to gain market share. This is known as *market penetration*. Much of the previous discussion is relevant to this option, since, for example, competences which sustain or improve quality or innovation or increasing marketing activity could all be means of achieving market penetration. So too are the arguments concerning the long-term desirability of obtaining a dominant market share. However, the ease with which an organisation can pursue a policy of market penetration will be dependent on the nature of the market and the organisation's resources and core competences, and the extent to which these can be developed:

▨   When the overall market is growing, or can be induced to grow, PIMS evidence shows that it is *relatively* easy for organisations with a small market share, or even new entrants, to gain share. This is because the absolute level of sales of the established organisations may still be growing, and in some instances those companies may be unable or unwilling to meet the new demand. Import penetration into some industries has occurred in this way.

▨   In contrast, market penetration in static *markets* can be much more difficult to achieve. The PIMS evidence on the cost of building market share is a reminder that it can be a costly process for weakly positioned

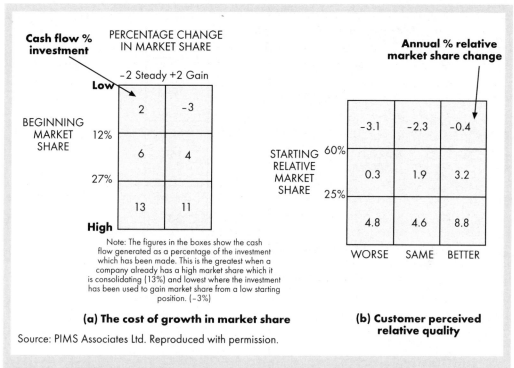

Figure 7.6   PIMS findings concerning strategies of market penetration

businesses (see Figure 7.6(a)). Short-term profits are likely to be sacrificed, particularly when trying to build share from a low base.

▨ However, the complacency of market leaders may allow smaller-share competitors to catch up. Or a low-share competitor may build a reputation in a market segment of little interest to the market leader, from which it penetrates the wider market. Figure 7.6(b) shows that perceived quality (relative to competitors) is a key determinant for rapid market penetration by lower-market-share companies and helps high-share business resist this penetration. The PIMS database suggests that this relationship may have been strengthened recently either because markets have become more sensitive to quality, or because buyers and sellers are better at measuring it (including the emphasis on performance indicators in the public services).

7.2.2 Product development

There are many reasons why companies might have a preference for product development. For example, retailers follow the changing needs of their customers by a continuing policy of introducing new product lines; and

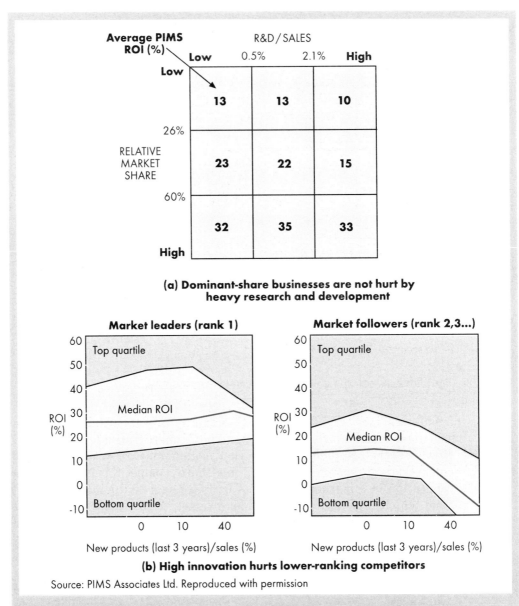

(a) **Dominant-share businesses are not hurt by heavy research and development**

(b) **High innovation hurts lower-ranking competitors**

Source: PIMS Associates Ltd. Reproduced with permission

Figure 7.7 The PIMS findings relating to product development

public services need to shift their pattern of services as needs change. In both these cases, a core competence for successful organisations is the ability to analyse and understand the changing needs of a particular group of customers or clients. Strategic development can be built around such a core competence. Similarly, product development may be preferred because the company has core competences related to R&D. When product life cycles are short — as with consumer electronics — product development becomes an essential requirement of an organisation's strategy, built around a core competence in R&D and/or the ability to acquire new products from elsewhere.

Despite the attractiveness of product development, it may often raise uncomfortable dilemmas for organisations. While new products may be vital to the future of the organisation, the process of creating a broad product line is expensive, risky and potentially unprofitable, because most new product ideas never reach the market; and of those that do, there are relatively few which succeed. Product development may require a commitment to high levels of spending on R&D. Figure 7.7(a) shows that, while high-market-share companies may benefit in profit terms from relatively high levels of R&D expenditure, companies in a weak market position with high expenditure may suffer.

Figure 7.7(b) also confirms that profitability can be depressed by overrapid rates of new product introductions, as organisations struggle to learn new competences needed to debug production, train sales people, educate customers and establish new channels. The evidence shows that this is even more important for market followers, where more than moderate rates of innovation dramatically worsen profitability.

In the long term, product development is unlikely to be sustainable without the development or acquisition of new competences. For example, there may be a need to respond to a *change of emphasis* among customers concerning the importance of product/service features. This can occur because customers become more experienced in judging value for money — for example, through repeat purchase or because new choices become available in the market. One of the stated purposes behind the privatisation measures in the public services (described in Chapters 6 and 10) was to empower customers in this way — through increasing choice and/or raising consumers' awareness and expectations about value for money from public services.[8]

These shifts at the customer end require responses from the organisation. These may be concerned not with the basic features of the product or service, but with the need to improve other aspects of the customer experience: for example, the quality of information provided to clients, the clarity of billing, the ease of payment methods and so on. So the organisation needs *complementary competences* in aspects of the business which have been regarded as peripheral. As mentioned in Chapters 4 and 5, even the recognition that this is necessary can prove difficult, since the dominant culture and distribution of power are not attuned to such radical thinking.

Competence development may not only be concerned with ensuring a continued 'fit' with the changing needs of the existing markets (box B in Figure 7.1). It may be possible — or necessary — to stretch the organisation's resources and competences to enter new markets (box D). This will be discussed more fully in section 7.2.4 below.

The need to develop competences and/or products even to survive in existing markets is underlined by the consequences of not doing so. It is likely that the performance may become so poor in relation to competitors or other providers that the organisation becomes a target for acquisition, particularly by organisations which have core competences in *corporate turnaround*.[9]

7.2.3 Market development

Most organisations have developed in ways which have resulted in *limited* coverage of the market by their products. It was emphasised in Chapter 6 that careful thought needs to be given to the way in which an organisation *positions* its products in markets — which inevitably means selectivity of market coverage. However, if the organisation's aspirations outstrip the opportunities in existing markets, it is natural to look for opportunities to exploit the current products in other markets. Three common ways of doing this are as follows.

1. *Extension* into market segments which are not currently served — although this might require some modification of the product to suit it to new segments. For example, a manufacturer of branded grocery products for the premium market may enter the mainstream market through 'own-brand' sales to supermarkets. This will require the development of new competences in (for example) key account selling.

2. Development of *new uses* for existing products. For example, manufacturers of stainless steel have progressively found new applications for the products which were originally used for cutlery and tableware. Nowadays, the uses include aerospace, automobile exhausts, beer barrels and many applications in the chemical manufacturing industry. Again, competences were needed in analysing each potential market and assessing the particular requirements of the product.

3. *Geographical* spread either nationally or internationally into new markets. Again, this may require some adjustment to product features or marketing methods. For example, it may be necessary to use agents for these new territories while sales volumes are low. It will also require other competences — for example, in market analysis and language/ cultural awareness. Chapter 3 discussed how in many industries there are increasing pressures for globalisation and that companies need to know how to respond and have the resources and competences to do so. Increased global market participation — as against simply selling more goods into a few new countries — requires the organisation to consider three main elements[10] (as seen in Figure 7.8):

Source: Based on G. Yip, *Total Global Strategy*, Prentice-Hall 1995, chapter 3.

Figure 7.8   Three elements of a globalisation strategy

- The benefits of high market share (in a single country) have already been discussed in section 7.2.1 and illustrated in Figures 7.3 to 7.6. These benefits of global market share can be even more important in global markets — for example, by concentrating manufacturing on a small number of locations, both cost and quality benefits may result.
- High global market share is important, but not sufficient for global market participation. There also needs to be a *global balance* of revenues within the global market. This is one feature which has tended to distinguish Japanese companies in global markets from their competitors. For example, in the automobile industry, companies like Toyota and Nissan have a significant presence in all three of the major 'arenas' (North America, Europe and Asia/Pacific). In contrast, the major American companies (Ford and GM) are strong in two arenas (North America and Europe), while the major European players (e.g. Peugeot) tend to be strong only in Europe.
- There is also a need to be participating in *globally strategic markets*. These are countries which are important beyond their stand-alone attractiveness. This could occur for a number of reasons. For

example, to be involved in at least one *large* market may be essential to get the cost structure or experience which are to be exploited elsewhere; it may be necessary to have a presence in the *home market of global customers* to gain access to, or credibility with, their global divisions or subsidiaries; in order to gain advantage over competitors there may be a need to operate in *competitors' home countries* or the countries where *competitors have a major presence*. Finally, a market may be strategically important because it is a source of industry innovation — for example, the USA for computer software, Germany for industrial control equipment, or the UK for popular music.

There are clearly important practical implications for organisations planning to increase their global participation, including the need to reassess the way in which the organisation's structure, design and control will need to change. These issues will be discussed in Chapters 9 and 10.

Illustration 7.2 shows how McDonald's expanded internationally by identifying new types of location as well as new countries. This continued, profitable growth also required competences in reducing opening costs of new outlets.

7.2.4 Diversification

Types of diversification

Diversification is a term used in many different ways. In this chapter, the word will be used to identify directions of development which take the organisation away from its present markets and its present products at the same time (i.e. box D in Figure 7.1). It has been traditional to divide the consideration of diversification into two broad types — related and unrelated diversification.

1. *Related diversification.* This is development beyond the present product and market, but still within the broad confines of the 'industry' (i.e. value chain) in which the company operates. For example, Unilever is a diversified corporation, but virtually all of its interests are in the fast-moving consumer goods industry. Related diversification may take several forms (see Figure 7.9).

   Backward integration refers to development into activities which are concerned with the inputs into the company's current business (i.e. are further back in the value chain). For example, raw materials, machinery and labour are all important inputs into a manufacturing company.

Illustration 7.2   McDonald's into new markets

International growth may require the identification of new market segments as well as new countries.

In March 1996, McDonald's announced plans to accelerate its rate of expansion to a record high, adding between 2,500 and 3,200 restaurants to the 1995 total of 18,380. Although McDonald's still has more restaurants in the USA than abroad, the overseas side is growing more quickly, and in 1995 international operating profits exceeded US operating profits for the first time. International growth appears to be changing the company's shape, with the opening of markets in eastern Europe, India and China reportedly producing a wave of enthusiasm.

The international market is attractive for a number of reasons. First, international sales are more profitable than those at home due to the lower level of competition. McDonald's is able to get more customers through its doors and charge higher prices. Another attraction is that growth has seemingly limitless potential. On any given day, McDonald's still serves barely half a per cent of the world's population. Its vision is to put everyone within easy reach of a Big Mac.

One reason why McDonald's has the potential to do this is that since 1990 it has slashed the cost of opening a typical restaurant by 30 per cent through the use of more efficient building designs, standardised equipment packages and global sourcing. This means that it can now open restaurants in locations that would have been hopelessly uneconomical five years ago. There are now McDonald's restaurants in more than 30 hospitals worldwide; in Wal-Mart discount stores across the USA; in the National Museum of Natural Science in Taichung, Taiwan; on the MS Silja Europa, a Swedish cruise ferry; in airports, schools and military bases; and on trains in Germany and Switzerland.

A new market development became operational in April 1996 when the first airborne McDonald's, dubbed McPlane took off from Switzerland. The experimental project is a joint venture of McDonald's Switzerland, the Swiss tour operator Hotelplan, and Crossair, the charter subsidiary of the Swiss national airline, Swissair. Hotelplan uses the Crossair-operated aircraft as part of its programme of package tours taking holidaymakers from Swiss airports to Disneyland Paris and Mediterranean resorts.

Also, in spring 1996, McDonald's announced its biggest international acquisition with an agreement to buy the 80-strong chain of Burghy restaurants in Italy. The move was considered unusual for McDonald's because the company had only previously expanded by building its own restaurants. However, a company spokesman said the Burghy acquisition represented a 'unique opportunity' to treble its size in Italy.

Source: *Financial Times*, 11, 18 and 22 March 1996.
Prepared by Sara Martin, Cranfield School of Management.

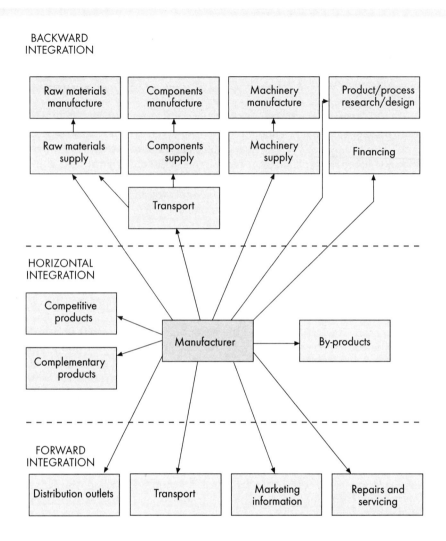

Figure 7.9   Related diversification options for a manufacturer

■ *Forward integration* refers to development into activities which are concerned with a company's outputs (i.e. are further forward in the value chain), such as transport, distribution, repairs and servicing. Illustration 7.3 shows how motor insurance companies were taking a more direct involvement in motor repairs — either through

Illustration 7.3   Forward integration: the British insurance industry

Sometimes reconfiguring the value chain, perhaps through forward integration or licensing arrangements, is essential to improving value for money.

In a bid to reduce premiums and improve customer service, in 1995 insurance companies were establishing their own chains of motor-repair centres. In a similar approach to that taken by Direct Line, which cut out insurance brokers by dealing direct with the public, insurers were hoping to bypass garage owners and repair damaged vehicles themselves. While in essence each of the insurance companies was attempting the same thing, they were going about it in various ways.

Churchill Insurance
Churchill Insurance, one of Britain's largest telephone-based insurers, had opened a wholly-owned repair centre in Rotherham, South Yorkshire. When fully operational it would be able to repair up to 60 cars a week using the latest technology. Vehicles belonging to customers who had accidents within a 50 mile radius of the centre would be picked up and taken in for repair. Owners were given a courtesy car to use until their vehicle was returned. All repairs were guaranteed for five years and there was no charge for the service, which the company said paid for itself. Customers avoided the nuisance of having to pay and claim the cost of the repair back, as this was done automatically.

Direct Line
Direct Line had taken a slightly different tack. They were intending to set up a limited number of wholly-owned 'repair and development' centres. These would eventually represent centres of excellence, and would be supported by a much larger network of recommended, but independently owned garages. As the network grew, franchised garages bearing the Direct Line name would also be established.

Prospero Direct
Prospero Direct, another telephone-based insurer, already had a network of approved repair centres, but it had no plans to set up its own garages. Rather, it had chosen to control costs and thus offer lower premiums by installing video cameras throughout the network that were directly linked to Prospero's claims centre. Using this live link, company claims experts could more accurately assess damage and repairs and so ensure that the garages were not overcharging.

In all three instances, the customer benefited from reduced costs and an improved level of service.

Source: *Sunday Times*, 25 June 1995.
Prepared by Sara Martin, Cranfield School of Management.

Illustration 7.4 Exploiting core competences: the Automobile Association — the 4th emergency service

In attempting to differentiate itself from the competition, the AA is becoming more efficient, less bureaucratic and more focused in its new position as the 4th emergency service.

The Association was founded in 1905 as a members' club for motorists, soon afterwards extending into the provision of rescue services in the event of breakdowns. By 1995 it had become a multimillion-pound organisation, with its membership standing at eight million. The array of services offered had become so diverse as to include the provision of both motor insurance and horse insurance. Despite this, the AA's market share of its traditional vehicle rescue service was falling as aggressive specialist competitors such as Green Flag and National Breakdown established themselves.

To reverse this trend, the AA restructured and actively sought to improve its general level of service. Furthermore, it attempted to differentiate itself from the competition and to extend into new markets by exploiting its new image as the 4th emergency service. The launch of 'AA Homeline' was one example of these efforts. A subscription to this new home assistance service gives members the assurance of finding help with a range of common household problems, including plumbing, electrics, roofing, glazing, general building and household appliance repairs. In the event of an emergency situation, the member simply phones the hotline and is given the name of a recommended firm and a specific rate for the job. Once the job has been completed, the AA collects the money from the member and pays the firm. The customer is asked to complete a job satisfaction sheet which enables the AA to monitor each job and ensure the same level of quality service again and again.

In providing this service, the AA staked its reputation on its ability to vet firms and individuals thoroughly enough to keep the 'cowboys' off the list. However, by using its experience and competence in call handling, resource management and problem solving, the AA could ensure that each member received a quality service. Indeed, for a firm to be accepted on to the list, it must show sufficient public liability insurance, satisfactory credit checks and six recent customer references.

The AA denied that this new service was a move away from the travel and financial services offered in recent years, stating that it simply extended the AA's expertise in delivering and monitoring quality emergency services, and controlling costs for the benefit of members.

Source: Excerpts from the national press and the AA Handbook.
Prepared by Sara Martin, Cranfield School of Management.

ownership or a 'licensing' scheme. *Vertical integration* is a broader term used to describe either backward or forward integration.

- *Horizontal integration* refers to development into activities which are competitive with, or directly complementary to, a company's present activities. For example, many organisations have realised that there are opportunities in other markets for the *exploitation* of the organisation's core competences — perhaps to displace the current providers as a new entrant. Illustration 7.4 shows how the Automobile Association (AA) had been founded as a members' club for motorists in the UK and extended into providing rescue services for breakdowns. As this market came under fierce attack from specialist breakdown organisations, the AA extended into new markets by exploiting its expertise in *rapid response to crisis*. It launched a home service for electrical and plumbing emergencies, a development pioneered by similar motoring organisations in Australia.

Figure 7.10 summarises some of the detailed reasons for related diversification or, in reverse, reasons why highly diversified companies might divest activities to increase their degree of specialisation. For example, it may be decided that supplies of raw materials have become available from a reliable low-cost source and this provides a good reason to cease the manufacture of those materials within the company.

It needs to be recognised that increased ownership of more value activities within the value chain does not guarantee improved performance for the organisation or better value for money for the consumer or client. Indeed, there has been some degree of disillusionment with related diversification as a strategy, and more emphasis on improving performance within the value system through external linkages and the management of relationships with the various parties in the supply and distribution chains.

Another example of the need to assess these issues of diversification/specialisation is the locational decisions for the separate activities of international companies, and the extent to which separate locations should specialise or diversify their activities. The logic of gaining competitive advantage through building competences in separate activities suggests that the separate activities of design, component production, assembly and marketing may be optimally located in different countries. For example, in consumer electronics, component design and manufacture tend to be located in more advanced economies (e.g. Japan), while assembly is carried out in lower-wage economies (Korea, Taiwan, etc.).

Gaining advantage through specialisation needs to be balanced against the need for well-managed linkages between these separate activities, which proves more difficult the more geographically

Possible advantages	Examples/comments
• Control of supplies	
Quantity	Tea processors own plantations to secure continuity of supply.
Quality	Components for motor cars may need to be manufactured by the company.
Price	Printing facility can be cheaper if in-house.
• Control of markets	UK shoe manufacturers own retail outlets to gain guaranteed distribution.
• Access to information	Shoe manufacturers are involved in machinery companies to keep abreast of developments.
• Cost savings	Fully integrated steel plants save cost on reheating and transport.
• Building on	
Core competences	Firm of accountants moving into tax advice or corporate recovery.
Technology	Precision engineering equipment manufacturer in one market entering another with similar technical requirements.
• Spreading risk	Avoids overreliance on one product/market, but builds on related experience.
• Resource utilisation	Manufacturer acquiring company for compatible products to fill capacity.

Figure 7.10   Some reasons for related diversification

dispersed are the separate activities. The most successful international companies are those which can develop organisational arrangements to exploit the advantages of specialisation and dispersion, while managing linkages successfully. These issues were introduced in Chapter 6 and will be discussed more fully in Chapter 9.

2. *Unrelated diversification.* Historically, the literature on diversification has been dominated by an environment-led perspective of strategic options. So relatedness has tended to be defined in somewhat narrow terms: that is, opportunities beyond the current product and market base of the organisation and outside the current industry (i.e. value chain). However, as discussions in previous sections have revealed, this narrow definition tends to hide important differences in the degree of relatedness of diversification opportunities. Again, this is where the resource-led perspective is so important. Unrelated diversification really needs to be divided into three categories:

■ It may involve extension into new markets and new products by *exploiting* the current core competences of the organisation. For example, the global development of conglomerate businesses is more likely to work if these subsidiaries are similar or related — in the sense that they are conducive to the management (parenting) 'formula' from the centre (as discussed in Chapter 6). This is often crucial, since the core competences may be linked to the tacit knowledge and routines of the organisation (as discussed in Chapters 4 and 5) and hence difficult to imitate. So some conglomerates are good at buying lame ducks, turning them around and selling them on as going concerns. They would not be good at managing a diversified empire which did not share these common characteristics. These issues about the roles and relationships between the corporate centre and the divisions or subsidiaries of the organisation are concerned with parenting, have previously been raised in Chapter 6 and will be discussed fully in Chapter 9 (section 9.4).

■ Diversification by the exploitation of core competences may go beyond simply moving into markets which already exist: it may involve the *creation* of genuinely new markets. There are some elements of this in Illustration 7.4, in the sense that it was the absence of an efficient and reliable means for individual households to access the fragmented suppliers of electrical and plumbing services which created the AA's opportunity. Another example is the way in which research and development based on microelectronic technology has progressively spawned whole new markets which did not exist even 20 years ago (personal electronic organisers, interactive video games and so on).

■ The most extreme form of unrelated diversification is where *new competences* are developed for new market opportunities. Not surprisingly, this extreme end of the diversification spectrum is less common. In fact, if an entirely pedantic definition of unrelatedness were taken, it might never be observed at all — it usually proves possible to identify some degree of relatedness in the market or resources/competences in any development opportunity. So this issue is really about *degrees of relatedness*, and the discussions which follow should be seen in that light. Figure 7.11 summarises some of the detailed reasons for unrelated diversification. Perhaps one of the reasons why diversification strategies run into difficulties is that organisations misjudge the degree of relatedness involved. This is a clear danger in vertical integration, which moves the organisation into activities that are adjacent in the value chain (e.g. supply or distribution), but which are entirely unrelated to the organisation's current competences.

Possible advantages	Examples/comments
• Need to use excess cash or safeguard profits	Buying a tax loss situation.
• Personal values or objectives of powerful figures	Personal image locally or nationally may be a strong motive.
• Exploiting underutilised resources/competences	Farmers use fields for camp sites. Local authorities use plastic waste for new materials.
• Escape from present business	A company's products may be in decline and unrelated diversification presents the only possible 'escape'.
• Spreading risk	Some companies believe that it is good sense not to have all their 'eggs in one basket' and so diversify into unrelated areas.
• Even out cyclical effects in a given sector	Toy manufacturers make subcontract plastic moulded products for industry.
• Benefit from synergistic effects	See text.

Figure 7.11   Some reasons for unrelated diversification

Synergy[11] is a commonly cited reason for both *related* and *unrelated* *diversification*. Potentially, synergy can occur in situations where two or more activities or processes complement each other, to the extent that their combined effect is greater than the 'sum of the parts'. Figure 7.12 outlines the conditions that need to be satisfied if strategies based on exploiting synergy are to be successful. This provides a useful link between the logic of synergy (opportunity to improve and the appropriateness of synergy) and the practical realities of adopting such a strategy (determination, acceptance and compatibility with the systems and culture of the organisation). This latter agenda is concerned with the issues of parenting which were discussed in Chapter 6.

Illustration 7.5 shows how Benetton claimed that there were synergies resulting from its diversification, while acknowledging that diversification may simply be *necessary* to achieve continuing growth once saturation occurs in current markets.

Diversification and performance

Diversification has been one of the most frequently researched areas of business. Much of this research has been undertaken within the 'disciplines' adjacent to strategic management (e.g. economics, finance, law and marketing). There have also been a number of research studies which

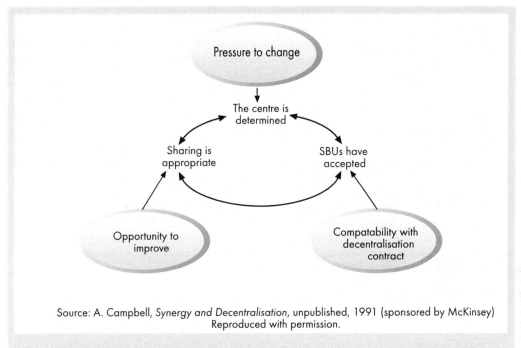

Source: A. Campbell, *Synergy and Decentralisation*, unpublished, 1991 (sponsored by McKinsey)
Reproduced with permission.

Figure 7.12   Conditions for synergy

specifically attempt to investigate the relationship between the choice of diversification as a strategy and the performance of the organisation in financial terms.[12] Overall, it needs to be said that the various attempts to demonstrate the effects of diversification on performance are inconclusive. Early research[13] suggested that firms which developed through *related diversification* outperformed both those that remained specialised and those which developed through *unrelated diversification*. These findings were later questioned.[14] The sum total of all of the research work linking patterns of diversification to financial performance is unclear apart from one important message. Successful diversification is difficult to achieve in practice. Some of the specific findings of the various research studies are as follows:

▨ The concept of diversity should not be interpreted too narrowly as relatedness in product terms. Diversity is also an issue on other dimensions, such as market spread or competence, as mentioned above. As stated in Chapter 6, there is some evidence[15] that profitability does increase with diversity, but only up to the *limit of complexity*, beyond which this relationship reverses. This raises the issue of whether managers can cope with large, diverse organisations — an issue which was raised in Chapter 6 and will be discussed further in Chapter 9. The PIMS database also supports the view that complexity, as measured by

Illustration 7.5 Synergy from diversification? The Benetton empire

After years of focusing on its core products of leisurewear, the Benetton family began diversifying in several unexpected directions through its family holding company, Edizione Holding. Such action was seen as Benetton's tacit acknowledgement that its traditional activities were close to saturation.

By 1995 the Benettons had amassed an empire with aggregate sales of £4 billion, making it one of the five biggest companies in Italy. However, 30 years after the first knitwear shop was opened, growth in the group's traditional clothing core had peaked, and the family was attempting to fuel growth by finding new frontiers in old markets, but also by diversifying into completely new markets. 1994/5 was a big year for acquisitions, and the family now controls a company that spans Formula 1 racing, roadside restaurants, hypermarkets, merchant banking and big-name sporting goods such as Nordica, Prince and Rollerblade.

Despite the diversity of these acquisitions, Luciano Benetton explained that synergy existed between them. In the case of the original shops, the supermarkets and the hypermarkets, the synergy occurred in the consumer who buy from all three. As a contrast, there are unique production and operational synergies that have been maximised within the group's sports activities by the creation of the Benetton Sportsystem umbrella. For example, Nordica ski boots and Rollerblade in-line skates are both made from the same plastic composite material. Furthermore, at the Nordica production plant in Italy, the same machines that make Nordica boots can easily switch components to manufacture Rollerblade skate shells. Synergies also existed at the distribution end of both the food and sports businesses.

Gilberto Benetton explained that the group wanted to expand, but existing operations promised only 'normal' rate growth. The only solution, therefore, was to diversify.

Prepared by Sara Martin, Cranfield School of Management.

customer numbers or communication costs, reduces profit potential. The evidence on this is particularly stark for service-based businesses.[16]

- The theoretical benefits of synergy through diversification are often difficult to achieve in practice. This is particularly supported in the research on diversification through acquisition. For example, a study[17] of 33 major corporations between 1950 and 1986 concluded that more acquisitions were subsequently divested than retained, and that the net result was usually a dissipation of shareholder value and the company left vulnerable to corporate raiders. Other research suggests that the management of the process of diversification[18] may be a more important influence on performance than the type or mode of diversification itself.

Illustration 7.6   Back to basics: splitting up diversified companies

In the mid-1990s, many large, diversified organisations were choosing to split into separate companies, each with a much more clearly defined core business and/or market focus.

The UK building industry
In 1996, two of the most vertically integrated companies, Wimpey and Tarmac, swapped some of their businesses to each reduce their diversification. Wimpey took over Tarmac's house-building business in exchange for the latter's quarries and contracting. A major spur for these moves was the fact that the diversified companies were significantly outperformed by specialist builders in the 1990s recession.

Hanson splits into four companies
Once the epitome of the successful conglomerate, Hanson plc decided in 1996 to split into four separate companies, specialising in energy, tobacco, chemicals and building materials. One of the cited reasons for this change was the issue of succession to Lord Hanson. Although he was seen as possessing the skills to create and hold together a diversified empire, his potential successors were seen as 'operating people' who lacked these 'parenting' skills.

Lonrho de-merger
In December 1995, Dieter Bock, the CEO of Lonrho, embarked on a process of convincing investors that shareholders would benefit from an end to Lonrho's conglomerate status. The plan was to split the company into two separate, stock market-quoted companies: a mining business and a business dealing with Lonrho's African trading and agricultural interests.

Thorn EMI de-merger
In February 1996, Sir Colin Southgate, the chairman of Thorn EMI, announced plans to split the company into EMI Music — one of the world's largest recording companies — and Thorn Rental Businesses. The company hoped that the rental business would benefit from the de-merger in terms of its public profile, which had long been overshadowed by the glamorous music division.

Illustration 7.6 shows that in the mid-1990s many large diversified organisations were choosing to split into separate companies, each with a much more clearly defined core business and/or market focus.

- An important conclusion of many research studies is that a universal prescription of the benefits of diversification is unlikely to be found. The likely success of diversification is extremely dependent on the circumstances of an organisation, such as the level of industry growth, market structures and the firm's size. Some studies[19] have also demonstrated that the relationship between performance and diversity will vary with the period of time studied (e.g. the point in the business cycle). For example, related diversification might be more suited to firms when there are opportunities for expansion in a growing economy. On the other hand, in times of little or no growth, a concentration on mainline products and/or seeking more market diversity might make more sense.

▧ Other studies[20] argue that a key factor is the resource situation of the organisation — particularly the area of underutilised resources. Underutilisation of physical resources or intangible resources (brand name, etc.) is likely to encourage related developments, whereas excess financial resources may well be used to underwrite unrelated developments (e.g. through acquisition), particularly if the other resources and competences are difficult to develop/grow quickly. This raises the question of whether successful performance is a *result* of choosing diversification or if the relationship is, in fact, the reverse. Perhaps successful organisations *choose* diversification because opportunities in their current product/market domain look limited.

7.3   Alternative methods of strategy development

The previous chapter was concerned with strategic choices at the broad or generic level — the *basis* on which the more detailed strategies are constructed. The previous section of this chapter reviewed the *alternative directions* in which organisations might develop. However, for any of these directions there are different potential *methods of development*. These methods can be divided into three types: *internal development, acquisition (or disposal)* and *joint development (or alliances)*.

7.3.1 Internal development

For many organisations, internal development (sometimes known as 'organic development') has been the primary method of strategy development, and there are some compelling reasons why this should be so. Particularly with products which are highly technical in design or method of manufacture, businesses will choose to develop new products themselves, since the process of development is seen as the best way of acquiring the necessary core competences to compete successfully in the market place. Indeed, it has been seen above that these core competences may also spawn further new products and create new market opportunities.

A similar argument applies to the development of new markets by direct involvement. For example, many manufacturers still choose to forgo the use of agents, since they feel that the direct involvement gained from having their own salesforce is of advantage in gaining a full understanding of the market. This market knowledge may be a core competence in the sense that it creates competitive advantage over other organisations which are more distant from their customers.

Although the final cost of developing new activities internally may be greater than that of acquiring other companies, the spread of cost may be more favourable and realistic. This is a strong argument in favour of internal development for small companies or many public services which may not have the resources available for major investment. The slower rate of change which internal development brings may also minimise the disruption to other activities.

An organisation may, of course, have no choice about how new ventures are developed. Those breaking new ground may not be in a position to develop by acquisition or joint development, since they are the only ones in the field. But this problem is not confined to such extreme situations. Organisations which would prefer to develop by acquisition may not be able to find a suitable target for that acquisition. For example, this is a particular difficulty for foreign companies attempting to enter Japan. Internal development also avoids the often traumatic behavioural and cultural problems arising from post-acquisition integration and coping with the different traditions and incompatibilities of the two organisations.

7.3.2 Mergers and acquisitions[21]

Development by acquisition tends to go in waves (for example, 1898–1900, 1926–9, 1967–73, 1985–7 and the early 1990s in the UK). It also tends to be selective in terms of industry sector. For example, in the UK, the 1960s activity was particularly important in electrical engineering and textiles, whereas between 1985 and 1987, high street retailing takeovers were common. The early 1990s saw a wave of mergers in professional service organisations, such as solicitors, property services, accountancy firms and financial services. International developments through acquisition have been critically important in some industries, such as newspapers/media, food and drink, and many sectors of the leisure industries.

A compelling reason to develop by acquisition is the speed with which it allows the company to enter new product/market areas. In some cases the product and/or market are changing so rapidly that this becomes the only way of successfully entering the market, since the process of internal development is too slow. Another reason for acquisition is the lack of resources or competence to develop a strategy internally. For example, a company may be acquired for its R&D expertise, or its knowledge of a particular type of production system. International developments are often pursued through acquisition (or joint development) for reasons of market knowledge. Illustration 7.7 shows that, in rapidly changing global industries in the 1990s, a combination of these factors led to a rapid growth in acquisition activity.

The competitive situation may influence a company to choose acquisition. In markets which are static and where market shares of companies are reasonably steady, it can be a difficult proposition for a new company to enter the market, since its presence may create excess capacity. If, however, the new company chooses to enter by acquisition, the risk of competitive reaction is reduced. The same arguments also apply when an established supplier in an industry acquires a competitor either for the latter's order book to gain market share, or in some cases to shut down its capacity to help restore a situation where supply/demand is more balanced and trading conditions are more favourable.

There are also financial motives for acquisitions. If the share value or P/E ratio of a company is high, then a firm with a low share value or P/E ratio may be a tempting target. Indeed, this is one of the major stimuli for the more aggressively acquisitive companies. An extreme example is asset stripping, where the main motive for the acquisition is short-term gain by buying up undervalued assets and disposing of them piecemeal.

Sometimes there are reasons of cost efficiency which make acquisition look favourable. This cost efficiency could arise from the fact that an established company may already be a long way down the experience curve and have achieved efficiencies which would be difficult to match quickly by internal development. In public services, cost efficiency is usually the stated reason for merging units and/or rationalising provision.

Many of the problems associated with acquisition have been hinted at in the discussion of internal development. The overriding problem with acquisition lies in the ability to integrate the new company into the activities of the old. This often centres around problems of cultural fit. Where acquisition is being used to acquire new competences, this 'clash of cultures' may simply arise because the organisational routines are so different in each organisation. For example, a company which has grown and succeeded by dominating a particular segment of the market may feel the need to extend into the 'mainstream' and decide to do this by acquisition. It is likely that most of the routines of these two organisations will be very different: in manufacture, continuous flow versus batch production; in customer communications, advertising versus personal selling; in distribution, the use of intermediaries versus direct delivery, and so on.

Reasons for mergers may be similar to those for acquisitions. However, mergers are more typically the result of organisations coming together voluntarily. This is likely to be because they are actively seeking synergistic benefits, perhaps as a result of the common impact of a changing environment in terms of either opportunities or threats.

Illustration 7.7   Mergers and acquisitions in global industries

Survival in globalising industries requires reduction in unit costs and/or an improvement in products or services. Mergers and acquisitions may be one way of achieving this.

IT industry

In 1995, almost 3,000 deals were tracked by Broadway Associates — a US consultancy — some 57 per cent higher than 1994. The total value of deals was US$134 billion. The telecommunications sector saw the largest deals with 98 transactions worth over US$20 billion. This included the acquisition of 49.99 per cent of Belgacom (Belgian) by a consortium of Ameritech, Singapore Telecom and Tele Denmark, and the alliance between Cable and Wireless of the UK and Veba of Germany.

The most active sector was software and services with 356 deals. A significant proportion of these acquisitions were of 'national champions' being purchased from abroad by companies looking for critical mass to operate globally. For example, ADP — a US payroll systems specialist — bought GSI, its French equivalent, while Ceridian — number two in payroll — bought Centrefile from the Natwest Bank in the UK.

Many acquisitions were driven by the pace of technological change. Companies with expertise in the Internet or ISDN (transmission technology) were prime targets for takeover, with more than ten European specialists being acquired by US companies seeking their expertise.

Pharmaceutical industry

The pharmaceutical market has also seen a series of acquisitions and mergers:

- *The first wave of acquisitions* in the late 1980s (e.g. Bristol Myers Squibb and SmithKline Beecham) aimed to improve revenue by combining field forces to increase coverage and expand into new geographic areas. By the mid-1990s, the role of the traditional representative has been reduced and salesforce downsizing is commonplace.
- The second wave of *horizontal acquisitions* (American Home/Cyanamid, Roche/Syntex, Glaxo/Wellcome, Hoechst/MMD and Upjohn/Pharmacia) and cashless mergers (Pharmacia/Upjohn and Sandoz/Ciba) attempted to pool interests as well as benefit from cost synergies.
- *Vertical integration* (Merck/Medco, SB/DPS and Lilly/PCS) were seen as an attempt to diversify into faster-growing segments of the healthcare market. All three mergers took place in 1993/4, when the pharma market averaged only 3–4 per cent growth.
- *Technological acquisitions* (Roche/Genetech, Ciba/Chiron and Astra/Fisons) added long-term shareholder value by importing exclusive technology or products.
- *De-mergers* (ICI/Zeneca and Sandoz/Clariant) enabled corporations to conserve cash for more productive investment. (There is even an opinion that some companies may invest directly in healthcare insurance.)

Source: IT industry, *Financial Times*; pharmaceutical industry, PMSI International Consulting.
Prepared by Tony Jacobs, Cranfield School of Management.

The research evidence on the financial consequences of acquisitions is again inconclusive, in a similar way to the research on diversification (of course, diversification is often achieved through acquisition). However, some of the findings do act as a reminder that acquisition is not an easy or guaranteed route to improving financial performance. It may take the acquiring company some considerable time to gain any financial benefit from acquisitions.[22] Some studies confirm the importance of non-economic factors such as previous experience of acquisitions;[23] decisions on whether to remove or retain executives of the acquired company;[24] and the management of post-acquisition cultural issues.[25]

7.3.3 Joint developments and strategic alliances[26]

Joint development of new strategies has become increasingly popular particularly since the early 1980s.[27] This is because organisations cannot always cope with increasingly complex environments (such as globalisation) from internal resources and competences alone. They may see the need to obtain materials, skills, know-how, finance or access to markets, and recognise that these may be as readily available through co-operation as through ownership.

There are a variety of arrangements for joint developments and alliances. Some may be very formalised interorganisational relationships; at the other extreme, there can be very loose arrangements of co-operation and informal networking between organisations, with no shareholding or ownership involved. The reasons why these different forms of alliance might occur are varied, but they are likely to be concerned with the assets involved in the alliance. (It should be remembered here that the assets may not just be financial or physical, but could also include access to market, skills and intellectual property.) The form of the alliance is likely, therefore, to be influenced by the following:

- Asset *management*: the extent to which assets do or do not need to be managed jointly.
- Asset *separability*: the extent to which it is possible to separate the assets between the parties involved.
- Asset *appropriability*: the extent to which there is a risk of one or other of the parties involved appropriating the assets for themselves.

Figure 7.13 summarises the different forms of alliance that exist and how different factors might influence the form of the alliance.[28] In addition, the figure shows how the same factors might also affect the decision to acquire or merge, rather than to create an alliance.

Joint ventures are typically thought of as arrangements where organisations remain independent, but set up a newly created organisation jointly

	Loose (market) relationships	Contractual relationships	Formalised ownership/ relationships	Formal integration
FORMS OF ALLIANCE	Networks Opportunistic alliances	Subcontracting Licences and franchises	Consortia Joint ventures	Acquisitions and mergers
INFLUENCES Asset management	Assets do not need joint management	Asset management can be isolated	Assets need to be jointly managed	
Asset separability	Assets cannot be separated	Assets/skills can be separated		Assets cannot be separated
Asset appropriability	High risk of assets being appropriated	Low risk of assets being appropriated		High risk of asset appropriation

Source: Based on A. Gupta and H. Singh, 1991.

Figure 7.13   Types of and motives for strategic alliances

owned by the parents. The joint venture was a favoured means of beginning collaborative adventures between eastern and western European firms in the early 1990s, with eastern European firms providing labour, entry to markets and sometimes plant; and western companies providing expertise and finance.

Consortia may well involve two or more organisations in a joint venture arrangement, and will typically be more focused on a particular venture or project. Examples include large civil engineering projects, such as the Thames flood barrier, or major aerospace undertakings, such as the European Airbus. They might also exist between public sector organisations: for example, following the dissolution of the UK metropolitan county councils in 1986, functions such as public transport were taken over by co-ordinating consortia often involving both private and public sector organisations.

Joint ventures or consortia usually involve formalised interorganisational relationships in the form either of shareholding or of agreements specifying asset sharing and distribution of profits. Such formalised arrangements are likely to occur when the following conditions hold:

- The assets involved need to be jointly managed: for example, as with the setting up of a production unit.
- However, the assets can be separated from the parent companies without damaging knock-on effects on those companies: for example, expertise

can be specifically devoted to the joint venture without its removal harming the parents.

▪ At least in theory, there is a low risk that the assets could be appropriated by one or other party involved. Having said this, it has been argued that some firms enter joint ventures specifically to obtain know-how and expertise for their own internal development.

At the other extreme, *networks*[29] are arrangements whereby two or more organisations work in collaboration without formal relationships, but through a mechanism of mutual advantage and trust. Such networks can be enduring and provide considerable mutual benefit to the organisations involved. Network organisations are discussed more fully in Chapter 9 (section 9.2.7). Illustration 7.8 shows how networks have been created in the airline industry by 'code-sharing' arrangements, allowing passengers to use several 'partner' airlines while travelling on a single ticket. *Opportunistic alliances* might also arise focused around particular ventures or projects, but again may not be highly formalised. In this sense, these arrangements are much nearer to market relationships than to contractual relationships. They may exist for a number of reasons:

▪ Assets do not need joint management — capital, expertise, know-how and so on can come together more informally.

▪ Assets cannot be separated easily from the firms involved, or without harm being done: for example, it may be that one partner is providing access to distribution channels which are part of the company's operation as a whole.

▪ If the assets involved were split off into a separate organisation, there would be a high risk of their being appropriated by another party. This would be particularly the case for the know-how and skills of the different parties involved.

Many intermediate arrangements exist. One such is *franchising*, perhaps the best-known examples of which are Coca-Cola and McDonald's. Here the franchise holder undertakes specific activities such as manufacturing, distribution or selling, but the franchiser is responsible for the brand name, marketing and probably training. *Licensing* is common in science-based industries, where, for example, the right to manufacture a patented product is granted for a fee. With *subcontracting*, a company chooses to subcontract particular services or part of a process: for example, increasingly in public services responsibility for waste removal, cleaning and so on may be subcontracted to private companies.

All these intermediate arrangements are likely to be contractual in nature, but are unlikely to involve ownership. They typically arise for two reasons:

▪ Particular assets can be isolated for the purposes of management: for example, manufacturing under licence.

Illustration 7.8   Strategic alliances in the airline industry

Many forms of co-operation exist in the airline industry. These range from total takeover, through partial equity swaps, franchising and code-sharing deals, to simple marketing alliances on a particular route.

Code-share, where airlines of a similar type sell each other connecting services on a single ticket, has become so popular that it has been dubbed the 'poor man's takeover'. *Airline Business* magazine identified 320 such alliances, which include nearly all the world's top airlines and exclude many of the poorer or up-and-coming players.

The fashion began when the well-established Swissair–Delta–Singapore Airlines alliance, which covered three continents, bolstered by a token equity swap, contributed to the failure of the ambitious merger between KLM Royal Dutch, Scandinavian Airlines, Swissair and Austrian. This collapse marked the end of the fashion for equity purchases. In its wake came the birth of the code-share.

Sir Michael Bishop, Chairman of British Midland Airways (BMA), who always distrusted the grandiose takeover despite the fact that 40 per cent of his airline is owned by Scandinavian Airlines, has led the way in code-sharing deals. British Midland now has ten such partnerships, the latest with Virgin Atlantic. All are supposed to be similar in service standards, and all have their own further partnerships, to which they would be expected to 'on-sell' the passenger.

For example, a business person with a British Midland ticket might fly from Glasgow to London on BMA, to New York with Virgin, on to Dallas with Virgin's friends at Delta, pick up its partner Aeromexico before heading south, switch to Aeromexico's friend Japan Airlines to the Far East, and fly Thai and Lufthansa on the way home.

The EU is concerned that such deals discourage airlines from starting their own new routes, and if left unchecked will over time recreate the cartels of the 1960s, where cosy understandings helped state-owned monoliths avoid head-to-head competition for 30 years to the detriment of both service and price. While the EU cannot force private companies to open new routes, recent moves suggest that it may address issues like code-sharing as a warning to some carriers not to get lazy.

Source: *Sunday Times,* 2 July 1995.
Prepared by Sara Martin, Cranfield School of Management.

- These assets can be separated from the parent firm to their advantage: for example, by setting up distribution or manufacturing in a country in which it would find difficulty operating.

Licensing or franchising is likely to take place, however, where there is a low risk of the assets involved being appropriated: for example, patent protection would prevent such appropriation for a licence holder. A less durable arrangement may be more appropriate if there is a risk of appropriation, as with a subcontracting arrangement, where the sub-contractor may already be operating in the sphere of activity involved.

In passing, it is worth noting that reasons for taking on full ownership in the form of acquisitions and mergers can also be explained in similar ways. Acquisitions and mergers are likely to take place where: (a) assets need joint management; (b) assets cannot be separated readily from either firm in-volved; and (c) there is a high risk of asset appropriation. Indeed, arguably the last two reasons are why an acquisition might be more attractive than a joint venture.

One research study of international strategic alliances[30] confirmed that the primary motivation to form alliances was the need for specific resources and competences to survive and succeed in globalising markets — particularly where technologies were changing too. Partners were chosen with these issues in mind. However, the success of alliances tended to be more dependent on how they were managed and the way in which the partners fostered the evolution of the partnership. For example, the following were found to be important:

- Proactive attitudes to commitment, trust and cultural sensitivity. An example would be the relationships between family companies — based on long-standing business and social relationships between the families.
- Clear organisational arrangements — particularly concerning activities which crossed or connected the partners.
- The desire of all partners to achieve organisational learning from the alli-ance rather than to use partners to substitute for their lack of competences.
- Allowing the alliance to evolve and change rather than prescribing it too parochially at the outset.
- Efforts by partners to achieve strong interpersonal relationships, including bonding and flexibility to changing circumstances.

7.4 Summary

This chapter has been concerned with both the *directions* in which an organisation's strategy might develop and the *methods* through which this might be achieved.

The choice of *direction* will be influenced by a number of factors:

- The extent to which the organisation is competitive within its current field of operation, and therefore has real opportunities to *protect* its current position into the future.
- Whether there are opportunities for *improvement* within the current field of operation. This may be about consolidating the organisation's position through improving performance in key areas of competence, such as

quality or innovation. It may be that this improved performance could provide opportunities to gain market share (market penetration).

- The extent to which the organisation is able to gain advantage through creating new products within its current competences, or to develop new competences to perform better within current markets.
- Whether the organisation's products and core competences can be exploited further in new markets. This may mean extension into new segments of the market, new uses for current products or geographical expansion.
- It may also involve diversification in several ways: by developing new products for new markets on the basis of the current core competences of the organisation; by creating new markets through exploiting current core competences; or — the most challenging form of diversification — by the development of new competences and their exploitation in new markets.

Organisations also have choices on *how* they will pursue new directions. Internal development has the major advantage of building the resource and competence base of the organisation as part of the strategy implementation. This might include the important competence of gaining market knowledge for new arenas of operation. In contrast, acquisitions can be appropriate provided the organisation is able to avoid the very real problems of post-merger integration and the difficulties of cultural fit mentioned above. The track record on this is not good.

Strategic alliances provide a variety of development methods which bridge these two extremes. These range from loose market-like relationships, such as networks, to tight formalised contractual relationships, such as joint ventures. The appropriateness of each method needs to be judged in relation to a number of factors regarding the asset base of the alliance. These are concerned with practical issues about the management of the assets and the risk of appropriation of those assets by the separate partners. The most successful alliances appear to be those where partners have positive attitudes to managing and evolving the relationship, and are concerned with using the alliance to improve their own competences through learning, rather than simply substituting for competences which they lack.

Together, Chapters 6 and 7 have provided a framework against which strategic options can be identified. Each development strategy for organisations consists of three strands concerning the *basis*, *direction* and *method* of development. Chapter 8 will look at ways in which strategic options can be evaluated as part of the process of strategic choice.

References

1. This figure is an extension of the product/market matrix: see H. Ansoff, *Corporate Strategy*, Penguin, 1988, chapter 6.

2. Downsizing can be difficult to achieve for a variety of reasons, as discussed in W. Cascio, 'Downsizing: what do we know? What have we learnt?', *Academy of Management Executive*, vol. 7, no. 1 (1993), pp. 95–104.

3. Divestment has been of concern in an international context for some considerable time. See J. Coyne and M. Wright (eds.), *Divestment and Strategic Change*, Philip Allan, 1986; M. McDermott, *Multinationals: Foreign divestment and disclosure*, McGraw-Hill, 1989.

4. M. Wright, B. Chiplin and S. Thompson, 'The market for corporate control: divestments and buy-outs', in M. Bishop and J. Kay (eds.), *European Mergers and Merger Policy*, Oxford University Press, 1993.

5. The PIMS data are collected from organisations which subscribe to the services offered by the Strategic Planning Institute. The data shown here are aggregate data, but subscribers are able to access data more specific to their industry sector. More details of the PIMS methodology can be found in R.D. Buzzell and B.T. Gale, *The PIMS Principles*, Free Press, 1987.

6. PIMS, 'Marketing: in pursuit of the perfect mix', *Marketing*, 31 October 1991.

7. A. Clayton and C. Carroll, 'Building business for Europe', *Panorama of EU Industry*, 1995. This was a study of competitiveness undertaken jointly by PIMS Associates and the Irish Management Institute for the European Commission.

8. For a review of the effect of these changes in the public sector, see P. Jackson and C. Price, *Privatisation and Regulation: A review of the issues*, Longman, 1994.

9. Turnaround is discussed in S. Slatter, *Corporate Recovery*, Penguin, 1984. An approach to reshaping capabilities to achieve turnaround is provided by C. Baden-Fuller and J. Stopford, *Rejuvenating the Mature Business: The competitive challenge*, 2nd edition, Routledge, 1995.

10. For a full discussion of building global market participation, see G. Yip, *Total Global Strategy*, Prentice Hall, 1995, chapter 3.

11. See A. Campbell and K. Luchs, *Strategic Synergy*, Butterworth-Heinemann, 1992.

12. V. Ramanujam and P. Varadarajan, 'Research on corporate diversification: a synthesis', *Strategic Management Journal*, vol. 10, no. 6 (1989) pp. 523–551, is a comprehensive review article on this topic.

13. R.P. Rumelt, *Strategy, Structure and Economic Performance*, Harvard University Press, 1974.

14. C.A. Montgomery, 'The measurement of firm diversification: some new empirical evidence', *Academy of Management Journal*, vol. 25, no. 2 (1982) pp. 299–307.

15. R.M. Grant, A.P. Jammine and H. Thomas, 'Diversity, diversification and profitability among British manufacturing companies, 1972–84', *Academy of Management Journal*, vol. 31, no. 4 (1988) pp. 771–801.

16. See T. Clayton, 'Services in focus', *PIMSletter no. 49*, PIMS Europe Ltd, 1992.

17. M.E. Porter, 'From competitive advantage to competitive strategy', *Harvard Business Review*, vol. 65, no. 3 (1987) pp. 43–59.

18. P. Varadarajan and V. Ramanujam, 'Diversification and performance: a re-examination using a new two-dimensional conceptualisation of diversity in firms', *Academy of Management*, vol. 30, no. 2 (1987), pp. 380–93.

19. See A. Campbell and K. Luchs, 'Towards some new propositions on synergy', Ashridge Strategic Management Centre, 1990, for a summary of findings.

20. S. Chatterjee and B. Wernerfelt, 'The link between resources and type of diversification', *Strategic Management Journal*, vol. 12, no. 1 (1991) pp. 33–48.

21. Good discussions of the reasons for, and problems with, mergers and acquisitions can be found in D. Jemison and P. Haspeslagh, *Managing Acquisitions: Creating value through corporate renewal*, Free Press, 1991; J. McTaggart, P. Kontes and M. Mankins, *The Value Imperative*, Free Press, 1994; and J. Kay, *Foundations of Corporate Success*, Oxford University Press, 1993, chapter 10. A number of useful case studies are included in A. Grundy, *Breakthrough Strategies*

for Growth, Pitman, 1995.

22. C. Loderer and K. Martin, 'Postacquisition performance of acquiring firms', *Financial Management*, vol. 21, no. 3 (1992), pp. 69–79.

23. G. Bruton, B. Oviatt and M. White, 'Performance of acquisition of distressed firms', *Academy of Management Journal*, vol. 37, no. 4 (1994), pp. 972–89.

24. A. Cannella and D. Hambrick, 'Effects of executive departures on the performance of acquired firms', *Strategic Management Journal*, vol. 14, (Summer 1993), pp. 137–52.

25. H. Ingham, I. Kran and A. Lovestam, 'Mergers and profitability: a managerial success story?', *Journal of Management Studies*, vol. 29, no. 2 (1992), pp. 195–208.

26. Two useful books on strategic alliances are: D. Faulkner, *Strategic Alliances: Co-operating to compete*, McGraw-Hill, 1995; and P. Lorange and J. Roos, *Strategic Alliances: Formation, implementation and evolution*, Blackwell, 1992.

27. K. Glaister and P. Buckley, 'UK international joint ventures: an analysis of patterns of activity and distribution', *British Journal of Management*, vol. 5, no. 1 (1994), pp. 33–51.

28. This figure is from A. Gupta and H. Singh, 'The governance of synergy: inter-SBU co-ordination versus external strategic alliances', Academy of Management annual conference, Miami, 1991.

29. Networks are discussed fully in J.C. Jarillo, *Strategic Networks: Creating the borderless organisation*, Butterworth-Heinemann, 1993.

30. See Faulkner (reference 26 above), chapter 16.

Recommended key readings

- M.E. Porter, *Competitive Advantage*, Free Press, 1985, discusses the logic of how strategies can be chosen dependent on the situation of the organisation.

- The work of the PIMS project and many of the findings are summarised in R.D. Buzzell and B.T. Gale, *The PIMS Principles*, Free Press, 1987.

- A good discussion of the reasons for, and problems with, mergers and acquisitions can be found in D. Jemison and P. Haspeslagh, *Managing Acquisitions: Creating value through corporate renewal*, Free Press, 1991, and A. Grundy, *Breakthrough Strategies for Growth*, Pitman, 1995.

- A useful book on strategic alliances is D. Faulkner, *Strategic Alliances: Cooperating to compete*, McGraw-Hill, 1995.

- Networks are discussed fully in J.C. Jarillo, *Strategic Networks: Creating the borderless organisation*, Butterworth-Heinemann, 1993.

Work assignments

7.1 Referring back to Figure 6.2, identify possible development strategies in terms of their combination of *direction* and *method* of development in one of the following:
   (a) The Brewery Group (Denmark)*
   (b) Coopers Creek*
   (c) an organisation of your choice.

7.2 *Given incursions by Japanese firms in the automobile industry (or an industry of your choice), evaluate the strategic positioning of two competing western firms (e.g. PSA Peugeot Citroën* and Rover/Honda*).*

7.3   **In the case of Kronenbourg,* Laura Ashley* or an organisation of your choice, write a brief for the management explaining how the PIMS findings should influence their choice of strategies.**

7.4   **Illustration 7.3 shows organisations which are committed to vertical integration within their industry. Make a critical appraisal of the advantages and disadvantages of vertical integration and explain the circumstances in which it is most likely to succeed or fail.**

7.5   With reference to Figure 7.9, map the development direction of the diversified interests of The News Corporation,* Laura Ashley* or an organisation of your choice in terms of backward, forward or horizontal integration. Explain how and why these have been changed over time.

7.6   *It has been argued that diversification in many companies has not led to better performance. Indeed, as seen in Illustration 7.6, many organisations are now restructuring and/or divesting in order to create more focused companies or business units. Discuss the potential benefits and dangers of diversification and refocusing by drawing on these examples and others with which you are familiar.*

7.7   *Referring to Illustration 7.3 and using additional examples of your own, criticise the argument that 'Synergy is a sound basis for acquisition.' Refer to P.C. Haspeslagh and D.M. Jemison, Managing Acquisitions, Macmillan, 1991, to assist with this assignment.*

7.8   In the light of your analysis and discussion in assignment 7.6, write a short (one paragraph) statement to a chief executive who has asked you to advise whether or not the company should diversify. Write a similar statement to the chief executive of a hospital.

7.9   Referring to section 7.3 and Figure 7.13 in particular, examine the reasons for the following:
   (a) the mergers and acquisitions in the IT and pharmaceutical industries (Illustration 7.7)
   (b) code sharing in the airline industry (Illustration 7.8)
   (c) the Rover/Honda alliance*
   (d) two acquisitions or alliances of your choice.

7.10   *'Strategic alliances will not survive in the long term if they are simply seen as ways of "blocking gaps" in an organisation's resource base or competences.' Discuss this in relation to any alliances with which you are familiar, or Rover/Honda.**

*This refers to a case in the Text and Cases version of this book.

CHAPTER 8

Strategy evaluation and selection

8.1 Introduction and evaluation criteria

The previous two chapters have discussed the strategic options available to organisations. This chapter will discuss how strategic options can be evaluated and the processes by which organisations might select strategies for the future. It is not the intention of the chapter to describe in detail a whole plethora of analytical techniques. Rather, the aim is to help readers understand the contribution that different types of technique can make in evaluating and selecting strategies.[1]

In assessing strategies — whether by formal or informal processes — there are three types of *evaluation criterion* which can be used:

▫ *Suitability* is a broad assessment of whether the strategy addresses the circumstances in which the organisation is operating (perhaps identified in a strategic analysis): for example, the extent to which new strategies would *fit* with the future trends/changes in the environment; or how the strategy might exploit the core competences of the organisation. This can often be the basis of a *qualitative* assessment concerned with testing out the *rationale* of a strategy and, as such, can be useful for *screening* options, as seen below.

▫ *Acceptability* is concerned with the expected *performance outcomes* (such as the *return* or *risk*) if the strategy were implemented, and the extent to which these would be in line with the *expectations of stakeholders*.

▫ *Feasibility* is concerned with whether the strategy could be made to work in practice. Assessing the feasibility of a strategy requires an emphasis on more detailed — often *quantitative* — assessment of the practicalities of *resourcing* and strategic capability.

Figure 8.1 shows how these various aspects of evaluation and selection can be fitted together, and builds on the issues previously discussed concerning strategic analysis and strategic options.

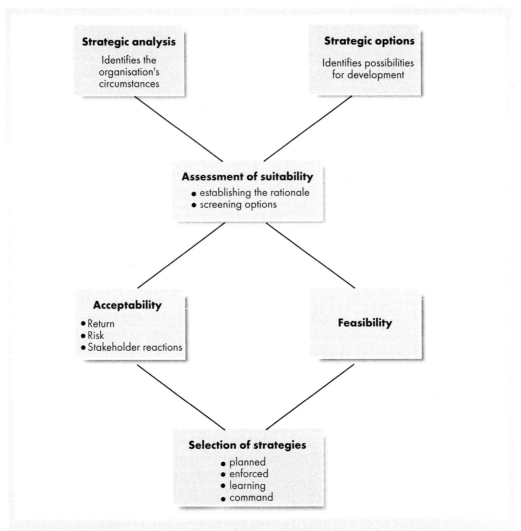

Figure 8.1   A framework for the evaluation and selection of strategies

8.2   Assessing suitability

Assessing the suitability of strategic options can be a useful basis on which to screen options before more detailed analyses are undertaken concerning the acceptability and feasibility of those options. This process can consist of two stages: first, establishing the rationale/strategic logic for each strategic option *in its own right*; and second, establishing the *relative* merits of an option when a number of choices are available through processes for *screening* options for further evaluation. This section looks at each of these aspects of evaluation.

8.2.1 Establishing the rationale

The assessment of suitability of a particular strategy is concerned with whether it addresses the circumstances in which the organisation is operating and/or wishes to operate. It can be a useful discipline to ask the 'champions' of new strategies to describe, clearly and succinctly, *why is this a good idea?*

This clearly relates back to the discussions in Part II of this book, since the main purpose of strategic analysis is to establish an understanding of the basis on which the suitability of strategies can be judged. For example, it will consist of assessing the extent to which a strategy:

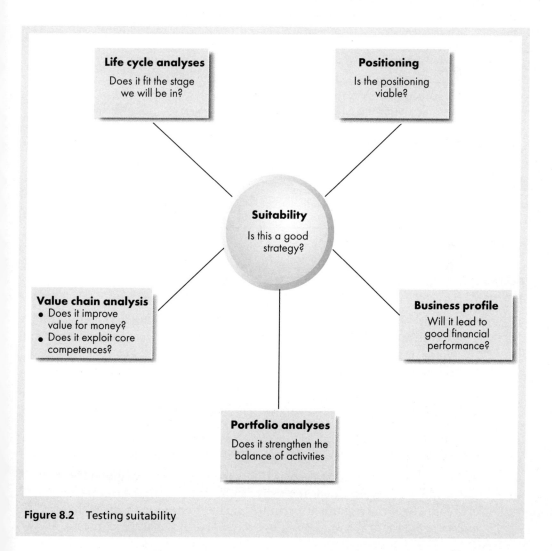

Figure 8.2   Testing suitability

STAGES OF INDUSTRY MATURITY

	Embryonic	Growth	Mature	Ageing
Dominant	Fast grow Start-up	Fast grow Attain cost leadership Renew Defend position	Defend position Attain cost leadership Renew Fast grow	Defend position Focus Renew Grow with industry
Strong	Start-up Differentiate Fast grow	Fast grow Catch-up Attin cost leadership Differentiate	Attain cost leadership Renew, focus Differentiate Grow with industry	Find niche Hold niche Hang-in Grow with industry Harvest
Favourable	Start-up Differentiate Focus Fast grow	Differentiate, focus Catch-up Grow with industry	Harvest, hang-in Find niche, hold niche Renew, turnaround Differentiate, focus Grow with industry	Retrench Turnaround
Tenable	Start-up Grow with industry Focus	Harvest, catch-up Hold niche, hang-in Find niche Turnaround Focus Grow with industry	Harvest Turnaround Find niche Retrench	Divest Retrench
Weak	Find niche Catch-up Grow with industry	Turnaround Retrench	Withdraw Divest	Withdraw

COMPETITIVE POSITION

Source: Arthur D. Little

Figure 8.3   The life cycle/portfolio matrix

- exploits the *opportunities* in the environment and avoids the *threats*.
- capitalises on the organisation's *strengths* and *core competences* and avoids or remedies the *weaknesses*.
- addresses the cultural and political context (as discussed in Chapter 5).

Figure 8.2 summarises different categories of analytical technique and the main contribution which they make to assessing the suitability of strategies.

Life cycle analyses[2]

These assess whether a strategy is likely to be appropriate given the stage of the product life cycle. Some analyses combine this with the relative strength or weakness of the organisation in its market to produce a *life cycle/portfolio matrix* (see Figure 8.3). The life cycle/portfolio matrix consists of two dimensions. The *market situation* is described in four stages ranging from embryonic to ageing; the *competitive position* in five categories ranging from weak to dominant. The purpose of the matrix is to establish the appropriateness of particular strategies in relation to these two dimensions. The crucial issue is establishing where an organisation is currently positioned on the matrix, and therefore what types of strategy are most likely to be suitable:

▓   The *position within the life cycle* can be determined in relation to eight external factors or descriptors of the evolutionary stage of the industry. These are: market growth rate, growth potential, breadth of product lines, number of competitors, spread of market share between these competitors, customer loyalty, entry barriers and technology. It is the balance of these factors which determines the life cycle stage. For example, an embryonic industry is characterised by rapid growth, changes in technology, fragmented market shares and pursuit of new customers. In contrast, ageing industries are best described by falling demand, declining number of competitors and, often, a narrow product line.

▓   The *competitive position* of the organisation within its industry can also be established by looking at the characteristics of each category in Figure 8.3. A *dominant* position is rare in the private sector and usually results from a quasi-monopoly. In the public sector, this may be a legalised monopoly status (e.g. public utilities). *Strong* organisations are those that can follow strategies of their own choice without too much concern for competition. A *favourable* position is where no single competitor stands out, but the leaders are better placed (as in grocery retailing in France or the UK). A *tenable* position is that which can be maintained by specialisation or focus. *Weak* competitors are ones which are too small to survive independently in the long run.

The danger is that such a detailed matrix can suggest that strategic choice is a simplistic affair; it is not and so, the A.D. Little matrix can only be helpful in guiding strategic choice.

Positioning

Positioning is a key test of suitability and was discussed in Chapter 6. The choice of generic product/market strategies forms the basis or framework within which the more detailed directions and methods of development are constructed. So assessing whether current and future positionings are viable can be done by asking whether *demand* is likely to grow or decline. For example, in mature markets, the size of the core market is often reduced by the development of a number of smaller viable 'niches'; the degree of *competitive rivalry* which exists; and the *relative competence* of the

A	B1	B2	C			
Resources and competences underpinning strategy	Which of these resources/competences are likely to create:		Which will be sustainable/ difficult to imitate			
	Cost reduction	Added value in terms of needs perceived by customers	Valued	Rare	Complex	Tacit

Figure 8.4 Assessing the suitability of a product/market strategy

organisation in facing these competitive rivals with a particular product/ market positioning. For example, the extent to which the organisation's unit costs are better than competitive rivals will determine the long-term viability of a low-price positioning. The uniqueness of the competences which underpin the value-added features of a product or service will determine the suitability of a positioning of differentiation. The extent to which an organisation is capable of supporting a particular positioning in its markets can be tested as follows:

- The first step in assessing the suitability of a particular strategy would be to list out the key resources and competences underpinning the strategy (column A in Figure 8.4).
- Second, these are 'scored' against the different bases of the product/ market strategy. Column B1 (cost reduction) is particularly important for route 2 or 3 in the strategy clock discussed in Chapter 6 (Figure 6.4). Column B2 (perceived added value) is particularly important for positionings on the strategy clock of 3, 4 or 5. So the question is asked: would this particular resource or competence underpin cost reduction (B1) or add to perceived value (B2)? A score (1–5) is then given in each column. For example, a competence in bulk purchasing may score highly in B1, but quite low in B2. In contrast, in-house R&D activities, although costly, may be the source of unique product features which are highly valued by customers.

▪ Finally, each of these resources and competences is revisited to establish whether it is sustainable and/or difficult to imitate: in other words, whether it is a genuinely unique resource or core competence (as seen in Figure 4.2) and hence provides competitive advantage to the organisation. The criteria used to judge this would include: whether it is valued by buyers; if it is rare; if it is complex to reproduce; and if it is embedded in the tacit knowledge of the organisation. Usually, this analysis reveals that very few resources and competences are difficult to imitate. Rather, it is likely to be the ability to manage linkages between separate activities and the tacit knowledge of the organisation that provides competitive advantage, as highlighted in Chapter 6.

▪ Assessing the relationship between the generic product/market strategy and the strategic capability of the organisation (resources and competences) will also be useful in a more detailed assessment of the feasibility of one or more strategies. This is often called *resource deployment analysis* and is discussed below (section 8.4.3). It is also a central consideration in preparing resource plans for implementing strategies, and *critical success factors analysis* is designed to ensure that the key resources and core competences will actually be in place to match the product/market positioning. This is part of establishing and maintaining the appropriate strategic architecture for an organisation, and is discussed in section 10.3.1 of Chapter 10.

Value chain analysis

Chapter 4 emphasised that understanding how cost was controlled and value created within the value system is very important when assessing the strategic capability of an organisation. It has also been mentioned above that an assessment of the type shown in Figure 8.4 usually reveals that the key to sustainable success can be found in the way the value system is *configured* — that the *linkages* between value activities are just as important as the competence in the separate activities. Therefore, the suitability of strategic developments may *also* be tested by the extent to which the strategy will reconfigure the value chain in a way which improves value for money and the competitive position of the organisation, as shown in Illustration 8.1.

The concept of *synergy*[3] is concerned with assessing how much extra benefit (value for money) can be created from reconfiguring the linkages in the value chain. Synergy can be sought in several circumstances, as is illustrated by the three strategies under consideration for the grocery retailer in Illustration 8.1:

▪ *Market development* (buying more shops) may improve performance in the value system, since it provides a further opportunity to exploit a good

Illustration 8.1   Value chain analysis: a worked example

Due to recent success, a grocery retailer has a large cash reserve and is considering expanding his operations. However, he is unsure whether he should buy more shops, expand into the alcoholic drink market, or open a cash-and-carry wholesaler. He undertakes a value chain analysis to assess what extra synergistic benefits would be obtained if each strategy were adopted by providing linkages within the current value system.

Degree of synergy with present activities	Strategy 1: Buy more shops	Strategy 2: Expand into alcoholic drink	Strategy 3: Open cash-and-carry wholesaler
Use of cash	Produces profit from idle cash	Produces profit from idle cash	Produces profit from idle cash
Use of premises	None	More turnover/ floor space	None
Use of stock	Perhaps small gains from moving stock between shops	None	Reduction of stock in shops as quick delivery guaranteed
Purchasing	Possible discounts for bulk	None	Reduced prices to shops
Market image	Good name helps launch (i.e. cost of launch reduced)	None	Little

corporate image, and hence 'launch costs' are minimised compared with a new entrant. Buying power should also increase.

- *Product development* (into alcoholic drinks) would improve the use of a key resource (floor space), and cash is available to fund initial stock.
- *Backward integration* (into wholesaling) may well produce cost advantage if better stock planning can be achieved between the wholesale and retail partners.

Synergy could arise through many different types of link or interrelationship: for example, in the market (by exploiting brand name, sharing outlets or pooling selling or promotional activities); in the company's operations (by shared purchasing, facilities, maintenance, quality control, etc.); and in product/process development (by sharing information/know-how). Synergy is often used as a justification for product/market *diversification*, particularly through acquisition or merger.

Portfolio analyses[4]

Chapter 6 discussed how portfolio analysis can be used to establish the basis for an organisation's approach to diversity. Therefore, when evaluating *specific options* for the future, they can be plotted on to a matrix (see, for example, Figure 4.11) and the long-term rationale of business development can be highlighted. For example, if the original BCG matrix were used, the following questions could be asked:

- Will the strategy move the company to a dominant position in its markets? Which strategies are most likely to ensure a move from *question marks* through to *stars* and eventually to *cash cows*?
- Since stars generally require an investment of funds, will there be sufficient cash cows to provide this necessary investment? A major reason for company bankruptcies is that a firm may invest heavily in the promotion and stocking policy for products in rapid growth, without profitable and well-established products from which it can fund these new ventures.
- The matrix can also help in thinking about *acquisition* strategy. Companies that embark on acquisition programmes may forget that the most likely targets for acquisition programmes are not the stars and cash cows of the business world, but the question marks or dogs. There may be nothing wrong with acquiring a question mark, provided the resources and competences are there to move it towards stardom, bearing in mind the need for parenting skills as discussed in Chapter 6, and the real costs and difficulties of acquisition as pointed out in Chapter 7.

Business profile

The PIMS database discussed in Chapter 7 can be used to profile the strategy of a strategic business unit against the parameters which PIMS has researched in relation to the strategy/performance match.[5] Illustration 8.2 shows how this profiling is done.

- The current strategic position of the frozen food business is 'scored' against the eleven parameters in Illustration 8.2(a). Evidence from the PIMS database shows that there are several factors associated with this business which serve to lower its expected financial performance, such as weak relative market share, poor relative quality position, high marketing intensity and complex logistics. Some parameters, on the

Illustration 8.2 Profiling an acquisition

The PIMS database can be used to profile the strategy of an SBU against the parameters which PIMS research in relation to the strategy/performance match. Sometimes it can suggest that a particular strategy, such as an acquisition, would weaken the business profile (of the combined company).

Bad ←——————————————————→ Good

Parameter	Bad							Good
Relative share	Weak		■					Strong
Relative quality	Inferior			■				Superior
Capital intensity	High						■	Low
Capital mix	Fixed					■		Liquid
Capacity utilisation	Low						■	High
Productivity	Below par					■		Above par
Real market growth	Decline					■		Growth
New products	Many				None			Some
Marketing intensity	High	■						Low
Bargaining power	Weak					■		Strong
Logistics	Complex	■						Simple

➡ Par ROCE ∼ 15%

(a) A frozen food marketing business, considering buying its supplier

Bad ←——————————————————→ Good

Parameter	Bad							Good
Relative share	Weak	■						Strong
Relative quality	Inferior				■			Superior
Capital intensity	High	■						Low
Capital mix	Fixed			■				Liquid
Capacity utilisation	Low			■				High
Productivity	Below par				■			Above par
Real market growth	Decline					■		Growth
New products	Many				None			Some
Marketing intensity	High						■	Low
Bargaining power	Weak	■						Strong
Logistics	Complex						■	Simple

➡ Par ROCE ∼ 10%

(b) The freezing business

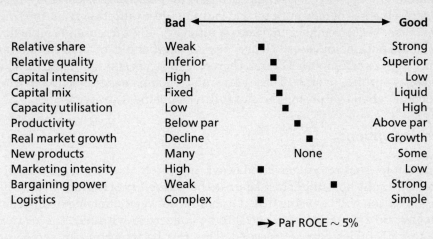

	Bad ◄————————————————————► Good			
Relative share	Weak	■		Strong
Relative quality	Inferior	■		Superior
Capital intensity	High	■		Low
Capital mix	Fixed	■		Liquid
Capacity utilisation	Low	■		High
Productivity	Below par	■		Above par
Real market growth	Decline	■		Growth
New products	Many	None		Some
Marketing intensity	High	■		Low
Bargaining power	Weak	■		Strong
Logistics	Complex	■		Simple

➤ Par ROCE ∼ 5%

(c) The combined business

Source: PIMS Associates Ltd. Reproduced with permission.

other hand, are more positive, such as asset flexibility, low capital intensity, high capacity utilisation and strong bargaining power with suppliers. This results in an above-average position overall and a likelihood of this business being able to cover its cost of capital.

▪ The company is considering backward integration through the acquisition of its major supplier of frozen food. The strategic position of this business is profiled separately (see Illustration 8.2(b)). It can be seen that, although there are some parameters which may give the business some strength (low marketing intensity and simple logistics), the overall profile is relatively weak, largely due to a combination of high capital intensity and low share. A business like this, based on comparison with others, would normally earn returns below the cost of capital, but still better than break-even.

▪ Illustration 8.2(c) shows how the combined businesses would look after an acquisition which merged the activities into a single integrated company. The result is a business with no real strengths and the weak characteristics of both businesses. Its expected performance would be worse than both its component parts — not a surprising conclusion in this case, since the managers were planning to pit the newly integrated business against the might of Unilever! A clear case of negative synergy.

▪ The important issue, however, is that these drivers of profitability are interconnected, and building a strong business profile is more difficult than might appear. For example, a gain in relative market share may require the use of new outlets, and gaining these outlets may, in the first instance, require higher marketing intensity and increased complexity in distribution logistics. Hence any strengthening of one parameter may well weaken others and therefore not necessarily improve the business profile overall. These interrelationships need to be taken into account when evaluating the suitability of business strategies.

8.2.2 Screening options

The previous section summarised ways in which the merits of specific strategies might be established against the *suitability* criterion. Typically, an organisation will be trying to make choices between a number of different strategies. So evaluation also needs to be concerned with how the *relative* merits of strategies can be assessed. This can be important in screening options before a more detailed assessment of acceptability and feasibility is undertaken.

This is not to suggest that options eliminated at this stage of evaluation should be excluded from further consideration, since the process tends to be iterative in practice. This section begins by reviewing the basis on which specific strategies can be assessed — whether options are to be judged on an absolute basis, against each other, or against the 'do nothing' situation.

The section outlines three contrasting approaches to the screening of options (see Figure 8.5):

- *Ranking* options against a set of predetermined factors concerning the organisation's strategic situation. The extent to which specific options fit these criteria determines their position in this 'league table'.

The relative suitability of strategic options can be assessed by:

METHOD	APPROACH
Ranking	• Options are assessed against key factors in the environment, resources and stakeholder expectations. • A score (and ranking) is established for each option.
Decision trees	• Options are progressively 'eliminated' by introducing further criteria.
Scenario planning	• Options are matched to different future scenarios. • Contingency plans are prepared.

Figure 8.5   Screening strategic options

■ *Decision trees*, which also assess specific options against a list of key strategic factors. However, options are ranked by progressively eliminating others.

■ *Scenarios*, which attempt to match specific options with a range of possible future outcomes and are particularly useful where a high degree of uncertainty exists (say, in the environment, as discussed in Chapter 3). Scenarios provide a means of keeping many more options under consideration.

Bases for comparison

Chapter 4 has already discussed the importance of establishing an appropriate basis for comparison when assessing strategic capability. This is also needed during evaluation. If strategies are assessed only in absolute terms or against industry norms, this does not address a central issue in

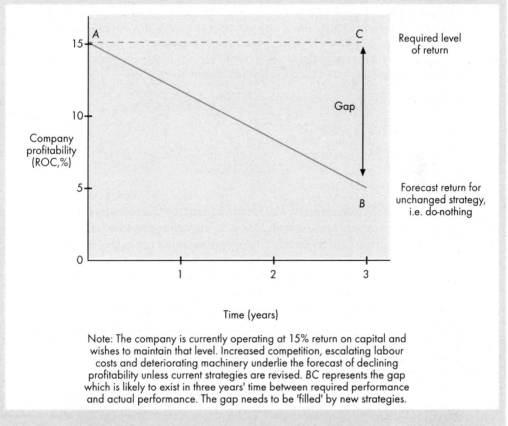

Note: The company is currently operating at 15% return on capital and wishes to maintain that level. Increased competition, escalating labour costs and deteriorating machinery underlie the forecast of declining profitability unless current strategies are revised. BC represents the gap which is likely to exist in three years' time between required performance and actual performance. The gap needs to be 'filled' by new strategies.

Figure 8.6   Gap analysis

Illustration 8.3 Ranking options: Churchill Pottery

In 1990 Churchill Pottery, based in Stoke-on-Trent, UK, was one of the subjects of a BBC series entitled *Troubleshooter*, where the management teams of a number of companies were invited to discuss their organisation's strategic development with Sir John Harvey-Jones (ex-Chairman of ICI). Like many traditional manufacturing companies at the time, Churchill found itself under increasing pressure from cheaper imports in its traditional markets, and was considering whether to move 'upmarket' by launching a new range aimed at the design-conscious end of the market. The ranking exercise opposite was done by a group of participants on a management programme having seen the Churchill Pottery video.

The results of the ranking are interesting. First, they highlight the need to do *something*. Second, the radical departures in strategy — such as moves into retailing or diversification — are regarded as unsuitable. They do not address the problems of the core business, do not fit the capabilities of Churchill and would not fit culturally. This leaves related developments as the front runners — as might be expected in a traditional manufacturing firm like Churchill. The choice essentially boils down to significant investments in cost reduction to support an essentially 'commodity' approach to the market (options 2 and 5) or an 'added value' attack on the growing 'upmarket' segments. The company chose the latter and with some success — presumably helped by their wide television exposure through the *Troubleshooter* series.

strategy evaluation: namely, the need to identify the *incentive to change* from the present strategy to a new strategy. It may therefore be helpful to use the 'do nothing' situation to assess the organisation's incentive to change.

The 'do nothing' situation represents the likely outcome if the organisation were to continue with current strategies, disregarding any changes occurring in the environment or the resource position of the company. The easiest way to incorporate this situation into an evaluation is by including it as a strategic option to be evaluated alongside others. However, it must be remembered that 'do nothing' is not usually an option *per se* — it merely provides a valuable base line against which to assess the incentive to change.

A useful technique which incorporates this approach is *gap analysis*, which can be used to identify the extent to which existing strategies will fail to meet the performance objectives in the future.

Figure 8.6 outlines the analysis for a single product/single market

Strategic options	Key strategic factors						Ranking
	Family ownership	Investment funds	Low price imports	Lack of marketing/ design skills	Automation low	Consumer taste (design)	
1. Do nothing	✓	?	✗	?	✗	✗	C
2. Consolidate in current segments (investment/ automation)	✓	✗	✓	?	✓	?	B
3. Expand overseas sales (Europe)	✗	✗	✗	✗	✗	?	C
4. Launch 'upmarket' range	✓	✓	✓	✗	?	✓	A
5. Expand 'own-label' production (to hotel/catering industry)	✓	✓	✓	?	✗	?	B
6. Open retail outlets	✗	✗	?	✗	?	?	C
7. Diversify	✗	✗	?	?	?	✓	C

✓ = favourable; ✗ = unfavourable; ? = uncertain or irrelevant.
A = most suitable; B = possible; C = unsuitable.

Source: Authors, based on *Troubleshooters* series, BBC, 1990, 1993.

situation. This is a simplified example which illustrates the general approach. The analysis follows several steps:

- First, decide on key *performance criteria* — in this case, company profitability (ROC).
- Second, agree the required performance year-on-year into the future — in this case, 15 per cent ROC.
- Third, forecast the likely performance if strategies are unchanged — in this case, a steadily declining ROC because of increasing labour costs and deteriorating machinery.
- Finally, establish the *gap* between the forecasted and required performance levels — this has to be 'filled' by new strategies.

Readers need to bear in mind that, like other forecasting techniques, gap analysis can be a difficult and time-consuming process. It is also usually necessary to apply measures other than profitability. Some of these may be

Illustration 8.4 A strategic decision tree for a sweet manufacturer

A sweet manufacturer wants to consider the range of future strategies he could pursue. Using a strategic decision tree, he is also able to eliminate certain options by identifying a few key elements or criteria which future developments would incorporate, such as growth, investment and diversification.

Analysis of the tree reveals that, if the sweet manufacturer wishes growth to be an important aspect of future strategies, options 1–4 are ranked more highly than options 5–8. At the second step, the need for low-investment strategies would rank options 3 and 4 above 1 and 2, and so on.

The sweet manufacturer is aware that this technique is limited, in that the choice at each branch of the tree can tend to be simplistic. For example, answering 'yes' or 'no' to diversification does not allow for the wide variety of alternatives which might exist between these two extremes. Nevertheless, as a starting point for evaluation, the decision tree provides a useful framework.

easily quantifiable, such as productivity or volume of sales, whereas others may be more subjective but nonetheless very important, such as levels of quality or service.

Gap analysis is also used extensively in public sector planning.[6] Here the strategic problem is often concerned with whether the future demands on a public service are likely to change to such an extent that the current resource provision will prove wholly inadequate. This is particularly important when considering the statutory obligations of many public services, such as hospitals, education and social services. Demographic information is often of central importance in attempting to assess the likely future gaps in provision: for example, whether hospitals or social services can cope with an ageing population.

Ranking

Ranking is a systematic way of analysing specific options for their suitability or fit with the picture gained from strategic analysis. As seen in Illustration 8.3, each option is assessed against a number of key factors which the strategic analysis identified in the organisation's environment, resources and expectations. One of the major benefits of ranking is that it helps the analyst to think through mismatches between a company's present position and the implications of the various strategic options. More sophisticated approaches to ranking assign weightings to each factor, in recognition that some will be of more importance in the evaluation than others.

Decision trees[7]

Although decision trees have been widely used in operational decision making, their use in strategy formulation has not, in general, received a great deal of attention. A typical strategic decision tree is shown in Illustration 8.4. It can be seen that the end-point of the tree is a number of discrete development opportunities, as discussed in Chapter 7. Whereas ranking assumes that all options have equal merit (in the first instance), the decision tree approach ranks options by progressively eliminating others. This elimination process is achieved by identifying a few key elements or criteria which future developments are intended to incorporate, such as growth, investment and diversification. For example, in the illustration, choosing growth as an important aspect of future strategies would automatically rank options 1–4 more highly than 5–8. At the second step, the need for low-investment strategies would rank options 3 and 4 above 1 and 2, and so on. Decision trees combine the identification of options with a simultaneous ranking of those options.

Perhaps the greatest limitation of decision tree analysis is that the choice at each branch on the tree can tend to be simplistic. For example, answering 'yes' or 'no' to diversification does not allow for the wide variety of options which might exist between these two extremes (see Chapter 7). Nevertheless, as a starting point for evaluation, decision trees can often provide a useful framework.

Scenario planning[8]

Ranking evaluates options against a specific list of items or criteria derived from a strategic analysis; decision trees achieve the same outcome by eliminating options through progressively introducing additional criteria to be satisfied. A third approach to screening is that of *scenario planning*, which was explained in Chapter 3 (see Illustration 3.3) as an important tool for assessing an organisation's environment in conditions of high uncertainty. It can therefore be used to screen strategic options by matching them to the possible future scenarios.

The outcome of this process is likely to be not a single prioritised list of options (as with ranking and decision trees), but a series of *contingency plans* which identify the preferred option for each possible future scenario. For example, a company planning international expansion may be uncertain about a number of key economic factors, such as exchange rates or tariff barriers. One scenario might be relatively stable exchange rates and reducing tariff barriers. In these circumstances, the company might choose to develop by manufacturing in the UK and exporting. In contrast, a scenario of a strengthening pound and increasing barriers would make a strategy of overseas-based manufacture more favourable.

Equally important is the organisation's ability to monitor the onset (or otherwise) of the elements of a particular scenario in time to implement appropriate strategies. Many public sector organisations have made extensive use of scenarios and contingency planning.

8.3 Analysing acceptability

Establishing the suitability of options is a useful starting point to an evaluation as it establishes the *rationale* or *strategic logic* behind a particular strategy. However, strategies also have to be acceptable to a variety of different stakeholders, as discussed in Chapter 5.

The acceptability of strategies can be assessed in three broad ways: *return*, *risk* and *stakeholder reactions*. Figure 8.7 summarises some of the approaches to assessing acceptability together with some of the limitations of particular analytical techniques. The general advice is to use more than one approach or technique in building up a picture of the acceptability of a particular strategy.

Approach	Used to assess	Examples	Limitations
Analysing return			
Profitability analyses	Financial return of investments	Return on capital Payback period Discounted cash flow (DCF)	Apply to discrete projects Only tangible costs/benefits
Cost–benefit analysis	Wider costs/benefits (including intangibles)	Major infrastructure projects	Difficulties of quantification
Shareholder value analysis (SVA)	Impact of new strategies on shareholder value	Mergers/takeovers	Technical detail often difficult
Analysing risk			
Financial ratio projections	Robustness of strategy	Break-even analysis Impact on gearing and liquidity	
Sensitivity analysis	Test assumptions/robustness	'What if?' analysis	Tests factors separately
Simulation modelling	Aggregate impact of many factors	Comprehensive models Risk analysis	Quality of data on causal relationships
Stakeholder reactions	Political dimension of strategy	Stakeholder mapping Game theory	Largely qualitative

Figure 8.7   Assessing the acceptability of strategies

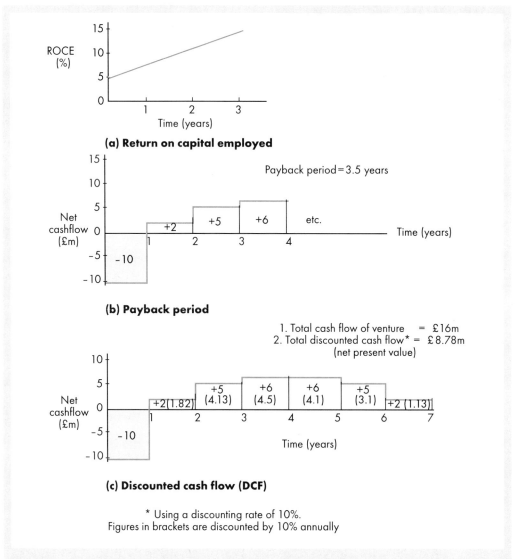

Figure 8.8   Some measures of profitability for strategy evaluation

8.3.1 Analysing return

An assessment of the returns likely to accrue from specific options is a key measure of the acceptability of an option. However, there are a number of different approaches to the analysis of return. This section looks briefly at three different assessments.

Profitability analyses[9]

Traditional financial analyses have been used extensively in the evaluation of the acceptability of strategies. Three of the more commonly used approaches are as follows (see Figure 8.8):

1. Forecasting the *return on capital employed* (ROCE) a specific time after a new strategy is implemented (e.g. the new strategy will result in a return on capital of 15 per cent by year 3). This is shown in Figure 8.8(a).

2. *Payback period* has been used where a significant capital injection is needed to support a new venture. In Figure 8.8(b), the payback period is calculated by finding the time at which the cumulative net cash flow becomes zero — in the example, three and a half years.

    The judgement is then whether this is regarded as an adequate outcome and if the organisation is prepared to wait that long for a return. This will vary from one industry to another. Major public sector ventures such as bridge building may well be assessed on a payback period of up to 60 years.

3. *Discounted cash flow* (DCF) analysis is perhaps the most widely used investment appraisal technique, and is essentially an extension of the payback period analysis. Once the net cash flows have been assessed for each of the years (see Figure 8.8(c)), they are discounted progressively to reflect the fact that funds generated early are of more real value than those in later periods (years). In the example, the discounting rate of 10 per cent reflects the value placed on money tied up in the venture. So the projected net cash flow of £2m in year 2 is discounted to £1.82m and so on. The net present value (NPV) of the venture is then calculated by adding all the discounted annual cash flows (after taxation) over the anticipated life of the project. DCF analysis is particularly useful for comparing the financial merits of strategies which have very different patterns of expenditure and return.

Although the evaluation of strategies may be assisted by the use of one or more of these financial techniques, it is important to recognise some of the implicit assumptions which inevitably limit their use as comprehensive techniques of strategy evaluation. In particular, the analyst should not be misguided by the tidiness or apparent thoroughness of these methods. The major issues to be aware of are as follows:

■   These methods were developed for the purposes of capital investment appraisal and, therefore, focus on discrete *projects* where the incremental costs and cash flows are easily predicted. Neither of these assumptions is necessarily valid in many strategic developments. The precise way in which a strategy might develop, and the costs and income flows, tend to become clearer as the implementation proceeds rather than at the outset.

Illustration 8.5   Sewerage construction project

Investment in items of infrastructure — such as sewers — often requires a careful consideration of the wider costs and benefits of the project.

In the early 1990s, Britain's recently privatised water companies were monopolies supplying water and disposing of sewage. They needed to invest in new sewerage systems to meet the increasing standards required by law. They often used cost–benefit analysis to assess projects. The figures below are from an actual analysis carried out in 1991.

Benefits

Benefits result mainly from reduced use of rivers as overflow sewers. There are also economic benefits resulting from construction. The following benefits are quantified below:

- The multiplier benefit to the local economy of increased spending by those employed on the project.
- The linkage benefit to the local economy of purchases from local firms, including the multiplier effect of such spending.
- Reduced risk of flooding from overflows or old sewers collapsing — flood probabilities can be quantified using historical records, and the cost of flood damage by detailed assessment of the property vulnerable to damage.
- Reduced traffic disruption from flooding and road closures for repairs to old sewers — statistics on the costs of delays to users, traffic flows on roads affected and past closure frequency can be used to quantify savings.
- Increased amenity value of rivers (e.g. for boating and fishing) can be measured by surveys asking visitors what the value is to them or by looking at the effect on demand of charges imposed elsewhere.
- Increased rental values and take-up of space can be measured by consultation with developers and observed effects elsewhere.
- Increased visitor numbers to riverside facilities resulting from reduced pollution.

Also, there are often significant time lags between *revenue* expenditures and income benefits. Nor are strategic developments easy to isolate from the on-going business activities in accurately assessing costs and projected income.

- Financial appraisals tend to focus on the *tangible* costs and benefits, and do not set the strategy in its wider context. For example, a new product launch may look unprofitable as an isolated project, but may make real strategic sense through the market acceptability of other products in the company's portfolio. Or, in reverse, the intangible cost of losing *strategic focus* through new ventures is readily overlooked.

Construction cost
This is net of the cost of unskilled labour. Use of unskilled labour is not a burden on the economy, and its cost must be deducted to arrive at opportunity cost.

Net benefits
Once the difficult task of quantifying costs and benefits is complete, standard discounting techniques can be used to calculate net present value and internal rate of return, and analysis can then proceed as for conventional projects.

Cost/benefit	£m	£m
Benefits		
Multiplier/linkage benefits		0.9
Flood prevention		2.5
Reduced traffic disruption		7.2
Amenity benefits		4.6
Investment benefit		23.6
Encouragement of visitors		4.0
Total benefits		42.8
Costs		
Construction cost	18.2	
Less: unskilled labour cost	(4.7)	
Opportunity cost of construction		(13.5)
Present value of net benefits (NPV)		29.3
Real internal rate of return (IRR)		15%

Note: Figures discounted at a *real* discount rate of 5% over 40 years.

Source: G. Owen, Policy Research Centre, Sheffield Business School.

▪ Overall, it is advisable to use a number of financial techniques in order to build up a picture of the financial attractiveness of various strategic options. Just as important is that managers surface those assumptions with greatest uncertainty in order to perform truly testing sensitivity analysis.

Cost–benefit analysis[10]

In many situations, the analysis of profit is too narrow an interpretation of return, particularly where intangible benefits are an important consideration. This is often the case for major public infrastructure projects, such as the siting of an airport or a sewer construction project, as shown in Illustration 8.5. *Cost–benefit analysis* attempts to put a money value on all the costs and benefits of a strategic option, including tangible and intangible returns to people and organisations other than the one 'sponsoring' the project or strategy.

Although monetary valuation is often difficult, it can be done, and despite difficulties cost–benefit analysis is an approach which is valuable if its limitations are understood. Its major benefit is in forcing people to be explicit about the various factors which should influence strategic choice. So, even if people disagree on the value which should be assigned to particular costs or benefits, at least they are able to argue their case on common ground and decision-makers can compare the merits of the various arguments.

Shareholder value analysis[11]

During the 1980s, attempts were made to address many of the limitations and criticisms of traditional financial analyses. At the same time, renewed attention was paid to the primary legal responsibility of company directors: namely, the creation of value/benefits for the shareholders. The takeover boom of the 1980s caused both corporate raiders and victims alike to look at how corporate development strategies were, or were not, generating shareholder value.

Together, these factors spawned *shareholder value analysis* (SVA). Applying this within the strategic management process requires a new mindset which is called *value management*:

- It emphasises that discounted cash flow analysis should concentrate on evaluating strategies at the strategic business unit level and not just separate investment projects. Because of complex interdependencies, it may not be sensible to evaluate a project separately using incremental cash flow analysis. For example, BP's 'project 1990' for culture change was inseparable from many other strategic initiatives and was not feasible to evaluate financially in isolation.
- The financial analysis must be driven by an understanding of the value creation process and the competitive advantage which the organisation derives from this process. In particular, it is critical to identify the key cash generators of the business, which are called the *value drivers*. One very important *external* value driver is competitive rivalry, which has a direct impact on margins. Ultimately, the net present value (NPV) of a strategy or strategic decision is likely to be critically dependent on a relatively small number of these factors. Value management's big contribution is to emphasise how important managing value drivers is to making strategic decisions, and in implementation and control.

Illustration 8.6   Strategy evaluation at BP and Rolls-Royce

Companies need to find a use for financial analysis which reflects their specific circumstances and provides information to managers when choosing new strategies.

Shareholder value at British Petroleum (BP)

Between 1986 and 1991, the BP Group shifted its corporate decision-making processes towards *value-based management* with the aim of enhancing BP's shareholder value. This change occurred because BP top management were dissatisfied with measuring performance through return on capital employed (ROCE), which was based on financial accounting measures and was backward-looking.

BP looked to value-based management to:

- Align all of its financial decision-making processes with its corporate financial objective of creating value for its shareholders.
- Give management a top-down check on where BP was adding to shareholder value and also where it might be dissipating value among its business portfolio.
- Enable managers within the businesses to evaluate strategies in detail using economic bases of appraisal (looking at SBUs as projects or bundles of projects).
- Set business performance targets and indicators in a way consistent with these strategies.

Over the five-year period, many major benefits had been secured. However, the process of implementation and of learning was still continuing. An important factor was that from the start the process had the firm commitment of top BP management, who refused to allow any sacred cows to dilute the changes needed.

Strategic project appraisal at Rolls-Royce Aeroengines

As a major player in a high-technology international market, Rolls-Royce Aeroengines had invested substantial sums in product development. Typically, it would take many years to recoup the value of these investments. Rapid growth in the past had resulted from airline deregulation, economic growth and changes in consumers' leisure patterns. However, this growth proved vulnerable to a variety of factors: for instance, recession, overcapacity of the airline industry and cutbacks in defence spending. In addition, aerospace companies competed fiercely to win orders for major new projects to ensure that (a) the requirement of a single major customer could be met, (b) there would be some winners so that manufacturing capacity would be well utilised, and (c) synergies were gained in development spend where possible.

The evaluation of individual projects was thus clouded by external uncertainty and by interdependency within the product range. Financial measures of project value were therefore seen as indicative rather than precise and definitive.

Rolls-Royce had also experimented with mapping the value-creating profiles of all its major projects in order to explore the interdependency effects and key vulnerables.

Source: Research undertaken by Tony Grundy, Cranfield School of Management. Reproduced with permission.   Also published in A.N. Grundy, *Corporate Strategy and Financial Decisions*, Kogan Page, 1992.

Illustration 8.7   Sensitivity analysis

Sensitivity analysis is a useful technique for assessing the extent to which the success of a preferred strategy is dependent on the key assumptions which underlie that strategy.

In 1997 the Dunsmore Chemical Company was a single-product company trading in a mature and relatively stable market. It was intended to use this established situation as a cash cow to generate funds for a new venture with a related product. Estimates had shown that the company would need to generate some £4 million cash (at 1997 values) between 1998 and 2003 for this new venture to be possible.

Although the expected performance of the company was for a cash flow of £9.5 million over that period (the *base case*), management was concerned to assess the likely impact of three key factors:

- Possible increases in *production costs* (labour, overheads and materials), which might be as much as 3 per cent p.a. in real terms.
- *Capacity fill*, which might be reduced by as much as 25 per cent due to ageing plant and uncertain labour relations.
- *Price levels*, which might be affected by the threatened entry of a new major competitor. This could squeeze prices by as much as 3 per cent p.a. in real terms.

It was decided to use sensitivity analysis to assess the possible impact of each of these factors on the company's ability to generate £4 million. The results are shown in the graphs.

From this analysis, the management concluded that its target of £4 million would be achieved with *capacity utilisation* as low as 60 per cent, which was certainly going to be achieved. Increased *production costs* of 3 per cent p.a. would still allow the company to achieve the £4 million target over the period. In contrast, *price* squeezes of 3 per cent p.a. would result in a shortfall of £2 million.

The management concluded from this analysis that the key factor which should affect their thinking on this matter was the likely impact of new competition and the extent to which they could protect price levels if such competition emerged. They therefore developed an aggressive marketing strategy to deter potential entrants.

- Value management involves a mastery of a complex system of value drivers (the value system) with many interdependencies. For example, quality of service in a supermarket may allow price premiums to be maintained. But this service level is dependent on and sustained by a number of other factors and investments — for example, staff training and check-out systems. This is needed right down to the level of having supermarket trolleys which run straight.
- Increasing customer value does not necessarily mean that value (to the

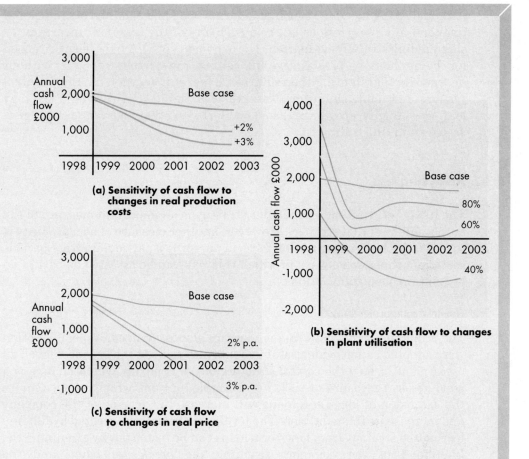

(a) **Sensitivity of cash flow to changes in real production costs**

(b) **Sensitivity of cash flow to changes in plant utilisation**

(c) **Sensitivity of cash flow to changes in real price**

Source: The Dunsmore example is from the authors. The calculations for the sensitivity test utilise computer programs employed in the Doman case study by P.H. Jones (Sheffield Business School).

company) is added. Increased quality of service may simply *protect* existing cash flow streams and avoid loss in value to the company. However, superior value to the customer may result in higher margins or capturing market share ('value capture'). So managers need to make many judgements on how value may be created, protected or exploited. Value management thus requires genuine and complex assessment of the competitive environment, operational options and their financial impact.

Although SVA has done much to address the shortcomings of traditional financial analyses, it does not remove many of the inherent uncertainties surrounding strategy evaluation. The exponents of SVA have been criticised for being heavily prescriptive in selling the virtues of SVA without necessarily highlighting the required changes in decision making, control systems and implementation. Nevertheless, the idea of valuing a strategy may serve to give greater realism and clarity to otherwise vague strategies, as shown in Illustration 8.6.

8.3.2 Analysing risk

The likely return from a particular strategy is an important measure of the acceptability of that strategy. However, another measure of acceptability is the *risk* which the organisation faces in pursuing a particular strategy. This section outlines some ways in which this risk can be assessed as part of an evaluation of specific options.

Financial ratio projections[12]

The projection of how key financial ratios would change if a specific option were adopted can provide useful insights into risk. At the broadest level, an assessment of how the *capital structure* of the company would change is a good general measure of risk. For example, options which would require the extension of long-term loans will increase the gearing of the company and increase its financial risk. The level of financial risk created by funding a proposed strategy from long-term loans can be tested out by examining the likelihood of the company reaching the *break-even point*, and the consequences of falling short of that volume of business while interest on loans continues to be paid.

At a more detailed level, a consideration of the likely impact on an organisation's *liquidity* is important in evaluating options. For example, a small retailer eager to grow quickly may be tempted to fund the required shopfitting costs by delaying payments to suppliers and increasing bank overdraft. This reduced liquidity increases the financial risk of the business. The extent to which this increased risk threatens survival depends on the likelihood of either creditors or the bank demanding payments from the company — an issue which clearly requires judgement.

Sensitivity analysis[13]

Sensitivity analysis is a useful technique for incorporating the assessment of risk during strategy evaluation. It is sometimes referred to as *what if?* analysis. Its use grew with the availability of computer spreadsheet packages, which are ideally suited to this type of analysis.

The technique allows each of the important assumptions underlying a particular strategy to be questioned and changed. In particular, it seeks to test how sensitive the predicted performance or outcome (e.g. profit) is to each of these assumptions. For example, the key assumptions underlying a strategy might be that market demand will grow by 5 per cent p.a., or that the company will stay strike-free, or that certain expensive machines will operate at 90 per cent loading. Sensitivity analysis asks: what would be the effect on performance (in this case, profitability) if, for example, market demand grew at only 1 per cent, or by as much as 10 per cent? Would either of these extremes alter the decision to pursue that particular strategy? A similar process might be repeated for the other key assumptions. This process helps management develop a clearer picture of the risks of making particular strategic decisions and the degree of confidence it might have in a given decision. (Illustration 8.7 shows how sensitivity analysis can be used in strategy evaluation.)

Simulation modelling

Strategic simulation models attempt to encompass all the factors considered by the separate analyses discussed in this chapter into one quantitative simulation model of the company and its environment. It should be no surprise that such global models have been virtually impossible to build. Nevertheless, the principle of *simulation modelling*[14] is a useful one in strategy evaluation, in those aspects which lend themselves to this quantitative view.

Financial models are often used to assess strategic options. *Risk analysis*[15] is a technique which seeks to assess the overall degree of uncertainty in a particular option by mathematically combining the uncertainties in each of the elements of the option. For example, the likelihood of a particular profit projection is governed by the uncertainties surrounding costs, prices and volume forecasts.

One of the limitations on the use of strategic modelling is the need for large amounts of high-quality data concerning the relationship between environmental factors and company performance. In this respect, the work of the Strategic Planning Institute (SPI) using the Profit Impact of Market Strategy (PIMS) database[16] has been interesting (see Chapter 7). Research at SPI has tried to build a number of quantitative causal models (using multiple regression) which explain how companies' performance has been influenced by up to two dozen different factors — such as those seen in business profiling, discussed in section 8.2.1 above and Illustration 8.2.

In general, the use of modelling in strategy evaluation is limited to well-structured problems. Particular care needs to be taken for the following reasons:

- There is a danger that the model will become a gross oversimplification of reality, and fail to encompass the most important uncertainties and risks.
- Attempts to incorporate a very large number of variables make the model highly complex, and all the critical interrelationships need to be included, which is in practice very difficult, if not impossible.
- Some key data, such as competitor reactions, are difficult to assess and/ or incorporate in the model. The overriding danger with models of all types is that they can result in less insight for managers/decision-makers than much simpler techniques (such as sensitivity analysis), as they hide the analysis away in a 'black box' which managers do not feel they can open. The model-builders create a level of detail which starts to conceal the important strategic questions and issues.

8.3.3 Analysing stakeholder reactions

In Chapter 5, the importance of understanding the political context of strategic change was emphasised, and the concept of *stakeholders* was introduced. *Stakeholder mapping* (Figure 5.5) was presented as a way of analysing and prioritising the 'political agenda' for an organisation. Readers are reminded that stakeholder maps can be usefully drawn only in relation to specific strategic options. They are therefore a valuable tool in assessing the likely reactions of stakeholders to new strategies, the ability to manage these reactions, and hence the acceptability of a strategy.

There are many situations where judgements of stakeholder reactions could be crucial. For example:

- A new strategy might require a substantial issue of *new shares*, which could be unacceptable to powerful groups of shareholders, since it dilutes their voting power.
- Plans to *merge* with other companies or to *trade* with new countries could be unacceptable to unions, government or some customers.
- A strategy of market development might require the cutting out of *channels* (such as wholesalers), hence running the risk of a backlash which could jeopardise the success of the strategy.
- Changes in competitive strategy in static markets might upset the status quo to such an extent that competitors will be forced to retaliate in a way that is damaging to all parties, but which would undermine the assumptions on which the strategy's acceptability had been assessed. The most common example of this would be a price war.

Stakeholder mapping is a useful technique for encouraging managers to predict both the degree of interest that stakeholders are likely to exhibit

Illustration 8.8   Funds flow analysis: a worked example

Kentex Industries plc is considering pursuing a strategy of expansion, which in the immediate future will involve the opening of a new production facility. To evaluate the financial feasibility of his proposal and so establish what funds would be required and how these funds may be sourced, the company decides to undertake a funds flow analysis.

Stage 1: Identification of sources
Opening of the new production facility has been estimated to increase the sales revenue from the current £30 million to £31.65 million per annum over the next three years. This is expected to generate funds from operations totalling £15 million over the three years. This is the estimate of future profits corrected for non-fund items such as depreciation, and represents real flow of funds into the company for a three-year period.

Sources	£	Uses	£
Funds from operations	15,000,000	New fixed assets	13,250,000
		Working capital	550,000
		Tax	1,200,000
		Dividends	500,000
Sub-total	15,000,000	Sub-total	15,500,000

Note: Shortfall between sources and uses amounting to £500,000.

Stage 2: Identification of uses
There would be a number of costs associated with the new production facility. First, there would be the direct costs of the capital investment required for new buildings, machines and vehicles. This is anticipated to be £13.25 million. Also, there will be additional working capital costs as sales are expected to increase. This has not been calculated by separate consideration of each element (e.g. stock increases, increased creditors), but in this instance has been based on a simple pro-rata adjustment. On the previous sales level of £30 million, a working capital level of £10 million was required, so the increase in sales of £1.65 million would require an additional £0.55 million in working capital. Tax liability and expected dividend payments have been estimated at £1.2 million and £0.5 million respectively.

Stage 3: Identification and funding of shortfall
The calculation so far leaves a shortfall in funds of £0.5 million. The company then finalises the forecast by looking at alternative ways of funding the shortfall. While it could raise funds through the issue of new share capital, it chooses to seek a short-term loan of £0.65 million. It should be noted that this in turn will incur interest payments of £0.15 million over the three-year period, assuming simple interest at 7.5 per cent per annum, hence leaving a net income of £0.5 million.

Prepared by Sara Martin, Cranfield School of Management.

for or against a strategy, and whether they have the power to help or hinder the adoption of that strategy.

Since an important issue may be the likely reactions of competitors to particular strategic changes, *game theory*[17] should, in principle, have some use as an evaluation technique. This is an approach to decision analysis which assumes that competitors are likely to react to any moves which the company makes (and/or that the company will need to react to their moves). The technique lays out and quantifies the costs and benefits of the various combinations of the company moves and competitor reactions. For example, a product modification option has four possible outcomes or combinations, ranging from neither the company nor the competitor modifying the product to *both* companies modifying the product. This helps in comparing these various strategies or courses of action. However, the difficulties of coping with the complexity of the strategic situation have limited the use of game theory to largely qualitative applications. The biggest difficulty lies in the assumption that the strategic competitive behaviour of companies can be predicted and categorised into a small number of clearly defined categories — this is rarely true in practice.

8.4   Analysing feasibility

Assessing the *feasibility* of options is concerned with whether an organisation has the resources and competences to deliver a strategy. A number of analytical approaches can be used to assess feasibility.

8.4.1 Funds flow analysis[18]

The assessment of financial feasibility should normally be an important part of any strategy evaluation. A valuable piece of analysis is a *funds flow forecast*, which seeks to identify the funds which would be required for any strategy and the likely sources of those funds, as shown in Illustration 8.8.

It should be remembered that funds flow analysis is a forecasting technique, and is subject to the difficulties and errors of any method of forecasting. Such an analysis should quickly highlight whether the proposed strategy is likely to be feasible in financial terms, and it could normally be programmed on to a computer spreadsheet should the model be repeatedly required during evaluation. This would also assist in identifying the *timing* of new funding requirements.

Illustration 8.9 Using break-even analysis to examine strategic options

A manufacturing company was considering the launch of a new consumer durable product into a market where most products were sold to wholesalers which supplied the retail trade. The total market was worth about £4.4 million (at manufacturers' prices) — about 630,000 units. The market leader had about 30 per cent market share in a competitive market where retailers were increasing their buying power. The company wished to evaluate the relative merits of a high-price/high-quality product sold to wholesalers (strategy A) or an own-brand product sold directly to retailers (strategy B). The table below summarises the market and cost structure for the market leader and these alternative strategies.

Market and cost structure	Market leader	Strategy A	Strategy B
Price to retailer	£10.00	£12.00	£8.00
Price to wholesaler	£7.00	£8.40	—
Total variable costs (TVC)	£3.50	£4.00	£3.10
Contribution to profit per unit sold (= Price sold − TVC)	£3.50	£4.40	£4.90
Fixed costs (FC)	£500,000	£500,000	£500,000
Break-even point: no. of units to sell (= FC/Contribution to profit)	142,857	136,363	81,633
Total market size (units)	630,000	630,000	630,000
Break-even point: market share (= Break-even point units/mkt size)	22.6%	21.6%	13.0%
Actual market share	30.0%	—	—

The table shows that the company would require about 22 per cent and 13 per cent market share respectively for strategies A and B to break even.

8.4.2 Break-even analysis[19]

Break-even analysis is a simple and widely used technique which is helpful in exploring some key aspects of feasibility. It can be used to assess the feasibility of meeting targets of return (e.g. profit) and, as such, combines a parallel assessment of acceptability. As shown in Illustration 8.9, it also provides an assessment of the risk of various strategies, particularly where different strategic options require markedly different cost structures.

8.4.3 Resource deployment analysis[20]

The previous two methods have concentrated on the assessment of feasibility in *financial* terms. It is often helpful to make a wider assessment of the resources and competences of the organisation in relation to *specific* strategies. This can be done through a *resource deployment analysis*, which is a way of comparing options with each other using the kind of framework already shown in Figure 8.4 (for separate options).

The requirements of alternative future strategies should be laid out, indicating the key resources and competences for each strategy. For example, a strategy of geographical expansion in the home market might be critically dependent on marketing and distribution expertise, together with the availability of cash to fund increased stocks. In contrast, a different strategy of developing new products to sell to current customers is dependent on engineering skills, the capability of machinery and the company's reputation for quality in new products.

The 'scoring' system described for Figure 8.4 can be used to compare various strategic options against the current resources and competences of the organisation in order to judge two things: first, the extent to which the current resources and competences represent sufficient capability to pursue each strategy; and second, the extent to which these resources and competences would need to change for each strategy.

There is a danger that resource deployment analysis will simply result in organisations choosing strategies which most closely fit the configuration of their present resources and competences. It should be remembered that the real benefit of such an analysis is the identification of those necessary changes in resources and competences which are implied by any strategy, and an analysis of whether these changes are *feasible* in terms of scale, quality of resource or timescale of change.

It will be seen in Chapter 10 that this broad process of assessing the resource requirements of specific strategies provides a link to a detailed assessment of the critical factors for success of any strategy and the kind of resource configuration which will be necessary to ensure success. Chapter 11 will look at how a remapping of an organisation's cultural web can be

Approach	Dominant processes	Elements of good practice	Dangers
Planning	Analytical techniques Tested against objectives Quantified where possible	Involve line managers Analyse 'holistic' picture Build in flexibility Communication between analysts and decision-makers	No ownership Fragmented analysis Rigidity — lost opportunities Decision-makers disown analysis
Enforced choice	Bend to environmental 'pressure'	Assess risk Prepare contingencies	'Victims of circumstances' Evaluation not done
Learning from experience	Reactive moves in separate parts of organisation Cultural/political context important	Processes need credibility Avenues of challenge Promote inter-unit learning	Fragmented/inefficient Pragmatism Risk of strategic drift
Command	Dominant stakeholder selects strategies	Inform/educate decision-maker Need 'completeness' Challenge the paradigm	Incomplete vision Vision institutionalised

Figure 8.9 Processes for selecting strategies

used to assess the need for cultural change and the extent to which such changes are likely to be feasible.

8.5   Selection of strategies

Chapters 6, 7 and 8 have so far explored, described and provided a critique of the literature, research evidence and managerial 'wisdoms' regarding the merits of a range of strategic options for organisations. This has been done in terms of the broad bases of an organisation's strategies as well as the more detailed choice of directions and methods of development.

This final section is concerned not so much with *what* those choices are, but with *how* the *process* of strategic choice and *selection* of strategies are and can be undertaken within organisations. This relates back to the discussions of strategic development processes in Chapter 2, which will be used as the framework against which to look at these process issues. This section reviews how strategic choice and selection are likely to occur within different processes of strategic development. The important question is: what role will be played by the types of analytical approach covered in Chapters 6, 7 and 8? Figure 8.9 provides a summary of the following discussions.

8.5.1   The planned approach: formal evaluation

This could be a view of how a 'rational' selection of future strategies should occur. Here the organisation's objectives, quantified where possible, are used as direct yardsticks by which options are assessed (for example, whether strategies are likely to meet target for return on capital or market share). The types of evaluation technique discussed above are therefore central to the decision-making process, and are expected to provide quantified 'answers' regarding the relative merits of different courses of action and to come up with the 'right' strategies. Such an approach might avoid too much of the 'gut feeling' which other approaches can represent.

The view taken throughout this book is that formal planning and evaluation can be valuable tools for strategic managers, but they should not be regarded as an exclusive process through which strategies are selected. So the critical issue for strategic managers is to ensure that the organisation's formal planning and evaluation activities assist whichever is the dominant approach to strategy selection. For example, *sensitivity analysis* (section 8.3.2 above) is a useful technique for allowing decision-makers to understand the risks and uncertainties surrounding specific strategies, but it does not select strategies for those decision-makers. Formal planning and evaluation are useful means of *raising the level of debate* among the decision-makers during the selection process. Strategy workshops or future search conferences[21] can fulfil a similar purpose and allow many more people in the organisation to contribute to the quality of thinking about future strategies.

8.5.2 Enforced choice

It was stated in Chapter 2 that there are some circumstances where the strategic development of the organisation is largely imposed from outside. This may be because major changes in the environment overshadow other considerations — as with a major technological breakthrough. Imposition may occur because of the dominant influence of an external stakeholder — say, in the case of small companies and their dependency on a few major customers, such as Ford or Marks and Spencer. It may be that a particular set of circumstances — perhaps a crisis — dictates the immediate priorities for strategic choice (e.g. the loss of a customer or a major product failure).

It could be concluded that in these situations the organisation is largely a victim of circumstance, so there is no role for strategy evaluation by managers. However, this is not the conclusion which should be drawn for two reasons. First, a danger of enforced choice is that the risk profile of the organisation becomes too great. Strategy evaluation should reveal this in the ways described earlier in the chapter, and should perhaps lead to a medium/longer-term strategic reorientation with the specific purpose of reducing this risk — for example, through spreading the customer base, repositioning the product, or even withdrawing from some products or markets. Second, techniques of evaluation, such as *scenario planning* (section 8.2.2 above), can be helpful in reminding strategic managers of the need for *contingency plans* if enforced choices are likely to lead to unacceptably poor performance. They help managers prepare for a change in direction.

8.5.3 Learning from experience

An incremental view of strategic development might see strategy evaluation and selection as a fragmented process occurring within the 'operating units' of the organisation as they reactively adapt to a changing environment. It was suggested in Chapter 2 that such a view of an organisation's development has much to commend it, providing the process is 'managed' in the organisation. Otherwise it is likely to lead to inefficiency, to different parts of the organisation pulling in different directions and to *strategic drift*.

The strategy evaluation and selection processes need to counteract these dangers. For example, it is important to ensure that organisational *learning* occurs between various parts of the organisation. An example of how this would occur in a large multinational is shown in Figure 8.10. New developments are encouraged within local (national) divisions and this is where most evaluation of strategic options occurs. However, the corporate centre is monitoring these local initiatives for ones which might be potential winners internationally. This could then be followed by two or more divisions regionally (e.g. Europe) being encouraged to test the wider acceptability of the product or strategy and/or any modifications or variants which might be required. If this proves successful, the product or strategy could then be adopted by all European divisions. The same process can then be repeated internationally, culminating in a formal acceptance of a new international product or strategy.

This incremental approach means that selection of new strategies for wide adoption is strongly influenced by the experiences of successes and failures within parts of the organisation. Illustration 8.10 shows how Asda, a grocery retailer operating in fast-moving markets, changed its approach to strategy selection to focus it more on the experience of those running the separate departments.

GEOGRAPHICAL SPREAD OF ADOPTION

Figure 8.10 Organisational learning in a multinational

Illustration 8.10   Asda's open plan

In fast-moving businesses, a 'command and control' approach to strategy selection may be too inflexible. There may be a need to focus selection of strategies much more at the business unit (or departmental) level.

In 1991, when Archie Norman became CEO of Asda (the UK grocery retailer), he inherited dwindling customers and mounting debts, and the company looked ready to close its doors. However, by 1996 it had become a much more open business with a management team that claimed to listen to both customers and staff. Performance had been transformed — with the company back in the black and a 30 per cent rise in customers.

The new approach was nurtured by de-layering management to shorten the line between stores and head office, but also by changing the way that departments were organised. For example, each in-store department, such as bakery or fishmongery, had its own profit and loss account. Head office functions were also split into business units (e.g. for meat, drink, clothing), each of which, in turn, was split into smaller categories (e.g. spirits, wines, soft drinks). In each category, the buyers and the Head of Marketing work with category (product) managers to develop their category business.

The overall aim had been to move away from a 'command and control' (by senior management) approach to what they called an 'inform and involve' culture. This took several forms. There were 'listening groups' on current issues and listening surveys of staff and customer opinion. Instead of the old-style weekly managers' meetings, they had twice-daily 'huddles' between managers and their work teams to plan ahead. There was a 'tell Archie' suggestions scheme which attracted 14,000 ideas in the first 18 months.

The style of senior management combined a high degree of approachability with the readiness to take (informed) decisions. Colleagues were expected to challenge management decisions and to take decisions of their own. Communication had also been improved in many small ways from newsletters to customer compliments, and an ample number of open and inviting meeting rooms.

The working environment was open, with plenty of opportunity for informal meetings, stimulating creativity and sparking off ideas. It was all part of 'getting rid of the treacle' of the old approach.

Source: *Management Today*, December 1995.

There are, of course, dangers in allowing too much freedom for unauthorised experimentation and adoption of new strategies within the organisation. In the extreme case, it could result in the organisation only ever developing by tinkering around at the edges and never really making fundamental evaluations or reappraisals, and never selecting strategies which would *transform* the organisation's performance (strategic drift, as discussed in Chapter 2).

Therefore, formal planning and evaluation processes can play an important part in organisations which are developing and selecting strategies through these fragmented, incremental processes. They can be an important device to ensure that best practice is communicated through the various parts of the organisation, and that managers are aware of the wider organisational context when making their 'local' decisions. Planning can be about changing minds, not just making plans.[22] This would be close to the stereotype of *logical incrementalism*, discussed in Chapter 2, where managerial intentions guide and steer the fragmented processes of evaluation and selection.

8.5.4 Command

In some organisations, the dominant process for the selection of strategies is *command*, since the decision is taken at the highest level with involvement/ advice from inside (and outside) the organisation to varying degrees. The efforts of those involved in formal evaluation are concerned to ensure that selections made through this command process are *well informed*. The discussion in Chapter 2 emphasised that there are many circumstances in which this command process is essential in counterbalancing the risk of strategic drift, which is likely to occur because of the power of the *paradigm* of the organisation. This is particularly evident where command is of the visionary type, providing 'shock' and impetus to the organisation by pursuing transformational strategies — or great leaps forward.

It is important that, if strategies are selected in this way, they have some *completeness* and are workable in practice. For example, it may be helpful for a CEO to declare his or her *intentions* that the organisation should develop as a centre of excellence (i.e. focused differentiation). But without some detailed substance in terms of specific strategic choices of development directions and methods (as discussed in Chapter 7), the vision and intentions are not a basis on which strategy selection can proceed. A dangerous combination can be powerful visionary stakeholders who are able to dominate the processes of strategic choice, but who are badly informed about the practicalities of making strategies work. This is a situation familiar to many public sector managers in their relationship with politicians, and raises the critically important issue of how the formal evaluation processes ensure good *policy advice* to politicians from their executive advisers (officers or civil servants).

8.6 Summary

This chapter has been concerned with the evaluation and selection of strategies. Evaluation requires *criteria*, and the chapter has been structured around the three evaluation criteria of *suitability*, *acceptability* and *feasibility*.

Suitability is largely concerned with establishing the rationale of a strategy and the extent to which it addresses the situation in which the organisation is operating (perhaps as detailed in a strategic analysis). It is also useful for comparing the relative merits of various options: that is, as a set of criteria against which strategies can be *screened* before undertaking more detailed analyses. Several approaches to screening were reviewed.

Acceptability can be assessed in a number of different ways which fall into three main categories: the likely *return*, the assessment of *risk* and the likely *reaction of stakeholders*.

Feasibility is concerned with whether a strategy can be made to work and has largely to do with the availability of the necessary resources and competences for successful implementation. There is a strong link with more detailed discussions of resource allocation and control in Chapter 10.

The final section of the chapter looked at how strategies are *selected* in organisations by relating back to the discussions in Chapter 2 of the processes of strategic management in practice.

There are important links between the discussions in this chapter and the practicalities of implementation. Indeed, an important reason for not selecting a strategy would be doubt about some of these practicalities: for example, whether the organisation structure will hinder implementation; whether resources will be available; or whether the organisation will be able to manage the change process adequately. These are issues which will now be discussed in detail in the final part of the book.

References

1. For a companion book which explores techniques more fully see V. Ambrosini with G. Johnson and K. Scholes (eds.), *Exploring Techniques of Analysis and Evaluation in Strategic Management*, Prentice Hall, 1998.

2. The techniques built around the life cycle concept have been developed and explained by the consultants Arthur D. Little in a series of booklets, the first of which was R. Wright, *A System of Managing Diversity*, 1974. Life cycle analyses are also covered in A. Hax and N. Majluf, *Strategic Management: An integrative*
approach, Prentice Hall, 1984. Some of the limitations of this and other portfolio analyses are discussed by Faulkner (see reference 4 below).

3. See A. Campbell and K. Luchs, *Strategic Synergy*, Butterworth-Heinemann, 1992.

4. Portfolio analyses are discussed in a number of books. See, for example, D. Faulkner's chapter on portfolio matrices, in Ambrosini with Johnson and Scholes (see reference 1); A. Hax and N. Majluf, in R. Dyson (ed.), *Strategic Planning: Models and analytical techniques*, Wiley, 1990; C.

Bowman and D. Asch, *Managing Strategy*, Macmillan, 1996, chapter 8.

5. This example is taken from T. Clayton, *An Introduction to Benchmarking*, PIMS Europe Ltd, 1996.

6. See Billsberry's chapter in V. Ambrosini with G. Johnson and K. Scholes (eds.), see Ref 1.

7. Decision trees are discussed in many books on management science and operational research. See, for example, W. Stevenson, *Introduction to Management Science*, 2nd edition, Irwin, 1992, chapter 10; S. French, *Readings in Decision Analysis*, Chapman and Hall, 1989.

8. The use of scenarios by Shell is described in P. Beck, 'Corporate planning for an uncertain future', *Long Range Planning*, vol. 15, no. 4 (1982), pp. 12–21, and more recently in D. Lane, *System Dynamics in Shell*, Wiley, 1996.

9. Useful texts on financial analyses for both strategic analysis and strategy evaluation are: A.N. Grundy with G. Johnson and K. Scholes, *Exploring Strategic Financial Management*, Prentice Hall (1998); J. Ellis and D. Williams, *Corporate Strategy and Financial Analysis*, Pitman, 1993; and A.N. Grundy, *Corporate Strategy and Financial Decisions*, Kogan Page, 1992. R. Butler, L. Davies, R. Pike and J. Sharp, *Strategic Investment Decisions*, Routledge, 1993, looks at several financial aspects of strategy development.

10. Cost–benefit analysis is discussed in A. Williams and E. Giardina, *Efficiency in the Public Sector: The theory and practice of cost–benefit analysis*, Edward Elgar, 1993. (Despite the title, the book covers the private sector too.) See also G. Owen's chapter, 'Cost/benefit analysis' in V. Ambrosini with G. Johnson and K. Scholes (see ref. 1).

11. The main proponent of shareholder value analysis was A. Rappaport, *Creating Shareholder Value: The new standard for business performance*, Free Press, 1986. See also J. Kay, *Foundations of Corporate Success*, Oxford University Press, 1993, chapter 13, and A. Grundy, *Breakthrough Strategies via Growth*, Pitman, 1995. See also R. Mill's chapter, 'Understanding and using shareholder value analysis', in V. Ambrosini with G. Johnson and K. Scholes (see ref. 1).An interesting article is

H. Kay, 'More power to the shareholders', *Management Today*, May 1991.

12. See Ellis and Williams (reference 8 above), part III.

13. B. Taylor and J.R. Sparkes, *Corporate Strategy and Planning*, Heinemann, 1977, discusses the use of sensitivity analysis. Computer spreadsheet packages are ideally suited for simple sensitivity analysis. Ellis and Williams (reference 8 above) give an example on pp. 348–9 in relation to share price.

14. T.H. Naylor, 'A conceptual framework for corporate modeling', *Operational Research Quarterly*, vol. 27, no. 3 (1976) pp. 671–682; reprinted in Dyson (reference 4 above).

15. See D. Hertz, 'Risk analysis in capital investment', *Harvard Business Review*, vol. 57, no. 5 (1979) p. 169; reprinted in Dyson (reference 4 above).

16. The PIMS database is discussed more fully in Chapter 7. Their approach is explained in R.D. Buzzell and B.T. Gale, *The PIMS Principles*, Free Press, 1987.

17. G. Saloner, 'Modeling, game theory and strategic management', *Strategic Management Journal*, vol. 12 (Winter 1991), pp. 119–36, discusses the uses and limitations of game theory in strategic evaluation. See also A. Brandenburger and B. Nalebuff, 'The right game: use game theory to shape strategy', *Harvard Business Review*, vol. 73, no. 4 (1995), pp. 57–71.

18. See Ellis and Williams (reference 8 above), pp. 188–93, for a discussion of the funding of strategies.

19. Break-even analysis is covered in most standard accountancy texts. See, for example, M. Broadbent and J. Cullen, *Managing Financial Resources*, Butterworth-Heinemann, 1993, chapter 7.

20. This relates to the idea of 'resource-based strategies' discussed in Chapter 4. Useful references are B. Wernerfelt, 'A resource-based view of the firm', *Strategic Management Journal*, vol. 5, no. 2 (1984), pp. 171–80, and D. Collis and C. Montgomery, 'Competing on resources: strategy in the 1990s', *Harvard Business Review*, vol. 73, no. 4 (1995), pp. 118–28.

21. Future search conferences are discussed by M. Weisbord, *Productive Workplaces*, Jossey-Bass, 1987, p. 285.

22. A. De Geus, 'Planning as learning', *Harvard Business Review*, vol. 66, no. 2 (1988), pp. 70–4.

Recommended key readings

- A companion book which explores techniques more fully is V. Ambrosini with G. Johnson and K. Scholes (eds.), *Exploring Techniques of Analysis and Evaluation in Strategic Management*, Prentice Hall, 1998.
- Useful texts on financial analyses for both strategic analysis and strategy evaluation are: A.N. Grundy with G. Johnson and K. Scholes, *Exploring Strategic Financial Management*, Prentice Hall (1998); J. Ellis and D. Williams, *Corporate Strategy and Financial Analysis*, Pitman, 1993; and A.N. Grundy, *Corporate Strategy and Financial Decisions*, Kogan Page, 1992.

Work assignments

8.1   Referring to Figure 8.2, explain how any of the broad approaches to assessing suitability might assist in establishing the rationale for particular strategies in the case of PSA Peugeot Citroën* or an organisation of your choice.

8.2   **Explain how the life cycle/portfolio matrix (Figure 8.3) might assist an organisation of your choice in mapping out its preferred strategic direction for the next few years. Are there any dangers with this approach?**

8.3   Undertake a ranking analysis of the choices available to Cooper's Creek,* Peugeot Citroën* or an organisation of your choice similar to that shown in Illustration 8.3.

8.4   Choose a specific strategy for Peugeot Citroën,* Kronenbourg,* Cooper's Creek* or an organisation of your choice, and explain which financial measures you would regard as most appropriate in assessing the anticipated return.

8.5   Criticise the cost–benefit analysis in Illustration 8.5 by commenting on:
(a) the appropriateness of the listed benefits
(b) the ease/difficulty of assigning monetary values to the benefits.

8.6 Using Illustration 8.7 as an example, what would you propose as the most important parameters to include in a sensitivity analysis in the case of each of the following organisations:
(a) The News Corporation*
(b) Sheffield Theatres*
(c) Kronenbourg*
(d) Peugeot Citroën*
(e) an organisation of your choice?
What general conclusion can you draw about the use of sensitivity analysis by comparing your answer for each organisation?

8.7 For an organisation of your choice (or Asda — Illustration 8.10), describe the dominant processes by which strategies are selected in the organisation. Now look at Figure 8.9, make your own assessment of whether you would wish to change these processes and justify your proposals.

8.8 *Using examples from your answer to previous assignments, make a critical appraisal of the statement that 'Strategic choice is, in the end, a highly subjective matter. It is dangerous to believe that analytical techniques will ever change in reality.' Refer back to the recommended key readings by Johnson and Stacey (Chapter 2), who between them conclude that strategic decision making neither is, nor should be, driven by analysis.*

*This refers to a case in the Text and Cases version of this book.

PART IV

Strategy implementation

Strategic analysis and choice are of little value to an organisation unless the strategies are capable of being implemented. Strategic change does not take place simply because it is considered to be desirable; it takes place if it can be made to work and put into effect by members of the organisation. Part IV deals with the vital issues of implementing strategy, the planning of that implementation, and the difficulties and methods of managing strategic change. Chapter 1 made it clear that one of the main characteristics of strategic decisions is that they are likely to give rise to important changes. It is therefore vital to consider the types of change required, how they can be managed, and the strategic architecture which needs to be in place to ensure success. This discussion of architecture includes a range of related issues:

- Chapter 9 is about organisation design at various levels of detail. It looks at various types of organisation structure and the circumstances in which they might sensibly be adopted. However, the important issue of organisation design from a strategic viewpoint is where within this structure strategic and operational decisions will be made. This is the issue of centralisation and devolution, and will include a discussion of the 'parenting' role of the corporate centre in relation to divisions, as introduced in Chapter 6. The most detailed issues of organisation design are concerned with the configuration of the organisation — its building blocks and co-ordinating mechanisms — and how these need to vary from one organisation to another depending upon its circumstances.

- Chapter 10 discusses resource allocation and control within organisations as critical issues of implementation. The discussion includes the impact of improvements in information technology on these processes and business process re-engineering and internal market mechanisms. Overall, an important theme of the chapter is the need for managers to steer strategy through the way in which they influence the context in which other people work, rather than simply being the masterplanners of the organisation. Resource allocation and control is one of the most important ways in which this 'shaping of context' can be achieved.

■ Chapter 11 examines more specifically how strategic change might be managed. This is done by considering different explanatory models of change; means of diagnosing blockages to change; and different approaches to managing change, including the styles of management and techniques which can be employed in managing change. These include the management of political and symbolic issues, the importance of communication, changes to organisational routines and other specific tactics of managing change. The chapter concludes by linking its contents to other issues raised in the rest of the book.

CHAPTER 9

Organisation structure and design

9.1 Introduction

Perhaps the most important resource of an organisation is its *people*, so how people are organised is crucial to the effectiveness of strategy. Traditional views about regulation through organisation can be traced back to early twentieth-century management scientists and beyond.[1] These approaches are commensurate with a view of strategy making which is essentially top-down. Strategy is formed at the top and the rest of the organisation is seen as a means of implementation, so organisation design becomes a means of top-down control. Such principles of control are known as *bureaucratic* or *mechanistic*.[2] However, as was seen in Chapter 2, the idea that strategy is formulated in a top-down way is questionable, and the extension of this, that mechanistic structures and controls are necessarily appropriate, is therefore also questionable.

This chapter considers organisational structure/design in the context of the strategic management of organisations. It is accepted that there is a need to regulate the implementation of strategy, but this needs to take account of many influences. For example, what are the *types* of problem that the organisation faces in constructing strategy? Is it in a highly *complex* or *changing* environment, or in a fairly stable environment? How *diverse* is the organisation?: for example, the needs of a multinational company are different from those of a small local firm. To what extent is the organisation reliant on simple or complex technologies? How answerable are the top executives to *external stakeholders*: for example, is the organisation a public body, perhaps answerable to a government minister; is it a privately owned firm; or is it perhaps a charity or a co-operative? It has already been seen in Chapter 6 that all these different influences have a bearing on strategic choices made by organisations. In turn, they also impact on the way the organisation needs to be designed. It is not possible to have a simple set of rules which can prescribe organisational structures and systems.

This chapter examines these issues, first by reviewing *basic structural forms*, and second by looking at how the authority to make strategic and operational decisions is mapped on to the structure — the issue of *centralisation/devolution*. Finally, the chapter looks at how the detailed design — or *configuration* — of an organisation needs to match its circumstances. Chapter 10 will complete the discussion of organisation design by exploring how the processes of *resource allocation and control* relate to the circumstances and structural arrangements of the organisation.

9.2 Structural types

Managers asked to describe their organisation usually respond by drawing an organisation chart, in an attempt to map out its structure. These structures are like skeletons: they define the general shape and facilitate or constrain certain activities. This chapter begins with a review of these basic structural types, and their advantages and disadvantages. It should be remembered that an organisation's performance will be mainly influenced by how the 'flesh' is built on to this skeleton. This is the area of organisational design which will be discussed in sections 9.3 to 9.5 and in Chapter 10.

9.2.1 The simple structure

A simple structure can be thought of as no formal structure at all. It is the type of organisation common in many very small businesses. There may be an owner who undertakes most of the responsibilities of management, perhaps with a partner or an assistant. However, there is little division of management responsibility, and probably little clear definition of who is responsible for what if there is more than one person involved. The operation is run by the personal control and contact of an individual.

The main problem here is that the organisation can operate effectively only up to a certain size, beyond which it becomes too cumbersome for one person to control alone. This threshold size will depend on the nature of the business: an insurance broker may personally handle a very large turnover, whereas a similarly sized business (in terms of turnover) in manufacturing and selling goods may be much more diverse in its operations and therefore more difficult to control personally because of the wider range of competences needed within the business.

9.2.2 The functional structure

A functional structure is based on the primary tasks that have to be carried out, such as production, finance and accounting, marketing and personnel. Figure 9.1 represents a typical organisation chart for such a business, and Illustration 9.1 shows the importance of the functional structure in a multinational company. This structure is typically found in smaller companies, or those with narrow, rather than diverse, product ranges. However, within a multidivisional structure, the divisions themselves are likely to be split up into functional management areas.

Figure 9.1 also summarises the advantages and disadvantages of a functional structure.[3] There are advantages, mainly in so far as it allows greater operational control at a senior level in an organisation; and linked to this is the clear definition of roles and tasks. However, there are disadvantages, particularly as organisations become larger or more diverse. In such circumstances, senior managers can be burdened with everyday operational issues, or rely on their specialist skills rather than taking a strategic perspective on problems.

In previous chapters there have been a number of discussions about *strategic business units* (SBUs) as the level at which an organisation should construct its product/market strategy, in terms of the choice of *generic strategy* and the *positioning* in its markets. In organisations of any size, there

Figure 9.1　A functional structure

Illustration 9.1   Scandinavian Airlines System (SAS)

Even when ownership and governance is split across three countries, the operational effectiveness of the company may require a single functional structure.

Scandinavian Airlines System (SAS) was formed in 1946 as a consortium of three national airlines — Denmark's DDL, Norway's DNL and Sweden's SILA. However, over the years the pressure from competition required SAS to operate as a single uniform company — at least in terms of the customer perception and experience. This dominant need for integration led to a functional structure for the company as a whole, despite the separate ownership of the three member companies.

The 1995 annual report explained how this functional structure worked across the three countries:

'SAS's central organisation has five operational line functions and five staff functions.

The line functions are Business Systems (Routes/products, SAS Trading and Cargo), Marketing and Sales, Station Services, Production (service on board, technical and flight operations), and Information Systems.

The five staff functions are Corporate Finance and Control, Human Resources, Public Relations and Government Affairs, Safety and Quality Control, and Information Systems Strategies.

This functional organisation was refined in 1995, among other things in order to guarantee good local support in the three parent countries. In the SAS Management Team (SMT), which comprises nine people, Vagn Sørensen is responsible for strategically important Danish issues and Gunnar Reitan has a similar responsibility for Norway. Since SAS has its head office in Sweden, it was not considered necessary to appoint someone to be responsible for Swedish issues.'

Source: Company Annual Report, 1995.

is likely to be a diversity of product/service and/or market/client group, which may lead to a diversity of positioning decisions for the different SBUs: for example, an airline or a hotel wishing to differentiate between its business and 'family' customers. A functional structure can be very problematic in coping with this diversity, since the structure is built around *business processes* which cut across the various SBUs, and there is often an attempt to impose an unhelpful uniformity of approach between the SBUs. So lead times in production, debt control in finance, advertising expenditure

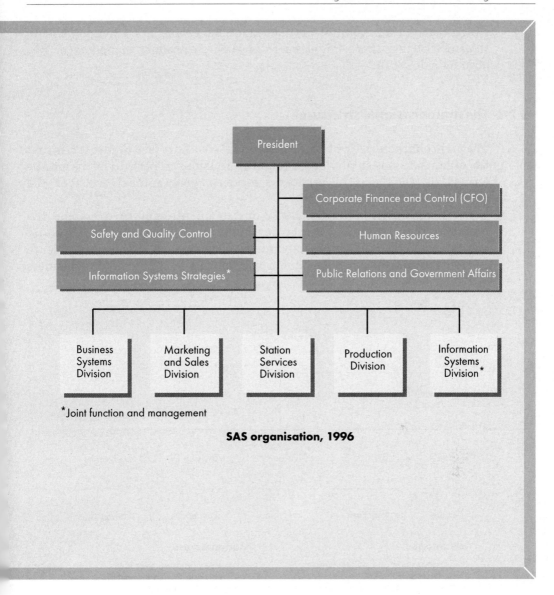

*Joint function and management

SAS organisation, 1996

in marketing, bonus systems in personnel, are too rigid to reflect the diversity which the organisation faces. The work of individuals is planned around a specialist business process and no one (other than the most senior managers) has any real ownership of the whole product or client group.

Of course, there are ways of minimising these problems with the functional structure, and they will be discussed more fully below (section 9.2.6). They are of two broad types: first, improving *co-ordination* between functions; and second, creation of a *substructure* within a business function which brings ownership of product or client group. For example, within sales/marketing, there might be roles such as product managers or key account sales staff.

9.2.3 The multidivisional structure

The main characteristic of a multidivisional structure (see Figure 9.2) is that the organisation is subdivided into units (divisions). These divisions may be formed on the basis of products, services, geographical areas or the processes of the enterprise.

Divisionalisation often comes about in an attempt to overcome the problems that functional structures have in dealing with the diversity mentioned above.[4] Its main advantage is that each division is able to concentrate on the problems and opportunities of its particular business

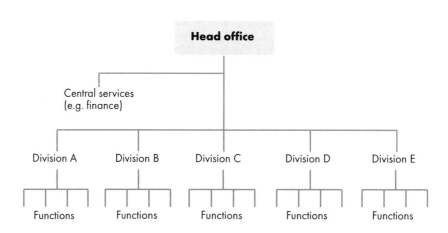

Advantages

- Concentration on business area (e.g. product market)
- Facilitates measurement of unit performance
- Ease of addition and divestment of units
- Facilitates senior management's attention to strategy
- Encourages general management development

Disadvantages

- Possible confusion over locus of responsibility (centralisation/ devolution confusion)
- Conflict between divisions
- Basis of intertrading
- Costly
- Divisions grow too large
- Complexity of co-operation if too many divisions

Figure 9.2 A multidivisional structure

environment. The product/markets in which the company operates may be so diverse that it would be impractical to bring the tasks together in a single body. So divisions can be created which relate closely to the SBUs, allowing a tailoring of the product/market strategy to the requirements of that SBU and improving the ownership of the strategy by divisional staff. A similar situation exists in many public services, where the organisation is structured around *service departments* such as recreation, social services and education.

In practice, the creation of divisions which closely match SBUs can prove difficult — for example, for reasons of size and efficiency (there would simply be too many divisions). So the divisional structure, in reality, is usually much broader than any one SBU. However, while the diversity within a division is less than in the company as a whole, nevertheless diversity still exists and can be difficult to manage. One way of coping with this in larger divisions is for divisionalisation to be rolled down to a next tier of subdivisions — sometimes by geography, sometimes by client group. A police force usually has territorial divisions. An education department often has subdivisions for primary, secondary and tertiary education.

A common problem in creating divisions is in deciding the *basis* of divisionalisation — should it be based on products or markets or technologies? The result can, of course, be a complex organisation: for example, a company may decide that it needs a number of levels of divisions in order to break up business activities sensibly. Figure 9.3 shows this. The company might be broken into a first level of divisions based on broad product groups. Within each of these divisions, there may be separate businesses which in turn have their own divisional structure. At some level in the organisation, a division will then be split into functionally based departments dealing with the specialist tasks of that business.

This raises the problems of which businesses should be in each division, which functions are to be included at each level of divisionalisation, and which functions are properly placed within the corporate head office rather than within any one of the divisions. For example, in Figure 9.3, where should a function such as financial planning be placed? Presumably, this is required both at a corporate level and at some level within an operating business; but should this be at level 1, 2 or 3? This issue will be discussed more fully in section 9.4 below, and is the aspect of organisational design concerned with choices about centralisation or devolution.

The advantages of divisional structures mainly centre on the ability to operate and monitor the activities of a division as a separate business (or business unit). There are disadvantages and difficulties, however, since the operation and control of multidivisional organisations is often far from straightforward. These issues are discussed more fully in section 9.4 below. Figure 9.2 also summarises the advantages and disadvantages of a multidivisional structure.

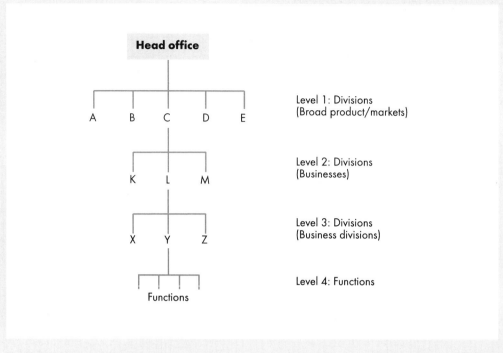

Figure 9.3 Levels of divisions

9.2.4 The holding company structure

In its most extreme form, a holding company is really an investment company. It may simply consist of shareholdings in a variety of separate business operations, over which the corporate centre exercises little detailed control. Although part of a parent company, these business units operate independently and probably retain their original company names. As mentioned in Chapter 6, the role that the parent company takes may be limited to decisions about the buying and selling of such companies with little involvement in their product/market strategy. Arguably, this is the situation as far as Lonrho or BTR is concerned.

An example of a holding company structure is given in Figure 9.4. The business interests of the parent company are likely to be varied: some of them may be wholly owned and some not, and there may be many business units within the group.

The advantages that a holding company can offer are based on the idea that the constituent businesses will operate their product/market strategy to their best potential if left alone, particularly as business environments become more turbulent. They should not have to carry the burden of a high central overhead, since the head office staff of the parent is likely to be

Parent company head office

| Company A (wholly owned) | Company B (wholly owned) | Company C (90% owned) | Company D (75% owned) | Company E (25% owned) |

Advantages

- Low central overheads
- Offsetting of individual business losses
- Availability of cheaper finance for individual businesses
- Spreading of risk for holding company
- Ease of divestment for holding company
- Facilitates devolution

Disadvantages

- Risk for individual business of divestment by holding company
- Unavailability of skills at group level to assist individual businesses
- Lack of synergy
- Difficulties of centralised control

Figure 9.4   A holding company structure

small. However, the business units can benefit from their membership of the group in such ways as the offsetting of profits against others' losses and the benefits of cheaper finance for investment from the parent company. The holding company itself may also claim benefits, such as the spreading of risk across many business ventures and the ease of divestment of individual companies.

Perhaps the greatest weaknesses of this structure are the risk of lack of internal strategic cohesion and duplication of effort between business units. It is one thing to say that business units operate better if they are given the profit responsibility to do so on their own; but in a large, perhaps multinational, operation there may be very considerable pay-offs from having some sort of overall product/market logic to the activities. These issues will be discussed more fully in section 9.4 below.

9.2.5 The matrix structure[5]

A matrix structure is a combination of structures. It often takes the form of product and geographical divisions or functional and divisional structures operating in tandem. Figure 9.5 gives examples of such a structure.

(a) Multinational organisation

(b) School

Advantages	**Disadvantages**
<ul><li>Quality of decision making where interests conflict</li><li>Direct contact replaces bureaucracy</li><li>Increases managerial motivation</li><li>Development of managers through increased involvement in decisions</li></ul>	<ul><li>Length of time to take decisions</li><li>Unclear job and task responsibilities</li><li>Unclear cost and profit responsibilities</li><li>High degrees of conflict</li><li>Dilution of priorities</li><li>'Creeping bureaucracy'</li></ul>

Figure 9.5 Two examples of matrix structures

Matrix structures may be adopted because there is more than one factor around which a structure could be built, so that pure divisional or functional structures would be inappropriate. For example, if a company extends its operations on a multinational scale and also develops new product lines, it may regard geographically defined divisions as the operating units for the purpose of local marketing, and product divisions as responsible for the worldwide co-ordination of product development, manufacturing and distribution to these geographical divisions.

Matrix structures do not occur only in large, complex organisations; they are sometimes found in quite small organisations and are very common in professional service organisations (both public and private sector).

It is claimed that matrix structures improve the quality of decision making in situations where there is a risk of one vital interest of the enterprise (e.g. a geographical area) dominating strategy at the expense of others (e.g. worldwide co-ordination of manufacturing). Formal bureaucracy is replaced by direct contact between individuals. The matrix structure is also supposed to increase managerial motivation and development because of the wider involvement in strategies.

However, matrix structures also have problems associated with them:

- There is a high risk of a *dilution of priorities*, whereby the message to those in the organisation is that everything matters equally and deserves equal debate.
- The *time* taken for decisions to be made may be much longer than in more conventional structures.
- It can be unclear who is *responsible* for what; while the idea of joint responsibility may conceptually be laudable, it can give rise to problems.
- Organisations with matrix structures may have to cope with a good deal of *conflict* because the lack of clarity of role definition and responsibility.

A summary of advantages and disadvantages is provided in Figure 9.5. The critical issue with any organisation structure in practice is the way in which it is operated. This is particularly important in the case of matrix structures, and the following guidelines should be considered:

- In practice, one arm of the matrix needs to *lead* in order to minimise the risk of paralysis. For example, the key issue for many major global manufacturing companies is the development and production of products in volumes which achieve financial viability. Although local 'tailoring' of products and marketing is also important, it is not the lead-edge of the company's global strategy.
- The allocation of workloads and/or duties for individuals should not normally be spread evenly across the matrix. So, for example, within a central personnel function there will be some degree of matching of individuals with the separate divisions to provide the *ownership* which

can be lost in a matrix structure. In the extreme form, the matrix structure will shade through into project teams of dedicated individuals from central functions seconded to divisions.

▧ Senior managers must be capable of *collaborating* across the matrix. It does not suit managers who are fiercely competitive (internally) and who cannot cope with *ambiguity*.

▧ There should be a clear means of breaking stalement. Usually, this is through referral to the chief executive. If this mechanism needs to be used too frequently, it is a sign that the matrix structure is not working sufficiently well.

9.2.6 Intermediate structures and structural variations

In reality, few organisations operate entirely like one of the pure structural types discussed above. The skill is in blending structure to the organisation's circumstances. There exists a whole range of 'shades of grey' between these pure types of structure, through which an organisation's structures might emerge and change over time in an attempt to reflect its changing circumstances. For example, a company may move from a functional structure to a divisional structure by a series of smaller incremental changes, and through changes in the approach to resource allocations and control (discussed in Chapter 10). Problems first arise within the functional structure as new products/markets compete for resources. Initially, these conflicts might be resolved by pushing the decision upwards until a sufficiently *senior executive* makes the decisions. When too many conflicts need to be resolved in this way, new *rules*, guidelines and procedures may develop to guide how resources are to be shared between products. The next step may be to *formalise* these procedures in the planning process by, for example, allocating a budget to the new product/markets. Up to this stage the problem has been dealt with by manipulating methods of control and operation rather than by structural changes.

As the new products/markets become more important and create competition for resources, it may be necessary to create *interdepartmental liaison roles*: for example, a committee or a temporary taskforce may be set up to advise on priorities. This may lead either to permanent teams of co-ordinators or special *co-ordinating jobs* (the product manager is a good example). Another step which may prove necessary to maintain the functional structure is the creation of departments with the sole function of co-ordination: *centralised planning departments*, for example. Ultimately, as the diversity increases, the organisation will divisionalise because the 'costs' of maintaining the functional structure will be unacceptably high. Or alternatively, the 'new venture' is created as a new division or even subsidiary, and the functional structure in the 'parent' reverts to its previous *modus operandi* as the 'problem' of diversity is removed.

9.2.7 Network and virtual organisations

The various intermediate structures discussed above are essentially an illustration of the importance of *horizontal integration* between the various activities within an organisation. In Chapter 4, it was emphasised that sustainable competitive advantage is likely to be gained by organisations which are able to 'manage' *linkages* between the separate activities in the organisation and, importantly, into the supply and distribution chains too.

Recent dramatic developments in the cost and effectiveness of telecommunications and the convergence with computer technology have opened up possibilities for many organisations to improve their management of these linkages. So the issue is how they might restructure the organisation (internally) to reflect and exploit these developments, and how they might relate (externally) to other organisations within their value chain. This has been of particular concern to many international organisations.[6] Some of the more detailed implications for organisation design will be discussed in later parts of this chapter and in Chapter 10 (for example, business process re-engineering). At this stage it is important to note some important trends in restructuring.

1. The drive to make organisation structures *flatter* through *de-layering* — although also driven by other factors like slowness in response of multitiered hierarchies — is now a real possibility for more organisations. Improvement in the speed and quality of management information allows for *spans of control* wider than was hitherto regarded as desirable.

2. The nature of work in many organisations has now changed such that it is less dependent on a particular place of work. The result is that many more people are able to carry out their work *independently*, but remain connected to key corporate resources (such as databases and specialist advice) and to colleagues, suppliers and clients through the telecommunications and computing infrastructure. The exploitation of the Internet is a major strategic issue for many organisations and will be discussed more fully in Chapter 10. It allows formal structures to be dismantled and replaced with well-functioning networks, supported by this information infrastructure. An example of a network organisation is given in Illustration 9.2.

3. Many organisations are debating and implementing (to a greater or lesser extent) concepts of *virtual organisations*,[7] where an organisation

Illustration 9.2   The network organisation: Asea Brown Boveri (ABB)

Network organisations need to have a well-developed and effective communications infrastructure to promote sharing and organisational learning.

With over 200,000 employees and operations worldwide, ABB is a vigorous and successful company in the 'electrotechnical business'. Between 1988 and 1992, revenues grew from $17 billion to $30 billion, with return on assets simultaneously improving from less than 10 per cent to almost 19 per cent.

ABB is organised as a federation of 1,300 companies. Each company, employing an average of 200 people and generating annual revenues of $25 million, is structured as a separate and distinct business and, to the extent possible, as a free-standing legal entity. In addition, each company has responsibility for its complete balance sheet, and it is company policy to permit each unit to retain a third of its net profits. This gives managers substantial financial independence by limiting their need to rely on corporate management for funding. Only one intermediate level of management exists between these front-line companies and the corporate executive committee. The entire headquarters of this $30 billion company, including the CEO and seven group executives who comprise the executive committee, and the various corporate staff groups, together number fewer than 100 people.

In ABB there is a clear recognition that those with the specialised knowledge and expertise most vital to the company's competitiveness are usually located far away from the corporate headquarters — in the front-line research laboratories, marketing groups or engineering departments. By decentralising assets and resources into these small specialised operating units, ABB is trying to create an environment in which this scarce knowledge can be developed and applied most appropriately. However, this decentralised structure has itself created a need for a powerful horizontal integration process to ensure that the entire organisation benefits from the specialised resources and expertise developed in its entrepreneurial units. Indeed, ABB's own 'Mission, Values and Policies' document states that 'a decentralised organisation will only work effectively with a good reporting system that gives higher level managers the opportunity to react in good time'.

The centrepiece of ABB's commitment to this information-sharing approach is ABACUS (Asea Brown Boveri Accounting and CommUnication System), a sophisticated, fully automated information system. Governed by strict rules concerning definition, format and timing, this democratic system provides accurate and timely data to the filed operations, ensures that managers around the company receive the same information at the same time regardless of their hierarchical level, and helps the group executives evaluate performance. As such, it allows the company to co-ordinate and control its diverse operations, keeping managers at all levels equally well informed.

Source: C. Bartlett and S. Ghoshal, 'Beyond the M-form: toward a managerial theory of the firm',
Strategic Management Journal, (1993), pp. 23–46.
Prepared by Sara Martin, Cranfield School of Management.

is held together not through formal structure and physical proximity of people, but by partnership, collaboration and networking. The important issue is that this organisation feels 'real' to clients and meets their needs at least as adequately as other organisations which are 'real' in the sense described here. Of course, this is *not* essentially a new issue about structures — as mentioned in Chapter 4, it is *normal* for organisations to decide to *specialise* by undertaking only some of the value activities in-house and to rely on other organisations to perform other tasks (in the supply or distribution chain). A major concern is the extent to which activities can be subcontracted. It has been argued[8] that extreme forms of subcontracting are likely to result in serious strategic weakness in the long run, as the organisation becomes devoid of core competences (see Chapter 4) and cut off from the learning which can exist through undertaking these activities in-house. This is now an important consideration in many industries such as civil engineering, publishing and specialist travel companies, all of which are highly dependent on subcontracting aspects of their business which hitherto were considered as core.

4. Networks can be organised in different ways, particularly in relation to how the interface with customers is structured (see Figure 9.6):

    ▪ A *one-stop shop* is where a 'real' and physical presence is created through which all client enquiries are channelled. The function of the one-stop shop is to put together a complete package of services by co-ordinating the various services provided. A 'turn-key' contractor (say, in civil engineering) might operate in this way — using its own expertise in project management and managing a network of suppliers, but not actually undertaking any of the detailed work itself.

    ▪ A second option is a *one-start shop*, again involving a real and physical presence dealing with client enquiries. However, the role here is essentially one of *diagnosing* the client's needs and *referring* them to the most appropriate provider. This is often referred to as 'pigeon-holing'. The role of primary health care practitioners (GPs) has traditionally been concerned with this process. Many advice services for small businesses have been established in this way — whether it be by banks or by government-sponsored agencies (e.g. Business Link in the UK).

    ▪ The *service network* is where there is no single starting point for clients in the network. The customer may access all of the services of the network through any of the constituent members of the network. A well-functioning network may not be easy to achieve, since it requires all members of the network to be fully informed, capable and willing to 'cross-sell' other people's products and to act

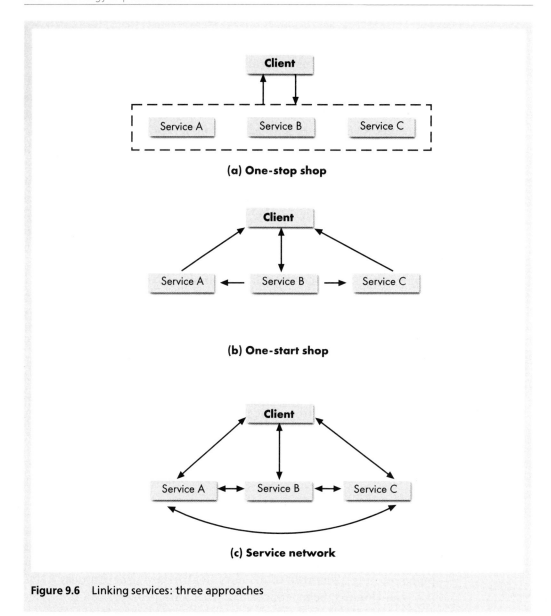

Figure 9.6 Linking services: three approaches

collaboratively. Some service networks also have a one-start shop facility. For example, Best Western is an international network of independent hotels, where customers can receive information or make bookings at any hotel in the network or through central booking points. This facility has the clear advantage of encouraging travellers to 'book on' their next destination with Best Western.

9.2.8 Structural types in multinational companies[9]

The growth in the size and importance of multinational businesses warrants some special mention, since the structural implications can be significant. A basic form of structure for a multinational is the retention of the 'home' structure and the creation of overseas subsidiaries which are managed through *direct contact* between the top manager of the subsidiary and the chief executive of the parent company. This is most common in single-product companies or where the overseas interests are relatively minor. Beyond this simple structure, the critical issue is the extent to which local independence and responsiveness should take precedence over global co-ordination (see Figure 9.7). In other words, it is an example on a global scale of the more general problems of co-ordination discussed in the previous three subsections. How this co-ordination is achieved will vary with circumstances and over time.

1. A common form of multinational structure is the *international division*. Here the home-based structure may be retained at first — whether functional or divisional — and the overseas interests managed through a separate international division. This draws on the products of the home company with the disadvantage of lack of local tailoring of

Source: Based on C. Bartlett and S. Ghoshal, *Managing Across Borders: The transnational corporation*, Harvard Business School Press, 1989.

Figure 9.7   Structural types in multinational companies

Illustration 9.3   3M's structures for Europe

Changing circumstances — both inside and outside companies — may require structural changes. Often, these changes will occur incrementally over time.

The Minnesota Mining and Manufacturing Company (3M) is based at St Paul, Minnesota, USA. Over an 80-year history (from 1914), it had diversified into leadership positions in seemingly unrelated fields such as adhesive tape, medical supplies, traffic signs and electrical equipment. In the mid-1990s, its turnover was about US$14 billion and it employed 87,000 people worldwide. The growth and development of the company had required many changes in structure, as shown by its approach in Europe. Some of the most significant changes were as follows:

■ 3M originally formed international divisions to exploit US products overseas.
■ By the 1950s, as 3M expanded its international presence, it created country subsidiary organisations (CSOs) in Europe with their own managing directors. The approach and product range of each CSO varied considerably, and the local language and culture prevailed in each CSO.
■ Although CSOs were very autonomous, strong links to headquarters were encouraged by not appointing a country national as the head of a CSO.
■ Once sales volumes justified investment, European manufacturing was allowed to substitute for imports from the USA. These plants were owned by one CSO and products sold to other CSOs in Europe.
■ By the early 1970s, 3M was experiencing fierce competition from the Japanese and needing to strengthen its technical and management capabilities. The status of MD of CSOs was raised considerably, becoming a role through which high flyers were expected to progress.
■ A 3M Europe office was established. Although this had no direct authority over CSOs, it was expected to co-ordinate activities between CSOs.
■ By the late 1970s, the need for European-designed and developed products had increased and technical directors were appointed to CSOs to achieve this.

services. Such structures tend to work best where there is a wide geographical spread and a portfolio of closely related products.

2.   Geographically based *international subsidiaries* often evolve from the previous structure (as seen in the case of 3M in Illustration 9.3). These subsidiaries are part of a multinational whole, but operate independently by country. In these companies, virtually all the management functions are nationally based, allowing for higher degrees of local responsiveness. Many of the multinationals founded in colonial days operated this way, such as Inchcape, Shell or Burmah. In such circumstances, the control of the parent company is likely to be

- In the early 1980s, the need to co-ordinate the efforts of CSO-based laboratories for the benefit of all European CSOs was reinforced by creating a reporting relationship of the technical directors to the appropriate laboratory head in the USA. Global potential of products started to dominate local considerations.
- To foster European/US exchange further, a whole series of informal and formal networks and relationships were developed between technical teams, including annual (global) technical planning meetings.
- In 1982 the European management team in Brussels was extended to include a European director for each product group. They functioned in an advisory capacity to CSOs.
- European management action teams (EMATs) were formed by pulling together sales/marketing managers from the larger CSOs. The heads of EMATs became product managers for 3M Europe.
- Conflict emerged for these heads of EMAT if the MDs of CSOs refused to implement the European product strategy in their division.
- As a result of these tensions, in 1986 a taskforce recommended that a formal pan-European structure based on product lines should be adopted, while keeping CSOs to support the local needs of business. The US parent decided not to accept the recommendations.
- By the end of the 1980s, many large customers (e.g. Ford Europe) were demanding a single access point to service their pan-European operations. It was also clear that the EMAT structure was not powerful enough to solve inefficiencies in CSOs.
- In 1990, another taskforce looked at the European organisation of 3M and its recommendations were similar to the 1986 report.
- Over the next two years, the company went through a major change process to adopt the new structure. They created European business centres (EBCs) which were product divisions reporting back to the US Group Vice-President; the 17 CSOs were reshaped to become ten regional subsidiaries (RSOs) (most covering more than one country) and reported to the Vice-President (Europe). Finally, a European operating committee was created as a forum to oversee the new European organisation. This included the heads of both EBCs and RSOs.

Source: M. Ackenhusen, D. Muzyka and N. Churchill, 'Restructuring 3M for an integrated Europe, part one: initiating the change', *European Management Journal*, vol. 14, no. 1 (1996), pp. 21–36.

dependent on some form of planning and reporting system, and perhaps the ultimate veto over national strategies; but the level of global co-ordination is likely to be low.

3. In many industries there has been a move away from the international division or subsidiary structure to what has become known as a *global product* or integrated structure. Here the multinational is split into product divisions which are then managed across the world. The logic of such an approach is that it should promote cost efficiency (particularly of production) on an international basis, and provide enhanced transfer of resources (particularly technology) between

geographical regions. The network of plants, each one in a separate country, may be making parts of cars, for example, which are assembled in yet another country: this manufacturing network may be supported by an international research and development network. The international development of many Japanese companies — for example, in electronics — has been managed in this way. A key requirement to support this structure is planning mechanisms to co-ordinate the various operations, and it is in these organisations that the planning and control systems are likely to be most sophisticated.

The obvious danger with a global product strategy is that local needs and differences may be ignored. Also, it is likely that the multinational will have several companies or divisions selling into the same country and these may be uncoordinated — perhaps creating inefficiencies through duplication of effort and/or confusing customers.

4. More recently, some organisations have developed structures which attempt to combine the local responsiveness of the international subsidiary with the advantages available from co-ordination found in global product companies. These have been called *transnational corporations*.[10] The key lies in creating an integrated *network* of interdependent resources and competences. Specifically, the transnational exhibits the following features:

- Each national unit operates independently, but is a source of ideas and capabilities for the whole corporation.
- National units achieve global scale through specialisation on behalf of the whole corporation.
- The corporate centre manages a global network by first establishing the role of each subsidiary, then sustaining the culture and systems to make the network operate effectively.

The success of a transnational corporation is dependent on the ability *simultaneously* to achieve global competences, local responsiveness and organisation-wide learning. This requires some degree of clarity as to the roles which the various global managers need to perform.[11] For example:

- Those responsible for *global products or businesses* have the overriding responsibility to further the company's global competitiveness, which will cross both national and functional boundaries. They must be the *product/market strategist*, the *architect* of the business resources and competences, and the *co-ordinator* of transnational transactions.
- Managers of *countries/territories* must act as a *sensor* of local needs. They must be able to *build* unique competences: that is, become a centre of excellence which allows them to be a *contributor* to the company as a whole.

- Managers of *functions* such as finance or IT have a major responsibility for ensuring worldwide learning across the various parts of the organisation. This requires the skill needed to recognise and spread best practice across the organisation — a form of *internal benchmarking*. So they must be able to *scan* the organisation for best practice, *cross-pollenate* this best practice and be the *champion* of innovations.
- The critical issue is the role played by the *corporate managers*, which is vital in the transnational corporation in integrating these other roles and responsibilities. Not only are they the *leaders*, but they are also the *talent spotters* among business, country and functional managers, facilitating the interplay between them. They are responsible for the *development* of a strong management centre in the organisation.

These issues about the role of the corporate centre and the way in which it adds value to the activities of the various parts of the organisation are issues about organisational design which will now be discussed (sections 9.3 to 9.5). It will be seen in Chapter 10 that there are also responsibilities concerned with ensuring that the processes of resource allocation and control of the organisation are adequate for the challenges of the future.

5. There are interesting differences between countries in the way that global strategies have tended to develop.[12] Companies which originated in many European countries (such as Unilever or Nestlé) needed to internationalise their activities at an early stage, owing to the small size of their home markets. This typically took the form of international subsidiaries (see Figure 9.7). Their challenge now is to reduce local autonomy and increase global integration.

   In contrast, US companies with a large domestic market tended to favour international divisions. They now face two challenges in globalisation: first, the issues of local autonomy; and second, the barriers between their separate strategic views of the domestic and international business. Japanese companies had traditionally been strongly domestically focused, and their international activities first developed through exporting. This resulted in strong global product strategies, and the subsequent need to relocate some production facilities overseas strengthened this position. The challenge is currently one of increasing local autonomy without losing the benefits of the global product strategies.

   Illustration 9.4 shows that organisations in practice may need to adopt a mixture of structures — in particular, the structures within different divisions may differ.

Illustration 9.4   BICC Group: structures within structures

Many large multinational organisations choose to cope with diversity through a mixture of structures. In particular, the structures within divisions may differ — some providing global coverage, while others have geographical territories.

BICC was formed in 1945 through the merger of two of the UK's leading electrical cable companies. For the next 25 years, the company developed its international interests, largely in the Commonwealth, and in 1969 it acquired Balfour Beatty, at that time predominantly a power construction and power engineering company. In the 1980s and 1990s, the group had developed its cables interests through acquisitions in North America, continental Europe, Asia and Australia. It had also broadened the base of Balfour Beatty's activities to encompass a major capability in civil engineering and other contracting businesses.

The structure of the organisation reflected these two principal businesses in different ways. First, one division encompassed the whole of Balfour Beatty with all of its operations in North America, the Middle East and the Asia-Pacific region. However, its cables businesses were managed through four separate divisions. Each had a geographic focus encompassing operations in Europe, North America, Australia or the Asia Pacific. Two further divisions existed in which non-core businesses sat.

Balfour Beatty

Balfour Beatty	Is a major international engineering and construction company. Its activities encompass civil, railway and power engineering, building and building services, maintenance and facilities management and housing. It also has a number of specialist manufacturing operations that support its power and railway engineering businesses.

9.3   The elements of organisational design

It should be clear from the previous sections that structure in itself will not ensure the success of strategy, although an inappropriate choice of

Cables Divisions

BICC Cables	Markets, designs, manufactures and installs a comprehensive range of cables and cable systems. It serves markets throughout Europe and the Middle East, Africa and South America.
BICC Cables Corporation	Is one of North America's leading producers of energy cables. It manufactures in Canada and the United States. Its principal business is in the supply of power cable to the US and Canadian utility and industrial markets. It also manufactures control, instrumentation, data communications, electronic and other speciality cable types.
Metal Manufacturers	Is one of Australia's leading industrial groups. It is the largest manufacturer of energy and communication cables, copper rod, copper and brass tubes and PVC pipes and fitting systems in Australasia. It is also the leading manufacturer of optical fibre in Australia and has an Australia-wide network of electrical wholesaling businesses.
BICC Cables Asia-Pacific	Was established in 1994 and is responsible for manufacture, marketing and marketing co-ordination of cable products in Asia-Pacific region.

Other Divisions

BICC Developments	The property development business consists of a number of completed properties offered for rental occupation and available for sale.
Other businesses	Andover Controls is a leading designer and manufacturer of advanced electronic building automation systems.

Source: Company Annual Report 1994

structure could impede success. The successful implementation of strategies will be influenced strongly by how the 'flesh' is hung on the structure. This is the province of organisational design and consists of three elements:

■ *Centralisation/devolution* — deciding where within the structure the responsibility for operational and strategic decision making should lie. This has also been referred to as *management styles*.[13]

■ *Organisational configurations* — the need to match the *detailed* structure with the context within which the organisation is operating.

■ *Resource allocation and control processes*, and how they influence the behaviour of people and assist or impede strategic developments.

The first two elements will be discussed in the following sections. Resource allocation and control is the subject of Chapter 10.

9.4   Centralisation vs devolution

One of the most important debates since the late 1980s in both public and private sector organisations has been concerned with *devolution*.[14] This is the extent to which the centre of an organisation delegates decision making to units and managers lower down in the hierarchy.

It is probably no accident that this interest in the importance of devolution coincided with a sustained period of market and financial pressure for most large organisations. Public services in many countries had seen their budgets significantly curtailed, while large private sector companies felt the bite of the market brought about by an extended recession in many parts of the world. This triggered senior managers to take action to address a number of issues which they were, perhaps, avoiding:

■ Top managers were becoming out of touch with the 'sharp-end' action in the markets and operations of the business. In fast-moving markets, or during periods of significant change in the public services, there was a feeling that more authority was needed *close to the action* in order to improve corporate performance.

■ Overcentralisation had resulted in organisations losing their way and becoming too concerned with internal matters at the expense of serving the customer or client.

■ Some would say that the drive towards greater devolution was largely a reaction to the previous era of overcentralisation. The issue of centralisation vs devolution is best discussed as a *continuum* from highly centralised to highly devolved and not as a black and white choice.

9.4.1 The role of the centre

In large organisations, most of the managerial activity which occurs between the centre of the organisation and its parts — departments, divisions or subsidiaries — has tended to be concerned with targeting and controlling the activities of those managing the parts. If organisations are to benefit from increased devolution, these activities of assessing the performance and value added by each part of the organisation remain important. However, a critical question which also needs to be answered is: what value does the centre of the organisation add to the activities of these separate parts? So asking the radical question, 'Do we need a centre at all?' can be a valuable discipline in understanding the role of the centre of the organisation and the centre/parts relationships. This is now referred to as the *parenting* role, as introduced in Chapter 6, particularly in organisations structured into divisions or operating a holding company model.[15] There are many different ways in which the centre (as a good parent) can add value (see Figure 9.8):

- Improving *efficiency* — perhaps through scale advantages from resource sharing, particularly in the use of infrastructure, support services and other overhead items. The corporate centre may have more *leverage* in either purchasing or market access.
- Providing *expertise* and *services* not available within smaller units — for example, personnel and financial services, estates management and IT infrastructure. Some of the most successful corporate parents have competences in market analysis, or cost analysis, which help fundamentally reassess the role and future of divisions or subsidiaries. Human resource and management developments and succession planning may be important ways in which the centre adds value.
- Providing *investment*, particularly during the early days of new ventures. This investment could be in resources and infrastructure, but also could be concerned with developing or changing the core competences within divisions. This could be linked to structural decisions — for example, the need to develop different specialist competences in the different divisions of a transnational corporation, as discussed in section 9.2.8 above.

Increasing value for money through

- Efficiency/leverage
- Expertise
- Investment and competence building
- Coaching/learning
- Mitigating risk
- Image/networks
- Collaboration/co-ordination/brokerage
- Standards/performance assessment
- Intervention (e.g. acquisition, disposal, change agency)

Figure 9.8   The role of the centre

- *Coaching* of people and managers in divisions may also be essential to improving competences. This would include the important role of providing a larger *peer group* through which individuals improve their own knowledge and skills: that is, fostering organisational *learning*, and the transfer of competences between divisions or subsidiaries.
- *Mitigating risk* which smaller units inevitably run, and easing the problems created by the variety and variability of demands from customers. Bigger units can smooth out these problems more easily.
- Providing a strong *external image* from which smaller units can benefit, and accessing *external networks* better than any separate unit.
- Encouraging *collaboration* and *co-ordination* of effort — in the ways discussed in sections 9.2.6 to 9.2.8 above — but not at the expense of diluting the core competences which are essential to separate strategic business units. This can often result in products or services which a single unit could not deliver. The corporate centre may also be able to *broker* external linkages or collaborations.
- Setting *standards*, assessing *performance* of individuals/units and *intervening* to improve performance (for example, by replacing managers, selling off businesses or ensuring turnaround of poor-performing divisions or businesses).

9.4.2 Dividing responsibilities

It has already been mentioned that the critical issue is a proper definition of the role of the centre of the organisation and its various parts. This is essentially concerned with how responsibilities for decision making are *divided* between the centre and the divisions or departments. Goold and Campbell provide three valuable *stereotypes* (or management styles) of different ways of dividing these responsibilities (see Figure 9.9). The parenting approach is very different in each case and requires very different competences at the corporate centre.

Strategic planning

Strategic planning (Figure 9.10) is the most centralised of the three approaches. Here the centre of the organisation operates as a parent who is the *masterplanner* and prescribes detailed roles for divisions and departments. The latter are seen as *agencies* which *implement* part of the organisation's plan. Their role is confined to the operational delivery of the plan. In the extreme form of strategic planning, the centre is expected to add value in *all* the ways outlined above. The centre orchestrates, co-ordinates and controls all of the activities of the departments/divisions, resulting in the extensive use of the management devices shown in Figure

Approach	Key features	Advantages	Dangers	Examples
Strategic planning	'Masterplanner' Top-down Highly prescribed Detailed controls	Co-ordination	Centre out of touch Divisions tactical	BOC Candbury Lex STC Public sector pre-1990s
Financial control	'Shareholder/ banker' Financial targets Control of investment Bottom-up	Responsiveness	Lose direction Centre does not add value	BTR Hanson plc Tarmac
Strategic control	'Strategic shaper' Strategic and financial targets Bottom-up Less detailed controls	Centre/ divisions complementary Ability to co-ordinate Motivation	Too much bargaining Culture change needed New bureaucracies	ICI Courtaulds Public sector post-1990

Source: Based on M. Goold and A. Campbell, *Strategies and Styles*, Blackwell, 1987.

Figure 9.9   Centre–division relationships

9.10. This is the classic bureaucracy familiar to many managers in large public and private sector organisations. Many of the multinational fast-food chains, such as McDonald's, would arguably come closest to this stereotype.

A follow-up study by Goold, Campbell and Luchs[16] of organisations categorised as strategic planning in the original study concluded that strategic planning can be a useful approach and one in which corporate managers add value, but only if they are able to have an in-depth detailed working knowledge of each 'core business'. Where attempts are made to extend beyond this arena, strategic planning as a management style becomes difficult to operate and often dysfunctional. Essentially, corporate managers run the risk of holding back the development of business areas which they do not understand or, even worse, steering them in inappropriate directions. The potential costs of bureaucracy are also dangers with this style, both in money and in lost opportunities.

The problems experienced with this approach have encouraged many organisations to devolve further (as seen in the case of IBM UK — Illustration 9.5). In particular, the relationship between the centre and divisions/departments tends to become entirely tactical and characterised by a 'special pleadings' mentality in the divisions/departments.

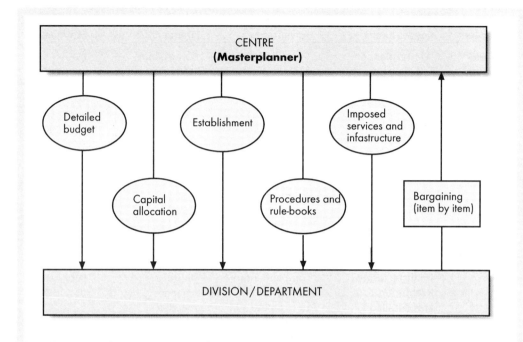

Figure 9.10   Strategic planning

Financial control

Financial control (Figure 9.11) is the most extreme form of devolved structure — short of complete dissolution of the organisation. The centre behaves as a parent who is like a *shareholder or banker* for divisions. There is little concern for the detailed product/market strategy of divisions — even to the extent that they can compete openly with each other. They might even have authority to raise funds from outside the company.

Here the role of the centre is confined to allocating capital (against bids), setting financial targets, appraising performance and intervening to avert or correct poor performance (e.g. by replacing divisional managers). The centre is attempting to add value in only a few of the ways listed earlier — in particular, through its corporate image and leverage (particularly in money markets) and/or mitigating the risk of individual divisions through the management of a portfolio of activities. Importantly, the centre is bringing managerial core competences (say, in turnaround of poor performance) which add value to the various businesses, by setting standards and reviewing performance.

This extreme is rarely found — even in the private sector. Some public sector managers appear to hold this as their ideal of what devolution means,

Illustration 9.5   A change of role for the centre: IBM UK Ltd

Historically, IBM had a centralised command and control structure supported by a strategic planning style at the corporate centre. However, as the structure has changed to a federation of individual businesses, the strategic style of the centre has also changed to one of strategic control.

Between 1991 and 1993, IBM UK was forced to take radical action in response to falling revenue and profitability levels. A review of the market place revealed that it was developing so fast and into so many niches that the old centralised planning and control structure was incapable of reacting fast enough. Within this structure, the company was largely product and technology driven, and product strategies were primarily developed at corporate headquarters. Countries were responsible for short- and medium-term targets, and for managing their resources and skills to achieve these targets. Within the country, sales branches had no strategic flexibility. They were given annual revenue, headcount and expense targets, with the main focus being on the achievement of revenue.

Under increasing pressure, a decision was taken to restructure the organisation into a federation of businesses, so devolving decision making closer to the customer to get the responsiveness needed. Further actions included changing the management system and substantially increasing the focus on quality. In this new environment, where there was considerable interdependence between the businesses, retaining the strategic planning style would have damaged the federal concept and a pure financial control style would have suboptimised the interdependencies between businesses. The adoption of a strategic control style was the optimal choice.

The adopted strategic control style means the individual businesses are free to experiment and to display the entrepreneurial characteristics necessary for rejuvenation. Power is placed as low down in the organisation as practical, with the sales branches and functions having both profit responsibility and the power to exercise that responsibility. Some power remains centralised, but only where there is good reason to do so. The centre's role has thus changed to:

- Deciding the allocation of limited financial resources between members of the federation.
- Investing in new opportunities and areas not being covered by existing businesses.
- Divesting those markets and systems which are no longer integral to the success of the whole.
- Establishing shared values and a style to bind the federation.
- Adding value through provoking strategic thinking and reviewing strategies.
- Optimising performance by not granting 'licences' for unattractive markets. Licences are obtained from the holding company when a business wants to operate in a specific area. Normally this will be an exclusive licence, although in some cases it may be appropriate for more than one business to be licensed.

Source: G. Lloyd and M. Phillips, 'Inside IBM: strategic management in a federation of businesses', *Long Range Planning*, vol. 27, no. 5 (1994), pp. 52–63.
Prepared by Sara Martin, Cranfield School of Management.

Figure 9.11 Financial control

but in reality, such extreme devolution is likely to remain unacceptable within the public sector for reasons of political accountability.

The follow-up study led to some interesting further observations about this style. First, it seems most appropriate to organisations operating in stable markets with mature technologies, and where the decision-making cycle (cause and effect) is short term: for example, organisations dealing with basic products. Second, there needs to be sufficient similarity between the divisions or subsidiaries for the core management competences to apply in similar ways to all divisions/subsidiaries. Otherwise, the parent may not have the competence to cope with a widely diverse set of subsidiaries. In terms of discussions earlier in the book, the management paradigm needs to be genuinely transferable from one organisation to another. Third, the target-setting and performance-appraisal regime needs to be applied consistently and tightly — an issue which proved difficult for some companies in the recession. Finally, the issue was raised of whether this style runs out of steam after a period of time, and is therefore most applicable to organisations which take a shortish-term view of their ownership of subsidiaries — where financial control is used to turnaround companies which are divested once in good shape.

Strategic control

Strategic control (Figure 9.12), which lies between these two extremes, necessarily defines the way in which most organisations operate. In a sense it is not a single stereotype, since it bridges all of the space between strategic

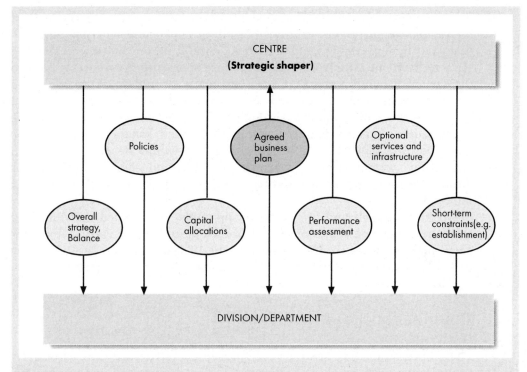

Figure 9.12 Strategic control

planning and financial control. So Figure 9.12 provides the *checklist* against which an organisation can establish its own particular brand of strategic control.

Here the centre operates as a parent who is a *strategic shaper*, and this defines the *minimum core role* of the centre as follows:

- Defining and shaping the *overall* strategy of the organisation — particularly through the resource allocation and control regime (to be discussed in Chapter 10).
- Deciding the *balance* of activities and the *role* of each division/ department.
- Defining and controlling organisational *policies* (on employment, market coverage, etc.).
- Assessing the *performance* of the separate divisions/departments and intervening to improve performance.

However, the centre does not fulfil these roles through an imposed masterplan. Rather, strategic control is built through the process of agreeing business plans produced by divisions — but within central guidelines. The important issue about 'shaping' is that the corporate centre is less concerned with developing strategy through structuring the *tasks* of its various departments or divisions. It is concerned with shaping the *behaviour* in departments and divisions.[17] And it is concerned with shaping the *context* within which other managers are operating. So, referring back to the earlier discussion and Figure 9.8, the centre would expect to add value through facilitating links and collaborations between divisions and departments — for example, through internal suppliers or collaborative product developments. Gaining advantage through *synergy* would often be an important objective in organisations. It would be concerned with promoting organisational learning by internal benchmarking and disseminating best practice. Central services may be optional rather than imposed.

Goold, Campbell and Luchs' follow-up study[18] concluded that fulfilling this particular type of parenting role is difficult unless the various divisions show similar characteristics. They cite the 1990s de-mergers in Courtaulds and ICI as examples of the difficulties of coping with too much diversity.

9.5 Organisational configurations

The discussions in section 9.2 presented structure as essentially synonymous with levels in a hierarchy. The discussions in the previous section have shown that organisational design is in practice more complex than this. It is better thought of as a number of *building blocks* and *co-ordinating mechanisms* which together make up the detailed *configuration* of an organisation.

Mintzberg[19] has suggested that there are essentially six pure configurations which can be adopted (or emerge) to fit the context which different types of organisation face. Before considering these configurations, it is necessary to describe the building blocks which make up each configuration.

Figure 9.13 shows Mintzberg's six basic building blocks of organisational design:

- The *operating core*, where basic work is produced — the factory floor, the operating theatre, the retail outlet.
- The *strategic apex*, where the general management of the organisation occurs.
- The *middle line* — all those managers who stand between the strategic apex and the operating core.
- The *technostructure* — staff analysts who design the systems whereby the work processes of others are delivered and controlled. Included here are engineers, accountants and computer specialists.

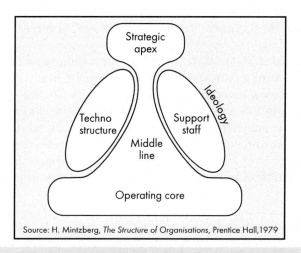

Source: H. Mintzberg, *The Structure of Organisations*, Prentice Hall,1979

Figure 9.13   The six building blocks of organisations

- The *support staff*, who support the work of the operating core, such as secretarial, clerical and technical staff, and catering.
- The *ideology* or culture of the organisation, consisting of the values, beliefs and taken-for-granted assumptions.

The relative size and importance of these building blocks will vary with circumstances — as discussed below — as will the methods by which activities are *co-ordinated* within the organisation. The following methods of co-ordination exist:

- *Mutual adjustment* through informal contact between people in the operating core. This is very common in small, simple organisations where people work closely and informally together. It is also common in very complex situations, such as R&D projects.
- *Direct supervision* through the hierarchy. Work is supervised by instruction from the strategic apex, through the middle line to the operating core.
- *Standardisation of work processes* through systems which specify how work should be undertaken. It is usually the job of the analysts in the technostructure to design and develop these systems of work standardisation.
- *Standardisation of outputs*: for example, through product or service specifications. This is particularly important where responsibility for separate activities is divided within the organisation. Many organisations are now developing *service-level agreements* between departments in order to clarify the parameters of service expected from,

say, computer services, credit control, etc. The corporate centre may also specify levels of output performance which are expected of divisions or subsidiaries — particularly in devolved organisations, as discussed above.

* *Standardisation of skills*, including knowledge and competences. This is an important co-ordinating mechanism in many professional service organisations (private and public sector). So the operating core of a professional service such as a hospital or an architect's practice functions smoothly because the operators share the same core knowledge and competences through their professional training.

* *Standardisation of norms*, where employees share the same core beliefs. This is particularly powerful in many voluntary organisations.

9.5.1 Configurations in practice

The choice of configuration to support an organisation's strategies can best be thought of in terms of matching the organisation's configuration to its strategic situation through the choice of the two design parameters discussed above: the *building blocks* and *co-ordinating mechanisms*. It should be clear from previous discussions in this book that this match is likely to *emerge* over time as an organisation finds ways of adjusting to the context in which it is operating. So it is unlikely to be a carefully considered choice as such. Nonetheless, it is useful for managers to reflect on the extent to which they see a match or mismatch between their organisational configurations and the context in which they are operating.[20]

Figure 9.14 summarises the key features of Mintzberg's six configurations, in terms of the circumstances or situations to which each is best suited and also the 'shape' and *modus operandi* of the organisation — its building blocks and co-ordinating mechanisms.

* The *simple structure* is in many senses a 'non-structure'. Few of the activities are formalised, and it makes minimal use of planning. It has a small management hierarchy, dominated by the chief executive (often the owner) and a loose division of work. The organisation is driven forward by the vision and personality of the chief executive. This configuration can prove highly effective in small entrepreneurial organisations where flexibility to changing circumstances is critical to success.

* The *machine bureaucracy* is often found in mature organisations operating in markets where rates of change are low. It is characterised by a large staff function — or *technostructure* — which develops systems and work routines to standardise work. The major improvements in cost efficiency in manufacturing industries early in the twentieth century were largely achieved through machine bureaucracies. This

Configuration	Situational factors		Design parameters	
	Environment	Internal	Key par of organisation	Key co-ordinating mechanism
Simple structure	Simple/dynamic Hostile	Small Young Simple tasks CEO control	Strategic apex	Direct supervision
Machine bureaucracy	Simple/static	Old Large Regulated tasks Technocrat control	Technostructure	Standardisation of work
Professional bureaucracy	Complex/static	Simple systems Professional control	Operating core	Standardisation of skills
Divisionalised	Simple/static Diversity	Old Very large Divisible tasks Middle-line control	Middle line	Standardisation of ouitputs
Adhocracy	Complex/dynamic	Often young Complex tasks Expert control	Operating core Support staff	Mutual adjustment
Missionary	Simple/static	Middle-aged Often 'enclaves' Simple systems Ideological control	Ideology	Standardisation of norms

Source: Based on H. Mintzberg, *The Structuring of Organisations*, Prentice Hall, 1979.

Figure 9.14   Mintzberg's six organisational configurations

configuration is still very appropriate for organisations producing commodity products or services where cost leadership is critical to the organisation's competitive performance (mail services would be an example).

- The *professional bureaucracy* is bureaucratic without the centralisation found in the machine bureaucracy. Professional work is complex, but it can be standardised through ensuring that the professionals operating in the core have the same core knowledge and competences. An emphasis on training and peer group interaction and learning is important to sustaining this standardisation.

- The *divisionalised* configuration is often found as a response to diversity in the product and/or markets of the organisation, as discussed earlier in the chapter. The important organisation design issues are concerned with centre/division relationships, as discussed in section 9.4. In particular, the corporate centre will specify levels of performance output expected from divisions or subsidiaries. These might be generic, such as overall profit performance, and might be found when *financial control* is the management style. In contrast, in organisations closer to *strategic control*, this specification of outputs is more likely to be expressed as a series of *performance indicators*, such as market share, efficiency ratios and a 'league table' position.

- The *adhocracy* is found in organisations whose competitive strategy is largely concerned with innovation and change. This configuration is highly organic, relying on direct interaction between workers in the operating core and a management style which assists and promotes this 'mutual adjustment'. Many professional service organisations (when providing tailor-made services rather than standard or routine services) may configure themselves in this way.

- *Missionary* organisations are dominated by cultural issues which are clear, focused, inspiring and distinctive. These ideals dominate the organisation's purposes and its *modus operandi*. Many voluntary organisations operate in this way: they attract like-minded individuals who share the missionary vision, and as such rely little on structures and systems to drive the organisation along.

Although few organisations will fit neatly into just one of these stereotypes, they can be used to think through some important issues concerning the structure/strategy fit in an organisation. Managers can check out in Figure 9.14 which stereotype their organisation currently most resembles. More importantly, they can describe the situational factors (both external and internal) for their organisation and see how closely these match the situation for which that particular configuration is best suited. For example, the simple structure is particularly appropriate for small companies in simple but dynamic environments.

9.5.2 Changing configuration

It is quite possible that changing circumstances will have created a mismatch between the configuration and the situation. This is where many difficulties occur in practice, not least for cultural reasons, as will be seen in Chapter 11. For example, the small company may have grown and diversified so that the simple structure can no longer cope. Many public services took on features of professional bureaucracies during a period of little change, and then experienced considerable difficulty in adjusting parts of their organisation towards an adhocracy as a necessary response to a dynamic environment which required more flexibility and customisation of services.

From	To	Reason	Example
Simple	Machine bureaucracy	Growth	Manufacturing companies
Machine bureaucracy	Divisionalised	Growth and diversity	Many companies
Professional bureaucracy	Adhocracy	Changing environment	Many service organisations
Missionary	Professional	Growth	Not-for-profit organisations
Professional bureaucracy	Network organisation	Dynamic environment	Professional service organisations
Single configuration	More than one type	Dynamic/complex environment	Many

Figure 9.15   Changing configuration: some examples

Figure 9.15 shows some of the situations which create the need to change an organisation's configuration.

An issue which most large organisations face — because of their diversity in product/market positioning — is the need for different configurations to support different SBUs or areas of the organisation's work. So the machine bureaucracy may be ideal for delivery of the commodity products or services, while the specialist product division positioned in a niche market may well need to operate like an adhocracy. For example, in a legal practice, for the *routine* legal work — say, wills or house conveyancing — the legal experts can design standard systems of delivery and the day-to-day work can be undertaken by other staff (or even partly by computer-based systems). *Standard* services require the experts to perform 'pigeon-holing' or diagnostic work (referred to in section 9.2.7 above) with clients to decide which standard services best suit their needs and circumstances — this can then be progressed by other staff. For *tailor-made* legal work, the legal expert needs to work with the client all the way through, since the work is genuinely unique to that client. The organisational configuration therefore needs to be a mix or a hybrid of the pure stereotypes, since the legal experts have different roles and contributions to make to these different types of service.

9.6   Summary

Making strategies work in practice can be a complex business. This chapter has been concerned with how the organisation's structure and design can influence the ease or difficulty of strategy implementation. The organisation structure *per se* is merely the skeleton of the organisation. An inappropriate structure can certainly impede strategy implementation, particularly where change in strategy is involved. However, structure in itself will not ensure successful implementation. It is how the detailed aspects of the organisation design are 'hung' around the structure which really matters.

The latter parts of the chapter considered two important issues of organisational design. First, the centralisation/devolution issue is concerned with where the authority for strategic and operational decisions should reside within the structure. This involves an understanding of the strategic roles of the divisions, departments or subsidiaries of the organisation, as well as the role of the corporate centre. There are different styles of managing the *parenting* role of the corporate centre, ranging from the centralised 'masterplanner' approach through to a highly devolved approach more akin to that of the shareholder or banker. Whichever style is adopted, the key issue to resolve is the way(s) in which the corporate centre will add value to the efforts of the divisions so that together they achieve more than they could do separately.

The second issue discussed was the detailed organisation *configuration* — how this is made up of different building blocks and co-ordinating mechanisms. Again, the issue is the extent to which a particular configuration best fits or supports different kinds of strategy. Organisations often need to change their configuration to support changing strategies, but this can be a difficult and sometimes painful process, since these detailed aspects of organisational life are ingrained into the culture. They are 'the way we do things round here'.

Chapter 10 will now consider how the processes of resource allocation and control within organisations can affect strategy implementation.

References

1. Some of these early writings are to be found in D. Pugh, *Organisation Theory*, Penguin, 1984.
2. These definitions come from T. Burns and G. Stalker, *The Management of Innovation*, Tavistock, 1968.
3. The advantages/disadvantages of functional structures are discussed in H. Mintzberg, *The Structuring of Organisations*, Prentice Hall, 1979.
4. This view of divisionalisation as a response to diversity was put forward by A.D. Chandler, *Strategy and Structure*, MIT Press, 1962, and supported by others, such as D. Channon, *The Strategy and Structure of British Enterprise*, Macmillan, 1973.
5. Matrix structures are discussed by C. Bartlett and S. Ghoshal, 'Matrix management not a structure, a frame of mind', *Harvard Business Review*, vol. 68, no. 4 (1990), pp. 138–45.
6. Network organisations are discussed in: J.C. Jarillo, *Strategic Networks: Creating the borderless organisation*, Butterworth-Heinemann, 1993; R.E. Miles, C. Snow and H. Coleman, 'Managing 21st century network organisations', *Organisational Dynamics*, vol. 20, no. 3 (1992),

pp. 5–20; R. Miles and C. Snow, 'Causes of failure in network organisations', *California Management Review*, vol. 34, no. 4 (1992), pp. 53–72; H.H. Hinterhuber and B.M. Levin, 'Strategic networks — the organisation of the future', *Long Range Planning*, vol. 27, no. 3 (1994), pp. 43–53; W. Ketelhohn, *International Business Strategy*, Butterworth-Heinemann, 1993, chapter 4; D. Cravens and N. Piercy, 'Relationship marketing and collaborative networks in service organisations', *International Journal of Service Industry Management*, vol. 5, no. 5 (1994), pp. 39–53. Also interesting is G. Redding, 'Overseas Chinese networks: understanding the enigma', *Long Range Planning*, vol. 28, no. 1 (1995), pp. 61–9.

7. Virtual organisations and the extensive use of subcontracting have been widely discussed. For example, W. Davidow and M. Malone, *The Virtual Corporation*, Harper Business, 1992; T. Peters, 'Get innovative or get dead', *California Management Review*, Fall 1990, p. 13; Jarillo (reference 6 above).

8. Jarillo (reference 6 above).

9. Good general texts on multinational corporations are G. Yip, *Total Global Strategy*, Prentice Hall, 1995; J. Ellis and D. Williams, *International Business Strategy*, Pitman, 1995.

10. C. Bartlett and S. Ghoshal, *Managing Across Borders: The transnational solution*, Harvard Business School Press, 1989; and 'Tap your subsidiaries for global reach', *Harvard Business Review*, vol. 64, no. 6 (1986) pp. 87–94.

11. C. Bartlett and S. Ghoshal, 'What is a global manager?', *Harvard Business Review*, vol. 70, no. 5 (1992), pp. 124–32.

12. Yip (reference 9 above), chapter 8.

13. M. Goold and A. Campbell, *Strategies and Styles*, Blackwell, 1987.

14. K. Scholes, 'Making the most of devolution', Sheffield Business School Occasional Paper No. 11, 1994. This issue of the centre/division relationship has also had a good deal of debate in the public sector context of the 1990s. See, for example, M. Clarke and J. Stewart, *The Enabling Council*, Local Government Management Board, 1988, and *The Role of the Centre*, Local Government Management Board, 1991.

15. Parenting has been discussed in Chapter 6. The key references are: M. Goold, A. Campbell and M. Alexander, *Corporate-Level Strategy: Creating value in the multibusiness company*, Wiley, 1994; A. Campbell, M. Goold and M. Alexander, 'Corporate strategy: the quest for parenting advantage', *Harvard Business Review*, vol. 73, no. 2 (1995) pp. 120–132. S. Ghoshal and H. Mintzberg, 'Diversification and diversifact', *California Management Review*, vol. 37, no. 1 (1994), pp. 8–27, discuss the implications of diversification on organisation design and the role of the corporate centre.

16. M. Goold, A. Campbell and K. Luchs, 'Strategies and styles revisited: strategic planning and financial control', *Long Range Planning*, vol. 26, no. 5 (1993), pp. 49–60.

17. C. Bartlett and S. Ghoshal, 'Changing the role of top management: beyond strategy to purpose', *Harvard Business Review*, vol. 72, no. 6 (1994), pp. 79–88; S. Ghoshal and C. Bartlett, 'Changing the role of top management', *Harvard Business Review*, vol. 73, no. 1 (1995), pp. 86–96.

18. M. Goold, A. Campbell and K. Luchs, 'Strategies and styles revisited: strategic control — is it tenable?', *Long Range Planning*, vol. 26, no. 6 (1993), pp. 54–61.

19. H. Mintzberg, *The Structuring of Organisations*, Prentice Hall, 1979. These configurations are also discussed fully in H. Mintzberg and J.B. Quinn, *The Strategy Process: Concepts, contexts and cases*, 3rd edition, Prentice Hall, 1995.

20. For further reading on the relationship between configuration and organisational context, see D. Miller, 'The genesis of configuration', *Academy of Management Review*, vol. 12, no. 4 (1987), pp. 686–701, and 'Organisational configurations: cohesion, change and prediction', *Human Relations*, vol. 43, no. 8 (1990), pp. 771–89; D. Jennings and S. Seaman, 'High and low levels of organisational adaptation: an empirical analysis of strategy, structure and performance', *Strategic Management Journal*, vol. 15, no. 6 (1994), pp. 459–75. In addition, a collection of research papers on configuration and strategy is included in the *Academy of Management Journal*, vol. 36, no. 6 (1993), pp. 1175–361.

Recommended key readings

- The different organisational structures are explained in J.R. Galbraith and R.K. Kazanjian, *Strategy Implementation: Structure, systems and process*, West, 1986.
- The centralisation/devolution considerations are discussed in M. Goold and A. Campbell, *Strategies and Styles*, Blackwell, 1987.
- Parenting is discussed fully in M. Goold, A. Campbell and M. Alexander, *Corporate-Level Strategy: Creating value in the multibusiness company*, Wiley, 1994.

- Organisational configurations are covered comprehensively in H. Mintzberg, *The Structuring of Organisations*, Prentice Hall, 1979, and H. Mintzberg and J.B. Quinn, *The Strategy Process: Concepts and cases*, 3rd edition, Prentice Hall, 1995.
- Organisational design issues in multinational corporations are covered in C. Bartlett and S. Ghoshal, *Managing Across Borders: The transnational corporation*, Harvard Business School Press, 1989, and G. Yip, *Total Global Strategy*, Prentice Hall, 1995.

Work assignments

9.1 Draw up organisation charts for a number of organisations with which you are familiar and/or any of the case studies in the book. Why are the organisations structured in this way?

9.2 Do you feel that the networking approach of ABB (Illustration 9.2) could be adopted by other organisations? What are the circumstances in which it would be most and least useful?

9.3 Compare the structure of 3M (Illustration 9.3) and BICC (Illustration 9.4). To what extent do you think they are in line with current thinking on organisational structure for multinational corporations (see Figure 9.7)? Would you recommend any changes in approach?

9.4 *Make a critical appraisal of the importance of the centre/division relationship in underpinning the strategic development of organisations (see Figures 9.9 to 9.12). Illustrate your answer by describing (with justification) the relationships which you feel would be most appropriate for the following organisations:*
   (a) The News Corporation*
   (b) Burmah/Castrol*
   (c) PSA Peugeot Citroën*
   (d) IBM (Illustration 9.5)
   (e) an organisation of your choice.

9.5 Referring to Figure 9.8, choose an organisation with which you are familiar and discuss the following two situations:

  ▪ increasing centralisation
  ▪ increasing devolution.

  In each case, explain and justify:

  (a) examples of the circumstances in which you would recommend each change
  (b) which specific items in Figure 9.8 you would centralise or devolve further
  (c) how the change would assist the organisation to improve its performance
  (d) any potential dangers of the change and how these might be avoided.

9.6 By referring to Figures 9.13 and 9.14, explain which of Mintzberg's organisational configurations best fits the situation of each of the organisations in assignment 9.4. To what extent is the actual configuration of the organisation in line with this expectation, and what are the implications of any mismatches?

9.7 *By using specific examples from your answers to the previous assignments, explain how the various aspects of organisational design need to fit together to support an organisation's strategies. How close are theory and practice? Refer to Mintzberg and Quinn in the recommended key readings to assist with your answer.*

Resource allocation and control

10.1 Introduction

The previous chapter looked at how people and other resources of an organisation might be organised, first in terms of the basic *structure* of the organisation; and second in terms of where within this structure operational and strategic *decisions* are made. Finally, the detailed way in which organisations might be *configured* in order to support their strategies was discussed in terms of the *building blocks* and *co-ordinating mechanisms* which make organisations work in practice. These are all important aspects of the *architecture*[1] of the organisation, as discussed in the introduction to Part IV.

This chapter is concerned with pushing the discussion of architecture to a further level of detail by looking at the ways in which resources are *allocated* to create and sustain the competences needed to succeed. There is an important link back to the framework and discussions in Chapter 4, which was concerned with analysing and understanding strategic capability. In this chapter, the emphasis is on ensuring that the resources and competences are in place to deliver the particular strategies that the organisation is wishing to pursue. The chapter will also be concerned with the processes of control and information handling which sustain the resources and competences of the organisation.

It is also important to emphasise again that, in thinking through how strategy will be put into effect, detailed thought is, in fact, being given to the *feasibility* of its implementation. As such, the planning of resource allocation and competence development is also part of the evaluation of strategy. Since much of strategic management is concerned with how an organisation will survive and prosper in a changing world, there is also an important link to the issues in Chapter 11, which is concerned with *management of change*.

Figure 10.1 illustrates how the planning and control of resources influences the success or failure of the organisation's strategies, and provides a framework for this chapter:

1. The *resource configuration* of the organisation is concerned with both the *identification* of resource requirements and how those resources will be deployed to create the *competences* needed to underpin particular strategies. These competences are usually created through allocating a *mixture of resources* to a particular activity, as discussed in Chapter 4, and the *processes* which link these activities together. Referring back to Figure 4.2, the resource configuration will define the broad mix of resources and competences — both necessary/threshold requirements, and also the unique resources and core competences on which competitive advantage will be built. It needs to be remembered that this will include the way in which the separate activities of the organisation are linked together and the management of linkages in the wider value system in which the organisation is operating. Since few strategies are developed in a 'greenfield site' situation, there are usually important practical issues about how existing resources are redeployed and/or developed into new competences.

2. The resource configuration will define the broad shape of requirements for the future resources and competences of the organisation. There will also need to be specific *resource plans* for new developments (or strategic projects) which identify the critical success factors, priorities, schedules and budgets: in other words, how the resource configuration will be operationalised.

Figure 10.1   Resource allocation and control — to support successful strategies

3. *Control* of these aspects of strategy implementation can be achieved in a variety of ways, depending on how the organisation is designed and the situation which it faces. This could range from an emphasis on *systems* of planning and co-ordination, through *performance targets* and *rewards*, to looser *'market' forces, cultural control* or *personal motivation.* These various mechanisms for sustaining the necessary competences for the future will be discussed in relation both to the *internal* activities of the organisation and also to linkages *outside* the organisation into the wider value system.

4. The *information capability* of the organisation will have a considerable influence on each of these previous aspects, and in that sense should be regarded as a key resource. For some organisations, information in the form of knowledge or intellectual property may be central to the organisation's competitive strength. New information technologies may also have been exploited to improve competences in, for example, purchasing or selling processes. This could be especially important as organisations globalise and face more complex situations. Similarly, the processes through which control of strategy is exercised can change if the information capability changes. For example, the rapid

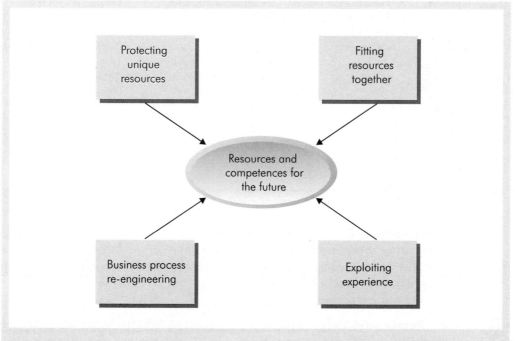

Figure 10.2   Resource configuration: creating capabilities for the future

Illustration 10.1   Skandia: creating competences for the future

Competences for the future must relate to value-creating processes.

'The future of Skandia is in creating new work methods, competences and value-creating processes, not just in following the beaten path ... Through these processes emerges an accelerated growth of hidden, intangible, value. This is Skandia's intellectual capital — a combination of human and structural capital.'

This was Bjorn Wolrath, the President and Chief Executive of Skandia — one of Europe's largest insurance groups — in a supplement to the company's annual report in 1995. The supplement was designed to demonstrate the variety of ways in which business units were addressing these issues of competences for the future. The table below summarises some examples.

Business unit	Value-creating processes	Organisational capital	Business effects
Vesta Processes for profitable customer relationships	• Systematised risk assessment and selection • Development of distribution channels to extend the duration of customer relationships • Development of IT-based support systems	• Database with overview of customer categories, so-called observation risks, no-risks, authorisation system • Routine manuals and systems for sales, customer care, customer renewal, operations, claims handling • Offer handling and analysis system	• Risk level (claims ratio) better than average • Improved distribution effectiveness • Growing market share • Increasing customer loyalty • Decreasing overhead ratio • Growing sales via alliances

development of the internet means that high-quality information is becoming increasingly available at the level of the 'operator', and does not need to be accessed, analysed and interpreted by specialist planning departments and/or managers. The importance of these changes will be discussed in section 10.5.

The chapter concludes with a short section which looks at how the circumstances of an organisation might determine or influence the structure and organisational design issues described in both Chapters 9

Business unit	Value-creating processes	Organisational capital	Business effects
Mexico Processes for risk management	• Risk assessment, management and selection • Relationship development, customer care • Competence co-operation	• Guidelines, manuals for risk management • Work procedures for relationship development and customer care • Packaged, communicated strategy	• Greater customer loyalty • Higher contract renewal rate • Greater number of offers handled • Falling administrative expense ratio
Industry Division Competence centres	• Development of IT-based **support systems** • Customer care and customer development teams • Knowledge sharing, competence co-operation	• INDRA, computer systems • Customer team manual • Competence centres • Network of global competence through co-operation agreements	• Streamlined, more effective work methods • Decreasing expense ratio • More satisfied customers • Doubling in premium volume through added and new sales
SkandiaLink Learning processes	• Automated fund switching • Transaction processing and telephone accessibility • Staff reward system • Augmentation of customer care	• SkandiaLink investment Analysis (SIA) • Value development process • Automatic fund-switching service, Telelink • FLINK index (administrative routines for business handling) • Routine handbook for transaction processing • Customer centres • Customer care groups	• Shorter processing times • Decreasing expense ratio • Growing volume of assignments/ representative • Increased number of automatic fund switches • Greater staff commitment

Source: 'Intellectual capital — value-creating processes', a supplement to Skandia's Annual Report, 1995.

and 10. It will also consider the difficulties of changing organisations (as a precursor to a fuller discussion in Chapter 11).

10.2 Resource configuration[2]

The deployment of resources and development of competences for the future is an issue of central importance to successful implementation of strategies (see Figure 10.2 and Illustration 10.1). The discussions in Chapter 4 have some important practical implications for the way in which resources and competences underpin the competitive advantage of an organisation. In particular, the risk of imitation was stressed (see Figure 4.2) and this becomes an important consideration when thinking through the resources and competences for the future. In addition to protecting resources, competences for the future will need to be created by fitting together separate resources and activities of the organisation, and by managing linkages in the wider value system (e.g. with customers). This may require a reconfiguration of current resources and competences, and relationships outside the organisation (business process re-engineering). Finally, this section will look at the importance of exploiting experience to underpin successful implementation.

10.2.1 Protecting unique resources

Where a strategy is dependent on the *uniqueness* of a particular resource, it is important to ensure that this uniqueness is protected. This may be possible through the legal or *regulatory framework* (such as the patenting of products). It may involve *lobbying* to secure protection from competitors who may undermine the uniqueness (for example, import restrictions). It may involve plans for *continued investment* — for example, in R&D — which should be a high priority in terms of using the improved margins that the uniqueness should be creating (for example, through price premiums, as discussed in Chapter 6, or higher budgets for 'centres of excellence').

For some organisations, their uniqueness is difficult to imitate because it lies in the tacit knowledge[3] of a number of individuals or groups. In other words, the capability of the organisation is found in *personal competence* and is not formally owned by the organisation, as discussed in Chapter 4. This is true in many knowledge-based organisations,[4] such as software houses and biomedical companies, particularly where technology and product life cycles are short. Although the organisation may have ensured ownership of current products and developments (through patents or copyright), it is impossible to own the tacit knowledge which underpins the next generation of developments. So the retention of those individuals or groups with this knowledge becomes a key implementation issue: for example, through the development of suitable policies on pay, promotion and working conditions.

10.2.2 Fitting resources together

The organisation must be able to bring together an appropriate *mix* of

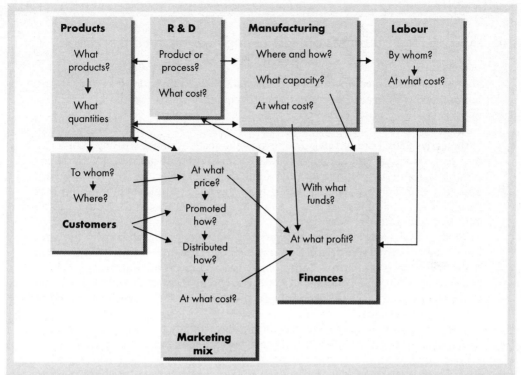

Figure 10.3   Resource integration in a new product launch

resources to create competences. This can be a complex matter in many situations. For example, Figure 10.3 shows some of the resources and activities which need to be integrated by an organisation hoping to gain competitive advantage through its competence in bringing new products to the market more quickly than competitors. A competence in new product launches results from an ability to integrate and co-ordinate the separate activities of R&D, manufacture, etc. — each of which, in turn, involves bringing together a complex mixture of resources. It is not sufficient simply to own these resources or to be competent in these separate activities. It is the ability to link these together effectively and quickly which determines the success or failure of the strategy and could be a source of real competitive advantage.

10.2.3 Business process re-engineering

Few strategic changes are introduced in a greenfield site situation, and therefore a central question in resource allocation is how the *existing* resources and competences of the organisation can be adapted to fit new

Illustration 10.2   Business process re-engineering at Ford and MBL

Business process re-engineering is concerned with reconfiguring resources and business activities to achieve dramatic improvements in performance.

Ford

In the early 1980s, Ford put its accounts payable sections under scrutiny in order to save costs. Management aimed to reduce the existing headcount of 500 by 20 per cent. This seemed a reasonable goal until they looked across at Mazda, which operated with only five people rather than the 400 Ford planned, implying that Ford's accounts payable section was five times the size it should be. Nothing to do with Japanese culture either!

Analysis of the existing system showed that the major problem was with the work required on purchase order/receipt document/invoice mismatches. Rather than *dealing* with these mismatches, Ford *stopped* them happening. It did this by initiating and storing orders on an on-line database, with no *physical* copies going to anyone. When the goods come in, someone checks the database; if they match, okay, if not they are simply sent back.

The old process required the accounting department to match fourteen data items; the new process needed only three, a part number, the unit of measure and a supplier code, and all of this matching is done automatically by the computer system, whereupon it automatically prepares the cheque, which accounts payable sends to the vendor. There are *no* invoices in the new system, since Ford told vendors not to send them. Ford gained two major benefits, a 75 per cent reduction in headcount and financial information that is significantly more accurate. Ford had completely *re-engineered* its accounts payable.

Mutual Benefit Life (MBL)

MBL completely *re-engineered* its insurance applications processing by taking a radical approach that was enabled by IS. This meant moving from a situation where 5 departments, 19 specialists, 30 internal checks, 7 different computer systems, 225 administrative staff and many months of elapsed time were required to issue a life insurance policy, to a situation that only required 1 case manager, 1 computer system, only 100 administrative staff and 1 day of elapsed time to issue a policy (and more being issued at that). This was done by sweeping *away* specialisation and the fragmentation of the task, and replacing it with IS-empowered single-person decision making. Since this redesign crossed many department boundaries, senior management resolution of disputes was vital to the success of the redesign process.

Source: Wendy Robson, *Strategic Management and Information Systems*, Pitman, 1994. Reproduced with permission.

strategies. This process of reconfiguring activities to create a dramatic improvement in performance is now generally referred to as *business process re-engineering* (BPR).[5] It will be seen in section 10.5.2 that increased capabilities in information technology have been an important driving force behind BPR (and examples are given in Illustration 10.2).

Sometimes a company will choose to manufacture and market a new product range through a new division or even a new company to avoid problems of conflict or incompatibility with existing operations. So the planning of resources also leads back into structural considerations (Chapter 9) and into issues of managing change which will be discussed more fully in the next chapter. An assessment of this fit between the strategy and the existing resources and competences begins to establish the extent to which implementation is likely to require major changes within the organisation, or is achievable by an adjustment of the current resource base and competences.

An important consideration about an organisation's resource configuration for the future is which activities it continues to undertake in-house and which should be bought in or subcontracted. This would include a review of *strategic alliances* (Chapter 7) and the *external networks* of the organisation (Chapter 9, section 9.2.7). Readers are also reminded of the discussions in Chapter 4 (section 4.3.6) about the dangers of subcontracting activities which are core competences, and this should be a guiding principle in reshaping these external relationships. So a global fast-food company like KFC is happy to franchise the operation of outlets, but maintains its core competences of product development and marketing in-house. These are the cornerstones of the business's success.

10.2.4 Exploiting experience

An important way in which organisations improve their competences is through the experience of undertaking activities repeatedly and learning how to do them better (i.e. with lower cost and/or better value). The concept of the *experience curve*, introduced in Chapter 4 (section 4.3.3), underlines this point. There are some important implications for strategy implementation. First, other organisations are likely to imitate the leaders and catch up through their own learning. So learning and improvement needs to be a permanent feature of successful implementation. This is the Japanese philosophy of *Kaizen*[6], and is fundamental to the idea of gaining competitive advantage by stretching resources and competences to achieve levels of performance which others cannot match.[7] It is about designing a misfit between aspirations and current resources in order to create this stretching.[8] This also means that resources will need to be available to sustain this continued improvement, so investment for the future is a permanent feature of successful organisations.

Another implication is that resource allocation decisions for the future should be driven by the expectation that efficiency gains (within limits) can be achieved without loss of quality (value); or alternatively, that value improvements can be achieved with the same 'unit of resource' (again within limits). Where organisations do not face free market situations (for example, many public services), the issue of efficiency gains tends to be a central issue for debate (and friction) during the resource allocation (budget-setting) process. The justification for year-on-year efficiency gains is that such gains through experience are essential to the survival of organisations in a free market situation, so this should be the benchmark against which continuous improvement in the public services is judged.

10.2.5 Sustaining competitive advantage

The discussion so far in this section has looked at a range of ways in which organisations might create the resources and competences for successful implementation of strategy. However, the relative importance of these resources and competences will vary depending on the type of strategy being implemented. For example, Figure 10.4 shows how the competences needed by an organisation will vary depending on whether the generic strategy is one of low-price positioning or differentiation.

1. A *low-price positioning* will need to be underpinned by real cost advantages on one or more of the items listed in Figure 10.4.[9] For example, a business purchasing large quantities of a given material from

LOW-PRICE STRATEGY	DIFFERENTIATION STRATEGY
Underlying competences	**Underlying competences**
'Process' design	'Product' design
Labour supervision	Marketing
Easily produced 'products'	Creative flair
Low-cost distribution	Research capability
	Corporate image
Requiring	**Requiring**
Tight cost control	Looser control
Detailed reporting	Simpler reporting
Highly structured	Strong co-ordination
Quantitative targets	Market-based incentives

Figure 10.4   Competences and management styles to support different strategies

Illustration 10.3   **Marks and Spencer**

Differentiation through added value products and customer service is difficult to imitate if sustained through the management of linkages in the value chain.

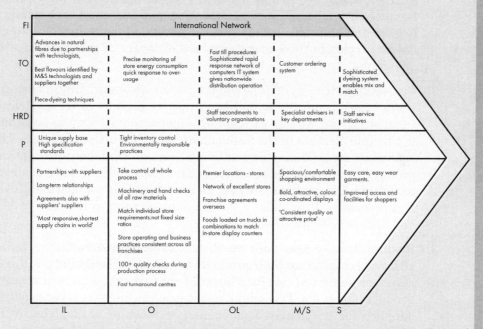

Marks and Spencer had built its reputation through consistency in product quality and levels of customer service. This differentiated M & S from many of its competitors in both food and clothing retailing (its two main areas of activity). The value chain above shows the importance of managing linkages to sustain this competitive advantage:

■ All aspects of the 'customer experience' worked well together. So the quality of the products themselves was reinforced by the premier location of shops, in-store display, spacious shopping environment, and consistency of store layouts and business practices (e.g. environmentally responsible practices).

■ The relationship with suppliers was a model of a genuine long-term partnership, involving a commitment to assisting suppliers to improve.

■ This supply chain management was supported by tight systems for inventory control and the development of high standards of specification.

■ Customer service standards in the stores required considerable efforts in systems development, exploitation of available technologies and the development of staff.

■ There was commitment to improving access for customers — both physical access and ordering systems.

Source: Company Annual Report, 1994.

a supplier is likely to obtain better prices, have greater negotiating power to ensure that deliveries are on time (and therefore reduce stocks), and build up knowledge and experience among its buyers that leads to greater internal efficiencies. The same business might be able to identify other activities in which it can also gain cost advantage. Further, it may be possible to identify where competitors are vulnerable because they have a lower market share and therefore higher unit cost (e.g. in distribution). It may then be possible for the business to drive down its costs in these areas as a further means of gaining competitive advantage.

2. Crucial to a strategy of *differentiation* is the understanding of customers' needs[10] and the ability to build appropriate product or service features. Competitive advantage through differentiation is likely to be achieved not by one element of the value chain, but by multiple linkages within the value chain. It may be relatively easy for a competitor to imitate a product, or an aspect of technology. It is more difficult for a competitor to imitate differentiation based on a multitude of compatible linkages and processes throughout a value chain, as seen in the case of Marks and Spencer (Illustration 10.3).

3. Businesses may also improve their competitive standing by building *switching costs*[11] into their products or services. Switching costs are the actual or perceived cost for a buyer of changing the source of supply of a product or service. This might be because the buyer is dependent on the supplier for particular components, services or skills. The business which can create significant switching costs is therefore achieving a differentiated position in the market.

    It is important to identify bases of such switching costs. Managers might do this by considering how their own value chain might link into the value chain of buyers — a point made previously in Chapter 4 (section 4.3.5). For example, it could be that a manufacturing company is following a low-price strategy and therefore that low stock levels are of significant strategic importance. A supplier might choose to work closely with the manufacturer to ensure speed of delivery and information on availability of components. The supplier is seeking to build linkages between different parts of the value chain, to gain experience in so doing, and therefore to build switching costs into the service provided. This strategy is being followed by Unipart, the UK-based automobile component manufacturer.

4. Difficulties tend to occur when there is a need for SBUs to *reposition*, requiring the development of new competences while the old competences become either redundant or of less importance. Figure 10.4 also shows that the approach to management control may need to

vary for different types of strategy. A low-price strategy may be well supported by a centralised bureaucratic approach, while differentiation usually requires a more flexible style. This will be discussed more fully in section 10.4 below.

10.3 Preparing resource plans

The discussion so far should help with defining, in broad terms, the resourcing/competence requirements for the future. However, it does not identify in detail the requirements of specific strategic developments. For this more detailed purpose, an organisation needs resource plans. The importance of these resource plans is to identify the critical factors for success of a particular strategy, and therefore the consequent priorities, schedules and budgets.

10.3.1 Critical success factors[12]

One of the major shortcomings of strategy implementation in organisations is a failure to translate statements of strategic purpose, such as gaining market share, into an identification of those factors which are critical to achieving these objectives, and the resources and competences which will ensure success. Chapter 4 introduced the idea of *critical success factors* (CSFs) as those components of strategy where the organisation must excel to outperform competition. These are underpinned by competences which ensure this success. A critical success factor analysis can be used as a basis for preparing resource plans.

Illustration 10.4 is an example of how a critical success factor analysis can be undertaken for an information systems company planning to improve its competitive position in a part of the market which requires complete 'turn-key' systems of hardware, standard software and customised information systems applications. It can be seen that the steps in a CSF analysis are usually as follows:

- Identify the critical success factors for the specific strategy, keeping these to a manageable list (preferably fewer than six). These might be factors such as *developing a global network, supply chain management and 'agile' production.*
- Identify the underpinning competences which are essential to gaining competitive advantage through each of these CSFs. These may be related to *separate activities* (e.g. after-sales service), support activities (e.g. training and development) or the management of *linkages between activities* (e.g. stock control linked to point-of-sale IT systems).

Illustration 10.4 Critical success factors for an information systems supplier

Success depends on identifying those components of strategy in which the organisation must excel in order to outperform competition. This also requires a clear understanding of the competences which will be needed to underpin these critical success factors (CSFs).

An information systems supplier was planning to improve its competitive position in the part of the market which required 'turn-key' systems (hardware, standard software and customised information systems applications). The approach of most companies currently supplying this market was typified by an overemphasis on 'supplier-led applications' and very poor after-sales support of customers, particularly in the crucial three months after installation. It was also felt that many current customers had now 'matured' in their understanding of their information systems needs and were ready to 'trade up' to more sophisticated applications with a much greater level of customisation to their own particular circumstances.

In order to prepare for this new strategy, the company undertook a critical success factor analysis using the value chain to identify the underpinning competences needed for each CSF.

Critical success factors	Underpinning competences and performance targets						
	Inbound logistics	Operations	Outbound logistics	Marketing and sales	Service	Support activities	Managing linkages
Software features	Royalty payments (5% premium)						Customer feedback (monthly)
Customer care		Responding to enquiries (24 hrs)			Speed of response (3 hrs)	Installations database	Customer feedback (monthly)
New business opportunities				Salesforce reports (monthly)		Competitor profiling (top 10)	Customer feedback (monthly)

■ Scrutinise the list to ensure that it is *sufficient* to give competitive advantage.

■ Identify *performance standards* which need to be achieved to outperform competition: in the illustration, 24-hour turnaround of enquiries, or 5 per cent royalty 'premium'. It is important to remember that competitors are likely to attempt to match or beat these standards and erode competitive advantage. Therefore, these performance standards need to be

Their analysis proceeded as follows:

- It identified three CSFs where it felt it would need to outperform competition. These were *customised software features, customer care* and *identification of new business opportunities*.
- The *underpinning competences* which were essential to gaining competitive advantage through each of these CSFs were identified. So the CSF of *customer care* needed to be underpinned by two competences: responding to *enquiries* and the speed of breakdown *maintenance service*. In turn, these were dependent on competences in key support activities, particularly the *database* on customer installations. Some underpinning competences related to managing external linkages: for example, the highly developed system for customer feedback (both directly and via salesforce reports) and its use in informing both software feature developments and new business opportunities.
- It scrutinised the list to ensure that it was *sufficient* to give competitive advantage.
- It identified *performance standards* which needed to be achieved in each of the underpinning competences to outperform competition: for example, 24-hour turnaround of enquiries and 5 per cent royalty 'premium'. It knew that competitors were likely to attempt to match or beat these standards and erode competitive advantage. Therefore, these performance standards needed to be constantly reviewed (and changed).
- It assessed the extent to which competitors could *imitate* each underpinning competence and any actions needed to counteract this imitation (continual improvement/revision of standards was one approach — it also considered whether to offer longer-term exclusive contracts to a few selected freelance writers).
- Competitors could, of course, also try to shift the competitive ground by identifying different critical success factors which were valued by (at least some) customers and developing their own competences to underpin these CSFs. For example, they might identify that *global coverage* was of special importance to multinational companies and build a network of support (through strategic alliances) to provide this and gain competitive advantage with that particular group of customers.
- The company took the view that *at this stage* it would not attempt to counteract such a move, since it would overstretch the resources and competences of the organisation. Instead, it would concentrate its efforts on the parts of the market where this CSF analysis showed it could gain real competitive advantage.

constantly reviewed (and changed). The use of performance standards to control strategy implementation will be discussed more generally in section 10.4.1 below.

- Assess the extent to which competitors can *imitate* each underpinning competence. As discussed in Chapter 4, this is a critical question in determining the core competences of an organisation.
- Decide on the impact of potential competitive moves and how these

might need to be *counteracted*. Continual review of performance standards has already been mentioned. In the illustration, the company took the view that there were certain possible moves which they would *not* attempt to counter (providing global coverage for multinationals).

It is important when implementing strategies that the *responsibility* for each of the activities from the CSF are properly identified. In the illustration, the area where this could go badly wrong is database maintenance. Although this responsibility is assigned to the customer service department, the linkages with both the sales and software systems departments are crucial in ensuring accurate information.

10.3.2 Planning priorities[13]

A resource plan sets out what resources and competences need to be created and which disposed of. This may well be in the form of a *budget*, but might also be usefully expressed as a sequence of actions or a timetable of *priorities* in a written plan. For example, an organisation introducing a new product line would need a plan of action to co-ordinate the sequencing of the various aspects of its resource plan. On-the-job production line retraining cannot begin until a production facility exists. Until the company has examined in detail the timing of development, installation, commissioning and completion of plant, it is not possible to examine fully the flow of funds required to finance the venture. Until it is known at what rate production is to be geared, a sensible view cannot be taken about the extent of the product launch; that in turn means that there will not be a clear idea of expected revenue flow, making it difficult to think sensibly about the requirement for funds.

The circularity of the problem is quite usual in developing a plan of action, and raises the question of where to start — with a market forecast, an available level of funds, a production-level constraint, or what? The answer is that it may not matter too much where the starting point is, since the plan will have to be reworked and readjusted several times. A useful guideline is to enter the problem through what appears to be the major change area. An organisation planning new strategies of growth may well start with an assessment of market opportunity. Someone starting a new business may well begin with a realistic assessment of how much capital they might have available.

Network analysis,[14] also known as *critical path analysis*, can be useful in this detailed planning of implementation. It is a technique for planning projects by breaking them down into their component activities and showing these activities and their interrelationships in the form of a network. By considering the times and resources required to complete each

	Activity	Preceding activity	Duration (weeks)
A	Pilot Survey	~	2
B	Investigation of computer requirements	~	1
C	Preliminary data analysis	A	1
D	Write initial report	B,C	1
E	Program design	B	1
F	Program testing and debugging	E	2
G	Main data collection	C	4
H	Data Collation	G	1
I	Run program on collated data	F,D,H	1
J	Discussion and analysis of results	I	1
K	Final report	J	2

Source: G. Worsdale, Sheffield Business School. Reproduced with permission

Figure 10.5 Network analysis for a customer survey project

of the activities, it is possible to locate the critical path of activities which determines the minimum time for the project. The network can also be used for scheduling materials and other resources, and for examining the impact of changes in one subarea of the project on others. The technique is particularly relevant to projects which have a reasonably definite start and finish, and where completion in the shortest possible time might gain competitive advantage.

It has been used very effectively in new product or service launches, construction of plant, acquisitions and mergers, relocation and R&D projects — all the sorts of activity relevant to strategy implementation. Figure 10.5 is an outline network analysis diagram for a customer survey project, which was of major importance in underpinning a drive for improved customer service standards.

10.4 Processes of allocation and control

Identifying the appropriate resources and competences to support strategy implementation is important, but it will not result in successful implementation unless the organisation is also able to allocate resources and control performance in line with the strategy. There are three broad types of control[15]: *administrative control*, through systems, rules and procedures; *social control*, through the impact of culture on the behaviour of individuals and groups; and *self-control*, which people exert over their own behaviour. These can be related to the six co-ordinating mechanisms suggested by Mintzberg (see Chapter 9, section 9.5). Direct *supervision* and the *standardisation of work processes, outputs* or *skills* are essentially administrative controls. *Standardisation of norms* and *mutual adjustment* are social controls, although the latter invariably involves a measure of self-control in the way that individuals choose to interact with others in and around the organisation.

This section looks at how the circumstances of an organisation might determine the most suitable approach to allocating and controlling resources. Although these circumstances are complex and varied, there are one or two broad issues which should most influence the approach to resource allocation and control: first, the extent of the *perceived need to change*, whether future strategies will be incremental developments from the past or more transformational in the sense discussed in Chapter 2; and second, the extent to which the organisational design is *centralised or devolved*, as discussed in section 9.4 of Chapter 9.

Figure 10.6 is a framework for this section and can be used as a checklist against which readers can assess whether the dominant processes in any organisation (perhaps your own) actually fit the circumstances of the organisation in relation to these two parameters. It may be that strategy implementation is being impeded by a mismatch such as a continuation of a 'strategic planning' style (top-down plans and formula allocations) in circumstances where the organisation is facing a real need to change its strategies significantly, and has committed itself to increased devolution as part of the change process (i.e. a move to 'strategic control').

10.4.1 Control through planning systems

This is the archetypal administrative control, where implementation is achieved through *systems* which plan and control the allocation of resources and monitor the actual utilisation against this plan. Many of the major strides forward in manufacturing efficiency and reliability in the early parts of the twentieth century were achieved through this 'scientific

PERCEIVED NEED FOR CHANGE

	Low	High
Low 'Strategic planning'	'Top-down' planning Formula allocations Direct supervision	Direct supervision Imposed targets
EXTENT **OF** **DEVOLUTION** 'Strategic control' 'Financial control **High**	'Bottom-up' planning Bargaining Performance targets Social/cultural control	Market mechanisms Self-controls

Figure 10.6   Approaches to resource allocation and control

management', which is still a dominant approach in many such organisations. Control through planning is particularly useful where the degree of change is low, but will need to operate differently in centralised as against devolved regimes.

Centralised regimes

In centralised regimes ('strategic planning'), planning is usually 'top-down' and accompanied by *standardisation of work processes* or *outputs* and an organisational configuration similar to Mintzberg's *machine* or *professional bureaucracies* (see Chapter 9, section 9.5). Even in service organisations, such 'routinisation' has been achieved (e.g. in insurance work and some legal services), leading to deskilling of service delivery and significant reductions in cost. This can give competitive advantage where organisations are positioning on low price with commodity-like products or services. Further advantage can be gained if these systems of allocation and control can stretch more widely in the value-system beyond the boundaries of the organisation into the supply and distribution chains. Fully integrated IT systems for inventory control into suppliers or the use of EPOS (electronic point of sale) systems into outlets are good examples.

Centrally planned systems often use a *formula* approach to resource allocation. For example, the advertising budget might be 5 per cent of sales, or in the public services revenue might be allocated on a per-capita basis (e.g. doctors' patients). There may then be some room for *bargaining* and fine tuning around this formula position — for example, in *redefining* the formula — by weightings or introducing additional factors.

Devolved regimes

In devolved regimes ('strategic control' or 'financial control'), planning systems can still be used as a primary mechanism for resource allocation and control. However, it is more likely to be centred around 'bottom-up' plans from divisions being developed within central guidelines, as discussed in section 9.4.2. It is important that the corporate centre and the divisions are clear on their respective responsibilities for planning and implementation. It is also essential that there are processes of *reconciliation*

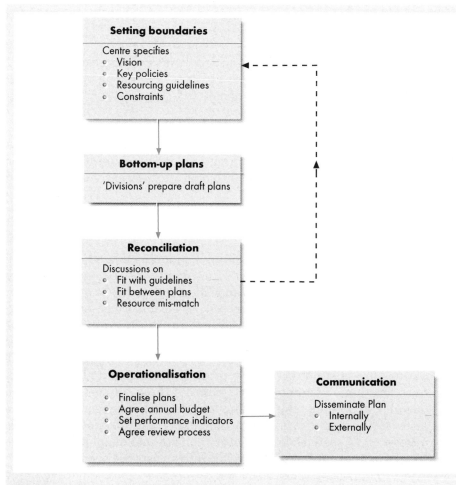

Figure 10.7   Resource allocation through the strategic planning process

between the divisions and the corporate centre to ensure that the sum total of divisional plans can be resourced. This may be resolved through processes of *bargaining* between the corporate centre and each division, and hopefully a revisiting of some of the central policies and guidelines, which should be regarded as movable (to a greater or lesser extent) through these planning processes. There may need to be several iterations of this process, as shown in Figure 10.7.

10.4.2 Control through direct supervision

Direct supervision is a common form of control in small organisations. It can also exist in larger organisations where little change is occurring and if the complexity of the business is not too great for one or a small number of managers to control the organisation *in detail* from the centre. This is often found in family businesses and in parts of the public sector with a history of 'hands-on' political involvement (often where a single political party has dominated for a long period). This situation also prevailed in many parts of the centrally planned economies of eastern Europe prior to 1990.

Direct supervision may also be appropriate during major change — for example, an organisational *crisis*. Here the survival of the organisation may be threatened and autocratic control through direct supervision may be necessary. The appointment of receivers to companies in financial difficulty by their creditors is a good example.

10.4.3 Control through performance targets

Another response to high levels of change — whether this is rapid growth, decline or simply reshaping of the organisation's business — is control through *centrally imposed targets*. For example, in the absence of a genuine market, many of the recently privatised utilities in the UK and elsewhere are controlled through the appointment of regulators.[16] These regulators control the organisations through a mechanism of *price-capping*[17] (the so-called K-factors), which imposes a ceiling on prices related to the retail price index (RPI). For example, in the UK, British Telecom in 1995 was subject to a K-factor of RPI − 7.5% imposed by its regulator, Oftel.

However, control through performance targets is not confined to situations of major change or crisis. It is becoming increasingly used in organisations which are wishing to gain some of the benefits of devolution and not necessarily experiencing high degrees of change. Illustration 10.4 (critical success factors) has already shown the importance of understanding the level of performance needed to outperform competition. A common first step is to move to a system of measurement of *outputs* through a series of agreed *performance indicators* (PIs).[18] This may be accompanied by *incentives and rewards* which relate to the achievement of targets — either for groups or individuals. Readers are reminded of the discussion in Chapter 4 about the importance of establishing PIs which relate to *benchmarks* of best performance — even if these are outside the industry or public service.

Many managers find the process of developing a useful set of PIs for their organisations difficult. One reason for this is that many indicators give a useful but only partial view of the overall picture. Also, some indicators are qualitative in nature, while the hard quantitative end of assessing performance has been dominated by financial analysis. In an attempt to cope with this very heterogeneous situation, *balanced scorecards*[19] have been proposed as a way of identifying a useful, but varied, set of key measures. They combine both qualitative and quantitative measures, acknowledge the expectations of different stakeholders and relate an assessment of

FINANCIAL PERSPECTIVE	
CSF*	**Measures**
Survival	Cash flow

CUSTOMER PERSPECTIVE	
CSF*	**Measures**
Customer service (standard products)	○ Delivery time ○ Maintenance response time

INTERNAL PERSPECTIVE	
CSF*	**Measures**
IT systems development ○ Features ○ Cost	Performance per £ invested (vs. competitors)

INNOVATION AND LEARNING PERSPECTIVE	
CSF*	**Measures**
Service leadership	○ Speed to market (new standards) ○ Speed of imitation (robustness)

* CSF = critical success factors

Figure 10.8   The balanced scorecard: an example

Illustration 10.5   The balanced scorecard: Rockwater

Rockwater, a wholly owned subsidiary of Brown and Root/Halliburton, a global engineering and construction company, is a worldwide leader in underwater engineering and construction. The table below shows how the company transformed its vision and strategy into a balanced scorecard with four sets of performance measures. The ultimate aim of this exercise was to create value for the whole organisation.

THE VISION

'As our customers' preferred provider, we shall be the industry leader. This is our mission.'

STRATEGY

Services that surpass needs
Customer satisfaction
Continuous improvement
Quality of employees
Shareholder expectations

OBJECTIVES

Financial
Return on capital
Cash flow
Project profitability
Reliability of performance

Customer
Value for money
Competitive price
Hassle-free relationship
High-performance professionals
Innovation

Internal
Shape customer requirement
Quality service
Safety/loss control
Superior project management
Tender effectiveness

Growth
Product and service innovation
Empowered workforce
Continuous improvement

BALANCED SCORECARD

Financial perspective
Return on capital employed
Cash flow
Project profitability
Profit forecast reliability
Sales backlog

Customer perspective
Customer ranking survey
Customer satisfaction index
Market share
Pricing index

Internal business perspective
Hours with customers on new work
Tender success rate
Rework
Safety incident index
Project performance index
Project closeout cycle

Innovation and learning perspective
Revenue per employee
% revenue from new services
Staff attitude survey
Rate of improvement index
Staff attitude survey
No. of employee suggestions

Source: R.S. Kaplan and D.P. Norton, 'Putting the balanced scorecard to work', *Harvard Business Review*, vol. 71, no. 5 (1993), pp. 134–47.

performance to choice of strategy (as shown in Figure 10.8 and Illustration 10.5).

Figure 10.8 is an example of a balanced scorecard for a small start-up company supplying standard tools and light equipment into the engineering industry. The owner-manager's financial perspective was simply one of survival during this start-up period, requiring a positive cash flow (after the initial investments in plant and stock premises). The strategy was to compete in customer service both on initial delivery and on maintenance back-up. This required core competences in order processing and maintenance scheduling underpinned by the company's IT system. These core competences were open to imitation, so, in turn, the ability to improve these service standards continuously was critical to success.

If performance targets are to be a useful form of control, it is important to decide the *basis* on which each part of the organisation will be assessed. This must relate to the degree of devolution in the organisation and can be achieved through establishing divisions or departments as *responsibility centres* of one or more of the types shown in Figure 10.9. Which type of responsibility centre is used should be determined by the other issues of organisational design. So a *financial control* organisation (see section 9.4.2) is likely to establish divisions or subsidiaries as profit or investment centres, since the responsibility for product/market strategy will be substantially devolved to divisions or subsidiaries. In contrast, *strategic planning*

Type	Examples	Control exerted over	Typical controls
Revenue	Sales dept	Income	Sales targets
Cost centre (a) Standard cost centres	Production dept (manufacturing) R&D	Cost of labour, materials, services, etc.	Detailed budgeting Standard product costing
(b) Discretionary expense centres	Administrative dept	Total expenditure	Budget
Profit centre	Internal services (e.g. design) Product or market division Subsidiary company	Profit	P&L accounts
Investment centre	Subsidiary company	Return on capital	Complete financial accounts

Figure 10.9   Different types of responsibility centre

organisations are likely to use cost or revenue centres, since the responsibility for many aspects of product/market strategy will be at the corporate centre. Divisions or departments will have devolved responsibility only for particular aspects of strategy, such as production costs or sales revenue.

10.4.4 Social/cultural control[20]

Historically, too much emphasis may have been placed on administrative controls as ways of delivering the co-ordination needed to implement successful strategies. In reality, the performance of an organisation will also be determined by the 'softer' controls within organisations — the social controls and self-controls. This section will look at how social controls can play an important part in the resource allocation and control processes in an organisation. It is largely concerned with what Mintzberg calls *standardisation of norms* (see section 9.5). It is important that social controls are working well in organisations with highly devolved structures ('financial control' or 'strategic control'), since they may be the primary mechanism for co-ordination in the organisation.

Social controls can also create *rigidities* if the organisation is needing to change.[21] Resistance to change may be 'legitimised' by the cultural norms. For example, plans to de-skill service delivery through routinisation and the use of 'non-professional' staff may be a logical strategy to pursue in terms of increasing value for money, but it is likely to be resisted by the professional staff. The social controls may work against such a change. However, this need not be the case. Since the professionals are likely to be strongly influenced by the behaviour of their peer group in other organisations, they may accept the need to change if they see it working successfully elsewhere. It is for these sorts of reasons that many organisations commit significant resources to maintaining *professional social networks*, both inside and between organisations, as a method of keeping in touch with best practice.

Training and development is another way in which organisations invest in maintaining the social controls within the organisation. It provides a common set of reference points to which people can relate their own work and priorities, and a common language with which to communicate with other parts of the organisation.

10.4.5 Control through market mechanisms[22]

Increasing levels of devolution have in many large organisations been accompanied by the introduction of *quasi* market mechanisms for the allocation and control of some or all of the organisation's resources. This has been particularly useful for those parts of the business that are needing to change substantially.

It might start in small ways with *competitive bidding* — perhaps through the creation of an *investment bank* or 'top-sliced' resources from which divisions or departments can bid for additional resources to support particular projects or developments. This can be a particularly successful way of supporting new ventures in their early phase, where otherwise they may be starved of resources.

Over the recent past, many organisations have introduced some form of *internal market* as a mechanism for 'regulating' the allocation of resources between the various parts of the organisation, and encouraging improvement in the value for money of the organisation's products or services. For example, a customer–supplier relationship may be established between a central service department, such as personnel, and the operating divisions or departments. It then becomes an important management task to regulate and manage this internal market.

However, an internal market is not the same as an external market. A key difference is that an internal market will always be subject to some degree of *constraint*. The extent of these constraints clearly depends on the degree of devolution. Organisations operating close to the stereotype of *financial control* may limit the constraints to issues of the internal availability of capital, and closely approach the external market situation. However, for many organisations, *strategic control* will require policies, rules and guidelines which constrain the internal market. For example, a pharmaceutical manufacturer which owned its own supplier of a strategically crucial ingredient naturally disallowed any third-party sales of the ingredient to competitive companies.

An important feature of internal markets is the 'right' of the internal customer to specify its requirements (in terms of the value for money it expects from the services (or products) it is receiving). This may be done in the form of a *service-level agreement* with the internal supplier. It can be particularly helpful if the agreement reflects the best performance which would be achieved from third-party suppliers outside the organisation.

At a practical level, there are some problems which can be created by internal markets and which are to be discouraged. First is the escalation in *bargaining* between units, which can consume important management time. Second is the creation of a new bureaucracy monitoring all of the *internal transfers* of resources between units. An overzealous use of market mechanisms can also have a profound impact on the dominant culture of an organisation, shifting it from one of collaboration and relational processes to competition and contractual relationships, which may prove dysfunctional.

10.4.6 Self-control and personal motivation

With the increased devolution and de-layering of organisations, the self-control and motivation of individuals is becoming critically important to the performance of organisations, and raises some important issues about resource allocation and control:[23]

- Self-control is closely related to Mintzberg's co-ordinating mechanism of *mutual adjustment* (see section 9.5), whereby resource allocation and control is largely determined by the direct interaction of individuals without supervision. The contribution of senior managers to this process is to ensure that individuals have the *channels* to interact (perhaps by improving the IT/communications infrastructure), and that the social/cultural controls which this process of interaction creates are properly *regulated* to avoid the rigidities mentioned in section 10.4.4 above. So senior managers are concerned with shaping the *context*[24] in which others are working.
- If individuals are to have a greater say in how they perform their work and achieve the organisation's goals, they need to be properly *supported* in the way in which resources are made available to them. One of these key resources is likely to be information, and it will be seen below that the organisation's IT strategy is a critical ingredient in this process of supporting individuals.
- There are important implications for how the credibility of managers/leaders is maintained. For example, credibility may arise from being a member of the peer group — this is why so many seniors in professional service departments or organisations are professional themselves. So the head of the design department undertakes assignments personally as well as overseeing the work of others.

10.5 Information: a key resource

The previous sections have discussed in detail how the resource configuration and the processes for allocating and controlling resources might sustain the ability of an organisation to implement its strategies successfully. Often, managers are disappointed by the results of their changes in organisational structure, design and control processes because they fail to realise that another key ingredient of implementation is information. If information is not available in the right format at the right time, the potential gains of other changes may be lost. This is increasingly important as many organisations become more complex and geographically dispersed through processes of globalisation.

This section looks at the information requirements of the various aspects of resource allocation and control discussed in this chapter, and how the management of information might provide competitive advantage.[25]

10.5.1 Information on individual resources

It was argued earlier in the chapter (section 10.2) that, if competitive advantage is built on individual resources, it is important to ensure that these resources cannot be imitated. If a key resource is knowledge, the 'intellectual property' needs to be protected. Although legal protection has increased, particularly for knowledge stored on electronic media, it is clearly a concern that the vastly increased capability and reducing cost of IT networks is likely to erode this protection. This may occur in legal ways simply by competitors knowing about new developments more quickly, and hence being able to bring out alternatives or plan a defensive strategy.

IT developments may also erode competitive advantage in other ways by undermining the importance of *tacit knowledge*. IT vastly improves the way in which data can be searched, sifted, sorted and packaged to increase the pace of learning of potential competitors. The improved sophistication of software packages in some arenas is partly able to replace professional skill — for example, in currency trading and medical diagnosis. This software can also include fully programmed controls and limits over the freedom of action of the operators (e.g. by limiting the size of financial deal, or excluding certain medical conditions in the two examples above).

10.5.2 Creating competences through information

Improved availability and quality of information can improve an organisation's competences in several ways:

- By reducing the cost of processes — for example, the telecommunications costs of the selling activities of international companies.
- By improving their quality — for example, the speed and accuracy of real-time booking systems.
- In retailing, the recording of sales by electronic scanning (EPOS) has not only improved efficiency and service in the store, but provided high-quality information on which to plan stocking, purchasing and sales promotions.

Since the wider availability of information can accelerate the learning of competitors, advantages gained through experience may be shorter lived than hitherto. This will inevitably mean that more organisations will need to revisit and redefine the *positioning* of their products/services in the market place more often, which in turn will put different information demands on the organisation.

As mentioned in section 10.2.3, this reshaping of business processes to create new and better-matched competences has generated a great deal of interest and effort since the early 1990s under the banner of *business process re-engineering (BPR)*.[26] It has become a central plank of IT strategy in many organisations, and has been derived by a philosophy that business processes which suited centrally driven bureaucratic organisations are no longer adequate for organisations competing on quality and service delivered at the 'sharp end' of the organisation. Illustration 10.2 showed how BPR can require quite radical changes in both outlook and resource deployment.

10.5.3 Information, performance targets and market mechanisms

The recent advances in the speed and (lower) cost of information processing should — in principle — improve the capability of control systems to measure performance against targets. Therefore, in exploiting this potential, it is important not to lose sight of some principles of good practice for performance measurement already discussed in sections 10.4.3 and 10.4.5. It has already been mentioned that market mechanisms are often introduced into organisations in order to encourage a new emphasis on value for money and increasing performance against the best external standards. However, internal markets are 'information hungry' if they function effectively, and therein lie dangers which need to be avoided when planning management control and information systems. In particular, *cost* of monitoring and effecting all the new transactions (cross-charging) can be prohibitive, or the organisation may simply not have the systems to achieve this without a considerable capital investment.

10.5.4 Information, cultural and self-controls

Many believe that the 'IT revolution' will genuinely transform the balance of the various processes of resource allocation and control discussed in this chapter.[27] They paint a picture of de-layered organisations, with IT taking the place of middle management, and cultural and self-control being the dominant control processes in organisations populated by 'knowledge workers', whose performance is vastly improved by their direct, personal and on-line access to information (section 10.4.6 above).

The internet will not respect many of the boundaries which are currently taken for granted, and will increase the ability of individuals low down in the hierarchy to communicate directly without having to go through the *information gatekeepers* and the corporate centre. This gatekeeping role has been a key source of power for managers in steering coherent strategies and allocating resources in organisations. Importantly, this means that social controls, including those provided by key external frames of reference, will need to take on a heightened importance. For example, the need for ethical standards and codes of practice as key regulators of behaviour among professions and industry bodies could prove more crucial.

10.6 Influences on organisational design and control

Together, Chapters 9 and 10 have discussed the various elements of organisational design and control: namely, centralisation/devolution, organisational configurations and the various processes of resource allocation and control. These elements need to work well together to support the successful implementation of an organisation's strategies. The

		MANAGEMENT STYLE		CONFIGURATION				ALLOCATION and CONTROL		
		Centralised	Devolved	Simple	Bureaucratic	Divisionalised	Adhocracy/ missionary	Administrative	Social/cultural	Self-control
STRATEGIES/ POSITIONING	Low price	x			x			x		
	Differentiation		x			x	x		x	x
TECHNOLOGY	Mass production	x		x	x			x		
	Complex technology		x				x		x	x
TYPE OF ORGANISATION	External accountability	x			x			x		
	Owner control	x		x					x	
	Defenders	x			x			x		
	Prospectors		x				x		x	x
NATURE OF ENVIRONMENT	Simple/static	x			x			x		
	Complex		x			x	x		x	x
	Dynamic		x				x		x	x

Figure 10.10 Influences on organisational design and control

important issue is how this 'package' will be influenced by the organisation's circumstances. In other words, the 'best' package is contingent on a number of different factors, and these are discussed below. Readers can use this section to assess the degree of 'match' between the circumstances of an organisation and the approach to organisational design and control. Figure 10.10 provides a checklist for this purpose.

10.6.1 Type of strategy

The discussion of organisational configurations in Chapter 9 acknowledged the importance of matching organisational design to the types of strategy that the organisation was pursuing. It also pointed out that this is a two-way process: organisational configuration also influences preferences for particular types of strategy. So different product/market strategies may require different forms of organisational design, as previously summarised in Figure 10.4.

The organisation following a low-price strategy will need to find a means of ensuring a cost-efficient operation with an emphasis on cost control, whereas the organisation following a differentiation strategy may need higher degrees of creativity to develop and sustain the aspects of the product or service which provide competitive advantage. The likelihood is that the low-price strategy will require a more *mechanistic* system of control, with clear job responsibilities, frequent and detailed reports on organisational efficiency and cost, and a clear delineation of responsibility for budgets and expenditure: in other words, a strong emphasis on administrative controls.

An organisation following a differentiation strategy, on the other hand, might need to have looser controls, a greater encouragement of informality and creativity within a more devolved structure, but a good deal of co-ordination between its various activities. The emphasis may be more on groups relating to problems and opportunities rather than on individual departments being concerned with specific job functions. So cultural and self-control processes are of greater importance. An organisation that seeks to follow differentiation and low-price strategies for different parts of its business may experience conflicts in terms of organisational design and the need to have different types of control system.

10.6.2 Operational processes and technology

The nature of the tasks undertaken by the operating core of an organisation has an important influence on the various aspects of organisational design and control, as discussed in section 9.5. It is known that there are links between the type of production process and the approach to management.

Mass production systems require the standardisation of processes (i.e. the *machine bureaucracy*), a tendency towards centralisation resulting in greater direction and control by senior managers either through formal planning systems or by direct supervision. Organisations with less standardised operational processes are likely to have more devolved and informal decision-making processes.

The more sophisticated and complex the technology of an organisation, the more elaborate the structure becomes for a number of reasons. It is likely that a good deal of responsibility and power is likely to devolve to those specialists concerned with the technology itself. The organisation may tend to operate as an *adhocracy*. In turn, this may create the need for liaison between specialists and the operating core of the business, giving rise to an increase in integrating and co-ordinating mechanisms such as committees, joint working groups and project teams, or an emphasis on social control through professional networks.

10.6.3 Organisational ownership and accountability

The nature of an organisation's ownership and *accountability* will also affect organisational design and control. Where government involvement is high (e.g. with a nationalised industry), the issue of public accountability becomes an important influence; it is likely to give rise to a centralised structure of decision making, where both power and accountability are in the hands of an easily identifiable team or individual at the centre. However, the price that has often been paid for this ease of public accountability is an inability to respond quickly to market and other environmental changes (hence many of the recent moves towards de-regulation and market mechanisms), while still maintaining an accountable centre to the organisation. *Owner control* will usually have an important influence on organisational design and control. For example, many companies which are owner-controlled operate a *simple* structure and retain a high degree of centralisation and direct supervision even when they grow quite large, as the influence of the owner-manager continues. This may provide a limitation to their continued successful development.

10.6.4 The environment

In an environment which is simple and static (as discussed in Chapter 3), organisations may gear themselves for operational efficiency. They standardise operations and processes of control. Examples are some mass-production companies and raw material producers. Increasing complexity is handled by devolving decision responsibility to specialists. This means

Illustration 10.6   Xerox: the entrepreneurial giant?

Many large organisations have learnt that size can breed inertia and loss of competitive advantage in changing environments. Some are trying to rebuild organisations to keep the benefits of size, while bringing back the entrepreneurship, innovation and responsiveness of smaller organisations.

By the early 1990s, Xerox was a $17 billion business operating as a 'document company' at the intersection of the two worlds of paper-based and electronic information. The spectacular growth which followed the introduction of the plain-paper copier in 1959 faltered in the 1980s as they were caught up by lower-cost Japanese competitors. Major improvements in quality together with radical business process re-engineering helped Xerox to gain back some of the lost market share. Nevertheless, with the advent of Paul Allaire as CEO in 1990, the company embarked on a radical process of redesigning its 'organisational architecture'. In particular, there were major changes in the approach to resource allocation and management control, aimed at putting back a more entrepreneurial and responsive *modus operandi* — even in such a large company. Allaire regarded this as essential if Xerox were to survive in a complex and rapidly changing business environment. Some of the changes were as follows:

- They changed from a functional structure to a type of matrix structure. The 'lead edge' of the matrix was nine relatively independent and profit accountable business units based around specific products and markets. These were supported by company-wide activities such as R&D and three geographically based sales and service teams (to ensure a single 'Xerox' face to the customer).
- Target setting started 'bottom-up' from the divisions, and the relationship with the corporate centre has moved away from 'strategic planning' to 'strategic control'.
- The new appointments to head business divisions were people who could 'think in terms of their own division but also in terms of Xerox as a whole': for example, on new technology development or customer interface/services.
- The reward and recognition system was completely redesigned. In particular, the rewards of the top 50 business executives were much more closely tied to business targets for the company as a whole and their own division or unit.
- The stated long-term aim was to increase delegation further, to the level where the whole company was organised as a 'federation' of self-managed work teams — what Xerox called 'productive work communities'.
- One of the main platforms of the changes was to replace much of the traditional formal processes by more informal resolution of problems and decision making, and for top management and the corporate departments to see their primary role as creating the context within which these 'productive work communities' could succeed and supporting them in doing so.

Source: R. Howard, 'The CEO as organisational architect', *Harvard Business Review*, vol. 70, no. 5 (1992), pp. 107–21.

that organisations in complex environments tend to be more devolved, at least for operational purposes.

In dynamic conditions, it is necessary to increase the extent to which managers are capable of sensing what is going on around them, identifying change and responding to it. It is unlikely that bureaucratic styles of management will encourage such behaviour, so their style is likely to place more emphasis on cultural and self-controls. However, this may not be the only response to dynamic conditions. In situations of high levels of competition, which require rapid response but also overall control at a strategic level (the extreme example being a *crisis*), it may be necessary to revert to highly centralised decisions by a dominant leader, if only temporarily.

Where the environment is both complex and dynamic — for example, among firms operating at the frontiers of scientific development — the situation is changing so fast that there is a need for speed and flexibility, and the level of complexity is such that responsibility and authority must be devolved to specialists. So self-control and the personal motivation of individuals has to be the dominant control process in the organisation. Illustration 10.6 shows how Xerox radically changed its approach in the 1990s, in the face of an increasingly complex and dynamic environment.

10.6.5 Reinforcing cycles

So far the discussion in this section has tended to suggest that structures, configurations and controls tend to 'follow' strategy. In reality, this is not an accurate description of the relationship between strategy and these factors. It also works in the opposite direction: that is, organisations operating in particular configurations tend to seek out strategies which best fit this configuration and reject those which require change. Also, the fact that it is possible to identify a limited number of stereotypes for organisational configurations, as described in Chapter 9, is a reminder that the factors listed in the sections above are not independent variables — they tend to occur in particular groupings. Indeed, configurations found in practice tend to be very *cohesive, robust* and *difficult to change*.[28]

The explanation of this draws together the issues which have been identified above. It is concerned with the *dynamic interaction* between the various factors of environment, configuration, systems, etc. to form *reinforcing cycles*, which tend to preserve the status quo. Figure 10.11 shows two examples. The *machine bureaucracy* is a configuration which is adopted in stable environmental conditions and can help create a position of cost leadership. This can underpin a positioning of 'low price' (or cost efficiency in the public services), requiring standardised work processes which, in turn, are well supported by a defender culture. This culture seeks

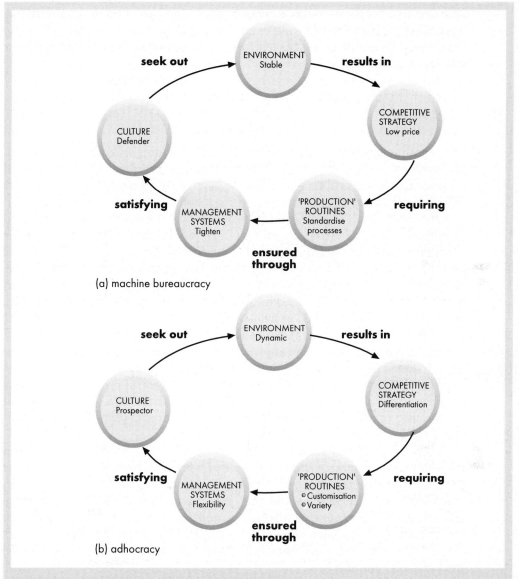

(a) machine bureaucracy

(b) adhocracy

Figure 10.11   Reinforcing cycles: two examples

out stable parts of the environment and the whole cycle is self-perpetuating. A similar reinforcing cycle can occur with the *adhocracy*, as seen in the same figure.

None of this may be a problem for the organisation — in fact, the matching of these various organisational issues to each other may prove to be a source of great strength to the organisation. However, it should be remembered from Chapter 2 that this is also likely to be an explanation of why *strategic drift* is so common. The organisation may need the capability to 'break out' of these reinforcing cycles if it is to survive and succeed in the long term. This will be discussed fully in Chapter 11, which is concerned with managing change.

10.7 Summary

This chapter has been concerned with understanding how the processes of resource allocation and control will influence the success or failure of strategy implementation. This consists of several related aspects. The first issue is whether the organisation is clear about the resources and competences it will need for the future, and how they can be developed and sustained. At this broad level, we are concerned with the resource configuration of the organisation. This includes the way in which linkages and relationships are managed both inside the organisation and in the wider value-system of suppliers, customers and collaborators. Within this broad framework, there will be a need for detailed resource plans as to how specific strategies will be resourced and sustained.

There are many different processes by which resource allocation and control can be managed. The approach taken by an organisation is likely to be influenced by the extent of change needed in resources and competences, and the 'management style' in relation to the extent of devolved authority over resource allocation decisions. Therefore, there is a wide variety of approaches ranging from centrally imposed resourcing plans to competitive 'market-like' processes within the organisation.

The information capability of the organisation has a major influence on its resource competences and processes of control. Given the rapid changes that many organisations are currently experiencing in their information capability, it is to be expected that many will fundamentally reappraise their approach to resource allocation and control. Even if managers are reluctant to undergo such change, they may be forced to do so as competitors outperform the company through their exploitation of this enhanced information capability.

References

1. Strategic architecture is discussed by G. Hamel and C.K. Prahalad, *Competing for the Future*, Harvard Business School Press, 1994, chapter 10, and J. Kay, *Foundations of Corporate Success*, Oxford University Press, 1993, chapter 5.
2. Detailed resource identification is often started by looking at the implications of each functional area of the business. G.A. Steiner, *Strategic Planning*, Free Press, 1979, is a useful guide. Readers who are unfamiliar with resource analysis in any functional area may wish to consult one of the following standard texts: P.

Kotler, *Marketing Management: Analysis, planning, implementation and control*, 8th edition, Prentice Hall, 1994; N. Slack and S. Chambers, *Operations Management*, Pitman, 1995; R. Wild, *Production and Operations Management*, 5th edition, Nelson, 1995; M.W.E. Glautier and B. Underdown, *Accounting Theory and Practice*, 5th edition, Pitman, 1994; D. Torrington and L. Hall, *Personnel Management: A new approach*, 3rd edition, Prentice Hall, 1995; C. Fombrun, N. Tichy and M. Devanna, *Strategic Human Resource Management*, Wiley, 1990.

3. Tacit knowledge is discussed in T. Nonaka and H. Takeuchi, *The Knowledge Creating Company*, Oxford University Press, 1995. The importance of people as a unique strategic resource is also argued in: P. Boxall, 'Strategic human resource management: beginnings of a new theoretical sophistication?', *Human Resource Management Journal*, vol. 2, no. 3 (1992), pp. 60–79, and 'Placing HR strategy at the heart of business success', *Personnel Management*, vol. 26, no. 7 (1994), pp. 32–4.

4. For examples, see J.B. Quinn, 'Managing the intelligent enterprise: knowledge and service-based strategies', *Planning Review (USA)*, vol. 21, no. 5 (1993), pp. 13–16; S. Davis and J. Botkin, 'The coming of knowledge-based business', *Harvard Business Review*, vol. 72, no. 5 (1994), pp. 165–70.

5. Business process re-engineering has been of considerable interest to both practitioners and academics. For example, see W. Robson, *Strategic Management and Information Systems: An integrated approach*, Pitman, 1994, pp. 203–14; M. Hammer and S. Stanton, *The Re-engineering Revolution*, HarperCollins, 1995 and R. Talwar's chapter, 'Business process re-engineering', in V. Ambrosini with G. Johnson and K. Scholes (eds) *Exploring Techniques of Analysis and Evaluation in Strategic Management*, Prentice Hall, 1998. A *Business Process Re-Engineering and Management Journal* was launched in 1995.

6. See I. Masaaki, *Kaizen: The key to Japan's competitive success*, Random House, 1986; R. Hannam, *Kaizen for Europe: Customising Japanese strategies for success*, IFS Publications, 1993. The Europe–Japan Centre staff have also published a series of books on the application of Kaizen (through the National Book Network).

7. G. Hamel and C. Prahalad, 'Strategy as stretch and leverage', *Harvard Business Review*, vol. 71, no. 2 (1993), pp. 75–84.

8. G. Hamel and C. Prahalad, *Competing for the Future*, Harvard Business School Press, 1994.

9. Cost advantage is discussed in R. Grant, *Contemporary Strategy Analysis*, 2nd edition, Blackwell, 1995, chapter 7, and B. Karlof, *Strategic Precision*, Wiley, 1993, chapter 3.

10. See S. Prokesch, 'Competing on customer service: an interview with British Airways' Sir Colin Marshall', *Harvard Business Review*, vol. 73, no. 6 (1995), pp. 101–12.

11. The importance of switching costs is explained in M.E. Porter, *Competitive Strategy*, Free Press, 1980, p. 19.

12. See M. Hardaker and B.K. Ward, 'Getting things done', *Harvard Business Review*, vol. 65, no. 6 (1987) pp. 112–120, for a fuller discussion of how critical success factors can be identified and used.

13. For a fuller discussion of the planning of priorities, see K. Scholes and M. Klemm, *An Introduction to Business Planning*, Macmillan, 1987, chapter 5.

14. Network analysis is explained in Wild (reference 2 above) and K. Howard, *Quantitative Analyses for Planning Decisions*, McDonald and Evans, 1975.

15. A good general reference for issues of control is P. Johnson and J. Gill, *Management Control and Organisational Behaviour*, Paul Chapman Publishing, 1993. Also of interest are R. Simons, 'Strategic orientation and top management attention to control systems', *Strategic Management Journal*, vol. 12, no. 1 (1991), pp. 49–62, and 'How new top managers use control systems as levers of strategic renewal', *Strategic Management Journal*, vol. 15, no. 3 (1994), pp. 169–89.

16. See P. Jackson and C. Price, *Privatisation and Regulation: A review of the issues*, Longman, 1994, chapter 3. M. Bishop, J. Kay and C. Mayer, *Privatisation and Economic Performance*, Oxford University Press, 1994, provides a number of in-depth case studies of de-regulation.

17. Price-capping as a regulatory mechanism is discussed in R. Rees and J. Vickers, 'RPI – X. Price – Cap Regulation' in M. Bishop, J. Kay and

C. Mayer (eds.), *The Regulatory Challenge*, Oxford University Press, 1995, chapter 15.

18. Performance indicators are discussed in several different contexts in Jackson and Price (reference 16 above), e.g. pp. 17–18. See also N. Carter, in D. McKevitt and A. Lawton (eds.), *Public Sector Management: Theory, critique and practice*, Sage, 1994.

19. See R. Kaplan and D. Norton, 'The balanced scorecard: measures that drive performance', *Harvard Business Review*, vol. 70, no. 1 (1992), pp. 71–9, and 'Putting the balanced scorecard to work', *Harvard Business Review*, vol. 71, no. 5 (1993), pp. 134–47.

20. See Johnson and Gill (reference 15 above), chapter 5.

21. For example, D. Leonard-Barton, 'Core capabilities and core rigidities: a paradox in managing new product development', *Strategic Management Journal*, vol. 13, (Summer 1992), pp. 111–25.

22. Market mechanisms of several types have been introduced into previously administered monopolies in the public sector in many countries. See Jackson and Price (reference 16 above), chapters 5 and 8.

23. G. Morgan, *Imaginization*, Sage, 1993, advocates an approach to strategic management which uses the creativity of people more.

24. The idea of top managers as 'shapers of context' is discussed in S. Ghoshal and C. Bartlett, 'Linking organisational context and managerial action: the dimensions of the quality of management', *Strategic Management Journal*, vol. 15, (1994), pp. 91–112; C. Bartlett and S. Ghoshal, 'Changing the role of top management: beyond strategy to purpose', *Harvard Business Review*, vol. 72, no. 6 (1994), pp. 79–88; S. Ghoshal and C. Bartlett, 'Changing the role of top management', *Harvard Business Review*, vol. 73, no. 1 (1995), pp. 86–96.

25. The important relationship between information strategy and competitive advantage is discussed in W. Robson, *Strategic Management and Information Systems: An integrated approach*, Pitman, 1994, chapter 7.

26. See reference 5 above.

27. A special edition of *Organisation Science*, vol. 6, no. 4 (1995), is devoted to how new electronic communications are changing organisational design. M. Morton, 'Emerging organisational forms: work and organisation in the 21st century', *European Management Journal*, vol. 13, no. 4 (1995), pp. 339–45, looks at how IT and other environmental influences are changing organisational design.

28. This idea of configurations being cohesive is discussed in D. Miller, 'Organisational configurations: cohesion, change and prediction', *Human Relations*, vol. 43, no. 8 (1990), pp. 771–89. There is also a collection of research on configurational approaches to organisation in the *Academy of Management Journal*, vol. 36, no. 6 (1993), pp. 1175–361.

Recommended key readings

- C.K. Prahalad, *Competing for the Future*, Harvard Business School Press, 1994, chapter 10, and J. Kay, *Foundations of Corporate Success*, Oxford University Press, 1993, chapter 5, for a discussion of strategic architecture.

- G.A. Steiner, *Strategic Planning*, Free Press, 1979, is a useful guide on translating strategic plans into functional plans.

- M. Hardaker and B.K. Ward, 'Getting things done', *Harvard Business Review*, (1987), is an excellent guide to how critical success factors can be identified and used.

- Business process re-engineering and the relationship between information systems management and strategic management are discussed in W. Robson, *Strategic Management and Information Systems: An integrated approach*, Pitman, 1994, pp. 203–14; M. Hammer and S. Stanton, *The Re-*

engineering Revolution, HarperCollins, 1995 and R. Talwar's chapter, 'Business process re-engineering', in V. Ambrosini with G. Johnson and K. Scholes (eds) *Exploring Techniques of Analysis and Evaluation in Strategic Management*, Prentice Hall, 1998.

- A good general reference for issues of control is P. Johnson and J. Gill, *Management Control and Organisational Behaviour*, Paul Chapman Publishing, 1993.

- P. Jackson and C. Price, *Privatisation and Regulation: A review of the issues*, Longman, 1994, is useful for readers interested in how approaches to resource allocation and control have changed in the public sector.

Work assignments

10.1 **Choose two strategic developments for an organisation with which you are familiar and compare the resource configuration implications (Figure 10.2). How would this analysis influence your choice of strategy?**

10.2 By referring to Illustration 10.4, undertake an analysis of the critical success factors and the associated underpinning competences for an important strategic development in an organisation of your choice.

10.3 **(a) Choose an organisation which is shifting its generic competitive strategy from low price to differentiation (or supplementing the former with the latter). Describe any resource planning difficulties which are occurring as a result of these changes and how they are being tackled (refer to Figure 10.4).**
   (b) Choose an organisation which is attempting the opposite shift (differentiation to low price) and undertake the same analysis.

10.4 Draw up a network analysis for a strategic development in an organisation of your choice (refer to Figure 10.5). How could the 'time to completion' be shortened, and what risks would the organisation be taking?

10.5 By referring to Figure 10.6, characterise how corporate allocation of resources works in an organisation of your choice. Assess whether or not you would regard the current approach as appropriate.

10.6 **Referring to Figure 10.6 and Illustration 10.5, write a short executive brief to the CEO of a multidivisional organisation explaining how they could use balanced scorecards to monitor and control the performance of divisions. Be sure you present your critique of both the advantages and pitfalls of this approach.**

10.7 Referring to Figure 10.9 and using an organisation with which you are familiar, identify the various responsibility centres within the organisation and make your own assessment of whether the organisation is controlled in the best way. What changes would you recommend? Why? What might be some of the dangers of these changes, and how could they be avoided?

10.8 *By referring to the key readings (Robson; Hammer and Stanton), argue the case for and against the contention that 'The IT revolution will fundamentally transform the way that all organisations go about their business. Those who deny the self-evident truth will not survive!' Use examples to illustrate your answer.*

10.9 By referring to the issues of organisation design in Chapter 9, and resource allocation and control in this chapter, compare the key difference you would expect to find between the approach of an organisation operating in a relatively simple/static environment and the approach of another organisation operating in a complex/ dynamic environment (see Figure 10.10, Illustration 10.6).

10.10 *By using specific examples from your answers to the previous assignments, explain how the various aspects of organisational design and control need to fit together to support an organisation's strategies. How close are theory and practice? Refer to Mintzberg and Quinn in the recommended key readings (Chapter 9) to assist with your answer.*

CHAPTER 11

Managing strategic change

11.1 Introduction

This book has been concerned with two key themes: (1) the ways in which issues relating to strategic management can be considered through tools of analysis and evaluation, commonly associated with a *planning* approach to managing strategy; and (2) the *processes* of managing the development of strategy. In considering the management of strategic change, the subject of this chapter, these two approaches are also evident. Some writers, and some practitioners, approach strategic change as an extension of the planning process. The emphasis here is on getting the *logic* of the strategy right and then *persuading* people of that logic; designing *structures and control systems* appropriate to the strategy and using them as mechanisms of change; putting in place the *resources* required; and planning *timing and sequencing* of change in detail. Much of this has already been discussed in Chapters 9 and 10.

However, ultimately the success of strategic change in an organisation depends on the extent to which people change their behaviour: for example, towards customers or each other. It is therefore necessarily concerned with the *beliefs and assumptions* that they hold and the *processes* in their organisational lives. Those who emphasise a *process* view of strategy tend to highlight these other aspects of the change process. While not dismissing the need for planning, they stress the importance of achieving the *commitment* of people in the organisation to change, and the need for *behavioural* change not only in terms of that which is formally controlled, but also in terms of *everyday aspects* of organisational life. Indeed, there are those who would argue that in a rapidly changing environment, organisations cannot rely on formal planning of change, but rather need to become *learning organisations*, continually sensitive to changes in the environment and able to adapt continually to those changes.

These organisational processes are the main focus of this chapter, which builds on four underlying premises:

▨ It is important that there is a clear view within an organisation of the strategy to be followed. This issue has been emphasised in much of the book, and will be re-emphasised in parts of this chapter.

▨ However, this is not enough. Change will not occur unless there is *commitment* to change in the organisation. It is vital that managers consider how such commitment can be achieved.

▨ The approach taken to managing strategic change is likely to be *context dependent*. It will not be the same for all situations in all types of organisation. Managers need to consider how to balance the different approaches to managing strategic change according to the circumstances they face. Some guidelines are given on this as the chapter progresses.

▨ Whatever the emphasis and approach, it must address the powerful influence of the *paradigm* and the *cultural web* on the strategy being followed by the organisation. As explained in Chapters 2 and 5, these can result in strategic inertia and resistance to change.

Figure 11.1 provides a structure for the chapter. The chapter begins by providing some explanatory frameworks of strategic change and linking these to the explanations of strategy development provided in Chapter 2. A framework of *types of strategic change* is provided, which shows that change events may differ in scale. Next, different explanations are provided of how change might occur in organisations: one which is more suited to explaining *managed change*; one which is more to do with the notion of the *learning organisation*; and one which acknowledges that *imposed* or *forced* change does occur.

Section 11.3 then moves on to discuss more specifically the management of change. First, some important points about the formulation of strategy are re-emphasised. This is followed by a discussion of the *diagnosis* of strategic change *needs*, considering the signs and symptoms of *strategic drift*, how *forces blocking and facilitating change* can be identified, and how the *cultural web* can be used to map the sorts of change that might be needed.

Section 11.4 considers the *processes* which can be employed *for managing change*. Elements of the cultural web including organisational *routines*, *symbols*, *political activity* and *structure and control* are used to show how they can all contribute to achieving change. Different *styles of managing* change, the role of *communication* and more specific *tactics* for managing change are also discussed.

Section 11.5 examines the role of different players in the change process. The role of the *strategist* is considered as the architect of the change to be followed, as is the role of the *change agent*, the person or group taking the lead in effecting strategic change (who may or may not be the same as the strategist). The role of *middle managers*, often faced with the difficult task of translating the intentions of change by top management into the everyday

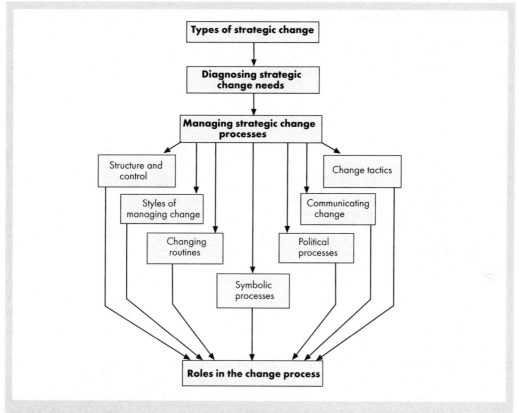

Figure 11.1   A framework for managing strategic change

reality of change, is also discussed. The role of *organisational members* who may be the recipients of the change process is also considered, for it is here, in the end, that change will be successful or not. Finally, the role of *external stakeholders* in the change process is considered.

The chapter concludes with an integrating section which pulls together the arguments in this chapter, and links them to themes running through the book.

11.2 Understanding types of strategic change

Different types of strategic change and different approaches to managing strategic change are observable in organisations. Which approaches are likely to make more or less sense are considered in this section.

11.2.1 Types of strategic change

Chapter 2 showed that strategies develop in different ways. In the main, strategy development in organisations is *incremental*, with occasional more *transformational* changes.[1] Figure 11.2 relates these types of change to how they might come about.

Arguably, it is beneficial for an organisation to change incrementally. In this way it will build on the skills, routines and beliefs of those in the organisation, so that change is efficient and likely to win their commitment. As explained in Chapter 2, there are those who argue that such incremental development can and should be proactively managed, and that, by so doing, the organisation will keep in touch with its environment and anticipate needs for change which can be achieved through a process of *tuning* current ways of operating. Others argue that, while it is not possible always to anticipate the need for change, organisations *react* to external competitive or environmental pressures. Managers may not perceive the need for major strategic changes, but rather may *adapt* the existing paradigm and current ways of operating.

Both proactive tuning and reactive adaptation may therefore result in incremental change. One way in which incremental change is explained is by conceiving of organisations as 'learning systems', continually adjusting their strategies as their environment changes. This has given rise to the idea of the *learning organisation*, which is discussed in section 11.2.2 below.

However, Chapter 2 also points out that within incremental change may lie the dangers of strategic drift because change is based on, or bounded by, the existing paradigm and routines of the organisation, even when environmental or competitive pressures might suggest the need for more fundamental change. There are, then, circumstances when more fundamental or *transformational change* is needed, either because incremental change has been inadequate or because the external pressures for change are extreme — for example, if sales decline or takeover threaten the continued existence of a firm.

Transformational change means change which cannot be handled within the existing paradigm and organisational routines: it entails a change in the taken-for-granted assumptions and 'the way of doing things around here'. Such transformational change may also come about as a result of either reactive or proactive processes. If strategic drift has occurred and has led to deteriorating performance or an uncompetitive position in its markets, or if external stakeholders (e.g. major shareholders) are not happy with the current strategy, management may be in a *forced transformational* position. Such a position may also be reached if other changes in the organisation's environment are so evidently significant or severe that the organisation is forced into such transformational change. It may, however, be that managers anticipate the need for transformational change, perhaps through

EXTENT OF CHANGE

		Incremental change	Transformational change
	Proactive	Tuning	Planned transformational
TYPE OF CHANGE			
	Reactive	Adaptation	Forced transformational

Adapted from D.A. Nadler and M.L. Tushman, 'Organizational frame bending: principles for managing reorientation', *Academy of Management Executive*, vol. 3, no. 3 (1989), pp. 194–204.

Figure 11.2   Types of strategic change

the sort of analytic techniques described earlier in the book. They may then be in a position of *planned transformational* change, which may provide them with more time in which to achieve it. However, implementing such change may be difficult to achieve if others in the organisation are resistant to it.[2]

There are, then, different explanations of how strategic change occurs in organisations. In this book, however, we are mainly concerned with exploring how the process can be managed. In doing this, it is helpful to consider different views about the role of management in change processes (see sections 11.2.2 and 11.2.3 below); then in the rest of the chapter we will consider the means whereby change might be managed.

11.2.2 Change and the learning organisation

Traditionally, organisations have been seen as hierarchies and bureaucracies set up to achieve order and maintain control: as structures built for stability rather than change. Arguably, this conception of the organisation is not suited to the dynamic conditions and often global forces for change of the late twentieth century (see Chapter 2, section 2.8.3, and Chapter 8, section 8.5.3). The organisation needs to be seen not as a stable hierarchy, but as an adaptive, continually changing *learning organisation.*

Advocates of the learning organisation point out that the collective knowledge of all the individuals in an organisation usually exceeds what the organisation itself 'knows' and is capable of doing: organisations typically stifle organisational knowledge and creativity. As suggested in Chapter 10 (section 10.4.6), in certain contexts the aim of management should be to encourage processes which unlock the knowledge of individuals, and encourage the sharing of information and knowledge, so that each individual becomes sensitive to changes occurring around them and contributes to the identification of opportunities and required changes.

The organisation then becomes capable of taking an holistic view of its environment rather than being reliant on partial, filtered information from its various functions. There is an absence of power plays and blocking routines, so that a shared vision of the future can be created and reinforced by mutual support by organisational members. Such an organisation, it is argued, will be creative and continually changing, and it will be able to cope with the ambiguity and contradictions it is likely to face. These will be seen not as threats, but as opportunities for creating synergies.[3]

It might be argued that some of the organisational forms (e.g. adhocracy) explained in Chapter 9, section 9.5.1, aspire to this rather than to the more traditional notions of stability and control. Clearly, if such organisations exist, they are well positioned to manage strategic change through continual *tuning*, such that proactive incremental change — the ultimate logical incrementalism — might come about. As an aim for managers, this is commendable. However, perhaps regrettably, there is little evidence of the common existence of such organisations. One reason for this, as shown in Chapter 2, is the forces for compliance with current ways of doing things and the current paradigm exerted by the cultural web.

11.2.3 Managed change

While a learning organisation is, then, a worthy aspiration, managers are typically faced not with a continually changing learning organisation, but with resistance to change. How can managers overcome such resistance and manage change?

If resistance to change and organisational inertia are the result of the organisation becoming trapped in its own paradigm and routines, there is a need for an 'unfreezing' of the paradigm. Figure 11.3 describes how such change might take place.[4] However, it needs to be recognised that at the different stages described in Figure 11.3, there is a likelihood that the powerful effect of the paradigm may act to promote conformity around the existing strategy. There are, then, challenges to the proactive management of change.

1. A significant change in the environment of the organisation — for example, new technology, changes in customer tastes, or the arrival of new competitors leading to a deteriorating market position — may act over time as an *unfreezing mechanism* and lead to an increasingly *felt need for change*. It is often said that 'a crisis is an opportunity' when it comes to managing change because it can provide a catalyst for unfreezing. However, in its absence, or in the absence of a clear and

dramatic external force for change, there is likely to be a need to *manage the unfreezing process.*

Managing the unfreezing process is not easy. Managers may seek to persuade people of the need for change (see section 11.4.6 below), emphasise — even exaggerate — external signs of problems or threats, make internal changes such as the removal of long-established management, or find ways of signalling symbolically the need for change (see section 11.4.4 below). However, there is a tendency for signals of change to be made sense of within the paradigm. For example, as one senior executive in a retail business commented, after five years of changing customer tastes had led to the decline of his company: 'We must be patient: when the market comes back to its senses, we will be in a good position.'

2. There may develop a situation of *flux* in the organisation, in which competing views surface about causes of, and remedies for, the problems. It is likely to be a time of high political activity (see section 11.4.5 below) and rumour spreading. While such processes give rise to conflict and appear to be disruptive, they can be useful in managing change because they can facilitate the debate of different points of view and help surface and challenge what is taken for granted.[5]

3. This debate may give rise to and be fed by *information building*, as executives attempt to check, test or find means of supporting their position — a stage which is likely to be a lengthy, iterative process. Again, however, it may be that this information building is constrained by the organisational paradigm — that information is deemed meaningful when it 'makes sense' and overlooked when it is outside the experience of people in the organisation. Market research information might be interpreted very selectively, for example.

It may therefore be especially important to manage this stage of information building. For example, *strategy workshops* could be useful, in which groups of managers debate needs and options for change. Or project teams may be set up to gather information and consider options. In such ways, the taken for granted may be questioned and challenged, advocates of new ideas may be provided with a platform, and those resistant to change may be identified.

4. Conflict and new information may contribute to individuals or groups arguing for different strategic ideas. These may then be tried out in practice — a process of *experimentation*. If successful, this could lead to the emergence of a change in strategy and changes in the organisation's paradigm and accompanying ways of doing things. Change managers may therefore deliberately try to involve key individuals in the organisation in such experiments (see section 11.4.2 below).

Illustration 11.1   A framework for planned strategic change

Gemini Consulting's process for managing change.

Gemini views organisations as living organisms with a mind, body, spirit and interaction with the environment. It believes that business transformation occurs through a four-dimensional process: reframe, restructure, revitalise and renew.

Gemini's four R's of transformation

5. Members of the organisation, faced with such disruption, may require a 'safety net' for the future. It may be that they will be ready to relate to the emerging new paradigm, although there are still dangers that they will revert to the old. *Refreezing* processes may be needed to confirm the organisational validity of the changed paradigm, so managers may need to consider ways of signalling this: for example, by changing

Reframing

Reframing is associated with the organisation's 'mind'. Questioning what the organisation is and what it can achieve opens up new possibilities and challenges. The first stage of the process is to *achieve mobilisation*; to create the will and the desire of individuals within the organisation to change. Next is to *create the vision* of a shared mental framework of where the organisation is going and then to *build a measurement system* which sets targets and defines the actions needed to achieve them.

Restructuring

Restructuring deals with the organisation's 'body' or structure, and is usually associated with lay-offs and cultural change. Their first stage is to *construct an economic model* of the organisation's processes, to give a detailed view of where and how value is created, and to ensure that resources can be provided to different parts of the organisation as and when required. Next is the *alignment of the physical infrastructure* of the organisation, to ensure that it fits with the strategic direction of the company, and then to *redesign of the work architecture* or processes of the organisation so that they add value by all interacting together in a seamless way.

Revitalising

Revitalising is associated with the need for a good match between the organisation and its environment; a 'good fit' will allow the company to grow and prosper. The first stage is to *achieve market focus*. A customer focus will enable the organisation to *invent new businesses* — the next stage. This breathes life into the organisation and enables it to use existing capabilities in new or enhanced ways. The third stage is to *change the rules* of competition through technology. Information technology, in particular, can provide new bases for competition, perhaps through product/process differentiation.

Renewal

Renewal deals with the 'spirit' of the organisation and ensures that individuals acquire the necessary skills to take the company forward and that a culture of acceptance of change is present. The first stage is to *create a reward structure* to provide a powerful motivating force and then to *build individual learning* — the encouragement for individuals to acquire the new skills necessary for the success of the transformed company. The final stage is to *develop the organisation*, in particular its learning capacity, to adapt constantly to changed circumstances.

Source: F.J. Gouillart and J.N. Kelly, *Transforming the Organisation*, McGraw-Hill, 1995.
Prepared by Tony Jacobs, Cranfield School of Management.

organisational structures, by finding symbols of change (see section 11.4.4 below) or by changing everyday routines (section 11.4.3 below).

In practice, change programmes often utilise approaches to managing strategic change which utilise similar concepts and may recognise the need to build a learning organisation. Illustration 11.1 shows the approach taken by Gemini consulting.

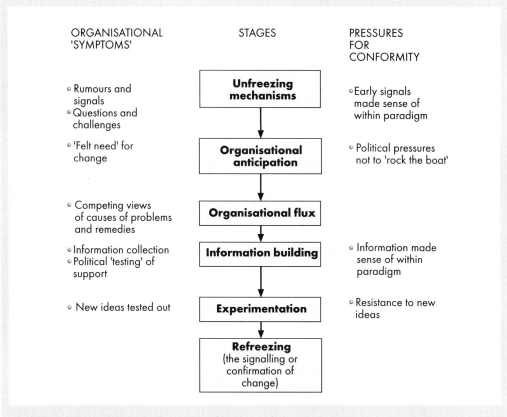

Figure 11.3 'Unfreezing' and the management of change

11.2.4 Imposed (or forced) change

There are, of course, situations where change is imposed on the organisation (see Chapter 2, section 2.5, and Chapter 8, section 8.5.2). This could either be because changes in the industry environment are so marked that the organisation has no choice; or because some external agency forces change. For example, many of the changes that have occurred in public sector organisations throughout the world, either in the form of de-regulation or privatisation, have been forced on those organisations. An external agency, perhaps government, may impose different structures of organisation or different regulatory devices to effect change.

In the case of the National Health Service in the UK, the government imposed an *internal market*, which separated the providers of health services from the purchasers of those services in what had previously been an integrated system (see Chapter 10, section 10.4.5). This was a significant structural change, not arising from a gradual, incremental adjustment based on organisational learning, and not planned by the management of the NHS, but rather imposed from outside. However, in such circumstances, an individual or group of managers will need to carry through such changes;[6] and again, the frameworks for managing change and the concepts and techniques discussed in this chapter will be useful in considering how this might be achieved.

In the rest of this chapter, the emphasis is on the role of managed change processes, both tuning and transformational. The question posed is: what can the manager do when faced with managing strategic change? Section 11.3 commences by looking at ways of diagnosing strategic change needs, and section 11.4 moves on to consider mechanisms for change.

11.3 Diagnosing strategic change needs

It is important to remember that, in managing strategic change, much of what has been written in previous chapters in this book is an essential precursor in identifying the need for and direction of strategic change. It will not be repeated in any detail here, but it is important to remember the need for clarity on the following points:

- Why strategic change is needed (discussed in Part II of the book).
- The basis of the strategy in terms of strategic purpose, perhaps encapsulated in the form of a clear statement of strategic intent and bases of competitive advantage (discussed in Chapter 6).
- The more specific directions and methods of strategy development (discussed in Chapter 7).
- The changes in strategic architecture required (discussed in Chapters 9 and 10).

However, there is also a need to understand the magnitude of the challenge faced in trying to effect strategic change. It can be useful to assess the extent to which *strategic drift* (see Chapter 2, section 2.8.2) has occurred and therefore the extent to which incremental or transformational change is required. It is also helpful to identify the specific blockages to change that exist and what forces might exist to help the change process. It can then be useful to map the sorts of change that might be required.

11.3.1 Detecting strategic drift

Incremental strategic change is more typical within an organisation, and much less disruptive, than transformational strategic change. However, it is important to gauge when incremental change has given rise to strategic drift and therefore in what circumstances more fundamental change may be required. Determining this is problematic because there is no absolute set of conditions which describe a state of strategic drift — this is a matter of managerial judgement. However, there are a number of possible symptoms:

- A highly homogeneous organisational culture and paradigm: the sort of organisation in which there are few differences of beliefs and assumptions about the organisation and its place in the external world; established routines which are not deviated from; powerful symbols and stories of an historical and conservative nature; and so on. If there is little toleration of questioning or challenge in the organisation and a readiness to dismiss new ideas with 'we've tried this before and it didn't work', an avoidance of debate of really difficult or sensitive issues and few avenues for challenging existing norms (see section 11.3.3 below), the observer might well be seeing signs of drift.

- Major power blockages to change, either because of resistant dominant leaders or because some group or layer of management is resistant to change. As one executive put it in a manufacturing company: 'Our problem is our senior managers: they've been there years and most of them are going nowhere and know it; but they can block anything if they choose. They are our "concrete ceiling".'

- An organisation with little focus on its external environment, particularly its markets. This might take the form of a lack of market information in a company; a reliance on price or cost control as a basis of competing, rather than delivering added value to customers; or a bias towards 'selling what we make' rather than responding to market and customer requirements. Such organisations are likely to be building their strategy on internalised views of the world and skill bases. This can be checked by means of research comparing managerial and customer perceptions of the organisation. Sometimes, however, it is quite evident to the external observer, as in some technologically obsessed firms or in the arrogance manifest in some professional service firms.

- Deteriorating relative performance: for example, is the performance of a business unit keeping pace with or outstripping its rivals; or has there been a gradual decline in relative performance? This may be detected, for example, by benchmarking, discussed in Chapter 4 (section 4.4.3).

11.3.2 Identifying forces blocking and facilitating change

Given that the overall strategic direction of the organisation has been identified, it is helpful to consider the forces within the organisation that could help or hinder change. Chapters 2 and 5 have already shown how the many aspects of the culture of the organisation work to shape and guide strategy, and how its influence can result in strategic drift. The *cultural web* is therefore a useful way of considering forces for and against change.[7] Illustration 11.2 shows how this exercise was undertaken in Hay Management Consultants, the international human resources consultancy firm.[8]

Although operating near to full capacity, by 1994 Hay realised that it would have to grow considerably just to meet demand and would need to become better at co-ordinating a range of services, rather than concentrating on its historical strength of job evaluation. Its executives used the framework of the cultural web to map out the existing culture (shown in Illustration 11.2(a)). While this confirmed that the firm had a focus on clients, it flagged up a number of concerns. The dominance of job evaluation as the 'core business' was very strong and potentially worked against the development of a greater range of services. The autonomy and individualism of consultants — the 'lone rangers' of the organisation — worked against co-ordination: these consultants tended to see themselves as generalists, which worked against the development of depth expertise. Change had become almost institutionalised to the point where people in the organisation tended not to take the latest change seriously. Indeed, there was a perception that, although decisions were taken, not much changed.

It can also be useful to consider the sort of culture that would exist if the required strategy were being followed effectively. This amounts to drawing a picture of an ideal. Again, the cultural web can be used because it not only provides a basis upon which the formal structures and systems of the organisation can be considered, but also requires managers to consider the day-to-day aspects of the organisation represented by routines, symbols and so on. Moreover, some of these aspects of culture — for example, organisational rituals and routines — are capable of being managed and can provide powerful messages of change (see sections 11.4.3 and 11.4.4 below).

Illustration 11.2(b) also shows how Hay managers redrew their cultural web. Here is an organisation much more integrated not only in terms of structures, but also in terms of systems and routines, and one in which the stories and symbols of the organisation represent that integration successfully. The core business is HR consultancy not just job evaluation; it is more team oriented as an approach, with group rather than individual bonuses, better information flows across departments, stories of successful teams and a lot of informal interaction. Many aspects of the existing web remain and can be built on, but the redrawn web can provide clues as to how change might be managed.

Forces for and against change can be represented in terms of a *forcefield analysis* (see Figure 11.4). This is a representation of the sort of forces for and

Illustration 11.2   Using cultural webs to identify forces blocking and facilitating change

Hay Management Consultants used cultural webs as a means of identifying required changes in culture.

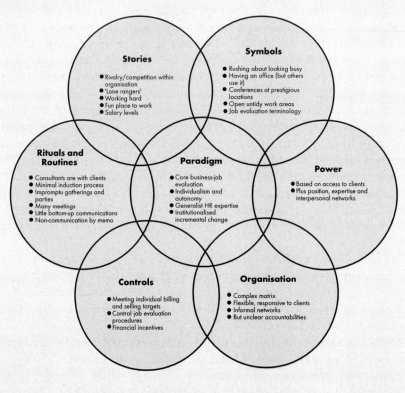

Stories
- Rivalry/competition within organisation
- 'Lone rangers'
- Working hard
- Fun place to work
- Salary levels

Symbols
- Rushing about looking busy
- Having an office (but others use it)
- Conferences at prestigious locations
- Open untidy work areas
- Job evaluation terminology

Rituals and Routines
- Consultants are with clients
- Minimal induction process
- Impromptu gatherings and parties
- Many meetings
- Little bottom-up communications
- Non-communication by memo

Paradigm
- Core business-job evaluation
- Individualism and autonomy
- Generalist HR expertise
- Institutionalised incremental change

Power
- Based on access to clients
- Plus position, expertise and interpersonal networks

Controls
- Meeting individual billing and selling targets
- Control job evaluation procedures
- Financial incentives

Organisation
- Complex matrix
- Flexible, responsive to clients
- Informal networks
- But unclear accountabilities

(a) The cultural web in 1994

against change discussed above, and which may have been identified in the web. A forcefield analysis can provide an initial view of the problems that need to be tackled, by building on the forces that might work for change and reducing the forces against change. For example, in Hay the existing culture raised problems — the embeddedness of job evaluation, the individuality, autonomy and power of individual consultants, complacency about change and so on — but it also highlighted existing forces for change: in particular, the client orientation of the firm and the fact that consultants spent a lot of time with clients, the flexible structure and approach to work in the firm,

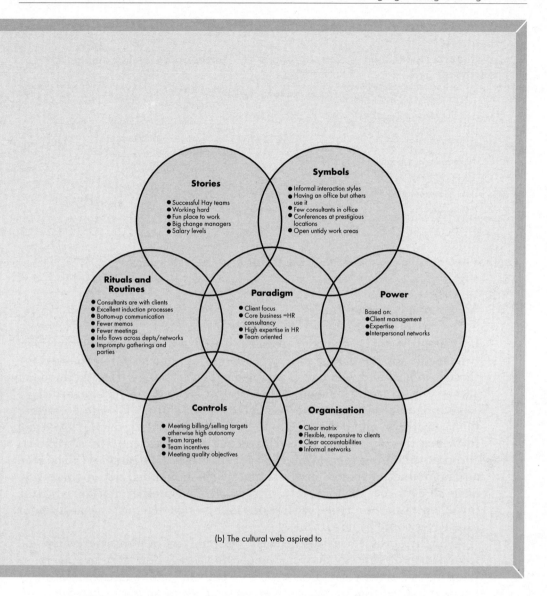

Stories
- Successful Hay teams
- Working hard
- Fun place to work
- Big change managers
- Salary levels

Symbols
- Informal interaction styles
- Having an office but others use it
- Few consultants in office
- Conferences at prestigious locations
- Open untidy work areas

Rituals and Routines
- Consultants are with clients
- Excellent induction processes
- Bottom-up communication
- Fewer memos
- Fewer meetings
- Info flows across depts/networks
- Impromptu gatherings and parties

Paradigm
- Client focus
- Core business =HR consultancy
- High expertise in HR
- Team oriented

Power
Based on:
- Client management
- Expertise
- Interpersonal networks

Controls
- Meeting billing/selling targets otherwise high autonomy
- Team targets
- Team incentives
- Meeting quality objectives

Organisation
- Clear matrix
- Flexible, responsive to clients
- Clear accountabilities
- Informal networks

(b) The cultural web aspired to

the fact that change was 'normal' in the organisation, the informal interaction that existed between people, and the fact that it was a fun place to work.

What emerges is that the routines, control systems, structures, symbols and power or dependency relationships can be both important blockages and facilitators to change. Changes in the structure, design and control systems of organisations have already been reviewed in Chapter 9. In the next two sections (11.4 and 11.5), processes for managing change are discussed and the different roles in the change process are reviewed.

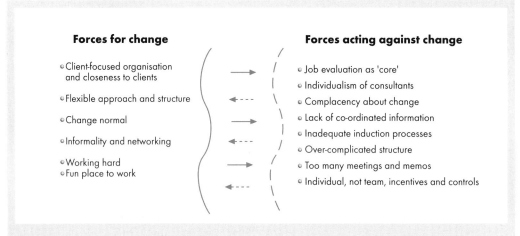

Figure 11.4 An example of forcefield analysis (based on the Hay cultural webs)

11.3.3 An openness to change

If strategy is to be changed, it needs to be not only debated by those responsible for its change and implementation, but also 'internalised' by those it affects and who have to implement the strategy. The likelihood of success in strategic change is low if the strategy is just regarded as something imposed on people — something which they have to do, rather than something which they relate to themselves in their everyday lives and for which there is 'ownership'. This is one of the reasons why traditional corporate planning approaches can be ineffective: the strategies can be seen as the product of remote analysis and decision making, not of those who have to put the strategy into effect. This is another reason why the involvement in the change process of wider groups than just the most senior executives could be important.

A further problem arises because the analysis of strategic issues and formulation of strategy may challenge the vested interest of managers, so there may be an unwillingness to tackle really difficult questions. Bowman[9] has highlighted this by referring to *zones of comfortable and uncomfortable debate* (see Figure 11.5). Managers are readily able to debate strategy in what he calls the *zone of comfortable debate*. Here they may well employ the techniques of strategic analysis and formulation, perhaps in formal corporate planning procedures or by hiring consultants to address strategic issues. However, the *zone of uncomfortable debate* encompasses aspects of the organisation and managerial attitudes and beliefs which, while they may be talked about informally, are not raised in formal meetings, planning reviews and the like. They are the sensitive areas of organisational life, which may touch on vested interest, bases of power, reputation and so on. If real

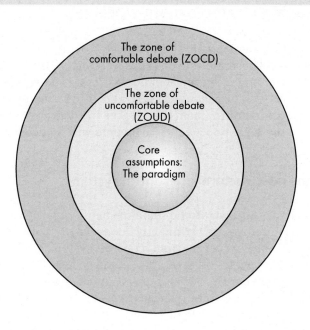

The zone of
comfortable debate (ZOCD)

The zone of
uncomfortable debate
(ZOUD)

Core
assumptions:
The paradigm

Source: Adapted from C. Bowman 'Strategy workshops and top team commitment to strategic change',
Journal of Managerial Psychology Vol 10, 1995 pp. 42-50

Figure 11.5   ZOCD and ZOUD

strategic change is to be effective, managers have to enter this zone of uncomfortable debate and be prepared to discuss and challenge such issues. Given the defence mechanisms they can employ, this can be difficult to achieve.

There are, however, some ways in which this may happen. Managers may perceive the risk of avoiding uncomfortable debate to be greater than that of pursuing it. For example, this may be the case if the organisation is in crisis. Managing entry into the uncomfortable is more problematic. It may be possible to enter through accessing a discussion about the core assumptions of the organisation — the paradigm. Mapping out the cultural web of the organisation may provide a visual image of the very aspects of the organisation which are often not discussed — the underlying power structures, the day-to-day routines, the symbols and stories, and the taken-for-granted assumptions which guide everyday life — and therefore facilitate debate about that which is rarely brought out into the open. Without such an openness of debate about the really significant blockages to change, it is unlikely that they will be tackled.

11.4 Managing strategic change processes

This section deals with the processes, or approaches, which need to be considered. These include changes in *structure and control systems*, *styles* of managing change, organisational *routines*, the use of *symbolic* and *political* activity, means of *communication* and other *change tactics*. While each of these is important in itself, the greater the degree of change, the more likely it is that multiple approaches to change will be needed.

11.4.1 Changes in structure and control systems

Many books on strategic management regard the implementation of strategic change as primarily concerned with changing aspects of organisational structure and control systems.[10] These are regarded as important aspects of strategic change here too, but they have been covered elsewhere (see Chapters 9 and 10) and so will not be discussed in further detail here. These aspects of change may have received particular attention because they tend to position top managers as the paramount agents or controllers of change, with organisational members responding to the systems imposed by them. It is a top management, top-down, view of change. The danger is that changes in structure and control systems may not affect the everyday existence of members of the organisation; that there will be a conformity towards such structures and systems, but that people will just carry on doing what they previously did on a day-to-day basis. Top management may think they have set up systems to implement strategy, but behaviour and assumptions may not have changed.

11.4.2 Styles of managing change

There are more or less appropriate styles of management for those faced with managing change.[11] These styles are summarised in Figure 11.6 and examples are given in Illustration 11.3.

1. *Education* and *communication* might be appropriate if there is a problem in managing change based on misinformation or lack of information. However, there are problems here. If large numbers of people are involved in the change, managers may try to communicate by mass briefings. But they are likely to find this ineffective, not least because those being briefed may not get a chance to assimilate the information, or because there is a lack of mutual trust and respect between managers and employees. Relying on processes of communication in a top-down

Style	Means/context	Benefits	Problems	Circumstances of effectiveness
Education and communication	Mutual trust/respect Small group briefings	Overcoming lack of (or mis)information	Time consuming Direction or progress may be unclear	Incremental change or long time horizontal transformational change
Participation	Small group/taskforce involvement	Increasing ownership of a decision or process May improve quality of decisions	Time consuming Solutions/outcome within existing paradigm	
Intervention/ manipulation	Change agent retains co-ordination/control: delegates aspects of change	Process is guided/controlled But involvement takes place	Risk of perceived manipulation	Incremental or non-crisis transformational change
Direction	Use of authority to set direction and means of change	Clarity and speed	Risk of lack of acceptance and ill-conceived strategy	Transformational change
Coercion/edict	Exploit use of power through edict or imposition of change	May be successful in crises or state of confusion	Least successful unless crisis	Crisis, rapid transformational change or change in established autocratic cultures

Figure 11.6 Styles of managing strategic change

Illustration 11.3   Styles of managing change

Executives use different styles of managing change.

Education, communication and participation in the electrical industry

In the early 1990s, Jan Timmer, the chief executive of Philips NV, was seeking to move the company from its cumbersome technologically focused, organisationally complex past to a more market, customer-focused future. A 'customer day' was organised in January 1992 on which Timmer communicated by satellite with 80,000 Philips employees throughout Europe. He spoke to every employee in their local workplace for an hour. This was followed by groups of employees locally identifying what a customer-oriented organisation and a customer-responsive employee should be like. Views on these local deliberations, together with questions for Timmer, were sent to the Eindhoven head office that same day. In the afternoon, Timmer again spoke to employees by satellite, answering the questions, commenting on the views and taking live questions from an audience in Eindhoven.

Intervention in the oil industry

A Dutch executive of an oil company was appointed as chief executive in a national subsidiary in southern Europe which had long been subject to government regulation on prices. 'I faced a sleepy management team which had simply managed the distribution of oil products; there was no thought about competition. Within a year we had to face a free market and all that meant in competitive terms. It was tempting to try and tell them what to do, but it would not have worked. They knew they had to change, but they did not know what it meant or how to do it. I set up project teams to tackle some of the major issues. I gave them the questions; they had to come up with the answers. I made it clear that the questions were based around the performance levels achieved in other companies in the group, so they knew they could be achieved. For example, how do we reduce costs by 30 per cent; how do we increase share by 50 per cent; and productivity by a similar amount? Members of the project team visited companies in other countries to see what they were doing; they came to me and asked questions, and I offered some suggestions; consultants I brought in argued with them and challenged them. Their task was to come up with recommendations for the future within a six-month period. This they did and we debated them. I then led a team to pull it all together and identify specific plans of action to make it happen.'

fashion may therefore be problematic: involvement of those affected by changes in strategy development and planning change processes may therefore be important.

2. A consultative approach through *participation* in the change process can be helpful in increasing ownership of a decision or change process, and in increasing commitment to it. This may entail the setting up of project teams or task forces. Those involved are then able to make a meaningful contribution to the decision-making process, the outcome of which may be of higher quality than decisions taken without such an approach. In the late 1980s, when British Airways effected major and successful change, there was widespread involvement across all levels of management in the critique of current practices and workshops proposing new ideas and appraising proposed solutions.

   Strategy workshops can also usefully cross levels of management to work on particular strategic problems, provide proposed solutions within a broad strategic framework, and drive change mechanisms down to routine aspects of organisational life. However, there is the inevitable risk that solutions will be found from within the existing paradigm. Anyone who sets up such a process, therefore, may well need to retain the ability to intervene in the process.

3. With the *intervention* approach, the co-ordination of and authority for processes of change remain with the change agent, but he or she delegates aspects of the change process. For example, it might be that particular stages of change, such as idea generation, data collection, detailed planning, the development of rationales for change and the identification of critical success factors, are delegated to project teams or task forces. Such teams may not take full responsibility for the change process, but they do become involved in it and see their work building towards it. The sponsor of the change ensures the monitoring of progress and that change is demonstrated.[12] An advantage here is that it involves members of the organisation not only in originating ideas, but also, in effect, in the *partial implementation* of solutions. For example, those who originate ideas might be given responsibility for co-ordinating or overseeing the implementation of such aspects of the strategic change. This involvement is likely to give rise to greater commitment to the change.

4. A *directive* style involves the use of managerial authority to support clear direction about future strategy and how change will occur, established at the top of the organisation. It is essentially top-down management of strategic change. It may be associated with a clear vision or strategic intent developed by someone seen as a leader in the organisation; but it will also be accompanied by similar clarity about the sort of critical success factors and priorities discussed in Chapter 10.

5. In its most extreme form, a directive style becomes *coercive*, involving the imposition of change or the issuing of edicts about change. This is the explicit use of power and may be necessary if the organisation is facing a crisis, for example.

There are some overall observations that can be made about the appropriateness of these different styles:

- Different styles are likely to be suited to different contexts and circumstances. For example, strategic change for an organisation has implications for different stakeholders. Education and communication may be highly appropriate for some stakeholders, such as city institutions in the case of a public corporation. However, at the same time other styles may be more appropriate to galvanise change internally within the organisation.
- Different stages in the change process should, perhaps, also be regarded in different contexts. Clear directions may be vital in the unfreezing and refreezing stages, whereas participation or intervention may be especially helpful in information building and experimentation.
- The evidence is that participative styles are most appropriate for incremental change within organisations, but that where transformational change is required directive approaches are more common. It is also worth noting that even where top management see themselves adopting participative styles, their subordinates may perceive this as directive and, indeed, may welcome such direction.[13]

11.4.3 Changes in organisational routines

Routines are the institutionalised 'ways we do things around here'[14] which tend to persist over time and guide how people do their jobs. As has been seen in the discussion on the value chain in Chapters 4 and 10, it may be that an organisation which becomes especially good at carrying out its operations in particular ways achieves real competitive advantages. However, there is also the risk that the same routines act to block change and lead to strategic drift (see Chapter 2, section 2.8.2).

The power of such routines is clear enough when they need changing in order to accommodate a new strategy. Managers often make the mistake of assuming that because they have specified a strategy which requires operational changes in work practices, and explained to more junior management what such changes are, the changes will necessarily take place. They may find that the reasons which emerge as to why such changes should be delayed or cannot occur have to do with the persistent influence of long-standing organisational routines.

Illustration 11.4   Changes in organisational routines

Changes in organisational routines can be a powerful signal and stimulus of change.

- The management of a transport and distribution firm, seeking to emphasise rapid response to customer needs, established a routine of telephone answering in the head office. No phone was allowed to ring more than twice before being picked up by someone; and no one was allowed to ignore a ringing phone — 'it might be a customer'.
- Public sector organisations have been obsessed with the stewardship of public funds, often resulting in very risk-averse cultures. Some have tried to break this by setting up internal 'investment banks' so that staff can 'bid' for the funding of new ventures.
- The activities of branch personnel in many UK banks were dominated by manual form-filling procedures. The effect was that these procedures were often seen as more significant than dealing with customers. In the late 1980s, the banks moved to computerised systems: this was not just to reduce staff costs, but also to remove the paperwork from remaining staff. As one manager put it: 'If you haven't got a form to fill in, you have to attend to customers, and that is at the heart of our strategy.'
- The chief executive of a long-established Danish company, manufacturing hearing aids, sought to transform the organisation into a 'knowledge-based' company. He introduced an open-plan office with mobile seating arrangements, and put everyone to work in project-based teams. Traditional job responsibilities were broken down and all head office staff were required to do up to five jobs, deciding themselves what they should prioritise and working in frequently changing project teams. The new office had no walls, but only workbenches with computer terminals. People moved between desks according to the projects they were working on, taking a set of drawers with them. Incoming mail was scanned on to the computer; if someone wanted to view something on paper, they went to the mail room, and it was then shredded.

A manager in a hospital trust in the UK, determined to make the hospital services more 'client friendly', tried to persuade a medical consultant to adhere to appointment times so as to cut down waiting time; and not require patients to change into the white gowns traditional in that hospital. 'People could be sitting or lying around for an hour in very scanty gowns; it was embarrassing for them.' After much debate the consultant agreed to more diligent appointment timing, but insisted the gowns were imperative. The manager instructed the white gowns to be removed from the consulting room. The following week, the consultant had purchased his own gowns and was bringing them into the hospital every morning.

Chapter 10 (see section 10.3.1) argued that it is important to drive the planning of strategic change down to the identification of critical success factors and competences underpinning these factors. In so doing, the planning of the implementation of the intended strategy is being driven down to operational levels, and it is likely this will require changes in the routines of the organisation. It is at this level that changes in strategy become really meaningful for most people in their everyday organisational lives. Moreover, as mentioned above, routines are closely linked to the taken-for-grantedness of the paradigm, so changing routines may have the effect of questioning and challenging deep-rooted beliefs and assumptions in the organisation. It is vital that managers who are trying to effect strategic changes take personal responsibility not only for identifying such changes in routines, but also for monitoring that they actually occur. The changes may appear to be mundane, but they can have significant impact. Illustration 11.4 gives some examples.

11.4.4 Symbolic processes in managing change[15]

Change processes are not always of an overt, formal nature: they may also be symbolic in nature. Chapter 2 explained how symbolic acts and artefacts of an organisation help preserve the paradigm, and Chapter 5 explained how their relationship to culture and strategy can be analysed. Here the concern is how they can be managed to signal change.

'Mundane tools that involve the creation and manipulation of symbols over time have impact to the extent that they re-shape beliefs and expectations'[16] because meaning becomes apparent in day-to-day experience in the organisation. This is one reason why changes in routines (discussed above) are important, but other such everyday or 'mundane' aspects include the stories that people tell, the status symbols such as cars and sizes of office, the type of language and technology used, and organisational rituals.

■ Many of the *rituals* (or rites) of organisations are implicitly concerned with effecting or consolidating change. Figure 11.7 identifies such rituals.[17] They are often capable of being managed proactively: new rituals can be introduced or old rituals done away with. Using the terminology in Figure 11.7, change agents can consider the rituals which may be useful. *Rites of enhancement* might include the spreading of 'good news' of transformation and the rewarding of those contributing to it. Corporate newsletters are often used for this purpose. There could be *rites of integration*, such as conferences which applaud change and 'change heroes', or which involve or associate members of the organisation with new approaches, activities or belief systems. *Rites of conflict reduction* to minimise or contain disunity may take the form of structural change or personnel appointments that demonstrate which executive groups have significant influence and which have been marginalised. *Rites of passage* can signal change from one stage of the organisation's development to another: for example, the departure of the old and introduction of new management, perhaps the replacement

Types of ritual (rite)	Role	Examples
Rites of passage	Consolidate and promote social roles and interaction	Induction programmes Training programmes
Rites of enhancement	Recognise effort benefiting organisation Similarly motivate others	Award ceremonies Promotions
Rites of renewal	Reassure that something is being done Focus attention on issues	Appointment of consultants Project teams
Rites of integration	Encourage shared commitment Reassert rightness of norms	Xmas parties
Rites of conflict reduction	Reduce conflict and aggression	Negotiating committees
Rites of degradation	Publicly acknowledge problems Dissolve/weaken social or political roles	Firing top executives Demotion or 'passing over'
Rites of sense making	Sharing of interpretations and sense making	Rumours Surveys to evaluate new practices
Rites of challenge	'Throwing down the gauntlet'	New CEO's different behaviour
Rites of counter-challenge	Resistance to new ways of doing things	Grumbling Working to rule

Figure 11.7   Organisational rituals and culture change

of senior board members or even a whole board, can signify much more than individual personnel changes as an indication of the passing from one era to another.

- Symbolic significance is also embedded in the *systems* discussed elsewhere in this chapter and in Chapters 9 and 10. For example, reward systems, information and control systems, and the very organisational structures that represent reporting relationships and often status are also symbolic in nature. Even budgeting and planning systems come to take on symbolic significance in so far as they represent to individuals the everyday reality of organisational life.

To take an example of such systems, the way selection interviews are conducted is likely to signal to those being interviewed the nature of the organisation, and what is expected of them. A highly formal interview procedure may signal a mechanistic, rather hierarchical organisation, whereas a more informal dialogue, perhaps preceded by open questioning of potential colleagues, is likely to signal an environment and expectation of challenge and questioning. If selection processes are changed, different types of manager are appointed, and visible encouragement to challenge and questioning is given, this can signal within the organisation the commitment to strategic change. In this sense, selection processes are symbolic in nature.

■ Changes in *physical aspects* of the work environment are powerful symbols of change. Typical here is a change of location for the head office, relocation of personnel, changes in dress or uniforms, and alterations to offices or office space.

■ The most powerful symbol of all in relation to change is the *behaviour of change agents* themselves. The behaviour, language and stories associated with such executives can signal powerfully the need for change and appropriate behaviour relating to the management of change. Too few senior executives understand that, having made pronouncements about the need for change, it is vital that their visible behaviour is in line with such change because for most people in an organisation, their organisational world is one of deeds and actions, not of abstractions. In one major retail business with an espoused strategy of customer care, the chief executive, on visiting stores, tended to ignore staff and customers alike: he seemed to be interested only in the financial figures in the store manager's office. He was unaware of this until it was pointed out; and his change in behaviour afterwards, insisting on talking to staff and customers on his visits, became a 'story' which spread around the company, substantially supporting the strategic direction of the firm.

■ *Stories* themselves can be managed to some extent. The use of corporate newsletters and newspapers is an example. There are, however, more subtle examples. One chief executive claimed that the most effective way of spreading a story in his business was to get his secretary to leave a memo from him marked 'strictly confidential' by the photocopier for ten minutes: 'Its contents would be all over the office in half an hour and round the regions by the end of the day.'

■ Also important in effecting change is the *language* used by change agents.[18] Either consciously or unconsciously, change agents may employ language and metaphor to galvanise change. Some examples are included in Illustration 11.5. In this context, language is not simply concerned with communicating facts and information; language is also powerful because it is symbolic and is simultaneously able to carry several meanings at once. For example, it may link the past to the future:

Illustration 11.5   Symbolic activity and strategic change

Symbolic aspects of management can aid the change process in organisations.

Language which challenges and questions
The chief executive of a retailing firm facing a crisis addressed his board: 'I suggest we think of ourselves like bulls facing a choice: the abattoir or the bull ring. I've made up my mind: what about you?'

In another company, the chief executive described the threat of a takeover in terms of pending warfare: 'We've been targeted: they've got the hired guns [merchant bankers, consultants, etc.] on board. Don't expect chivalry: don't look for white knights; this is a shoot-out situation.'

Physical objects such as clothing which signal change
The head nurse of a recovery unit for patients who had been severely ill decided that, if nurses wore everyday clothes rather than nurses' uniforms, it would signal to patients that they were on the road to recovery and a normal life; and to nurses that they were concerned with rehabilitation.

However, the decision had other implications for the nurses too. It blurred the status distinction between nurses and other non-professional members of staff. Nurses preferred to wear their uniforms. While they recognised that uniforms signalled a medically fragile role of patients, they reinforced their separate and professional status as acute care workers.[19]

Confirmatory action signalling change
In a textile firm in Scotland, equipment associated with the 'old ways of doing things' was taken into the yard at the rear of the factory and physically dismantled in front of the workforce.

When the new president of Asaki Breweries in Japan introduced Koku-Kire beer, he signalled a fundamental shift in product policy and required commitment to the new product, not only with a high publicity launch and a change in company logo, but also by dumping all stocks of the old product and recalling it from 130,000 stores.[20]

it may attack or undermine an image of the past, and therefore carry a very serious message, yet do so in a playful way; and it may evoke emotional feelings more strongly than rational understanding. Of course, there is also the danger that change agents do not realise the power of language and, while espousing change, use language that signals adherence to the status quo, or personal reluctance to change. Those involved in change need to think carefully about the language they use, and the symbolic significance of their actions.

Illustration 11.5 gives other examples of such symbolic signalling of change.

11.4.5 Power and political processes in managing change[21]

It is likely that there will be a need for the reconfiguration of *power structures* in the organisation, especially if transformational change is required. In order to effect this reconfiguration of power, it is likely that the momentum for change will need *powerful advocacy* within the organisation, typically from the chief executive, a powerful member of the board or an influential outsider: indeed, an individual or group combining both power and interest, as described in Chapter 5 (see section 5.3.2 and Figure 5.5).

However, political activity is not relevant only at the chief executive or senior executive level. Any manager faced with managing change needs to consider how it might be effected from a political perspective. Managers also need to realise that analysis and planning may themselves take on political dimensions. A new marketing director of a company commissioned market research on customer perceptions of service, and the results were highly critical. However, he found that the presentation of the findings to the board gave rise not to analytical debate, but to systematic 'rubbishing' of the research report. He failed to realise that his work had been seen 'not so much as an analytical statement, as a statement of political threat': it had threatened the very bases of the business upon which many on the board had built their authority and power in the organisation. So managers need to be sensitive to the political dimensions of their activities, both because there might be blockages to apparently rational behaviour and because political activity might, itself, help effect change.

Chapter 5 discussed the importance of understanding the political context in and around the organisation. Having established this understanding, there is also a need to consider the implementation of strategy within this political context. The approach developed here draws on the content of Chapter 5 and also some of this chapter to provide a framework. Figure 5.6 in Chapter 5 lists sources of power in organisations. These also provide indicators of some of the mechanisms associated with power which can be used for change. Summarised in Figure 11.8, these include the manipulation of *organisational resources*; the relationship with powerful groupings and/or *élites*; activity with regard to *subsystems* in the organisation; and again, *symbolic activity*. All of these may be used to: (1) build a power base; (2) encourage support or overcome resistance; and (3) achieve commitment to a strategy or course of action.

- Acquiring additional *resources* or being identified with important resource areas or areas of expertise, and the ability to withdraw or allocate such resources, can be a valuable tool in overcoming resistance or persuading others to accept change.

- Powerful groupings in the organisation are of crucial importance and

Activity areas	Mechanisms				Key problems
	Resources	Élites	Subsystems	Symbolic	
Building the power base	Control of resources Acquisition of/identification with expertise Acquisition of additional resources	Sponsorship by an élite Association with an élite	Alliance building Team building	Building on legitimation	Time required for building Perceived duality of ideals Perceived as threat by existing élites
Overcoming resistance	Withdrawal of resources Use of 'counter-intelligence' information	Breakdown or division of élites Association with change agent Association with respected outsider	Foster momentum for change Sponsorship/ reward of change agents	Attack or remove legitimation Foster confusion, conflict and questioning	Striking from too low a power base Potentially destructive: need for rapid rebuilding
Achieving compliance	Giving resources	Removal of resistant élites Need for visible 'change hero'	Partial implementation and participation Implantation of 'disciples' Support for 'young Turks'	Applause/ reward Reassurance Symbolic confirmation	Converting the body of the organisation Slipping back

Figure 11.8   Political mechanisms in organisations

may, of course, correspond to powerful *stakeholder groups*. Association with such groupings, or their support, can help build a power base, and this may be necessary for the change agent who does not have a strong personal power base from which to work. Similarly, association with a change agent who is respected or visibly successful can help a manager overcome resistance to change.

- It may be necessary to remove individuals or groups resistant to change. Who these are can vary: from powerful individuals in senior positions, to loose networks within the organisation and sometimes including external stakeholders with powerful influence, to whole layers of resistance perhaps in the form of senior executives in a threatened function or service — the 'concrete ceiling' referred to earlier in the chapter.

- Building up *alliances* and a *network* of contacts and sympathisers, even though they may not be powerful themselves, may be important in overcoming the resistance from more powerful groups. Attempting to convert the whole organisation to an acceptance of change is difficult: it is likely that there will be parts of the organisation or individuals in it more sympathetic to that change than others. The change agent might sensibly concentrate on these to develop momentum, building a team strongly supportive of the activities and beliefs of the change agent. He or she may also seek to marginalise those who are resistant to change.

  The danger is that powerful groups in the organisation may regard the building of such a team, or acts of marginalisation, as a threat to their own power, and that this may lead to further resistance to change. An analysis of power and interest similar to the stakeholder mapping described in Chapter 5 might, therefore, be especially useful to identify bases of alliance and likely political resistance.

- As has been seen, the employment of *symbolic mechanisms* of change can be useful. From a political point of view, this may take several forms. To build power the manager may initially seek to identify with the very symbols which preserve and reinforce the paradigm — to work within the committee structures, become identified with the organisational rituals or stories that exist and so on. On the other hand, in breaking resistance to change, removing, challenging or changing rituals and symbols may be a very powerful means of achieving the questioning of what is taken for granted. Symbolic activity can also be used to consolidate change: by concentrating attention or 'applause' and rewards on those who most accept change, its wider adoption is more likely; and there may be means of confirming change through symbolic devices such as new structures, titles, office allocation and so on, so that the change is to be regarded as important and not reversible.

COUNTERMOVES TO CHANGE

- **Divert resources**. Split budget across other projects, give key staff other priorities/other assignments.
- **Exploit inertia**. Request everyone to wait until a key player takes action, reads a report, or makes an appropriate response; suggest the results from another project should be assessed first.
- **Keep goals vague and complex**. It is harder to intiate appropriate action if aims are multidimensional and specified in generalised, grandiose or abstract terms.
- **Encourage and exploit lack of organisational awareness**. Insist that 'we can deal with the people issues later', knowing these will delay or kill the project.
- **'Great idea — let's do it properly'**. Involve so many representatives or experts that there will be so many different views and conflicting interests it will delay decisions or require meaningless compromise.
- **Dissipate energies**. Conduct surveys, collect data, prepare analyses, write reports, make overseas trips, hold special meetings . . .
- **Reduce the change agent's influence and credibility**. Spread damaging rumours, particularly among the change agent's friends and supporters.
- **Keep a low profile**. Do not openly declare resistance to change because that gives those driving change a clear target to aim for.

COUNTERING COUNTERMOVES TO CHANGE

- **Establish clear direction and objectives**. Goal clarity enables action to proceed more effectively than ambiguity and complexity, which can slow down action.
- **Establish simple, phased programming**. For the same reasons as having clear goals.
- **Adopt a fixer–facilitator–negotiator role**. Resistance to change can rarely be overcome by reason alone, and the exercise of these interpersonal skills is required.
- **Seek and respond to resistance**. Take a proactive approach to resistance in order to overcome, mitigate or block it: appeal/refer to high values/standards or powerful authorities; warn them off; use influential intermediaries; infiltrate meetings and supporters; wait them out or wear them down.
- **Rely on face to face**. Personal influence and persuasion is usually more effective in winning and sustaining support than the impersonal memo or report.
- **Exploit a crisis**. People will often respond more positively to a crisis which they understand and face collectively than to personal attempts to change behaviour.
- **Co-opt support early**. Build coalitions and recruit backers, of prior importance to the building of teams; co-opting opponents may also be tactically useful.
- **The meaningful steering committee/task force/project team**. Include in its membership key players in the organisation who carry 'weight', authority and respect.

Adapted from D. Buchanan and D. Boddy, *The Expertise of the Change Agent: Public performance and backstage activity*, Prentice Hall, 1992, pp. 78–9.

Figure 11.9   Political manoeuvres and change

Illustration 11.6 Machiavelli on political processes

It should be borne in mind that there is nothing more difficult to handle, more doubtful of success, and more dangerous to carry through, than initiating changes in a state's constitution.

'The innovator makes enemies of all those who prospered under the old order, and only lukewarm support is forthcoming from those who would prosper under the new. Their support is lukewarm partly from fear of their adversaries, who have the existing laws on their side, and partly because men are generally incredulous, never really trusting new things unless they have tested them by experience. In consequence, whenever those who oppose the changes can do so, they attack vigorously, and the defence made by the others is only lukewarm. So both the innovator and his friends come to grief.'

The Prince, Penguin, p. 51; OUP, p. 22

Machiavelli's Prince is precariously balanced between four interest groups: the army, the nobility, the populace and the state. Gauging the relative power of these and devising strategies which take this into account become crucial, as Machiavelli illustrates.

Scipio's *army* rebelled against him in Spain for allowing too much licence. Commodus and Maximinus (two Roman emperors) both exhibited excess cruelty, and both were killed by their armies.

The *nobility*'s desire is to command and oppress the people. Bentivogli, Prince of Bologna, was killed by the Canneschi (nobility) who conspired against him. However, after the murder, the people rose up and killed the Canneschi. The Canneschi misjudged the goodwill of the people toward Bentivogli.

It is necessary for a prince to possess the friendship of the *populace*, particularly in times of adversity. Nabis, prince of the Spartans, sustained a siege by the rest of Greece and a victorious Roman army, defended his country against them, and maintained his own position through unifying the populace.

Machiavelli commends three principles:

■ Establish whether you are in the position, in case of need, to maintain yourself alone, or whether you need the protection of others.
■ Esteem your nobles, but don't make yourself hated by the populace.
■ Follow the example of Ferdinand, King of Aragon and Spain, who 'continually contrived great things which have kept his subjects' minds uncertain and astonished, and occupied in watching their result'.

Source: Machiavelli, *The Prince*, Penguin, 1961.
Prepared by Roger Lazenby, Cranfield School of Management.

■ Change agents also have to cope with the tactical political manoeuvring of other managers resistant to change. The sort of tactics typically employed to counter change are identified in Figure 11.9.[22] The figure also identifies some of the actions that might be taken in countering such countermoves: many of these build on the discussion in this chapter of styles of managing and symbolic and political aspects of management.

Political aspects of management in general, and change specifically, are unavoidable; and the lessons of organisational life are as important for the manager as they are, and always have been, for the politician (see Illustration 11.6). However, the political aspects of management are also difficult, and potentially hazardous. Figure 11.8 summarises some of the problems.

A problem in building a power base is that the manager may have to become so identified with existing power groupings that he or she either actually comes to accept their views or is perceived by others to have done so, thus losing support among potential supporters of change. Building a power base is a delicate path to tread.

In overcoming resistance, the major problem may simply be the lack of power to be able to undertake such activity. Attempting to overcome resistance from a lower power base is probably doomed to failure. There is a second major danger: in the breaking down of the status quo, the process becomes so destructive and takes so long that the organisation cannot recover from it. If the process needs to take place, its replacement by some new set of beliefs and the implementation of a new strategy is vital and needs to be speedy. Further, as already identified, in implementing change the main problem is likely to be carrying the body of the organisation with the change. It is one thing to change the commitment of a few senior executives at the top of an organisation; it is quite another to convert the body of the organisation to an acceptance of significant change. The danger is that individuals are likely to regard change as temporary: something which they need to comply with only until the next change comes along.

11.4.6 Communicating change

Managers faced with effecting change typically underestimate substantially the extent to which members of the organisation understand the need for change, what it is intended to achieve, or what is involved in the changes. Some important points to emphasise are as follows.

■ The reasons for a change in strategic direction may be complex, and the strategy itself may therefore embrace complex ideas. However, to be effective it is important that it is communicated in such a way that

Source: Based on R.H. Lengel and R.L Daft, *The Selection of Communication Media as an Effective Skill*. The Academy of Management Executive, 1988, vol.2, no. 3, pp. 225–232.

Figure 11.10   Effective and non-effective communication of change

complexity has a meaning and vitality which can be assimilated across the organisation. This message has already been discussed elsewhere in the book, when considering the importance of *vision* and *strategic intent* in Chapters 5 and 6. These should not be banal statements of strategy, but rather should encapsulate the significance and challenge of that strategy.

It may be important to clarify and simplify further the priorities of the strategy. Some writers argue[23] that a *three themes* approach is useful, emphasising a limited number of key aspects of the strategy, rather than expecting to be able to communicate overall complexity and ramifications.

There are *choices of media* by which to communicate the strategy and the elements of the strategic change programme.[24] Figure 11.10 summarises some of the choices and the likely effectiveness of these in different circumstances. Choices of media richness vary from face-to-face, one-to-one communication through to routine bulletins on notice boards and circulars sent round the organisation.

The extent to which these different forms of media are likely to be effective depends on the extent to which the nature of the change is routine or complex. To communicate a highly complex set of changes, it would be inappropriate to use standardised bulletins and circulars with no chance of any feedback or interaction. In situations of strategic change, members of the organisation not involved in the development of the strategy may see the effects of change as non-routine even when senior executives regard them as routine. So communication which provides interaction and involvement is likely to be desirable.

* The *involvement* of members of the organisation in the strategy development process or the planning of strategic change is also, in itself, a means of communication and can be very effective. Those who are involved might be used to cascade information about the change programme into the organisation, in effect becoming part of the change agency process themselves. This is an important element of the *intervention* style described in section 11.4.2.

* Communication needs to be seen as a two-way process. *Feedback* on communication is important, particularly if the changes to be introduced are difficult to understand, threatening or critically important to get right. It is rare that changes have been thought through in ways which have meaning to or can be put into effect at lower levels in the organisation. In addition, the purpose of the changes may be misunderstood or misconstrued at such levels.

  These problems can be tackled in various ways. If there has been a cascading process in the organisation, this can also be used to obtain feedback. It may be useful to set up 'focus groups' which give feedback to senior executives on the implementation and acceptance of change. Some organisations employ survey techniques to check the extent to which change processes are being followed, understood or welcomed. In other organisations, senior executives invite feedback by 'walking the talk', ensuring that they meet with those responsible for implementing change, perhaps on an informal basis in their workplace.

* There is, however, another reason why communication is very important. Communication occurs in organisations not simply because managers trying to effect change wish to communicate, but because members of the organisation need to make sense of what is happening for themselves. They therefore communicate with each other. This takes the form of *rumours*, *gossip* and *story telling*. Indeed, it has been noted that at times of threat and change, such story telling increases in importance.[25] In managing change, the task is not only to communicate change, but to do it sufficiently powerfully to overcome the inevitable *counter-communication* which is likely to take place.

11.4.7 Change tactics

There are also some more specific tactics of change which might be employed to facilitate the change process.

Timing

The importance of timing is often neglected in thinking about strategic change. To some extent this has already been covered in Chapter 10, when considering issues such as network analysis. However, network analysis has mainly to do with the scheduling tasks within a change project. Timing also refers to choosing the right time tactically to promote change. For example:

- The greater the degree of change, the more it may be useful to build on actual or perceived *crisis*. If members of the organisation perceive a higher risk in maintaining the status quo than changing, they are more likely to change. For example, the management of a company threatened by takeover may be able to use this as a catalyst for transformational strategic change, as ICI did when threatened with takeover by Hanson in the early 1990s. It is said that some chief executives seek to elevate problems to perceived crisis in order to galvanise change.
- There may also be *windows of opportunity* in change processes. For example, the period following the takeover of a company may allow new owners to make more significant changes than might normally be possible. The arrival of a new chief executive, the introduction of a new highly successful product, or the arrival of a major competitive threat on the scene may also provide such opportunities. These windows of opportunity may, however, be brief; and the change agent may need to take decisive action during these periods.
- It is also important that those responsible for change do not provide conflicting messages about the timing of change. For example, if they see that rapid change is required, they should avoid the maintenance of procedures and signals which suggest long time horizons. For example, managers may exhort others to change while maintaining the same control and reward procedures or work practices that have been in place for many years. So the *symbolic signalling of time frames* becomes important (see section 11.4.4 above).
- Since change will be regarded nervously, it may be important to choose the time for promoting such change to avoid unnecessary fear and nervousness. For example, if there is a need for reduction in personnel or the removal of executives (see below), it may make sense to do this before rather than during the change programme. In such a way, the change programme can be seen as a potential improvement for the future rather than as the cause of such losses.

Job losses and de-layering

Change programmes are often associated with job losses, from the closure of units of the organisation, with hundreds or thousands of job losses, to the removal of a few senior executives. In the 1990s, in some countries change was associated with de-layering: the removal of whole layers of management. As indicated above, the timing of such job losses in relation to the change programme can be important. There are other considerations which can affect a change programme:

- The tactical choice of where job losses should take place related to the change programme may be important. For example, it could be that there is a layer of management or particular individuals who are widely recognised in the organisation as *blockers* of change. Their removal may indicate powerfully the serious nature and intent of the change. The removal of one layer of management may also provide perceived opportunities to management below. As one chief executive commented: 'If I have to lose people, then I will choose the most senior levels possible: they're the ones most usually resistant to change; and it provides a wonderful incentive for those below.'
- It may also be important to avoid 'creeping' job losses. If the change programme is continually associated with a threat to security, it is less likely to be successful. The same chief executive continued: 'It is better to cut deeply and quickly than hack away remorselessly over time.'
- It is also important, however, that if job losses are to take place, there is a visible, responsible and caring approach to those who lose their jobs. Not only are there ethical reasons for this, but tactically it signals to those who remain that the organisation cares. There are now many examples of companies which have successful redeployment, counselling services, outplacement arrangements, retraining facilities and so on. Indeed, British Coal Enterprise was set up with this purpose and was very successful in helping past employees in the coal-mining industry in all these respects.

Visible short-term wins

Strategy may be conceived of as having to do with long-term direction and major decisions. However, the implementation of strategy within a change programme will require many quite detailed actions and tasks. It is important that some of these tasks are seen to be put into place and to be successful quickly. This could take the form, for example, of a retail chain quickly developing a new store concept and demonstrating its success in the market; the effective breaking down of old ways of working and the demonstration of better ways; the speeding up of decisions by doing away with committees and introducing clearly defined job responsibilities; and so on.

In themselves, these may not be especially significant aspects of a new strategy, but they may be visible indicators of a new approach associated with that strategy. The demonstration of such wins will therefore galvanise commitment to the strategy.

11.5 Roles in the change process

While it is very important to identify blockages to change and understand mechanisms of change, it is also necessary to consider the roles that individuals or groups of individuals play in the change process, and the sorts of skill they require. A good deal of the literature on leadership emphasises the personal, individualistic aspects of change management in organisations. Such literature sometimes suggests that strategic change is heavily dependent on the activities of charismatic leaders.[26] These views can be misleading because they fail to identify the context in which change agency occurs, the fact that change usually depends on more than one individual, and the extent to which skills in managing change can be developed.

In the sections below, a number of roles in the management of strategic change are reviewed. However, it should be emphasised that this is not meant to suggest that these roles are mutually exclusive. For example, the creator of a strategy may, or may not, also be the change agent; and it may be that a middle manager is also a recipient or indeed a change agent in a different context. So these are roles that different people in organisations may find themselves in at different times and in different contexts.

11.5.1 The change agent

The person or people who develop a strategy may or may not be the same as those who take a lead in actually managing strategic change. Some strategists may be especially good at creating a vision for the future, but may need to rely on others to take a lead in effecting the changes. It may be that there is a group of change agents from within the organisation or perhaps from outside, such as consultants, who have a whole team working on a project, together with managers from within the organisation. So change agency does not necessarily correspond to one individual, though it may.

Those faced with effecting change need to consider the extent to which the various components of change agency discussed in this chapter are in place or can be developed, and how these components match the context of change. The successful change agent will therefore:

- Be sensitive to the *external context* of change — for example, the triggers in the environment giving rise to change, or the pressure from external stakeholders.
- Be sensitive to *organisational context*, building on or relating to the values and beliefs of those in or around the organisation who advocate or feel sympathy towards the need for change and the history of the organisation.[27]
- Understand the overall strategy in terms of required *strategic architecture* (see Chapter 10) and therefore the magnitude and *type of change* necessary (see section 11.2).

■ Employ an appropriate *style* of managing change, adapting that style to the circumstances rather than imposing his or her style without regard for the specific context of change.

In a study carried out on the perceived effectiveness of change agents, many of these aspects of managing change were shown to be important. They are reflected in fifteen key competences identified from that study (see Figure 11.11).[28]

Goals
1. Sensitivity to changes in key personnel, top management perceptions and market conditions, and to the way in which these impact the goals of the project in hand.
2. Clarity in specifying goals, in defining the achievable.
3. Flexibility in responding to changes without the control of the project manager, perhaps requiring major shifts in project goals and management style, and risk taking.

Roles
4. Team-building abilities, to bring together key stakeholders and establish effective working groups, and to define the delegate respective responsibilities clearly.
5. Networking skills in establishing and maintaining appropriate contacts within and outside the organisation.
6. Tolerance of ambiguity, to be able to function comfortably, patiently and effectively in an uncertain environment.

Communication
7. Communication skills to transmit effectively to colleagues and subordinates the need for changes in project goals and in individual tasks and responsibilities.
8. Interpersonal skills, across the range, including selection, listening, collecting appropriate information, identifying the concerns of others, and managing meetings.
9. Personal enthusiasm, in expressing plans and ideas.
10. Stimulating motivation and commitment in others involved.

Negotiation
11. Selling plans and ideas to others, by creating a desirable and challenging vision of the future.
12. Negotiating with key players for resources, or for changes in procedures, and to resolve conflict.

Managing up
13. Political awareness, in identifying potential coalitions, and in balancing conflicting goals and perceptions.
14. Influencing skills, to gain commitment to project plans and ideas from potential sceptics and resisters.
15. Helicopter perspectives, to stand back from the immediate project and take a broader view of priorities.

Source: From D. Buchanan and D. Boddy, *The Expertise of the Change Agent: Public performance and backstage activity*, Prentice Hall, 1992, p. 92–93.

Figure 11.11   Fifteen key competences of change agents

Personal traits of change agents may, however, be relevant. To what extent do successful change agents demonstrate special or different personal traits from others, and are the personal traits of the change agent appropriate to the context of change? The literature on *leadership* typically argues that they have visionary capacity, are good at team building and team playing, are self-analytical and good at self-learning, have mental agility and 'constructive restlessness' while also being able to concentrate for long periods, and are also self-directed and self-confident.[29]

There is a tendency here to overemphasise such personal attributes. However, managing the complexity of strategy development and strategic change certainly places special demands on change agents. One of the more telling commentaries on change agency arises from Peters and Waterman's[30] argument that the successful manager of change in organisations is a 'master of two ends of the spectrum'. By this they mean that the change agent is simultaneously able to cope with potentially conflicting ways of managing.

- In strategy creation, they have an ability to undertake or understand detailed analysis, and at the same time to be visionary about the future.
- In achieving organisational credibility for a strategy, they need to be seen as insightful about the future, and yet action orientated about making things happen.
- In challenging the status quo in an organisation, they need an ability to maintain credibility and carry people with the change, while attacking the taken-for-granted and current ways of doing things.
- In communicating strategic intent, they need an ability to encapsulate often quite complex issues of strategy in everyday ways which people can understand.
- In consolidating a strategy, and making it happen, they need an ability to maintain performance of the organisation while breaking down old assumptions and old ways of doing things, which potentially could jeopardise the efficiency of the organisation.

It is a challenging task, demanding the abilities to cope with ambiguity, to demonstrate flexibility, insight and sensitivity to strategic context, and to relate to others.

However, not all change agents are the same. Their personal traits and orientations lead to different approaches to strategic change. It is therefore important for them to understand that such personal orientations may or may not be appropriate to the context in which they are working. The change agent might, for example, have a personal inclination towards a *planning* view of strategic change, with a bias towards analysis, expert knowledge, control and persuasive logic; or a reliance on a *directive* style, having worked through his or her own logic for change.

Other change agents may, in processes of change, emphasise *participation* and feedback systems, so that people in the organisation can contribute to and develop the change process. Here, then, the change agent may be more sympathetic to the notion of the *learning organisation*, trying to improve relationships between organisational members and the environment in which they work, such that learning can take place and change be adaptive. Others may lean towards a more *interventionist* or manipulative approach, seeking to identify signals and symbols of change by which taken-for-granted assumptions can be challenged and questioned, and routines changed so as to require changes in behaviour.[31]

The important point is that the perspective that the change agent brings to the situation may not always be the same as the organisational context in which he or she is operating. For example, the change agent who takes a planning approach may find that members of the organisation are adept at using the systems associated with this to avoid tackling the really difficult questions or issues that may be necessary (see section 11.3.3 above). Or the change agent who leans towards a learning perspective may find it is necessary to move towards this gradually, within a context which emphasises formal planning systems and is not used to questioning, challenging and open debate. Sensitivity to context is therefore important.[32]

11.5.2 Middle managers

A top-down approach to managing strategy and strategic change sees middle managers as implementors of strategy: their role is to put into effect the direction established by top management by making sure that resources are allocated and controlled appropriately, monitoring performance and behaviour of staff and, where necessary, explaining the strategy to those reporting to them. Those who take such an approach view middle managers not as facilitators of the strategy, but as blockages to its success. Indeed, this is sometimes seen as one reason for reducing the numbers and layers of management, so as to speed up communication between top management and organisational members, and to reduce potential blockages and filters.

However, there is evidence that middle managers can and do provide a real benefit in both the development and the implementation of strategy.[33] Their involvement in strategy development is important first because in their role they are likely to be intimately associated with the processes which represent the competences of the organisation (see Chapter 4); and also because they are likely to be in day-to-day contact with aspects of the business environment (see Chapter 3). If they are committed to helping develop effective strategy, they can help to interpret the extent to which such processes can provide advantages, and help to identify strategic opportunities.

Such involvement is also likely to mean that they have both a greater understanding of strategy and a greater commitment to it. This is important in effecting strategic change because they can play three vital roles. The first is the systematic role of implementation and control. The second is the reinterpretation and adjustment of strategic responses as events unfold (e.g. in terms of relationships with customers, suppliers, the workforce and so on). The third is as the crucial bridge between top management and members of the organisation at lower levels.

Middle management are likely to contribute substantially either to galvanising commitment to strategy and the change process; or, indeed, to blocking it. Commitment through involvement is likely to result in a positive role here. Lack of commitment can result in serious blockages and resistance. As suggested earlier, then, the involvement of middle management in strategy development, the planning of strategic change programmes and feedback on strategic change can be vitally important.

11.5.3 Other organisational members

The critical measure of the effectiveness of a strategy is the extent to which it affects the behaviour of those who interact with the organisation — for example, by customers buying more products, becoming more aware of a firm's benefits or using the services of a hospital or library more. If this is to happen, people perhaps in very junior roles in organisations play a crucial role because they are usually the interface between the organisation and those affected by the strategy outside the organisation. A critical question is how their commitment and understanding can best be gained at that level.

The point has already been made that relying on intellectual persuasion or assuming that changes in structure and control procedures are enough to effect strategic change is a mistake. A senior executive in a bank, who understood the powerful blockages within the bank's culture built up over decades, had just heard the chief executive present the new strategy to 200 employees. The presentation had included a careful explanation of the strategy and the new structure demonstrated with videos, slides and glossy handouts. The presentation was heard in respectful silence, but as the audience left for lunch, he remarked: 'There really is no contest between a 35 mm slide show and 100 years of culture: this is a bank; no matter how well intentioned, that talk will not change things.' The point he was making is that the day-to-day procedures and routines operating in the bank would persist. So how can change be effected at junior levels in the organisation?

Illustration 11.7   **The Unipart University**

Unipart sees its university — the U — as an aid to building a learning organisation through the involvement of its members.

Unipart's objective when setting up the U was to 'provide the physical environment that would permit a learning organisation and a continuous reskilling culture to flourish in our company'. This objective was supported by the U's mission statement: to develop and inspire people to achieve world class performance within the Unipart group of companies and amongst its stakeholders.

John Neill, group chief executive officer, stated: 'There is a good commercial argument for the U: it's a support route to commercial advantage, and it enhances shareholder value by helping to prevent us from becoming obsolete.' He continued:

> The U is also a platform from which we will be able to see future possibilities in a way which might not otherwise have been possible. It has a fundamental role to play in inspiring the learning that will be essential to getting us safely into the next century ... It is by working with all our stakeholders in long-term shared-destiny relationships, and by using the best learning, that we can eliminate waste and improve quality and customer service. Learning and training are fundamentally and inextricably linked with the very being of our company.

The U consists of ten faculties, each of which relates directly to an area of the company's business operations. Divisional managing directors form part of the U's staff and each have their own faculty. Having been schooled in how to teach, they write and present training courses at the U and are responsible for ensuring that they are relevant to business goals. Certainly, the philosophy underlying the U's courses is 'what you learn in the morning you can use in the afternoon to do your job better'.

The fact that employees design most of the courses sets the U apart from other learning centres. However, it is not just a top-down process: the U encourages the sharing of knowledge across the company, and virtually all of the group's employees, irrespective of age or position, have attended the U's four foundation courses. Unipart believes that all employees can make a contribution to teaching; managers and employees from all levels, as well as the divisions' managing directors, have become teachers, sharing their knowledge and learning from each other to bring Unipart's mission and vision alive.

Source: Company data and annual report, 1994.
Prepared by Tony Jacobs, Cranfield School of Management.

Running through this chapter, indeed through the whole book, has been the theme that changing strategy requires making changes in the taken-for-granted assumptions and the taken-for-granted routines and ways of doing things that are the elements of culture. Richard Pascale argues:[34] 'It is easier to act your way into a better way of thinking than to think your way into a better way of acting', easier to change behaviours and thus change taken-for-granted assumptions than to try to change taken-for-grated assumptions and therefore change behaviour. This is the distinction between what is known as *programmatic change*, by which is meant the attempt to convince people by persuasion and logic of the need for change; and *task alignment*, by which is meant changes in behaviour and routines.[35] The argument is that task alignment is a more powerful way of achieving change than the programmatic. Those who take this view would argue that the style of the change agent (see section 11.5.1 above) needs to take this into account.

As explained earlier (see section 11.2.2), others argue that long-term change is best achieved by trying to create a *learning organisation*, in which, in effect, all its members need to become strategic thinkers, aware of the strategic impacts of the environment around them, questioning and challenging their colleagues and contributing to the development of strategy. Clearly, this is a challenging task, requiring a major commitment and investment in intellectual resources and, for most organisations, a significant change in organisational culture. Few organisations have succeeded in this, but some take it seriously. For example, organisations such as Motorola and Unipart have set up organisational 'universities' which are serious attempts to develop such a capacity (see Illustration 11.7).

11.5.4 External stakeholders

Just as it is important to tailor approaches to change according to different organisational contexts, the same may be required for different stakeholders. Figure 5.5 in Chapter 5 shows how different stakeholders can be identified according to their level of interest and political influence. It also suggests that the approach to managing change with regard to these different stakeholders will differ. For example, those with a high level of interest in the organisation but low power may simply need to be kept informed of change requirements and processes, so careful thought needs to be given to means of communication here. Others, with a low level of interest but high actual or potential political influence, need to be kept satisfied. They may not be so concerned about understanding the details of the change process or wanting to be involved in it, but serious attention needs to be paid to convincing them of its effectiveness and its benefits for them.

The key players are those with high power and high interest. These may differ by organisational context. Indeed, as shown in Illustration 11.3, within the same organisation there may be different stakeholder groups requiring different approaches. For example, it may make sense to deal with fund managers representing key investments in an organisation by adopting an essentially logical approach and a style of education and communication. The approach taken towards managers or other organisational members may need to vary according to existing culture or time available for the change process. Others — for example, in the public sector — may find more explicit uses of political influence necessary: for instance, if the chief executive of a local government authority has to deal with different political parties or, indeed, central government.

11.5.5 Outsiders

The use of outsiders in the change process can be productive.

- A new chief executive from outside the organisation may be introduced into a business to effect change. He or she brings a fresh perspective on the organisation, not bound by the constraints of the past, or the everyday routines and ways of doing things which can prevent strategic change. *Hybrid* new chief executives seem to be especially successful. These are chief executives who are not part of the mainline culture of the organisation, but who have experience and visible success from within the same industry or even the same company. For example, they might have been a successful change agent with a competitor or some other part of a conglomerate.

- The success of introducing outsiders in middle and senior executive positions is likely to depend on how much explicit, *visible backing* they have from the chief executive. Without such backing they are likely to be seen as lacking authority and influence. With such backing, however, they can help galvanise change in the organisation.

- *Consultants* are often used in change processes. This may be to help formulate the strategy or plan the change process. However, consultants are increasingly used as facilitators of change processes: for example, in a co-ordinating capacity, as facilitators of project teams working on change, or of strategy workshops used to develop strategy and plan the means of strategic change.

  The value of consultants is twofold: first, they too do not inherit the cultural baggage of the organisation and can therefore bring a dispassionate view to the process; and second, they signal symbolically the importance of the change process, not least because their fees may be of a very high order. For example, a consultancy project undertaken by Gemini, one of the leading strategic change consultancies in the world, might involve large numbers of consultants on a worldwide basis and fees running into millions of pounds.

11.6 Summary

This chapter has emphasised a number of key points in the management of strategic change:

- There are different *types of strategic change* observable in organisations, varying from incremental change which is reactive (adaptation) or proactive (tuning), to transformational change which also can be reactive (forced) or proactive (planned). Different approaches may be required for different types of change, and these are discussed in the rest of the chapter.
- There are also different views about the management of change. At the beginning of this chapter, the distinction was made between change processes which are intentionally *planned change*, changes resulting from *learning*, and *imposed change*. Later sections in the chapter focused on ways in which the intended change might be managed.
- The importance of diagnosing the need for and means of change was discussed in section 11.3, where symptoms of *strategic drift* were described along with ways of using the *cultural web* and *forcefield analysis* as means of identifying blockages of change and potential levers for change.
- Processes for managing strategic change were then discussed, including the importance of changes in *structure and control*, appropriate *styles of managing change*, the need to change organisational *routines* and *symbols*, and the importance of *political processes*, *communication* and other change *tactics*.
- The final section of the chapter reviewed different *roles in the change* process, including those of change agent, middle managers, other members of the organisation, different stakeholder groups and outsiders. Again, the point was made that different approaches to change are likely to be necessary according to different contexts and in relation to the involvement and interest of different groups.

In their study of firms which had managed change successfully, Pettigrew and Whipp[36] summarise their findings in a way which usefully integrates much of the material in this chapter with other chapters in this book. They argue that organisations which manage change successfully demonstrate five important characteristics.

11.6.1 Environmental assessment

Chapter 3 explained the importance of understanding the business environment. However, this does not mean simply employing techniques of analysis, or hiring analysts to do this. Organisations which manage change effectively are more like open learning systems: the sensitivity to the environment is organisation wide; it is not dependent on a set of techniques or specialists. Managers and staff in the organisation see their role as keeping close to, being sensitive to, and responding to signals in the environment. The external orientation is, therefore, part of the culture of the organisation; it is 'taken for granted' that this is an important orientation, and it is championed visibly by senior management. Further, the structural characteristics of the organisation are such that there is an emphasis on external rather than internal orientation (see Chapter 10).

11.6.2 Leading change

It is a mistake to think of the management of change as a prescribed set of activities. The way in which change is led by change agents must depend on contexts which will differ by organisations, or perhaps by market. However, the ability of the change agent to establish, or develop, a context for change is crucial, both in cultural terms and also in terms of the capabilities of the organisation. It is also necessary to tailor the agenda for change specifically in terms of the organisational context and the values and beliefs of those in the organisation. This chapter has emphasised this point, discussed methods of managing strategic change and indicated that these need to be drawn upon in ways which are specific and relevant to context.

11.6.3 Linking strategic and operational change

Organisations which have successfully managed change have been able to link strategic change with operational change and the everyday aspects of the organisation. This emphasises the importance not only of translating strategic change into detailed resource plans, critical success factors and key tasks, and the way the organisation is managed through control processes (Chapter 10), but also of how change is communicated through the mundane and symbolic aspects of the organisation discussed in this chapter. This is more likely to be effective if change can be continual and incremental, occurring in the everyday aspects of the organisation, rather than being implemented in major one-off steps.

So successful change may not be as dramatically observable as transformational change. The problem arises, of course, when an organisation has not been changing continually and arrives at a point where more transformational change is necessary. Then the bridging between strategic change and operational and mundane aspects of the organisation is much more difficult.

11.6.4 Strategic human resource management

Organisations which successfully manage change are those which have integrated their human resource management policies with their strategies and the strategic change process. As discussed in this final part of the book, training, employee relations, compensation packages and so on are not merely operational issues for the personnel department; they are crucially concerned with the way in which employees relate to the nature and direction of the firm, and as such they can both block strategic change and also be significant facilitators of strategic change.

11.6.5 Coherence in managing change

The final point that needs emphasising in a sense summarises the whole thrust of this book. Strategic change is much more likely to work if it is coherent across all aspects of the organisation. By this we mean the following:

- There is a consistency between the intended strategy, the stated strategic objectives, their expression in operational terms and, very important, the behaviour of executives to reinforce the strategy.
- The direction of strategic change is consistent with what is happening in the environment, and the way in which this is understood in the organisation. It is also managed with due regard to stakeholders, including suppliers and customers, on whom the organisation is critically reliant.
- The strategy is feasible in terms of the resources it requires, the structuring of the organisation, and the changes that need to occur in organisational culture and operational routines.
- The strategic direction is clearly related to achieving competitive advantage or excellent performance; and internally it is understood how this is so.

Overall, such coherence means that there needs to be an ability to hold the organisation together as an efficient, successful entity, while simultaneously changing it.

There are a growing number of studies on the reasons why some organisations are more successful than others. All make it clear that the clarity of strategy direction and its relevance to a changing environment are crucial. The wiser researchers and writers realise, however, that it is not possible to reduce the explanations of how this is done to simple do's and don'ts. This book has aimed to provide an insight into some of the ways in which managers might contribute to this. It has done so by describing research which tries to explain success, and by explaining techniques of analysis, evaluation and planning which can help organisations understand bases of success and plan for the future. But most of all, it has stressed that it is the processes of management, the skills of managers and the ability of managers to relate to their external environment, their internal culture and the people around them, that will ensure success.

References

1. See E. Romanelli and M.L. Tushman, 'Organisational transformation as punctuated equilibrium: an empirical test', *Academy of Management Journal*, vol. 37, no. 5 (1994), pp. 1141–61.

2. This discussion is based on an adaptation of the framework used by D.A. Nadler and M.L. Tushman in their paper 'Organisational frame bending: principles for managing reorientation', *Academy of Management Executive*, vol. 3, no. 3 (1989), pp. 194–204.

3. See P. Senge, *The Fifth Discipline: The art and practice of the learning organisation*, Century Business, 1992.

4. This framework of 'organisational learning' builds on the work of K. Lewin, *Field Theory in Social Science*, Tavistock, 1952. The framework is used by a number of writers to discuss strategic change. See, for example, L.A. Isabella, 'Evolving interpretations as a change unfolds: how managers construe key organisational events', *Academy of Management Journal*, vol. 33, no. 1 (1985), pp. 7–41; and E.H. Schein, *Organisational Culture and Leadership*, Jossey-Bass, 1985. A number of other writers on strategic change employ similar models: for example, F. Gouillart and J. Kelly describe Gemini Consulting's approach in *Transforming the Organisation*, McGraw-Hill, 1995.

5. The argument that conflict can bring about useful debate is developed by J.M. Bartunek, D. Kolb and R. Lewicki, 'Bringing conflict out from behind the scenes: private informal and non-rational dimensions of conflict in organisations', in D. Kolb and J. Bartunek (eds.), *Hidden Conflict in Organisations: Uncovering behind the scenes disputes*, Sage, 1992.

6. For an account which shows the role of managers in such circumstances, see A. Pettigrew, E. Ferlie and L. McKee, *Shaping Strategic Change*, Sage, 1992.

7. See G. Johnson, 'Managing strategic change: strategy culture and action', *Long Range Planning*, vol. 25, no. 1 (1992), pp. 28–36. See also the chapter, 'Mapping and re-mapping organisational culture', in V. Ambrosini with G. Johnson and K. Scholes (eds) *Exploring Techniques of Analysis and Evaluation in Strategic Management*, Prentice Hall, 1998.

8. The illustration is based on a description of the use of the cultural web by L. Heracleous and B. Langham, 'Strategic change and organisational culture at Hay Management Consultants', *Long Range Planning*, vol. 29, no. 4 (1996), pp. 485–94.

9. See C. Bowman, 'Strategy workshops and top team commitment to strategic change', *Journal of Managerial Psychology*, vol. 10, no. 8 (1995), pp. 4–12.

10. For example, see L. Hrebinrak and W. Joyce, *Implementing Strategy*, Macmillan, 1984, and the chapters on implementation in G. Greenley, *Strategic Management*, Prentice Hall, 1989.

11. See, for example, J.P. Kotter and L.A. Schlesinger, 'Choosing strategies for change', *Harvard Business Review*, vol. 57, no. 2 (1979) pp. 106–114.

12. The intervention style is discussed more fully in P.C. Nutt, 'Identifying and appraising how managers install strategy', *Strategic Management*

Journal, vol. 8, no. 1 (1987) pp. 1–14.

13. Evidence for this, as well as a discussion of different styles, is provided by D. Dunphy and D. Stace, 'The strategic management of corporate change', *Human Relations*, vol. 46, no. 8 (1993), pp. 905–20.

14. T. Deal and A. Kennedy refer to 'the way we do things around here', in *Corporate Cultures: The rights and rituals of corporate life*, Addison-Wesley, 1982.

15. For a fuller discussion of this theme, see G. Johnson, 'Managing strategic change: the role of symbolic action', *British Journal of Management*, vol. 1, no. 4 (1990), pp. 183–200.

16. This reference is taken from one of Tom Peters' early papers, 'Symbols, patterns and settings: an optimistic case for getting things done', *Organisational Dynamics*, vol. 7, no. 2 (1978), pp. 3–23.

17. See H.M. Trice and J.M. Beyer, 'Studying organisational cultures through rites and ceremonials', *Academy of Management Review*, vol. 9, no. 4 (1984), pp. 653–69; H.M. Trice and J.M. Beyer, 'Using six organisational rites to change culture', in R.H. Kilman, M.J. Saxton, R. Serpa & associates (eds.), *Gaining Control of the Corporate Culture*, Jossey-Bass, San Francisco and London.

18. The importance of the language used by corporate leaders has been noted by a number of writers, but particularly L.R. Pondy, 'Leadership is a language game', in M.W. McCall, Jr and M.M. Lombardo (eds.), *Leadership: Where else can we go?*, Duke University Press, Durham, NC. See also J.A. Conger and R. Kanungo, 'Toward a behavioural theory of charismatic leadership in organisational settings', *Academy of Management Review*, vol. 12, no. 4 (1987), pp. 637–47.

19. From M.G. Pratt and E. Rafaeli, 'The role of symbols in fragmented organisations: an illustration from organisational dress', presented at the Academy of Management Meeting, Atlanta, GA, 1993.

20. The paper by T. Nakajo and T. Kono, 'Success through culture change in a Japanese brewery', *Long Range Planning*, vol. 22, no. 6 (1989), pp. 29–37, is an interesting account of strategic change in a quite different culture, but which draws many lessons parallel to this chapter.

21. This discussion is based on observations of the role of political activities in organisations by, in particular, H. Mintzberg, *Power in and around Organisations*, Prentice Hall, 1983; and J. Pfeffer, *Power in Organisations*, Pitman, 1981.

22. The figure is based on D. Buchanan and D. Boddy, *The Expertise of the Change Agent*, Prentice Hall, 1992, pp. 78–80.

23. See reference 2 above.

24. See R.H. Lengel and R.L. Daft, 'The selection of communication media as an executive skill', *Academy of Management Executive*, vol. 2, no. 3 (1988), pp. 225–32.

25. Both Isabella (see reference 4) and Johnson (reference 15) note this.

26. For example, see W.G. Bennis and B. Nanus, *Leaders: The strategies for taking charge*, Harper and Row, 1985; and Conger and Kanungo (see reference 18).

27. The importance of context in relation to the leadership of change is a theme running through B. Leavy and D. Wilson, *Strategy and Leadership*, Routledge, 1994.

28. See reference 22 above.

29. For a review of the support characteristics and traits of successful corporate leaders, see C. Garfield, *Peak Performers: New heroes in business*, Hutchison Business, 1986.

30. Peters and Waterman argue that 'An effective leader must be the master of two ends of the spectrum: ideas at the highest level of abstraction and actions at the most mundane level of detail.' See *In Search of Excellence*, Harper and Row, 1982, p. 287.

31. For a fuller discussion of these observations, see P. Felkas, B. Chakiris and K. Chartres, *Change Management: A model for effective organisational performance*, Quality Resources, 1993.

32. See reference 27 above.

33. See S. Floyd and W. Wooldridge, 'Dinosaurs or dynamos? Recognising middle management's strategic role', *Academy of Management Executive*, vol. 8, no. 4 (1994), pp. 47–57; W. Wooldridge and S. Floyd, 'The strategy process, middle management involvement and organisational performance', *Strategic Management Journal*, vol. 11, no. 3 (1990), pp. 231–41.

34. This quote is taken from R. Pascale, *Managing on the Edge*, Viking, 1990.

35. The argument for a task alignment approach is given by M. Beer, R.A. Eisenstat and B. Spector, 'Why change programmes don't produce change', *Harvard Business Review*, vol. 68, no. 6 (1990), pp. 158–66.

36. This integrating framework is from the research on strategic change undertaken by Andrew Pettigrew and Richard Whipp: see *Managing Change for Competitive Success*, Blackwell, 1991.

Recommended key readings

* For a discussion of styles of managing strategic change, see D. Dunphy and D. Stace, 'The strategic management of corporate change', *Human Relations*, vol. 46, no. 8 (1993), pp. 905–20.

* The task alignment view of strategic change argues for concentrating on changes in routines and tasks so as to promote behaviour change. This is explained by M. Beer, R.A. Eisenstat and B. Spector, 'Why change programmes don't produce change', *Harvard Business Review*, vol. 68, no. 6 (1990), pp. 158–66.

* For a fuller discussion of symbolic aspects of change management, see G. Johnson, 'Managing strategic change: the role of symbolic action', *British Journal of Management*, vol. 1, no. 4 (1990) pp. 183–200.

* G. Johnson, 'Mapping and re-mapping organisational culture', in V. Ambrosini with G. Johnson and K. Scholes (eds.), *Exploring Techniques of Analysis and Evaluation in Strategic Management*, Prentice Hall, 1998.

* There are surprisingly few readings which focus on aspects of political management. The best book remains Machiavelli's *The Prince*, published by Penguin.

* Finally, for a discussion of the management of strategic change in the context of wider aspects of strategic management, see A. Pettigrew and R. Whipp, *Managing Change for Competitive Success*, Blackwell, 1991.

Work assignments

11.1 Based on cultural webs you have drawn up (e.g. for assignment 5.8 in Chapter 5), or on the basis of the cultural web in Illustration 2.7, identify the main blockages to change in an organisation.

11.2 Draw up a cultural web and use forcefield analysis to identify blockages and facilitators of change for an organisation (e.g. one for which you have considered the need for a change in strategic direction in a previous assignment). Redraw the web to represent what the organisation should aspire to given the new strategy. Using the cultural webs and forcefield analysis, identify what aspects of the changes can be managed by a change agent and how.

11.3 With reference to section 11.4.2 and Figure 11.6, identify and explain the styles of managing change employed by different change agents (e.g. Colin Sharman in KPMG* or Rupert Murdoch in the News Corporation*).

11.4   Using Figure 11.7, give examples of rituals which signal (or could be used to signal) change in an organisation with which you are familiar.

11.5   *Consider a process of strategic change that you have been involved in or have observed. Map out the steps in the change process in the following terms:*
        (a) new rituals introduced or old rituals done away with, and the impact of these changes;
        (b) the means of communication employed by change agents, and how effective they were.

11.6   *In the context of managing strategic change in a large corporation or public sector organisation, to what extent, and why, do you agree with Richard Pascale's argument that 'It is easier to act ourselves into a better way of thinking than it is to think ourselves into a better way of acting'? (References 33 and 34, and also 15 and 17 will be useful here.)*

11.7   **Using the frameworks for managing change discussed in Part IV of the book and Chapter 11 in particular, compare and evaluate the approaches to strategic change followed by two change agents of your choice. Bear in mind their strategic and organisational contexts in your evaluation.**

11.8   **There are a number of books by renowned senior executives who have managed major changes in their organisation. Read one of these and note the levers and mechanisms for change employed by the change agent, using the approaches outlined in this chapter as a checklist. How effective do you think these were in the context that the change agent faced, and could other mechanisms have been used?**

        *This refers to a case study in the Text and Cases version of this book.

Case studies

A guide to using the case studies

The main text of this book includes about 70 short illustrations which have been chosen to enlarge specific issues in the text and/or provide practical examples of how business and public sector organisations are managing strategic issues. The case studies which follow allow the reader to extend this linking of theory and practice further by analysing the strategic issues of specific organisations in much greater depth — and often providing 'solutions' to some of the problems or difficulties identified in the case.

The case studies are intended to serve as the basis for class discussion and not as an illustration of either good or bad management practice. They are *not* intended to be a comprehensive collection of teaching material. They have been chosen (or specially written) to provide readers with a *core* of cases which together cover most of the main issues in the text. As such they should provide a useful *backbone* to a programme of study, but can sensibly be supplemented by other material.

Some cases are written entirely from published sources, but most have been prepared in co-operation with and have the approval of the management of the organisation concerned. We would ask readers to respect the wishes of 'host' companies not to be contacted directly. Case studies can never fully capture the richness and complexity of real-life management situations and we would encourage readers and tutors additionally to take every possible opportunity to explore the live strategic issues of organisations — both their own and others.

A continuing feature of this edition is the inclusion of *work assignments* at the end of each chapter. These relate issues in the text to illustrations and the readers' own experience or choice of organisations but also to the case studies in this section of the book. The format of work assignments is explained in the preface.

The following brief points of guidance should prove useful in selecting and using the case studies provided:

- The summary table which follows indicates the main focus of each of the chosen case studies — together with important subsidiary foci (where appropriate). In general, the sequence of cases is intended to mirror the chapter sequence. However, this should not be taken too literally because, of course, many of these cases cover a variety of issues. The 'classification' provided is therefore for guidance only. We expect readers to seek their own lessons from cases, and tutors to use cases in whichever way and sequence best fits the purpose of their programmes.

- Where cases have been chosen to illustrate the issues of strategic choice and implementation covered later in the book, it will normally be a prerequisite that some type of strategic analysis of the case material is undertaken. When planning the use of these cases within programmes, care needs to be taken to balance the time taken on strategic analysis so as to allow the time required to analyse the main issues for which the case has been chosen.

- Where the text and cases are being used as the framework for a strategy programme (as we hope they will), it is essential that students are required to undertake additional reading from other sources and that their 'practical' work is supplemented by other material as mentioned above.

A Guide to the main focus of cases

TEXT

Case	Page no.	1 Intro-duction	2 Strategic manage-ment process	3 Business environ-ment	3 Five Forces	4 Com-petence analysis	5 Expec-tations Objectives Purpose	3–5 Overall strategic analysis	6 Cor-porate strategy
British Steel	503	**							
New Town	510		**						
Castle Press	518		**						
Pharma-ceuticals	525			*	**				
European brewing	533			**	*				
Kronenbourg	558							*	*
Brewery Group Denmark	574					*			
Laura Ashley	585					**	*		
Iona	600						**		
Sheffield Theatres	615					*	**		
Fisons	630						**		
World automobile industry	637			**					
Peugeot	654							*	
Rover/ Honda	670								
BMW	683								
Coopers Creek	691					*			
News Corporation	703		*				*		
Nokia	731					*			
ISS	752					*			*
Doman	780								
Royal Alexandra Hospital	793						*		
UNDP	811		*						
KPMG	820		*				*		
Burmah Castrol	840					**			**

Note: ** = Major focus
      * = Important subsidiary focus

CHAPTERS

6	7	7	8	3/6/9	9	10	11
Competitive strategies	*Strategic options*	*Diversification*	*Evaluation*	*Global management*	*Structure, design*	*Resource planning*	*Managing change*
				★			
	★		★★				
	★★		★	★★			
				★			
					★		
★★	★				★		
★	★★						
★	★★			★			
				★★	★		
		★★			★	★	
★		★★					
				★★	★★		
		★★				★★	
					★		★
				★★	★★		
					★		★★
				★	★★		

British Steel

KEVAN SCHOLES

In the past, excess steel making capacity in Europe has been sustained by a high level of exports to regions where local capacity was either insufficient or inefficient. This source of demand cannot be relied upon in the longer term. In areas where there is insufficient capacity, such as Asia, new competitive capacity is being installed locally, while the efficiency of capacity in the United States, for example, has improved dramatically. At the same time, import pressures in western European markets are intensifying, most notably from eastern Europe.

While I believe that the western European industry can continue to compete successfully in its key markets, it is very likely that over time net exports will diminish. Thus, the pressures on European Union companies to restructure will continue. The changes in the industry structure relate to both ownership and concentration. In the past, the western European steel industry has been very fragmented and has had a high level of state ownership. The process of privatisation is reducing state ownership, and there are signs that mergers and joint ventures, some of them across national boundaries, are accelerating.

In this environment, British Steel is well placed. The company's UK assets are in good shape and we have no major capital expenditure requirements in the near term. We are strongly placed in the European market, with very low costs, high quality of product and service and a very competitive range of products.

We expect this region to provide the profitable core of our business for many years to come. However, for the company to grow, we are looking to reduce dependence on the UK and European markets and we are seeking to shift the balance of our assets into other regions.

This was Ted Denham, British Steel's director of corporate planning, speaking in September 1995 about the future challenges for a company which over the previous decade had achieved one of the most remarkable turnarounds in corporate history.[1] From being a near-bankrupt state-owned

---

This case study was prepared by Professor Kevan Scholes, Sheffield Business School, from published sources. It incorporates information from the previous British Steel case studies. It is intended as a basis for class discussion and not as an illustration of either good or bad management practice. © Kevan Scholes, 1996.

[1] *American Metal Market*, vol. 103, no. 182 (1995), p. 14.

corporation (BSC) with cumulative losses of some £7bn between 1975 and 1984, the company had been transformed into the super-fit privatised British Steel.

At the time of privatisation in 1989, the ingredients of the transformation could be clearly seen. For example, labour costs had fallen from 31 per cent to 20 per cent of total costs since 1980 as the workforce was reduced from 140,000 to 51,000 (this had declined to 41,000 by 1995); and in terms of productivity, by 1987 the UK steel industry produced around 320 tonnes per man-year against West Germany's 279 — a remarkable change from 1981 when Germany led the UK by 227 tonnes to 167. These improvements in performance were dependent on a number of important changes and management decisions made during that period:

- An investment programme of £985m for modernisation and re-equipping was undertaken. For example, by early 1989, the company produced about 80 per cent of its output by the efficient continuous casting method rather than the ingot method. This represented savings of about £14–18 per tonne. However, the French, Italian and West German industries well all nearly 90 per cent committed to continuous casting by 1988. The company itself believed that it needed about £250m annually to maintain the necessary investment programme.
- British Steel had completely revamped its management structure, reducing central overheads considerably and devolving responsibility for operations and profit to a substantial degree.
- There was a revolution in working practices. Up to 18 per cent of pay became bonus related, giving British Steel room to curb its wage bill during fluctuating demand (by 1995 this variable element of pay had risen to 25–30 per cent).

The period immediately prior to and following privatisation was one of growing international demand and impressive financial performance from British Steel, as shown in Appendix 1. However, by 1991 the recession and overcapacity in Europe had forced both prices and volumes down by more than 10 per cent. The economics of British Steel's position were harsh. A 10 per cent reduction in price took some £300m off profits; and 10 per cent off volumes reduced profits by a further £500m, transforming a healthy profit of £773m in 1989/90 to losses in both 1991/2 and 1992/3.

In 1993/4, although turnover continued to decline marginally, the company made a small (but rare among steel-makers) profit. The company's market share in the UK was still declining to between 50 and 65 per cent (depending on sector). However, its spread of sales had also increased with only 53 per cent of turnover being from the UK; 30 per cent came from continental Europe, 10 per cent from North America and the remainder from elsewhere. The year 1994/5 showed a strong recovery in both sales and profits as the general economic climate improved. This once again underlined the harsh economic equation in such a cyclical industry. The £330m rise in half-year profits from the same time in the previous year could be traced to £130m from increased volumes, £130m from increased prices and £70m from efficiency gains.

By 1996, under the leadership of chairman Brian Moffat, the company had an ambitious and well-communicated vision to be a genuinely internationally based steel company — which did not exist anywhere in the world so far. Its formula for achieving this vision was also spelled out:[2]

- To continue to achieve efficiency gains and remain one of the most cost-efficient producers globally.
- To build the business in a market-led way rather than simply increasing capacity and trying to fill it.
- To target capital investment carefully — for example, with a strong emphasis on flexible 'mini-mills' — and to reuse or relocate assets where possible, as it was doing in the construction of a joint venture mini-mill in Tuscaloosa (USA) using 'mothballed' production units from the UK.
- To use a range of different approaches to global development, such as joint ventures (western Europe and USA); overseas transplants (USA, eastern Europe and possibly Asia and South America); and continued exports of high added value products.
- Above all to keep a strong balance sheet (good cash management and low gearing) to ride out the fierce cycles in demand.

This globalisation of the company's activities was the culmination of many years of recognising and adjusting to a changing business environment. Exchange rates were of critical importance to international businesses, and the combination of a strong pound against the US dollar and weakness against the German Mark was almost an ideal situation for British Steel (as an exporter to continental Europe and an 'offshore' manufacturer in the USA). Although process technologies in steel marking were long established, there were still important competitive advantages to be gained by both product development and the management of the logistics of the supply and distribution chains. The 'steel intensity' in many products (e.g. motor cars) had declined remarkably over 20–30 years, with average steel thickness (for the same performance) reducing from 2 mm to 0.8 mm. In the reverse direction, improvements in cost and metallurgical properties were allowing steel beams to make major inroads into the construction market at the expense of concrete.

Perhaps the greatest problem for British Steel in the UK had been the poor international performance of UK-based manufacturing industries using steel. As they lost out in world markets, their need for steel declined. The advent of Japanese transplants in the UK had reversed this trend. The

[2] *Management Today*, June 1995, pp. 42–6.

most encouraging aspect of the mid-1990s was the new willingness — at least in Europe — of national governments to remove their subsidy of state-owned steel firms and to move towards privatisation. Over the previous decade, British Steel had cited this as a major problem — the unwillingness to tackle the 20 per cent excess capacity in Europe.

Following acquisitions in the late 1980s, British Steel was also a major player in the distribution (stockholding) of steel in the UK, with over 30 per cent market share. Here the exploitation of information technology to reduce costs and increase customer service was critical to success.

So by 1996 the vision of the next five years for British Steel was clear. This was fighting talk indeed for a company which (by value) was only a quarter the size of the market leader, Nippon Steel, and half that of the German Krupps. However, it was now some 50 per cent bigger than the one-time US giant, Bethlehem Steel (see Appendix 2). This was a rapidly changing world in which the old 'pecking order' was very much up for challenge. Could British Steel fulfil its dream?

Appendix 1   Turnover and pre-tax profits (£m)

	Revenue	Pre-tax profits (loss)
1980/1	2,954	(1,800)
1981/2	3,443	(492)
1982/3	3,231	(866)
1983/4	3,358	(253)
1984/5	3,736	(378)
1985/6	3,735	(42)
1986/7	3,461	177
1987/8	4,116	419
1988/9	4,906	593
1989/90	5,113	733
1990/1	5,000	254
1991/2	4,600	(55)
1992/3	4,300	(149)
1993/4	4,190	80
1994/5	4,780	578
1995/6	7,050*	1,100

*This figure includes about £1,800m as a result of the reincorporation of United Engineering Steels (UES) and 51% ownership of Avesta Sheffield.

Appendix 2   Major steel producers by volume of sales, 1994

	Company	Country	Output*
1	Nippon Steel	Japan	26.2
2	POSCO	Rep of Korea	22.1
3	Usinor Sacilor	France	18.5
4	British Steel	UK	12.9
5	Arbed	Luxembourg	11.9
6	NKK	Japan	11.6
7	USX	USA	11.5
8	Thyssen	Germany	10.7
9	Kawasaki	Japan	10.6
10	Sumitomo	Japan	10.4
11	SAIL	India	10.3
12	Bethlehem Steel	USA	8.9

* Million metric tons.
Source: *World Steel in Figures 1995* (International Iron and Steel Institute).

Strategy development at
New Town Council

ANDY BAILEY and JULIE VERITY

I'm not really comfortable with the way we develop strategy here, but I'm not sure I know how to manage the process to make it more coherent either.

Chief executive, New Town Council, 1995

New Town Council formed one part of a two-tier system of local government responsible for the provision of services within a geographical area of the UK; the other part was the county council. Both authorities operated under Acts of Parliament, with specific duties laid down by these Acts and with central government controlling many of the activities of local authorities. The county council had responsibility for school education, fire and police services, highways and social care, while the council had responsibility for environmental health, housing, planning, recreational facilities and refuse collection.

Local authorities consist of councillors (Members) and paid employees. The councillors are elected representatives and decide the council's policy and priorities. The paid employees are responsible for implementing policy, with the role of senior officers (the senior ranks of the paid employees) being to advise the councillors on policy and to implement the policy decided.

New Town Council grew up alongside New Town as it was built on its greenfield site in the 1970s. Central government decreed that New Town would exist and the Development Corporation designed, planned and built it. As the bricks, mortar and amenities were developed, the council 'followed on behind, picking-up the litter, literally. I mean the Corporation built it and we provided the refuse collection systems for the people when they arrived to live here. When the Corporation was wound up and we had to take over, it was a lot to cope with. I think we are still learning to cope in some respects,' explained a senior officer at the council.

When the Development Corporation ceased activities in the early 1990s, New Town Council took responsibility for housing, environment, recreation, economic development and community development services. It did not assume control of education or social services, which remained with the county council, an arrangement which by 1995 was under review. Since 1979, the Conservative Party had been in central government and had made frequent and significant changes to local authority legislation.

It was against this backdrop that some of the top management team of New Town Council described how they thought strategy came about in their organisation.

Making sense of strategy

The chief executive had been in his role for ten years:

> For the majority of my time here we have had a hung council.[1] My 'management board', therefore, is a group of elected representatives who are generally interested in a common aim — the greater good of the community — but who are totally split about the way to achieve it. They also rarely make a clear decision; they simply delegate, and when they don't like the proposed solution, they block implementation. Hence, my role is to act as an interface between the party political processes of the Members of Council and my management organisation [the officers]. I have to seek to understand the party political process, interpret it and help manage things via that process. At the same time, I have to understand the strengths and weaknesses of my management organisation [the officers], repair the weaknesses and build on the strengths.

Two senior officers had been recruited to the organisation within the last five years. One was head of personnel services:

> Our focus is the local community. Our strategy is based on the combined expectations of these people. Being a new town, taking over from the Development Corporation, you would expect us to have a defined vision to do with the social and physical development of New Town. The vision we have is not our own vision, we have inherited it. It is the vision of the government who decided to build New Town 30 years ago.

The other was commercial director of the direct services directorate. This was one of six main directorates within the council with responsibility for those services which the government had decreed should be subject to compulsory competitive tendering (CCT).[2] This included services

---

[1] No political party in overall control.

[2] Central government legislation which compelled local authorities to invite competitive tenders for the provision of certain types of work, with in-house teams bidding against private sector competitors for a specified task.

such as landscape, highways, building, vehicle maintenance and leisure management, and accounted for about a fifth of the council's workforce:

> From my perspective, strategy develops in fits and starts. Since I've been here we have had a hung council, which has meant that no one political party has been able to stamp its views firmly on the whole organisation. In strategy terms, that has left us floundering because it has been very unclear whether an initiative will get approval or not.
>
> As a group of officers, we have had to say that, regardless of the party political situation, there are certain things we are going to have to cope with: one is the extension of CCT, another is the Local Government Review[3] and lastly is our struggle with the budget, whereby the money that we get from government has been held at the current level or reduced, year-on-year, while they have mandated we provide extra services!

Finally, there was the central services director, with responsibility for 200 people who largely provided services internally, to council departments. This directorate included computer services, estates management, the law division and central administration:

> In 1987 we held a conference to think about the future. We coupled that with a large public consultation exercise and as a result, the elected Members were asked to approve a strategic plan which had six main objectives in it. The process since then has been yearly reviews conducted by a small team within the policy directorate, which has reported back to the management team on the changes that have occurred in the environment and sought endorsement from Members. As a result of this review process, this year there are some fairly significant changes to the strategy document.
>
> Strategies also arise through the various council directorates: for example, Housing or Environment. Directorates produce their service plans each year, reviewing the external and internal influences and reacting to changed circumstances, revising their objectives for the current year in line with these changes.
>
> Therefore, the council's strategy is a series of very broadly based objectives which express the aspirations of the community. This is meant to be supplemented by the council's short-term objectives, its policies and the directorates' service plans. It is an interaction between these two sets of objectives that determines the way we go.

Planning is desirable, but . . .

> Traditionally the organisation has not been focused on planning or developing policy. There was actually an anti-policy line. Instead, strategy developed in an ad-hoc manner, with the council being able to do as it wanted because it was well

---

[3] A review of local government structure from which recommendations are made for either the retention of the present two-tier system or the creation of a single unitary authority to provide services within a geographical area.

resourced. In the late eighties, we developed a community strategy — New Town 2000. This was perhaps a first for a local authority: that is, to try and devise a corporate strategy. After that, I think we got blown off course by events of the time: massive inflation, couldn't find staff or keep staff, so I spent a lot of time reorganising and looking internally. When we did find time, we tried to get the individual businesses of the council (because we are a series of services) to project their own services into the future and formulate their own plans.

Now we are back to trying to realise the community strategy. So strategy to us is about determining where we are principally in our community, the key influences which are pushing us around within this, and trying to make sense of the steps we are taking, knowing that we are going to falter on some and going to be accelerated on others.

Chief executive

The chief executive went on to conclude that planning was desirable and something he had tried to introduce into the organisation by bringing in facilitators and training his people to become skilled in planning processes and techniques. He admitted, however, that the organisation was still struggling to plan effectively. Some issues were easier to plan for than others. The Local Government Review, for example, 'had encouraged officers to come together and realise that, despite the political differences, you can have planning for the future'.

Others in his team, however, stressed that strategies had to be built around a theme of flexibility. With strategies liable to change at any point, there were doubts about the value of planning in this sort of organisation.

What strategic objectives we have do not emerge from inside the organisation, they emerge from outside the organisation [from central government].

Head of personnel services

The strategic objectives and priorities of New Town do not really come out of planning. Whatever is particularly powerful at the time will get attention first, and then next week it could be something different. This creates cynicism in the organisation because this week something is important and the week after it is something else entirely, and all the time we are required to keep picking up the bits and pieces and delivering them.

Commercial director, direct services

New Town Council is action orientated

The culture is not about restricting actions. Even in times of severe financial constraint — which we have at the moment — the culture about this place is always to develop and try something new.

Central services director

The chief executive believed that, in the past, the council would have grasped every opportunity, a situation influenced by Members who saw everything as a priority. Things were changing. Now it was not realistic to try and put everything first on the priority list; budgets were shrinking and central government's list of demands was growing. However, despite an environment apparently littered with obstacles, there were opportunities to get things done and his council did deliver. After all, local authorities were essentially independent. There was a choice:

> You have to look at what you want to achieve, understand what is limiting and what is possible. A classic example is how we were capped[4] on capital projects in every area except for housing. Despite this we have just built a £6m recycling facility which we persuaded the government was in line with their ideas about the environment. There is no doubt that we have to accommodate ourselves to deliver what central government want, but there are ways and means of getting what you want as well. Another example is to get your community supporting you. If you can stand together, you can be vastly influential — if you ignore them, you are dead!
> Chief executive

Power is not evenly distributed

While all the officers agreed that political behaviour was common at New Town Council, there were differing views on how this influenced the development of strategy. The chief executive said:

> No one individual has dominated New Town. Individuals and groups do, however, determine the nature of the organisation and the way it does its business, and heavily impact on strategy.

Power was held in certain directorates because of the size of their budgets, the nature of the service or the strength of the director's personality:

> There is some internal competition where one director is more powerful than another. These people tend to get more resources and perhaps develop their services at a faster pace. That often goes along with having more party political support. For example, housing is traditionally a strong department. It is an important concern of the council, and strong Members have chaired that committee. So resources do tend to move in that direction.
> Head of personnel services

> We had an extremely powerful finance director, for example, because he was a very powerful individual. But, finance was also a key issue for us, so the function was important. Now, since this particular director left, finance is still an important issue, but the department does not have the same amount of power. By definition, the directorate structure tends to isolate us; communication does not happen across directorates. It is only through corporate working groups that we have been able to get people together.
> Commercial director, direct services

> From my position, we are divided into two camps. Those who provide a central service (in a co-ordinating corporate role) and those who provide specific services like housing and recreation. In effect, we at the centre think we always compromise in favour of the direct services. Those in direct services always say that they find

---

[4] Limits placed on the amount which can be spent.

themselves compromising in favour of the centre. But I don't think this has a big impact on strategy.   Central services director

The way to win the game of influence in this organisation was described by officers and chief executive alike as being close to Members. However, only the chief executive thought he was good at bridging the divide between Members' ideas and the organisation's ability to deliver. The central services director knew that, on the rare occasions that he had been particularly close to Members, he had been very effective at influencing decisions. Influencing fellow officers was a matter of being 'in on the network' or leading a working group on a specific issue.

The head of personnel did not like 'politicking' with Members, but realised that while she resisted indulging in this behaviour she was liable to remain less effective at getting her view heard. Talking with people was how the commercial director of direct services tried to get her ideas adopted — talking with colleagues on the top management team who might be sympathetic to her cause, or influential Members and other senior managers. This took the form of informal preparation before the formal process. By the time the formal process was in action, she would have a good idea of the likelihood of her initiative being successful.

A democratic chief executive

New Town officers were in agreement about the chief executive's style. He was a leader, but not a domineering one. He sensed the issues and hot spots: he was very conscious of what Members were thinking; he was a facilitator and someone who moderated the power of different interest groups.

> He is not the most powerful person in the organisation. There are others with more outright power. He doesn't lay down the law or anything like that. But he is very good at making sure all interests are met, and when you look back, you can see what he has achieved even though it was difficult to appreciate at the time.
>
> Commercial director, direct services

> The previous CE was an extreme autocrat, in complete contrast with our current CE, who is a democrat. The power is not institutionalised in the position.
>
> Head of personnel services

> He is the counterbalance between the power of two or three of the service chiefs and their committees on the one hand and, the Members of the council as a whole. He is a facilitator who uses his personality to manage the process.
>
> Central services director

A clarity of purpose?

> If you asked people working here if they had a good understanding of what this organisation was trying to achieve, then I predict their answer would be 'no'. This is partly because we are very poor at communicating about these issues.
>
> Chief executive

Other members of his team agreed. The commercial director of direct services said:

> I don't think there is a strong shared assumption about what New Town Council is here for — other than to provide services. I doubt if you would even get people to agree on what those services should be on a priority list. When the Development Corporation was dissolved, New Town Council was suddenly responsible for everything and it struggled to cope and is still not taking a lead. Members in particular have found it quite difficult to become strategic thinkers and develop long-term plans, particularly given that none of them have overall responsibility anyway.

The head of personnel disagreed, believing that there was a unifying theme:

> We have managed to hold on to being something other than what the government requires us to be. That is the over-riding *raison d'être* of the organisation. This makes organisational life difficult, because we are fighting against the government's direction and trying to set a strategic direction of our own.

In pursuit of the ideal

How would members of the top management team like to improve the strategy process?

> I don't think strategy is about forecasting the future. I think strategy is about setting out to say what do I want to do, what are we seeking to do, what are the guidelines that are going to take us in this direction. It's like playing football; you need to know if the strategy is to attack or defend.
>
> Also, because we are all rational, well most of us are, we want a strategy to be rationally based on some sort of hard evidence. What we have not done in organisations like this is develop a very rational basis of thinking. Our thinking is based partly on principle, partly on political philosophy and partly on the way you interpret what your local community might want in the future. The rationality comes when we try and bring these three together. Then something changes, as it always does, and we have to be prepared for that change as well.
>
> If we could forecast it rationally, it would be ideal. That is what we should strive for.
>
> Chief executive

> My criticism is that we spread ourselves too thin, that if we focused our strategy and concentrated on two or three very important goals then we might make more impact. On the other hand, by spreading ourselves thinly we have achieved an amazing amount. Maybe the downside of that though is that we have not all been

pulling in the same direction, which means there could be room for improvement.

Central services director

There is scope for improvement. We need to develop strategic skills and redefine the Members' role. We need to prevent the debate from slipping into the nitty gritty, operational details and move it into the arena of developing policy and the strategic direction of the council.   Head of personnel services

In the top management team, we spend a lot of time talking about strategy, but we don't talk much about the implications of the strategy. So, we all may leave the room, having spent three hours together, with different interpretations of what the strategy means. Therefore, how we implement it may actually vary.

What we need is general agreement as to what our purpose is. Some people might call it a vision. Something which says this is what we are trying to achieve and this is the direction we are trying to pursue.

I don't believe we have this, but we need it. Why? Because we have lots of conflicting demands that we can't meet. A lot of our time therefore, is spent fire-fighting. I don't know if there is an alternative. Fire fighting might not be a bad thing if there is no clear system to direct you otherwise. You just try and keep as many balls in the air as is possible until it becomes clearer. It's just that we seem to have been doing that for such a long time now!

Commercial director, direct services

One view was that they should make a virtue of their system, given the hostile and volatile environment:

In a way it works. It is very flexible and we may be doing exactly the wrong thing in trying to fit a rigid framework on to something that is inherently unstable. In which case we need to try and get this message over to staff, who see the process as it currently is as a mess and difficult to work in.

Strategy development at Castle Press

ANDY BAILEY and JULIE VERITY

> I am not a commanding manager. I seek consensus, I am methodological, I'm a
> planning type of manager.
> Managing director

Castle Press is a specialist publisher of educational materials and the
largest subsidiary of a significant, UK-based publishing and media group.
Despite the company's long history in the UK and a strong tradition in its
specialist field, it markets its products and related services to an
increasingly global audience. Castle Press is the largest company of those
in the corporate group, with 200 people working from the UK office
creating an annual turnover of £30m in 1995 and accounting for more than
40 per cent of total group revenue.

Changing times

For more than a decade, prior to 1995, Castle Press was the market leader in
its field, but it had slipped into second place. This change in market status
provided a new incentive for organisational change, after a long period of
relative internal stability (some now say, complacency). Internal
determination to regain market dominance was supported by a new strong
message from corporate headquarters to 'go for growth', with the stated
objective of doubling turnover by the year 2000.

> Because we didn't change in the past, now we are having to make major changes.
> We were locked into the past and into the way we did things before. If an area had a
> certain level of resources one year, it would get more of the same next year. That
> was the business approach, more of the same and building on what we already had.
> Publishing director

> We have been too conservative, too slow to respond to the market, too conservative in the way we progress careers, too slow to embrace new technology.
>
> Managing director

Changing markets

Castle Press found the global market place to be increasingly challenging. Since the late 1980s the company had been exposed to recession-bound Europe, the growth prospects of the Pacific Rim and newly opened communist countries, and the highly volatile and regulation-prone South American markets. Overall, demand for its products was growing, but competition was strong and the competitive map was also changing.

> From an international perspective the market is becoming more competitive as the result of smaller companies being bought-up by (mainly) UK and American groups whose aspirations are to become truly global. As far as the local perspective is concerned, we're getting ferocious competition, as we have done for many years, but it is now in our core markets from local publishers who are becoming experts in producing this material, and they are becoming more effective because they're learning the tricks.
>
> Marketing director

Changes in the top management team

The top management team (TMT) consisted of five executive directors (the managing director, finance director, publishing director, marketing director and production director) and one non-executive director from the corporate group. With the exception of the finance director (who was relatively new to the organisation), all TMT members were promoted from the business, either from within the subsidiary or from the group. Only two years before, however, the team was much bigger:

> Two years ago, I inherited a TMT of twelve people. It was impossible to discuss strategy with that number of people. Six months later, three key people and myself 'retreated' for a few days and thought about what we needed rather than what we had. The outcome was implemented about eighteen months ago. We now have a TMT of six people and the focus of our meetings is higher level discussions and strategic planning.
>
> Managing director

As a group, the TMT thought that they were compatible and rarely in conflict with each other. The collective criticism of team meetings was the danger that discussions gravitated towards the operational rather than the strategic, since this was the one time that team members found themselves together in one place at one time. The finance director (only two years with Castle Press) noted that he could bring a different contribution to the team's discussion:

I think we were very internally focused. It is easier when you come from outside the organisation and from this position I can be constructive. I'm the only person on the Team who hasn't been with Castle Press for the past twenty years, so I do have some useful external benchmarks.   Finance director

A tradition of planning

Planning had a long history at Castle Press and was an established part of the yearly routines of the TMT. The five-year planning horizon did, however, have its critics, as did the emphasis and reliance on the planning process:

> We have a five-year business plan. We revise it every year, so it's ongoing. It is continuous, changing annually as we progress.   Production director

> The strategy process is mainly planning. But because we are dealing with global markets and there are always things happening, like economic changes in various parts of the world, we have to react to these rather than plan for them! We might be able to plan that something could happen, but to predict when and where is not so easy — we have to react to these external influences.   Publishing director

> We are commissioning new books now that will reach a peak of sales in the year 2000. So I think there is too much emphasis on the short term. We need to force ourselves to think longer term, not just five years down the line.
>   Marketing director

> In my view, the information for strategy development tends to be more informal than formal. We are not very good at collating centrally what is key information about the external environment. It tends to be much more in people's heads rather than having a resource that can be consulted and information taken from there.
>   Publishing director

A parental drive for planning

The strong emphasis on planning, while driven from within Castle Press, was reinforced by the corporate group. At this group level, a recent change in TMT make-up had changed the style of downward communication to Castle senior management. New planning formats were being imposed with clearer monitoring and review systems. In general, the Castle top team looked on these changes favourably, but also felt that strategy was a very 'downward' (rather than upward) process and that there was a lot of time spent making plans.

> The group require each of their Strategic Business Units [SBUs] to prepare a strategic planning document, once every two years. Derived from that is the operating plan, and from that the budgets. The group have actually imposed a new strategic planning and implementation structure, which we think is going to work very well. For once we agree with what our parent company has said.

What is good about the new planning system is that it provides us with a clear evaluation document that we can use in the future to measure whether we've done what we said we would do, whether it's been successful or not.

Managing director

However, despite a clear requirement for planning from corporate headquarters, what was planned was largely down to the Castle Press team. Where parental constraint was obvious, it was in the financial demands made by the parent and in agreeing budgets and profit expectations.

Apart from the 'go for growth' message, no one limits what we can do, anything can be considered.

One of the key things is that our part of the business is very profitable and cash generative. We are also big relative to the other parts of the group. These factors allow us a lot of freedom.

Finance director

The group do constrain us in the level of profit they demand. They have the power to tell us to make 5% or 15% profit this year; this limits what we can do.

The divisional structure does mean we operate in a fairly well-defined area of operation. When we have suggested operating outside these areas, we have been told it is not our responsibility. So while there is a lot of discussion about going for growth and being entrepreneurial, there are constraints placed on individual business units which perhaps go against that.

Marketing director

A consensual approach

Formal planning activities were associated with more informal team needs, such as the need to arrive at a consensus, coupled with a strong sense of community, respect and belonging. Once agreed at this level, the strategy was cascaded down through the organisation and more consensus was sought from employees. Without this, the TMT argued, little of the plan would be implemented.

I think there is an element of tradition. We have our plans every year, we continue to do them every year, and I think it's also a reflection of the function of doing everything by consensus, and the planning approach we take here is very much about developing a consensus view.

Publishing director

We are very consensual and we like to debate everything and then reach an agreement. If somebody is in disagreement with something, it is unlikely that it will proceed very far.

Production director

Because we employ people who are intellectual and academic, we take into account that they will have strong opinions on how the business is run and ignoring them will mean trouble. It is the nature of the people we employ that means that we have to have a more consensual and sensitive approach to management

At the beginning of this year we decided within our management board what our key objectives were. We took twenty of our senior managers away for two days and spent time explaining our key strategies. Then we asked them to work out action plans for how they would implement those strategies within the units. This is important because we have had problems with implementation before. We assumed that senior managers understood what we were trying to do after a short briefing! Now we are involving the senior guys more. This is a very traditional and conservative division and people are resistant to change, so we spend a lot of time trying to get people thinking in a different way.   Managing director

Politics and power

Because of the drive towards consensus, the issues of power and politics were not seen as very strong, although they were not absent:

> I don't think there is really any conflict. I think there are differences — we all know where we're trying to get, but the difference is about how we should get there.
>
> Publishing director

> At board level I think we are quite well balanced power wise; people respect each other. I don't see that there is any one dominant player. However, influence comes about because of the business we're in — publishing and selling your product. So it is these groups who have influence ... at the end of the day decisions come down in their favour rather than on the processing side like my department. My area is only here on sufferance, because they need the product to be produced.
>
> Production director

Cultural influences

Employees at Castle Press were proudly professional and passionate about publishing quality books — the best in their specialist area. These commonly shared values about their trade directed strategy by keeping Castle Press away from certain areas of business and certain markets.

> There is a strong feeling here and within the group of 'we have always done things this way'. It is an even stronger culture in Castle Press where, in its specialist area of publishing, it is very much in a world of its own. I think people in this area of publishing around the world are just a family apart from the rest. They are very committed to this area rather than to publishing. I think people have this work in their blood and that is one of the things that gives it a very strong culture. Wherever you go worldwide, we get sucked into that culture.
>
> Production director

Long service among the workforce was common in Castle Press. This helped to reinforce the common culture of the organisation. Even when new people were recruited from outside the organisation, the tendency was that these were selected from the publishing arena and publishing houses which were very similar to Castle Press.

In the top management team and more generally, we are limited [in terms of experience] to Castle and then to a slightly wider level of publishing. We have deliberately recruited people who don't have any experience in either, but there aren't many of them at the moment.   Publishing director

I think our strategy is principally historical, to some extent dictated by our wish to be the number one and our assumption that we can be that. In order to be number one, we have got to have fairly high objectives and to some extent that assumption dictates the overall strategy that we've got to be a major player wherever we operate.

There are accepted industry ways of producing, selling and promoting materials in our business. There are common strategies, and following these is only restrained by size — the bigger and closer in size the competitors are to us, the more similar the strategies are.   Marketing director

Reacting to a changing environment

While there had been a strong focus on strategy development through planning processes, the changing nature of the operating environment, changes in economic conditions and the speed of environmental change were dictating a different response from the organisation.

This incremental approach — that's what we're getting more of now and it's because the environment is changing. New opportunities are arising. Before, we never really took them. Over the last couple of years we have started to take more risks in the hope that they will work. We try to set things up in a way where we can keep it low key and we can withdraw if it doesn't work, but if it looks as if it's a success, we can build on it.   Publishing director

I think that we should experiment more and when there's an opportunity we should take it. This has happened on a small scale and I think there will be more of it. But there will always be pressure on us not to waste the money, so having a flutter will always be a bit of a problem.   Production director

Participating at the top and the ideal future

One reason the process is as it is, is that it is the way I like to do it. I suppose in that sense, that is power and that is what I have done. Also the business we are in is quite straight forward in the materials we produce, and in other respects it's a big, global, complex business. Therefore, we need a whole variety of inputs from people in order to agree our strategic goals and implement actions. The other reason is of course we are required to plan by the group.   Managing director

The managing director is very much a member of the team rather than a leader of the team.   Publishing director

The TMT at Castle Press envisaged the future of the strategy process to be more of the same, with some different emphases: more involvement, for example, of people who will deliver the strategy. Their role was seen not necessarily as a direct contribution to the strategy debate, but as greater ownership and commitment to making it work. There was also recognition that the TMT would have to be swifter-of-foot, to counter new competition and unpredictable environmental changes. A new focus on formal information gathering would be essential to try and read future trends and be sensitive to external changes sooner. The planning process itself needed to be pushed further into the future, five years being too short a time frame to promote informed, creative strategic thinking. Finally, there was a voice of challenge against the consensual approach:

> There is a strong argument for less of the consensual, democratic approach. At times we should say 'let's do it' and actually just go and do it!

The pharmaceutical industry

GERRY JOHNSON[1]

The origins of the pharmaceutical industry are primarily post war and during that time it has been driven greatly by technological innovation. For example, if we go back to the early 1950s, the discovery of tetracycline by such companies as Pfizer and Lederle led to them becoming numbers one and two in the market. You can then see a progression of drugs that have made or broken companies over time. For example, the betablockers were largely discovered by ICI, who formed major franchises out of the treatment of cardiovascular diseases. Companies such as Syntex and Boots were based primarily on the discovery of the non-steroidal inflammatory drugs. Smith-Kline was based on the success of Tagamet, and Zantac formed the base for the global success of Glaxo, going on to be the world's number one product with sales in excess of £2 billion per annum. Technological new product success has therefore fuelled the growth of the industry.

In the UK, the general practitioner (GP) — the local doctor — did not really know the price of products, so pharmaceutical companies tended to make their money out of minor adjustments or 'me-too' adjustments to existing products or a copy of a competitor's product, traditionally priced at a premium to the existing market on the back of 'muscle marketing'. The doctors would accept a premium price for a new product because it was a new product, offering a minor advantage. For example, it might be a less frequent dosage or it might have a slightly improved side-effect profile; but with regards to its therapeutic outcome, it was very similar to the product which it was competing with. The doctors really acted as gatekeepers. The

[1] In 1996 Graham Leask of Astra Pharmaceuticals was engaged in a review of the firm's strategy. This case study is based on extracts from his briefing to consultants on the background to developments in the pharmaceutical industry. The comments made represent the views of Graham Leask and not necessarily those of Astra Pharmaceuticals.

patients consumed the product, the health authorities paid for the product. All the doctors did was diagnose the problem and prescribe the product. The industry therefore was one which achieved its profitability through constant production of minor product improvements, strong marketing and selling which financed the breakthrough R&D discoveries.

It used to be said that to develop a world-class capability in R&D cost in excess of $100 million a year. Now the cost of bringing a new drug to market is approximately $300 million. Every day lost in bringing a new drug to market probably loses you approximately $1 million in sales, if the product is successful. If we go back to the early 1960s the time from discovery to launch was probably only 3–5 years, whereas now because of increased safety standards and the requirements of clinical testing brought about by such disasters as thalidomide, it takes approximately 12 years from patent of drug to bringing that drug on the market. In the past you probably had 6–7 years' lead on your nearest competitor. Now because of improved chemistry and computer generation of analogues, you see the lead times down to about 18 months. So the time you have to establish a viable market position prior to meeting your first competitor is much reduced. So it takes 12 years to develop a drug, but when you have got it on the market there is likely to be a competitor in 18 months. Patents only relate to your own process and the discovery of the drug. What people are doing very cleverly now is coming up with similar products. However, overall the chances of success of a new product are very low. Approximately 1–4 per cent see the market, and of those that reach the market, approximately 60 per cent fail to achieve sufficient sales to justify their R&D expenditure.

One of the other things that the industry has had to watch out for is substitute products. This could be an alternative at a much lower cost: a generic product, for example, or a new way of gaining a better clinical outcome, for example with surgery, which makes intervention by drugs unnecessary.

Going back to the industry in the early 1980s, success in the market place was driven by having good product supply, but also by having a successful sales and marketing operating. This meant achieving an optimal visit frequency of about 6 visits a year to each general practitioner and gaining sufficient coverage or seeing sufficient GPs. Over time, sales forces have increased very sharply in size. In 1985, there were approximately 3,000 representatives in the UK, calling on approximately 30,000 doctors. By 1992 there were 36,000 GPs being called on by 7,000 representatives. So the ratio had changed from 1–10 down to nearer 1–5, a trend which has been mirrored in a lot of other countries, notably Germany, Italy and France.

Threats and changes in the UK

The industry of the early 1980s was driven by premium-priced product improvement, strong sales and marketing, calling on a customer group which was not responsible for purchasing drugs and did not have a high awareness of drug prices. It was an industry which traditionally produced returns in excess of 20 per cent on investment. The National Health Service in the UK was established in 1948, and for a long time very little happened to change the original statement, which was quality healthcare as required, free at point of need, irrespective of status. There have been marked changes. In the 1980s there was a realisation that patients' expectations were increasing, the cost of healthcare was increasing and at the same time the capability of the country to sustain such spending was not increasing. That has been common worldwide, with the highest problem occurring in countries like the United States. In fact, it is said that in America, General Motors spends more on healthcare for its employees than it does on steel to make its cars. But it is the same for all the larger pharmaceutical markets in Europe too.

For some time within the UK there had been an agreement with government, the pharmaceutical price regulation scheme, which limited the level of profit which pharmaceutical companies were allowed to make in the UK. From the mid-1980s, though, government started to take more direct intervention. Prescription prices were raised, though bear in mind that the majority of the population was exempt, being under 16, elderly or unemployed. Then in 1985, the UK government introduced its blacklist. This delisted certain groups of products, some anti-hypnotics, such as valium, and some cough syrups. This had a tremendous differential effect on the industry. For example, Roche, which was in the top ten within the pharmaceutical industry, very rapidly fell to the 40s or even 50s within the industry as its two major products were delisted.

The next significant change was signalled in 1989 when the Conservative government introduced a white paper entitled *Working for Patients*. *Working for Patients* was put together on the premise that, through competition, patients would gain better services and value for money would be increased. There were four main changes within *Working for Patients*. The first was that for the first time the cost of drugs and other services on both the GP side in the community and on the hospital side were brought under control of the local regional health authority (of which there were then fourteen in England and Wales). The second change was that for the first time responsibility was linked with accountability within the management of the NHS, and NHS managers were recruited from outside on short-term performance contracts. The third change was the splitting of the so-called purchaser, who bought the service, from the provider, who provided it, with the result that competition among providers for money held by purchasers was encouraged. An internal market was thus created. The fourth main change was that all hospitals were no longer part of the district health authority. If they were sufficiently large and had the right managerial resources, they could become NHS trust hospitals, which meant that they were able to raise their own independent sources of finance and operate more independently. This affected competition because hospitals for the first time could specialise. They didn't have to provide all the services to the community which they had traditionally. In the past, hospitals were paid on the basis of their resident population, now they were being paid on the basis of the amount of work they did, as money followed the patient.

The government was also very worried about the cost of prescribing drugs and the fact that their cost was steadily increasing year on year, at a rate greater than the rise in GDP. Two key measures were introduced: the first was the introduction of indicative prescribing amounts which rapidly became changed to prescribing budgets, which produced a ceiling beyond which GPs were not supposed to go. The second change was the introduction of a new type of GP, a fund-holding GP, who was given a fund to cover staff, prescribing and certain specified hospital procedures: for example, hip replacements and cataracts. The advantage to the fund-holder was that they could move money from one budget to another and, if they saved money on the budget, could keep 50 per cent of those savings towards improvements in their own practices. Concomitant with this and as a requirement of fund-holding was that the GP practice installed an approved computer system, which had two benefits. The first one was that it held all the patients' records, but the second was that it often allowed the computer to set a formary, a limited list of drugs, that they used routinely. At the same time it also allowed the practice, if it wished, to print all prescriptions in their generic form, rather than a branded form, which meant that if an alternative cheaper generic drug was available, the pharmacist could prescribe it and hence save the practice money. The result was that the old brand loyalty, which the pharmaceutical industry had spent so much time and money developing, disappeared. Within the UK this fund-holding scheme has been very marked in its success in controlling prescribing costs. For example, in the first year of operation, fund-holders were 0.7 per cent below their expected budget, whereas non-fund-holding GPs had exceeded their budget.

By 1996, given the far more price-sensitive market, GPs were far more aware of the cost of drugs and they have a number of reminders from medical advisers, pharmaceutical advisers and their local PACT data which detail exactly what they have spent and where they have spent the money. Competition has also increased because it is no longer viable to introduce me-too products at a premium price because they simply won't sell; so new products are, for the first time, being introduced at a price discount and hence becoming early generics. This further increases the pressure on the industry's profitability, while as access to GPs declines, the viability of large sales forces becomes increasingly called into question.

Changes in Europe

In other European countries, companies faced the same fundamental issues: a rise in patient expectation, increasing costs of healthcare and the fact that GDP is not increasing at a rate sufficient to offset rises in costs. In other European countries, therefore, there have been similar changes. For example, in Germany in 1993, the government introduced a system called 'reference pricing'. Government took a series of products and said that the price that they were willing to reimburse for those was the mid-point. As a result, patients had to pay extra in order to obtain a product listed above the cost of the reference price. The result of this was that the value of the pharmaceutical market fell by 25 per cent in three months. In Germany, in common with the UK and several other European countries, there was also a price freeze. For example, in the UK pharmaceutical companies had to reduce prices by $2\frac{1}{2}$ per cent. In Germany similar price freezes were put in place alongside reference pricing. However, what worried the Germans most was the imposition of 'global budgets'. A global budget was introduced for doctors. If it was exceeded, the excess would be paid half by the pharmaceutical industry and half by the doctors. Doctors reacted very quickly by using cheaper products because they didn't know how much they would be charged and feared high costs being passed on to them. The result was that in Germany a number of pharmaceutical companies reacted quickly by cutting the size of their sales forces and looking for ways to decrease their costs.

In Sweden reference pricing was also introduced, and by 1996 it was rumoured that the county councils, who administer healthcare, had been given budgets for drugs and were starting to set up drugs and therapeutics committees to evaluate which products they would endorse within their local community.

In Italy they have imposed a number of price freezes, followed by a banding system for drug reimbursement in 1994. Drugs in band A are classified as being essential and fully reimbursed, drugs in band B are 50 per cent reimbursed and drugs in band C are not reimbursed at all. There is also band H which is hospital drugs, which tend to be reimbursed at 50 per cent of the cost. The interesting thing here is that a drug can move from band A to band C without a pharmaceutical company being given prior warning. Price changes are sometimes imposed with such rapidity that you don't have time to change the printing on your packaging, so you have to do it with labels. The Italian government has tried to set the price fairly. They have taken an average of two high-cost markets — for example, the UK and Germany — and two low-cost markets, Spain and France. Unfortunately they have not set exchange rates which are realistic.

There are, then, a number of different cost containment measures and most governments have tried some or all of them to some degree with some success. We've had negative lists, we've had positive lists, we've had price freezes, we've had price reductions, we've had reference pricing, we've had price banding, we've had patient co-payments, and all these factors have made the environment more difficult.

On top of all this, distribution, which in the past used to be seen as very much a given within the pharmaceutical industry, is now becoming more important. As large distribution companies begin to become pan-European in their operation, they can source products from the lowest point of supply in Europe through the medium of parallel imports. These are products which are available at a cheaper price in lower fixed cost countries. Within Europe the higher-priced markets are Germany, the UK, Sweden and Holland; and the lower-priced markets, Spain, Portugal, France, Italy and Greece; and it's from the lower-priced markets that parallel imports are coming. The price differences can be significant.

Another difficulty has been the growth of a strong generic industry, particularly in the UK and Germany. In Germany the market has become far more price driven because of 'branded generics'. A generic product is a product manufactured after patent expiry by another manufacturer, normally at a cheaper price. These are normally at the bottom of the market. It is not developed and manufactured by the original manufacturer and is not backed by the manufacturer's quality control and medical information department. To a lot of GPs that makes little difference. Between these two price points there is an opportunity to have branded generics; these are generic products which offer a small advantage and which are sold at a price above the lowest-priced generics. In Germany you have original branded products at the top of the market, high-priced high-quality generics, middle-priced generics and low-priced generics.

It is often said that the pharmaceutical industry is a global industry. I'm not sure I would agree with that. In Europe, production facilities tend to be strategically placed and hence are often not present in each country. With respect to advertising and methods of marketing, however, it can differ from country to country. For example, a colleague of mine in Germany asked me why in the UK the industry holds so many doctors' meetings. The answer became obvious when I spent some time in Germany; going out with a German representative for a day, you might see ten doctors for face-to-face conversations. In the UK access is declining and the average now is probably about 3.3 calls per day; so to see sufficient customers, it's important to find other ways in which to see them — for example, through postgraduate education meetings. In Sweden, on the other hand, access to doctors is again difficult, but unlike the UK, where the average conversation is five to ten minutes, in Sweden you make appointments to see the doctor and they expect to spend half an hour with you. So whereas you don't see them so easily or so frequently, you do get a decent length of time in which to discuss your product. One of the major differences which the NHS changes in the UK have brought about is that the demands on doctors' time have become much more severe. Five years ago a doctor planned on a five-minute patient consultation on average. Now that patient consultation is 8–10 minutes, hence to see the same number of patients takes almost twice as long. In the UK there is also a larger requirement for paperwork from the health authority, which has meant that GPs have to spend more time on administration. Fund-holding has also meant that GPs have to become more professional in terms of buying goods and services and running their surgeries more like a business. In the rest of Europe they don't face quite the same pressures, but access to doctors is starting to decline. Certainly in Sweden getting satisfactory access to doctors at a reasonable frequency is difficult, especially bearing in mind that it may take 3–6 calls a year to convince a doctor of the benefits of a product, depending upon its complexity and the perceived risks.

The result of all this is that, whereas operating costs have remained the same, sales growth of products has slowed, and increasingly you can no longer cover the costs of innovative R&D through incremental me-too product modifications. Profitability is starting to fall quite sharply, and in some cases it is reaching 10 per cent or lower and is predicted to fall to between 3 and 5 per cent by the end of the century. A change would put pharmaceuticals very much in line with the average profitability of many other manufacturing industries who do not face such risks in new product discovery and development.

The corporate response

There are increasingly three types of company: those that make things happen, those that watch things happen and those that wonder what the hell happened! Within the pharmaceutical industry there have been several major trends. The first has been towards mergers and acquisitions, as companies have sought to merge with other companies in order to become larger to leverage economies of scale, and exercise the benefits of critical mass in exploiting more efficient R&D and better sales and marketing practices; and at the same time hopefully gain improved geographical reach. Examples here are Glaxo Wellcome, Smith Kline Beecham, Hoechst and Marion Rousse. Other strategies have included the building of distribution systems to gain information on product usage, parallel imports and generics such as the Glaxo distribution initiative. Another strategy aimed at gaining better control of distribution and getting closer to customers is the purchasing of pharmacy benefit managers[2] in the USA, led by Merck who purchased Medco for $6 billion, followed by Smith Kline who purchased DPS and Eli Lilly who purchased PCS. So this is vertical integration. Another approach has been that taken by Rhone Poulenc, who have started to form alliances with several small R&D companies and biotechnology companies on the basis that by funding research in a number of small companies, which are small and innovative, chances of coming up with a new product lead are improved. Other strategies have been very much to stick to the knitting, as with Astra, while some other companies have moved to disease management, such as Zeneca, with Salick for cancer.

There are of course other changes that could happen which are much less certain. Perhaps it is surprising that some of the large Japanese pharmaceutical companies have not made more inroads into Europe and the USA. They have not; but that is not to say that they will not. After all, they have in many other industries. And if they did, the further increase in competition could very well prompt even more mergers and acquisitions. We should also remember that most of the major pharmaceutical markets are currently in the West and Japan. There are other potentially huge markets for pharmaceuticals that are, as yet, underdeveloped — China, India, South America to name but a few. Who knows the extent to which they might develop as market opportunities? And then there are the advances in biotechnology: the media hype this up as a major development for the future. I suspect that that is an exaggeration, but we just do not know at the moment.

---

[2] PBMs arose when managed core organisations in the USA developed. In principle they 'carve out' the prescription benefit from the healthcare maintenance organisations and manage it. Mechanisms such as drug utilisation review, start formularies and direct telephone intervention to both prescriber and patient in order to encourage switching to lower-cost alternatives are commonly employed.

The European brewing industry

TONY JACOBS and MURRAY STEELE

Europe is the major centre of beer consumption and production in the world. As a production entity, European output is more than 50 per cent greater than that of the USA, the world's largest beer-producing country. However, significant differences exist from country to country, in terms of both industry structure and market characteristics.

This case study is in three parts:

- A general description of the European brewing industry.
- Characteristics of the principal brewing countries.
- A description of major European brewers.

A general description of the European brewing industry

In terms of value, the European alcohol market is dominated by beer, which accounts for over 50 per cent of the total alcohol market.

Industry structure

Table 1 shows the top fourteen European brewing companies by their output in 1994. The European market, taken as a whole, is not very concentrated; the top five brewers have a combined market share of 35.2 per cent. The European brewers are also relatively insular. Only four of the top fourteen have sales of any significance outside Europe (i.e. over one million

Table 1   Top fourteen brewers in Europe, 1994

	Estimated European beer sales	Estimated market share (%)	Estimated rest of world sales	Estimated total sales
1. Heineken (Holland)	30.0	10.1	30.4	60.4
2. Carlsberg (Denmark)	24.4	8.2	5.8	30.2
3. Danone (France)	20.9	7.0	5.8	26.7
4. Guinness (Eire)	13.7	4.6	11.9	25.6
5. Bass (UK)	15.9	5.3	0.5	16.4
6. Interbrew (Belgium)	14.3	4.8	0.4	14.7
7. Courage (UK)	12.2	5.3	–	12.2
8. Oetker (Germany)	9.4	3.2	0.2	9.6
9. Bräu & Brunnen (Germany)	9.4	3.2	0.1	9.4
10. Maerz (Germany)	8.9	3.0	0.4	9.3
=11. Whitbread (UK)	7.8	2.6	–	7.8
=11. Holsten (Germany)	7.3	2.5	0.5	7.8
13. S & N (UK)	6.8	2.3	0.1	6.9
14. Grolsch (Holland)	2.0	0.7	0.1	2.1

Notes:
1. All figures are in millions of hectolitres.
2. Volumes include those companies in which the relevant brewer has a financial interest.

Source: Annual reports and trade sources.

hectolitres per annum) and for the majority of them, the bulk of their output is produced in their country of origin.

On a global comparison, only two of the brewers listed in Table 1 are in the top ten brewers of the world (1994 figures). Heineken is the second largest, and Carlsberg is the eighth. To put this further in context, Anheuser-Busch of the USA, the largest brewing company in the world, had an annual output of nearly 107 million hectolitres in 1994, and Heineken, Europe's largest brewing group, produced just over 60 million hectolitres in the same year.

Industry concentration

Individual European countries have substantially different industry structures. They vary from the highly concentrated to the highly fragmented. Some countries, such as the United Kingdom, have regulations which limit the degree of concentration allowed in industries. Other countries do not have these rules, and in fact may encourage concentration to help the creation and development of significant international competitors. Table 2 shows the varying degrees of concentration in the principal European brewing countries.

Table 2   Estimated industry concentration by country, 1994

Country	Industry situation	Number of competitors	Degree of concentration (%)
Denmark	Monopoly	1	71
Holland	Monopoly	1	74
Italy	Monopoly	2	61
Belgium	Monopoly	2	86
France	Monopoly	2	71
United Kingdom	Concentrated	5	84
Spain	Concentrated	5	87
Germany	Fragmented	5	26

Notes:
1. The degree of concentration relates to the combined market share held by the number of competitors indicated.
2. Estimates for 1994. Mergers and acquisitions within the industry have led to further concentration in several key markets.

Ownership

There is little ownership of breweries by other European companies in Germany and none in Denmark. However, significant proportions of the Italian and Spanish industries are owned by foreign brewers as a result of cross-border acquisitions since the 1970s, driven by small domestic markets causing ambitious brewers to seek international expansion. Table 3 shows the major European cross-border ownership stakes.

There is little ownership in Europe by non-European brewers. There are, however, licensing arrangements whereby brewers in one country brew a brand from another country. This principally takes place in the United Kingdom. A good example is Whitbread, which brews and sells both Stella

Table 3   Cross-European ownership stakes

	Heineken	Danone	Carlsberg	Interbrew
France	*	**		*
Germany			*	
Belgium		*		**
Holland	**			
Denmark			**	
Spain	*	*	*	
Italy	*	*	*	*
Greece	*	*		
United Kingdom			*	
Ireland	*			

Note: ** denotes country of origin. * denotes an ownership presence.

Table 4   Consumption (litres) per capita

	1994	1993	1992	1991	1990	1989	1988	1987
Germany	140	138	144	143	143	143	144	144
Czech Republic	161	155	167 ⎫	131	135	132	130	130
Slovakia	93	56	72 ⎭					
Denmark	127	126	128	126	127	127	126	125
Belgium/Luxembourg	106	108	113	112	121	115	121	121
Austria	117	117	123	124	121	119	118	116
United Kingdom	102	101	105	109	113	114	114	111
Hungary	81	77	98	101	107	103	101	100
Ireland	113	123	124	123	124	118	111	108
Holland	86	85	90	91	90	88	83	84
Spain	67	67	71	71	72	71	69	67
Portugal	62	64	65	67	65	64	53	47
Greence	42	42	42	37	41	39	41	38
France	39	39	41	41	42	41	39	39
Italy	26	25	24	23	23	22	23	23

Sources: BLRA and CBMC.

Artois and Heineken under licence in the UK. This provides them with an expanded portfolio of brands with which to compete.

Consumption

Table 4 shows the consumption per capita in litres per annum for the major European markets for the years 1987–94.

Brands

With low growth, or declines, in consumption in the European markets, branding has become increasingly important. Brewers have intensified their brand development policies and a very high brand awareness exists among consumers, principally due to high-profile (and high-cost) advertising. As one British brewing manager put it:

> You have got to own your own brands, and they have got to be good brands, or else you are going to be dead in the water.

Figure 1 shows the top ten selling beer brands in millions of hectolitres in Europe. Not surprisingly, the top three brands are marketed by the three largest companies which have the most extensive operations across Europe.

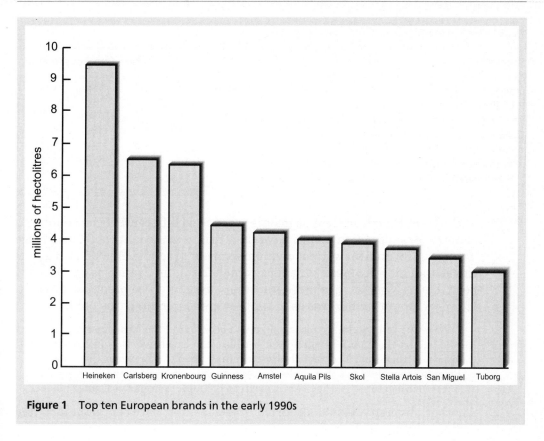

Figure 1 Top ten European brands in the early 1990s

Heineken has two of the top five brands — Heineken and Amstel — and Carlsberg has two of the top ten brands — Carlsberg and Tuborg.

Market segmentation

In a saturated market there is segmentation. In a growing market beer is beer, in a segmented market this is not the case. Dutch brewing manager

An example of a growing segment in a mature market is the increase in lager sales in the United Kingdom. Since the 1970s the total volume of beer sold in the UK has not fluctuated substantially, but in the same period lager's share of the market has increased from 7.5 to 55 per cent, before falling back to 50 per cent in 1993. Distinct segments of the European market appear to be developing. These are shown in Table 5.

The segments which have been growing and are expected to continue to grow are at either end of the market: the low- and no-alcohol beers and particularly the premium and speciality beers. Also seen as growing are the supermarket chain own-label beers as a result of their low price and the distribution power of the supermarket chains.

Table 5   European market segments in the early 1990s

Segment	Estimated market share (%)
Low and no alcohol	7
Premium or strong	25
Speciality — aperitif or special occasion beers	5
Ordinary — the major volume sector	63
of which:	
Branded products	50
Supermarket chain low-price, own-label beers	13

Different brands in their segments are viewed differently from country to country. Brands which do not have their origin in a country, i.e. which are 'foreign', are often viewed as premium segment products. A good example of this is Danone's Kronenbourg 1664, which is sold in France as an ordinary beer, but is viewed in almost all other markets as a premium product. However, potential hazards exist for brewers in pursuing this policy.

> In Great Britain, Stella Artois is a premium beer, one of the most expensive beers you can get there, and people buy it because it is expensive. It is marketed and promoted that way. The British are travelling people, now when they come to Belgium, they discover that Stella Artois is a cheap beer, so they ask themselves if it is justified to pay so much for it in Great Britain.   French brewing manager

Another diversity exists in price relationships between premium and ordinary beers and by region:

> In southern Europe the price differential is high between the premium/speciality segment and the ordinary segment — of the order of 40%. In northern Europe the difference is much lower, only 15%.   French brewing manager

A possible source of explanation for this wide discrepancy could be the widely differing duty and taxation rates on beer across Europe.

Duty

The duty levied on beer in Europe is calculated by one of two methods — the wort system and at the brewery gate (BG). The latter, as its name implies, means that tax is levied at the 'brewery gate' on point of shipment to the next stage in the distribution channel. The wort system is more complex and dates from the last century. Duty is calculated during the brewing process, at the point of fermentation.

Rates of duty vary dramatically across Europe from the equivalent of 2.8 pence per pint of beer in Luxembourg to 71 pence per pint in Finland. Tax rates vary between 15 and 25 per cent. This variation in duty rates impacts on the economics of brewing. In the UK, for example, raw materials, salaries, packaging, etc. are one-third of total manufacturing costs, the other two-thirds is duty.

The anticipated harmonisation of rates of duty throughout the EU member countries since the introduction of the single market has, so far, yet to materialise. One British manager summed up the present duty situation:

> The harmonisation of duty is a mess in Europe, frankly. There are very wide duty differences across Europe. You have the situation where there is a potential price difference between France and the UK of 25 per cent in a very saleable commodity. The UK government are saying that there won't be any need to harmonise duty, because they will be able to control it one way or the other, they will capture it at the border. I really don't think that is realistic, because if you can make £25,000 profit bringing a tanker of beer across the Channel, you will bring a tanker of beer across the channel, whether it is legal or illegal, and if you get caught once or twice it is probably still worth it.

Distribution

European consumers purchase their beer in two main ways. They either purchase beer in stores to drink at home (known as the 'off trade') or they purchase it, principally on draught, in an outlet such as a bar, pub, caf³, restaurant or hotel to be consumed immediately. Table 6 shows the percentage of beer purchased in draught form in recent years in the major European markets.

The type of container in which beer is purchased also varies significantly from country to country. The four principal types are: draught, where the

Table 6 Percentage of beer consumed on draught by country

	1994	1992	1989	1988	1987	1985
Germany	22	22	28	28	29	29
Denmark	7	6	5	4	4	3
Belgium	40	40	44	45	40	40
United Kingdom	67	70	72	73	75	77
Ireland	82	83	86	86	88	88
Holland	31	30	29	30	31	31
Spain	37	37	40	40	n/a	35
Portugal	32	34	25	25	24	19
Greece	4	4	3	3	n/a	n/a
France	24	25	25	25	24	22
Italy	16	14	16	16	16	16

Source: CBMC.

Table 7 Consumption patterns by country, 1994

	Draught beer	Returnable bottles	Non-returnable bottles	Cans
Germany	22	78*	0	0
Denmark	7	93	0	0
Belgium	40	53	4	3
United Kingdom	67	4	6	23
Ireland	82	4	4	10
Holland	31	64	6	0
Spain	36	38	19	7
Portugal	32	55	9	4
Greece	4	76	4	16
France	24	16	55	5
Italy	16	15	58	11

* Includes all bottles and cans.

Source: CBMC.

beer is served in a glass and drunk immediately, normally in a bar; returnable bottles, where the bottle is returned to the point of sale or some other point after the beer has been drunk; non-returnable bottles, where the bottle is discarded after consumption of the beer; and cans, which are also normally discarded after consumption of their contents.

Table 7 shows the percentages of consumption by the different types of container for the major European countries in 1994. With the exception of the United Kingdom and Greece, beer sold in cans is not a significant feature of the European market, and for environmental reasons beer cannot be purchased in cans in Denmark by law.

There is a growing tendency throughout Europe for premium beers to be sold by the bottle rather than by the can, as bottles are perceived to be of higher quality by many consumers.

Channels of distribution also vary, which is to be expected given the different consumption characteristics of each market. The channels of distribution which exist in France, Holland, Spain, Italy, Belgium and Denmark are similar. What does vary from country to country is the proportion of beer sales which flows through each channel.

In the aforementioned countries, the brewers do not own many of the retail outlets and tend to distribute through wholesalers, which may or may not be owned by the brewers. The supermarket chains have substantial power in the distribution channels and offer the brewing companies attractive economies of scale. Brewers can deliver large volumes to a central point in the supermarket chain distribution system. This power is growing across Europe as more beer is sold through supermarkets.

In the UK and to a lesser extent Germany, the brewing companies owned a significant proportion of the retail outlets — 44 per cent in the United Kingdom and 22 per cent in Germany — distributed direct to the pubs and bars. However, since the Monopolies and Mergers Commission report into the UK brewing industry in 1989, there has been a substantial change in ownership patterns and some estimates suggest that the number of retail outlets owned by brewers will drop to around 19 per cent by the year 2000. In both the UK and Germany, supermarket chains are increasingly becoming important channels for distribution.

Production

Table 8 shows the production output of the major European beer-producing countries during recent years in millions of hectolitres.

Imports and exports

Tables 9 and 10 show imports as a percentage of consumption and exports as a percentage of production respectively for the major European brewing countries.

Table 8   Brewing output (millions of hectolitres) by country

	1994	1993	1992	1991	1990	1989	1988	1987
Germany	118.6	115.8	120.2	118.0	104.3	93.0	92.6	92.8
Czech Republic	18.1	17.8	19.5 ⎫	22.3	23.5	22.8	22.7	22.2
Slovakia	4.5	3.0	3.8 ⎭					
Denmark	9.4	9.4	9.8	9.7	9.0	8.8	8.7	8.2
Belgium	14.7	14.2	14.2	13.8	14.1	13.2	13.8	14.0
Austria	10.1	9.8	10.0	10.2	9.6	9.2	9.0	8.9
United Kingdom	58.3	56.7	57.6	59.6	61.8	62.1	61.9	61.0
Hungary	8.3	7.9	9.9	9.6	9.5	9.7	9.5	9.1
Ireland	7.2	6.9	6.7	6.4	6.4	6.1	5.6	5.5
Holland	22.2	20.4	20.7	19.9	20.0	18.8	17.5	17.5
Spain	25.0	24.3	26.1	26.4	27.3	27.3	26.6	25.8
Portugal	6.6	6.6	6.9	6.9	7.0	6.8	5.6	5.0
Greece	4.3	3.9	3.9	3.7	4.1	3.9	4.1	3.8
France	20.4	20.8	21.3	21.0	21.4	20.9	20.1	19.9
Italy	12.1	11.7	10.9	10.7	11.1	10.4	11.3	11.1
Total	339.8	329.2	341.5	338.2	329.1	313.0	309.0	304.8

Sources: BLRA and CBMC.

Table 9   Imports as a percentage of consumption

	1994	1993	1992	1991	1990	1989	1988	1987
Germany	2.4	2.4	2.6	2.5	1.8	1.7	1.5	1.5
Denmark	0.7	0.3	0.3	0.3	0.4	0.3	0.4	0.3
Belgium/Luxembourg	5.1	4.4	4.3	4.3	5.2	5.8	4.5	4.7
United Kingdom	8.7	7.9	9.3	8.8	8.0	7.2	6.9	6.5
Ireland	9.8	13.4	17.0	15.0	11.7	10.2	12.6	10.9
Holland	4.1	4.3	3.9	5.7	4.5	4.5	5.6	4.3
Spain	7.7	6.2	6.6	5.0	4.2	3.3	2.8	2.8
Portugal	2.7	2.2	1.8	2.0	1.6	1.5	0.7	0.7
Greece	4.7	5.4	5.6	4.6	3.8	2.3	3.6	1.0
France	17.3	13.3	12.0	12.7	13.0	12.0	11.3	11.3
Italy	21.0	19.7	20.3	19.0	18.2	16.7	13.7	16.4

Source: CBMC.

Table 10   Exports as a percentage of production

	1994	1993	1992	1991	1990	1989	1988	1987
Germany	6.7	6.3	5.4	5.2	5.6	5.7	5.7	5.8
Denmark	28.4	26.8	28.0	26.5	25.8	23.7	23.8	22.8
Belgium/Luxembourg	31.2	26.1	23.6	23.1	18.5	17.8	18.3	18.0
United Kingdom	5.3	3.8	3.7	3.2	2.7	2.2	2.1	1.9
Ireland	45.3	45.3	42.9	40.9	39.2	37.7	38.8	37.7
Holland	42.2	38.2	35.6	34.6	36.0	33.3	33.1	32.0
Spain	1.4	1.2	1.2	1.0	0.8	0.7	0.5	0.5
Portugal	9.2	6.5	7.0	4.3	4.4	2.8	2.2	1.5
Greece	5.9	3.4	3.3	1.6	0.7	1.8	1.0	0.7
France	6.3	4.8	4.8	4.8	5.1	4.0	3.6	3.4
Italy	2.0	1.8	1.3	1.4	1.7	0.8	0.5	0.6

Source: CBMC.

Characteristics of the principal brewing countries

The characteristics of some of the major markets are now reviewed briefly.

Denmark

The Danish brewing industry is dominated by Carlsberg, which has a 71 per cent share of its home market and is a major global competitor, being, in 1994, the eighth largest brewer in the world. Its brand is the second most popular beer in Europe, selling almost 7 million hectolitres annually. Carlsberg's majority shareholder is a charitable trust.

There are 15 breweries in Denmark divided among 9 brewers. In 1989 a merger created the Brewing Group Denmark (BGD), making it the second largest brewer in Denmark, supplying roughly 15 per cent of the beer consumed there. However, a significant amount of their production is exported.

Danish brewers are also the largest producers of soft drinks in Denmark, with Carlsberg having a 50 per cent market share. This has been useful in gaining access, for beer, to channels of distribution.

Danish beer drinkers are by nature conservative. Most of the beer sold in Denmark is brewed domestically, and attempts to introduce foreign beer, even when brewed under licence in Denmark, have been unsuccessful.

A particular feature of the Danish beer market is the 'border trade' on the German–Danish border, where Danes cross to buy cheap beer. The price differential is principally due to differences in the rates of duty on alcohol between the two countries. The 'border trade' beer is likely to be supplied by Danish breweries to German retailers.

Border trade sales once contributed significantly to total sales and caused the Danish government to lose tax revenue. However, since Denmark joined the EU in 1993, the Danes have dramatically reduced duty on beers — by about 46 per cent — which has led to a reduction in the border trade in beer.

Roughly 70 per cent of beer is sold through retailers such as the supermarket chains. These are therefore extremely important customers of the brewing companies. The big supermarket chains have introduced their own beer brands, which are sold as cheap discount beers. These beers are also brewed by Danish brewers and are estimated to have 10–20 per cent of the market.

An important feature of the Danish beer market is the bottle reuse system. Beer and soft drinks must be sold in reusable bottles; cans are banned. It has been claimed that the bottle reuse system is a major barrier to foreign brewers entering the Danish market. With these barriers in mind, the ban on the use of cans was up for reconsideration in 1996, with the EU trying to balance environmental considerations with fair trade.

Holland

Holland is one of the world's largest producers of beer and has increasingly concentrated on exporting to overcome the lack of growth opportunities in its home market. Indeed, Holland is one of the largest exporting countries in the world for beer and the most international, exporting to 170 countries, principal of which is the USA, taking 37 per cent of Holland's beer exports in 1994. The proportion of its production exported has grown from 23.7 per cent in 1980 to 42.2 per cent in 1994, while imports remain relatively static at 4.1 per cent in 1994. Some 93 per cent of beer imports come from Belgium.

Like Denmark the brewing industry in Holland is dominated by one brewer, in this case Heineken, which is the largest brewer in Europe and the second largest in the world. Although Heineken only produces 6.7 million hectolitres of beer in Holland, it produces over 60 million hectolitres (1994 figures) worldwide.

Heineken also has ownership stakes in brewing companies in Spain, France, Italy, Greece, Holland, Hungary, Poland, Switzerland and Ireland, and has a licensing agreement with Whitbread in the UK to brew Heineken for sale there. Heineken is the largest imported beer brand in the USA, with 1.5–2 per cent of the total market.

Approximately 70 per cent of beer purchased in Holland is from the supermarket chains for consumption at home, making these retailers an important part of the distribution channel in Holland.

There are three mid-size Dutch brewing companies: Bavaria, Interbrew Netherland and Grolsch. Their sales, in millions of hectolitres, for 1993 were 3.4, 2.0 and 1.5 respectively. Grolsch, despite its relatively small output, has carved out a strong niche market position in many of the world's major beer markets.

Belgium

The Belgian brewing industry produces a large number of beers: 420 different brands of 18 different types. Belgian brewers claim that no other country offers such a wide variety.

Belgium is one of the world's leading exporters of beer. In 1994 it exported over 31 per cent of its production, almost all to other EU countries. The biggest export market was France, which took 63 per cent of Belgian exports. Imports account for less than 5 per cent of consumption and are in slow decline.

The Belgian beer industry is dominated by Interbrew and Alken-Maes. Between them they have approximately 85 per cent of the Belgian market. Interbrew was formed in 1986 by a merger between Artois and Piedboeuf, and now incorporates Lamot. The company is also a significant producer of soft drinks, owns production and bottling units in France, Italy and a number of African countries, and has licensing agreements in the UK and Canada and distribution companies in Holland, France, Italy and the USA.

Alken-Maes is 85 per cent owned by the French brewer Danone, having been created in 1988 by a merger of Alken Kronenbourg and Maes. It has subsidiaries in France, Italy, Spain and Holland, and a presence in many other markets. It has 20 per cent of the Belgian market.

Principal among the distribution channels in Belgium is the specialist dealer or 'negociant', who provides home delivery of beverages, operates beverage discount outlets, delivers to the hotels, restaurants, caf³s and bars and deals as a wholesaler.

The home delivery system is a typically Belgian approach to distribution and highlights the importance of drinking to the Belgian consumer. The growth in supermarkets which offer a wider range of beers at lower prices, and changes in lifestyle such as increased car ownership, rising real disposable income and more working women (who are therefore not available to take deliveries at home during the day) have led to the decline of the home delivery system in recent years.

By the 1990s there were around 1,000 discount outlets for beverages. These combined a large choice of products with a fast service and lower than average prices. The hotels, restaurants, caf³s and bars sector also represents a large part of the market. In this sector the negociant still plays a large role. It is estimates that 49% of beer sales are distributed through negociants, 27% through supermarkets and 6% through direct sales in caf³s and bars.

Italy

In Italy, beer became a popular drink only recently and Italy still has the lowest consumption per capita of all European countries. This consumption is concentrated in the north of the country. Traditionally, beer was produced with a low alcohol content and was seen as a refreshing drink, frequently accompanied by snacks, pizzas or fast food.

Because of their comparatively high alcohol content, imported beers were almost always classified as 'special' beers. However, recent EU legislation (a decree passed in 1992 defined what might constitute a beer) has led Italian brewers to raise the level of alcohol to the EU average, and this might change consumers' perceptions over time.

Beer imports have increased steadily for a number of years, reaching 20 per cent in 1992. This figure rises significantly when foreign beers brewed under licence in Italy are included. Principally imports come from Germany, Holland, Belgium and Denmark. Their products are seen as being of higher quality and constitute the upmarket segment of the market. Exports are negligible.

The main competitors and their domestic output in 1993 are shown in Table 11. Peroni is the largest brewery group in Italy and is 75 per cent owned by the Peroni family; the remaining 25 per cent is owned by Danone, the French brewer. It produces a wide range of beers and has a strong sales network, giving it national coverage. Dreher-Heineken is the second largest brewer in the country and is fully owned by the Heineken Group. Poretti is half owned by Carlsberg and half by Bassetti, and Italian group of

Table 11   Domestic output of main Italian beer producers, 1993 (million hectolitres)

Peroni	4.5
Dreher-Heineken	3.5
Poretti	1.4
Moretti	1.1

Source: BLRA.

companies. Moretti was formed when it and Prinz, another brewer, were bought and merged together by Labatts of Canada, which has now itself been bought by Interbrew of Belgium.

Distribution is similar to other European countries, with roughly 40–50 per cent being through hotels, restaurants, cafªs and bars. Supermarkets and hypermarkets take a further 20 per cent and traditional grocery outlets about 16 per cent. Door-to-door distribution is a small but growing channel. Traditionally used by wholesalers of soft drinks, in recent years this channel has extended its service to include beer. Only the supermarkets buy directly from the breweries.

France

Wine is the French national drink and, of the major European countries, consumption of beer is only lower in Italy. Despite this, Danone is the second largest brewing company in Europe and eighth largest in the world.

At the end of the Second World War, there were 1,000 breweries in France. Since then there has been considerable concentration. By the mid-1990s there were three main breweries and another two brewers which had production of around 1.3 million hectolitres. Additionally, France has approximately twenty smaller, specialist breweries. The main competitors and their domestic output in 1993 are shown in Table 12.

France is not a major exporter of beer. In 1994 it exported 6.3 per cent of its output, principally to its neighbours, Italy and Spain. In the same year, 17.3 per cent of its consumption was imported, principally from Belgium.

The brewing and drinking of beer in France is essentially a northern activity. Average consumption in the north is 80 litres per capita compared to the French national average of 41 litres.

Distribution patterns have remained static throughout the 1980s. Supermarkets and hypermarkets account for over 63 per cent, with hotels, restaurants and cafªs accounting for roughly 36 per cent. Breweries do not own bars or cafªs but will provide them with cheap finance deals in return for a contract to sell their beers for a fixed period of time, typically 5–10 years.

Table 12 Domestic output of main French beer producers, 1993 (million hectolitres)

Danone (Kronenbourg)	9.8
Brasserie Heineken	5.2
Interbrew France	2.2
Brasserie Fischer	1.3
Brasserie St Omer	1.3

The market is segmented similarly to other European countries, with light or low-alcohol beers, ordinary beers and stronger speciality beers. The low-alcohol and strong/speciality beers are the fastest-growing market segments in the 1990s.

The five countries already discussed, i.e. Denmark, Holland, Belgium, Italy, and France have much in common in their brewing industries. They have similar degrees of industry concentration and distribution systems. Spain, the United Kingdom and Germany exhibit considerably different characteristics from the first five.

Spain

The brewing industry in Spain is not dominated by any one company. The major brewing companies with their domestic output in 1993 and their ownership are shown in Table 13. There are three other small breweries with a local focus and small production outputs.

The Spanish market is regionally oriented with three very strong regional groups which have been able to develop strong production economies of scale and distribution power. These three are Cruzcampo, Mahou and Damm. Only San Miguel markets its brand successfully on a national scale at the moment, although this is expected to change as the international brewers take more interest in the Spanish market.

An interesting feature of the Spanish industry is the high degree of foreign ownership compared to other European countries (see Table 13), and there are also many licensing agreements to produce beer locally. For example, in 1995 Damm announced that it had signed an agreement with

Table 13 Domestic output of main Spanish beer producers, 1993 (million hectolitres) and their ownership

Cruzcampo	6.5	89% Guinness 11% Carlsberg
El Aguila	4.2	65% Heineken
Mahou	4.2	33% Danone
Damm	4.0	16% Oetker 5% San Miguel
San Miguel	3.5	Affiliated to San Miguel in the Philippines and 25% Danone

Anheuser-Busch to produce Budweiser beer for the national market. One explanation for this is that importation from any country other than France is difficult due to the distances involved. The Spanish market is not as well developed as other European markets, and Spanish consumption is almost entirely satisfied by domestic production. In 1994 Spain exported 1.4 per cent of its output and imported 7.7 per cent of its consumption.

It is only in recent years that the market segments well established in other European countries have begun to develop in Spain. There are three basic market segments — ordinary, special and strong beers. However, the consumers' perception of these segments can vary from region to region, so strong are the three regional brewers. The market is developing rapidly, forced mainly by the foreign brewers such as Carlsberg and Heineken through strong advertising and brand development campaigns. The 'new' market segments, i.e. special, strong and a small non-alcoholic segment, are the fastest growing.

Distribution in Spain is currently split 25 per cent through supermarkets and 75 per cent in caf³s, bars, hotels and restaurants. However, there is a definite move towards increased sales through supermarket grocery chains, as in the rest of Europe. This development has to do with the changing lifestyles of the Spanish. More of them are now buying beer in supermarkets for consumption at home. Packaging trends are also changing, from returnable bottles to non-returnable bottles and cans.

United Kingdom

In the UK there are three principal types of beer — lagers, ales and stouts. Lagers are served chilled, ales are brown in colour and are drunk at an ambient temperature, and stouts are heavy, dark-coloured beers, principal among which is Guinness. Most of the beer drunk in the UK is produced domestically, with imports standing at 8.7 per cent of consumption in 1994. In the same year, 5.3 per cent of output was exported.

In 1970, ales dominated the beer market, having an 85 per cent share. However, in the following two decades, lagers became increasingly popular, accounting for 55 per cent of the market in 1990. By 1993 their market share had declined to about 50 per cent as ales regained some of their popularity.

A growing trend is the increased sale of beer from grocery supermarket chains. Their share grew from 12 to 18 per cent during the 1980s and is predicted to be 25 per cent by the year 2000. Personal imports of beer from France are also increasing since the removal of trade barriers in 1993. The popularity of this cross-border trade is due to beer duty being seven times higher in the UK than in France. In 1994 personal imports of beer, principally from France, accounted for 16.5 per cent of the off-trade (take-home) market — approximately 4 per cent of total beer sales in that year.

In 1994 over two-thirds of beer sold was through on-trade licensed outlets, principal of which are the pubs. This figure shows a decline of about 5 per cent since 1989, due in part to off-trade prices being reduced and changing consumer lifestyles. Traditionally, the British brewing industry was highly vertically integrated, with brewers owning production and retailing facilities and even, in some cases, the sources of raw materials. In many independent pubs a supply agreement, known as a 'tie', existed. This meant that, in return for preferential loans, they would only sell beer provided by the brewer they were 'tied' to.

This level of integration changed dramatically after the Monopolies and Mergers Commission report into the industry in 1989. It concluded that a complex monopoly existed which restricted competition at all levels of the industry, and its findings led to brewers being restricted to owning no more than 2,000 pubs plus 50 per cent of their original holdings, the elimination of the loan tie arrangement and the enabling of pubs to buy at least one brand of beer from a brewer other than its usual supplier.

The report effectively forced brewers to decide between brewing or retailing activities, and the takeovers and asset swaps that followed have led to the UK brewing industry becoming increasingly concentrated in the 1990s. In 1990 Courage and Grand Metropolitan merged their brewing interests. Courage acquired Grandmet's breweries and concentrated on brewing. Grandmet focused on retailing and property management, acquiring Courage's pubs. In 1995 Courage was bought by Scottish and Newcastle, whose brewing division, now known as Scottish Courage, became the largest brewer in the UK. Another example of consolidation occurred in 1991 when Carlsberg (UK) combined with Allied Lyons in a 50/50 joint venture to form Carlsberg-Tetley, then the third largest UK brewer.

Despite a growing number of small regional breweries, which sell beer on a local basis, four large brewing companies had the majority of the market in 1995 (see Table 14).

In the UK, beer consumption is in long-term decline. Some 25 per cent of brewing capacity is in excess of demand. This has left some companies as uncertain holders of brewing or pub assets and the potential for further concentration within the industry. Allied Lyons, now known as Allied Domecq following the 1994 takeover of the world's biggest producer of

Table 14   Market share of the largest UK brewers, 1995

Brewer	Market share (%)
Scottish Courage	25
Bass	23
Carlsberg-Tetley	15
Whitbread	14

sherry, Pedro Domecq, decided to focus on spirits and in 1996 entered into negotiations with Bass concerning the sale of its 50 per cent share of Carlsberg-Tetley, a deal which would give Bass around 38 per cent of the UK market and leave Whitbread in a distant third place in terms of market share.

Germany

Germany is the largest beer-producing nation in Europe and has not experienced concentration of its brewing industry on the same scale as the rest of Europe. There are approximately 1,200 breweries in Germany, with 800 in Bavaria alone. The German brewing industry produces 5,000 different brands of beer, accounting for nearly half the world's total.

German drinkers are very conservative and loyal to their favourite beer, normally a beer brewed locally. Ninety per cent of breweries sell their products within a 30-mile radius. This is encouraged by the *Reinheitsgebot* or 'purity laws', which were first introduced in 1516. The law states that only malted cereals, hops, yeast and water can be used in the brewing process. Artificial additives are not allowed to improve quality or extend shelf life, thus clearly inhibiting imports or the transportation of local products over any significant distances.

In 1987 the European Court of Justice ruled that the *Reinheitsgebot* could not be used to prevent the sale of imported beers. Germany compromised, allowing beers with additives to be sold, but they had to be clearly labelled and could not be called beer. Despite this ruling, only a few foreign companies have entered the German market and imports are negligible, standing at 2.4 per cent of total consumption in 1994.

The proportion of beer production exported grew during the 1980s from 3.2 to 6.7 per cent. The principal countries exported to were the UK, France, Italy, Spain, Austria and Switzerland.

Another feature of the German brewing industry is the low profitability of the brewing companies. The margin is about 1 per cent, compared to approximately 10 per cent in the UK. This is another factor contributing to the low importation of beer brands.

Distribution channels have some similarities to the rest of Europe, but also some differences. The major similarity is that 60 per cent of beer sales are made through supermarkets for consumption in the home. The German brewers sell and deliver direct to the supermarket chains. It is estimated that 60 per cent of all beer sales across Europe are now made through supermarkets. The remaining 40 per cent of German beer sales are sold through cafés, bars, hotels and restaurants.

Where Germany differs from the rest of Europe, with the exception of the UK, is that about 22 per cent of cafés and bars are owned by the breweries. In addition, many cafés and bars that are not owned directly by the breweries have agreements with breweries to sell only their products in return for cheap loans. It is a strategy which helps breweries to maintain a strong hold in their local market place.

A description of major European brewers

Heineken

The Dutch brewer Heineken is essentially a family controlled business, with the family holding 51 per cent of its shares. With more than 90 breweries worldwide, Heineken is the second largest brewer in the world and the most international, with activities in every continent. It is possible to buy Heineken in 150 countries.

The main area of activity is Europe, where Heineken is the leading beer brand. It is also the biggest import beer brand in the United States — its biggest market outside Europe. Current estimates suggest that the USA accounts for 6 per cent of total production and 30 per cent of profits. In 1993 Heineken sold over 60 million hectolitres of beer worldwide.

Due to the small size of its home market, Heineken began international operations as early as 1928, although the major move towards internationalisation took place in the 1980s with a series of acquisitions in France, Spain, Italy and Greece. In the UK, Whitbread brews 2.6 million hectolitres of Heineken beer under licence. Heineken owns 1 per cent of Whitbread and has a seat on the board. The company's international brands are Heineken, Amstel, Buckler and Murphy's Irish Stout. They play a central role in the brand policy and are supported by a large number of national brands.

In eastern Europe, Heineken is developing activities to increase brand awareness and the distribution of Heineken beer. Despite the difficult economic situation during the early 1990s, Heineken exports show a sizeable growth, though the volumes are still modest. In 1994 Heineken bought a 25 per cent stake in the Polish brewer, Zywiec Brewing, to facilitate the introduction of Heineken in Poland, and increased its stake in the Hungarian brewer, Komaromi Sorgyar, from 55 to 100 per cent following considerable rises in its sales. Also in 1994, Heineken boosted its stake in El Aguila, the Spanish brewer, from 51 to 65 per cent. In 1995 Heineken bought Interbrew Italia, a subsidiary of the Belgian brewer Interbrew, which raised its share of the Italian beer market to 30 per cent. Heineken is also looking to expand its operations in the Far East and South America.

The financial history of Heineken between 1990 and 1995 is summarised in Table 15.

Table 15   Financial history of Heineken, 1990–5 (millions of guilders)

	1995	1994	1993	1992	1991	1990
Turnover	10,443	9,974	9,049	8,944	8,696	8,210
Operating profit	1,006	895	798	733	730	613
Net profit	664	662	519	463	410	366
Total assets	9,641	8,919	8,132	7,834	7,925	7,484

Note: Exchange rate, August 1996: £1 = 2.55 guilders.

Source: Company annual reports.

Carlsberg

Carlsberg is the second most international brewer in the world after Heineken, with operations in 38 countries selling more than 80 per cent of its beer outside its home market of Denmark.

Carlsberg sought international expansion for the same reasons as Heineken, i.e. the small size of its domestic market. In the UK Carlsberg-Tetley, the 50/50 joint venture with Allied Lyons, became operative at the turn of 1992/3 after a lengthy approval process by the British authorities and the European Commission. Carlsberg has a 5.6 per cent share of the UK market.

Carlsberg's most significant businesses outside Europe are in Hong Kong, where it has 15–17 per cent of the market, and Malaysia, where its share exceeds 50 per cent. Exposure is also strong in the remainder of the Far East, with further breweries soon to open in Thailand and China. Carlsberg brews about 0.5 million hectolitres in Africa.

The largest shareholder in the company is the Carlsberg Foundation, which is pledged to possess a minimum of 51 per cent of the shares. The Danish Labour Market Supplementary Pension Scheme accounts for more than 10 per cent of the shares and the Tuborg Foundation has 6 per cent.

The Carlsberg Foundation was established by Carlsberg's founder in 1876 and its income goes to support Danish natural and social sciences as well as the humanities. In 1991 the Carlsberg and Tuborg Foundations merged in order to improve Carlsberg's ability to raise new capital.

Carlsberg derives approximately 30 per cent of sales from non-beer-related activities. These include wines and spirits, soft drinks, supplying complete processing plants to the beverage and food industries, and Royal Copenhagen, which manufactures and sells porcelain, glassware, silverware and plastic and glass packaging.

The financial history of Carlsberg between 1990 and 1995 is summarised in Table 16.

Table 16   Financial history of Carlsberg, 1990–5 (millions of kroner)

	1994/5	1993/4	1992/3	1991/2	1990/1
Turnover	17,072	16,919	15,595	14,957	14,462
Operating profit	1,203	1,153	1,086	1,161	957
Net profit*	1,003	802	910	854	802
Total assets	18,599	18,018	17,798	14,921	13,108

* After minority shareholder's share of profit in subsidiaries.
Note: Exchange rate, August 1996: £1 = 8.88 kroner.

Source: Company annual reports.

Grolsch

Grolsch is a 'super premium' niche brewer, selling its Grolsch product in draught and in the very distinctive and identifiable swing-top resealable bottles in its primary market of north-west Europe. Grolsch is one of the leading brewing groups in Holland, where it has a market share of 17 per cent. In 1994 it was estimated to have produced 2.1 million hectolitres of beer. Its reputation for product differentiation was enhanced by the recent introduction of Grolsch Special Malt and Grolsch Meibok.

Grolsch began exporting in the mid-1970s for two reasons — the small size of the Dutch market and its dominance by Heineken. Exports increased from 14 per cent in 1985 to 31 per cent in 1989. However, export sales represent only 20 per cent of Grolsch's volume, showing the higher-price premium it can command in overseas markets.

Its principal foreign markets are the USA and the UK, estimated at 25 and 40 per cent of its export volume respectively, but it is available in a total of 35 markets worldwide. Duty-free sales are estimated to account for another 25 per cent of sales by volume.

In 1991 Grolsch acquired Germany's Rheinisch-Bergischen Brauerei, doubling its sales. However, this was sold on to the German brewer Bräu und Brunnen AG in 1994, which then signed a distribution agreement for Grolsch's products, giving Grolsch entry to 6,000 cafés across Germany.

In 1992 Grolsch purchased the Ruddles real ale brand and brewery from Courage for £40 million. The move was part of a strategy to create a 'Europe of Brands', as opposed to one pan-European brand, and to develop a strong north-west European brewing group.

In 1994 Grolsch set up a distribution joint venture with Bass, then the UK's largest brewer, to boost sales in Britain and Ireland. This gave Bass the right to produce Grolsch beer locally, although not in Grolsch's trademark swing-top bottles. The move was a departure for Grolsch, which

Table 17   Financial history of Grolsch, 1990–5 (millions of guilders)

	1995	1994	1993	1992	1991	1990
Turnover	630.5	554.1	793.5	866.7	791.5	793.5
Operating profit	88.4	80.2	65.6	64.3	55.7	48.9
Net profit	58.8	52.4	43.5	43.4	41.9	37.9
Total assets	545.4	523.7	675.6	635.4	704.1	430.4

Note: Exchange rate, August 1996: £1 = 2.55 guilders.

Source: Company annual reports.

had previously been keen to set itself apart in the UK by being a foreign-brewed beer. This venture, coupled with the Bräu und Brunnen distribution deal in Germany, was predicted to lead to significant improvement in the company's results. Its next marketing thrust will be to further its market penetration in southern and eastern Europe.

The first three brewing companies we have considered have beer as their principal activity. For the next two — Bass and Danone — beer is only a constituent part of a range of diverse activities. However, the brewing activities are significant on a European scale.

Bass

Bass is one of the leading brewing companies in Europe, and in 1994 had a market share of 23 per cent in the UK. Bass reorganised in 1989 to a divisional structure separating brewing and pub retailing, primarily to comply with the UK's Monopolies and Mergers Commission directives. There are now five divisions:

- Bass Brewers — which owns and markets a portfolio of brands of beer.
- Bass Taverns — the leading UK pub retailer with 4,200 outlets.
- Britvic Soft Drinks — a soft drinks company with brands such as Pepsi, Tango and 7-Up.
- Holiday Inn — the single largest hotel brand in the world, with more than 1,770 hotels and 338,000 guest rooms.
- Bass Leisure — one of the UK's leading leisure retailers, with bingo, betting and bowling operations.

Bass Brewers has strengthened its market share by targeting the fast-growing take-home sector in the UK, and by increasing sales to the free on-trade, including the emerging chains of pub multiples. In 1993 Bass successfully launched a number of new brands, including premium lagers such as TAG, Zeiss and Carling XD, an extra-dry bottled lager.

Table 18   Financial history of Bass, 1990–5 (£m)

	1995	1994	1993	1992	1991	1990
Turnover	4,541	4,452	4,451	4,307	4,383	4,461
of which:						
Brewing	1,251	1,295	1,202	1,191	1,056	929
Pub retailing	1,121	1,079	1,024	1,100	1,173	1,089
Operating profit	672	633	603	602	616	673
of which:						
Brewing	144	140	154	173	148	177
Pub retailing	240	220	205	218	238	245
Net profit	396	364	329	318	263	216
Total assets	3,697	3,582	3,413	3,343	3,622	2,935

Source: Company annual reports.

In the same year, Bass Brewers acquired a 34 per cent share in Prague Breweries, the second largest brewer in the Czech Republic, and increased its shareholding further in 1995 — a year which also saw the company take a majority stake in two further Czech brewers and the setting up of a brewing joint venture in northern China. Bass also took up its option to brew Grolsch in the UK, although the flip-top bottled version was still to be imported from Holland.

Its portfolio of alcoholic drinks was further extended with the introduction of Hoopers Hooch — an alcoholic lemonade drink which had immediate success in the UK market.

In early 1996, Bass entered into negotiations with Allied Domecq concerning the possible acquisition of the latter's 50 per cent stake in Carlsberg-Tetley. This deal which would give Bass around 38 per cent of the UK beer market and make it the largest brewer in the UK — a position lost when Scottish and Newcastle bought Courage in 1995.

The financial history of Bass between 1990 and 1995 is summarised in Table 18.

Danone Group

Danone changed its name from BSN in 1994 and is France's largest consumer product company and Europe's largest mineral water, dairy products, glass bottle and biscuit company, with significant positions in beer, pasta and champagne.

Danone's beer division accounted for only 9 per cent of the group's total sales in 1993. Total production was 26.7 million hectolitres in that year, placing it third in Europe after Heineken and Carlsberg and making it the eleventh largest brewer in the world.

Its principal brands are Kronenbourg, Kanterbräu, 1664 and Tourtel, a no-alcohol beer. Since the mid-1980s it has promoted these brands as pan-European. However, France remains the main area of operations, accounting for 46 per cent of group sales. Danone has almost a 50 per cent market share, double that of Heineken, its nearest rival. Its Kronenbourg and 1664 brands have benefited significantly from the trend towards premium beers. It has also been successful with its light beer, Kronenbourg Light, and Tourtel, its no-alcohol beer, which together now account for 400,000 hectolitres of production. In 1990 it introduced 1664 Brune, a dark beer to complement the traditional 'blond' 1664. The end of 1993 brought a string of new product launches, which included Kronenbourg Tradition Allemande, Kronenbourg Tradition Anglaise and Wel Scotch, the last based on whisky malt.

Danone brews approximately 16.5 million hectolitres outside France, principally in Italy, Spain, Belgium and Greece. In Italy it merged its interests with Peroni, giving it a share in 4.9 million hectolitres of production or nearly 40 per cent of the market. In Spain the company owns one-third of Mahou, which produced 4.2 million hectolitres in 1993 and has an efficient distribution system concentrating on the Madrid area. In Belgium it has an 85 per cent stake in Alken-Maes, which sells 1.2 million hectolitres. This is equivalent to a 17 per cent market share, in a market which is dominated by Interbrew with a 60 per cent share.

In 1989 Danone entered the Greek market with the acquisition of a 19 per cent stake in Northern Breweries, formerly known as Henninger Hellas. With 1.1 million hectolitres of production or a 27 per cent market share, Danone is well behind Heineken's share of 65 per cent. Northern has three

Table 19 Financial history of Danone, 1990–5 (millions of Ffr)

	1995	1994	1993	1992	1991	1990
Turnover	79,450	76,820	70,108	70,840	66,069	52,897
of which:						
Brewing	7,423	7,222	6,395	6,552	6,599	6,598
Operating profit	7,018	6,832	6,351	7,117	6,701	5,675
of which:						
Brewing	973	912	808	899	806	843
Net profit	2,133	3,527	3,422	3,638	3,445	3,091
Total assets	93,233	87,181	78,777	71,712	70,188	59,303

Note: Exchange rate, August 1996: £1 = Ffr7.74.

Source: Company annual reports.

breweries and some rationalisation may be needed. Danone's other major brewing business in Europe is the licence of the Kronenbourg brand to Courage in the UK, which in 1994 accounted for 700,000 hectolitres of production.

The financial history of Danone between 1990 and 1995 is summarised in Table 19.

Brasseries Kronenbourg

ROLAND CALORI and PHILIPPE MONIN

The company

In 1994 Kronenbourg SA was number two in the European beer market. Kronenbourg SA was the holding company of the beer division of the Groupe Danone, and Brasseries Kronenbourg was the main department of the beer division based in Alsace, a region with a strong brewing tradition.

Brasseries Kronenbourg had been formed from the merger of Kronenbourg and Kanterbräu, two companies acquired by the BSN Group (the former name of Danone) in the 1970s. By 1986 the two firms shared their production units, functional departments (human resources, administration and finance) and top management. In 1994 the two marketing departments and sales forces were merged, and Brasseries Kronenbourg produced and marketed a unified set of 28 brands.

By 1994 Brasseries Kronenbourg had a strong leadership position in the French market, with over 40 per cent market share. The number two was Brasseries Heineken with 23.1 per cent; third was the Belgian Interbrew-Stella with 8.3 per cent; and number four was Fischer (a French independent firm) with 7.7 per cent of the market (19 other brewers shared the rest of the market).

In 1994 the French market represented 22.7 million hectolitres, including 1.5 million hectolitres bought by British citizens crossing the Channel to buy cheaper beer in France and on the cross-Channel ferries (due to lower taxation). According to the Nielsen panel, such cross-border trade was increasing (it was estimated at around 0.8 million hectolitres in 1993), while French consumption was decreasing (21.9 million hectolitres in 1993, 21.2 million hectolitres in 1994).

This case study was prepared by Roland Calori and Philippe Monin, professors at the Groupe ESC Lyon. The authors would like to thank the Brasseries Kronenbourg for their assistance in the writing of this case study. It is intended as a basis for class discussion and not as an illustration of either good or bad management practice. © R. Calori and P. Monin, 1996.

Kronenbourg beer was also produced under licence in the UK and in Ireland, although production under licence in Africa (about 1 million hectolitres in Congo and Nigeria) ceased in 1994. Through Kronenbourg SA, Danone was also represented in several other European markets and its beer brands were distributed in 80 countries in the world. In 1994, the volume sold by the breweries in which Danone had dominant or significant stakes was around 26 million hectolitres.

The turnover and sales volumes of Brasseries Kronenbourg itself are shown in Tables 1 and 2. In France the original brands from Kronenbourg represented about two-thirds of sales and those from Kanterbräu about one third.

At the beginning of the 1990s, some of the foreign breweries controlled by Danone started to brew locally the international brands of Brasseries

Table 1   Kronenbourg SA: balance sheets and statements of income (simplified)

(Simplified) balance sheets (Ffr000)

	1994	1993	1992
Assets			
Net property plant, equipment and intangible assets	1,885,533	1,899,148	1,971,609
Financial assets	2,727,774	2,632,093	2,350,600
Current assets	1,795,484	1,689,190	1,677,479
Miscellaneous	7,568	12,131	15,422
Total assets	6,416,359	6,232,562	6,015,110
Liabilities			
Equity	2,103,721	2,126,514	2,085,827
Provisions	101,982	136,690	199,031
Debts	4,087,379	3,856,620	3,627,541
Miscellaneous	123,277	112,738	102,711
Total liabilities	6,416,359	6,232,562	6,015,110

(Simplified) statements of income (Ffr000)

	1994	1993	1992
Net sales	5,709,108	5,838,607	5,926,784
Operating costs and expenses	4,814,146	5,029,719	5,111,258
Operating profit*	894,962	808,888	815,526
Net profits	496,038	456,898	428,942

* Before financial revenues and expenses, before extraordinary items and before income tax.

Source: Annual reports, 1993, 1994.

Table 2   Volumes sold by Brasseries Kronenbourg and other companies under control of Kronenbourg SA (hectolitres, beer)

	1994	1993	1990
Brasseries Kronenbourg			
France	9,733,000	9,838,000	10,698,000
(incl. Kronenbourg)		(6,400,000)	(6,769,000)
(incl. Kanterbraü)		(3,438,000)	(3,929,000)
Direct export sales*	541,000	510,000	873,541
Total	10,274,000	10,348,000	11,571,541
Production under licence abroad	766,000	1,095,000	1,030,000
	(UK and Ireland)	(UK, Ireland and Nigeria)	(UK and Nigeria)
Subsidiaries and companies in which Kronenbourg was a significant stakeholder			
Alken-Maes (Belgium)	2,167,000	2,010,000	2,377,000
Peroni (Italy)	4,549,000	4,522,000	5,369,000
Mahou (Spain)	4,366,000	4,196,000	4,316,000
San Miguel (Spain)	3,516,000	3,527,000	–
Northern Breweries (Greece)	520,000	491,000	617,000
Congolaise de Brasseries		577,000	368,000
Total	15,118,000	15,323,000	13,047,000

* Including Switzerland: 110,000 hl; Spain: 10,000 hl; Germany: 6,000 hl; Belgium: 5,000 hl; USA: 5,000 hl, etc.

Sources: Annual reports, 1990, 1993, 1994.

Kronenbourg: for instance, Tourtel and Kronenbourg were brewed in Italy and in Spain (by San Miguel) and 1664 was brewed locally in Italy. (This evolution explains the decrease of direct export sales as compared to 1990.) The Kronenbourg 1664 upmarket beer and Tourtel (a non-alcoholic beer) were particularly successful. However, during this period, the market share of Kronenbourg SA in France decreased slightly (from 43.5 per cent to 42.9 per cent), whereas the share of private labels increased, particularly in the mass market. Indeed, all the major beer brands suffered from the growing power of food retail chains.

In 1994 Brasseries Kronenbourg invested Ffr292 million in industrial plant and equipment to modernise production sites, improve productivity and launch new packaging. Financial investment amounted to Ffr292.6 million in 1993, in order to increase the shares of the group in the companies under its control and to take over wholesalers. In 1994 the holding company of the beer division started to increase its shares in the Spanish brewery San Miguel, so as to hold 100 per cent of the equity by the end of 1997 (i.e. a financial investment of Ffr2 billion in four years 1994–7). By completing this acquisition, Danone (which already had a minority stake in Mahou) will become the leader on the Spanish beer market. At the end of 1994 some important commercial investments were made in order to merge the sales forces of Kanterbräu and Kronenbourg and sell a unified product range. (Table 4 presents an overview of brands in each market segment.)

Kronenbourg, the beer division and the Danone Group

BSN (the former name of the Danone Group) was primarily a glass manufacturer when it acquired Kronenbourg in 1970. The BSN Group then began a radical diversification from glass making to the food and drinks industries. In 1973 it acquired Gervais Danone, a major dairy products business, followed by other food companies. From Ffr300 million in 1966, the turnover of the group went up to about Ffr53 billion in 1990, and Ffr76.82 billion in 1994 (packaging representing 8.1 per cent). Table 3 breaks down the sales turnover and the operating income of the Danone Group by division and geographical zone.

The goal of Antoine Riboud, président directeur général of the group, was to become the leader or the number two in each area of business, first at the European level, then at the world level. The stated strategy of Danone was:

- to strengthen the leadership in Europe in growth business (such as *plats cuisinés*);
- to accelerate international extension;
- to innovate and strengthen the corporate image.

At the end of 1990, Danone sold its champagne business, Lanson and Pommery, to LVMH for Ffr3.1 billion in order to focus on the businesses in which leadership or number two positions could be reached. By 1995 Danone was the third leading food marketer in Europe, challenging Nestlé and Unilever. It was also the world's largest seller of dairy products (under the Danone brand and with Galbani Italian cheeses); the second in the world for mineral waters (Evian, Volvic, Badoit, Lanjaron), pasta sales (Panzani) and biscuits (Lu, Jacob's, leader in Europe and in Asia); the leader in Europe in sauces and condiments (Amora, Maille); the number two in Europe in the beer industry and in the glass packaging business (bottles and pots); and the number three in Europe in *plats cuisinés* (Vivagel).

Danone was the biggest food marketer in France, in Italy and in Spain, and the number six worldwide. The international division (i.e. outside Europe, cf. Table 3) included businesses and exports in Asia, Oceania, America and Africa which represented about 10 per cent of the total sales turnover in 1994 and showed high growth potential.

Between January 1993 and June 1995, Danone acquired a number of food and drink concerns worldwide. The most significant acquisitions included:

Table 3 Sales turnover and operating income, Danone Group (1992–4), by division and by geographical zone (Ffr000,000)

	Sales turnover			Operating profits		
	1994	**1993**	**1992**	**1994**	**1993**	**1992**
Europe						
• Dairy products	22,624	22,067	23,041	2,181	2,123	2,412
• Epicerie, pasta	14,689	13,142	13,081	940	970	1,027
• Biscuits	12,837	12,949	13,457	807	862	1,126
• Beer	7,222	6,395	6,552	912	808	899
• Mineral waters	7,000	5,898	5,716	1,060	955	898
• Packaging	6,368	6,663	7,046	624	556	730
Total Europe	70,740	67,114	68,893	6,524	6,224	7,092
International	7,804	4,608	3,605	387	180	111
Internal sales	(1,724)	(1,614)	(1,658)			
Other profits				(79)	(103)	(86)
Group total	76,820	70,108	70,840	6,832	6,351	7,117

Bagley (biscuits, Argentina), Campineira de Alimentos (biscuits, Brazil), Vivagel (*plats cuisinés*, France), Serdika (joint venture, dairy products, Bulgaria), Keletpest BTV (dairy products, Hungary), Bolshevik (biscuits, Russia), Britannia Group (biscuits, Asia), Aquaterra (mineral waters, Canada), Bonafont (mineral waters, Mexico), San Miguel (beer, Spain), Aguas de Lanjaron (mineral waters, Spain), Volvic (mineral waters, France), Deslile (dairy products, Canada) and Jiangmen (biscuits, China). Franchise agreements were also signed in Malaysia and Singapore in order to develop the Danone brand locally.

1994 was the year when the group changed its name to Danone: 'Our image will benefit from the influence of our most global brand, a symbol of quality, innovation, taste and health' (Antoine Riboud, Assemblée Générale Ordinaire, July 1994).

Belonging to a large, diversified group meant shared responsibilities between the headquarters and the companies. Antoine Riboud explained the relationships in *Le Figaro* (9 September 1991):

> You have to limit the number of hierarchical levels, avoid complicated procedures, avoid barriers to the free circulation of information, cash flow and people. You have to delegate operational decisions. At BSN [Danone] the managers of divisions and departments are free with regard to the management of operations, but each one knows his limits. On the other hand, strategy must be centralised, it is the responsibility of the 'Premier Rond' of BSN [Danone].

The 'Premier Rond' of Danone consisted of Antoine Riboud (président), the vice-president and chief executive (Franck Riboud) and three vice-chief executives. The 'Deuxième Rond' consisted of the managers of the product divisions (among whom was the manager of the beer division), three regional managers (Asia, America-Africa-Oceania and exportation), and two functional managers (finance and human relations). The 'Troisième Rond' included 86 general managers of the departments and of the subsidiaries of the group, among them the managing director of Brasseries Kronenbourg.

Each year, the managing director of each department/company in the group presented the previous year's results and the future scenarios for the company to the Premier Rond. The Premier Rond responded with general objectives for the coming year. It was then the responsibility of the manager of the corresponding division to monitor the achievement of the objectives of the department. The headquarters left the managing directors of departments/companies free to manage their businesses, as long as the objectives were achieved. In the beer division, Brasseries Kronenbourg in France, Alken-Maes in Belgium, and Mahou and San Miguel in Spain were four departments. The participations in Peroni (Italy) and Northern Breweries (Greece) were managed directly by the director of the beer division.

Even the companies in which Danone did not have a dominant financial stake participated in the Danone planning system. The division level helped in restructuring companies joining the group when needed, and was also in charge of transferring skills between the departments.

In 1994 Danone employed 68,181 persons. The management style of the group, personified by Antoine Riboud, also influenced Kronenbourg. The cornerstone of this philosophy was a double economic and social intent: *Pas d'économie sans social, pas de social sans économie.* Indeed, the group won the Palme d'Or for the best corporate institutional image among managers in an Ipsos-L'Expansion study conducted in 1990 in France. 'Dialogue' at work and with strong unions, 'participation of the personnel in the profits of the firm' and 'mutual support' were the key characteristics of the management at Danone.

The strategy of Brasseries Kronenbourg

The top management of Brasseries Kronenbourg saw brewing as a 'heavy industry' with the emphasis on the capacity of production units and increasing capital intensity due to the development of automatic processing. They therefore believed that there were three key success factors for the business:

- Managing the high level of investments with a tight control of the debt/equity ratio.
- The achievements of economies of scale — the high level of fixed costs required a focus on lower production costs through larger units to cover bigger geographical areas (up to 1,000 km for mass-market beer).
- Improvements in productivity and quality through effective human resource management to keep up with new techniques (e.g. automation and quality control).

The management of inventories and production planning were also seen as critical functions, as beer consumption was seasonal, especially in southern Europe.

Compared to many other food-processing businesses, the beer industry dealt with two distinct distribution channels: cafés and restaurants; and food retailing for home consumption. Each distribution channel required a specific approach.

The food channel was taking an increasing share of the market: 58 per cent in 1990 and 62.8 per cent in 1994, 70 per cent of which was through the major retail chains. Dealing with the food channel, especially with large retail chains, demanded both high expenditure and management skills in advertising and merchandising. Brasseries Kronenbourg had strengthened partnerships by developing a merchandising system, called 'Pluton', that improved the presentation of beers and adapted it to each retail chain, each region and each season.

Selling to cafés, hotels and restaurants (37.2 per cent of the French market in 1994) required investment in the place of consumption, and long-term contracts were concluded with cafés. This channel offered higher margins and an opportunity to advertise beer brands — the main opportunity in France since the *Loi Evin* forbade advertising of alcoholic drinks in most other places. The distribution to the 150,000 sales points was done by wholesalers (*entrepositaires*), a profession which had undergone a high concentration (about 1,000 wholesalers in 1994 compared to 2,000 in 1985). In order to strengthen their positions and increase their market share, Kronenbourg and other brewers had started to develop downstream activities in wholesaling. For instance, in its division France Boissons, Heineken had a particularly strong distribution network of 35 wholesaling subsidiaries and 70 warehouses. Merging the sales forces and commercial assets of Kronenbourg and Kanterbräu contributed to a better positioning of brands and a more effective distribution in the traditional channel. Since 1993, through a wholly owned subsidiary, Elidis, Brasseries Kronenbourg had acquired 60 warehouses (half of which were wholly owned). In 1994 Elidis distributed about 20 per cent of the volumes sold to cafés and restaurants. Elidis and France Boissons had a reciprocal distribution agreement of their respective ranges of bottled beer, in order to complement their coverage of the French territory.

In both channels the image of the product and the brand name were viewed as key success factors, and marketing skills and financial support were seen as critical to strengthen and expand the brand image. Finally, in order to grow in a mature market and to cover the company's high fixed costs, international development was considered crucial.

Productivity, quality and human resource development

One of the objectives of Brasseries Kronenbourg was to be among the best brewers in the world in terms of productivity; this was vital given overcapacity of around 30 per cent in the industry. High investments in automation were made during the 1980s. Between 1989 and 1991 a *restructuration* plan was implemented to improve productivity. Staffing levels were reduced by 570 jobs during this period,[1] mostly by voluntary departures (an agreement was signed between the top management and the unions to organise the re-employment of the workers).

---

[1] In 1994 Brasseries Kronenbourg employed 2,127 persons (53 per cent in production; 30 per cent technicians, supervisors and administrative staff; and 17 per cent managers).

The number of hierarchical levels was also reduced. At the same time, professional development was strengthened, and Brasseries Kronenbourg became involved in an extensive qualification and apprenticeship programme for young people. Personnel training represented 3.5 per cent of the wages, and the company distributed Ffr130 million to the personnel *au titre de la participation des salariés aux fruits de l'expansion* (shares) in 1994.

Marketing, innovation and image

The company strategy was to develop several brands, to address all the market segments according to quality and alcohol levels.

1. *Bières de luxe* for the mass market represented 64 per cent of the total French market (branded beers 39 per cent and lower-priced products and beer sold under retailers' names about 25 per cent).[2] Brasseries Kronenbourg dominated this segment in France, with two labels: Kronenbourg and Kanterbräu (which amounted to 70.9 per cent of the sales turnover of the company in 1994). The main competitor was the 33 Export from Heineken. However, the competition from lower-priced retail private labels at one end and from upmarket *bières spéciales* at the other end was increasing. Brasseries Kronenbourg responded by launching new products and labels such as Kronenbourg Tradition Allemande, Kronenbourg Tradition Anglaise, 'K' and new packaging. Brasseries Kronenbourg also brewed beer for a major French retail chain (about 600,000 hectolitres a year) selling under private label.

   According to the top management of Brasseries Kronenbourg, there was a particular phenomenon in the brewing industry: a beer positioned in the mass market in its country of origin tended to become an upmarket beer in the foreign countries to which it was exported. For instance, Heineken was seen as a *bière spéciale* in France (competing with Kronenbourg's 1664), and Kronenbourg was seen as an upmarket beer in several foreign countries. Actually the differences between the two products (in terms of taste and quality) were minimal.

2. Upmarket beers, *spéciales* and *spécialités*, together represented 21 per cent of the French market (of which about two-thirds were *spéciales* and one-third *spécialités*), and 21.7 per cent of the sales turnover of Brasseries Kronenbourg in 1994. The company had two *bières spéciales* — 1664 from Kronenbourg and Gold from Kanterbräu — and imported Carlsberg in France. *Spécialités*, even further upmarket, included beers

---

[2] Percentages are estimations of volumes sold.

with higher levels of alcohol and premium imported foreign beers. The demand for *spécialités* was growing rapidly. Brasseries Kronenbourg distributed some Belgian beers produced by Alken-Maes — Blanche de Bruges, Mort Subite and Grimbergen. It also imported Guinness stouts and Kilkenny, and launched a new product in 1994: Wel Scotch (a whisky malt beer). Kronenbourg 1664 was seen as a premium beer in foreign countries.

3. Non-alcoholic beer had developed rapidly in Europe in the late 1980s, but by 1994 it had reached maturity, representing 5 per cent of the market. Brasseries Kronenbourg was the leader in France, Belgium and Italy with its brands Tourtel (originally from Kanterbräu, with sales of around 1 million hectolitres) and Silver (originally from Kronenbourg, launched in 1991). This segment was characterised by being more international or pan-European, and Brasseries Kronenbourg competed with the Buckler brand from Heineken.

4. Low alcoholic beer or 'light beer' represented about 5 per cent of the market. Brasseries Kronenbourg had two brands: Kronenbourg Light and Obernai.

5. *Panachés* were a mix of beer and lemonade, and they represented about 5 per cent of the French market. Brasseries Kronenbourg had two brands — Force 4 and Chopp, competing with Panach from Heineken.

Non-alcoholic beer, light beer and panachés amounted to 7.4 per cent of the sales turnover of Brasseries Kronenbourg in 1994. Table 4 summarises the main products and brands of the company.

Product innovation was seen as important in Brasseries Kronenbourg. Tourtel was the first non-alcoholic beer launched in the European market, and Kanterbräu was the first to expand the range of non-alcoholic beers to dark beer with Tourtel Brune (1989), Tourtel Ambrée (1990) and Tourtel 100% pure malt (1994). In 1993 and 1994 Brasseries Kronenbourg launched several new products in order to 'de-banalise' beer in the French mass market: Kronenbourg brewed in the German tradition, Kronenbourg brewed in the English tradition, and Christmas beer. These were followed in 1995 by a non-bitter beer called 'K' (Mexican style).

Innovations in packaging were also seen as important. For instance, Kronenbourg had won an award for packaging with its 'prestige' bottle for cafés and restaurants — thin, with angles and an encrusted label, and preserving the brilliance of the glass after several uses. It had also equipped its bottles of 1664 with a label that changed colour when the optimal consumption temperature was reached. Moreover, it adopted a variety of presentations (bottles and packaging) for the French market and for the international market. This policy was supported by the links with the packaging division of the Danone Group.

Table 4 Main product lines and brands of the Brasseries Kronenbourg

Main product lines and brands sold on the French market

Segments	Brands	
Bières de luxe (mass market)	Kronenbourg K Kronenbourg Tradition Anglaise Kronenbourg Tradition Allemande	Kanterbräu
Bières spéciales	1664 Blonde 1664 Brune	Gold
Spécialités	Blanche de Bruges	Grimbergen Mort Subite Wel Scotch
Non-alcoholic beer	Silver	Tourtel
Light beer	Kronenbourg Light Obernai	
Panachés	Force 4 Force 4 lemon	Chopp
Other imported beers	Carlsberg (spéciale) Guinness (spécialité) Kilkenny (spécialité)	

Main products/brands sold on foreign markets
by direct exportation or through the foreign companies controlled by the group

Segments	Brands
Spéciale Spécialité Non-alcoholic beer	Kronenbourg (Kronenbourg) 1664 Tourtel

From 1993 in France, the *Loi Evin* limited advertising of alcoholic drinks, TV advertising was forbidden, radio advertising was restricted to a few hours a day, press advertising was only permitted in magazines for adults, and street advertising was forbidden in many areas. Most of the other markets in Europe had less strict limitations. As a consequence, Brasseries Kronenbourg strengthened the promotion of its products in the cafés, and developed sponsoring to support its non-alcoholic brands (Tourtel and Force 4) with two main partners, the Paris Saint Germain and the Strasbourg football teams. The advertising campaigns for these products were based on conviviality. The concern for ecological issues also contributed to the company's image: 80 per cent of the bottles were made of recycled glass and Kronenbourg had the world record for low water consumption.

The international strategy of Brasseries Kronenbourg and the beer division of Danone

Given high relative costs of transportation and logistics and high marketing expenses, the geographical scope of the market was seen as limited around a production unit. The case of upmarket beers (at the top of the pyramid) was different: the higher margins of the premium products would cover the costs of distribution logistics and marketing. So Brasseries Kronenbourg started to export its premium products in the 1960s, selling to local importers and distributors, complementing their range of drinks to be sold mainly in the cafés, hotels and restaurants. This export mode was still employed in 1990 in the case of more distant foreign countries such as Japan, Hong Kong, Australia, Canada and Sweden.

However, this strategy would not lead to high volume, and volume sales required a significant position in a foreign market, a broader range of products, including lower-priced beers, and therefore higher costs of distribution and marketing. Given the overcapacity in the beer industry, the executives from Brasseries Kronenbourg believed that partnerships and acquisitions were the best way quickly to achieve a significant position in a foreign market.

As far as licences were concerned, Brasseries Kronenbourg had established a position in the United Kingdom by entering into a production agreement with Courage when the British market started to consume more and more continental/international lagers and reduce its consumption of traditional ale. The volumes of Kro 1664, a specific beer for the British market, increased to 766,000 hectolitres in 1994.

This strategy of entering into partnerships with other strong local breweries was also employed in Italy, Belgium, Spain and Greece. Several criteria were considered to select the priority countries for international development:

- A permeable upmarket segment.
- Growing demand for beer.
- Signs that the competitive structure of the industry might be beginning to concentrate.

The Mediterranean countries were typically in this situation at the end of the 1970s, and it was regarded as a priority to establish a position in these countries before international competitors did so.

The selection of the brands that Brasseries Kronenbourg would make international was based on the success of the brand in its home market. The leading brands in France were selected: namely, Kronenbourg (including 1664) and Tourtel. Selectivity was crucial because it was recognised that developing an international brand would require very high marketing investments. The formula applied to dealing with the product range overseas was to keep the strongest local brands of the partner (or the acquired company), but to add the Kronenbourg, 1664 and Tourtel brands from Brasseries Kronenbourg to the product range of the local partner, positioning them as upmarket beers.

In Italy, Kronenbourg SA first took control of Wührer, which had a 10 per cent market share and was particularly well established in the north of Italy. However, Peroni was the market leader and well established in the south. BSN arranged the merger of Wührer and Peroni, Kronenbourg SA having a 25 per cent stake in the company. Between 1991 and 1994 the Italian market stagnated (with good years and bad years). Peroni maintained its leadership position with a 40 per cent market share, sales around 4.5 million hectolitres a year, and a turnover around 470 billion lire. In 1994 Peroni sold four main brands: Peroni (mass-market), Nastro Azzuro (an Italian premium beer), Kronenbourg (with increasing sales) and Tourtel (the leading brand among non-alcoholic beers). By 1995 the Italian market had become very competitive, and large European brewers were involved in negotiations to strengthen their positions. For instance, Heineken increased its market share from 23 per cent to 30 per cent by taking over the Italian subsidiary of Interbrew.

The market in Belgium was nearly as big as the Italian market, due to a high consumption of beer per capita, but it was slowly decreasing. Kronenbourg SA first took control of Alken and of Anglo Belge, which together held 10 per cent of the market. Then, in 1988, a joint venture with Maes gave a 25 per cent share of the market to Alken-Maes, in which Kronenbourg SA had 50 per cent of the capital. In 1993 Kronenbourg SA increased its participation to 84.7 per cent. Interbrew (created after the merger of Stella Artois and Jupiter) was the leader in Belgium with a 50 per cent market share. Alken-Maes was number two with sales of 2.2 million hectolitres and a turnover of Bfr6,086 million in 1994. The company had a broad portfolio of brands: Maes on the mass market, Tourtel, and many Belgian specialities such as Blanche de Bruges, Grimbergen, Gueuze and Krick Mort Subite, Cristal, and Cuvée l'Ermitage. Exports of these *spécialités* were rapidly growing (18 per cent in 1994).

Spanish consumption had regularly increased by 3–4 per cent a year in the 1980s. From 72 litres per person per year in 1989, experts forecasted consumption of 100 litres per person per year by the end of the century. Actually, the consumption stopped growing at the beginning of the 1990s. Several major European competitors had taken over Spanish breweries and brands. Heineken was number three with its subsidiary El Aguila (17.3 per cent market share in 1993). Guinness was number two with its wholly owned subsidiary, Cruzcampo, acquired in 1991 (25.1 per cent market share in 1993). Kronenbourg SA first acquired 33 per cent of the capital of Mahou in 1988. As Mahou did not accept distribution of the international brands of Brasseries Kronenbourg in Spain, the company had to continue parallel distribution through a sales subsidiary. In 1992 Kronenbourg SA acquired 24.6 per cent of the capital of San Miguel, and started to distribute Kronenbourg and Tourtel with this partner. In 1994 the Danone Group announced that San Miguel would become a wholly owned subsidiary by 1997. Mahou had an 18 per cent market share in 1994, a brand new brewery and growing sales: 4.4 million hectolitres, 46 billion pesetas (a 10 per cent increase compared to 1993). San Miguel produced 3.5 million hectolitres in 1994 and its sales turnover amounted to 33.5 billion pesetas. With Mahou and San Miguel, Danone became the leader on the Spanish market with a 33 per cent share.

In 1989 Kronenbourg SA acquired 80.3 per cent of the equity of Henninger Hellas, the number two Greek brewery. Sales decreased during the commercial and industrial restructuring of the company, but started to grow when the Kronenbourg and Tourtel brands were introduced beside the Henninger. In 1992 Kronenbourg SA reduced its participation to 19.6 per cent of the capital when the Greek Boutari Group (involved in wholesaling) became a partner and acquired 67 per cent of Henninger Hellas. The company sold 520,000 hectolitres in 1994 (about 12 per cent of the Greek market) and started to export to Albania. In 1995 its name was changed to Northern Breweries. In Greece the leader was Heineken with its subsidiary, Athenian Brewery, having a 77 per cent market share.

With strong bases in southern Europe, Kronenbourg therefore planned to develop both local brands and the international brands of Brasseries Kronenbourg.

Acquisitions strategy

Acquisitions were prepared and implemented at the level of the beer division. The decision was shared between the Premier Rond and the Deuxième Rond of the Danone Group.

A constant effort was made to rationalise the industrial process. Before each acquisition, the specialists from Danone analysed the commercial value of the potential acquisition (brands, market shares, distribution network); but they also analysed the potential productivity gains after integration into the Danone industrial network.

The beer division would transfer skills in R&D, production and marketing, and if necessary help the restructuring of the company.

Brasseries Kronenbourg could also play a role in the process of international acquisitions and joint developments: by signalling opportunities to the beer division, by providing cash and by transferring its distinctive skills.

Brasseries Kronenbourg also retained marketing control over its international brands which were distributed by Alken-Maes, Peroni, San Miguel and Henninger. European marketing co-ordination functions were established at Brasseries Kronenbourg — one for Kronenbourg and one for Tourtel — in order to support the international development of these brands. However, the packaging of Kronenbourg, 1664 and Tourtel on foreign markets was slightly different from the packaging of these products in France, and pricing policy was different between countries for a given product.

The future

It was the view of the top management of Kronenbourg that, considering the positions taken by major brewers such as Heineken, Kronenbourg and to a lesser degree Interbrew and Carlsberg, and considering the constraints of anti-monopoly institutions, it would be hard for any major brewer to achieve any new significant acquisition in the EU. The major uncertainties concerned the British and German brewing industries, the latter still highly fragmented and with customers having a preference for local German brands.

The executives of Brasseries Kronenbourg believed that it was too early to try to move into the German market. It was impossible then to find a partner at a national level. In order to take a significant share, a foreign brewer would have had to take over several breweries, manage the diversity of the resulting product range and probably close some of the breweries. The idea was to let the Germans first restructure their industry. However, the German market was so large (about 119 million hectolitres in 1994) that several competitors had reached a significant scale. Bräu und Brunnen produced 14 million hectolitres a year (with the following brands: Brinkoff, Schlösser, Küppers, Henninger, Jever and Eichbaum), Binding produced 8.8 million hectolitres a year (DAB, Berliner, Kindl and Radebergen) and Holsten produced 6.6 million hectolitres.

The 57 million hectolitre British market was slowly declining. The British brewing industry was in the process of restructuring, with a vertical split between brewing and retailing (imposed by the Monopolies and Mergers Commission in the early 1990s) and large scale takeovers followed by capacity reductions.

Kronenbourg believed that the European single market would not bring radical changes, especially for the major brewers already established in several countries. However, the pricing policy would probably have to change between countries. The level of taxes (excise duties and VAT) were very different across Europe (for instance, high in the UK and low in France), and the same brand was often positioned differently in different countries. With customers travelling more and more across borders and comparing prices and quality, with the expected progressive harmonisation of taxes and duties across European countries, and with the free circulation of goods, international breweries were pushed to harmonise their prices across Europe, generally at a lower level. International logistics and co-ordination of marketing across Europe seemed to become crucial.

At the beginning of 1995 some major competitors increased their worldwide ambitions. Miller, the US-based number three brewer in the world (part of the Philip Morris Group) showed interest in an alliance with Heineken. Heineken preferred independence and continued to push its global product and spend fortunes on advertising (about three times as much as their competitors). Interbrew (previously number four in Europe) acquired the Canadian brewer Labatt for US$2 billion, to create the world's fourth largest brewing group.

When presenting the annual report of the Danone Group in June 1995, Antoine Riboud declared:

> Danone is now based on three main activities: dairy products, mineral waters and biscuits ... In the future the expansion of beer will be decided step by step. (*Les Echos*, 8 June 1995)

The Brewery Group Denmark: Faxe, Ceres and Thor

FLEMMING AGERSNAP

> It is better to be dominant in a small niche than to be a marginal supplier in a big market.　　　　　　　　　　　Claus Nielsen, international sales director, BGD

Denmark is a beer-drinking country with a long tradition of brewing beer. The Danish brewing industry is dominated by the Carlsberg Group, holding a market share of 70–75 per cent and a worldwide position with sales and production in many countries.

In the Danish market there are four midsize breweries and a number of smaller ones competing with Carlsberg. In 1989 two of the midsize breweries merged their brewing activities into a joint venture 'Bryggerigruppen', The Brewery Group Denmark (BGD). This made it the second largest brewer in Denmark and was the background to significant international expansion.

Brewery Group Denmark (BGD), Faxe, Ceres and Thor

Together BGD supplies about 15 per cent of the beer consumed in Denmark, although its share varies within the various Danish regions. Located in Aarhus, Jutland, Ceres has had a strong market position there for many years and over the last 30 years it has merged with breweries in neighbouring towns. One of these breweries was the Thor brewery in Randers. In 1996, Thor had a strong position in the northern part of Jutland. Located on Zealand, Faxe has only a small local market, but it had long been an important supplier to restaurants and retailers in Copenhagen.

At an early stage, both Ceres and Faxe felt a need for growth in order to obtain sufficient volume gains in production and subsequent reductions in costs. They first expanded in the domestic market to become national

This case study was prepared by Flemming Agersnap, Copenhagen Business School. It is intended as a basis for class discussion and not as an illustration of either good or bad management practice. © Flemming Agersnap, 1996.

Exhibit 1   Financial statistics for BGD, 1989–95

	1995	1994	1992	1990	1989
Turnover (mill. DKK)	2.274	2.204	1.977	1.607	1.624
Export share (%)	59	59	52	51	43
Profit before tax (mill. DKK)	103	93	46	16	−19
Return on equity (after tax) (%)	18	18	12	7	−8
Number of employees	1,089	1,005	1,039	824	930

distributors, but any substantial growth could be obtained only through exports.

Exhibit 1 shows the financial data for the years after the establishment of the joint venture.

Organisation and management

Exhibit 2 shows the organisation structure of BGD. After the merger in 1989, the positions of chief executive officer and of international sales director were filled with people without previous experience of breweries. Claus

Exhibit 2   Organisation diagram (simplified)

Nielsen came with a background from the international pharmaceutical industry. Hiring a manager from outside also solved the problem of choosing a candidate from one of the two existing sales organisations.

BGD was formed as a limited company, where the Faxe and the Ceres companies each owned 49 per cent and their common bank 2 per cent. All beer and soft drinks activities were transferred to BGD. The parent companies also had a few other small activities besides BGD. Both companies were listed separately on the Copenhagen Stock Exchange. The Faxe brewery had a controlling capital owned by the founding family, whereas the Ceres company had no such controlling shareholder group. Carlsberg owned 38 per cent of the predominantly non-voting B-shares of Ceres, but without a seat on the board of the company. Carlsberg declared that it had no wish for a more active role in the management of Ceres or BGD, rather its involvement was said to be an investment for financial reasons. Others argued that the investment could be seen as a defensive investment guarding against a foreign acquisition of Ceres.

International development

Despite the dominance of Carlsberg, in its annual report BGD could lay claim to being the largest Scandinavian beer exporter. This was because Carlsberg placed emphasis on licensing agreements or local production for its foreign markets, while BGD's strategy was export led: 'Eighty-three out of every hundred bottles of beer that we produce are sold in foreign markets.' By 1995 the percentage of export sales by region of the world was as follows: western Europe 63 per cent, the Americas 10 per cent, eastern Europe 22 per cent, others 5 per cent. The development of BGD's operations in some of these markets is now reviewed.

Italy

More than 30 years ago, Ceres entered into co-operation with a slaughterhouse for pork (Tulip) in a neighbouring Jutland town. This slaughterhouse specialised in select meat cuts and canned meat for different markets. The co-operation led to export to Italy based on the transportation of meat and beers in refrigerated vans. Ceres joined this co-operative venture at the invitation of the slaughterhouse, but in 1996 beer export accounted for 75 per cent of turnover and more than 95 per cent of profit — and the joint sales company in Italy had been bought fully by BGD, though still acting as agent for the slaughterhouse.

Claus Nielsen commented:

We are the largest exporter of beer to Italy and dominate the 'duplomolto' [strong beer] segment. Our success has been largely due to our marketing strategy. For the last 30 years we have been concentrating on the on-licence trade — restaurants, discos, bars and so on. We have achieved a very strong position in such outlets, which has given us a strong brand presence in Italy. In these outlets we have strongly promoted our bottled Ceres brand at point of sale. We would prefer people who go to restaurants and discos to be holding our bottle with our brand name on than drinking draught beer out of a glass without a brand name on it. In the last ten years we have also started to develop our presence in the off-licence retail trade — the shops selling beer. As in so many markets, the retailers have become more powerful, but a good indication of our brand strength is that we are able to resist the pressure they put on us for increased discounts. If they want to press us for such discounts, we simply refuse. They can delist us if they like, but they have to come back again because of the strength of the brand.

The Italian culture also helps us. Most young men do not get married until they are about 30 and live at home until then. This means that there is a great deal of disposable income for men in their early 20s; and they spend a lot of money in restaurants, discos and bars, where we are strongly represented. They also prefer our brand, which is a premium, strong beer. The trend in Italy away from wine drinking has also helped us. It has become less common to drink wine heavily at lunch, for example. But Italians do like to have a drink and our beer is a good deal stronger than Italian beer. So they can feel good about not drinking wine, but drink a couple of Ceres instead. It looks better, but has much the same effect.

The Ceres concept in export markets such as Italy has been to emphasise the origin of the beer, that the beer is imported, and to emphasise premium and strong lager beers.

The Caribbean

Ceres also found and developed a market in the Caribbean islands for malt beer. A Ceres manager on vacation in the Caribbean observed that some of the locals were drinking a rather distinct type of beer, dark and sweet. When it was analysed back at the brewery, it turned out that the beer was very much like Danish malt beer, an almost non-alcoholic beer. Exports started and a market niche was developed in that region.

The product, Vitamalt, is rich in vitamins B and D and proteins. Claus Nielsen explained:

In the Caribbean you have two markets for beer: those who drink alcoholic beer and those who do not drink alcohol at all. Our market is for the non-alcoholic market — people who do not drink because of their religious beliefs, as well as a significant percentage of women and children too. The product is also believed by some to have aphrodisiac properties.

In a few markets in the Caribbean, local production is beneficial because of high import duties, and Heineken produce Vitamalt in the Bahamas under licence. However, Vitamalt became so successful that both Heineken and Guinness approached BGD with a view to licensing the product for production elsewhere in the Caribbean.

In fact, Vitamalt has a market not only in the Caribbean, but also in many other parts of the world where there are people of Caribbean origin. Sales are high in London, Amsterdam and Paris, for example.

Germany

On the border between Germany and Denmark, a special border trade has developed, since Danes can avoid paying the high Danish duty on beer by purchasing it in Germany. At times this trade has accounted for approximately 10 per cent of Danish beer consumption. Ceres has dominated the border market.

Before the joint venture, Faxe also developed a market in the wider Germany for canned beer. In the 1970s Faxe bought tapping equipment for canned beer; for environmental reasons, canned beer was not allowed to be sold in Denmark, but it is accepted in Germany. And canned beer is especially suitable for supermarket chains. This development (plus bottled beers) created a comparatively strong position for Faxe in the German market — considering the low level of German imports of beer. Its beers were sold partly in ordinary retail shops and supermarkets, but increasingly also in restaurants.

The Baltic states

The changed political and economic situation in the former Communist bloc has opened up many sales opportunities. Following the break-up of the Soviet bloc, the Baltic states of Estonia, Latvia and Lithuania wished to become more closely linked to other Nordic states, a move encouraged by the governments of the Nordic countries. Trade delegations were organised from Denmark, and BGD took part in the first of these. 'We realised all the breweries were worn out and the quality of the beer was poor, but the population liked beer.' As a result, BGD appointed two distributors in Lithuania.

> We often appoint two distributors when we start up in a country to see which will be most successful. Here we agreed that both could import the Faxe brand and compete in Lithuania; one would also export to Latvia and the other to Estonia. It has been very successful. Unfortunately we also found that a good deal of the product was crossing the border into Russia, and we got complaints from our Russian distributors about this. We have to change the contract with our distributors in the Baltic states to prevent exporting Faxe to Russia. What we did

was to provide them with another brand each, providing they did not export Faxe to Russia. They also have the right to export the other brand to Russia.

Elsewhere in western Europe

In 1993 BGD bought a small British brewery, Cain's, located in Liverpool, England, and with an established local market. Besides involving a transfer of brewing technology, the acquisition of Cain's brewery opened up more possibilities for pub sales of BGD beers in that region, though still as imported beer. Similarly, Cain's traditional English beer was introduced into Denmark and other European countries as a supplement to the BGD range.

There are also markets for beers in Holland, Belgium, Austria and Switzerland. Yet, as Claus Nielsen said, 'Why bother when we know we won't get any result?' These beer markets are very competitive, but also stagnating. He continued:

> We were about to move into Spain, but I said: Stop, Stop. Look how much the others have invested. Carlsberg has lost 500 mill. DKK. Heineken and all the other big ones are there. Why enter that fight? Why not look to the nice neighbouring country, Portugal, where imported beers account for less than 1 per cent of beer consumption? They are an extraordinarily kind and pleasant people to work with. Let us focus on these 10 million people and try to gain a foothold there. So we were established there before anybody else with imported beer.

Brazil

A fast-growing market for BGD is Brazil. Traditionally, the Brazilian market has been protected by high import duty, varying from 8 to 60 per cent depending on the economic situation of the country. Furthermore, the Brazilian government has been very restrictive and avoided foreign capital. Big Brazilian breweries took advantage of the situation and set very high prices. But partly as a consequence of the GATT negotiations and partly to counteract inflation, the Brazilian government planned to open the country for imports. The entrance of American and European breweries into the market led to a price reduction of about 80 per cent. Claus Nielsen explained:

> There was an opening coming up and I could see there was an undersupply. We took the step with imported beer before anybody else and were successful. It was a combination of timing, of finding the right partner and of the change in regulations.
>
> We thought of using our Caribbean concept, malt beers, since the northern parts of Brazil resemble the Caribbean climate and population. However, a closer study and an awareness of the culture of Brazilian society led us to act differently.

Brazil is a multiethnic country, although many Brazilians get angry and agitated when one wants to distinguish between the European and African parts of the population. Such distinctions do not exist for the Brazilians. Now I have been there several times and differences do exist. For me it was like walking around in Africa and in the ethnic parts of London and Paris. Those who understand and adapt to the differences will obtain benefits in this market. And that is what we have done. So in the end we have emphasised a European approach — also because of the partner we found.

We were very lucky with the partner we found. Cafe Bom Dia is a company with a distribution network covering all relevant segments of the market. It is a modern coffee roaster with ISO 9000 certification of quality; the biggest in Brazil. They have a distribution network covering coffee shops and supermarkets and delivery to 90,000 restaurants. And today our beers are placed on their vans.

They know — or we tell them — that if they choose Heineken or Carlsberg, these breweries in a few years' time will start local production and take over the distribution. The big ones enter as 'big brothers'. They chose us — we have been very lucky and the sales volume is growing rapidly.

There is also a benefit with regard to the cost of distribution. They are one of Brazil's biggest coffee exporters and we have arranged to use their empty containers to ship product into Brazil at a lower cost than we would normally incur.

I have never — like other breweries — entered a market together with other breweries, not even local ones, in a joint operation. It may give an easy start if the partner has the set-up, knows how to distribute the beer — and has the same target group. But one only gets the share of the market the partner allows one to get. I want to find a partner where we complement each other instead of competing. It can be a soft drinks distributor — or a coffee distributor. In India we will enter a contract with the biggest tea distributor.

Russia

By 1996 BGD was also operating in Russia.

The Russian market is huge and the demand for beer very high; but there had been no investment in the breweries and they produced very low-quality beer. In 1993 we began with a number of distributors in order to handle the problems of distribution. However, eventually it became clear there were two performing really well and we were approached by both of them for sole distribution rights. Given the way in which business is done in Russia, this is not a straightforward matter. We eventually decided on one distributor who is also a major distributor of other food products to cash 'n' carries and small shops in the cities. It also has associates who can handle distribution elsewhere in Russia; and it is a very sophisticated operation in terms of the education of their management and their computer and distribution systems. It is proving to be immensely successful: for example, we have 80 per cent retail penetration in Moscow. Russia is now our biggest export market, in terms of volume.

Initially we found problems because of transport costs to Russia. There was one major container distributor from Denmark who quoted extremely high costs of distribution. We overcame this in a rather novel way. We decided in the summer to ship our products direct to Moscow by river using barges with loads of 2 to 6 million bottles. Keeping transport costs down in beer distribution is extremely important.

China

The Chinese market for beer is growing at around 10–20 per cent per annum, and Claus Nielsen sees it as one of the most attractive markets for the future.

> It is of course a huge market, but we had to be very clear about our positioning. Most of the people in China are not that wealthy, but there is a percentage of the population which is. China has become one of the largest markets for Rolex watches, Mercedes cars and French XO Cognac. We decided to position Faxe as a premium product and target geographic regions where there was high disposable income. Our distribution strategy was also important. Most western companies have tended to go through Hong Kong, where they can find English-speaking distributors. But of course it adds to costs of distribution. We wanted to export to China direct. Most organisations we contacted wanted a joint venture arrangement for manufacturing and the building of a brewery. This is of course not our strategy; we only deal with export beer, so we were not prepared to do this. We spent three years finding the right distributor and eventually did so. It is a government-owned organisation, regionally structured, selling mainly liquor and tobacco, but not beer until now, to tax-free shops throughout China. We began in September 1995 and we are doing well. We also distribute Ceres through the more traditional route via a Hong Kong distributor.

The marketing concept

BGD did not intend to compete directly with the big international breweries on their major markets, with standard-type beers. It looked for niches for special forms of distribution or special products. The core of BGD's international marketing concept has been to emphasise that its beers are *imported*. There was no local production of its brands outside Denmark and its beers are alike in all countries. As Claus Nielsen says: 'The big breweries adapt their brands to the various markets. Let them have these markets. If we are to get any distinction, it must be tied to the fact that our beer is always the same Danish beer.'

So BGD emphasised the development of its sales organisation in the various markets more than price and production costs. In this way, its beers could be seen as competing more with beers like the Dutch Grolsch beer than with widely sold beers from, for example, Heineken or Carlsberg. The consumer might think of the beer as something to be chosen for a special occasion and not as a daily standard product.

The types of customer and the consumption patterns of the standard beers and of special beers were quite different. Although in a specific country the market for expensive imported beer might be small, it could be an attractive size for BGD. Furthermore, imported beers were acquiring an increasing market share worldwide, even though by 1996 they exceeded 10 per cent of the total market in only a few countries.

BGD in Denmark

Like Carlsberg (and Tuborg), BGD had a wide assortment of beers, ranging from non-alcoholic beers and ordinary beers to premium beers and strong beers. Alongside their traditional beers the two breweries introduced a number of specialities, such as Dortmunder beer (Ceres), draught beer in cans or special bottles (Faxe), and Christmas and Easter beers. BGD had not produced and sold discount beers to the big retail chains.

In the Danish market, Faxe had intended to launch draft beer in cans. When distribution in cans was banned, Faxe launched draft beer in special dark bottles with a different shape than ordinary beers. The dark brown colour of the bottles was necessary because the draft beer was more sensitive to sunlight than ordinary beers. It was a success at the time, since many smaller restaurants and bars did not have beer-tapping equipment. Gradually the price on this equipment has fallen and many restaurants and bars have got beer taps, so this special market has almost vanished.

In 1996 the ban on canned beer was up for reconsideration. The EU understood the environmental reasons behind the ban. However, in Sweden, canned beer has been allowed provided there is a 'pawn' on each can which is refunded when the empty can is returned. This system, which is similar to the present Danish one for bottles, ensures that the cans are recycled. It is actively debated whether, by such a system, cans represent a heavier burden on the environment than bottles. The cans have a high return rate (to cash the pawn) and are reused through a melting process. The bottles are directly reused, but the washing of the bottles requires many chemicals and considerable amounts of water.

The major reason that the EU wanted the ban lifted was that it is seen as a trade barrier. It is difficult for a foreign brewery to tap beer in the special Danish bottles and to handle the bottle return system. If the ban is lifted, canned beers are expected to account for only about 10 per cent of the market. But it would be far easier for a German brewery to enter this market niche.

In the Danish market, BGD also sells a number of soft drinks, some under its own brands and others under licence to tap and sell, such as Pepsi Cola and 7-Up.

International management

With so many international opportunities to consider, Claus Nielsen commented:

> I have a well-functioning organisation with seven regional managers and their staff and the most efficient shipping/transportation department in Denmark, exporting more than 15,000 containers a year. I only want to expand at the pace of adding a new colleague each year. He or she has a chance really to get versed in the job and to get attention from the organisation. Then soon they may get their own independent area of responsibility. So physically we cannot enter all the potential markets, not even all the promising ones. We must focus on some and leave the others till we have the organisation to enter them. We aim at structured and well-studied approaches, but sometimes it is incidental information that tells us where the best potentials surface.
>
> I like to run a very flat structure. The regional executives have total operating control over their regions. It is my job to set up new businesses around the world — I spent a lot of time in China in 1995, for example — and deal with overall strategy, price setting and yearly budgets. They then run the businesses. It does mean a lot of travel; I try to visit all major markets at least once a year. In 1995 I spent 150 days out of Denmark.

Managing the BGD joint venture

The joint venture mainly had an impact on the organisation of sales and distribution, but not on production. In the domestic market, a number of depots were merged and considerable cost savings achieved. In the international markets where Faxe had a significant export market Ceres was virtually absent and vice versa. Faxe was positioned in one way and Ceres in another, so they complemented each other without overlap. The success was evident. In 1989 exports were 514 mill. DKK and in 1995 1,522 mill. DKK.

Although the sales organisation became fully merged, the production units remained separate according to the old company structures, with breweries in the towns of Faxe, Ceres and Thor, and brands exclusively brewed where they were first introduced. This was said to be necessary due to special requirements as to water and yeast as well as local knowledge of the brewing processes.

> Just for fun we have tried to let the Ceres people brew some Faxe beer. It didn't taste the same. Similarly, Faxe people have tried to make Ceres Dortmunder. It didn't work either. We do not want any risk of mixing of the yeasts, so they are kept apart. The water supply is also very different. Carlsberg has a brewery in Copenhagen and one in Fredericia, Jutland, where they brew the same beer brands, but experienced brewers can tell where one of these beers is brewed.

The absence of merged activity in production was also attributed to the existing cultures and loyalties among managers and workers. Traditionally, the two breweries have been staffed at the top levels by 'brewers' — people with a pharmaceutical, chemical or engineering background at university and later trained within the trade and with formal education from the special advanced Scandinavian Brewing High School. This tradition had created a high professional standard and intimate knowledge of the trade, but had also meant a certain level of closure to other forms of training and experience form other consumer goods industries. Similarly, the experienced brewery workers had developed a competence in, for example, adjusting the beer taste and a strong attachment to the specific brewery.

This has meant that the brewers have emphasised their wish to have full discretion in running a brewery and have been reluctant to consider more integrated operations. However, the expansion in sales volume required the full use of capacity, utilising established production patterns.

Laura Ashley Holdings plc

JOHN L. HEATH

Introduction

In the spring of 1996 Laura Ashley's shareholders began to believe, at long last, that better times really were on the way. The group had paid only nominal dividends since 1989 and had survived a cash crisis in 1990 and several years of indifferent performance and recovery attempts since then. Shareholders looked back on the company's heady successes of the 1980s and wondered what had gone wrong. How was it that the distinctive strengths on which the group's fortunes had been built were unable to sustain it in the 1990s?

Now, however, there were encouraging signs. Since Ann Iverson's appointment as chief executive in June 1995 the share price had doubled, and when results for the year to January 1996 were released in April it was clear that the turnaround she had instituted was already bearing fruit. The group announced a return to profit and the first dividend payment for six years. Pre-tax profit of £10.3m was the highest since 1989 and a strong turnaround from the £30.6m loss in the previous year.

Early history

In 1953 Bernard and Laura Ashley started printing tea towels and scarves to their own design in their flat in Pimlico, London. The success of these designs led the Ashleys to form their first company, Ashley, Mountney Ltd in 1954.

In 1960 the Ashleys decided to move their expanding business to Wales, where Laura Ashley was born and where in 1966 Laura Ashley designed her first clothing items, two apron dresses. These were not originally intended as fashion items but proved to be of profound significance to the subsequent development of the group. Encouraged by their success the Ashleys opened the first Laura Ashley retail shop in London, in 1968, and the subsequent growth and development of the group stems from this move into direct retailing. Within two years the group was concentrating primarily on producing goods for sale in its own shops. The basic structure of Laura Ashley as a vertically integrated business embracing design, fabric printing, clothing manufacture and retailing was thus established.

Laura Ashley's design philosophy, deeply rooted in traditional English country values, was the foundation for the group's designs. She created and trained teams of designers to develop her work. Laura Ashley died following an accident in September 1985, and although her death was a severe blow to the company, her design concepts had been thoroughly absorbed and understood throughout the group.

By 1985 the group's product range embraced both clothing and home furnishings, and as a vertically integrated group Laura Ashley manufactured around 85 per cent by value of these products itself. Clothing and home furnishing products were supplied directly to each shop in the United Kingdom, principally by the group's own vehicles, supplemented in continental Europe by arrangements with local carriers. Clothing for North America was dispatched weekly by airfreight to each shop.

A vital element in the group's organisation was its major commitment to information technology in all areas of its operations. By 1985 its three main computer centres — in Carno (Wales), Helmond (Netherlands) and Mahwah (New Jersey, USA) — were all linked through a communications network. Its IT capability was regarded by management as a crucial element in the effectiveness of the group's vertically integrated structure.

Laura Ashley shops were designed to create the same look and atmosphere throughout the world and played an important part in projecting the image of Laura Ashley. In its shops the group was an early adopter of electronic point of sale (EPOS) systems, whereby sales figures from each shop were analysed daily by product line.

The complementary talents of the Ashleys — Laura's design flair and Bernard's business acumen and interest in fabrics printing — had by 1985 transformed a cottage industry into an international group with 219 shops in Europe, the United States and the Pacific Basin, and worldwide sales exceeded £100m. Laura Ashley became a public company in November 1985. It was floated on the stock market to a rapturous City, and such was the enthusiasm for the company that the offer was oversubscribed 34 times. The flotation valued the Ashley family's 70 per cent stake at £292m.

Although the share offer was widely endorsed by the business press as an attractive investment, there were some notes of caution amid the general euphoria:

Although storming ahead in the USA, European performance is at best luke-warm. Mrs Ashley's death will be a severe loss.

Expansion in Europe, notably France, has not been a success.

Does a mish-mash of designing, manufacturing and retailing warrant a premium store rating?

International development

Acquisition

In 1986 the group began a series of acquisitions with the purchase of Sandringham Leather Goods Ltd of Llanidloes and Bryant of Scotland Ltd, a high-quality knitwear company. In August 1987, Willis and Geiger, a traditional outdoor clothing specialist with both wholesale and retail businesses in the USA, was acquired for $3m. In November, Penhaligons Ltd, an old established perfumery business offering an exclusive range of gentlemen's fragrances from five distinctive shops in London, was acquired for £1m. It was intended to develop the Penhaligon range of products and extend its business internationally. Since 1979 the group had also produced its own unique range of women's fragrances through its Swiss-based subsidiary, Parfums Laura Ashley. The group intended to extend the product ranges and shop openings of its acquisitions in their base countries and later internationally.

In March 1989 the purchase of Revman Industries Inc., a US home furnishings marketing company, was announced. The company was established as an important source of quality designer bedlinen selling to major department stores, specialist chains and catalogue houses across the United States.

Manufacturing investment

In August 1985 work commenced on a new 135,000 sq. ft textile factory in Wales. The following year work began on a new vinyl wallpaper plant on an adjacent site. These facilities represented an investment of some £7.5m, a significant part of the cost of which was offset by a grant from the Development Board of Rural Wales.

In 1987 a £1.3m computer-aided design system was installed in the textile design studios at Newtown, and in the following year a computerised garment-cutting room was opened at Carno at a cost of £1.7m. Other investments in manufacturing included a £670,000 computerised handling system for the Newtown garment factory. This was designed to reduce garment throughput times from several days to a few hours, and thereby allow more rapid response to retail demand.

1988 reorganisation

Early in 1988 the group was restructured into seven divisions in order to facilitate its growth over the next five years. Each division had a managing director separately accountable to the main board for his division's profit performance. The reorganisation was reported to reflect, in part, the group's decision to break away from the vertically integrated structure that had been a distinctive feature of the Laura Ashley organisation almost since its inception.

The new divisions were as follows:

- *Laura Ashley Group Services*, responsible for finance, legal work, informatics and strategic planning.
- *Laura Ashley Brand Management Group*, responsible for design, sourcing, image protection and licensing.
- *Laura Ashley Industries*, responsible for textile, wallpaper, and garment manufacture and distribution, together with leather goods and knitwear subsidiaries.
- *Laura Ashley UK Retail*, responsible for retail operations in the UK.
- *Laura Ashley BV*, responsible for retail operations in continental Europe.
- *Laura Ashley Inc.*, responsible for retail operations in the USA and Canada.
- *Laura Ashley Pacific Basin*, responsible for retail operations in Australia and Japan.

Major cost-cutting, restructuring and quality improvement initiatives were introduced within Industries Division as the group gradually reduced its dependence on its own manufacturing activities. Whereas around 85 per cent of products sold in 1985 were manufactured in-house, by 1988 this was down to 60 per cent and falling.

Retail developments

In 1987 the group took a 'major step towards segmentation' with the opening of six Laura Ashley Mother & Child shops in the USA. These sold a co-ordinated range of clothes and bedroom furnishing products for babies and children up to 12, and dresses for their mothers. Mother & Child collections were also launched in the UK and continental Europe the following year.

In 1989, 'Laura Ashley Home' shops were launched to sell a wider range of home furnishings than was available in existing Laura Ashley outlets. The range featured Laura Ashley designed furniture carrying the Laura Ashley brand name, but manufactured outside the group. This, together with the home furnishing range, offered customers a complete Laura Ashley lifestyle package.

Also in 1989 Laura Ashley opened the first of 50 'Units' shops it planned to open in the UK by 1992. These stores were operated under licence from a subsidiary of the J.C. Penney retailing group, and offered a range of unsophisticated women's knitted clothing items which could be co-ordinated into several different garments.

In the UK and Ireland, the number of Laura Ashley outlets increased from 87 in 1986 to 182 by early 1991. UK turnover over this period rose from £56.4m to £143.6m. An enlarged Mail Order Centre was opened in Newtown in December 1987. Mail order sales grew steadily over the period, increasing by 50 per cent in 1988, 45 per cent in 1989 and 40 per cent in 1990 to overtake the turnover performance of Laura Ashley's most successful UK store.

Laura Ashley's international expansion continued and by early 1991 there were over 500 outlets worldwide. Expansion in continental Europe, primarily through shop-in-shops, was slow at first but gathered pace towards the end of the period. In North America, garments and home furnishing sales accounted for 70 and 30 per cent respectively of 1990/1 turnover of £136.2m. In the Pacific Basin, Laura Ashley's principal markets were Australia and Japan. The number of outlets in Japan doubled from 12 to 24 in the year to January 1990, a further 13 were opened by January 1991 and 12 more were planned for the following year.

Retrenchment

By the end of the 1980s, Britain's economy was causing increasing concern in government and business circles alike. British business was bracing itself for a difficult start to the 1990s. High interest rates, combined with new restrictions on mortgage interest tax relief, brought a virtual standstill in the housing market. There were serious knock-on effects in the construction industry, and in home furnishing and home improvements markets. Sterling was under almost constant attack on foreign exchanges.

Among the casualties of the recession were a number of well-known competitors of Laura Ashley. At Next, the retail group that George Davies had made a high street star, many of the group's acquisitions were sold to reduce its debts and in December 1988 Davies was ousted. At Coloroll profits slumped and in March 1990 chairman John Ashcroft resigned. November saw Sir Ralph Halpern's departure from the Burton Group after a 39 per cent fall in profits.

Difficult times at Laura Ashley

In the year to January 1989, Laura Ashley reported its first fall in profits, down to £20.26m from the previous year's figure of £23.08m. This was blamed on a £1m start-up loss at Willis & Geiger, higher interest charges, and the strength of sterling. Chief executive John James said that, in spite of the exchange rate problems, the company had adopted an expansionist policy in the USA, which it saw as its biggest potential market.

For the year to January 1990, the group reported a net loss of £4.7m before tax, despite sales increases across all divisions. Sir Bernard Ashley acknowledged the need to reduce the group's high borrowing levels and in response a major rationalisation programme was set in motion. This, he warned, might include disposals of businesses and restrictions on new shop openings. Among the exceptional costs for the year were management consultants' fees of £1.5m. Press comment on the group's losses highlighted a series of problems: in particular, severe production difficulties, especially over supplies to the USA. 'The 1989 autumn range arrived three months late in the shops long after everyone's thoughts had turned to spring.'[1]

Some commentators wondered whether Laura Ashley was becoming dated. 'What has happened is that the typical buyer has simply grown up. Laura Ashley has failed to provide for the more discerning sophisticated 30-plus consumers — who don't want their homes or their clothes to evoke the design team of a chain store.'[2]

In June 1990 difficult refinancing negotiations were concluded and the company agreed to recruit two new non-executive directors and strengthen its top management. John James acknowledged that the company had been overstretching its executive talent. For more than a year, to May 1990, the group had been without a finance director, and Mr James had covered this responsibility in addition to his role as chief executive. His long association with the group ended with his resignation on 1 September 1990. Press reports suggested that John James's attempts to reorganise the group had been hindered by the company's somewhat insular family culture and a very conservative board. The Ashley family's 70 per cent stake in the company led one writer to comment, 'the upheavals at Laura Ashley must make investors wonder whether companies should ever be floated with such dominant shareholdings'.[3]

At the end of August 1990 the Aeon Group, Laura Ashley's partner in Japan, acquired a 15 per cent stake in the group in return for a cash injection of £39m. As part of the deal, Aeon secured exclusive rights to both sales and manufacture of Laura Ashley goods throughout Asia. The Aeon

[1] *Sunday Times*, 4/2/90.
[2] Quoted in the *Sunday Times*, 4/2/90.
[3] *Independent*, 25/8/90.

deal reduced Laura Ashley's gearing from 100 per cent plus to 30 per cent and Ashley family holdings fell to 59.2 per cent. Sir Bernard said he would allow his stake to fall below 50 per cent in the future as the company expanded. In September closure of seven UK factories was announced. 'It is no longer viable to source current levels of garments worldwide from our British factories when products of a similar quality can be bought at significantly lower cost from suppliers abroad,' said Sir Bernard.

The 1991 Report and Accounts highlighted actions taken to strengthen the group's financial position. Central controls over profit and cash management were implemented and new policies were introduced on capital expenditure and investment appraisal. A stringent stock control programme was implemented to reduce lead times, eliminate buffer stock and dispose of slow-selling lines. During the year net borrowings were reduced from £87m to £23m, and stocks from £105m to £40m.

Businesses that were not core to the Laura Ashley brand were closed or divested, including Penhaligon's, Bryant of Scotland and Sandringham Leather Goods. A programme to improve relations with the City, investors and the financial press was instigated to develop a better understanding of the company's plans and actions.

1991 reorganisation

In his 1991 report, Sir Bernard highlighted the international brand name 'Laura Ashley' as the company's most valuable asset, and in order to develop and exploit the brand more effectively worldwide, a new corporate structure was put into place with effect from February 1991.

> The Group Marketing Division is responsible for all aspects of marketing the brand, and for designing and sourcing products to satisfy consumer expectations.
>
> The UK and Continental Europe Retail Divisions have been amalgamated with the objective of obtaining synergies from shared marketing and a reduction of overheads. The intention is to retain regional marketing focus. The retail divisions use their knowledge and experience of their own markets to maximise opportunities for Laura Ashley branded products.
>
> The Group Operations Division is responsible for co-ordinating the logistical aspects of the business, moving product from the suppliers into retail and other distribution outlets. It accommodates the in-house manufacturing facilities which now comprise the print factories in Newtown, the Welsh-based garment operation (4 factories) and one home furnishing factory.

Chief executive officer

| Group Marketing | European Retail | North American Retail | Group Operations | Finance |

New leadership

In July 1991 the company announced the appointment of a new group chief executive, Dr Jim Maxmin aged 48, to take effect from 16 September 1991.

Jim Maxmin was born in the United States and lived in the UK from 1964 to 1988. After completing a PhD in Philosophy at King's College, London, he joined Unilever plc, working primarily in marketing roles. In 1971 he joined Lex Service Group plc, rising to chief executive and joint chairman of Volvo Concessionaires UK by 1979. In 1983 he moved to Thorn-EMI as chief executive of television rentals. In 1988 he moved to Boston to oversee the acquisition of Rent-a-Center Inc. and was also appointed president of Thorn-EMI Inc.

Taking stock

The new CEO's first few weeks were spent visiting Laura Ashley stores, manufacturing units and offices around the world. This confirmed to Jim Maxmin that the question of Laura Ashley's core identity had not been resolved. No one seemed to know whether its key strengths were in design, manufacturing or retailing, or resided primarily in the brand. The result was a lack of coherent strategy and operational and organisational confusion.

In Jim Maxmin's discussions with staff a common theme emerged — one of complexity, bureaucracy and people feeling impotent to act. They felt trapped within the group's 22 strategic business units, which forced them to think parochially rather than in global terms. Business units were managed vertically as profit centres with no integration of such key functions as warehousing, distribution, stock management and financial control.

Simplify, focus and act

Under the heading 'Simplify, Focus and Act', Jim Maxmin announced a major management reorganisation programme designed to refocus group activities. The changes would remove 100 management jobs and cost more than £5m. This included capital spending of £3m to upgrade and unify computer systems. Jim Maxmin said the group would be run as a single international business. 'Laura Ashley has suffered from a fragmented management structure that has prevented a clear global brand strategy from being developed and implemented.' He instituted a Global Operations Executive (GOE) which would meet monthly 'around the world'. On the marketing front, Global Collection Development (GCD) replaced Group Marketing. Its mission was 'single global image marketing', rather than five or six separate campaigns.

Prior to Jim Maxmin's appointment, Glenne Gibson, senior retail consultant with Coopers Lybrand & Deloitte, had been recruited to develop Laura Ashley's marketing strategy. She set up a programme of quantitative and qualitative market research, the first comprehensive survey of its customers that Laura Ashley had undertaken. This elicited a huge response from some 57,000 customers in the UK and USA. The overriding message of the research was the very strong customer loyalty that the brand continued to enjoy. Other aspects of the research were fed back into the design process and the marketing of goods in shops. Commented Jim Maxmin:

> To my way of thinking Laura Ashley is a brand. It is not a retailing company. It is not a fashion company. It is not a production or manufacturing company. I see the management task as simply unleashing the intrinsic strength of that fantastic brand.[4]

One of the chief executive's main aims was to implement and explain the change programme to staff quickly, in order to avoid as much speculation and worry as possible. He ran a week of roadshows for senior managers throughout the world, making presentations in the UK and at the group's overseas locations in Holland, the USA and Japan. Senior managers then briefed staff using a video of the roadshow to support the communication process. The message was further reinforced by a special edition of the staff newspaper, *LA News*, distributed to every Laura Ashley employee around the world. Jim Maxmin said:

> This isn't a one-off thing. Our business is all about communication — talking with each other, talking to our customers and listening to what people have to say. All staff will be kept fully in touch with the decisions being made which will affect the operations and future of the company.

Described variously as an effusive, highly active manager with a ready line in marketing jargon and an obsessive concentration on target customers, and a man guided by market research, financial disciplines and management consistency, Jim Maxmin's management style came as something of a shock to Laura Ashley staff. Maxmin was an 'enabling manager' who believed in empowering employees in order to enhance customer service. Incentive schemes were introduced to encourage employee suggestions for improving customer service. To encourage corporate staff to make contact with customers and better understand the demands on shop staff, Maxmin asked all managers to spend at least one day each month working in a Laura Ashley shop.

In January 1992 Andrew Higginson, group finance director, announced a new five-year, £50 million finance facility agreed with Laura Ashley's banks. This would replace the shorter three-year arrangement signed in November 1990 and was seen as 'a strong vote of confidence from our banks ... and reflects our success in putting the business on a sound financial footing'.

[4] *Financial Times*, 31/7/91.

Later that month Laura Ashley announced the appointment of Denise Lincoln as global human resources director. Recruited from Grand Metropolitan plc, where she had been group management development director, she was the first woman to join Laura Ashley's main board and her appointment reflected the importance attached by Jim Maxmin to 'the development of people in building a world class business'. A management development programme was put in place, designed to improve integration and understanding among the senior team. Significant changes were also made in the way in which the company recruited, trained and managed its shop staff. Older store managers were recruited to better match the age profile of Laura Ashley customers.

Logistics: a strategic alliance

On 19 March 1992 Laura Ashley and Federal Express Business Logistics announced a global alliance — reported as the first of its kind. The accompanying press release acknowledged that Laura Ashley's existing logistics were 'complex, costly and inefficient'. The agreement was seen as a critical step in Laura Ashley's 'Simplify, Focus and Act' programme. The benefits to Laura Ashley of the alliance were listed as follows:

- Savings from the simplification of the existing supply chain amounting to 10–12 per cent of total distribution costs (based on like-for-like service levels) as well as substantial reductions in working capital.
- Access to the global systems of Federal Express. This will provide Laura Ashley with leading-edge distribution systems within a short timeframe. At a minimum this will save Laura Ashley £3m in planned system development costs.
- The ability to improve customer service, with the objective of being able to deliver anywhere in the world within 24 to 48 hours if required, by September 1993.
- Enable Laura Ashley management to focus on areas of core competence.
- The key systems infrastructure to enable flexible response and the opportunity for new initiatives such as worldwide mail order.

The alliance was intended to be of indefinite duration, but had a minimum contract period of ten years. Over this period the estimated value to Federal Express was £150m. Commenting on the alliance, Jim Maxmin said:

> This alliance gives us access to management systems and logistics capacity that we could not dream of developing ourselves. It represents a quantum leap in our strategy of simplifying and focusing operations. We now have a unique opportunity to break new ground in developing a global mail order business with the objective of 48-hour delivery anywhere in the world. The alliance opens the

door to lower costs, enhanced delivery performance, higher stock turn and improved customer service. It also enables us to focus our own resources where we can add value to the core business.

Back from the brink

Results for the year to 25 January 1992, released in April, showed a recovery from a £6.7m loss to a profit of £2.7m before exceptional items. 'The extraordinary thing about Laura Ashley is not that it has been dragged back from the financial brink', commented the *Daily Telegraph*, 'it is that it was ever pushed there in the first place. It took a rare combination of management failure, over-ambition and bad luck to bring such a business to its knees.'[5]

Pre-tax profits for the year to 30 January 1993 were £1.8m, but the group continued to suffer badly in the USA where stock problems produced a £6.9m loss. 'We are rebuilding the business, but that takes time,' said Jim Maxmin.

In February 1993 it was announced that the Ashley family had reduced its stake in the business with the sale of 10 million shares. This reduced the family's holding to about 50 per cent and followed the sale of a similar amount fourteen months earlier, when Sir Bernard had relinquished his executive duties. A further 30 million shares were sold in May and Sir Bernard retired as chairman of the company.

Headaches in the USA

Laura Ashley's difficulties in the USA had been hidden to some extent by the rapid growth of sales through new shop openings. However, analysis showed that no store had produced year-on-year growth after the second year. The group's problems in the USA had persisted for more than two years despite the efforts of Jim Maxmin and others to turn the operation around. He found that there were no standard shop operating systems, and that the managers of US shops were not as capable as their UK counterparts. In the fiscal year 1993/4, 53 per cent of US shop managers were replaced.

To add to the US problems, heavy snowstorms in March 1993 led to a loss of 800 store days as the spring and summer collection was being introduced, which led to yet more discounting. Since 40 per cent of Laura Ashley turnover was in the USA, losses there were jeopardising the group's development elsewhere.

On 13 April 1994 Jim Maxmin abruptly announced his departure from Laura Ashley after a row over the group's American operations. The

[5] *Daily Telegraph*, 7/4/92.

Financial Times commented:

> His departure, accompanied only by a brief statement, is unsatisfactory. The appointment of Mr Hugh Blakeway Webb as executive chairman looks like a victory for the old guard, who have let down shareholders before.[6]

The group made an operating loss of £100,000 for the half-year to 30 July 1994, after a £3.3m first tranche of restructuring costs. This figure included a £1.2 million pay-off to Jim Maxmin.

Back to basics

More restructuring

In marked contrast to the previous management, whose priority had been to invest in the Laura Ashley brand, the new management team emphasised its determination to tackle costs in every area of the business. It believed that substantial savings could be made by cutting jobs and rationalising offices and stock levels.

For the year to 28 January 1995, the group made a loss of £30.6 million after absorbing £34.4 million of exceptional charges. Hugh Blakeway Webb acknowledged that the action being taken was hurting, but said that it was necessary to return Laura Ashley to acceptable levels of profitability. The restructuring measures were aimed at tackling the group's £44 million central overhead costs. Laura Ashley's ratio of sales to overheads stood at 14 per cent, whereas the average figure for comparable retailers was 10 per cent. The group's product range was also being rationalised to allow Laura Ashley to return to its core products and drive up margins. Ranges such as food, swimwear and furniture were to be scrapped.

With its share price languishing at around 75p, Laura Ashley was seen as vulnerable to predators seeking what, despite a decade of problems, remained a strong international brand.

A new chief executive

On 15 June 1995 it was announced that Ann Iverson had been persuaded to join Laura Ashley as chief executive after the top job had been left vacant

---

[6] *Financial Times*, 13/4/94. Hugh Blakeway Webb was appointed a non-executive director and deputy chairman in January 1991. A partner at accountants Coopers & Lybrand Deloitte from 1983, Mr Blakeway Webb was known to be close to Sir Bernard Ashley and had advised him on tax matters since the early 1980s. He resigned his partnership prior to joining the Laura Ashley board.

for almost a year. Ann Iverson came to Britain in 1990 from Bloomingdales, the American retail group, to join Storehouse as BHS stores director. Two years later she became managing director of Mothercare and revitalised the ailing company. Mrs Iverson's appointment eased rumours that a bid for Laura Ashley was in the offing, but also had a less welcome effect. Lazards, Laura Ashley's merchant bank, terminated its relationship with the company because it had not been consulted over Ann Iverson's appointment.

In September 1995 Ann Iverson presented her first review of the business and announced that she was bringing the design, buying and merchandising functions under one roof, reducing the product range by a quarter, and introducing a common look across the group.

> By re-establishing a 'retail culture' and a strong unified look in the product ranges, the Laura Ashley brand still has scope for significant expansion. It is a brilliant brand, it is resilient; we haven't killed it. It is fixable, and we have positioned it at the end of three years for double-digit operating margins.

Previous restructuring attempts had concentrated on cutting costs, without considering how to develop the brand, and improve sales and gross margins. 'You never heard anything about how we were going to grow the business', commented Mrs Iverson.

Her review of the company had shown that its clothing and furnishing products and its marketing lacked a 'single point of view'. The range was too broad, the supply chain was inefficient, and many shops — particularly in the USA — were too small. The group also lacked 'clear lines of accountability'. After tackling these problems, the next stage would be to make the supply chain more efficient. This would include a review of the role of manufacturing operations, which still supplied 25 per cent of Laura Ashley products. The store portfolio in the USA and UK would also be reviewed.[7]

Ann Iverson's observations came as the company reported a fall in pre-tax profits from £5.1m to £3m for the six months to 29 July 1995. As the group embarked on its targeted turnaround by the end of the decade, the company's shareholders kept their fingers firmly crossed.

Return to profit

In announcing a return to profit in April 1996, the company said that its turnaround would take another two to three years to complete. Ann Iverson said the group was embarking on an expansion programme in the USA and UK, but not in continental Europe. 'We are going after real estate and growth relative to our opportunities right now, which are in the US and the

---

[7] *Financial Times*, 22/9/95.

UK,' said Mrs Iverson. She planned to expand the group's sales in home furnishings to two-thirds of total sales and reduce the garment element accordingly. The store portfolio was being reshaped, with smaller stores being closed and replaced by larger outlets which could show a wider range of the home furnishings.

To the surprise of some commentators the group had decided to retain its manufacturing plant, but this was being radically overhauled. Finance director Jim Walsh said that the group's manufacturing plant in Wales had 'lost touch with economic reality'. Press reports spoke of 'horrific levels of seconds and utilisation running at a lowly 70 per cent'.[8] The 1,100 jobs in the Welsh operation would fall to around 700 over the next three years. Cost savings of £2m to £3m were expected.

The company also intended to cut costs in its distribution network, consolidating its use of Federal Express. Selling prices, which Ann Iverson said were too high, were also being scrutinised. The mail order business, which was reined back sharply in 1995 after a disastrous year, was to be relaunched.

'Analysts now believe the company has fallen into good retail hands,' commented the *Financial Times*.

> Mrs Iverson has already shown the light at the end of the tunnel by proving she can achieve cost savings, and has shrewdly latched on to the growth prospects of the home furnishings market in the US. It is possible the group will not even sell garments in 10 years' time.[9]

[8] *Independent*, 19/4/96.
[9] *Financial Times*, 19/4/96.

Appendix 1   Group financial record, 1991–6

	1996 (£m)	1995 (£m)	1994 (£m)	1993 (£m)	1992 (£m)	1991 (£m)
Profit and loss account						
Turnover	336.6	322.6	300.4	247.8	262.8	328.1
Operating profit/loss before exceptional operating costs	9.1	4.1	2.3	1.1	−0.6	3.4
Exceptional operating costs	0.1	−33.4	–	–	–	–
Operating profit/loss	9.2	−29.3	2.3	1.1	−0.6	3.4
Profit from associated undertakings	2.0	1.5	1.8	1.5	1.9	0.1
Exceptional items	–	−1.0	–	–	−8.1	−2.6
Net interest payable	−0.9	−1.8	−1.1	−0.8	−2.3	−12.4
Profit/(loss) on ordinary activities before taxation	10.3	−30.6	3.0	1.8	−9.1	−11.5
Taxation	−3.3	−0.9	−1.9	−1.0	–	2.5
Profit/(loss) on ordinary activities after taxation	7.0	−31.5	1.1	0.8	−9.1	−9.0
Dividends	−1.2	–	−0.2	−0.1	−0.1	−0.1
Retained profit/(loss) for the year	5.8	−31.5	0.9	0.7	−9.2	−9.1
Balance sheets						
Fixed assets	45.2	48.3	71.7	66.3	60.5	67.1
Net current assets	27.0	43.7	50.2	53.9	52.8	66.9
Long-term creditors	−0.9	−15.0	−35.1	−34.4	−28.0	−41.4
Provisions for liabilities and charges	−8.3	−21.3	−0.7	−0.3	−0.5	−0.4
Net assets	63.0	55.7	86.1	85.5	84.8	92.2
Issued capital	11.8	11.7	11.7	11.7	11.7	11.7
Reserves	51.2	44.0	74.4	73.8	73.1	80.5
Equity shareholders' funds	63.0	55.7	86.1	85.5	84.8	92.2
Statistics						
Earnings/(loss) per share (p)	2.97	−13.41	0.45	0.34	−3.86	−4.39
Dividends per share (p)	0.50	–	0.10	0.10	0.10	0.10
Operating profit as a percentage of sales (%)	2.7	1.3	0.8	0.4	0.2	1.0
Profit/(loss) on ordinary activities before taxation as a percentage of net assets (%)	16.3	−54.9	3.5	2.1	−10.7	−12.5
Net asset value per ordinary share (p)	26.6	23.7	36.6	36.4	36.1	39.3
Gearing (%)	–	−1	19	19	5	25

The Iona Community

PETER H. JONES

The Iona Community is an association of some 200 members committed to work out together a particular expression of their Christian beliefs. The movement, started in the 1930s, is popularly associated with the Abbey on Iona, a small island off the west coast of Scotland. Its leader, Norman Shanks, indicated the difficulties of giving concrete shape to its purpose as the early vision of its founder ceased to be so obviously relevant 60 years on.

> It was easy to see the Community's purpose being fulfilled when we were re-building the Abbey. Now it is less tangible; it is building the Church in the world; it is building lives of service and celebration in God's Kingdom. We still need to be linked to our centres in Iona, but we must be more than an agency which runs a spiritual conference centre.

An historical review of developments

The Iona Community was founded in 1938 by George MacLeod, a Church of Scotland minister. In the 1930s he had a parish in the shipbuilding area of Govan in Glasgow, but though preaching to a large congregation of middle- and upper-class people, he made little impact on the working-class men of Govan. He felt that his training had been irrelevant to the concerns and language of the industrial working class of his parish.

His vision to change this was to put ministers and craftsmen alongside each other in a long-term building project where they could work together and learn from each other. An opportunity to do just this arose on the tiny island of Iona, lying off the west coast of Scotland.

Why Iona? To understand this one must travel back 1,400 years, to ad 563,

---

This case study was written by Peter H. Jones, Sheffield Business School. The co-operation of the Iona Community is gratefully acknowledged. The study is for educational use and is not designed to portray either good or poor management practices. © P.H. Jones, 1996.

when Saint Columba with twelve followers landed from Ireland on Iona. Columba used Iona as a base for the establishment of Christianity and Christian colonies all over Scotland and as far afield as the east coast of England. During the following 1,400 years several monasteries were built, destroyed and rebuilt on the site. In 1899 the Duke of Argyll, who owns the land and the monastery, made a gift of the Abbey remains to the Iona Cathedral Trust, an independent trust body representing the established Church of Scotland. An appeal was launched and the Abbey cathedral was restored by the Trust between 1902 and 1910 through public subscription money. The monastery, however, remained in ruins.

In MacLeod's vision, rebuilding the monastery was fused with his passionate desire to find a way to renew the corporate life of the church in industrial settings. He resigned as parish minister of Govan. The Iona Community was born: 1938 saw it start with George MacLeod and twelve others. On Iona in the summer months, the pattern of living was simple, austere and communal: worship led by MacLeod himself — morning and evening — was part of the pattern; eight hours of manual labour rebuilding the monastery; communal sleeping accommodation; shared chores. At the end of the summer, the twelve returned to mainland Scotland — ministers to their work in their churches, craftsmen to seek scarce work.

Those first minister-members wished to remain as a community, and a pattern emerged in which the 'member' was the man who had been through an initial two years' training experience; the man still serving those two years was to be regarded as a novice. Even though the rebuilding of the Abbey was completed in 1967, those embarking upon a two-year initiation programme still attend a 'Work Week' when manual work of maintaining or improving a centre is done. Thus elements of the original concept of creating community through shared work is maintained.

As new members joined in the rebuilding work, the Iona Community began to grow. But what does community mean for members on the mainland of Scotland living apart from each other? The answer that evolved is embodied in five personal disciplines to which members commit themselves. It forms the 'five-fold rule of the Iona Community' or, more simply, 'The Rule'.

The five-fold rule calls each member to:

1. Daily Bible reading, and prayer for each other, common concerns, and the wider work of the church.
2. Share and account for the use of their money — the economic discipline. Members donate a tenth of their disposable income to the work of the Community and the wider work of the church.
3. Account for the use of their time to their 'Family group'.
4. Act for justice and peace in society. A full statement of the commitment in this area is given in Appendix 1.

5. Meet with and account to each other. Each member belongs to one of 28 geographically based Family groups which meet monthly, and is also expected to attend some of the four annual Plenary meetings.

Up to the mid-1960s members were almost exclusively male ordained ministers of the Church of Scotland, but that is no longer so. By 1995 there were 201 members; 95 were ordained, 120 were domiciled in Scotland, and 90 were women.

But if the Rule defines the Community, what does the Community do? There are three strands which have developed over the years. They are the Island Centres, the mainland work, and the Wild Goose Publishing arm of the Community. Each is described in turn.

The Island Centres

The *Abbey*, finished in 1967, can accommodate 44 guests, mostly in bunk-bedded rooms. During 1995 just over 1,500 people stayed, as is customary, for a week's programme, being charged £150 per adult for a week's full board. However, the Community did not see the Abbey as a holiday hotel. As early as 1939 lecturers had been invited to lead discussion with the new minister-members on topics concerning how spiritual and secular matters should relate. A programme on these broad lines has continued ever since. A week on Iona is thus focused on the experience of sharing 'the common life' through a combination of relaxation, worship, discussion and daily chores.

Young people's camps have also been a feature of the Community's work on Iona. However, by the mid-1980s the accommodation for these was becoming inadequate and inappropriate. With increasing numbers also coming to the Abbey, a decision was taken to celebrate the 90th birthday of the founder with the establishment of the *MacLeod Centre*. Opened in 1988, at a cost of £1 million, it has accommodation for 52 guests. The Mac, as it is known, is particularly geared to young people and families, and has residential facilities for the disabled (lacking in the Abbey). It is close to the Abbey and many events are shared. Charges are the same as at the Abbey. In 1995 just over 1,300 people stayed.

The centres are staffed by 24 full-time staff who look after the running of the Abbey, the Mac, a shop and a coffee house shop. About half are on one-year appointments, though some, including the warden of the Abbey and the director of the MacLeod Centre are three-year appointments. In addition some 30 extra volunteer staff are paid 'pocket money', and over 100 volunteers work on Iona over the season for periods of 6–12 weeks. There is a policy that the Abbey warden should be a member of the Community, so that the key leadership position should be filled by a person committed to the vision and purposes of the Community.

The centres are open from March to December, though there is minimal use in November and December. In the other eight months the Abbey has an occupancy of 99 per cent and the Mac just under 80 per cent. Though full details of potential bookings turned away were not kept, it was believed that the Abbey accommodation was oversubscribed three or four times over. It was hoped to increase total guests to 3,500 for 1996.

In 1994 just under half the guests came as part of a group, the remainder being individual bookings. Twelve groups (out of 90 group bookings) were brought by Community members, and there was a desire for this to be a higher proportion. However, fewer members were working in jobs where they had opportunities to take groups away for residential experiences. Thus increasingly guests came by word-of-mouth recommendations. No post was primarily responsible for publicity or marketing the centres.

A third much smaller residential centre operated by the Community was not on Iona, but on the adjacent larger island of Mull. The *Camas Adventure Centre* provides accommodation for sixteen. Its emphasis is on outdoor activities for young people.

Financial data for the centres are included in Appendix 2.

The mainland work

The work and initiatives of the Community on the mainland of Britain are many and varied. They arise from the concern of members to see their Christian beliefs and commitment to the purposes and ideals of the Community worked out in the wider society. Seven working groups seek to raise awareness of particular issues within the Iona Community, to influence outside agencies (including churches and government), and to network with other similarly concerned groups. In 1995 two of the working groups were supported by full-time paid workers.

The *Justice and Peace Planning* group aimed to create practical expressions of all members' general commitment to this area. There were a variety of initiatives: an exhibition on Iona on fair trade between nations; the promotion of a video 'The Invisible Wall', exploring how trade and debt are used to exploit the world's poorest people; a resources centre and a Peace House, with a full-time peace and justice worker, supported jointly with the Quakers.

The *Youth Work Planning* group supported and advised the Community's Youth Development worker, including the mounting of a Youth Programme on Iona and Camas. Some of the programme weeks had specific themes (e.g. exploring prejudice and reconciliation); others were open weeks attracting school parties. Both types sought to give a flavour of the 'Iona Experience'. Additionally, the group organised a range of opportunities in which young people who have been to Iona can maintain contact with each other.

The main purpose of the *Interfaith and Racism* working group was to raise awareness of the perceived need for change in the nationality and immigration laws of the UK.

The *Cause of the Poor* group acted to support and lobby for legislation on social and disability issues.

The *Rediscovery of Spirituality* group sought to refocus the Community's energy towards 'reflective activism'. Work included reviewing the training of new members, and encouraging members in their prayer discipline to fulfil item 1 of the Rule.

The *Sharing Communion by the year 2000* group aimed to encourage and support members in ecumenical activity.

The *Constitutional Matters* group dealt mainly with issues concerning Scotland's constitutional relationship within the United Kingdom.

Groups met on an *ad hoc* basis. Few members belonged to more than one group. Each group had a budget principally to cover travelling expenses of members on group matters. There was no fixed measure of a group's success, though most groups provided themes and leaders for Iona weeks. If a particular topic emerged, a new group could be created and a budget sanctioned, subject to the approval of Council. In 1995 there was the possibility of groups forming to deal with interfaith issues (as it was felt the existing group concentrated on race issues), and unemployment and work issues.

In addition to the working groups there was the *Wild Goose resource and worship group*. This comprised four full-time workers and sixteen volunteer young adults involved in developments in worship which 'capture the imagination and enable the participation of young people'. By 1995 funding for the group was mainly self-generated (70 per cent), with the Church of Scotland (20 per cent) and the Iona Community (10 per cent) making up the balance, although historically the self-generated funding proportion had been significantly lower.

Norman Shanks, the leader of the Community, summed up this aspect of the Community's work:

> Our primary emphasis is not what any full time staff can do, but what members do in their daily lives of work, worship and service. We are not out to build an Iona empire but to be a gift to the Church.

Wild Goose Publications

The publishing arm of the Community, Wild Goose Publications, sold books of Christian songs and associated cassettes, meditations and prayers, and collections of short drama pieces for use in worship. In 1994 it had sales of £112,000, making a loss of £6,000. Of those sales, 81 per cent were accounted for by material generated by the Wild Goose resource group. The main reason for the loss was a slowdown in new titles published, arising from several changes of personnel. Since 1995 there had been a move to broaden the scope of material published by Wild Goose to include more works dealing with the wider work of the Community.

A 'bias to the poor'?

In maintaining and running the centres on Iona, Community members wanted there to be a policy of a 'bias to the poor' in their use. This was felt to be consistent with one founding purpose of the Community, to blend together people from all walks of life. Thus in both centres there were special discounts for families, groups and young people. Those on benefit or low income could apply for special subsidised rates which were funded from the Subsidy Fund. £15,000 was available in 1994 for this purpose. This had enabled 204 guests to be subsidised at the two centres. £8,500 was used to allow four groups to come to the Mac at virtually no cost. The remainder was spread fairly evenly across all weeks at both centres. There was a general feeling among Community members that more subsidies should be given. Otherwise a fear expressed was that the centres would become 'middle-class spiritual Butlins offering a dose of quick fix spirituality'. Money for the Subsidy Fund came from the interest on the Islands Access Fund. This was a typical way in which charities turned capital gifts and legacies into income. The Fund had been set up in 1989 when interest rates were high and interest income was expected to provide a healthy amount for the purpose. But as interest rates fell in the 1990s, so had the Subsidy Fund. The Community had committed itself to increase the Access Fund from its 1994 level of £160,000 to £500,000. In 1994 applications to the Subsidy Fund were significantly oversubscribed.

However, there was considerable debate over the effectiveness of the mechanisms to achieve the aim of getting mixed socioeconomic groups at the centres. Of the £15,000 subsidy given in 1994, only £3,200 was to guests at the Abbey, the rest was to those going to the Mac. In members' eyes this reinforced the stereotypes that the Abbey catered mainly for 'middle-class English women', while 'younger Scottish males' went to the Mac centre. But according to Peter Macdonald, the convener of the Islands Committee:

> We don't want to perpetuate this situation. I hope we can move towards a greater mix of people at the Abbey. If we then have to say 'no' to repeat bookings from, for example, English middle-class areas I'd not worry. But I'm not happy about our procedures to make this greater mix happen through subsidy payments. Some may be put off by the high cost and by the impression this could give that the Abbey was not the place for folk like them. That 'cultural shift in guests' occurred

at the Mac when we went from a youth camp charging £20 per week to a purpose-built centre charging nearer £150; and then some people wondered why our client group changed!

Another convener echoed this thought.

We need to make the Mac centre much more of a youth centre — not a carbon copy of the Abbey. Unfortunately fewer of our members now work with the poor, or in churches in poor areas. There has been a shift in our members' jobs. Perhaps as a Community we are no longer seen as being on the cutting edge of new forms of church life; not seen as so relevant to younger church ministers. We need to be more proactive in seeking out what I call the 'multipliers'; those such as teachers, social workers, and youth workers who can bring groups of the disadvantaged to Iona. The state has taken over more responsibility in this area compared to 40 years ago, so we need to capture such people's interest. We have written a job description to appoint someone to market the centres to these groups — but not made an appointment yet.

The 'Robin Hood' mechanism of charging guests more than costs and using the excess to offer more subsidies drew mixed reactions.

I'd be happy with it, as long as it wasn't too blatant, especially in the Abbey. It would be a tragedy if we only got wealthy guests. It would be great to get more mixed groups.

I'd be reluctant to do this. I don't think you can mix people if they know they are paying different rates. I feel the younger Scots would end up saying 'they are no my kind of people'.

If the price went up too much, guests would expect a higher level of service — we'd end up just running a hotel.

There was a two-stage booking procedure. Draft brochures for the following year were sent in August to groups who had previously booked. Confirmed brochures were not sent to individual members and friends until December. Group bookings were accepted from November, but individuals could not apply until January. It was rare for people from poorer areas to apply as individuals. Thus the 'bias to the poor' was largely driven by groups that applied.

Island Centres ownership

Surprisingly, perhaps, the Community only owned one of the three centres it used: the Mac.

The Abbey was owned by the Iona Cathedral trustees. This body was set up in 1899 by the then Duke of Argyll to look after the Abbey, but had no endowment money. Since 1938 when the Community commenced the completion of the monastic buildings, the Community have effectively both occupied and looked after the buildings. Only since the early 1980s have the Trustees become active again in terms of both fund raising and buildings maintenance. It had become increasingly clear to them that some full-time management was needed to administer their responsibilities, and that any large donors or funding bodies would need to see a properly constituted management structure in place to administer moneys donated for the preservation or development of the Abbey. Thus in 1993 Iona Abbey Limited was formed.

The split of responsibilities was that the maintenance of the Abbey Cathedral, and of the exterior of all the Abbey buildings, grounds and monuments, was the responsibility of Iona Abbey Ltd, while the Community undertook the internal maintenance of the Abbey buildings. The Community had an agreement to use and occupy the Abbey buildings at zero cost. This agreement is due for renewal in 1999.

The chief executive of Iona Abbey Ltd was a successful architect and property developer. He maintained that the Community had assumed responsibilities for running activities such as the bookshop and coffee shop in a situation where the legal lease position was not clearly specified. The Cathedral trustees had not really been interested in such matters. He pointed out that the Community:

- Paid no realistic rent for use of the Abbey buildings.
- Repaired the interior of the Abbey buildings, but had no obligation to do so, other than a need to operate the accommodation.
- Paid only 20 per cent of their heating bills.
- Paid no rent on the coffee shop and bookshop, yet took the profits and used the shops as a 'shop window' where the Community's concerns were publicised.
- Took on responsibility for showing visitors round the Abbey cathedral.

He believed that this situation needed to be put on a 'proper footing' and wished to create an understood partnership between the Community and Iona Abbey Ltd.

Asked why the current 'murky situation' should not continue, he feared a renewal of what he called a 'giving-barrel war' as the financial needs of maintaining the Abbey increased. In such a 'war', visitors to the island could be confused and antagonised by separate requests for money from two bodies, each claiming jurisdiction over different parts of the Abbey.

> With over 120,000 visitors to Iona each year, this could be a real bone of contention. In 1997, it will be 1,400 years since the death of Columba. This can be a national tourist event, an opportunity not to be missed. Visitors from all over the world will be coming to Scotland and Iona. I have plans for several major events. There must not be open war between the Community and the Abbey during this period.
>
> I can see various undesirable outcomes which neither party wants unless we develop a realistic partnership. If the lease is not renewed, it could split the

Church of Scotland. There is a lot of goodwill towards the Community in Scotland as a whole. Besides, I personally don't want to see the Abbey becoming a luxury hotel only for wealthy guests. I support what the Community is doing, but not all the Trustees are sympathetic to the radical stances of the Community, especially on the nuclear issue. If we cannot come to some agreement, we could pull out of the monastery altogether, forcing the Community to take over all the exterior maintenance as well. I very much doubt they would be set up to or want to do that.

Community members, in general, saw a responsibility to co-operate with Iona Abbey Ltd. As one member said, 'We must not be confrontational, but on the other hand we must not let them walk all over us.'

Detailed discussions had not taken place over the issue of the lease renewal, but representative views included:

If the rent went up so high that we had to charge, say, £300 per week, I'd rather pull out.

There are very stringent rules on what one can do in such a historic building, but we have to live here. You cannot live in a monument; there needs to be a greater degree of sympathy to us.

Keeping up the monastery interior is a form of rent anyway. Normally landlords would do that for you.

Faced with the question of what would happen to the Community if the lease on the Abbey were not renewed at a satisfactory rent, reaction was fairly uniform. One said:

Losing it would be tragic, but not a death blow. We'd have the Mac centre on the island, and we could still worship in the Abbey itself. We might well develop a mainland base. Our Community is a community of the heart, whereas often the Church is a community of the mind. Losing Iona would be a blow to our heart, but I hope members see the Community as more than Iona — it is a movement of like-minded people.

Another commented:

Iona holds the key to vivid experiences in which we have encountered one another and God. I had a personal crisis just recently. To sort myself out I went 'home' — to Iona. It's my spiritual home, although I know God is not restricted to Iona.

The buildings used by the Camas Camp on Mull were owned by the Duke of Argyll and leased at a rent of £400 p.a. This lease was renegotiated in 1995 without difficulty.

Organisation and decision making in the Community

Legally the Iona Community was a company limited by guarantee, but the diverse set of activities undertaken by the members and full-time staff of the Community was co-ordinated by a structure of leader, Council and committees. The ultimate authority was a Plenary meeting.

The *Publishing* committee acted as an editorial board and gave policy direction to Wild Goose Publications.

The *Mainland* committee oversaw the working groups and outreach projects, including the Wild Goose resource group.

The *Islands* committee set policy for the three centres on Iona and Mull.

The *Finance and Staffing* committee acted in a co-ordinating role for matters relating to central administration and finance. It comprised the conveners (chairs) of the above three committees, six elected members, the Iona warden and four members of staff (the leader and three heads of department) from the Glasgow office of the Community. It met seven times a year in the afternoon, when in the evening the Council met.

The *Council* was the main executive body of the Community. It consisted of six elected members of the Community, the four conveners of the above committees — all as voting members — together with the leader, Iona warden and three heads of departments, who did not have voting rights.

The committees and Council involved just over 30 members of the Community. All positions were elected for a three-year term, and there was usually not too much difficulty filling vacancies, although ensuring knowledge levels adequate to the tasks was sometimes problematic. On occasions there had been the need to hold elections (particularly for the Islands committee) when more than one nomination was received, but this was not frequent.

The Community met in *Plenary* four times a year:

- Twice a year for a day to discuss a current topic of interest. There was an attempt to move these around the country, but geography and British Rail meant they were usually in central Scotland.
- Once (in Glasgow) for the AGM and the transaction of business formalities.
- For a week on Iona during Community Week.

Members shared their concerns at Plenary meetings, which provided a focus for opinion sounding and communal decision taking.

Although formally the Community's ultimate decision body, the Plenary meetings usually discussed only general strategy issues, setting down a policy framework within which Council worked out detailed decision making. Attendance at Plenaries varied. At the Community Week on Iona there were usually about 100–120 members; meetings in central Scotland attracted about 80, while a meeting in Newcastle in 1994 attracted only 40. One English member explained:

> There is a real barrier at the England/Scotland border. Few Scottish members travel south when we hold Plenaries in England, and English members feel put

out by this. We're expected to travel to Scotland, but it doesn't work the other way round.

The various committees wrestled with the extent to which they should be involved in day-to-day matters. The senior full-time administrator saw a distinction between the Community as a 'movement' and as an 'organisation'. He wanted a clear distinction between setting policy (the purpose of committees) and operational management (the remit of full-time staff). However, he acknowledged that longer-standing committee members found it difficult to let go of minor matters.

Among some committee conveners there was a wish to focus the energy of the Community.

> Some working groups do too little. We should be prepared to close down working groups or give them a limited life. We need to be clear what added value we give to activities as the Iona Community. For me that is the Iona experience of community, and our ability to link faith and spirituality with a concern for social justice.

In a Strategic Plan Review, the convener of Council wrote:

> Review of strategy is not first and foremost an opportunity to refine a structure, nor to oil the wheels of an organisation. It is rather the attempt to allow ourselves to be disturbed and challenged — even goaded — into new things to stay faithful to the same God.

The leader of the Community was elected by and from the membership, and had a seven-year term of office. Norman Shanks became leader in August 1995, having served on all four committees and Council since he became a member in 1980. He saw a variety of roles for the leader: as the public relations face of the Community, as a pastor to members, offering support and encouragement, and as the clarifier and embodiment of the purpose and direction of the Community. Looking out from what he saw as a basically healthy Community, he said:

> We must not lose our nerve or sense of direction. We must continue with a sense of adventure, faith and hope that God is at work in the world through us, as in so many other ways. We must also not lose our sense of togetherness. A Community of many more than the present 200 could easily become too fragmented, lacking cohesion and togetherness. Larger scale would change our character.

Relating to the wider world

The Community, through its members, had many informal contacts with the outside world. It was not a closed Community, a sect or a cult. The great majority of individual members were members of local churches.

As an entity, there was a formal link to mainstream churches through the Iona Community Board of the Church of Scotland. This board, appointed by the Church of Scotland, also contained representatives of other denominations to which Community members belonged (such as the Church of England, Roman Catholic, United Reformed, Methodist and Society of Friends). It received an annual report on the activities of the Community and acted as a formal channel of communication regarding the Community's concerns and activities.

The Community was affiliated to several other organisations, including the following:

- Church Action on Poverty.
- Christian CND.
- The Scottish Environmental Forum.
- The Ecumenical Association of Laity Centres.
- The Scottish Council for Voluntary Organisations.
- Strathclyde Community Relations Council.
- Action for Southern Africa.
- Ecumenical Committee for Corporate Responsibility.

Such affiliations provided networking possibilities for members, in addition to their own personal links to a whole range of bodies. This provided immense networking potential to the Community as a whole.

Iona was a popular place for visitors and pilgrims. This was a combination of the Abbey Church, its Benedictine and Columban antecedents, and the Community itself. On summer days there could be upwards of 1,000 visitors and over 120,000 per year. Visitors to the Abbey were asked by Iona Abbey Ltd to make a donation of £2 towards its upkeep and most did. This money went to the Abbey trustees. The Community operated both the coffee house and Abbey shop, which catered for day visitors as well as residents. In both these shops the work and concerns of the Community were publicised.

Over the years many people who had visited Iona, who had stayed at the Abbey or Mac centres, or who just wished to keep in contact with what the Iona Community stood for, had expressed a wish to be linked to the Community and support its work. There was an active network of just over 1,600 Friends of the Community, who received its bi-monthly magazine, *The Coracle*. Additionally there were around 1,400 Associates who were bound by the Prayer discipline of the Rule, and who could follow the other disciplines voluntarily. They were encouraged to participate in the economic discipline by donating 2 per cent of their disposable income to a 'Common Fund' whose disposition was decided by a sub-group of Associates.

A successful community?

Musing about success over a cup of coffee, the Islands convener said:

Over the last 10 years we've grown considerably. We've been scrambling to keep pace. Turnover has gone from tens of thousands to a million pounds. We've just started to get a grip on our finances and budgets. I suppose only now are we starting to answer the 'success' question. Up to now our answers have been anecdotal. We do believe lives have been changed; people tell us so. They tell us that in their struggles, they have found peace. Quantitatively, however, I don't think we have many measures. I sometimes wonder if we should?

Appendix 1   Statement on 'Justice and Peace commitment'

We believe:

1 that the Gospel commands us to seek peace founded on justice and that costly reconciliation is at the heart of the Gospel.
2 that work for justice, peace and an equitable society is a matter of extreme urgency.
3 that God has given us partnership as stewards of creation and that we have a responsibility to live in a right relationship with the whole of God's creation.
4 that, handled with integrity, creation can provide for the needs of all, but not for the greed which leads to injustice and inequality, and endangers life on earth.
5 that everyone should have the quality and dignity of a full life that requires adequate physical, social and political opportunity, without the oppression of poverty, injustice and fear.
6 that social and political action leading to justice for all people and encouraged by prayer and discussion, is a vital work of the Church at all levels.
7 that the use or threatened use of nuclear and other weapons of mass destruction is theologically and morally indefensible and that opposition to their existence is an imperative of the Christian faith.

As members and family groups we will:

8 engage in forms of political witness and action, prayerfully and thoughtfully, to promote just and peaceful social, political and economic structures.
9 work for a British policy of renunciation of all weapons of mass destruction and for the encouragement of other nations, individually or collectively, to do the same.
10 work for the establishment of the United Nations Organisation as the principal organ of international reconciliation and security, in place of military alliances.
11 support and promote research and education into non-violent ways of achieving justice, peace and a sustainable global society.
12 work for the reconciliation within and among nations by international sharing and exchange of experience and people, with particular concern for politically and economically oppressed nations.

Appendix 2 Financial performance: profit and loss by activity (£000)

	1991	1992	1993	1994
Shops on Iona	75	74	107	115
The Abbey	13	48	49	65
Mac centre	−13	12	−7	21
Camas	−7	−2	−3	−5
Islands admin.	n/a[1]	−65	−91	−99
Outreach projects	−9	−14	−29	−15
Wild Goose Publications	−16	−8	27	−6
Net HQ staffing[2]	−35	−53	−65	−86
Total	9	−8	−12	−10

[1] In 1992 the basis of accounting was changed. Islands Admin. is the cost of central administration of all the activities of the centres and shops, i.e. the four account categories above it.
[2] Donations from members are included in this category.

Sheffield Theatres Trust

GARETH MORGAN and KEVAN SCHOLES

Theatres face survival fight — subsidies in danger as audiences dwindle ... But Sheffield Theatres chief executive Stephen Barry and Board chairman John Cornwell said they welcomed Sheffield Council's call for a three year survival plan to ensure the future of live drama in the city. *Sheffield Star*, May 1996

Sheffield has two distinct theatrical traditions: a profile of high-quality production theatre (represented by the Playhouse and subsequently by the Crucible) and a strong history of touring theatre (for which the main venue is the Lyceum). This distinction is fundamental: a producing theatre, through its artistic director, commissions and finances its own productions and employs its own artistes. By contrast, a touring theatre enters into contracts with touring companies, which bring their productions (and their own artistes) to the theatre concerned.

Today, these traditions are brought together in a charitable company known as the Sheffield Theatres Trust, which is unique in the UK in running a producing house and a touring house in one complex. By 1995, Sheffield Theatres was hosting total attendances of over 350,000 per year across its three stages. Serving the population of the fourth largest English city outside London, it had almost £4.5m overall income, making it one of the largest 350 charities in the UK.

Theatre buildings in Sheffield

The Lyceum Theatre opened in 1897; it was designed by the leading theatre

---

This case study was prepared by Dr Gareth G. Morgan and Professor Kevan Scholes, Sheffield Business School, with the assistance of theatre management, external bodies and press reports. It incorporates information from the previous Crucible Theatre case studies (1976, 1988, 1992). It is intended as a basis for class discussion and not as an illustration of either good or bad management practice. © Gareth Morgan and Kevan Scholes, 1996. Please note: Sheffield Theatres regrets that it *cannot* respond to further enquiries related to this case study.

architect of the day, and is now a grade II listed building. It has the rare advantages among traditional theatres of having no pillars obstructing audience views and of having one of the deepest stages in the country. By the early part of the twentieth century it had established itself as one of the UK's leading touring venues, a reputation which grew further in the 1940s. In the 1950s and 1960s it was especially famous for pantomime. But lack of investment and modern amenities forced the Lyceum to close as a venue for music and drama in 1968; demolition was considered, but it subsequently became a bingo hall.

Modern producing theatre in Sheffield dates from the foundation of the Sheffield Repertory Company around 1923, which was renamed 'The Playhouse' in 1938. Initially its work was purely commercial, but it received an Arts Council of Great Britain grant (£5,000) in the 1960/1 season: 'to allow the Playhouse to undertake more prestigious productions than their own resources allow'. This grant marked the change from commercial to subsidised theatre, a transition completed in 1963 when the Playhouse became one of only eight theatres outside London to be taken into formal association with the Arts Council.

In 1966 Sheffield Council announced its intention to sponsor the building of a new theatre of 800–900 seats, and a board of trustees was appointed with representatives from Sheffield Council, the University of Sheffield, the Trades and Labour Council, and the Playhouse itself. This board was responsible for organising the public appeal and other decisions about building the new theatre. This would be mainly a producing house, although with the demise of the Lyceum, it would also host some touring productions.

The result was the Crucible Theatre, completed in 1971 at a total cost of £884,000, on a site next door to the old Lyceum. The 'Crucible' name was chosen to reflect the design of the building and Sheffield's historically famous steel industry. After some controversy, the final building comprised a main auditorium with 1,000 seats around three sides of a thrust stage (which critics complained limited its use for large-scale opera and ballet), and a smaller Studio Theatre with 250 seats (now increased to 400). Sheffield Corporation agreed to lease the site (valued at £250,000) and in addition agreed to contribute £350,000 to the capital cost. The Arts Council granted a further £300,000 from its 'Housing the Arts' fund. A further £150,000 was raised from the public appeal and £50,000 from the Gulbenkian Foundation.

The Playhouse completed its last season in 1970/1 and the Crucible opened in a blaze of local publicity. One of the most notable differences between the Crucible and the old Playhouse was the range of activities which were undertaken. Apart from the two stages, there was a restaurant, coffee bar, shop and licensed bar. Most of these services were operated throughout the day on the principle that the more people who could be enticed through the doors for whatever purpose, the stronger the theatre-going community would be. The foyer/bar was exceptionally large by most standards and was also used for exhibitions and for *ad hoc* folk music performances.

However, as early as 1981 there was a major local campaign to reopen the Lyceum as a theatre, and in 1987 Sheffield City Council agreed to redevelop it as part of the decision to build a number of first-class sporting and leisure facilities for the 1991 World Student Games. The building was by this time derelict and the renovation cost £12.4m. On completion in 1990, the restored Lyceum Theatre provided a superb example of a historic theatre, thoroughly refurbished to modern standards, and with seating for 1,100.

The Crucible and Lyceum stand physically together overlooking a paved square, and for reasons of economy of scale it was decided to form a new company, Sheffield Theatres, to run both venues. The distinctive role of each theatre was, however, to be retained with the Crucible as a producing house, and the Lyceum now hosting a new range of touring companies for the 1990s. The Studio theatre hosts a mixed programme of chamber music and drama, and is the resident home of the Lindsay String Quartet.

Controversies

The Crucible Theatre, and more recently Sheffield Theatres as a whole, have been no strangers to controversy. In September 1972, less than a year after the Crucible opened, it found itself heading for unprecedented losses and the centre of a public storm. Leaks from a confidential report by the city treasurer claimed that the theatre should slash costs and attract bigger audiences to improve its financial position. It was criticised for not staging enough popular shows, for inadequate use of the building, and for 'having too many chiefs and not enough Indians'. Sheffield Corporation was offering to bail out the Crucible provided it put its house in order on these lines, but the theatre administrator claimed that the vital artistic standards would be endangered.

At that time the theatre was run jointly by an administrator and an artistic director, but by 1975 the former had resigned and the latter had retired, and a new post of 'the Director' was created, filled initially by Peter James. However, this first season was a classical one with attendances below 50 per cent of capacity. Speaking to the *Sheffield Star* he said: 'There is a wealth of difference between what an audience thinks they want and what contemporary writers want to write about. The problem is trying to strike a balance.' In 1981 he was succeeded by Clare Venables, who said in an interview shortly after her arrival in the city: 'A theatre that isn't controversial is dead. If people aren't talking about it and getting excited about the theatre, even if it includes criticism, then you are having no impact.'

A further financial crisis in 1982 led to an investigation by the Arts Council and Sheffield City Council. According to the *Sheffield Star*, the subsequent report criticised the board for only meeting twice a year, not even enough to fit in with Arts Council rules for theatres they subsidise. The Management Committee was accused of failing to manage, and scathing comments were made about the 'ill-defined and ineffective' role of the Finance Committee.

Following this, structures were changed. The chair of the board resigned, and the board membership was widened to give greater representation of external and internal interests. For example, in 1986 Sheffield City Polytechnic (now Sheffield Hallam University) was represented on the board for the first time, and observers attended the board representing theatre staff and Yorkshire Arts Association. The board was by then meeting bi-monthly and the Finance and Management Committees were replaced by a new Executive Committee. Changes were made to budgets, to plan on an average of 50 per cent fill capacity instead of 70 per cent — the figure which had been used since the early 1970s despite the fact that 70 per cent had only been achieved once (in 1974). More recently this has been further refined, as even 50 per cent has been found over-optimistic for many Crucible productions, particularly with three theatres operational, and capacity fill is now estimated individually for each production.

However, such changes were not easily received. Clare Venables came close to resignation over the reduction in artistic freedom which arose from the more stringent financial policies. By the mid-1980s a new national climate of public finance had emerged, with no guarantees against loss from the Arts Council, and no scope for local authorities to advance substantial sums to bail the theatre out of difficulties.

Under Clare Venables the theatre enjoyed a considerable reputation — at least among its regular audiences — with productions that were both controversial and challenging artistically. By 1987 the Crucible reached a capacity fill of 74 per cent. But then, as the *Sheffield Telegraph* subsequently noted, 'attention began to focus on the Lyceum, and suddenly the Crucible started to take a back seat'.

With the reopening of the Lyceum, a new post of chief executive of Sheffield Theatres was advertised. In January 1990, Stephen Barry (previously with the Theatre Royal, Bath) was appointed to manage the overall Crucible/Lyceum complex. Clare Venables completed her final season as artistic director the same year, and a number of other staff changes took place.

The Lyceum brought big name touring productions and popular drama and musicals to Sheffield for much of the year. Previously the Crucible had hosted some touring productions (for up to 30 per cent of the year), but it was now able to concentrate almost entirely on its own work. Seats at the Lyceum sold well with average fill at over 60 per cent of capacity, and up to 80–90 per cent for some shows.

By 1991, a new crisis was emerging. In October, the *Sheffield Weekly Gazette* reported: 'The artistic director has resigned, attendances are down by 50 per cent, productions planned for the new year are cancelled, the company is heading for a £250,000 deficit.' This came after an emergency meeting of the directors of Sheffield Theatres Ltd to discuss the drastic fall in Crucible box office receipts following the opening of the Lyceum. However, Stephen Barry insisted that the situation could be managed. 'We are not asking for more money, nor are we trying to take audiences away from the Lyceum.' he said. 'There are different types of audiences out there and we must look at ways of attracting them to the Crucible.'

Two years later he reflected:

> In retrospect we were too defensive about the Crucible — narrowing our market appeal and attempting an over-specialist role. We did not capitalise on the single site thinking brought about by the management structure. We knew the Lyceum would inevitably have an initial effect on the Crucible audiences — which was no doubt deepened by the recession. However, by 1991/2 a balance between the two theatres' programmes had begun to emerge and the box-office turned upwards again.

Some relaxation of the split between the role of the two theatres was agreed, with a few touring productions being accommodated in the Crucible, and one local production (the annual pantomime) being staged at the Lyceum.

However, a new financial crisis emerged in 1993, this time unrelated to box offices sales or grants, but caused entirely from within. It emerged that the assistant head of the accounts department had, over a period of two years, embezzled nearly £0.5m of funds from the various companies under the Sheffield Theatres umbrella. The person responsible was charged and convicted by the courts, and around a third of the money was subsequently recovered. But the events of the fraud created a major trauma for everyone involved, and produced a large overdraft in the theatre accounts, with consequent ongoing interest charges.

Structures

Until the opening of the Lyceum, all the work of the Crucible was handled by one Trust Board. But from 1987 a separate Lyceum Trust was established, and until 1995, Sheffield Theatres actually comprised four separate companies, each with their own boards, under common management:

- Crucible Theatre Trust Ltd, which leased the Crucible site from the City Council and which had responsibility for the Crucible productions.
- Sheffield Lyceum Theatre Trust Ltd, which had responsibility for the Lyceum site.

- Sheffield Theatres Ltd (a management company owned equally by the boards of the two theatres, which employed most of the non-artistic staff).
- Offstage Ltd (a trading subsidiary company responsible for the bars, catering and commercial sponsorship).

Stephen Barry described this as 'an extraordinary structure based on a shotgun marriage of two charitable trusts, requiring in total no less than 22 board meetings per year'. The complexity was largely due to the separate charitable status of each building. This structure meant that few board members had a full picture of the overall financial situation, and grant aid might be increased to one company while being withdrawn from another.

In 1995, after extensive debate, the boards collectively agreed, and it was subsequently approved by Sheffield City Council, to transfer overall legal responsibility for the work of *both* theatres to one body, the Sheffield Theatres Trust. This took over the former responsibilities of the Crucible Trust and Sheffield Theatres Ltd, and assumed all responsibility for managing the Lyceum as a theatre.

Sheffield Theatres Trust is a registered charity and a company limited by guarantee (with permission to omit the word 'Limited' from its title). Its charitable objects, as stated in its Memorandum of Association, are:

- 'To promote, maintain, improve and advance education, particularly by the production of educational plays and the encouragement of the arts of drama, mime, dance, singing and music ...'
- 'To receive, educate and train students in drama, dancing, music, and other arts, and to promote the recognition and encouragement of special merit in students ...'.

The Lyceum Trust continues to exist, but it employs no staff and its role is simply as custodian of the Lyceum building. It leases the building to Sheffield Theatres Trust for use as a theatre for a payment of £90,000 per year — most of this money goes into a long-term building fund to cover future repairs and maintenance.

As with most charitable organisations of any size, it is necessary to have a trading subsidiary company to undertake non-charitable activities such as the sale of food and drink, and this role continues to be met by Offstage Ltd. Offstage is wholly owned by Sheffield Theatres Trust, and at the end of each year, Offstage undertakes a gift aid payment to transfer all its profits to Sheffield Theatres Trust. This means that no corporation tax is paid, and the theatres get the full benefit of all associated activities undertaken on their premises.

Thus, from April 1995, the Board of Sheffield Theatres was able to operate in effect as one organisation, with overall responsibility for management of professional theatre in Sheffield. The board membership is shown in

Appendix 2. The board members are both directors of the company and trustees of the charity; as such they are unpaid. The full board takes responsibility for the entire work; the only subcommittee is an Audit Committee. Staff of the two theatres, from the chief executive downwards, are employees of the board: they are not actually directors of the company, even if the job title 'director' is used.

The change to a single board meant that many long-standing members on one or other of the original boards had to be asked to retire in order to reduce the overall numbers to a workable size. However, a separate Advisory Council was formed, comprising most of those who stepped down. This meets two to three times per year to offer general guidance on the work of the two theatres.

Grant funding

Since the beginning of subsidised theatre in Sheffield in 1960/1, income had shifted from purely commercial sources towards a heavy dependence on grants, primarily from the Arts Council of Great Britain and the local authorities. By 1977 some 63 per cent of the income was in the form of grants; this declined to about 55 per cent by the 1980s, to 40 per cent in 1989, and to 27 per cent by 1995 (this last figure being calculated on both theatres together) — see Appendix 3. It should be noted that the Arts Council does not give grants to touring theatres, but instead gives grants to certain touring companies towards the cost of their productions. However, Sheffield City Council makes grants towards both theatres (in the case of the Lyceum, the bulk of the grant is simply to cover lease payments back to the Council).

The policy on public funding of the arts had changed substantially over the period of this case. In 1985 there was an attempt to build up genuine 'centres of excellence' in the regions, and the Crucible was one of thirteen regional theatres selected as a major beneficiary. The Crucible thus received significant increases in its Arts Council grant — for example, in 1986/7 the grant increased by £100,000, allowing the theatre to move to genuine 52-week operating, and to relaunch its 'Theatre in Education' programme, which organises extensive work with schools.

Another important policy change in the late 1980s was the introduction of 'parity funding', by which the Arts Council aimed that the total public funding of any theatre should be shared equally between the Arts Council and the local authority. However, Sheffield City Council was unable to reach agreement with the Arts Council on this issue as capping of local authority expenditure forced the council to make cuts. David Patmore, director of arts for Sheffield City Council, explained in 1992 that much of the problem was due to the internal structures of the Arts Council, which treated production theatre and touring companies completely separately. As a result, the substantial money which the city council was contributing to the Lyceum project was not recognised by the Arts Council in calculations of overall parity. 'From our point of view,' he stated, 'we'd prefer to talk to the Arts Council about our theatre policy as a whole — but their structure gets in the way of this.' The net effect was that the Crucible lost out substantially in the overall 'pecking order' of Arts Council grants, compared to other large provincial repertory theatres.

In the early 1990s, the Arts Council moved to a regional structure, which meant that the grant to Sheffield Theatres came from Yorkshire and Humberside Arts Board rather than direct from the Arts Council of Great Britain. This meant the Crucible was no longer in direct competition for funds with as many other theatres as previously (there being only one other production theatre in Yorkshire and Humberside of comparable size), but it also meant that the scope for Arts Council grants was influenced heavily by the initial split of the 'cake' into regional 'slices', over which the theatre had relatively little influence. The result was that in the years 1994–6, the Arts Council grant remained static in cash terms at around £650,000 — effectively a cut each year after allowing for inflation.

In 1991, Sheffield City Council commissioned a consultant's report on its funding of Sheffield Theatres. This recommended that the council should reaffirm its commitment to the vital roles which the theatres played in the city in relation to the strategy for regeneration, based on a growth in leisure facilities and increases in tourism. The theatres were seen as a primary focus for the city centre, and a contribution to the new image of the city.

The resultant recommendation was that the council's funding support should be directed to certain key *target investments* — funding only those aspects of the theatres' operations which were of key importance to the city, such as building maintenance, production support and audience development. (The city council was particularly concerned to widen the range of people attending the theatres, as surveys in the past had shown that some 70 per cent of all seats were sold to a core of around 20,000 regular theatre attenders, drawn largely from the professional classes.) At the same time, the theatres were encouraged to become more entrepreneurial, generating a wider range of commercial income.

These recommendations were accepted in general terms: the city council funding became focused on certain areas of the theatres' work, with a service-level agreement which specifies standards that the theatres were expected to achieve. However, the overall restrictions on the city council's budget made it difficult to develop this further, and in any case it was almost impossible to cost things like 'audience development' as a separate activity. The total funding from the city council (excluding grants related purely to the lease of the site) was some £732,000 in 1995, a figure which was actually reduced by £12,000 in 1996. A small amount of grant aid was also received from two neighbouring local authorities (Rotherham and Barnsley), but financial pressures meant that Rotherham entirely withdrew its £11,000 grant in 1996.

The static grant from the Arts Council, and the direct cut in local council funding, meant that in real terms the theatres lost some £66,000 of income from public sources between 1995 and 1996 — a trend which was likely to continue.

Attendances and pricing

The largest part of Sheffield Theatres' revenue is dependent on tickets sold at the box office, and this money must meet all the remaining costs not met by grants or ancillary income. Budgeting for this is dependent upon the three issues of: how seats are priced, what proportion of seats for any production are sold, and to what extent seats are sold at concessionary prices.

In 1995/6, seats in the Crucible ranged from £7 to £13.50 including VAT (with two slightly different scales for different productions). In the Lyceum prices varied widely according to the production, but could be as high as £34 for prime seats at opera performances. The Studio theatre prices were £5 to £10 when used for the theatre's own productions, but it also hosts many musical concerts and smaller outside production companies. In each theatre a wide range of discounts are offered for regular theatre-goers who belong to certain membership schemes which the theatres run; concessions are also available to those over 60, children, students, registered unemployed, disabled people and members of certain unions. Standby seats (£3 to £4 in 1996) were also offered in certain cases.

In the case of the Lyceum, the revenue from ticket sales is distributed between Sheffield Theatres and the touring company according to a contract which is negotiated individually for each production. In some cases quite complex formulae can be used, but a typical split is for 70 per cent of revenue to go to the touring company and 30 per cent to be retained by the theatre. The revenue figures in Appendix 3 show total box office receipts, which increased substantially when the Lyceum opened, but payments to touring companies form a very substantial cost to be met.

Although most performances at the Lyceum are well attended, many of the Crucible productions since 1994 failed to sell as well as hoped, and Sheffield Theatres as a whole had two very poor trading years in 1994/5 and 1995/6. Stephen Barry attributed this partly to the state of economy and partly to the fact that 'people are spending their leisure money on other things, such as the National Lottery'. The theatre has made many attempts over the years to widen its audience, but despite a high profile (a 1990 study found 95 per cent of the local population were aware of the Crucible) many people simply did not see themselves as theatre-goers. This situation — which was typical of theatres in general — was often referred to as 'threshold fear'. Other difficulties in the 1995/6 financial year included a very hot summer (which makes theatre less attractive in the main tourist season), a Christmas pantomime which lacked a well-known television actor, and a difficulty in finding 'touring productions of the required quality' to fill the entire 40–45 weeks needed at the Lyceum.

Other income

In addition to the grant and box office income, Sheffield Theatres worked hard, particularly after 1990, to generate other forms of income.

The most long-standing source of external income has been from hosting the World Snooker Championships. To many people in the UK, the Crucible became synonymous with the championships, which have been held there over three weeks in April/May every year from 1977, under the sponsorship of a tobacco company (which itself caused some controversy in the early days). Although the snooker brought in substantial revenue (around £160,000 in 1995, including extra catering profits), this decision was not without its critics. As the chair of the Advisory Council said in 1996: 'I don't like snooker. I really object to my theatre being used as a snooker hall and it breaks up the theatre season. But it does mean that five or six times a day the *Crucible, Sheffield* is mentioned on prime-time TV. And we do need the money!' The overall view of the board has been that the Crucible needed the revenue, and in 1996 the theatre was negotiating to continue hosting the championships.

The profits of the restaurant, bars and gift shop form an important source of additional income, which is generated via the trading subsidiary Offstage Ltd. By the mid-1990s, Sheffield Theatres became increasingly successful in attracting sponsors for many Crucible productions (and for some at the Lyceum, too, if not already sponsored through the touring company), although after a recession this income was harder to obtain, as sponsorship of the arts is an obvious area for companies to reduce in times of difficulty. The total profits of such commercial activities contributed about £250,000 to theatre funds in 1995/6, although the theatre does not charge Offstage any rental for the space used by bars, etc.

In addition, as a charity, Sheffield Theatres has been active in various forms of fundraising over the years. A Programme Development Fund launched in 1994 was due to generate around £100,000 over four years, from individuals who took out four-year covenants to support the development of new Crucible productions. The Friends of the Lyceum also made a small contribution to the costs of that building.

Certain capital projects have also been supported by fundraising — in particular, in 1994 the £400,000 enlargement of the Studio Theatre from 250 to 400 seats and improved access for disabled people was funded by money raised from the European Regional Development Fund, from a local trust committed to the arts, and from the Foundation for Sport and the Arts. In 1996 the theatre was seeking further funds from the arts distribution of the National Lottery in order to upgrade the Crucible with improved access to the main theatre and consequent better use of foyer space.

Employees

In 1996, Sheffield Theatres employed 161 staff on on-going contracts: 70 in selling and front of house, 53 technical (stage crews, etc.), 25 in maintenance and security, and 13 administrative and secretarial. A further 53 were employed by Offstage Ltd in catering and retailing. Actors and production staff are taken on individually for each production — the most recent average was 29.

Issues for the late 1990s

For Sheffield Theatres, the principal challenge as the Crucible approached its 25th birthday in 1996 was the on-going requirement to maintain the quality of output on the three stages, while attracting sufficient revenue to make this possible. In May 1996 this came to a head with Sheffield City Council calling for a three-year business plan to reverse the decline in Crucible attendances, as a condition of further grants.

Two very difficult years in 1994/5 and 1995/6 had led to major concerns that went beyond the board to outside funders. There was no doubt that, while attendances as a whole had increased dramatically since the opening of the Lyceum, numbers at the Crucible had fallen by roughly a third.

The declining external grants situation meant that the Crucible production budget is 'carved up into ever smaller slices', as Stephen Barry explained it. This had forced the artistic director into offering smaller productions: choosing plays with fewer actors and opting for simpler sets and costume design. Over a seven-year period, the theatre had seen a substantial reduction in the size of productions — at a time when it desperately needed big high-profile productions to win back audiences and influence critics.

But all those involved agree there is a limit to this: it is impossible to promote a 1,000-seat major regional theatre on the basis of small, underfunded productions, particularly when there is the Lyceum and Studio to fill as well. Some local commentators felt that Sheffield was simply unable to support 2,500 seats of professional theatre (although there was no attempt to use all three stages for productions for 52 weeks per year). In addition, attitudes take many years to change, and the city lacks the strong tradition of arts and commerce which is enjoyed by many regional theatres elsewhere in the UK.

On the income side, for many years the theatre had employed a development officer to attract further funding, as well as having a marketing department responsible for promoting productions to the public. In early 1996 a decision had already been taken to recruit for a new post of sales and marketing director to assume overall responsibility for marketing and for the box office. This led to a reorganisation of internal structures (see Appendix 1) following the extensive reorganisation of governance the previous year.

By 1996 the board was equipped with a unified structure to direct the three stages as one financial operation, and had established a new management structure to carry it out. The fraud which had caused so much anguish was moving into history. Yet public sector grants were falling, and fundamentally the future of the theatres would depend on their own marketing efforts, with funders even making this a condition of their support.

The ultimate challenge facing the new marketing director on appointment was to generate sufficient revenue (through ticket sales and other income) not just to enable Sheffield Theatres to survive, but to allow the Trust to maintain the quality and diversity of artistic output for which the Crucible, in particular, had always been known. The management were confident that it could be done — as the *Sheffield Star* reported:

> Stephen Barry and John Cornwell insisted that it was possible to reverse the downward trend: 'Trading last year declined in both theatres, mainly due to the failure of both Christmas shows, but the recently-announced programme for 1996 has the fastest-booking Christmas show ever.'

Appendix 1   Management structure as at May 1996

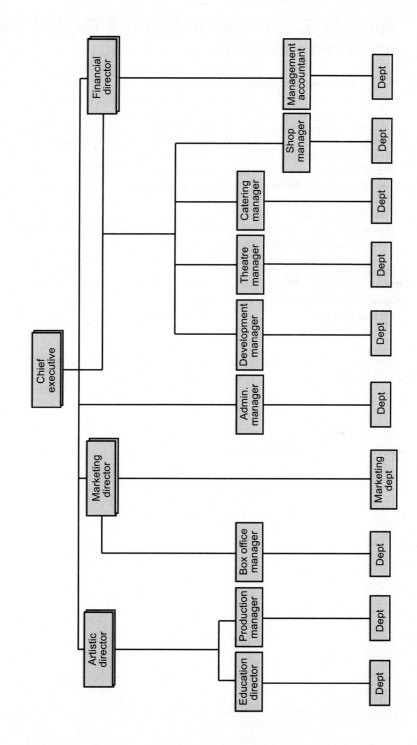

Appendix 2 Summary of Sheffield Theatres Trust board membership, May 1996

Directors/Trustees (15 persons)
Nominated by Sheffield City Council — three members, including the deputy chair of the board.
Elected — ten members, including the chair (John Cornwell) and company secretary. These members serve for periods of three years after which they may be re-elected for one further three-year period. The board elects its own successors.
Nominated by the Lyceum Trust — one member.
Nominated by the Advisory Council — one member.

Observers
Sheffield City Council Arts Department — two observers (officers of the council).
Yorkshire and Humberside Arts Board — one observer.

Officers in attendance
Chief executive
Artistic director
Finance director
Marketing director

Full papers for board meetings are also circulated to all members of the Advisory Council.

Appendix 3 Performance figures and summary revenue accounts (1972–95)

Measure	1972	1973	1974	1975	1976	1977	1978	1979	1980	1981	1982	1983	1984	1985	1986	1987	1988	1989	1990	1991	1992	1993	1994	1995
Attendances																								
Crucible total (000s)	190	221	246	215	227	197	183	174	201	193	176	182	176	186	232	222	192	173	180	110	139	131	92	84
Crucible —																								
capacity fill (%)	52	69	77	49	51	62	61	49	66	55	59	71	58	63	74	74	65	58	65	41	64	63	49	40
Studio total (000s)	13	15	20	32	22	18	21	15	13	19	17	13	8	18	21	15	17	13	5	10	9	15	28	22
Lyceum total (000s)	–	–	–	–	–	–	–	–	–	–	–	–	–	–	–	–	–	–	51*	316	288	299	253	219
Financial																								
Box office (£000s)	89	119	142	152	209	226	256	343	380	399	389	454	486	1145[1]	1306[1]	1330	1446	1596	2274[2]	4051	3929	4599	3789	3017
Grants (% of income)	64	58	56	60	63	58	58	53	53	53	55	55	55	45	45	44	43	40	36[2]	25	27[3]	23	27	30
Surplus/(deficit) (£000s)	(12)	(12)	(8)	(43)	(53)	(5)	(80)	(38)	(111)	(170)	40	(8)	(22)	54	82	(19)	40	(170)	98[2]	(31)	(36)	(115[4])	(228)	(318)
No. of productions																								
Crucible/Studio[5]	73	78	46	44	48	52	59	60	64	42	32	37	37	46	37	34	39	21	37	43	44	34	45	
Lyceum	–	–	–	–	–	–	–	–	–	–	–	–	–	–	–	–	–	–	4*	50	52	41	40	41

Note: Years shown relate to the financial year commencing with the season indicated: e.g. the column '1995' refers to the year Apr. 1995–Mar. 1996.

[1] Catering revenue accounted differently from 1985.

[2] Accounting principles again changed in 1990 (to a basis similar to that used in 1985). Also from 1990 the figures include box office sales and grants for the Lyceum (i.e. the figures from the Crucible Trust and Lyceum Trust have been amalgamated for this table).

[3] From 1992 the Lyceum site was the subject of a lease-back arrangement with the City Council — grants relating to lease payments are excluded from the calculation.

[4] The final surplus or deficit for each of the years 1990–3 is affected to some extent by the fraud referred to in the text.

[5] Figures for numbers of Crucible/Studio productions include: home productions, tours and concerts. However, concerts at the Lyceum (being generally one day events) are not included in the numbers of Lyceum productions.

* Part year only.

Source: Theatre records and published accounts.

Fisons: the fall from grace

HELEN PECK

During the early 1980s, John Kerridge, chairman and chief executive of Fisons, achieved one of the most remarkable business turnarounds in recent times. After selling off the company's loss-making core fertiliser business, he went on to create a highly profitable mini-conglomerate with three distinct areas of business. The Pharmaceutical Division, with its small portfolio of specialist asthma and anti-allergy drugs, was by far the most profitable part of the business. The Scientific Equipment Division was the largest non-American supplier of scientific equipment anywhere in the world. It occasionally outperformed Pharmaceuticals in terms of turnover, but never profits. The very nature of the Scientific Equipment business meant that it was vulnerable to recession. Then there was the tiny, reliable and modestly profitable Horticulture Division, specialising in lawn fertilisers and an array of value-added peat products.

By 1984, Kerridge's transformation of the business was complete. In January 1986, a poll conducted by stockbrokers James Capel had identified Fisons as the best managed company in its sector.[1]

As the 1990s dawned, Fisons was generally regarded as a superbly managed company; highly skilled in the art of mergers and acquisitions, and very efficiently run. Fisons' senior management saw, therefore, no need to give regular presentations to analysts (unlike its pharmaceutical competitors who communicated assiduously with the City), and field trips to view the company's sites and facilities were not permitted. Despite this tendency towards secrecy, the majority of analysts slept soundly in their beds at night, confident that Fisons' remarkable financial performance could be relied upon for the foreseeable future. But while the City fêted Kerridge and his management team, the company's reputation was

[1] The *Financial Times* Health and Household sector.

declining fast in other quarters. It seemed that the Horticulture Division's peat-cutting activities were rapidly developing into a *cause célèbre*.

Fisons was by far the largest cutter of peat in the UK. According to the conservationists, 90 per cent of its cutting was on land which had been designated at Sites of Special Scientific Interest (SSSIs). Fisons was legally entitled to continue working the sites where planning permission predated the award of SSSI status. It was, however, clearly sensitive about outside interest in its peat-cutting activities, and was rapidly acquiring a very bad reputation among sections of the local and national press. In 1989, a *Sunday Times* photographer had had to be rescued by police after being held against his will by Fisons' employees, who blocked in his car for 45 minutes, demanding that he hand over his film. But in March 1990, Fisons overstepped the mark when it illegally drained and severely damaged a 65 acre peat bog on the edge of Thorne Moor, a South Yorkshire nature reserve. The company admitted destroying the Thorne Moor bog, but claimed that it had been a 'genuine mistake'. Environmentalists were not convinced. Similar incursions had been made before when the company 'accidentally' cut peat from important conservation sites on neighbouring Snaith and Cowick Moor.

The Thorne Moor incident prompted ten highly influential conservation groups — including Friends of the Earth, the Royal Society for Nature Conservation, the Royal Society for the Protection of Birds and the Worldwide Fund for Nature — to take up the cause, banding together to form the Peatlands Campaign. The campaigners, led by the Prince of Wales, called for gardeners to boycott peat products and save the remaining peat bogs from total destruction. The Peatlands Campaign did not stop there. In May 1990, it contacted 50 investment managers controlling over £870m worth of Fisons' shares (around 42 per cent of the total) in advance of the company's forthcoming annual meeting. Institutional shareholder, the Borough of Lewisham, supported by the South Yorkshire Pensions Authority (SYPA) and the Pearl Assurance Pension Fund, agreed to press the company to end its peat-cutting operations, urging it to invest instead in the development of peat substitutes. Fisons refused, but its vocal opponents were rallying support from other quarters. The issue was debated in the House of Lords and in the House of Commons, where an early day motion in support of the Peatlands Campaign was signed by 25 Members of Parliament. Fisons remained firm, but 34 local authorities joined the Prince of Wales in banning the use of peat products on their properties. More worryingly for Fisons' shareholders, B&Q — Britain's largest DIY and gardening chain — announced that, 'on conservation grounds', it had decided to ban all peat cut from SSSIs from its stores. Its leading competitors quickly followed suit.

The row rumbled on, but the overall impact on the group's bottom line was negligible. The entire Horticulture Division accounted for only 7 per cent of the company's turnover and 5 per cent of its profits. However, the SYPA — holder of £1m worth of Fisons' shares — continued to demonstrate concern for its local bogs, requesting that it be allowed to visit the SSSIs in its own area where peat cutting was taking place. The SYPA received a letter from head of corporate affairs, Peter Woods, informing it that 'Relations between Fisons and major customers are operational and confidential and as such we would not comment on these to shareholders or any other third party.' Permission for the visit was refused. In the meantime, investors' attention focused on the forthcoming announcement of Fisons' results for the half-year to June 1991.

On 16 September, the eve of the announcement, analysts were still gleefully predicting an 11 per cent rise in interim profits. Little growth was expected from the Scientific Equipment or Horticulture businesses, but hopes were high for the seemingly recession-proof Pharmaceuticals Division. Sales of the anti-asthma drug 'Tilade' — Fisons' most important new drug for many years — were expected to have gathered momentum, and analysts were hopeful that the US Food and Drugs Administration (FDA) was about to approve the drug, granting it access to the world's most lucrative pharmaceutical market.

However, the results announced by Kerridge the following day were not quite as everyone had expected. For the first time in over a decade, Fisons' profits — while up by 6 per cent — had failed to meet expectations. The reason, explained Kerridge, was that £10m had been wiped off profits following supply problems with two of the company's older drugs — Imferon (a blood product) and Opticrom (an anti-allergy eye treatment). Kerridge went on to explain that the disruption to supplies was caused by the 'extremely pedantic' FDA. The City was stunned, and Fisons' share price took a 35p downward leap, closing at 464p on the day (see Appendix 1).

The analysts had rarely complained about Fisons' non-communicative manner while profits soared, but the company's continued reluctance to discuss key areas of the business now made them suspicious that the US problems were more serious than the interim statement had implied. Their worst fears were confirmed — and exceeded — on 11 December 1991, when Fisons announced that the drugs would not be reinstated as quickly as was originally thought, and that the result would be a £65m reduction in profits for 1991. Fisons stressed that the impact on profits would be short term in nature, and that US sales and market share of both drugs would be quickly recaptured, once full supply was resumed the following year. Fisons was nevertheless reportedly furious with the FDA, blaming the delay in clearing Imferon and Opticrom on a dispute between the FDA's Washington and Buffalo offices. Within minutes of the announcement, a further £340m was sliced off the value of the company. The affair had by now reduced the price of the company's stock by a third, wiping over £1bn off its stock market value. Fisons' longer-term growth prospects were now in doubt. As one analyst observed: 'They've been growing through acquisitions based on the strength of their shares, and with the shares so weak, they won't be able to keep it up.'

Two weeks later, as the stock markets reopened from the Christmas break, Fisons' share price nose dived again, as further revelations about its difficulties with the FDA swept the City. According to an article published in *FDC Reports* — an American technical magazine with close links to the FDA — there were long-standing leakage problems with the inhalers used to dispense the anti-asthma drug Intal — Fisons' best selling pharmaceutical product. The article claimed that the company had switched to an alternative design of valve without FDA approval, and that the company had allegedly produced deceptive test results on the new equipment. According to the magazine, Intal had been allowed to remain on the market only because of 'the medical necessity of the product'. The report went on to reveal that the FDA inspectors had also uncovered significant deviations from best practice at Fisons' Holmes Chapel manufacturing plant, including the practice of storing drug solutions for the manufacture of Imferon in what the inspector identified as 'beer kegs'.

The company's immediate reaction was to dismiss the allegations as 'scaremongering' and 'nonsense'. The City was unimpressed. Three days later, on 30 December, a detailed press statement was issued by the company. It stated that 'At no time did Fisons use "beer kegs" in the manufacture of Imferon', and refuted or explained in detail the background to each of the allegations made by the *FDC Reports*. The statement steadied the stock market, but for at least one institutional investor — the SYPA — this was one mishap too many. On 6 January 1992, in a letter to the *Financial Times*, the institution's clerk and financial officer expressed his concern over 'the board's failure to manage effectively both its business and its investor relations'. The SYPA was looking for institutional support for a motion to challenge the board at the forthcoming annual meeting. Fisons' shares were widely held, with the six largest shareholders controlling around 15 per cent of the equity. The following day, an article in London's *Evening Standard* revealed that the SYPA's letter had drawn a 'positive response'. Kerridge's resignation — with immediate effect — was announced one week later.

The man who stepped into Kerridge's shoes to become executive chairman was Patrick Egan, a non-executive director of the company since 1985. Egan stressed that, once a new chief executive had been appointed, he would be concentrating his energies on the company's strategic direction and on improving relations with the City and the company's shareholders. Promising a more open style of management, Egan acknowledged that Fisons' relationships with institutional investors and City opinion-formers had not always been well handled in the past. 'But if you think there are any further skeletons to come out of the cupboard, then you are wrong,' he said.

The respite was short-lived. On 16 January, the full report of the FDA's latest visit to the Fisons' Holmes Chapel plant became available under US freedom of information legislation. The report revealed that the FDA had identified a catalogue of faults during an inspection of the site in 1990. Several months later, a reinspection by the regulators had found that some of its recommendations had still not been put into practice. A spokesman for Fisons had dismissed the FDA's findings as 'not significant', adding that 'All drug companies get these reports. The FDA is ever increasing its quality standards.'

The FDA was incensed. The following day, Peter Smith, associate director of the FDA's International Programmes and Technical Support Branch — the department responsible for overseas inspections — made plain his views on the matter. In a statement in the *Guardian* newspaper, Smith insisted that 'The points in the inspection report were very significant from the FDA standpoint ... We have invested more time and money in Fisons than any other company ever and [they] keep failing inspections.' Smith went on to explain that an inspection usually takes two to five days, but visits to Fisons could take up to three weeks. 'And this is all at the expense of the FDA. There are always problems there.'

At the company's annual meeting on 12 May 1992, it became apparent that Opticrom was unlikely to be readmitted to the USA in time for the all important hay fever season. Worse still, it came to light that its US patent would expire early the following year. With sales of Opticrom disrupted, its market would quickly disappear as rival versions of the relatively simple drug entered the market. The company also confirmed that, due to the long absence of Imferon, the American drugs group Starius had just received FDA approval to market a similar product.

Fisons was at this point still awaiting final approval from the FDA for its new drug, Tilade. The shares took their now customary skip downwards. A profits warning was issued one month later, indicating that profits for the half-year to June 1992 would be only around half those for the same period last year. The shares crashed 77p on the day, wiping off almost a quarter off the company's value. Only speculation that a bid must now be imminent prevented them from falling further.

Fisons struggled through the next year, under a new chief executive, former head of the Scientific Equipment Division, Cedric Scroggs. The company continued its negotiations with the FDA, finally securing approval for Tilade on 31 December 1992. The difficulties surrounding Intal's dispensers were resolved, but discussions regarding the relicensing of Opticrom continued, in the hope that it might yet win back some of its market share. Imferon was formally abandoned. Scroggs' tenure as chief executive was short-lived. He was effectively sacked in December 1993, after recessionary pressures had plunged the Scientific Equipment

Division deep into the red, and some dubious (though not illegal) accounting practices were revealed in the Pharmaceutical Division.

Under a new chief executive, Stuart Wallis, Fisons sold off its Scientific Equipment and Horticulture interests, disposing of the troublesome peat bogs. By early 1995, all that remained of the mini-conglomerate was a cash-rich pharmaceutical shell which continued to turn in operating losses. The company was negotiating a possible merger with Medeva, a small and dynamic pharmaceutical company, and in the meantime speculation persisted that Fisons was a takeover target for a much larger player, Zenica.

Appendix 1 Fisons' share price, 30 December 1988 to 31 December 1993 (weekly)

High 510.00 21/6/91 Low 112.00 17/12/93 Last 134.00

Source: Datastream.

A note on the world automobile industry, 1996

RANJIT DAS

Introduction

The automobile industry is dependent on the state of the economy, and the early 1990s witnessed an economic depression in the three traditional vehicle markets: Japan, western Europe and North America. Between 1990 and 1993 new registrations of passenger cars across the three regions fell from 28.87m to 25.30m. In the same period, production dropped from 31.28m units to 27.6m. See Table 1 for a regional breakdown.

In comparison, during 1990–3, sales and production grew in the rest of the world — particularly in Asia, eastern Europe and Latin America. Sales of passenger cars in the rest of the world increased from 5.72m in 1990 to 6.85m in 1993, and production rose from 4.72m to 6.42m in the same period. However, the economic triad of NAFTA, Japan and the EU accounted for three-quarters of the world's vehicle sales, so while the newly developing Asian vehicle markets offered a higher growth rate, their volume sales

Table 1 Registrations and production of passenger cars, in Japan, western Europe and North America, 1990–3 (000s)

	Registrations		Production	
	1990	**1993**	**1990**	**1993**
Japan	5,100	4,200	9,950	8,500
Western Europe	12,230	11,450	13,580	11,300
NAFTA*	10,530	9,650	7,750	8.170

* NAFTA is the North American Free Trade Association and comprises Canada, Mexico and the USA.

Source: Industry journals.

were comparatively small. Also, many of the markets were closed to foreign producers: for example, South Korea and Taiwan and certain car-makers had established close links with some governments, so creating a barrier to entry for other car manufacturers, such as Volkswagen and Peugeot in China. Manufacturers also had to take into account the increased risk of entering Asian markets.

The worldwide demand for passenger cars grew in 1995 to 33.26m units and was predicted to reach 38.68m units by 2000 (see Table 2). Similarly, production had increased slowly from the low of 1993 and was predicted to increase by about 2 per cent a year (see Table 3). The world automobile industry was forecast to grow at about 3 per cent per year between 1995 and 2000. The largest growth rate was expected in Asia, where a 7–8 per cent growth rate was predicted between 1995 and 2000. However, during that period, growth in western Europe and the NAFTA region was forecast at less than 3 per cent a year, and in Japan sales were predicted to stagnate while production was expected to decrease as Japanese companies began to develop overseas production. The growing shift of production from Japan to overseas facilities had a major impact on exports from Japan, which in turn put pressure on domestic production, where most Japanese car-makers suffered from overcapacity.

In every market in the world, competition among the car manufacturers intensified during the 1990s. Although the Japanese trade barriers were being lifted, the nationalistic buying habits of the Japanese meant that that market would be very hard for US and European car-makers to enter.

Table 2   Actual and predicted new registrations of passenger cars by region, 1994–2000 (000s)

	1994	1995	1996	1997	1998	1999	2000
Western Europe*	11,838	12,018	12,475	12,770	13,110	13,470	13,705
NAFTA**	10,155	9,420	9,380	9,435	9,600	9,875	10,250
South America	1,600	1,720	1,900	2,100	2,250	2,400	2,575
Japan	4,210	4,443	4,600	4,700	4,625	4,575	4,525
Asia exc. Japan	3,072	3,179	3,425	3,665	3,915	4,220	4,615
Eastern Europe	1,456	1,488	1,580	1,627	1,738	1,814	1,904
Other	970	990	1,015	1,035	1,055	1,075	1,110
Total world	33,301	33,258	34,375	35,332	36,293	37,429	38,684
% change	n/a	−0.1	3.4	2.8	2.7	3.1	3.3

Note: Figures for 1994–5 are actual; figures for 1996–2000 are forecasts.
* Western European countries are Austria, Belgium, Denmark, Finland, France, Germany, Greece, Ireland, Italy, Luxembourg, Netherlands, Norway, Portugal, Spain, Sweden, Switzerland, UK.
** NAFTA countries are Canada, USA and Mexico.

Sources: Trade journals; author's forecasts.

Table 3 Actual and predicted production of passenger cars by region, 1994–2000 (000s)

	1994	1995	1996	1997	1998	1999	2000
Western Europe*	12,798	13,129	13,490	13,670	13,825	14,100	14,360
NAFTA**	8,672	8,370	8,030	8,315	8,475	8,670	8,895
South America	1,556	1,510	1,700	1,850	2,000	2,100	2,200
Japan	7,801	7,610	7,600	7,800	7,725	7,625	7,500
Asia exc. Japan	3,118	3,596	3,970	4,270	4,590	4,845	5,190
Eastern Europe	1,637	1,736	1,829	1,924	2,024	2,093	2,161
Other markets	90	92	94	96	99	102	105
Total world	35,672	36,043	36,713	37,925	38,738	39,535	40,411
% change	n/a	1.0	1.9	3.3	2.1	2.1	2.2

Note: Figures for 1994–5 are actual; figures for 1996–2000 are forecasts.
* Western European countries are Austria, Belgium, Denmark, Finland, France, Germany, Greece, Ireland, Italy, Luxembourg, Netherlands, Norway, Portugal, Spain, Sweden, Switzerland, UK.
** NAFTA countries are Canada, USA and Mexico.

Sources: Trade journals; author's forecasts.

The US market was dominated by the American manufacturers, General Motors (GM), Chrysler and Ford, as well as by Toyota, Nissan and Honda. Between them they accounted for 87.5 per cent of car sales. This oligopoly was not expected to change throughout the 1990s. The western European market was more balanced. Toyota, Nissan, Honda, Ford and GM had 32 per cent of sales in 1995 and the European manufacturers — Volkswagen, Renault, Peugeot and Fiat — had 50 per cent of the market. However, the government protection enjoyed by Renault, Peugeot and Fiat was predicted to disappear, leading to a more level playing field by 2000.

For ease of discussion the case has been divided into five sections. The first three sections consider the automobile business in the traditional trading regions of western Europe, NAFTA and Japan respectively. The final two sections review the developments in the regions of Asia-Pacific (excluding Japan) and eastern and central Europe.

Western Europe

In western Europe the passenger car market had reached maturity in about 1990/1. The expected downturn in the region was delayed by German unification in 1991, the former East Germans being responsible for an unpredicted 1.1m extra car sales. The boom was unsustainable and 1993 saw the overdue downturn with a 15.2 per cent drop in car sales.

Registrations in western Europe rose by just 1.5 per cent in 1995 (see Table 4). This slight increase was achieved by using expensive market-boosting measures, such as cheap finance and one-off special offers. Incentives were the crutch of the European car industry, with registrations in France and Spain almost all due to such schemes. The only significant sales rises in 1995 came in Germany, Europe's biggest car market, and the UK, the second biggest. In both cases, the increases had been driven by discounting and incentives. With the integration of Austria, Finland and Sweden into the European Union (EU) and the cyclical upturn in the region, a slight improvement in the economy was expected between 1995 and 2000.

As Table 5 indicates, there was an increase in supply in western Europe, due mainly to the establishment of Japanese factories in the UK. Nissan, Toyota and Honda had a joint capacity of more than 500,000 units a year in 1995, and further planned expansion would increase production to 650,000 by 1999. European car-makers also expanded. Fiat's southern Italian factory produced up to 450,000 cars a year; Ford and Volkswagen set up a new plant in Portugal; and Volvo and Mitsubishi expanded a factory in the Netherlands as part of their Nedcar joint venture.

The problem of oversupply worsened because of foreign imports into the region: for example, Hyundai and Daewoo of Korea, Proton of Malaysia and Tata of India. Oversupply was forecast to increase in 1996 with Chrysler's strategy to expand into Europe. The increase in supply had been partly mitigated by more sales outside western Europe. The Japanese, for example, shipped limited numbers of cars to Japan. Exports to eastern

Table 4   Actual and predicted new registrations of passenger cars in western Europe by country, 1994–2000 (000s)

	1994	1995	1996	1997	1998	1999	2000
Germany	3,209	3,316	3,430	3,490	3,590	3,700	3,800
France	1,973	1,930	1,970	2,000	2,100	2,150	2,200
Italy	1,610	1,704	1,740	1,810	1,925	2,100	2,150
UK	1,911	1,945	1,995	2,070	2,100	2,125	2,150
Spain	879	834	900	940	960	980	1,000
Netherlands	434	451	460	480	470	465	460
Belgium	387	360	380	400	390	380	375
Others	1,435	1,478	1,600	1,580	1,575	1,570	1,570
Total	11,838	12,018	12,475	12,770	13,110	13,470	13,705
% change	n/a	1.5	3.8	2.4	2.7	2.7	2.7

Note: Figures for 1994–5 are actual; figures for 1996–2000 are forecasts.

Sources: Society of Motor Manufacturers and Traders; trade journals; author's forecasts.

Table 5 Actual and predicted production of passenger cars in western Europe by country, 1994–2000 (000s)

	1994	1995	1996	1997	1998	1999	2000
Germany	4,094	4,320	4,360	4,460	4,560	4,650	4,725
France	3,175	3,050	3,130	3,160	3,190	3,250	3,300
Italy	1,341	1,422	1,510	1,570	1,550	1,560	1,575
UK	1,467	1,532	1,650	1,720	1,825	1,925	2,000
Spain	1,822	1,865	1,850	1,755	1,725	1,750	1,800
Netherlands	92	95	150	165	160	155	155
Belgium	408	390	375	360	350	340	340
Others	399	455	465	480	465	470	465
Total	12,798	13,129	13,490	13,670	13,825	14,100	14,360
% change	n/a	2.6	2.7	1.3	1.1	2.0	1.8

Note: Figures for 1994–5 are actual; figures for 1996–2000 are forecasts.

Sources: Society of Motor Manufacturers and Traders; trade journals; author's forecasts.

Europe were also increasing, and were estimated to increase further with the removal of local tariffs on imported cars.

With supply outstripping demand, manufacturers had to spend heavily on marketing and new product development. Niche buyers were targeted, such as four-wheel-drive sports utilities, convertibles and multipurpose vehicles (people-carriers). But the risk was that the strategy of targeting niches would be self-defeating as the niches became overcrowded. For example, Fiat and its Alfa Romeo subsidiary already had two models competing with Rover's MGF for the two-seater sports car sector, and in 1996 BMW, Mercedes-Benz, Porsche and Renault also introduced two-seaters. The same was happening with multipurpose vehicles: Renault's Espace was competing with two models from the Fiat Group and from Peugeot-Citroën. Ford and VW also launched products in 1995, and in 1996 Mercedes-Benz, Opel and Chrysler were all to produce their own models for this sector.

An alternative strategy to stimulate demand was through price cuts, but this would require rationalisation, meaning plant closures and possible mergers.

Table 6 gives a breakdown of manufacturers' market shares in the region. The top six manufacturers held 75 per cent of the market, but with the threat of entry of the US producer Chrysler, a rationalisation within the industry via mergers and acquisitions was a likely strategy: BMW had acquired Rover in 1995 and there had been a failed merger attempt between Renault and Volvo in 1993.

We will now examine specific western European markets.

Table 6   Market shares of passenger cars in western Europe by manufacturer, 1991–7 (%)

Manufacturer	1991	1992	1993	1994	1995	1996	1997
Volkswagen Group (Volkswagen, Audi, Seat, Skoda)	16.4	17.5	15.9	16.7	16.8	16.3	16.2
General Motors (Opel/Vauxhall, Saab)*	12.0	12.4	12.9	13.1	13.0	13.0	13.1
Ford Group (Ford, Jaguar)*	11.8	11.2	12.0	12.1	11.9	11.0	10.9
PSA Peugeot Citro·n	12.1	12.2	12.8	12.0	12.0	12.4	12.1
Fiat Group (Fiat, Lancia, Alfa Romeo, Maserati)	12.7	11.8	10.8	10.9	11.1	10.6	10.4
Renault	9.9	10.6	10.8	10.4	10.4	10.6	10.7
BMW Group (BMW, Rover)	3.1	3.3	6.5	6.2	6.3	6.7	6.7
Mercedes-Benz	3.4	3.1	3.6	3.4	3.3	3.3	3.1
Volvo	1.5	1.5	1.7	1.8	1.8	1.7	1.7
Nissan	3.2	3.2	3.3	3.1	3.1	3.4	3.5
Toyota	2.7	2.5	2.6	2.6	2.5	2.6	2.7
Honda	1.2	1.3	1.4	1.5	1.5	1.6	1.7
Mazda	1.3	1.4	1.5	1.4	1.4	1.5	1.5
Mitsubishi	1.4	1.2	1.0	1.1	1.1	1.2	1.3
Others	7.3	6.8	3.2	3.7	3.8	4.1	4.4
Total sales in western Europe (000s)	13,500	13,498	11,250	11,838	12,018	12,475	12,770

Note: Figures for 1991–5 are actual; figures for 1996–7 are forecasts.
* Includes cars imported from USA and sold in western Europe.

Sources: European Automobile Manufacturers Association; author's forecasts.

France

A dramatic drop of 18.3 per cent in the French car market in 1993, from 2.11m units to 1.72m, forced the government to introduce a temporary incentive scheme to boost registrations. Owners of cars over ten years old were given a cash incentive ($800) towards the cost of a new car in return for scrapping their old car. This incentive was matched by the car manufacturers. New car registrations rose sharply in 1994, but levelled out in 1995 as most of the potential buyers had bought replacement cars in 1994. Increases in new registrations were forecast for the late 1990s due to the natural replacement cycle.

Germany

German unification in 1991 boosted the German market, with a 37 per cent increase in new registrations between 1990 and 1991, from 3.04m cars to 4.16m. The demand for cars in former East Germany had never been met under Communist control, and the favourable exchange rates given to the East Germans following reunification led to a flood of new registrations. Demand for cars in the former West Germany was dictated by the economic conditions and the replacement cycle. The former West Germany had been entering a downturn in demand just as unification occurred, and this resulted in an unpredicted boost in demand. Thus, when the downturn came in 1992/3 a sharp fall was seen, from 3.93m in 1992 to 3.19m in 1993.

Demand grew in 1995, but predicted increases in taxes to pay for higher welfare spending and a levy to cover car recycling costs meant that the demand for cars was expected to grow only gradually between 1995 and 2000.

Italy

The Italian market fell sharply during 1992–4, from 2.38m cars to 1.61m, but a slight growth in new registrations was expected up to 2000. Low consumer confidence due to an expected rise in taxes, poor economic conditions and political instability meant that growth in the late 1990s would be due principally to the replacement cycle.

Spain

The underlying decline in the Spanish car market between 1991 and 1993 was only temporarily halted in 1992 because the government reduced the VAT rate on cars and many suppliers took that opportunity to cut prices.

This boosted sales from 0.87m units in 1991 to 0.98m in 1992, but sales fell to 0.74m in 1993. The rise in sales between 1993 and 1994 was again due to government cash incentives towards the cost of a new car in return for scrapping an old car. New car registrations were expected to grow slightly up to the year 2000 due to an economic upturn, lower income taxes and the normal replacement cycle.

UK

UK car sales peaked in the late 1980s with the registration of 2.35m vehicles in 1989. The 1990–2 recession caused a 30 per cent reduction in car sales, which fell to 1.59m in 1992. The rate of recovery in the mid-1990s was lower than expected, and growth was forecast to be low throughout the 1990s.

Some 45 per cent of the UK car market was made up of the company fleet car sector. As part of their remuneration package, most senior and middle managers received a company car leased from a fleet car operator. Companies had been able to negotiate favourable deals on the leasing of luxury cars and so distorted the registration figures of such cars in the UK. Government taxes on company cars meant that many employees had opted to take a financial payment in lieu of a company car, and then buy their own, typically smaller, vehicles directly. This trend was forecast to continue, so the demand for smaller cars was expected to rise.

The shift away from company cars may have been expected to increase private car sales. However, due to the large depreciation suffered by new cars, private buyers were buying low-mileage, used cars. Thus, it was forecast that the demand for new cars would be low, but that the market for used cars would grow.

Other western European markets

Austria's membership of the EU meant a fall in car prices. That, together with a peak in the cyclical replacement cycle in the mid-1990s, led to an increase in registrations in 1995, which were forecast to reach 300,000 cars a year in 1996. Demand was expected to fall beyond 1996 as the market was mature, the replacement cycle was expected to wane and expected new taxes on cars would make car ownership less appealing.

Due to steady economic growth, the car market in *Belgium* was predicted to grow, peaking at 0.4m cars a year in 1997, after which demand was expected to fall gradually. The market was saturated, the population was stable and possibility of new fuel and vehicle taxes meant that new registrations were predicted to reduce in the years leading up to the year 2000.

New registrations in the *Netherlands* were expected to rise to 0.48m by 1997, due to a peak in the replacement cycle and an improvement in the economy. Growth beyond 1997 was expected to be driven only by the replacement demand, since the population was stable and alternative forms of transport were fully developed.

The NAFTA region

In 1995 performance of the North America Free Trade Association region (NAFTA), comprising the USA, Canada and Mexico, was let down by Mexico. The USA and Canada had mature markets, but their growth rates during the late 1990s were expected to improve and their inflation was under control. Mexico, however, was thrown into an economic downturn when the currency was devalued by 40 per cent in 1994. Consumer confidence, buying power and savings were lost, and it was expected to take many years before consumer confidence and growth rates recovered and inflation fell. Car sales in Mexico had shown a dramatic drop in 1995 (see Table 7). Mexico's economic difficulties meant that the country's vehicle sales were expected to fall sharply in the mid-1990s and then recover by 2000.

Due to a combination of the General Agreement on Trade and Tariffs (GATT), the initiation of the North American Free Trade Agreement, the economic recovery and an upturn in the replacement cycle, the demand for passenger cars was forecast to grow steadily in Canada and the USA from the mid-1990s, but new registrations in 1995 were lower than in 1994. The industry was paying for price rises in 1994 and a flood of two-year-old cars on to the used car market — the product of the promotion of cheap short-term leases. Also, discounts and lease deals used to sell new vehicles in the early 1990s had encouraged customers to resist higher prices.

Table 7   Actual and predicted new registrations of passenger cars in the NAFTA region, 1994–2000 (000s)

	1994	1995	1996	1997	1998	1999	2000
Canada	749	670	690	750	790	900	1,100
Mexico	414	110	115	160	200	275	350
USA	8,992	8,640	8,575	8,525	8,610	8,700	8,800
Total NAFTA	10,155	9,420	9,380	9,435	9,600	9,875	10,250
% change	n/a	−7.2	0.4	0.6	1.7	2.9	3.8

Note: Figures for 1994–5 are actual; figures for 1996–2000 are forecasts.

Sources: AMIA; author's forecasts.

Table 8   Actual and predicted production of passenger cars in NAFTA, 1994–2000 (000s)

	1994	1995	1996	1997	1998	1999	2000
Canada	1,211	1,340	1,365	1,420	1,455	1,470	1,495
Mexico	856	700	665	720	770	850	950
USA	6,605	6,330	6,000	6,175	6,250	6,350	6,450
Total NAFTA	8,672	8,370	8,030	8,315	8,475	8,670	8,895
% change	n/a	−3.5	−4.1	3.5	1.9	2.3	2.6

Note: Figures for 1994–5 are actual; figures for 1996–2000 are forecasts.

Sources: AMIA; author's forecasts.

In the USA six manufacturers dominated the market in 1995: General Motors (33.9 per cent), Ford (20.7 per cent), Chrysler (9.1 per cent), Toyota/Lexus (9.2 per cent), Honda/Acura (8.6 per cent) and Nissan/Infiniti (6.0 per cent). There was a similar scenario in Canada, where the respective market shares of the main firms were: GM (33.9 per cent), Ford (16.9 per cent), Chrysler (14.5 per cent), Honda (9.9 per cent) and Toyota (8.5 per cent). The balance between the main manufacturers was not forecast to shift dramatically in the 1990s unless takeover or joint venture strategies were followed.

Passenger car production was forecast to dip in 1996, but then to grow steadily in the following years (Table 8). It was predicted that US growth would be due to the local US producers meeting the increased demand and the Japanese transplants coming on-line, and growth in Mexico due to the manufacturers developing their capacity.

Japan

Political scandals, the strength of the yen and concerns about interest rates and taxes had left consumer confidence in Japan weak at the start of the 1990s. A slowing down of the growth of GNP induced a rise in interest rates in the early 1990s, leading to a slowing of the economic boom. This was reflected in a 13.8 per cent fall in new registrations between 1991 and 1993, from 4.87m to 4.20m cars.

Although the economic prospects were improving in the mid-1990s, recovery was predicted to be slow. Aided by a cut in sales tax for cars in 1994, the following few years were predicted to show an increase in new car registrations. The stringent and expensive vehicle testing regime on older vehicles also acted to create an upturn in the replacement cycle in the mid-

1990s. The 1995 sales figures showed that Toyota was the market leader with 33.6 per cent market share, with Nissan's 18 per cent share placing it second. These two manufacturers dominated sales, with Mitsubishi (9.2 per cent), Honda (8.5 per cent), Suzuki (7.4 per cent) and Mazda (6.3 per cent) trailing behind.

Sales of foreign-produced cars, excluding models made by Japanese manufacturers overseas, accounted for only about 7 per cent of the market in 1995. For years US and European car-makers had complained about the barriers to entering the Japanese car market, ranging from high tariffs to superfluous safety checks. But trade negotiations have removed such barriers and as a result the big three US manufacturers forecast a sixfold increase in sales to 100,000 cars each by the year 2000. European car-makers also believed they could take a substantial share of the world's second largest market, with imports predicted to reach between 20 and 30 per cent of the market.

A key factor for the predicted surge in imports into Japan had been the strong yen, which allowed foreign manufacturers to reduce prices and offer additional features at no extra cost. Even prestige marques, such as Mercedes-Benz and Audi, were able to cut the differential between their prices in Japan and those in their domestic market. 1995 saw an increased demand for the less prestigious brands: almost half of Rover's sales were for the Mini and the Rover 100, and VW enjoyed a similar upturn. But some big European manufacturers, such as Fiat, Peugeot-Citroën and Renault, found Japan a hard market.

The Japanese government was becoming increasingly protective of the environment, with expectations that the use of alternative fuels and more environmentally friendly vehicles would be needed in the longer term. These were likely to be more expensive than the 1995 models. By 1995 the market for passenger cars in Japan was saturated. Although the number of cars per person remained low by world standards, congestion and parking restrictions made ownership of a car unattractive. Thus, sales were expected to flatten out in the late 1990s and then fall slightly by the end of the decade, due to the predicted tightening of environmental laws, parking restrictions and increases in sales tax (see Table 9).

Table 9 Actual and predicted new registrations of passenger cars in Japan, 1994–2000 (000s)

	1994	1995	1996	1997	1998	1999	2000
Japan	4,210	4,443	4,600	4,700	4,625	4,575	4,525
% change	n/a	5.5	3.5	2.2	−1.6	−1.1	−1.1

Note: Figures for 1994–5 are actual; figures for 1996–2000 are forecasts.

Source: DRI; author's forecasts.

Motor vehicles were Japan's largest export business. Although in the first half of the decade, exports to Malaysia and Indonesia had dropped sharply, shipments to China had increased. There was also a growth in exports to the Middle East and South America. In total, however, the volume of exports had fallen. Thus, vehicle production fell sharply in the first half of the decade.

Apart from falling exports, other factors like a shrinking home market, self-imposed cutbacks by the Ministry of International Trade and Industry (MITI), the appreciation of the yen and growth of overseas operations all led to a drop in local production in the early 1990s. Labour shortages and increasing production costs also gave manufacturers serious problems.

Production had fallen from 9.75m to 8.50m cars between 1991 and 1993, and further decreases were expected by the end of the decade due to a predicted fall in local demand and the further development of overseas transplant operations (Table 10). There had been an increase in such operations in order to avoid the impact of exchange rate fluctuations, which undermined the competitiveness of direct exports. Overseas production also helped allay trade frictions and allowed car-makers to respond more flexibly to local market needs.

The three largest Japanese companies, Toyota, Nissan and Honda, focused on the USA and the UK as their bases for overseas development. In the UK, Japanese car companies produced more than 500,000 units in 1995, and this was forecast to reach 650,000 units by 1999. Honda remained the most international of Japan's three leading car-makers. Honda expanded overseas output more rapidly than Toyota and Nissan because its home sales were smaller, and the company predicted that by 1996 it would make more cars overseas than in Japan. The company expected to build 996,000 vehicles overseas in 1996, compared with 975,000 units at home. Toyota increased overseas production by 20 per cent in 1995 and expected a 9 per cent rise in 1996 to 1.37m units. By contrast, Nissan, one of the first Japanese car-makers to shift production abroad, did not plan significant increases in overseas output.

Table 10   Actual and predicted production of passenger cars in Japan, 1994–2000 (000s)

	1994	1995	1996	1997	1998	1999	2000
Japan	7,801	7,610	7,600	7,800	7,725	7,625	7,500
% change	n/a	−2.5	−0.1	2.6	−1.0	−1.3	−1.6

Note: Figures for 1994–5 are actual; figures for 1996–2000 are forecasts.

Sources: DRI; author's forecasts.

Asia-Pacific excluding Japan

Asia-Pacific had one of the fastest growing economies in the mid-1990s and this was predicted to continue if the countries in Asia could keep inflation under control. The political uncertainty of many of the governments in the area and the risk of cross-border wars remained the key potential stumbling blocks in the region's growth.

Vehicle sales were predicted to grow by 7 per cent annually for the region (see Table 11). Vietnam, China, Indonesia, India, Thailand and the Philippines were all predicted high growth rates. However, slower growth was predicted in South Korea (5 per cent a year) and Taiwan (2 per cent a year), and demand in Australia was expected to fall by 0.2 per cent a year.

In 1995, South Korea was the largest producer of passenger vehicles in the region, with a 55.6 per cent share of production (see Table 12). With a rapid development of production operations in India and China predicted during the latter part of the decade, South Korea's share of the production market was expected to fall to 48.2 per cent of all the region's output. Australia's importance as a producer in the region was expected to decline.

China's automotive policy, announced in 1994, froze new car manufacturing ventures until 1997 and demanded that companies wanting to produce vehicles in China showed a commitment by investing in the components sector. China was clearly the biggest potential new market for the automobile industry, and Volkswagen of Germany led the early entry of European manufacturers into China: the company established its first manufacturing joint venture facility in 1985. The dominance of German companies was reinforced when the Chinese government selected

Table 11 Actual and predicted new registrations of passenger cars in Asia (excluding Japan), 1994–2000 (000s)

	1994	1995	1996	1997	1998	1999	2000
China	376	330	400	500	600	725	850
India	282	390	440	510	550	600	720
South Korea	1,140	1,150	1,220	1,250	1,320	1,400	1,490
Taiwan	435	455	465	475	485	495	505
Others	839	854	900	930	960	1,000	1,050
Total	3,072	3,179	3,425	3,665	3,915	4,220	4,615
% annual change	n/a	3.5	7.7	7.0	6.8	7.8	9.4

Note: Figures for 1994– 5 are actual; figures for 1996–2000 are forecasts.

Sources: DRI; author's forecasts.

Table 12 Actual and predicted production of passenger cars in Asia (excluding Japan), 1994–2000 (000s)

	1994	1995	1996	1997	1998	1999	2000
China	250	321	400	500	600	700	850
India	298	390	430	500	580	640	740
South Korea	1,760	2,000	2,220	2,300	2,390	2,450	2,500
Taiwan	283	308	320	340	360	375	390
Others	527	577	600	630	660	680	710
Total	3,118	3,596	3,970	4,270	4,590	4,845	5,190
% change	n/a	15.3	10.4	7.6	7.5	5.6	7.1

Note: Figures for 1994–5 are actual; figures for 1995–2000 are forecasts.

Sources: DRI; author's forecasts.

Mercedes-Benz and Porsche in preference to Chrysler and Ford for two important industry projects. Mercedes-Benz explored the possibility of building 60,000 multipurpose vehicles (also known as people-carriers) and 100,000 engines, and Porsche agreed to set up a technical and research centre for new car lines.

Japanese car-makers remained wary of the relatively undeveloped Chinese market and were cautious about large investments there. Japanese ventures in China included the Jinbel/Toyota joint venture and the General Motors/Daihatsu joint venture to produce the minibus model. Isuzu was also involved in a venture to produce vehicle bodies.

General Motors beat Ford to one of China's largest car manufacturing projects involving a foreign partner. General Motors planned to invest $1bn in a plant in Shanghai to produce a new company car for Chinese corporations. The joint venture with state-owned Shanghai Automobile Industry Corp. will build 100,000 vehicles a year by the end of the decade.

Ford had a clear strategy of establishing vehicle manufacturing in China, although it was not well represented there. The company had four joint venture agreements to produce automotive components with Chinese companies, and took a 20 per cent share of Jiangling Motors, a small company based in the southern province of Jiangxi, producing 120,000 light trucks a year.

In sharp contrast to China, Vietnam opened its doors and gave licences to twelve foreign car manufacturers ranging from Chrysler and Ford of the USA and Toyota of Japan to smaller, less experienced players such as Hyundai. The government seemed to have taken the philosophy of free-market economy to extremes. Fierce competition as well as neighbouring Thailand's ambitions of producing 1m cars by the year 2000 could force some car-makers out of Vietnam.

Japanese car-makers were well positioned to take advantage of growth in the Far East region; they were geographically close to the market and some companies had been in some of these markets for as long as 30–40 years. For example, in Thailand, Japanese brand names had a market share of more than 90 per cent. Japanese brands also dominated the markets in Indonesia, the Philippines and Malaysia: for example, Mitsubishi Motors had a 58 per cent share of the Malaysian car market. Mitsubishi planned annual car sales in the Asia-Pacific region of 900,000 units by the year 2000.

Japanese car-makers strengthened their position in the region with vehicles tailored specifically to regional needs. The companies took cars developed in Japan and modified them to suit local needs. Referred to as 'Asia cars', such models were viewed almost as 'national cars' by local consumers.

India was a very attractive market for foreign investment in the 1990s when the government abolished industrial licensing in the passenger car sector in 1993. For decades two companies had dominated the Indian car market: Hindustan Motors and Premier Automobiles. In 1983 a Suzuki–Indian government joint venture formed a third manufacturer, Maruti. Targeting the small-engined 'people's car', Maruti gained 71 per cent of the car market. However, numerous joint ventures (JVs) indicated a potential explosion in car sales and production in the years leading up to the end of the decade:

- Daewoo and DCM, an Indian heavy goods vehicle (HGV) maker, entered a JV to produce a small car called the Cielo.
- Mercedes and Telco, another HGV maker, entered a JV to make the Mercedes E220 saloons.
- A 50/50 JV between Hindustan Motors and General Motors planned to produce the Opel/Vauxhall Astra.
- Hindustan also had a licensing agreement with Mitsubushi to produce the Lancer.
- Premier Automobiles and Peugeot had a JV to build the 309 saloon.
- Premier also had a separate JV with Fiat to produce the Uno.
- Mahindra & Mahindra, the Indian utility vehicle-maker, had a JV with Ford to produce the Escort and Fiesta.
- Siel, the Indian engineering group, had a JV with Honda to make the latter's Civic.
- Volkswagen and Eicher, the Indian commercial farm vehicle group, planned to produce the Gold.

None of the new joint ventures aimed directly to challenge the low-price, high-volume sector of the market dominated by Maruti, but instead aimed to create a new upmarket sector.

Eastern and central Europe

Apart from an ailing Russian economy, in 1995 most of the economies of the countries in this region were growing, albeit at a slow rate. Poland's economy had grown every year since 1992, and Hungary, Romania, Bulgaria and the Czech Republic all showed signs of being over their economic decline. Russia's social and political instability meant that the trend of a declining economy since 1989 was not expected to change during the 1990s.

Following the collapse of the region's command economy, the low currency value in eastern Europe meant that, although many people aspired to own a new car, few could actually afford one. Between 1990 and 1995 demand had fallen from 1.1 million units to 0.69m units in the region's largest market, Russia and the Ukraine, which accounted for 65 per cent of the region's vehicle sales in 1990 (see Table 13). There was a similar trend in the other countries of eastern Europe, with the region's sales falling from 2.0m cars to 1.49m units between 1990 and 1995.

Production levels were on the decline in the early 1990s. In Russia and the Ukraine production had fallen from 1.1m units to 0.81m between 1990 and 1995. In the rest of eastern Europe production fell from 0.72m units to 0.68m between 1990 and 1992, but then recovered to 0.92m units by 1995. Foreign investment had boosted production: for example, Fiat in Poland and Volkswagen in the Czech Republic. The increase in production was predicted to continue between 1995 and 2000 (see Table 14).

Hungary led the way in market-led reforms in the former Communist bloc and was rewarded by attracting foreign investment. Between 1990 and 1994, the country attracted $8.49bn in foreign investment, more than was invested

Table 13   Actual and predicted registrations of passenger cars in eastern and central Europe, 1994–2000 (000s)

	1994	1995	1996	1997	1998	1999	2000
Russia and Ukraine	690	675	700	750	800	850	900
Czech Republic	95	110	115	120	125	132	140
Slovakia	15	25	28	33	38	42	50
Hungary	91	56	70	65	62	60	60
Poland	250	260	267	277	287	300	320
Others	315	362	400	382	426	430	434
Total	1,456	1,488	1,580	1,627	1,738	1,814	1,904
% change	n/a	2.2	6.2	3.0	6.8	4.4	5.0

Note: Figures for 1994–5 are actual; figures for 1996–2000 are forecasts.

Sources: Industry journals; author's forecasts.

Table 14 Actual and predicted production of passenger cars in eastern and central Europe, 1994–2000 (000s)

	1994	1995	1996	1997	1998	1999	2000
Russia and Ukraine	798	805	835	890	950	980	1030
Czech Republic	174	195	205	215	220	225	230
Slovakia	8	22	26	28	32	40	46
Hungary	32	51	58	66	72	78	85
Poland	338	364	375	385	400	410	420
Others	287	299	330	340	350	360	350
Total	1,637	1,736	1,829	1,924	2,024	2,093	2,161
% change	n/a	6.0	5.4	5.2	5.2	3.4	3.2

Note: Figures for 1994–5 are actual; figures for 1996–2000 are forecasts.

Sources: Industry journals; author's forecasts.

in all other eastern European countries combined. Hungary's geographic location between the European Union and the huge former Soviet market meant that the country was the natural route for western companies into eastern Europe, Ukraine, Russia and Romania. Ford moved its central European headquarters from Vienna to Budapest in order to give its executives a better understanding of market conditions in eastern Europe.

Hungary also had an agreement with the EU which abolished or provided for the phasing out of tariffs on goods produced in Hungary. Thus, western European companies could produce in Hungary and then sell the goods on the EU markets without incurring heavy import taxes. This reduction in production costs more than offset the cost of moving production to Hungary. Audi, for example, shipped components overnight to its engine plant at Gyor in western Hungary, and following assembly they were sent back via a train link which came directly on to the factory floor. Manufacturers from the USA and Asia, such as Ford and Suzuki, also moved production to Hungary because it was a low-cost base from which to export to the EU.

However, Poland and the Czech Republic were also competing for such investment. General Motors planned to invest $359.7m in a new east European car plant site in southern Poland, with a possible further $250m expansion to raise production capacity from 72,000 cars to 150,000. The Polish government offered corporate tax relief and customs duty incentives to encourage the investment in Poland. In some designated economic development zones, the Polish government offered complete relief from corporation tax for up to ten years, a further ten years in which corporation tax would be paid at half the normal rate, and relief on customs duty for imported plant and equipment.

PSA Peugeot Citroën

ROLAND CALORI, PHILIPPE VERY and MICHEL BERTHELIER

The PSA Group included two general car manufacturing companies: Automobiles Peugeot and Automobiles Citroën. The two were linked by strong technological, industrial and financial synergies, although each marque kept its identity, and its own marketing and sales. In 1994 the PSA Group was the third largest car manufacturer in Europe, with a 12.8 per cent market share.

The year 1994 showed improved performance of PSA, after difficulties in 1993: profitability rose from a Ffr1 billion loss to profits of Ffr3.1 billion, and the sales turnover increased from Ffr145.4 billion to Ffr166.2 billion (95 per cent of which was in car manufacturing). PSA employed 139,800 people and manufactured 1,989,000 vehicles, of which two-thirds were sold outside France in 150 countries and 22,000 sales locations. With export sales of Ffr74.9 billion, the group was the main French exporter.

The PSA Group

In 1976 Peugeot, a family owned company, took over Citroën. Then in 1978 it took over the European subsidiaries of Chrysler. At the beginning of the 1990s, the group (Peugeot and Citroën) was controlled by the Peugeot family, who owned 22.7 per cent of the equity, the largest other shareholder being Michelin. The rest of the equity was held by financial institutions and individual stockholders.

From 1980 to 1984 the PSA Group went through financial difficulties, its net debts rising to Ffr33.1 billion and its equity dropping to Ffr5.3 billion in 1984. In 1983 the group lost Ffr2.6 billion. The renaissance of PSA came with

This case was prepared by Roland Calori, Philippe Very and Michel Berthelier, professors at the Group ESC Lyon. The authors would like to thank the PSA Group for its support in writing the case study. It is intended as a basis for class discussion and not as an illustration of either good or bad management practice. © R. Calori, P. Very and M. Berthelier, 1996.

the hiring of a new top manager, Jacques Calvet, and with the growth in the European market (+4 per cent per year on average) between 1985 and 1989. Jacques Calvet became président directeur général of Peugeot, then président directeur général of Citroën in 1983 and président du directoire of the holding company in 1984. Formerly he had been directeur du trésor at the French Ministry of Finance and president of the Banque Nationale de Paris. Experts believed that his skills and the rigour of his management were at the centre of the recovery of the PSA Group. Losses were cut as early as 1984, and debts were reduced starting from 1987. At the end of 1989, the company announced net profits of Ffr10.3 billion (a net margin of 6.7 per cent of turnover); the sales turnover was about Ffr153 billion and debts had been reduced to Ffr1.9 billion.

Substantial progress in production methods was also achieved: productivity improvements were about 72 per cent between 1982 and 1987 (the best European performance according to the consulting company Luvigsen Associates), and 50 per cent during the period 1985–9. High investments were made to rationalise manufacturing and to develop the company's range of products.

In 1986 Jacques Calvet announced an ambitious goal for PSA: to become the leading car manufacturer in the European market in terms of number of vehicles sold. However, the aim of dominant market share was postponed with the recession of the western European market and the unexpected opening of the eastern European market, which was more favourable to competitors based in Germany (Volkswagen and GM-Opel). Indeed, from 1990 to 1993, with the economic recession, the European car market decreased and sales and profits of the PSA Group slowly declined before the 1994 revival.

Table 1 gives the main financial indicators of PSA between 1990 and 1994, and Table 2 gives information on the two main companies of the group, Automobiles Peugeot and Automobiles Citroën.

Table 1   PSA Group: main consolidated financial data

	1994	1993	1992	1991	1990
Net sales	166.2	145.4	155.4	160.2	160
Cash flow	15.2	8.3	13.7	15.4	16.2
Investments (tangible assets)	10.5	11.3	13.8	15.5	15.2
Net profit	3.1	(−1.4)	3.4	5.5	9.3
Shareholders' equity	53.5	50.5	53.1	51.7	47.2
Net financial debts	7.6	16.7	14.3	9.4	8.3
Earnings per share (Ffr)	62	(−28)	67	111	185

Note: Figures in millions of French francs unless stated.

Source: Adapted from annual report, 1994.

Table 2 The two main companies of the PSA Group: Automobiles Peugeot and Automobiles Citroën

AUTOMOBILES PEUGEOT

Group's holding: 100% (fully by Peugeot SA)
Plants in: Sochaux-Montbéliard, Mulhouse, Poissy, Ryton (UK) and Villaverde (Spain).
Plants in: Dijon, Lille, Saint-Etienne, Sept-Fons, Vesoul, Valenciennes and Villers la Montagne.

	1994	1993
Economic data		
Production (in number of vehicles)	1,202,000	1,058,100
Sales (in number of vehicles)	1,209,200	1,061,900
Employees		
Company	41,900	43,800
Group	69,200	73,000
Consolidated financial data (Ffr m)		
Net sales	101,778	89,968
Working capital provided from operations	7,545	3,102
Net income	1,394	(958)
Stockholders' equity	30,644	29,318
Capital expenditures	6,047	5,758
Dividend	280	—

AUTOMOBILES CITROËN

Group's holding: 100% (fully by Peugeot SA)
Production sites in: Aulnay, Rennes, Vigo (Spain) and Mangualde (Portugal).
Plants in: Asniéres, Caen and Charleville.

	1994	1993
Economic data		
Production (in number of vehicles)	787,800	693,500
Sales (in number of vehicles)	779,600	702,000
Employees		
Company	28,900	29,900
Group	45,700	46,800
Consolidated financial data (Ffr m)		
Net sales	70,653	64,592
Working capital provided from operations	4,416	1,540
Net income	184	(2,341)
Stockholders' equity	4,757	4,637
Capital expenditures	3,240	3,456
Dividend	—	—

Source: Annual report, 1994.

Markets

Western European market shares fluctuated depending on two main factors: significant changes in relative prices and the success of new models. The top management of the PSA Group was preoccupied with the price war that had been taking place since 1990. They were also concerned with monetary fluctuations within Europe, particularly with the competitive devaluations of sterling, the peseta and the Italian lira (about 38 per cent since 1992), which had upset sales at the beginning of the 1990s. PSA and several other car manufacturers were looking forward to the possibility of a single European currency. As Jacques Calvet remarked in the annual stockholders' meeting in June 1995:

> For Europe, which is now truly a single market, the worst wounds have come from within, with the breakdown of the European Monetary System and competitive devaluations, notably of the Italian lira. Europe will not hold up long if there is not a rapid solution to this problem.

Moreover, new competitors were emerging. The market share of Korean car manufacturers in Europe (about 3 per cent in 1994) was growing, particularly in the low-priced segment.

The eastern European markets had stagnated at around 1 million vehicles a year and experts forecast a maximum of 1.5 million vehicles by the year 2000. The Russian market was estimated around 2 million vehicles and moderate growth was expected.

The North American market grew in 1992 (5 per cent) and in 1993 (7.3 per cent), and it represented 16.5 million vehicles in 1994. 'Light trucks' (mini-vans, pick-ups, four-wheel-drives) represented 40 per cent of sales, with a high growth. General Motors, Ford and Chrysler had a 73 per cent market share, compared to the Japanese 23 per cent, and the European car manufacturers' 2.7 per cent. PSA had left the US market in 1985, since it could not establish a significant position in this highly competitive environment (on average the price of cars in the United States was 30 per cent lower than in Europe).

The Japanese market showed signs of revival in 1994 (an increase of 1 per cent) after three years of decline. It represented 6.5 million vehicles. In this market, dominated by Toyota (with a 41 per cent market share), imports from foreign OECD countries were marginal. German manufacturers together exported 121,000 vehicles in 1994, Americans exported 37,000 vehicles, and the French sold 6,800 units.

The African and Middle East markets remained marginal (stable at around a total of 1 million vehicles a year). Two other zones experienced high growth: South America (2.8 million vehicles a year, with a 6 per cent annual growth) and Asia (apart from Japan), which represented annual sales of 4.8 million vehicles (with a 9 per cent annual growth).

Table 3 shows the breakdown of the sales of the PSA Group in the world, and Table 4 gives the breakdown of market share for the group in Europe.

At the annual stockholders' meeting in June 1995, Jacques Calvet commented on the 1994 performance of PSA as follows:

> The market-share of Peugeot and Citroën in western Europe, 12.8 per cent, as compared to 12.1 per cent in 1992 and 12.4 per cent in 1993, has grown significantly. This commercial dynamism results both from the deployment of our ranges of vehicles ... and from the favourable evolution of European markets: those where Peugeot and Citroën have a high share have evolved more favourably than the European average.

The strategy of PSA

Jacques Calvet chose to be chairman of Automobiles Peugeot and chairman of Automobiles Citroën in order to stimulate synergies between the two companies, which had kept their own culture for several years after the merger. Peugeot and Citroën were both involved in the main segments of the market and adopted parallel market positioning (see Table 5). Automobiles Peugeot had a 7.7 per cent market share in western Europe (18.7 per cent in France) and Automobiles Citroën had a 5.1 per cent market share in western Europe (12.4 per cent in France).

Some other competitors also had more than one marque. The Volkswagen Group had several, with Seat and Skoda at the low end of the market, Volkswagen as a generalist and Audi at the top end of the market. The Fiat Group had Ferrari at the very top of the market, Alfa Romeo, Fiat itself and Lancia. Other car manufacturers such as Renault had only one marque.

At PSA, the standardisation of vehicles was relatively high between the two product lines, about 50 per cent of the components being common. These were the non-visible components – engines, gearboxes, etc. – while the elements of the car that could be seen were different. Joint purchasing of components through Sogedac, a group company (with an annual sales turnover of Ffr80 billion), was seen as a source of competitive benefit by the company.

Part of the R&D expenses were also shared: thanks to the two parallel model ranges, synergies in R&D had increased, particularly in the early phases of new product development. For instance, the Citroën XM and the Peugeot 605 were developed by a single 'technical platform' (multifunctional project team). Innovations concerning new materials and new methods were shared. Industrial teams also worked together on international operations.

Differences and separation between the two marques were apparent in product design and style, the development of production processes, and marketing and sales, with two distinct dealer networks competing with each

Table 3   Worldwide sales of the PSA Group (passenger cars and light commercial vehicles, 000s)

	1994	1993	1992
Western Europe			
France			
Peugeot	430	328	437
Citro·n	304	250	270
PSA Peugeot Citro·n	734	577	707
Other western European countries			
Peugeot	585	544	617
Citro·n	416	399	459
PSA Peugeot Citro·n	1,000	942	1,076
Outside Western Europe			
Eastern Europe			
Peugeot	14	20	15
Citro·n	8	10	6
PSA Peugeot Citro·n	22	30	21
Africa			
Peugeot	24	22	31
Citro·n	9	7	8
PSA Peugeot Citro·n	34	29	39
America			
Peugeot	99	71	59
Citro·n	11	8	8
PSA Peugeot Citro·n	110	79	67
Asia–Pacific area			
Peugeot	40	59	57
Citro·n	21	19	15
PSA Peugeot Citro·n	61	79	72
Special registrations			
Peugeot	19	18	19
Citro·n	10	9	13
PSA Peugeot Citro·n	29	28	33
Total worldwide			
Peugeot	1,209	1,062	1,235
(including small collections)	(40)	(42)	(27)
Citro·n	780	702	779
PSA Peugeot Citro·n	1,989	1,764	2,014

Source: Annual report, 1994.

Table 4   European sales of the PSA Group: share of passenger car registrations (%)

	1994	1993	1992
France	31.1	29.7	30.4
Austria	7.8	7.5	7.0
Belgium–Luxembourg	13.7	13.6	14.2
Denmark	14.8	14.8	12.3
Finland	8.4	6.9	5.7
Germany	4.5	5.1	4.5
Greece	11.3	11.5	11.2
Ireland	7.0	6.9	6.7
Italy	7.0	6.7	7.1
Netherlands	12.1	13.1	11.0
Norway	8.9	8.0	7.5
Portugal	13.3	14.0	16.2
Spain	19.9	20.3	20.7
Sweden	4.6	4.3	3.2
Switzerland	7.9	7.9	6.6
United Kingdom	12.1	12.6	11.8
Total Europe	12.8	12.4	12.1
Europe outside France	9.2	9.3	8.8

Note: Does not include light commercial vehicles registrations.

Source: Annual report, 1994.

other. There was no intention to merge the two distribution networks, since executives believed the weaker marque could be disadvantaged (a problem which occurred when Peugeot took over Chrysler-Simca in 1979). Besides, the view was that merging the two independent distribution networks could give an opportunity for foreign competitors to take over dealer networks.

Such a strategy required a significant effort to renew the range of models of the two companies. In order to renew eight basic models (four Peugeot and four Citroën) every six years, PSA would have to launch one or two new models every year. On average the investment to launch a new model was estimated at around Ffr10 billion.

The PSA Group was the world leader in diesel cars with 957,400 vehicles in 1994, and had a significant competitive advantage in this domain. It sold diesel engines to Rover and Ford. In general, French car manufacturers PSA and Renault had a particularly strong position in diesel cars, with a 38 per cent market share in western Europe. The top management of PSA argued that diesel engines consumed less and cheaper fuel, produced less pollution, and were more reliable and long lasting than petrol engines. The proportion of diesel cars was very low in Japan and in the United States, but it was significant and growing in Europe, particularly where the taxation of fuel was not unfavourable (see Table 6).

Table 5   Group production of Peugeot and Citro·n models (number of vehicles)

Sector	Peugeot		Citro·n	
	Model	1994	Model	1994
Mini	106	340,800	AX	198,700
Super mini	205	146,600		
Lower medium	306	380,850	ZX	251,600
	309	300		
Upper medium	405	214,300	Xantia	214,700
	504 Paykan	45,550	BX	100
	505	9,600		
Executive	605	19,050	XM	20,600
'Monospace'	806	10,900	Evasion	7,200
Utility and	J5, J9, Boxer	34,050	C15, C25,	94,900
miscellaneous			C35, Jumper	
Total		1,202,000	Total	787,800

Source: Annual report, 1994.

Table 6   Percentages of diesel cars in the main EEC countries

	1990	1994
France	33.0	47.6
Germany	9.8	16.6
Italy	7.3	8.7
United Kingdom	6.4	21.7
Netherlands	10.9	12.0
Belgium–Luxembourg	31.8	41.4
Spain	14.7	28.2
European Union (12 countries)	14.2	23.1

Source: PSA.

Renewal

Since the beginning of the 1990s, a particular effort was made to launch new models and renew existing models. In 1994 PSA launched the 806 monospace (Peugeot) and its brother, the Evasion (Citroën). At Peugeot the 605 was restyled and re-engined, and new versions of the 306 (a cabriolet and a 'tri-corps'), and new utility vehicles (Boxer and 205 van) were launched. At Citroën the XM was restyled and re-engined, new versions of the ZX (Break) and the Xantia (Activa) were produced, and a new utility vehicle (Jumper) was launched. Advertising and promotional budgets were increased so as to rejuvenate the image: warm and relaxed for Citroën, humorous and lively for

Peugeot. Peugeot reinvested in the Formula 1 Grand Prix and won eight podiums in 1994 with the McLaren team; they also won 'super tourism' competitions with the 405. Citroën won the world rally championship for the second time with its ZX.

The co-operation between Peugeot and Citroën was crucial in order to share the efforts in renewing products. For years PSA also co-operated with Renault in the development and manufacture of components as well as in research on environmentally friendly cars. At the beginning of the 1990s, the co-operation with Fiat was strengthened in order to share the development and manufacturing of a monospace. In 1994 the Sevelnord plant at Valenciennes (France) started to manufacture the monospace for the four companies: Peugeot 806, Citroën Evasion, Fiat Ulysse and Lancia Zeta. Sevelnord, a 50/50 joint venture between PSA and Fiat, required a Ffr6 billion investment and was to produce 130,000 vehicles a year. The same type of co-operation was set up in Italy in order to share the manufacturing of small utility vehicles: Peugeot Boxer, Citroën Jumper and Fiat Ducat. Sevelsud was to manufacture 190,000 vehicles a year. The top management of PSA viewed such focused alliances at the best way to compete in new market niches.

From 1988 to 1990 PSA spent 3.5 per cent of its turnover on R&D. In 1994 the budget for R&D was Ffr7.2 billion, representing 3.8 per cent of the consolidated turnover, a high percentage compared to other European competitors, but lower than the Japanese Toyota and Honda (both around 5 per cent). Most of the 9,200 persons employed in R&D worked for the two marques: on the development of new models, on market-driven technological innovations or on manufacturing technologies and methods. For instance, PSA participated in a joint European programme, Prometheus, to improve road traffic in Europe with the help of electronic systems. The group was also active in joint European programmes for the recycling of vehicles. The improvement of subsystems such as diesel engines and suspensions was also seen as a priority: for instance, the launch of the Xantia Activa in 1994 was based on a new system of active suspensions.

The electric car was one of the top research priorities for PSA. In 1991, PSA was the first car manufacturer to sell electric vehicles for urban use (to Electricité de France and to local government authorities and public institutions). The market was estimated by executives to be around 250,000 vehicles in Europe by 1995. The large-scale manufacturing and sale of the electric Peugeot 106 and Citroën AX was planned to start in 1996. The electric car was to become the second family car, for driving short distances mainly in towns. The PSA executives believed they were three years ahead of competition in this domain. The group co-operated with several townships so as to implant the necessary infrastructure to provide power for recharging batteries. PSA also launched the 'Tulip' project, a system of electric car rental for the town. Small two-seater Tulip cars would be rented by subscribers in several places in a town, and batteries would be recharged in a number of parking places with an electric terminal. The system was experimented with in Tours at the end of 1995, and PSA decided to continue its further development.

Productivity and effectiveness

Investment was particularly high at the beginning of the 1990s, about Ffr15 billion a year in 1990 and 1991. It represented about 9.5 per cent of the sales turnover, one of the highest ratios of the industry, and was financed internally rather than through borrowing. 'Investments are aimed at renewing the product range. They are also aimed at continuing the modernisation of the industrial assets of the group, in order to improve productivity, flexibility, efficiency and the quality of the products' (annual report, 1990). With the crisis in 1993, investment was reduced; however, in 1994 it still represented Ffr10.5 billion.

On average, productivity was improved by 10 per cent a year during this period, with a 12 per cent improvement in 1994 compared to 1993. Reductions in costs were vital. Jacques Calvet stated that the market reversals in 1990 and 1991 and the price war made them even more so.

Purchases represented 58 per cent of production costs in 1994. Cost cutting on procurement was a priority for the Sogedac, and productivity plans were implemented with suppliers. On average, suppliers increased their added value ratio by 5 per cent a year.

In PSA's plants the number of hierarchical levels was reduced and a price controller was named for each model. His or her role was to validate suggestions for technical simplifications and cost cutting, many of which came from the workers (128,765 suggestions were in 1994 compared to 78,434 in 1991). Progress was also made in logistics and manufacturing; and delivery times were reduced to a total of 25 days in 1994. Inventories were reduced by Ffr2,000 million in 1993 and Ffr759 million in 1994. When investments were made, the group tended to choose simple, reliable, less costly solutions. Cost cutting was seen as a priority, productivity improvement targets for the period 1995–2000 remained very ambitious, and the simplification of product ranges and assembly lines was seen as the way to achieve these goals and improve the quality of vehicles.

In order to improve the effectiveness of R&D, after 1994 every development process (subsystem or new model) was organised in a 'project team' based on a 'technical platform'. This form of organisation was begun in the 1980s by the Japanese in order to reduce the development time of new models and to improve the simplicity of manufacturing. A project leader was in charge of quality, cost, scheduling and specific performance targets (for a new model, he or she reported directly to the top management of PSA). All the professions and functions were represented within a 'technical platform': designers, process engineers, the manufacturing, quality and procurement functions as well as some key suppliers. Typically, the technical platform for a new model would include 20–30 permanent members and a total of 200–300 people working temporarily on particular phases of the project. In 1994 the new model development time had been reduced to 196 weeks at PSA (compared to 250 weeks in 1990); the objective was to reduce it further to 156 weeks by the year 2000. The Japanese car manufacturers and General Motors Europe (Opel Vauxhall) had the shortest new product development times in the industry (between 160 and 180 weeks). The only problem with independent project teams and technical platforms was the risk of overlooking potential synergies between models, creating new components and increasing their unit costs. At PSA the early phases of development of new models were shared between Peugeot and Citroën. The role of Sogedac (the group company in charge of components and procurement) also helped achieve such synergies. It was in the latter stages of product development, when design and the development of production processes dominated, that the two technical platforms for Peugeot and Citroën became more apparent.

Given the limited growth opportunities, productivity improvements led to a regular reduction in staff, particularly in France: 139,800 employees in 1994 compared to 143,900 in 1993 and 150,800 in 1992. The forecasts for the period 1995–2000 showed a continuation of this trend. Careful personnel planning and forecasts at PSA reduced the risk of crises in the long term. Indeed, work patterns were changing: between 1984 and 1994 the percentage of highly skilled workers rose from 10 to 25 per cent, the percentage of technicians from 9 to 13 per cent, and the percentage of supervisors and managers from 4 to 8 per cent. The group had developed an ambitious training programme, representing more than 4 per cent of the wages in 1994 (as compared to 2 per cent in 1984).

The international strategy of PSA

Europe

PSA had industrial units in several countries in Europe. In 1994, about 80 per cent of manufacturing was done in France. Indeed, France was considered a competitive country in terms of production costs. Peugeot Talbot España (with 205 and 306 manufactured at Villaverde) and Citroën España (with AX, ZX and C15 manufactured at Vigo) represented about 16 per cent of the production. Peugeot Talbot Motors, based at Ryton (United Kingdom), manufactured the 405 until 1993 and the 306 after 1993 (75,300 vehicles in 1994, representing about 3 per cent of the total). The Mangualde plant in Portugal manufactured 14,000 AXs. The Sevelsud joint venture with

Fiat in Italy manufactured small utility vehicles. Automobiles Peugeot and Automobiles Citroën made 87 per cent of their sales in Europe; and the European market was seen as a priority for the PSA Group, particularly the large countries (see Table 4). In the German market, seen as particularly attractive, PSA had tried to strengthen its position and had developed its network of dealers. Since Peugeot had taken over the chronically loss-making UK operations of Chrysler, production had risen from about 20,000 units in 1985 to 116,500 in 1990. It then started to decrease with the decline of the British market. However, PSA aimed at improving its UK market share for Peugeot and Citroën as the main export market of the group.

The relationships between the corporate centre in France and the foreign subsidiaries were becoming more complex as the international strategy developed. Research and development was centralised in France; product marketing, pricing and communication policies were also decided in France; but some adaptations to particular important foreign markets were negotiated between the headquarters and its subsidiaries.

Peugeot Talbot Motor Company Ltd (UK) also had a higher degree of autonomy than most of the Peugeot operating businesses. From 1982 onwards, PSA took over the marketing and design decisions for the UK, and disbanded the Ryton design centre. However, PSA Centre did realise the differences in the UK market, especially because of the importance of the fleet market (cars purchased centrally by companies for company personnel). There was therefore a marketing director in the UK, but with a strong functional reporting link through to marketing and design in PSA Centre. The degree of autonomy was less than had been expected by George Turnbull, the chief executive from 1978 to 1985, and he left. The increasing autonomy of the later 1980s had been 'earned' not only by the UK company delivering against its business objectives and the improvements made in industrial relations and productivity, but also by the 'diplomatic' style of the chief executive at that time, Geoffrey Whalen, towards the corporate centre.

Europe was seen as the domestic market of European car manufacturers, and Jacques Calvet was known for his defensive strategy against Japanese competitors. In *European Motor Business* (November 1989) he stated:

> We must develop a common foreign policy towards Japan. We must limit the imports of Japanese cars as long as we do not sell a significant number of cars in Japan, that is to say a ratio of at least one [European car sold to Japan] for two [Japanese cars sold in Europe]. We must also have a common policy concerning the Japanese transplants in Europe ... We need a significant proportion of local content [in Japanese transplants in Europe] — namely 80 per cent — because this relates to the problem of employment and to sustaining technological capabilities in Europe ... We should examine the suggestion made by Gianni Agnelli [president of the Fiat Group] who says that there should be an overall quota on the importations of Japanese cars — wherever they come from — and a limitation to the manufacturing of Japanese cars in Europe.

As far as the strategy of the PSA Group was concerned, Calvet also stated, in *Le Figaro Economie* (April 1991): 'As long as I am President of the Group, I will never accept an agreement with the Japanese.' It was a view he retained in 1995.

The PSA Group was actively lobbying at the EC level to defend the argument of protection against the Japanese, as stated in the annual report of the group in 1990:

> The group will continue its efforts of persuasion in order to avoid dangerous drifts in building Europe and in the negotiations, which are badly opened, between the twelve states of the EC and Japan ... Do we make Europe for the Europeans, for employment, for technology, for European wealth and power or do we abandon ourselves to a competition which is not truly based on free trade and which would lead to a weaker Europe?

With the exception (to some extent) of the Fiat Group, the other European car manufacturers had less intransigent positions towards Japanese competition. However, the attitude of the German companies and of the subsidiaries of the North American companies in Europe evolved towards more protectionism between 1989 and 1991. The attitude of the EC Commission also changed in this direction during the same period. The result was the EEC–Japan agreement of 1991. Japanese imports into Europe would be limited to their 1990 level — that is, to about 1.23 million vehicles a year — during a transitory period until the end of 1999. More precisely, the quotas limiting Japanese imports in some European countries (mainly France, Italy and Spain) would be increased progressively. With regard to Japanese transplants in Europe (not subject to the above limitations), both parties had agreed to limit the production of Japanese transplants to under 1.2 million vehicles until the end of 1999. Actually a complicated system of monitoring was put in place, taking into account the annual evolution of the European market in order to define limits to Japanese growth.

As far as eastern Europe was concerned, PSA had a prudent strategy. By 1990 the group had established a distribution network in most of the countries, but exports represented fewer than 22,000 vehicles in 1994.

New continents

In the 1990s PSA started to look for growth in other continents. As stated in the annual report (1990):

> The industrial projects target countries with a real potential of development for the group, considering the situation of the economy of the country, its industrial base, and the perspective of growth of the automobile market.

In his address to the annual stockholders' meeting in June 1995, Jacques Calvet declared:

We have made great strides in extending our international presence. Our ambitious goal in this area is for Peugeot and Citroën to progressively make 25 per cent of their sales outside western Europe. Advances in this area include the new phase in Citroën's manufacturing operations in China, Peugeot's recent co-operation agreement in India, our plans to begin production of the 306 in Argentina, and Citroën's negotiations with Proton in Malaysia, which may soon come to a conclusion.

Peugeot had a good reputation in Africa, but this continent offered limited growth opportunities. Morocco and Egypt were the only exceptions (the 405 and AX were assembled in Egypt). The further aim was to complete the group's representation around the Mediterranean basin (including Turkey and Tunisia). Iran was the main base of the group in the Middle East, but local assembly was limited to 8,400 vehicles in 1994.

In Asia, the Japanese market was too competitive to expect significant growth for PSA: 6,600 vehicles were sold in 1994. The Korean market was attractive (900,000 vehicles and 1.2 million expected in the year 2000), but it was tightly protected and dominated by local manufacturers (Daewoo, Hyundai). On the other hand, the sales of the group were growing in Malaysia (3,400 units in 1994), in Taiwan (4,500) and in Thailand. In most of these countries, Japanese car manufacturers already had dominant market shares and strong positions with their networks of local suppliers (for instance, Toyota produced diesel engines and electrical equipment in Thailand, gearboxes and transmissions in the Philippines, petrol engines in Indonesia, steering systems in Malaysia, and co-ordinated activities in Singapore). The Chinese market was less structured and experts forecast annual sales of 1.2 million vehicles in the year 2000 to be manufactured locally. In this market European competitors were more active, particularly Volkswagen and PSA. Peugeot had a joint venture with the Canton township. Guangzhou Peugeot Automobile had the capacity to produce 45,000 vehicles a year (505, pick-up 504). Actual production was around 20,000 units a year; however, there was a project to extend capacity and to manufacture the 405 (150,000 units in the year 2000). Dongfeng Citroën Automobile Company manufactured 8,000 Citroën ZXs in 1994 (compared to 5,000 in 1993), and new plants were being built in Wuhan and in Xiangfan in order to produce 37,000 ZXs and extend the capacity to 150,000 vehicles in the year 2000.

There were about 200 million individuals belonging to the middle and upper classes in India, and the 300,000 vehicle market was expected to become a 600,000 units annual market by the year 2000. The Indian car industry was dominated by Maruti, a joint venture between Suzuki and the Indian state which had a 70 per cent market share (particularly with the small Maruti 800). A number of international competitors were making agreements with local partners: Mercedes with the local Telco, Daewoo with the local DCM, Opel with Hindustan (objective: 12,000 vehicles) and

Volkswagen with Eicher Motors (objective: 30,000 vehicles of the Golf 4 and Audi). At the end of 1993, PSA had signed an agreement with Premier Automobile Ltd (the number two in India) to manufacture the Peugeot 309 in Kalyan, starting from 1995. After a Ffr1 billion investment, the objective of the joint venture PAL Peugeot Ltd was to produce 60,000 vehicles a year.

In the South American continent, Peugeot and Citroën had significant positions in Argentina (with a 15 per cent market share) and in Chile (8,000 vehicles in 1994). The industrial presence of Peugeot in Argentina through the Sevel joint venture was a key success factor in the context of the new Mercosur free-trade agreement in this zone. Peugeot and Citroën had just established sales subsidiaries in Brazil and sales grew from 3,000 vehicles in 1993 up to 10,300 in 1994.

Finally the top management of PSA was studying the opportunity of a 'come back' in the North American market. Like several other European car manufacturers, PSA had been pushed out of the US market in the late 1980s. At the time, it distributed the 505 and the 405 through a limited number of megadealers, in the east coast, the west coast and the south-east. A study conducted in 1994 recommended the following:

- Specific vehicles were needed (given the local norms and preferences).
- A complete sales network was needed (because cars travel all around the country).
- At least two and up to four models were needed in order to feed the sales network.
- It was necessary to have local production (given the evolution of the US dollar and the relatively low cost of manpower in this zone); plants could be located in the USA, in Canada or in Mexico (Volkswagen had plants in Mexico; BMW and Mercedes had plants in South Carolina).
- Such an investment was estimated around Ffr20 billion in four years, and the next 'high cycle' of the US market was expected in the year 2000 (after the 1994–5 high cycle).

Challenges for 1995–2000

Within western Europe the top management of PSA was concerned with the decrease in consumption, as shown by the estimation of sales for 1995. Price differentials between European countries, mainly due to competitive devaluations, stimulated the development of parallel distribution channels (for instance, the price of French cars in Italy was 30 per cent lower than in France for some models). This situation, combined with increased competition in a mature market, was driving down prices. Moreover, according to the EEC–Japan agreement, the competition with the Japanese would be free in Europe starting from the year 2000, and Korean competitors were expected to sell about 1 million vehicles in Europe by the end of the century.

Finally, the chairmanship of Jacques Calvet was supposed to come to an end in 1997, although some believed that, given his success at the head of PSA, he would continue. Indeed, the market value of the group had been multiplied by 15 in ten years, with the Peugeot family keeping control of the company.

In June 1995 Jacques Calvet concluded his address to the annual stockholders' meeting as follows:

> The challenges facing us are clear. The economic and monetary environment and the intense competition in our markets are serious threats. On the other hand, the Group's forward looking attitude and our employees' strong commitment to achieving our objectives — which I greatly appreciate — are precious, even crucial strengths. As a result we can face the future with confidence.

The Rover/Honda alliance

DAVID FAULKNER

The strategic alliance between the Rover Group and Honda was embarked upon after a meeting between the two companies at the Fairmont Hotel, San Francisco, in September 1978. From that time it evolved from a limited licensing agreement into a multifunctional relationship including joint development and production and a 20 per cent share exchange between the two companies.

Background

At the time of the approach to Honda, Rover was an ailing car manufacturer owned reluctantly by the British government, and still making large losses despite attempts by its then chief executive, Michael Edwardes, to modernise it through a major rationalisation plan, and a determination to curb the trade union power that had contributed in a major way to making BL an example of failing British industry.

By 1979, despite the rationalisation plan, the company was still losing money (£46 million in 1979), and was facing the prospect of a Tory government less likely to continue to finance unprofitable development. The world automobile market, after a number of years of growth, had shown signs of becoming less attractive. Rover had been pinning its hopes on the Metro, the Maestro and the Montego, but none of these models was reaching its targeted sales figures. The major problem seemed to be Rover's poor reputation for quality.

At the very least Rover needed a new product in the 'lower-medium' sector to plug a gap in its product range, but it lacked both the time and

This case was prepared by David Faulkner of Oxford University School of Management Studies and is intended for class discussion and not to illustrate either correct or incorrect handling of an administrative situation. © David Faulkner, 1996.

the finance to do this unaided. Still named the British Leyland Motor Corporation (BLMC), the company was facing a declining market share and had poor financial results. The world automobile industry was dominated by the multinational giants, and entry to this exclusive club did not seem to be available to Rover.

Furthermore, the Japanese were beginning to make their presence felt on the world automobile stage with their emphasis on quality, reliability, robotic methods of manufacture and fuel economy.

Among the Japanese car makers, Honda was something of a maverick. Having started its international life as predominantly a motor-cycle manufacturer, it did not develop a presence in the car market until 1963. In automobile company terms Honda was a medium-sized organisation, with a very high reputation for sound engineering, high quality and high productivity. It had a philosophy based on customer satisfaction and customer improvement, and aspired to be a global player.

Honda was a successful company, but in world automotive industry terms it was still regarded as principally a motor-cycle manufacturer. Honda's image was not sufficient at the time of the alliance formation for it to take its place naturally among the General Motors or even, in its own country, the Toyotas.

Honda had established itself well in the USA, but of the three legs of the Triad, the European leg was to Honda almost entirely undeveloped in 1979. Also Honda felt insecure in this area as it knew European tastes differed from American ones, but it did not trust its understanding of them. Furthermore, Honda did not believe it had the time to set up in Europe, and develop its own European arm from scratch. The development costs of new European models would be too great at that stage of Honda's development, and the time scale too long to be acceptable. As Mr Hayashi, managing director of Honda UK commented:

> At that time there were restrictions on exports to Europe, therefore there was no way to increase our exports there … Europe was suffering from over-capacity, so we had no chance to build our own factory there … We thought the Rover approach might help in Europe. It was company policy to be flexible with people who approached us, and to have international collaboration, so we agreed to license Rover to manufacture Honda products from knock-down kits.

However, they covered any reservations they might have had by limiting the first deal to an arm's length licensing arrangement, and some time later embarked on the building of the Honda Swindon factory to maintain their flexibility.

In 1978 Rover and Honda were approximately the same size, in terms of world sales, at about £4 billion turnover. Honda was profitable and growing fast, however, and Rover was loss making and possessed factories operating at a level substantially below capacity.

Development of the alliance

The 1978 meeting in San Francisco came about because BLMC had recognised that, if it wanted a successful future in the world automobile industry, it needed a partner. Roland Bertodo, Rover's strategic planning director, described how the BLMC top management tackled the problem:

> We consciously sat down and wrote down all the automotive companies and listed the pluses and minuses against each one. Honda was the one that came out top purely because it was a similar size to us, it had growth ambitions, and a reputation for high quality at a time when quality for us was the biggest problem. It was renowned for its management at a time when we were struggling for management know-how. We were therefore attracted to Honda.

Rover lacked the financial resources and the time to produce market-acceptable new models after the lack-lustre performance of the Maestro and the Montego. It also lacked a self-confident company culture after years of loss making, union restrictive practices disputes, and poor press. It knew that it was regarded as one of the major 'lame ducks' of British industry.

Rover had access to an acceptable UK and European network of component suppliers and subcontractors. It had ample spare capacity in its factories, and could manufacture as many cars for Honda as the Japanese company could manage to sell. Rover also had an understanding of European tastes, and it could contribute to the development costs of new models to make this necessary factor come within the financial reach of both companies.

Rover was a little concerned at the outset that Honda would absorb its know-how and then walk away. As Bertodo noted:

> We took steps to limit transparency and minimise informal transfer of knowledge by circumscribing a partner's opportunity to learn in an uncontrolled manner ...
> The challenge is sharing sufficient skill to create a competitive advantage for both partners while avoiding wholesale transfer of core ability.

The risk from Rover's viewpoint was at shopfloor level, where close discipline in relation to information transfer was unlikely to prevail. Honda faced little risk in this area since, as John Bacchus, Rover's director of collaborative strategy, commented, the Japanese are traditionally secretive and do not seem to feel the need to demonstrate their knowledge to show their abilities.

Rover was the driving force in bringing about the alliance, and was subsequently the active partner in proposing new avenues for collaboration.

Honda responded positively to Rover's initiative, and the first deal was signed in December 1979, which was a limited licensing arrangement for BLMC to manufacture the Triumph Acclaim from Honda 'knocked-down' kits at the BLMC factory in Longbridge in Birmingham. The Triumph

Acclaim was based on the Honda Accord and filled the vacant position in Rover's product range. 130,000 Acclaims were manufactured at Longbridge, and the brand achieved a regular position in the top ten UK sellers list, although it was in reality no more than a rebadged Honda.

The next phase of the partnership was the Rover 200 launched in 1984, of which 175,000 were built. This was the 'sister' model to the Honda Ballade. The 200 was a Japanese-designed car, but with Rover wheels, bumpers and interiors. Both the 200 and the Ballade were produced at Longbridge and equipped with different badges. The agreement was more than a simple licence this time. Rover had the right to change the basic design if it wished to do so for its version of the car, and there was also a manufacturing agreement to make cars for Honda. For the Ballade, Rover provided the missing European values in terms of styling that Honda needed.

In 1985, however, Honda announced its intention to build a factory in Swindon. This concerned the British press; *The Times* warned of a possible Rover takeover by stealth, and questions were asked in the House of Commons on the issue of whether this move heralded the decline of the alliance with Rover. This proved not to be the case. Honda proposed only to make engines in Swindon at first, and subsequently to make both Rovers and Hondas there. On the question of whether Honda might be in the market to buy Rover, Honda's president Mr Tadashi Kume claimed it lacked the resources. *The Times* concluded also that this was not generally how Japanese companies behaved. Organic development was much more the rule than acquisition. By 1985 Honda was still a very small player on the British market. It sold 19,000 cars in the UK that year for 1 per cent market share.

In 1986 the partnership evolved further with the launch of the Rover 800 and the Honda Legend. This was the first car that was the product of a joint development effort. The experience of working closely together on design made the relationship between the two companies much closer, and led to a substantial improvement in Rover's understanding of quality standards. At this time Rover and Honda signed a statement of understanding to extend the partnership, which dealt with the principles of the relationship. However, it was felt that the mutual trust that had developed during the work on Project XX, as the 800 was called, was much more important than any legal document.

By this time Rover's product life cycle for new models had become considerably shorter than it had traditionally been. Figure 1 illustrates this reduction from about seven years to nearer five. Rover's productivity was also on a steeply improving curve (see Figure 2), with average costs moving rapidly towards Japanese levels. These improvements followed from absorbing the Honda philosophy that it was not in the business of making excellent cars. Its aim was to make *perfect* cars!

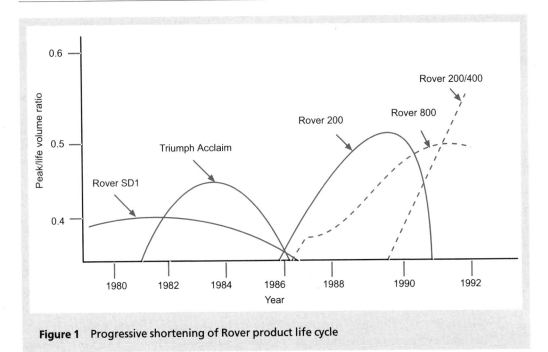

Figure 1   Progressive shortening of Rover product life cycle

A further maturing of the relationship occurred in 1988. Rover and Honda agreed to stop making the Rover 800 and the Honda Legend for each other at their respective factories. It was claimed by both companies that this was because both parties wanted to make refinements that could not be easily carried out at each other's factories. However, Honda had built only 1,600 Rover 800s at its Suyama works in Japan, and Rover only 3,500 Legends in Cowley, and these low volumes were probably a major factor behind the move. The decision did not appear to damage the relationship in any way.

1989 saw the next project, the Rover 200/400 with its twin the Honda Concerto. This heralded a further development, in that it was the product of joint development and co-production plus the cross sourcing of components. In 1990 Rover built more than 40,000 Concertos for Honda for sale in the UK and EC to a quality standard acceptable to the Japanese.

By 1990 Rover and Honda were engaged on a further collaborative venture involving integrated development and production, and demonstrated their further confidence in the future potential longevity of the alliance by concluding a 20 per cent share exchange between Rover and Honda Manufacturing (UK) Limited.

Thus from an arm's length licensing agreement in 1979 the alliance had progressed a long way in terms of mutual development and production, and had even reached the point of minority share exchange. However, there was no attempt to collaborate in merging marketing identity, or in management off the shop floor.

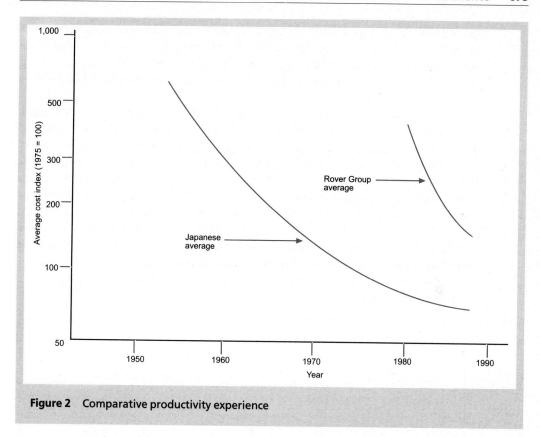

Figure 2   Comparative productivity experience

Honda was still clearly a Japanese company with its own aims and ambitions. Its objectives were wider than Rover's. It sought to provide a range of cars to meet all quality segments save the top and bottom, and to become a true global player. It had a distinct strategy and Rover featured in this only as a European partner. At the time the alliance was concluded, Honda was strong in the USA and a medium-sized player in Japan. Its European presence was negligible.

Rover was fairly strong in the UK, had 2.9 per cent share of the European market and had little presence anywhere else. In fact 95 per cent of its production in 1980 was for Europe, including the UK. Similarly, Rover had its distinct identity and showed no sign of losing it.

The companies by 1990

Despite trebling its size in turnover terms during the 1980s, Honda was still not among the giants of the motor world by 1990. In Europe its sales accounted for only 1.2 per cent of the European market, and Rover's accounted for 3.1 per cent against Volkswagen's 15 per cent and Ford of Europe's 14 per cent. However, much progress had been made in performance terms for both companies since 1979. Rover was back in profit and with a coherent strategy, and Honda had an established foothold in Europe.

Honda grew from a medium-sized player in 1978 with a turnover of around £4 billion to one with a worldwide sales level of more than £12 billion, of which 66 per cent was earned outside Japan, and a net profit after tax of more than £500 million in 1990. Honda was already large in the USA at the time of the alliance formation, and motor cycles, power products and parts accounted for a quarter of total revenue, as was still the case in 1990 (see Figure 3). However, in Europe, Honda's sales of cars increased from a negligible amount in 1978 to £700 million of 191,00 units in 1990 (see Figure 4). Not only had Honda raised its European direct sales, but it also benefited from part of Rover's sales of approximately 450,000 units.

Honda had the characteristic Japanese total quality control attitude to manufacturing, which by lengthy tuition had been able to elevate Rover into

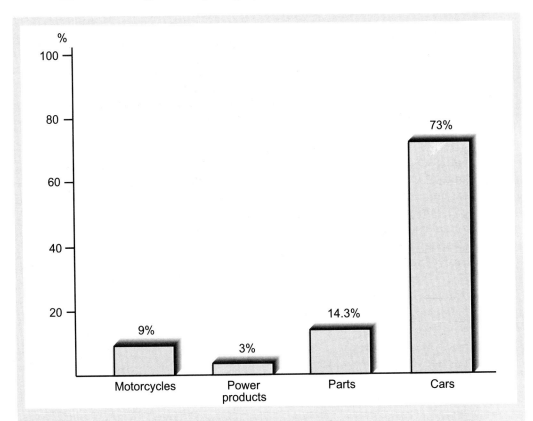

Figure 3   Percentage of total Honda sales by volume (1990)

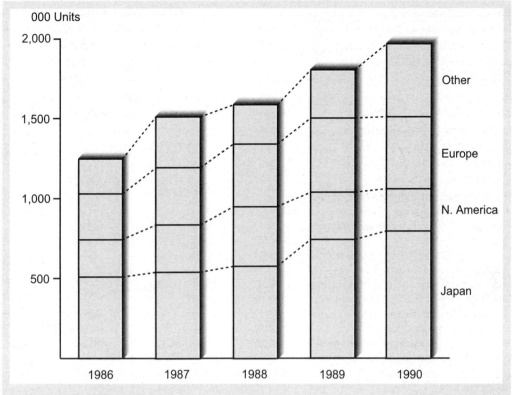

Figure 4 Honda car sales by geographical area

a quality performer. It had a pragmatic attitude to design that facilitated the creation of reliable marketable cars. It had the robotics-dominated methods of manufacture that could gain the necessary cost economies in unit terms. Also it had sufficient finance to collaborate with Rover in the production of new models and this was an important attraction.

Rover aimed to become an upmarket quality executive marque with a high reputation for style, quality and reliability; and priced at a level to make the senior management fleet buyer its natural customer. It now became unashamedly a niche marketeer under its chairman Sir Graham Day, and was no longer the largest UK car producer, coming third behind Ford and Vauxhall.

However, from its position as a regular loss-maker, Rover moved steadily into profit from 1986 onwards, and in 1990, as a subsidiary of British Aerospace plc, it contributed an annual profit in excess of £50 million to its parent. But that was not the whole of the picture. Rover's overall financial performance through most of the 1980s was pretty dismal. It only became profitable with financial restructuring after its acquisition by British Aerospace (Table 1).

Table 1 Summary of Rover Group results, 1983–7

	1983	1984	1985	1986	1987
Turnover (£m)					
UK	1,935	1,987	2,353	2,228	1,827
Overseas	1,486	1, 415	1,062	1,184	1,269
Total	3,421	3,402	3,415	3,412	3,096
Exports from UK (including above)	917	827	764	768	1,042
Profits and losses (£m)					
Operating profit (loss)	4.1	(11.7)	(34.6)	(246.4)	16.8
Exceptional losses	—	—	(15.0)	(109.2)	
Share of profits of associated companies, formerly subsidiaries	—	—	—	—	11.1
Profit (loss) before interest and taxation	4.1	(11.7)	(49.6)	(355.6)	27.9
Interest	(71.2)	(61.6)	(75.7)	(100.0)	(49.5)
Loss on ordinary activities before taxation	(67.1)	(73.3)	(125.3)	(455.6)	(21.6)
Taxation on ordinary activities	(7.2)	(7.7)	(4.1)	(6.5)	(5.2)
Loss on ordinary activities after taxation	(74.3)	(81.0)	(129.4)	(462.1)	(26.8)
Minority share of profits of subsidiaries	(3.8)	(1.8)	(1.4)	—	—
Loss before extraordinary items	(78.1)	(82.8)	(130.8)	(462.1)	(26.8)
Extraordinary profits (losses)	(64.8)	163.4	(7.2)	(430.0)	—
Profit (loss) after extraordinary items	(142.9)	80.8	(138.0)	(892.1)	(26.8)
Loss on translation and other movements	(8.6)	(6.7)	(25.8)	(6.9)	(0.1)
Transfer to (from) reserves	(151.5)	73.9	(163.8)	(899.0)	(26.9)
Balance sheets					
Fixed assets	1,014.6	908.5	939.2	772.8	703.7
Other net assets	500.2	434.7	447.1	26.3	190.2
Total	1,514.8	1,343.2	1,386.3	799.1	893.9
Net borrowings	(796.5)	(571.9)	(790.5)	(1,108.7)	(560.2)
	718.3	771.3	585.8	(309.6)	333.7
Called-up share capital	2,139.5	2,139.5	2,139.5	2,139.5	2,762.2
Reserves	(1,463.2)	(1,389.3)	(1,553.1)	(2,452.1)	(2,428.5)
	676.3	750.2	588.4	(312.6)	333.7
Minority interests in subsidiaries	42.0	21.1	9.4	3.0	—
	718.3	771.3	595.8	(309.6)	333.7
Net asset value per share (pence)	15.8	17.5	13.7	—	6.0
Capital expenditure including tooling (£m)	247.7	234.2	231.5	172.8	119.8
Depreciation and amortisation (£m)	177.9	147.2	154.5	160.3	135.7
Vehicle unit sales (000s)	564	511	542	494	513
Weekly average number of employees (000s)	103	96	78	73	49
Ordinary shareholders (year end) (000s)	67	65	63	62	60

Note: These figures include all divested businesses up to their effective date of leaving the group, including Jaguar to July 1984, and Unipart, Leyland Vehicles and Freight Rover to December 1986.

Source: Rover Group.

Sales turnover remained on a plateau at £3–4 billion and not growing, and in terms of assets Rover contracted dramatically from its bloated 1970s size. Rover's export sales were pretty stable in the late 1980s, and its UK sales showed little growth either (Tables 2 and 3).

But if quality and a regenerated reputation were prime objectives, these seemed to be established. The 800, the 200 and the 400 series were all generally acknowledged to be first-class cars from a quality viewpoint, and Rover's reputation was reflected in its profit figures. It was estimated also that the business between the two companies at that time was currently worth in the region of £500,000 annually. However, the Honda-related models accounted for only about a quarter of total Rover production (see Table 4). The much maligned Metro, Maestro and Montego were still responsible for a substantial tranche of Rover's sales.

Table 2 Total Austin Rover retail export sales, 1982–9 (units)

	1982	1983	1984	1985	1986	1987	1988	1989*
Passenger cars	110,328	100,165	89,709	101,821	117,963	139,289	132,720	130,500
Car derived vans	1,582	856	412	566	388	388	1,312	1,500
Total	11,910	101,021	90,121	102,387	118,351	139,677	134,032	132,000

* EIU estimates.

Source: Rover Group.

Table 3 Development of the Rover Group's car sales in the UK, 1980–9

	Units	Change on previous year		Market share (%)	Change on previous year (%)
		Units	%		
1980	275,798	−61,186	−18.2	18.2	−1.4
1981	285,071	9,273	3.4	19.2	1.0
1982	277,260	−7,811	−2.7	17.8	−1.4
1983	332,725	55,465	20.0	18.6	0.8
1984	312,054*	−20,671	−6.2	17.8	−0.8
1985	327,955	15,901	5.1	17.9	0.1
1986	297,466	−30,489	−9.3	15.8	−2.1
1987	301,811	4,345	1.5	15.0	−9.8
1988	332,607	30,796	10.2	15.0	—
1989	312,306	−20,301	−6.1	13.6	−1.4

* Excludes Jaguar.

Source: SMMT.

Table 4 Production of the Rover Group by model, 1985–9 (units)

	1985	1986	1987	1988	Jan.–Nov. 1989
Mini	34,974	33,720	37,210	34,574	37,193
Metro	174,466	158,546	161,285	144,701	128,930
Rover 200/Honda Ballade	65,844	63,167	80,263	95,859	84,355
New Rover 200 series	—	—	—	—	8,105
Maestro	88,848	63,722	58,280	67,406	56,032
Montego	95,874	70,623	73,447	79,316	71,221
Rover SDI	15,916	2,870	—	—	—
Rover 800 Series/Honda Legend	—	16,029	57,111	49,894	36,787
Land Rover	23,772	19,195	20,475	22,229	17,160
Range Rover	13,314	14,494	20,815	24,021	25,962
Discovery	—	—	—	—	2,632
Total	513,008	442,366	508,886	520,000	468,377

Source: Rover Group.

The 20 per cent share exchange between the companies was intended as a positive demonstration of commitment. On the issue Hayashi commented that the share exchange was most important for the manufacturing and development staff, since it engendered trust, in that it showed that the partnership was for the long term. Of course, the trust had not been naœve. Rover only released information on a 'need to know' basis; the Japanese likewise, and the two teams did not fraternise greatly at a social or shopfloor level. However, trust did develop as the two sides grew used to working together. Matters moved on successfully and as Hayashi said:

> The Legend, the joint Honda–Rover product, cleared the way for Honda to enter into the executive car sector of the market. Rover's interior design and European taste contributed to the success of the Legend . . . Now Rover is a truly integral part of Honda's strategy in Europe.

Thus the alliance with Honda had had a dramatic effect on Rover's quality performance, and as John Bacchus said, it no longer saw itself as a 'loser'.

The alliance in 1990

It was one thing to form an alliance; quite another to make it work. Two separate studies, one by Mckinsey, and one by Coopers and Lybrand, showed that more than 50 per cent of alliances foundered within five years. Rover also had some experience of disappointing alliances. As Bertodo recounted, they had been in fifteen previous alliances since 1921 with, among others,

Isuzu, BMW, Ferguson, Hindustani, AMC, Perkins and, at the time of the Honda negotiations, Nissan. Only seven could be judged successful, he commented, and only four outstandingly so.

In Bacchus's view if Honda were to exit the alliance, Rover would be unlikely to maintain the quality standards it had learned to achieve under Honda's discipline. Furthermore, Rover was still small in global terms, and its only hope would be to find another partner or establish a defendable niche. Also, some major issues appeared in 1990: Rover was losing market share in Europe and even in the UK, and the technological and financial power of Honda threatened to turn the alliance into one dominated by the Japanese company.

Hayashi saw it differently: 'If we broke apart, we would be in competition with the same technology, the same components, the same suppliers, and the same products: a duplicate of ourselves.' But an EIU article in *European Motor Business* in 1990 suggested that:

> Model development in the car programme has been shifted over largely to Honda, with Rover manipulating the available hardware to encompass its upmarket and niche model ambitions. This compromise will permit a more rapid updating of the model range than Rover could otherwise contemplate, but this attachment to Honda has also given rise to uninspired styling and uncompetitively bland designs.

If there were any validity to this criticism, the joint enterprise would need some rejuvenation to succeed in the next round of competition. Hayashi was confident, however:

> We have strong commitment to the alliance. Even when we start production in Swindon we will still benefit from the joint supply network, and Rover is still in need of Honda's capability in product development, and quality standards. In that sense both companies have a management policy of strong commitment, because competition in Europe is very keen, and since we are already established in the UK with suppliers and co-operation with Rover this confirms our commitment.

The inevitable early problems with contrasting cultures seemed to have been largely successfully handled, as Hayashi commented:

> Much endeavour and patience were needed to overcome many barriers ... in language, culture, ways of thinking and sense of value to name just a few. By overcoming these barriers, the people of Honda and Rover were able to generate mutual understanding and trust, which eventually led to close friendship.

Bertodo confirmed his belief in the future of the alliance similarly: 'Honda have compressed our learning curve and given us better value for money by sharing resources on R and D.'

There were joint design teams working on new models. Both companies' factories produced for the other partner. There was joint sourcing of components, and many compromises were made to accommodate the respective manufacturing needs of the two partners. However, from the outset the marketing arms of the two companies remained separate. Entry into Europe by Honda did not mean the use of Rover's sales network.

Bertodo saw the alliance as requiring constant refreshing, by both sides being ready with something extra to trade at each crucial point in what he called the 'collaboration vortex' to prevent the alliance flying off centrifugally into independence, or centripetally into one-sided dependency. He saw a key part of his job as preventing Rover, in particular, from doing the latter.

Some key issues remained, however: How would the parties to the alliance deal with the increasingly likely prospect of Rover being sold by its parent company? In the existing world automobile industry, was a strategic alliance a secure way to achieve competitive advantage that could be sustained in the face of keen competition by integrated corporations? And finally, do the undoubted costs involved in co-ordinating alliances lead to a competitive cost advantage in relation to the major world players in the global market place? Only the future would answer these questions.

The BMW acquisition of the Rover Group

NICK S. POTTER

Background

The strategic alliance between Rover and Honda had developed into a wide-ranging relationship by the early 1990s. British Aerospace (BAe) had acquired the Rover Group from the British government in 1988 and, under the terms of sale, Honda had the right to be informed of any intent to sell and offered first refusal over the balance of equity. BAe further undertook not to sell Rover until August 1993 at the earliest.

The recession in many parts of the world continued to be the dominant industry factor affecting both Rover and Honda during 1992 and 1993. Rover announced losses of £83 million in February 1992, including a £45 million write-off as a result of withdrawing from the US market. Honda's profits during 1992 fell by 32 per cent.

George Simpson, managing director of Rover, knew that although the company had gained immeasurably from its collaboration with Honda, there were still many problems to overcome if he was to create a business with sustainable profits. Although break-even was down from 530,000 to 450,000 units per year, sales were still running at fewer than 420,000. Simpson knew that international sales had to play an even greater role in the future.

A major restructuring of the business occurred early in 1992, and as a consequence the internal objectives regarding overseas sales were raised from 45 to 60 per cent of total turnover. Rover also signed Japanese-style agreements with its workforce which included a radical 'Jobs for life' guarantee. The restructuring split the company into three new trading divisions:

This case was prepared by Nick Potter of Birmingham Business School and is intended as a basis for classroom discussion rather than to illustrate correct or incorrect handling of an administrative situation. © N.S. Potter, 1996.

- Rover Europe — managing director, Graham Morris.
- Rover International — managing director, Chris Woodwark.
- Rover Marketing — managing director, Kevin Morley.

During this period, Rover continued to learn an enormous amount about quality and manufacturing techniques through the Honda alliance, and was even training BAe staff in lean manufacturing techniques. Other Japanese car manufacturers were, however, setting up operations in the UK, and Simpson felt that the restructuring and working agreements were necessary to compete with them on level terms.

The process begins

The first indication of what lay ahead came in March 1992. Volkswagen shocked the entire car industry by announcing that it would like to buy Rover in order to gain a foothold in certain markets. In reality, the company was impressed with the outcomes of the Rover/Honda agreement and extremely interested in an alliance with Honda. Ford also let it be known that it was interested in the possibility of acquiring Rover. BAe responded to these informal advances by simply restating that, under its agreement with the British government, Rover could not be sold until at least August 1993.

By late 1992, however, speculation about Rover's future was rife. BAe chairman John Cahill still repeated that he had no intention of selling Rover, although earlier in the year he had talked of a long-term strategy based around core businesses in aircraft and defence.

Volkswagen had bought both Seat and Skoda in the meantime and was no longer thought to be in a financial position to bid. Fiat and Peugeot were interested, although Jacques Calvet, chairman of Peugeot, was known to display an almost legendary hostility towards Japanese companies.

Honda had only purchased its 20 per cent stake in Rover as a sign of good faith. As far as it was concerned, the relationship was a complete success and had become the envy of the motor industry. It was based on trust, reciprocal need and mutual benefits. Honda's chief executive officer, Nobuhiko Kawamoto, was convinced that there were important political factors ruling out any increased shareholding, and Honda was, in any case, short of money.

Collaboration intensifies as competition increases

George Simpson continued to demonstrate his belief in collaborative deals by increasing Rover's stake in its joint venture with Lombard Finance, and entering into talks with the Bulgarian government about a 49.9 per cent stake in a joint venture to assemble and sell the Maestro range of medium-size 'hatchback' cars when UK production ceased.

Honda was by now building its own manufacturing facility in Swindon, and Rover had opened a new £200 million factory at Cowley. The collaborative agreement with Honda had played a significant part in the planning process for the new facility as the futures of the two companies became steadily more linked and interdependent.

At around the same time, the Economist Intelligence Unit published a report which concluded that Rover was too small to survive as an independent manufacturer and had insufficient volume to service such a wide model range. The report also stated that, by the year 2000, the car industry would be dominated by a group of only five global manufacturers: General Motors, Ford, Toyota, Volkswagen and Nissan.

In late 1993, the Rover 600 was jointly launched with the new Honda Accord. Engines and gearboxes were the same in both ranges and most other components were also shared. George Simpson restated Rover's joint strategy of co-operation with Honda and a continued move upmarket — Roverisation as he called it. He estimated that Rover had saved around £150 million in development costs on the 600 due to the alliance, and that this had further contributed to lower break-even volumes. Significantly, in the light of later developments, Nobuhiko Kawamoto was reported as saying that it would be difficult for Honda to continue the sharing of technology and designs if Rover were sold to another manufacturer.

In June 1993, the two companies reached an agreement to rebadge the Land Rover Discovery as the Honda Crossroad for sale in Japan. Honda was becoming increasingly interested in further alliance possibilities based on Rover's four-wheel-drive expertise, as it lacked the finance to develop the technology alone.

In July 1993, George Simpson explained in an interview why Honda would not increase its stake from the current level of 20 per cent. He repeated that the success of the alliance was based on mutual trust, and the creation and nurturing of relationships which facilitated synergies, and that this would not necessarily be enhanced by a larger shareholding. Simpson knew that Honda already considered Rover part of its 'empire' and did not therefore consider it necessary to use scarce resources to obtain full control. He felt the alliance would continue to expand along the value chain from process technology and product development into areas such as shared distribution.

Rover by mid-1993

The company had by this time successfully exploited the alliance to create a chic image combining British styling and Japanese reliability. Quality had improved to such an extent that Rover dealers complained they had insufficient work to carry out under warranty.

Rover's performance had even been instrumental in raising the share price of BAe. However, in March 1993, BAe was forced to repay £110 million to the British government after the European Commission ruled that the state aid or 'sweeteners' granted by the British government to BAe at the time of the original purchase was an illegal subsidy under EC law.

Sales performance continued to strengthen, with unit volumes up 20 per cent on the previous year. Sales of Rover cars in Japan were up 40 per cent for the same period, due to the penetration of middle and upper segments of the market, and the break-even point was falling to around 400,000 units per year as cost savings continued to accrue from the alliance. Sales of the Land Rover four-wheel-drive range were also running ahead of production capacity. Rover's gains compared favourably with the reductions in volume being experienced by the other car manufacturers (see Table 1).

Around this time, there was talk of a management buy-out (MBO), but with BAe maintaining an equity stake prior to eventual flotation. However, the dynamics of the car industry had moved on — Volkswagen was now thought to be in financial trouble and Ford was trying to digest its acquisition of Jaguar. The biggest question centred around whether BAe should sell Rover at all, particularly in the short term. Rover was poised to widen its joint venture policy even further by entering a development project with Kia of Korea to produce a new V6 engine for top-of-the-range models (this would also have the effect of slightly reducing Rover's dependency on Honda's engines).

Table 1 European car sales, 1993

Manufacturer	Volume (000s)	% change	Market share (%)
Volkswagen	1,886	−20.1	16.4
General Motors	1,489	−11.8	13.0
Peugeot/Citroën	1,405	−14.4	12.3
Japanese manufacturers	1,396	−12.8	12.2
Renault/Volvo	1,373	−16.0	12.0
Ford	1,316	−13.3	11.5
Fiat	1,272	−20.6	11.1
BMW	371	−15.0	3.2
Rover	363	+9.7	3.2
Mercedes	334	−14.0	2.9

Notes: Japanese category includes Nissan, Toyota, Mazda, Honda and Mitsubishi. The market for the year was down 15.1 per cent in total.

Source: Society of Motor Manufacturers and Traders.

BMW — the need for strategic change

BMW was less troubled by the recession of the early 1990s than most European car companies. It had not only avoided short-time working, but remained in profit throughout the period. The company had monitored Rover's progress for a period of years, as the two companies were of similar size in terms of unit volume and increasingly competed in certain market segments.

On 13 May 1993, Bernd Pischetsrieder succeeded Dr Eberhard Kuenheim as chairman of BMW, and his first task was to carry out a strategic audit of the whole business. The conclusion he reached was inescapable. Like Rover, BMW was too small to survive on its own as a manufacturer into the twenty-first century. The company needed to extend its range and achieve economies of scale in sourcing, production, distribution and R&D. By a process of eliminating alternatives, it appeared that Rover was of potential interest in this regard. On direct instructions from Pischetsrieder, BMW's R&D director visited all of Rover's facilities during September 1993 and drove every model in its entire range. Senior management of BMW then spent the period until Christmas digesting every piece of financial, marketing and strategic information available on Rover.

Rover had already been in discussions with BMW for some time about the possibility of using a BMW diesel engine in the new Range Rover, as Honda lacked diesel engine expertise. As this relationship and the investigations developed, Pischetsrieder began to realise that with Rover they could 'offer a comprehensive range of cars in virtually every category'.

In fact, as BMW's senior management studied future market trends and the joint capabilities, they realised that the two companies were a perfect fit. The Rover brands, in particular Land Rover, had considerable value. Having observed the efforts of Mercedes to develop four-wheel-drive during the 1980s, Pischetsrieder could see the synergies emanating from selling a range of off-road vehicles through BMW showrooms, with the added benefit of applying Land Rover's four-wheel-drive expertise across the BMW car range. The development and brand promotional costs involved in achieving these objectives organically would almost certainly be more than Rover's market value.

BMW made an informal approach to BAe in October 1993 about the possibility of acquiring Rover Group. It also contacted Honda in order to gauge reaction — but received no response at all. Honda was concerned at the prospect of a third party having open access to joint secrets, and was anxious not to lose its grip on Rover. However, under the cross-shareholding agreement, Honda had to be formally told that Rover was potentially for sale and was given first option to buy the remaining equity. Nobuhiko Kawamoto felt this afforded Honda a high degree of protection.

Privately, he was prepared to raise the stake to 40 per cent, but could see little benefit in going further. He had his own problems, as Honda was stuck halfway between mass market volumes and being a niche manufacturer. Moreover, pressure caused by the strong yen had seen Honda's profits fall by 32 per cent, and financially Honda was in no real position to bid for the whole of Rover.

On 6 November 1993, the first press speculation appeared linking BMW with Rover. Comment centred around similarities in size and the complementarity of product range, as well as the difficulties both would face in trying to stand alone. BAe responded by saying that Rover was now part of its core business and this, together with the announcement of George Simpson's departure to head Lucas Industries, seemed to indicate that no sale or flotation of Rover was imminent.

On 19 January 1994, however, at the first extraordinary meeting of the supervisory board in the history of the company, BMW made the decision to bid for Rover. The formal offer was made on Wednesday 26 January and, on the following day, after a meeting lasting five hours, the BAe board decided to accept the offer in principle. BMW would pay £800 million and take on around £900 million in net debt and off-balance-sheet finance.

Honda had raised its previous offer to £165 million for a further 27.5 per cent of Rover. George Simpson was told by BAe management, however, to take the next flight to Tokyo and to inform Honda that this latest offer had been refused. He was to offer Honda the opportunity to increase its shareholding to 51 per cent. BAe would continue to hold 49 per cent as long as agreement was reached on a market flotation within five years. But Honda refused to increase its offer and the meeting between Simpson and Kawamoto was described as 'extremely tense'.

The alliance — implications of the acquisition

John Towers, managing director of Rover Cars, did not find out about the bid until the day after the BAe board meeting. He was immediately concerned about the reaction of his Japanese partners and the possible implications for the company. On Saturday, however, in a meeting with Tim Sainsbury MP, a minister at the Department of Trade and Industry, BMW reassured the British government that its fears over job security and the impact on Anglo-Japanese relations were unfounded.

Following this meeting, and approval from the British government, the deal was concluded ten days after the formal offer. Honda was said to be 'surprised and humiliated', and threatened to sever all links with Rover, privately saying that it would never do business with BMW, its fiercest rival in the USA. Honda immediately set up a taskforce to assess the benefits of continuing the alliance, which, it was realised, would also allow a 'cooling off' period. John Towers attempted to explain to Honda that in the end it was BAe's problems that had set the agenda, regardless of the relationship built up during the alliance.

Neither BAe nor Honda had wanted ownership of Rover, and so BMW had won. By this move, it was to become the largest 'specialist maker' of cars in the world, with a range of potential synergies with its new subsidiary, including range extension, economies of scale across the board, access to front-wheel and four-wheel-drive technology, one of the best small car engines in Europe, and a selection of valuable and, in some cases, underdeveloped brands.

Although shaken by the acquisition, the reaction of Honda's senior management underlined the cultural differences involved in the original alliance. BAe had clearly been discharging its obligations to its shareholders. Even so, the behaviour shown in breaking trust was absolutely inexplicable to the management team within Honda.

On 17 February, a delegation from BMW and Rover, including both MDs, flew into Tokyo for talks with Honda. BMW wanted Honda to swallow its pride and to work along with both companies. The only response was a statement from Nobuhiko Kawamoto: 'We will accelerate our policy of establishing independent and self-reliant operations in Europe.' On existing relations with Rover, he went on to say:

> We will continue those that are beneficial from a business standpoint such as mutual sourcing of parts and components — although our relationship with Rover Group will continue, the acquisition by BMW has caused a fundamental review of our European strategy.

On 17 February, the cross-shareholding was formally dissolved with a net payment from BMW to Honda of £116 million. Toshio Ishino, head of Honda UK, said that the company would continue to honour its agreement to supply components to Rover, but hinted that there would be no further major collaborative projects. This conflicted with claims by John Towers that the alliance would continue beyond 2006.

Bernd Pischetsrieder made clear his intention to transform Rover into an exclusive upmarket producer, involving development of new models. The implication is that this leaves little scope for future collaboration with Honda. His plan was to turn Rover into a brand as strong and exclusive as BMW, and at the same time to double or even treble world sales. As part of this strategy, Pischetsrieder realised that BMW's logistics technology had to be transferred to Rover in order to build cars to individual customer specifications, as opposed to the Honda system of batch production of 30 identical cars.

BMW and Rover — facing the twenty-first century

Bernd Pischetsrieder always viewed the transformation of Rover as a long haul. By 1996, BMW was committed to an investment programme of £500 million per year in the UK until the year 2000, in order to counteract the effects of decades of low investment, and Rover was not expected to make a net contribution to the group until early in the next century. BMW had a target margin of 6–7 per cent pre-tax, and this was regarded as the minimum necessary to fund long-term growth in the industry.

BMW was positioned to appeal to successful, affluent buyers. However, companies such as Toyota and even Honda continued to attack this exclusive segment with some success. Questions inevitably arose regarding BMW's ability to withstand this sustained competition, while simultaneously funding Rover's future development.

In May 1996, the structure of Rover was totally reorganised. Emphasis was placed on design, by separating the engineering and manufacturing functions. Much of Rover's future design work would emanate from Munich, and sales and marketing were directly controlled by Tom Purves, head of BMW in the UK.

BMW attempted to reduce costs further by the standardisation of non-visible components where possible between both the Rover and BMW model ranges. Marketing objectives concentrated on the globalisation and focusing of the Rover brands, possibly including names such as Healey, Riley and Triumph.

In 1996, industry analysts predicted that the first joint BMW/Rover car would be a new 700, due out in 1998 to replace the 600 and 800, and this would be followed by a new mini range. The 200/400 range might be rebadged as Triumph and a new top-of-the-range flagship was planned, possibly using the Riley name.

Pischetsrieder argued that the core of BMW's thinking was not about brand names, but about brand identity. He went on to add: 'The first task is to build a Rover brand identity and a solid presence in the market. You cannot do this in a hurry, you must be properly prepared, because in this industry you only get one shot.' He also stated: 'Either you become a global player or you will be out of business in twenty years' time.'

The big question, given the increasing dynamism of the industry, was whether the company had the resources and competitive position to achieve these aims.

Coopers Creek and the
New Zealand wine industry

HEATHER WILSON and MAUREEN BENSON-REA

Coopers Creek, established in 1982, was one of New Zealand's more successful medium-sized wineries by 1996 in terms of sales of quality, award-winning wines. Andrew Hendry, the managing director, consciously managed the growth of the company in order to attempt to retain the benefits of small size. He did this by leveraging resources and managing networks of co-operative relationships with other New Zealand winemakers better to serve both local and export markets. As a result of this greater experience and success in domestic and international operations, Hendry was faced with questions of whether to pursue growth and, if so, how, given his lifestyle aspirations; and whether to maintain his commitment to network-based strategies and, if so, how to maintain and develop them.

Background

Andrew Hendry, an accountant by training, considered himself a good salesperson. Indeed, he had always been a bit of a trader, having dealt in jewellery and gold from the Middle East before setting up a small business producing home-made pâtés with his wife, Cyndy. Andrew maintained that his overall approach to business was seeing a good deal, while balancing this with the cautious, measured approach of an accountant. His aim has been to take advantage of opportunities without overextending himself or his financial situation. Andrew's first encounter with the wine industry was when he worked on behalf of a syndicate as a buyer at the auction houses of Sotheby and Christie in London. When he returned to New Zealand, he took a position with a finance company until he was headhunted to join the Penfolds Wine Group, which became part of Montana Wines, as financial director/general manager.

According to Andrew Hendry, he was essentially a sole trader and he operated best by himself. Hence the desire to run his own company. When he first established the company, he was determined to keep it small and not to get to the stage where his time was occupied by management tasks. He wanted the operation of the company to be a pleasurable experience which did not involve sitting behind a desk most of the time. By 1996, Andrew found that the company was a lot bigger than he ever thought it would be. From the production of 2,500 cases of wine in 1982, the company produced 57,500 cases in 1995. When Andrew first set up the business, he envisaged producing 30,000 cases, with 90 per cent of that comprising domestic sales by year 10.

The land for the Coopers Creek vineyard west of Auckland was purchased by the Hendrys in 1980 with seed capital from the home-made pâté business. Coopers Creek winery was established with 40 per cent loan capital from a local bank and 60 per cent equity capital (20 per cent from Andrew Hendry and 40 per cent from other shareholders). Andrew Hendry fostered relationships with grape growers to encourage them to invest as shareholders in the business. In addition, he fostered contacts with colleagues of his former life, partners in Coopers and Lybrand, and involved them in the partnership.

Finally, the most important relationship at start-up was with the winemaker, and Andrew arranged the ownership structure so that the winemaker owned one-third, he owned one-third and the other shareholders owned the final third of the company. A partnership was formed which enabled the company to enjoy tax write-offs, and the participants essentially earned a tax holiday until the company returned a profit.

Like most small businesses, Coopers Creek relied heavily on borrowed capital during the early years. This also coincided with rising interest rates from 1985 onwards, resulting in the interest bill being the second major disbursement after the grape bill. Later on, as profits were generated, Andrew Hendry bought out the partnership, and by 1996 he owned just under 75 per cent of the shares of the business, and the ratio of debt to equity was $1:3.3$. The original winemaker partner left the business, sold his shareholding to Andrew and returned to the USA. He has since been replaced by a New Zealander. Andrew maintained that the winemaker was key to the success of the various wines' labels. He recognised this contribution by paying one of the highest salaries for a winemaker in the New Zealand industry. The new winemaker, Kim Crawford, was offered shares in the company, but chose to operate on a contract basis rather than defer current earnings until some future dividend date. Only one grower has retained a shareholding in the Coopers Creek business, although all of the shareholder growers experienced capital gain. Essentially, the growers decided they could no longer operate on both sides of the fence: as growers they wanted to negotiate the highest price, but as shareholders they wanted to bargain for the lowest price.

When Hendry set up the winery in the early 1980s, the New Zealand environment was highly regulated. For example, the early development of Coopers Creek was severely limited by the local council's refusal to permit the new winery to press grapes from outside the region. However, this restriction did not apply to older wineries in the area. By 1984, the New Zealand government had initiated a programme of deregulation, which included devaluation of the New Zealand currency, exchange rate flotation and general anti-inflationary initiatives, with the aim of maximising sustainable medium-term growth within a framework of price stability. As a result, the small, protected and debt-burdened New Zealand economy was transformed into one of the most competitive in the OECD, ranking seventh in 1995.

The opening up of New Zealand's domestic market meant that businesses had to improve their efficiency substantially over a short period. Both industry and agriculture sought out new products and markets to replace the loss of their traditional dependence on the European market. While this dependence has declined, from 65 per cent of all New Zealand exports in 1965 to 15 per cent in 1994, exports to Australia, Japan and the rest of Asia increased over the same period. The make-up of these exports also changed considerably, from predominantly sheepmeat and dairy products to more fresh fruit, venison and wine. A further response to fiercer competition at home and in overseas markets was the increasingly strong focus on quality — of the product itself and of service responsiveness in support of the product. This had been the main thrust of strategies in the New Zealand wine industry since the beginning of its phenomenal growth in the 1980s and 1990s.

The New Zealand wine industry

The New Zealand wine industry accepted the consequences of the liberalisation of the domestic economy and, faced with the strength of the New Zealand dollar against sterling (an appreciation of 35 per cent during the two years to 1994), also recognised the need to understand how on-going changes in the international economic environment affected its prosperity and how to plan accordingly. Building from a low international base in the 1980s ($4.5 million in exports in 1987), New Zealand wine exports achieved phenomenal growth and accounted for $41 million in 1995. This was down slightly from $48 million in 1992/3 due to poor grape harvests. The industry has a target of $100 million in export earnings by the year 2000.

In 1995, the UK market was the most important export market for the industry, accounting for 64 per cent of New Zealand wine exports by value and 70 per cent by volume. This amounted to some $27 million in 1995 (see Figure 1). Since 1985, exports to the UK increased by almost 700 per cent, although since 1993, export dollar values had been disadvantaged by the appreciation of the New Zealand dollar.

The wine industry in 1996 was dominated by four large firms: namely, Corbans, Montana, Villa Maria and Nobilo. Between them, these four firms accounted for around 65 per cent of all exports, with another twelve medium-sized companies handling 25 per cent in combination. For the most part, industry participants exported between 10 and 25 per cent of their production, but a few producers had a much higher export intensity.

In 1996, the New Zealand wine industry was still considered to be young, and this was the key characteristic of its products and strategies. The main features of the industry were its small scale, its distinctive 'clean and green' growing conditions, high-cost structures and a focus on premium wines. This last point was in keeping with the trend for New Zealand producers to

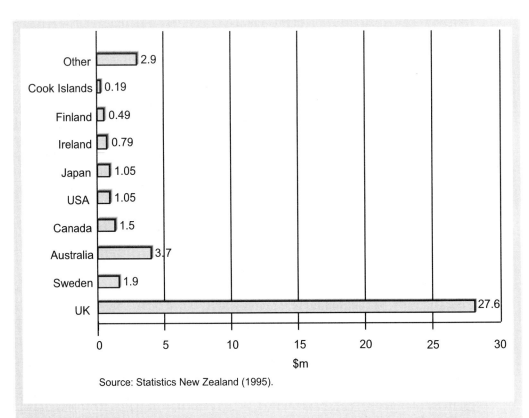

Source: Statistics New Zealand (1995).

Figure 1   New Zealand wine exports, 1995

move away from the commodity mentality to more value-added, quality products. New Zealand's range of international-quality products included New Zealand Sauvignon Blanc, Chardonnay and Riesling, red wines based on Cabernet Sauvignon, Merlot and Pinot Noir, and sparkling wines. Quality was maintained by high competitive standards domestically, protection of prime viticultural land, the fostering of close relationships between wineries and quality grape growers, improvement in winemaking standards, and certification of export wine quality. New Zealand wines competed with other 'new world' wines from Australia, California, Chile and South America primarily in advanced economies.

Investment in plantings had been important for the industry as a whole — rising grape prices followed poor yields in the 1992 and 1993 seasons. Some wine producers diversified away from high-priced contract grapes and invested extensively in their own vineyard plantings. After two relatively small harvests, the 1995 vintage produced a bountiful crop, the second largest ever for the New Zealand wine industry. However, the New Zealand wine industry was expecting to face an oversupply situation in 1996, given the stock of grapes in the ground and the winemakers' predictions. There was a concern among existing wine companies that the growers would form a co-operative to utilise the excess grapes and produce their own wine. This could be bought as supermarket own-label wine, and/or could be introduced into the New Zealand market place as a low-cost competitor. The introduction of a low-cost competitor would affect the export market more than the domestic market, because domestic customers value particular vineyard labels in the local market, while export customers were considered to be more price sensitive because they lacked this local knowledge. However, it should be borne in mind that, in the past, the liabilities of a small economic base and the vagaries of the New Zealand climate had left the industry without sufficient product to tackle the task of export market diversification, and an oversupply situation could be a temporary phenomenon.

The New Zealand Wine Institute, the Wine Guild and Country Action Groups

All New Zealand winemakers had to belong to the New Zealand Wine Institute. In order to sell wine, companies were legally obliged to acquire a licence and take out membership of the Institute. The Institute acted as a self-regulatory body for the wine industry. Among its regulatory activities, the Institute administered the Ministry of Health's export certification procedures, which involved chemical testing and blind tastings. Andrew Hendry was elected to the board in 1986 as a representative of small producers (the wineries were categorised according to size by annual litre sales). By 1993, however, Coopers Creek was categorised as a medium-sized company. In 1995, there were 204 members of the Wine Institute comprising 4 large producers, 12 medium-sized companies and 188 small, 'boutique' wineries.

Some Institute members with export interests in specific markets had established special interest groups: the Wine Guild was formed by those wineries either already established in the UK export market or interested in entering this market; and another four groups, termed Country Action Groups, were established to share information, experiences and promotional activities relating to Germany, the USA, Canada and Australia.

By 1996, the Wine Guild involved around 53 full members and about 25 associate members. Generally, the associate members were very small producers not currently exporting, but intending to at some stage. It is important to note that, of all the potential members of the Wine Guild, around 15 could be termed active participants of the network targeting the UK. The Guild, originally organised on an informal basis, was expected to become more formalised in future as government funding ran out. Tradenz (the New Zealand government body concerned with promoting overseas trade) provided a third of the Wine Guild's funds in order to facilitate New Zealand wine exports. This government funding would be available until 1997. After that, the Guild was expected to continue with Wine Guild membership funding only. Meanwhile, members of the Wine Guild provided the additional two-thirds funding, which was calculated as a percentage levy on sales (a 1 per cent levy on free-on-board sales). Thus, members felt that they paid in proportion to the individual company benefits. However, some increases in sales were not always a direct result of the Guild's initiatives; rather, they were due to single company marketing efforts. Individual firms paid for any additional exporting costs and extra promotion they wished to undertake beyond that provided by the Guild.

The overall Wine Guild administration, based in the offices of the Wine Institute in Auckland, was controlled by a board of directors, of which Andrew Hendry was deputy chairperson in 1996. At that time there were also two Tradenz representatives (one based in Auckland, the other in Wellington), as well as a rotating chairperson. Another director on the board of the Guild was the executive officer of the Wine Institute. In addition, the Wine Institute had seconded a part-time employee to work on behalf of the Wine Guild. These links with the Wine Institute facilitated information sharing, although the Institute had no voting rights in how the Wine Guild operated. Essentially, the board provided financial and marketing expertise for the successful operation of the Guild, as well as ideas for future developments. Although a voting system was in place, decisions were usually made by consensus.

The four Country Action Groups developed marketing plans to explore and, ultimately, exploit export opportunities within the chosen markets. The marketing plan was implemented through a semi-formal funding arrangement whereby individual companies contributed to costs on a project-by-project basis. For example, only those companies which were interested in a particular promotion contributed to the costs of mounting it. Coopers Creek was actively involved in the Canadian and US Country Action Groups in terms of joint promotional efforts.

Coopers Creek — export markets

In 1987, less than 1 per cent of Coopers Creek produce was exported (mainly to Australia). Indeed, Andrew Hendry's approach to exports was to delay efforts until the company had secured enough long-term commitments from suppliers of the grape and had established a firm foothold in the New Zealand market. Also, the aim was to consolidate, build the value of the label and establish wine styles before export commitments were made.

The first export market was Australia, which, according to Hendry, was a hard market in which to sell. This opportunity arrived almost by chance, or certainly ahead of Hendry's original export schedule. Entry to the market place was facilitated by the company's relationship with the Wine Institute of New Zealand, which co-ordinated a Wine Expo in Sydney in 1984. At the time, the opportunity to venture into this market proved irresistible because it coincided with the devaluation of the New Zealand currency and the resulting value for money prices in the Australian market place. Despite some initial difficulties associated with new market entry, this exporting experience proved to be invaluable in overcoming problems associated with selling New Zealand wines abroad.

Coopers Creek initiated a serious export strategy in 1989, having delayed for one year because 1988 was a bad season for the production of grapes. The UK was the next market targeted by the company, again in partnership with the Wine Institute (from which the UK Wine Guild evolved). This was followed two years later by excursions into other European countries (Holland, Belgium and Switzerland) and North America, principally because Andrew Hendry did not want to become too reliant on the UK market. In terms of volume in 1995, 65 per cent of exports were sold in the UK market, with around 5 per cent each for Australia, Canada, Holland and the USA (east coast states). Smaller markets where, according to Hendry, decent quantities of Coopers Creek wine were sold comprised Fiji, Belgium, Switzerland, Ireland, Hong Kong and Singapore. For the future, Coopers Creek was looking to expand in Hong Kong, Switzerland and the USA, and develop new export markets in Denmark, France, Germany, Norway and Sweden.

Coopers Creek's focused export strategy involved considerable collaborative and individual efforts. Collaboratively, Coopers Creek entered the Australian, UK, US and Canadian markets, although considerable individual effort was also expended in the process. For example, it took Andrew Hendry six months of negotiations with the Ontario Liquor Control Board to gain their agreement to distribute his wines to all of the Board's 630 stores throughout Ontario. Special labels and cartons had to be developed to meet local requirements; and, because the wine could be shipped in the depths of the Canadian winter, when temperatures can be as low as minus 20°C, the wine was transported in heated containers. This effort was recognised by the award of a Tradenz Export Commendation on the recommendation of the New Zealand Trade Commissioner in Canada. Markets which Coopers Creek has essentially developed on its own include Holland, Belgium, Ireland, Hong Kong, Singapore and Switzerland.

In those markets where collaborative efforts had been employed, the principal aim had been jointly and effectively to sell the New Zealand label ahead of individual wine company labels. Promoting the generic New Zealand brand in this way was seen as a way of benefiting all New Zealand exporters. For example, the network of wineries involved in the UK Wine Guild comprised 15 active participants in 1996. This Wine Guild, set up on the initiative of the Wine Institute in 1992, established an office in London with two full-time employees to promote and support sales of New Zealand wines. Basically, the agents of this Guild provided organised tastings of New Zealand wines, an information bureau, placement of advertisements, and travel arrangements for local wine writers and trade buyers to visit New Zealand.

In the UK market, sales and distribution remained the responsibility of the exporting firms and, typically, they used exclusive agreements with established agents and distribution networks. However, these relationships evolved from more co-operative structures. For example, in the UK, one firm was agent for several New Zealand wine companies initially until the volume of business became too large for the agent to handle. Subsequently, the wineries had to find agents able to handle increasing volumes, and the agency/distributor relationships began to fragment. In the German and US markets, where growth was at an early stage, the New Zealand companies tended to share the same agents. The Wine Institute and the Guild played a role in facilitating distribution processes by hosting visits by groups of agents.

Despite the fragmented distribution structure in the UK, Andrew Hendry was still able to develop a collaborative relationship with one major UK customer, the supermarket chain Tesco's. Both Andrew Hendry and Kim Crawford visited Tesco's, Coopers Creek was actively involved in the promotion of new vintage releases through the chain, and agents of the supermarket were invited to visit New Zealand and provide input into the development of wine styles. This relationship resulted from Hendry's basic inclination to conduct some personal selling in export markets in addition to his appointed agents. This approach also provided an opportunity to ensure that export customers were very clear about the amount of product they could expect from Coopers Creek in the coming years.

A new development for the company targeted the US market place. Coopers Creek and eight other members of the Wine Institute (not through the US Country Action Group) planned to take a joint New Zealand stand at the Boston Wine and Food Show in 1996. Wine would be promoted alongside seafood, venison and other produce. Hendry was actively seeking New Zealand government funding to support this initiative.

Andrew Hendry maintained that it was the export market which provided the major impetus to the growth experienced by his company and the wine industry in general. Coopers Creek had been experiencing around 25 per cent growth per year, compared with an industry average of 5–10 per cent growth. In 1995, exports comprised around 40 per cent of Coopers Creek's production level. So, instead of the company operating in the small New Zealand market as first envisaged, the developed economies of the world were presenting new and exciting opportunities. Nevertheless, the domestic market place was still important to the company. Indeed, the domestic market place alone was in 1995 accounting for more business than Hendry ever envisaged for the company (35,000 cases sold recently in the domestic market).

Domestically, Coopers Creek had established collaborative relationships with a group of local competitors in the West Auckland area. These competitors comprised Selaks, Kumeu River, Matua Valley and Nobilo. The relationships were established on the initiative of Andrew Hendry, who, on a visit to Australia, observed some local Australian winemakers collaborating locally. The group initially came together for joint advertising and promotions. For example, over Easter weekends, three of the companies arranged tours, special wines, meals and music, with the aim that visitors should sample a different food course at each vineyard. This initiative promoted custom, getting a larger proportion of people to visit the wineries than on normal weekends. This event had been operating since 1990. The grouping had also collaborated on trade tastings in Wellington, when they emphasised current releases and invited retailers, restaurant owners and wine vendors to sample the wine.

These companies regularly gathered as a group in an informal committee to decide on their next collaborative efforts. The situation had arisen where only two or three companies in the group had gone ahead with a particular promotion. Other times, all five companies had been involved. Beyond this committee, there had been co-operation on the production side of the companies' operations. For example, at key times, equipment had been shared and some key processes, like grape crushing during peak periods, had been performed on the competitors' sites. On the level of key inputs, the grouping had recently considered collaborating to negotiate discounts on purchases from bottle producers.

A feature of all the networks in which Coopers Creek was involved was horizontal or competitor-based co-operation. Competition in the domestic market place was considered to be intense. However, this did not impede collaborative efforts where these were deemed more efficient or beneficial (while paying heed to the need to avoid anti-competitive behaviour). In the international market place, once the customer had decided to purchase New Zealand wine, Coopers Creek considered itself to be in competition with all New Zealand wineries present, whether large or medium sized. The exception was the Canadian market place, where, because the company had been particularly successful, competition was centred around only the larger New Zealand wineries. Regardless of size, according to Andrew Hendry, the overseas perception of New Zealand wine was based on the development of personal relationships, and the quality and price of the wine.

In international markets, before the decision to purchase the New Zealand brand, the competition for sales and market share was seen by New Zealand wine companies to be from other countries rather than from individual firms. The newer producing countries, such as Chile, were perceived to be the bigger threat due to rapid advancements in production quality. However, even within the international market place there was co-operation, with industries across countries sharing information and learning about new techniques and processes. This international learning was achieved through informal means, such as exchange visits by producers and by New Zealand-based winemakers spending the off-season in northern hemisphere wineries to build connections and to benefit from low-level technology exchange.

In order to keep up with the growth, principally driven by exports, Coopers Creek had to increase its supply of grapes from the original 4 hectares west of Auckland. This was achieved by acquiring additional land for its own plantings in Hawkes Bay and West Auckland, as well as buying grapes from independent growers in Marlborough and Gisborne. This strategy enabled the company to spread the risk of adverse weather conditions in any of the four growing regions. By 1996 Coopers Creek sourced 90 per cent of its grape supplies from eighteen independent growers, basing the purchase decision entirely on the quality of the harvest. The company would have liked to have grown more of its own supplies, but decided to wait until prices stabilised before purchasing more land.

In addition, the company invested in plant to the extent that, by 1996, it was in a position to double production without further investment. This development meant that Coopers Creek was able to do all of its own crushing, processing, bottling and packaging. The company still intended to use local trucking companies as well as sourcing grapes, bottles, labels and corks from independent suppliers.

Andrew Hendry also recruited a marketing director in 1996 to free himself for some of the more pleasurable tasks he first envisaged when establishing the company, such as building direct relationships with top-class restaurants. The new marketing director was responsible for promotions, liaison with customers and agents, co-ordination of label design and point-of-sale material, and direct marketing. To a certain extent, Hendry felt that this step went against the grain of maintaining a controlled, rather than monolithic, lifestyle operation. However, his company at the time was operating with generally fewer staff than some winemaking companies of equivalent size. Filling this position enabled Andrew to pursue and cultivate relationships by doing more personal selling, spending one day a week on this task. For example, Andrew found that a particularly effective personal selling strategy was to visit restaurants in the domestic market place in order to encourage them to include the Coopers Creek label on their wine list. However, he avoided going down the route of supplying the wine directly to these customers and continued to utilise distributors.

Andrew Hendry's future strategy for the company was not to grow, but to become more effective. He wanted to protect the $3\frac{1}{2}$ million dollar turnover achieved in 1995, considering this to be sufficient for his purposes. However, Andrew recognised that, given the previous momentum, the company was likely to continue to grow by about 5 per cent each year, and that in ten years' time the company could be three and a half times the size he first imagined. This would pose some dilemmas for him personally. Although Andrew and Cyndy had four daughters, none of them had shown an interest in taking over the business in the future.

In terms of the further pursuit of network-based strategies, Andrew Hendry looked less than favourably on the links with other organisations which Coopers Creek was obliged to maintain, believing that relationships based on compulsion were difficult to assess in terms of outcomes. Even if the relationship with the Wine Institute was not a successful or beneficial one, Coopers Creek could not legally relinquish membership. The general benefits for the involvement of Coopers Creek were considered to be information from technical sub-committees, industry-level participation and lobbying. For example, the Institute has been a supporter of the New Zealand government's membership of the International Wine Office (Office International de la Vigne et du Vin) and the negotiating leverage that can bring in international trade.

The benefits of Coopers Creek's relationship with the UK Wine Guild were easier to gauge. From the time of inception to 1996, New Zealand wine sales to the UK had risen by around 200 per cent. The direct outcome for Coopers Creek was increased profitable sales, as the UK Guild helped to raise the number of case sales while also raising the perception of the quality of New Zealand wines, enabling Coopers Creek to command higher prices. The critical issue for the future was to ensure that the Guild efforts were maintained and, possibly, the momentum raised in terms of both the Guild and the Country Action Groups.

One possible impediment to this future momentum was the need to consider the individual company contributions to Guild operations as a result of a financial shortfall in 1994. A suggestion was on the table in 1996 that there should be a tiered flat fee structure (with larger exporters paying the higher fees). The potential danger was that these larger exporters would take the position that they were essentially supporting competitors' sales, and would refuse to accept the flat fee structure. At a more extreme level, they could even decide to initiate their own marketing efforts, thus endangering the viability of the Guild partnership.

The local network was considered to be 'very neighbourly considering we're all in competition'. Andrew Hendry had been involved in so many local network activities that assessment of mutual benefit for the networked wineries was an important consideration when developing his own company strategy. The overall benefit of the local network was the critical mass that a number of wine companies working together were able to achieve — basically being able to act big while retaining the benefits of small size.

Thus, in 1996, Andrew Hendry was faced with the potential dilemma of enforced growth resulting from continuing participation in networks. His strategic options were broad, but the key issue seemed to be how to balance sustaining and consolidating existing markets with developing new ones. The question was whether both approaches were sustainable and whether he should develop independently or in collaboration with other firms (by establishing either vertical or horizontal linkages). In addition, he had to consider whether he could balance his desire to stay small with the opportunities for growth which seemed to present themselves.

Bibliography

M. Cooper, *The Wines and Vineyards of New Zealand*, Hodder and Stoughton, 1994.

G.T. Crocombe, M.J. Enright and M.E. Porter, *Upgrading New Zealand's Competitive Advantage*, Oxford University Press, 1991.

New Zealand Trade Development Board, *Export News*, 30 January 1992 and 2 May 1994.

Wine Institute of New Zealand, *Annual Report 1995*.

World Economic Forum, *World Competitiveness Report*, 1995.

The News Corporation

JULIE E. NORTON and LESLIE P. WILLCOCKS

For the year ending 30 June 1995, turnover at The News Corporation (TNC) reached over £5bn. This made TNC the fourth largest media business in the world, eclipsed only by America's Time Warner and Disney/Capital Cities, and Germany's Bertelsmann. Yet there was no doubting who was the leader in the media industry. What was breathtaking about TNC was its global reach, its sweeping ambition and the extent to which it was the creation of one man. Rupert Murdoch has been the chief executive since 1953.

Early years and growth to 1980

The company was established in Australia in 1923 by Rupert Murdoch's father, Sir Keith, with the founding of *The News* in Adelaide. By 1980 the company was publishing that country's only national newspaper, *The Australian*, two national magazines and over twenty provincial newspapers. Interests in book publishing and television had also been acquired, along with film making, record production, farming and transport interests. The Murdoch family interest in the company, however, remained strong, through an equity holding of nearly 45 per cent.

The profitability of this Australian base was the springboard to multinational status. It provided the financial backing for the 1968 purchase of the UK-based News of the World Organisation, publishers of the *News of the World* (*NOTW*) Sunday newspaper. By 1980 News International Ltd, the UK subsidiary, was publishing not only the *News of the World*, but also the *Sun*, both newspapers with consistently the largest circulation in the UK, and had interests in magazine and book publishing,

This case was written by Julie E. Norton, University of Reading, and Leslie P. Willcocks, Oxford University. It is intended as a basis for class discussion and not as an illustration of either good or bad management practice. © Julie E. Norton and Leslie P. Willcocks, 1996. Not to be reproduced or quoted without permission.

printing, warehousing and transport. During the early 1980s this subsidiary was the major contributor to TNC's profits.

From 1973, with the purchase of the Express Publishing Company of San Antonio, Texas, the company also operated in the United States. During the 1970s, expansion in the USA occurred in the areas of local newspaper publishing (the *New York Post* was acquired in 1976) and in magazine publishing (the *Star*, a national magazine, was founded in 1974, and the *Village Voice* and *New York Magazine* were acquired in 1977).

In TNC's annual report for 1980, Rupert Murdoch outlined the company's approach to its early growth and development:

> Over the years expansion has been both by original start-up and acquisition. Typically, acquisition has been followed by a mobilisation of energies and talents to transform both the professional quality and the market performance of old or failing publications ... In virtually every market where [TNC] operates, it has achieved its position by first purchasing the weakest existing publication and slowly restoring its viability.

Television and film making

The 1980s saw TNC accelerate its real growth and development, with expansion continuing to focus on traditional product areas. Major acquisitions included Times Newspapers Limited in the UK and, in the USA, the *Boston Herald* and *Chicago Sun–Times* newspapers, *New Woman*, a general interest magazine, and a group of technical and travel magazines. By 1984, turnover had reached nearly £1.2bn. The financial results for the period of the case are summarised in Appendix 1, and Appendix 2 details the major acquisitions and disposals.

However, 1984 saw the beginnings of a major geographical and product shift. This expansion was US based. It aimed to transform TNC into an integrated global media group, with a place in all parts of that industry from newspapers to television, from magazines to film.

In 1984, TNC acquired the film company Twentieth Century Fox. This company was in a poor financial position. In 1984 it had lost £60m on revenues of £520m and was heavily indebted, and its net worth had fallen from £260m to just over £35m. A successful future would require large injections of cash. On the plus side, the purchase created an integrated entertainment company and provided access to studios for making films and television programmes, and to a film library valued at £700m.

In 1985, six television stations in the USA were acquired from the Metromedia broadcasting group. Though operationally very profitable, this company suffered from high interest charges on debt incurred from an earlier leveraged buy-out. Rupert Murdoch's purchase involved paying only £160m in cash, but taking over £1bn in high-interest debt.

These US acquisitions were restructured into three principal operating groups:

- Twentieth Century Fox Film financed, produced and distributed television programmes and theatrical motion pictures throughout the world. The company had a film library of more than 2,000 titles, including such classics as *Star Wars* and *Butch Cassidy and the Sundance Kid*, plus syndicated TV series such as *M*A*S*H* and *Dynasty*.
- Fox Television Stations owned and operated seven independent television stations, all within the top ten US television markets (and including the first three).
- Fox Broadcasting Company (FBC) provided first-run original entertainment programming by satellite to independent affiliated television stations.

For Rupert Murdoch, this consolidation confirmed that:

> The News Corporation is now a multi-national, multi-media, company ... at the forefront of global marketing, ready to encourage the cross-fertilisation of ideas between continents, and the different media within them ... The News Corporation is a citizen of the global village.

However, these purchases had two further significant implications for TNC. Revenues and operating profits increased, but so too did debt levels. Rupert Murdoch had to be careful that his acquisitions, and the debt associated with them, did not breach bank loan agreements, which required total borrowings not to exceed net assets by more than 10 per cent. Furthermore, as US law prevented foreign citizens from holding more than 25 per cent of any company with a broadcasting licence, in 1985 Rupert Murdoch became a US citizen.

The strategy of globalisation

In a speech to the International Institute of Communications in September 1988, Rupert Murdoch confessed that he did not have a very detailed strategic plan:

> If in 1980 we had attempted to chart on paper the destiny of our company, we would never have anticipated the 30 very diverse acquisitions we made on four continents, almost all of which arose from unique and unanticipated events. Business situations and business opportunities simply change too quickly for there to be much point in loading ourselves down with piles of strategic speculation.

He has, however, asked himself three questions about the globalisation of the media:

> Is a global communications network a reality? Yes. Are there really going to be

world-wide media networks? Yes. Is it really going to be possible for an advertiser to achieve, in practice, a single order with the media of his choice across the world? Yes.

Other media groups had come to similar conclusions. For example, in its 1988 annual report, Time Inc. stated that 'by the mid-1990s, the media and entertainment industry will consist of a handful of vertically integrated, worldwide giants'. In this period the media were seen as tremendous growth industries, with long-term growth encouraged by rising real incomes and new technologies, which, for example, saw US communications spending growing half as fast again as GNP between 1960 and 1990.

The attraction of globalisation was based on the belief that tastes, income levels, technologies and even political philosophies around the world were converging on the American model, producing strong demand for American-style films and television programmes. In 1988, for the first time in history, foreign television stations spent more on American movies than stations in the USA itself.

Combining globalisation with integration was expected to increase profits through economies of scale. For example, a group's publishing house could gain preferential access to authors for potential movie subjects. Through its cable or satellite television network, it would have a ready market for its film output and could pay more to attract best-selling authors or star directors by putting them to work on numerous related books, films or television projects under one roof.

Rupert Murdoch — The Wizard of Oz

He's an expansion minded person, he's wanted to buy assets, he's wanted to take over, to move around the world, to build his media empire. But he also wants to retain control.   Australian financial analyst

What was unique about TNC was that it was not a faceless multinational, but an organisation keenly linked to its chief executive — as a 1990 UK television programme commented, it was Murdoch's 'Empire', built on his 'vision, ruthlessness and daring'.

Rupert Murdoch himself managed the various businesses through the 'formulae' that he had for their products. As a former newspaper editor explained: 'He talks in formulae terms. He has formulae for newspapers. There is the broadsheet formula, the popular formula. There is the downmarket tabloid formula, and so on.'

The implementation of these 'formulae' was achieved through the appointment of known and trusted lieutenants to run key products or business segments. However, the whole management structure was very informal with no defined responsibilities. One aide suggested that TNC was 'an emotionally driven and bonded company, where executives don't spend time guarding territories because nobody has one nailed down'. Another suggested that Rupert Murdoch's idea of management was to put in a manager and put in someone beside him, and not quite tell either of them what they were doing. A News International executive confirmed: 'I think he does do that. I don't think he does it to undermine the original person. I think he thinks that if the two can work off each other things will improve.'

Rupert Murdoch disliked committees, bureaucracy and red tape. In the late 1980s, the worldwide headquarters in midtown Manhattan, USA, employed barely 60 people, with hardly a memo in sight and communications kept to a bare necessity.

At the same time, this management style was supplemented by an extremely efficient reporting system. This focused on a weekly document known as the 'Flash', for which each operating unit had to provide a summary of its operating results. These had to include the budgeted figures for every aspect of its affairs set against the actual figures for the week, and then compared with the same week in the previous year. Each Thursday it was passed to headquarters, with Rupert Murdoch studying it over the weekend. He might then casually ring to query a figure. The call might come only once in the year, but it kept everyone on their toes for the other fifty-one weeks. Control was also achieved by unannounced 'parachuting-in' trips to check in person on the details of a business's activities and management, or to take personal control at key moments. As a News International financial manager confirmed:

> He really is the driving force and most major decisions are made by him … even relatively minor decisions — like whether we start our TV burst of advertising now or do we put it back three weeks. Those are the sort of things that would be discussed with him before the final timings are decided. He does like leading from the front and where there's likely to be a bit of excitement he'll wade in … I think his biggest advantage is understanding the businesses that he's in. He can get down to the core of the business and has a lot of vision as to where that business ought to be going.

Maintaining control also required that Rupert Murdoch looked outside of the business to the regulatory environment that might constrain his activities. Most governments believed that the media was an industry whose importance required regulation, particularly regarding foreign ownership, cross-ownership and concentration. Controlling a business with a global reach, with several media products, Rupert Murdoch was likely to find himself affected by national regulatory systems. Many commentators have suggested that his political friendships have bought him influence in this area.

For example, in 1979 the Australian government amended the rules regarding the ownership of television stations, from a requirement that an owner be resident in Australia to one requiring only that an owner be an Australian citizen. This enabled Rupert Murdoch to acquire Channel 10 in Melbourne, even though he was no longer resident in Australia. These amendments were christened by the Australian press as 'the Murdoch amendments'. Again, it was suggested that the support of Murdoch's newspapers for Margaret Thatcher in the 1979 UK general election helped to ensure that his acquisition of Times Newspapers in 1981 was not referred to the Monopolies and Mergers Commission, and certainly the government called a three-line whip to stop any referral.

However, as one commentator has put it: 'His personal politics are right-wing ... but he's opportunistic in his business dealings. He doesn't support only right-wing leaders — he supports winners. And he supports people who are going to promote his business interests.'

Progress and conflict in Fleet Street

It is useful to return to the UK to examine in more detail the developments during the 1980s at the subsidiary that was the major contributor to TNC's profits.

Times Newspapers Ltd (TNL), in the UK, was acquired for £25m in 1981. The previous year, the company had reported losses in excess of £10m. Over the next four years, however, *The Times*'s circulation more than doubled to over 485,000 copies, and advertising revenues increased by over 30 per cent in both 1984 and 1985. This improvement was achieved on the basis of a traditionally loyal market, the appointment of new people in management and editorial, savings from economies of scale, some reduction in manpower, and aggressive selling of the paper. Profitability, however, required cutting production costs further, and maintaining uninterrupted production to make inroads into competitors' markets and to maintain advertising revenue.

The *Sun*, following earlier price-cutting campaigns and the introduction of 'Bingo' cards, increased circulation in 1985 to 4.165 million, and the *NOTW*, having introduced a free colour Sunday magazine and having been relaunched in tabloid format, increased to 5.2 million. These two papers were the dominant contributors from the UK to multinational profitability. The *Sun*'s production, however, was stuck at around 4 million due to limited printing press capacity.

In terms of increasing revenue and profits from increased circulation and advertising, Rupert Murdoch's strategies at News International had been fairly successful. The major problem in 1985 seemed to be how to secure continued stable growth for all of these titles. News International had invested nearly £100m in new plants at Wapping in Tower Hamlets,

London, and at Kinning Park, Glasgow. However, both remained idle due to the nature of industrial relations within the national newspaper industry.

In particular, over the years, Fleet Street management had shown a repeated failure to resist local union claims. This resulted from the weak position of supervisors and middle management, the short-term irrationality of resistance (suspension of production meant the loss of revenue from what was essentially a 'perishable' good — news) and the predominance of editorial, rather than financial, goals among senior management.

Management failure was coupled with strong union bargaining power due to the integratedness of the production system, and the fact that a point of maximum bargaining strength occurred nightly throughout most of the production shift and at each stage in the production cycle. The managing director of News International at the time, Bruce Matthews, indicated his frustration by saying that the company could 'no longer tolerate being bled to death by unnecessary industrial action' by employees who 'have the advantage of industrial blackmail each night'.

Given the opportunity, management would not wish to import into Wapping the same customs and practices that operated in Fleet Street. However, to bypass the old unions successfully required the introduction of a new computerised production system, a new workforce to run the machinery and journalists to write the copy, a new method of distribution and a means of neutralising the effect of any industrial action by the old unions. The assessment of such a project kept management away from negotiations during much of 1985.

Feasibility studies to determine the profitability of a new London evening paper masked the installation at Wapping of new technology and a new workforce, and the establishment of a new distribution system. This allowed management to put forward proposals for moving to Wapping that were so restrictive (as far as the unions were concerned) that acceptance was extremely unlikely, and a resort to industrial action the only likely response. On 24 January 1986, the unions declared strikes across News International's four titles. All production was transferred to Wapping and, although the dispute was a bitter one, the unions were unable to bring pressure to bear to disrupt production or distribution.

The accounts of News International to June 1986 included an exceptional item of £66m as the cost of moving to Wapping. However, operating profit at the subsidiary had nearly doubled to £81m during that year, and it increased again the following year by a further 65 per cent to £133m.

Towards the 1990s — the sky is the limit?

During the second half of the 1980s, TNC continued to expand and develop in its traditional product and market areas. The US book publishers Harper &

Row were acquired for £194m (outbidding rivals Harcourt Brace Jovanovich by £65m). More significant, however, were the acquisitions of the Australian *Herald and Weekly Times* (*HWT*) in 1987 and the American Triangle Publications in 1988. Although the acquisition of *HWT* was largely funded by the issue of convertible notes (classified as equity finance), the increased debt involved with the acquisition of Triangle Publications was of such magnitude that Rupert Murdoch was obliged, in 1988, to commit TNC to a significant debt reduction programme. This commitment, however, did not restrain the company from the launch in the UK on 5 February 1989 of Sky Television, a direct broadcasting by satellite European television network, offering four (initially) free-to-air, advertiser-supported channels.

The UK had regulations regarding the cross-ownership of media interests, including a requirement that no national newspaper proprietor may own more than 20 per cent of a television company. However, as Sky Television was beamed on channels rented from the Luxembourg-controlled Astra satellite, it fell outside the UK government's jurisdiction, even though its programmes were aimed almost exclusively at a UK audience. Rupert Murdoch, a non-UK national, was therefore able to own newspapers with 25 per cent of the national UK market, as well as his four television channels.

There were fewer subscribers than expected, resulting in lower subscription and advertising revenues. Although stringent cost reductions were implemented (one of Rupert Murdoch's maxims being that it was always easier to take a million off costs than add a million to revenues), the performance of Sky Television had marked financial consequences for TNC. In the year to 30 June 1990, £134m had been invested in the venture, yet losses of nearly £10m per month were being incurred, and it was estimated that £400m of investment would still be required through to the end of 1991.

Rupert bears the debt burden

In March 1989, Rupert Murdoch announced plans to launch a new investment company — Media Partners International (MPI). The aim was to raise approximately £850m in equity funds, which would then give the company access to £2.6bn when borrowings were included. This was to be spent on buying media and communications companies all over the world. The News Corporation was to hold only a minority (20 per cent) stake, but would have a ten-year management contract to run the company. The venture's first acquisition was to be HarperCollins, TNC's publishing interest.

By January 1990, however, MPI had been abandoned. There were reports of considerable resistance by potential investors to the idea of effectively making a 'blind bet' on Rupert Murdoch. HarperCollins was, therefore, put into a joint venture company established by TNC and its investment bankers, Credit Suisse First Boston. Effectively, the bank agreed to purchase, on a short-term basis, half of HarperCollins. The News Corporation was then able to equity account for this investment and so move the debt associated with it 'off' its balance sheet.

In November 1990, Rupert Murdoch announced the merger of Sky Television with its UK rival, British Satellite Broadcasting (BSB). BSB had begun broadcasting in March 1990. Start-up costs here had also been higher than expected and the purchase of satellite dishes lower than expected. The News Corporation and BSB each owned 50 per cent of the equity of the newly-created company, BSkyB (although, because BSB was a consortium, the next largest individual shareholder held only 11 per cent). However, the new company came to be dominated by Sky Television. The Astra satellite channels and the technology used by Sky Television were adopted, redundancies following the merger occurred mainly among the BSB staff, and Sky executives came to dominate senior management, giving it operational and editorial control of the new company.

These moves could not disguise the severe problems that had materialised for the company in 1990. These included a protracted strike at the 50 per cent owned Ansett Airlines and a poor year at Fox Film Studios. The News Corporation was also investing £500m in new printing presses in the UK. This was a heavy cash drain at a time when there was a slowing of the economies of each of TNC's three main markets. These problems resulted in a gap in working capital of £1.3bn, financed by highly expensive short-term borrowing. At the same time, banks worldwide experienced a liquidity crisis which resulted in TNC facing difficulty in refinancing maturing bank debt and in meeting working capital requirements.

By January 1991, in response to these problems, TNC's shares fell to a low of 156p — way below their peak of 850p, touched ahead of the stock market crash of 1987. Even during 1990 the shares had traded as high as 680p. The group's bonds were trading on yields of nearly 50 per cent and its debt had been downgraded by Moody's Investor Services, the US ratings agency, to near default levels. The News Corporation's market value of nearly £800m was a fraction of the £5bn net asset value of the 1990 accounts, and its borrowings of over £4.5bn were five times this stock market capitalisation. It became clear that, without some form of restructuring, the company would default on loans due for repayment in 1991.

Operation Dolphin

In October 1990, TNC called in Citibank of New York and began negotiations (codenamed Operation Dolphin) for the refinancing of its debt. At the time it was the largest and geographically most diverse corporate restructuring sought from international banks. For Rupert Murdoch it was a very different banking relationship to the one he was used to. As one commentator suggested, during the 1980s TNC had dominated the relationship:

> Sarazan [then chief financial officer] liked to use only banks who understood News Corp well ... The bank also had to accept Sarazan's clever global accounting practices, and the fact that News Corp would not secure loans with its own holdings and would brook very few restrictive covenants. In the end it seemed as if News Corp were doing the bank a favour by agreeing to borrow money.

Now Murdoch was flying between New York, Sydney and London, being grilled on TNC's figures, trying to sell himself and convince the bankers that he was a long-term survivor.

The banks faced a dilemma. Theoretically, they could push TNC to repay all its debts. However, with the exception of a small amount in Australia, none of the company's loans was secured on individual assets. The banks would be forced to liquidate the company to sell its assets and, although TNC was a strong business as a going concern, £6bn of assets were revalued intangibles. It was not clear how such values would hold up in a forced sale situation.

Many bankers discounted the possibility of calling in the company's loans from the start. They liked and respected Murdoch, he had a reputation among his business peers for honouring his commitments, he was also seen as a winner — if they pulled the plug on him, they did not believe that anyone else could run the business as well, in which case they could again wave goodbye to their money.

However, agreement to the restructuring was not automatic. The majority of problems developed following the discovery that original lenders had, quite legally, passed on some of their exposure to TNC to other banks, without TNC's knowledge. The result was that the company had to obtain unanimous agreement to the restructuring from a total of 146 banks. Some, particularly those with much less to lose, were not always supportive — on 6 December 1990, the £4bn (US$7.6bn) restructuring plan nearly collapsed and the company almost went into receivership when a modest US bank, Pittsburgh National, wanted to call in a US$10m loan.

In February 1991, TNC finally entered into a three-year, £3.8bn debt restructuring agreement and a £300m bridging loan agreement. Apart from the increased financial cost to TNC of these agreements, several strict financial covenants were introduced. Rupert Murdoch had to agree to quarterly meetings with the banks to discuss progress and to monitor the new covenants, and to guarantee to reduce debt levels by £1bn. He was also tied to the deal. One of the events of default related to a change in control of TNC, which would occur if Murdoch ceased to be chief executive or if the Murdoch family shareholding in the company fell below 20 per cent.

In explaining TNC's problems, Rupert Murdoch admitted: 'I had taken my eye off the financial side.' In retrospect, he concluded that the decision to modernise printing plants in Australia and the UK should have been delayed by three to four years, that the purchase of Triangle 'could have been a deal of US$1bn too much' and that he 'wasted time' with the MPI initiative.

On the rebound

By October 1991, TNC had raised £900m through asset sales, and had announced plans for the flotation of 55 per cent of its Australian printing and magazine interests to raise a further £314m. By the end of 1991, most of the £470m debt repayment due in February 1992 had been paid, and it appeared that further obligations could be met from existing cash flows without raising new money.

The important issues again lay with business directions. The perception of brokers Potter Warburg was that the company's profits in the 1990s would come from BSkyB, Twentieth Century Fox and Fox Broadcasting. Other market analysts saw consumers turning increasingly to film and television, perhaps reflecting the fact that newspaper circulation was in long-term decline. According to the UK's *Sunday Telegraph* newspaper, 'Murdoch's watchers say that while his heart is always in newspapers his head is increasingly in television.'

Rupert Murdoch himself set out his view of TNC's longer-term future in his chief executive's review of 1992. This involved 'steering a growth course' according to the following principles:

- Further strengthening the company's balance sheet.
- Improving and expanding existing businesses.
- Building new businesses.
- Nurturing and guiding the creative process as the foundation of the company's products.
- Strategic planning, involving examining opportunities for owning and operating media and entertainment ventures around the world. Particularly:

> We believe that our future is to be the pre-eminent supplier of first-rate creative and editorial product. The more we think about our businesses, and the more we look at the whole communications industry in all its facets, the more we define ourselves as a global supplier of what is now called 'software'. For us, the hardware developments that attract so much attention are secondary to our real business.

Elements of the implementation of Murdoch's five principles can be seen in the progress of the company through to early 1996.

A major refinancing of all borrowing took place. This resulted in short-term bank debt as a proportion of total debt falling from 80 to 8 per cent, and the average maturity of public debt being extended from less than three years to over ten years. Debt repayments due in 1994 under the agreement were paid early. In 1993, Standard and Poor's and Fitch Investors Service re-rated TNC's public debt securities investment grade.

In August 1995, MCI Communications Corporation, the second largest US long-distance telecommunications operator, agreed to pay £1.2bn in return for a 13.5 per cent stake in TNC. This, and other share issues, reduced the Murdoch family holding to just over 30 per cent (over which MCI was given first refusal should it be offered for sale). The terms of the alliance, however, limited MCI to a maximum 20 per cent investment in TNC and, although having voting rights, MCI was obliged to vote with the majority.

Existing newspaper businesses in Australia and the UK benefited from the reduced production costs resulting from the completion of capital investment programmes upgrading printing facilities. British newspapers added new sections which offered better-targeted advertising, and initiated aggressive price competition. In Australia, the company was at the forefront of the introduction of colour printing.

In 1995, the printed word of newspapers and magazines still provided over half of TNC's profits. But increasingly, profits were coming from the screen, from films and television.

On the box

Sky and BSB (and the subsequent merged company, BSkyB) were first marketed primarily as movie channels, for films receiving their first-time television screening. This was still seen as important, with BSkyB securing exclusive pay-television rights to all major Hollywood films until the year 2002, which increased subscribers to 1.7 million. In September 1992, BSkyB launched Sky Sports channel, having secured exclusive rights to broadcast English football Premier League matches for five years. In under six weeks, a million new subscribers were added. A gap in the market had been identified that was to revolutionise the nature of sport and the finances of BSkyB.

By 1996, BSkyB dominated the televising of English club football. It also had a stranglehold on international golfing championships, and live rights to all English overseas cricket and domestic one-day internationals. The company had also bought the rights to rugby union's Pilkington Cup and Courage Clubs Championship, and had offered £175m for five years' coverage of the Five Nations Championship. In contrast, the BBC's total sports budget stood at £100m.

The strategy was exported to other areas. In 1994 in the USA, Fox obtained the broadcast rights to the National Football League's NFC games for four years and the 1997 Super Bowl. A ten-year television deal was also made with the rugby unions of South Africa, New Zealand and Australia. In Australia, TNC even went so far as to create its own rugby Super League of ten teams, whose games would be shown exclusively on TNC-owned channels.

While advantages from increased payments have accrued to many sports, TNC's moves have not been without criticism. There were concerns that limiting sport to pay-television would have a detrimental effect on participation levels. Furthermore, when BSkyB's target was one of the sporting calendar's traditional highlights, or when the players involved were amateurs, arguments concerning sport as part of a 'national birthright' were evoked. These were influential enough to force an amendment to the UK's 1990 Broadcasting Act, ensuring that eight high-profile events were broadcast on terrestrial television. These were the Wimbledon finals weekend, the FA Cup Final, the Scottish Cup Final, the football World Cup Finals, domestic cricket Test Matches, the Olympics and the Derby.

The success of BSkyB's sports strategy increased subscribers to 3.6 million by September 1994. BSkyB was easily the most profitable television station in the UK. In December of that year, the company made a public offering of 20 per cent of its shares for over £4bn. This reduced TNC's interest in the company from 50 to 40 per cent, but its share of the flotation funds was a useful £600m.

By 1996, BSkyB was providing 28 channels, compared with the four it offered on launch and the four available on terrestrial television. Yet while the tenth-rated programme on Sky One, the most popular satellite channel, might win an audience of 350,000, the tenth-rated programme on ITV pulled in over 12 million. What provided the value in BSkyB was the fact that 80 per cent of revenues came from subscription. For the future, analysts believed that the company's exclusive rights to key programmes — films and sport — would drive the subscriber base forward:

> As critical mass is achieved and additional advertising revenues obtained, the strong cash flow generated will put the group in pole position to secure further sports rights and renegotiate the movie contract, which will in turn further stimulate subscriber interest.   Barclay de Zoote Webb

With subscription television, it was important to have in place a system that allowed for the correct collection of revenue. This required secure 'scrambling' and 'decoding' of the satellite signal. In the UK, the only established technology was controlled by News Datacom, a subsidiary of TNC. Using News Datacom's proprietary encryption code, BSkyB sent viewers a card which, when inserted into the decoder box connected to the television set, allowed programmes to be viewed.

Not only has this ensured full and appropriate payment for services provided by BSkyB, but, as one industry executive pointed out, for the future the company 'is in a position to skim off money from anyone who wants to start a satellite channel'. Control of encryption technology made BSkyB a channel 'gatekeeper'. For any channel operator, getting through the gate would require the payment of significant fees. However, by-passing the BSkyB 'gatekeeper' would require any new channel establishing its own encryption and marketing systems. Apart from the high investment and running costs, this would require viewers to buy a new decoder box to sit on top of their television sets.

In 1993, TNC moved into Asia with the acquisition of the Hong Kong-based company Star TV, which broadcast over China, India and 51 other countries containing approximately two-thirds of the world's population.

Murdoch's strategy in Asia was a variant of the 'be global, act local' philosophy that had come to dominate much thinking about international business. With the media, this was reflected in the realisation that, with the possible exception of Hollywood feature films, regional programmes in local languages were needed to make any impact outside English-speaking élites. To that effect, Star Television acquired Media Assets, which had a film library of approximately 550 Chinese-language motion pictures, and took a 50 per cent stake in Zee TV, a Hindi television channel in India. It was also clear that Star would not be profitable remaining as a free-to-air, advertiser-supported channel. While Sky moved from a free-to-air service to a pay-for-view network with surprisingly little difficulty, the cost of developing such a network in the immature Asian market was one reason Star was losing so much money.

Other problems stemmed from having to find a *modus vivendi* with Asia's political leaders. In September 1993, addressing an audience in London, Rupert Murdoch had claimed that 'advances in the technology of telecommunications have proved an unambiguous threat to totalitarian regimes everywhere'. Expansion in Asia by TNC was hindered by the authorities there, many of which were opposed to the free flow of information and the expansion of American cultural influence, recognising the truth of this statement. In response, Murdoch sold the embarrassingly anglophile *South China Morning Post* and Star removed the BBC World Service from its northern Asia channel. Murdoch also offered authorities the opportunity of controlling satellite programming through TNC's decoding technology. This would effectively allow censors to filter programmes to be broadcast.

In 1995 in Australia, TNC established a pay cable television joint venture, Foxtel, with Telstra, the country's national telephone company, utilising newly laid fibre-optic networks. In the USA, Fox Television, which had created a name for itself with youthful and irreverent programmes such as *The Simpsons* and *Married with Children*, repeated its success with *The X-*

Files, a detective-and-conspiracy series which attracted huge audiences of young males all over the world. By 1995, Fox Broadcasting had signed up nearly 200 independent stations as affiliates. Together with Fox television stations, this gave Fox Broadcasting the ability to deliver its programmes to 98 per cent of the total US network. A 24-hour general entertainment cable programming service and a cable movie channel were also launched in the USA. Murdoch then announced that TNC would set up a 24-hour global television news service and combine most of its sports interests with those of Tele-Communications Inc., the biggest cable TV group in the USA, to create a global sports network. In January 1996, TNC and MCI paid US$682m for the last unclaimed frequency slot for American satellite television.

In November 1995, TNC closed one of the last significant holes in its global TV coverage by joining with three other television, programming and distribution groups to create a satellite service covering Latin America. These partners were Globo, Brazil's biggest media group; the Mexico-based Grupo Televisa, the biggest Spanish-language programming provider in the world; and TCI International, a subsidiary of Tele-Communications Inc.

The superhighway

Traditionally, television, film, printing and publishing companies were considered independent entities, even if part of large national or multinational organisations. The 1980s, however, saw the emergence of a trend towards integration and globalisation, centred around television. The News Corporation was at the forefront of this with its acquisition of 20th Century Fox and Metromedia in the USA, and the development of Sky TV in the UK.

The 1990s saw the convergence and globalisation of media and entertainment industries with the information industry (creating the 'infotainment' industry), and of companies involved in content production and packaging with those involved with distribution. This convergence of media, information and computing, of electronics, satellite, cable and telecommunications, laid the foundations for the development of the 'superhighway' of interactive services to be accessed from every office and living room.

These moves were further fuelled by the arrival of digital compression technology, which allowed many more television programmes or channels to be broadcast and cut the cost of a broadcasting channel significantly. By the end of 1997, most parts of the world would have the opportunity to tune into at least 150 channels of digital television; in Europe, the total could easily be more than 500. Importantly, this digital technology could be utilised by all the differing methods of distribution — satellite, cable, terrestrial land-based transmission and the telecommunications network. Sir Iain Vallance, chairman of the UK telecommunications company British Telecom, spoke for all such distributors when he said: 'We are becoming retailers of anything that can be converted into digital form.'

The development of the superhighway initiated a string of strategic alliances, acquisitions, mergers and investments between media content providers and packagers, telecommunications operators, cable television companies and computer makers.

For example, in 1989 Time created the first fully-fledged 'supergroup' by merging its publishing and cable interests with Warner's film and music business, and in 1995 Time Warner also acquired Turner Broadcasting. In 1993, the regional telephone operator US West paid US$2.5bn for 25.5 per cent of Time Warner, and in 1995 Time Warner, US West and Toshiba of Japan announced a US$400m joint venture to develop cable television in Japan.

In 1995, Walt Disney paid US$19bn (£12bn) to acquire Capital Cities/NBC and formed a joint venture with three US regional telephone companies to create interactive videos. In the same year, Bill Gates's software group, Microsoft, announced plans to add to its Internet package with the launch of a 24-hour news channel in conjunction with the US television network NBC. The company also invested US$500m in Dreamworks, the entertainment group founded by the film director Steven Spielberg.

It is in this context that one should view MCI's investment in TNC, and both companies' subsequent commitment to joint ventures exploiting TNC's media resources and MCI's ability to distribute electronic information over its telecoms network.

MCI, like other telecoms operators at this time, was a significant cash generator, but was also under pressure to increase volume on its network and to add value to the traffic being transmitted, as increased competition would erode profitability by the end of the century. MCI needed a way to differentiate its version of what was quickly becoming a commodity service — long-distance transport of telephone traffic — from those of competitors, if it was to maintain profitability. Rupert Murdoch detailed the possibilities:

> Imagine being able to access the innovative Internet, MCI, and Delphi Internet shopping and on-line information over the same service that brings you first-rate original entertainment. Imagine being able to retrieve computerised information stored in the MCI network wherever you are, whenever you want, without limitation. That's the power of this relationship.

Having said that, however, Murdoch is also convinced that the superhighway, and the brave new world of interactive television, will take longer to develop than most people expect: 'That's 15 to 20 years away in the US and Europe — and 50 years in the rest of the world.' Furthermore, 'we don't know where technology is taking us in the delivery of content'. However, the MCI link 'opens up all these options as technology develops'.

And into the millennium

The possibility of Rupert Murdoch's retirement, with all its implications for TNC's future, seemed remote in 1996. This was perhaps fortunate, as the company had no senior, experienced executives capable of filling his shoes. Murdoch had repeatedly quarrelled with potential successors. He appeared to prefer the hereditary principle. Asked which of his two daughters and two sons he would like to succeed him, Murdoch, aged 65 in 1996, was quoted as saying: 'I hope we can work it out between us'; adding, however, that he would probably make a judgement about his successor in about twenty years. For the future, the activities of TNC will continue to be linked with the motivations, personality and perceptions of Murdoch himself. It is appropriate, therefore, that he should have the last word:

> News Corporation is institutionally committed to the proposition that fortune favours the brave. We believe it, and we act on it, and it works for us. It requires more intense management discipline and a more penetrating creative insight [but] I believe we have shown these qualities since our start against large odds in Australia forty years ago.
>
> News Corporation has helped to define the new world of media: our own internal evolution from primarily a newspaper publisher to an electronic media powerhouse is evidence of this shift ... Today, we are working to shape the media products of tomorrow.

Appendix 1 The News Corporation Ltd: financial data

Consolidated profit and loss accounts, 1982–95 (summarised)

	For year ending 30 June (£m)[1]					
	1982	1983	1984	1985	1986	1987
Turnover						
USA	136	198	319	525	909	1,233
UK	351	378	433	501	551	587
Australia	266	300	410	525	396	481
	753	876	1,162	1,551	1,856	2,301
Operating profit[2]						
USA	2	12	17	16	132	154
UK	7	39	39	48	83	145
Australia	30	25	40	40	33	49
	39	76	96	104	248	348
Interest charges	31	33	66	47	108	172
Profit after tax	22	51	60	61	118	159
Extraordinary items[3]	(2)	(25)	(38)	32	1	199
Profit after extraordinary items	20	26	22	93	119	358

[1] Trading results have been converted at the average exchange rates for the year.
[2] Operating profit is shown before interest payments.
[3] Extraordinary items include the following:

1982–4	Foreign exchange losses totalling £100m
1986	Costs of relocating production facilities £66m
1987	Profit on the sale of non-current assets £255m
1988	Write-off of new business start-up and termination costs £57m
1989	Profit on the sale of non-current assets £400m
1990	Profit on the sale of non-current assets £209m
	Previously capitalised start-up and development costs of Sky Television written off £134m
1991	Losses on the sale of non-current assets £82m
	Refinancing costs £91m
1992	Profit on sale of non-current assets £96m
	Refinancing costs £12m
1993	Profit on sale of non-current assets £27m
	Refinancing costs £18m
1994	Profit on sale of non-current assets £61m
1995	Profit on sale of non-current assets £314m
	Provisions £213m

1988	1989	1990	1991	1992	1993	1994	1995
1,050	1,780	2,321	3,105	2,831	3,128	3,404	3,590
698	808	819	1,064	860	841	835	893
740	1,140	986	1,023	763	656	664	655
2,488	3,728	4,126	5,192	4,454	4,625	4,903	5,138
155	288	376	487	385	417	455	493
153	191	62	93	167	174	125	137
100	208	200	157	144	146	94	71
408	687	638	737	696	737	674	701
245	448	474	577	431	357	281	251
192	235	133	152	232	424	419	446
3	316	29	(338)	(13)	(50)	37	24
195	551	162	(186)	219	374	456	470

Consolidated balance sheets, 1982–95 (summarised)

	As at 30 June (£m)[4]					
	1982	1983	1984	1985	1986	1987
Current assets						
Cash	3	11	12	74	29	95
Receivables, inventories and other items	206	248	336	394	746	887
Total current assets	209	259	354	468	775	982
Non-current assets						
Investments	110	136	255	300	213	1,156
Property, plant and equip.[5]	164	196	266	305	459	550
Publishing rights, titles and TV licences[6]	49	52	437	673	1,480	2,160
Goodwill					331	343
Other	12	21	37	44	447	434
Total non-current assets	335	405	995	1,322	2,930	4,643
Total assets	544	664	1,349	1,790	3,705	5,625
Current liabilities						
Borrowings	20	40	33	8	84	346
Creditors and accruals	143	202	359	382	637	800
Total current liabilities	163	242	392	390	721	1,146
Non-current liabilities						
Borrowings	162	154	266	607	1,068	1,626
Creditors and accruals	16	37	57	91	275	367
Total non-current liabilities	178	191	323	698	1,343	1,993
Total liabilities	341	433	715	1,088	2,064	3,139
Net assets	203	231	634	702	1,641	2,486
Shareholders' equity						
Share capital						
Ordinary[7]	16	16	16	32	32	70
Other[8]						600
Revaluation reserve			381	249	210	561
Other reserves	170	173	194	333	413	945
Minority interests[9]	17	42	43	88	986	310
Total shareholders' equity	203	231	634	702	1,641	2,486

[4–9] See page 724.

1988	1989	1990	1991	1992	1993	1994	1995
60	78	72	96	161	294	204	582
876	1,188	1,478	1,454	1,057	1,400	1,563	2,006
936	1,266	1,550	1,550	1,218	1,694	1,767	2,588
1,600	1,616	1,556	1,419	1,389	1,458	1,603	1,808
744	932	1,561	1,538	1,427	1,647	1,674	1,821
2,320	4,290	6,017	5,867	5,072	5,943	6,214	6,493
294	298	258	237	184	235	216	210
609	840	848	1,149	1,010	1,194	1,248	1,346
5,567	7,976	10,240	10,210	9,082	10,477	10,955	11,678
6,503	9,242	11,790	11,760	10,300	12,171	12,722	14,266
278	246	1,332	354	139	8	53	67
874	1,059	1,395	1,499	1,202	1,448	1,671	1,754
1,152	1,305	2,727	1,853	1,341	1,456	1,724	1,821
2,296	3,568	3,419	4,698	3,882	4,535	3,679	3,848
341	475	531	614	482	479	491	863
2,637	4,043	3,950	5,312	4,364	5,014	4,170	4,711
3,789	5,348	6,677	7,165	5,705	6,470	5,894	6,532
2,714	3,894	5,113	4,595	4,595	5,701	6,828	7,734
70	70	70	70	86	428	456	718
600	600	600	600			187	250
606	595	1,961	2,017	1,620	1,756	1,797	1,844
1,101	1,744	1,697	1,564	2,571	3,215	4,158	4,681
337	885	785	344	318	302	230	241
2,714	3,894	5,113	4,595	4,595	5,701	6,828	7,734

[4] The financial position has been converted at the exchange rate at balance sheet date.

[5] Including capitalised interest: £162m 1995

[6] Assets are stated at cost or, from 30 June 1984, at valuation. Where at valuation, assets are revalued triennially and are recorded at 70% of revaluation figure. Changes in value from the 1993 revaluation exercise have not been reflected in the financial accounts. No amortisation is provided since, in the opinion of the directors, they do not have a finite economic life.

[7] Changes include the following:

1985	1 for 1 bonus issue
1987	1 for 1 bonus issue
1993	3 for 1 bonus issue
1995	£232m preferred limited voting ordinary shares

[8] Convertible notes (1987–92) pay 5% semi-annually, and are convertible at any time at the option of the holder into ordinary shares. All notes not converted by 31 January 1992 were converted into ordinary shares. The difference between the face value and the market value of these shares was credited to the share premium account.

1994 includes issue of £172m $8\frac{5}{8}$% guaranteed perpetual preference shares only redeemable at the option of TNC.

1995 includes issue of £63m of adjustable rate cumulative preference shares only redeemable at the option of TNC.

[9] 1986 includes issue of preference shares by a subsidiary as a swap for Metromedia debt.

Consolidated source and application of funds, 1982–8 (summarised)

	1982	1983	(£m)[1] 1984	1985	1986	1987	1988
Source of funds							
From operations	23	62	83	95	207	279	292
Issue of shares:							
Ordinary					3	167	
Preference		31		93			244
Convertible						545	
Sales of assets	14	8	79	145	55	99	212
Gain on sale of businesses					39	240	5
Increase in liabilities:							
Current	23	91	94	38	380	436	48
Non-current	17	(2)	120	443	801	693	661
Increase in minority							
interest					1,007		
Other	8	7	56	40	140	21	181
	85	197	432	854	2,632	2,480	1,643
Application of funds							
Increase in assets							
Current	28	60	77	175	385	225	(22)
Property, plant and							
equipment	23	53	81	97	281	171	250
Investments	1	25	95	156	41	868	603
Publishing rights, etc.			37	321	992	404	210
Increase in goodwill					391		
Tax paid	18	8	4	31	20	20	28
Dividends paid	6	6	7	10	45	57	16
Redemption of preference							
shares		4		26		608	234
Other	9	41	131	38	477	127	324
	85	197	432	854	2,632	2,480	1,643

[1] See page 720.

Consolidated statement of cash flows, 1988–95 (summarised)

	For the year ended 30 June (£m)[1]		
	1988	1989	1990
Interest payments	(241)	(444)	(484)
Income tax payments	(28)	(24)	(17)
Cash provided/(used) by operating activity	0	(22)	441
Investing and other activity			
Property, plant and equipment	(138)	(295)	(835)
Investments	(747)	(2,348)	(572)
Proceeds from sale of non-current assets			
(incl. business entities)	255	1,233	505
Other	(38)	(26)	(16)
Cash provided/(used) in investing activity	(668)	(1,436)	(918)
Financing activity			
Issuance of debt	961	1,220	1,114
Repayment of debt	(323)	(264)	(405)
Issue of ordinary shares	–	–	–
Issue of other stock	244	575	188
Preference capital redeemed	(234)	(41)	(400)
Dividends paid	(10)	(14)	(14)
Other	(5)	–	(6)
Cash (used)/provided by financing activity	633	1,476	477
Net (decrease)/increase in cash	(35)	18	0
Opening cash balance	89	60	78
Exchange movement	6	0	(6)
Closing cash balance	60	78	72

[1] See page 720.

1991	1992	1993	1994	1995
(529)	(337)	(324)	(266)	(210)
(20)	(28)	(39)	(10)	(33)
222	170	505	583	474
(306)	(147)	(247)	(187)	(199)
(134)	(69)	(73)	(484)	(499)
461	275	168	439	423
(6)	—	—	—	—
15	59	(152)	(232)	(275)
418	361	3,753	595	509
(369)	(717)	(4,190)	(1,342)	(360)
—	175	408	4	59
—	80	—	361	—
(151)	(1)	(98)	—	—
(21)	(15)	(26)	(28)	(56)
(97)	(41)	(106)	(19)	(29)
(220)	(158)	(259)	(429)	123
17	71	94	(78)	322
72	96	161	294	204
7	(6)	39	(12)	56
96	161	294	204	582

Industry sector analysis, 1984–95

	1984	1985	1986	1987	(£m) 1988
Revenues[1]					
Newspapers	781	1,014	953	875	1,062
Magazines	141	216	222	247	252
Television	84	22	170	297	233
Filmed entertainment	–	–	267	601	490
Commercial printing	70	77	72	77	107
Book publishing	–	–	–	–	–
Other	86	122	172	204	344
	1,162	1,551	1,856	2,301	2,488
Operating income[1]					
Newspapers	47	50	74	150	198
Magazines	25	35	47	44	44
Television	5	6	26	50	34
Filmed entertainment	–	–	37	74	34
Commercial printing	4	4	8	8	9
Book publishing	–	–	–	–	–
Other	15	9	56	22	89
	96	104	248	348	408
Identifiable assets[4]					
Newspapers	619	686	647	1,367	1,754
Magazines	132	448	400	372	375
Television	169	133	1,332	1,324	1,249
Filmed entertainment	–	–	853	757	684
Commercial printing	28	36	35	56	141
Book publishing	–	–	–	–	–
Other	147	187	227	592	700
Corporate items	254	300	211	1,157	1,600
	1,349	1,790	3,705	5,625	6,503
USA	276	660	2,649	2,621	2,440
UK	348	442	463	911	989
Australia and Pacific Basin	471	388	382	936	1,474
Corporate items	254	300	211	1,157	1,600
	1,349	1,790	3,705	5,625	6,503
Capital expenditures[4]					
Newspapers	20	70	63	50	115
Magazines	3	10	3	10	4
Television	1	4	6	9	8
Filmed entertainment	–	–	3	6	5
Commercial printing	4	6	3	7	6
Book publishing	–	–	–	–	–
Other	6	8	12	9	18
	34	98	90	91	156
USA	6	15	20	25	23
UK	9	58	44	33	90
Australia and Pacific Basin	19	25	26	33	43
	34	98	90	91	156

[1] See page 720.
[4] See page 724.

1989	1990	1991	1992	1993	1994	1995
1,374	1,420	1,461	1,291	1,329	1,216	1,200
554	680	619	719	717	695	705
352	552	630	540	699	884	1,095
572	596	1,041	1,059	1,135	1,300	1,322
224	243	234	—	—	—	—
—	—	—	635	655	671	642
652	635	1,207	210	90	137	174
3,728	4,126	5,192	4,454	4,625	4,903	5,138
325	306	247	258	290	183	206
131	150	133	167	174	142	150
47	3	58	114	161	196	216
57	50	100	56	23	59	64
23	27	26	—	—	—	—
—	—	—	89	87	87	77
104	102	173	12	2	7	(12)
687	638	737	696	737	674	701
2,345	3,596	3,612	3,392	3,720	3,447	3,594
1,820	1,745	1,615	1,362	1,744	1,686	1,789
1,696	2,222	2,003	1,692	2,236	2,867	3,135
725	751	1,075	947	1,065	1,256	1,522
171	164	145	—	—	—	—
—	—	—	1,141	1,410	1,429	1,579
869	1,757	1,890	417	538	434	258
1,616	1,555	1,420	1,349	1,458	1,603	2,389
9,242	11,790	11,760	10,300	12,171	12,722	14,266
4,736	5,519	5,920	5,074	6,479	6,558	6,924
1,420	2,804	2,448	2,383	2,414	2,452	2,692
1,470	1,912	1,972	1,494	1,820	2,109	2,261
1,616	1,555	1,426	1,349	1,458	1,603	2,389
9,242	11,790	11,760	10,300	12,171	12,722	14,266
179	536	248	152	216	120	67
5	5	4	5	3	5	8
81	206	48	3	20	48	68
6	10	14	7	6	7	40
12	21	9	—	—	—	—
—	—	—	2	4	4	3
18	19	20	4	7	28	45
301	797	343	173	256	212	231
24	32	33	19	39	81	135
220	634	207	57	33	37	24
57	131	103	97	184	94	72
301	797	343	173	256	212	231

Appendix 2   The News Corporation Ltd: major acquisitions and disposals, 1984–95

Year	Acquisitions			Disposals		
1984	*Chicago Sun-Times*	(USA) ⎫	£16m			
	New Woman	(USA) ⎬				
	Ziff Davies Magazines	(USA)	£287m			
	Twentieth Century Fox	(USA)	£400m			
1985	Metromedia	(USA)	£160m			
1986	*South China Morning Post*	(Hong Kong)	£115m	*Chicago Sun-Times*[1]	(USA) ⎫	
				Houston Community	⎬ £101m	
				Papers	(USA) ⎭	
1987	*Herald & Weekly Times*	(Australia)	£1bn	Newspaper interests		
				and television stations[2]	(Australia)	£535m
1988	Harper & Row	(USA)	£194m	*New York Post*[1]	(USA) ⎫	
	Triangle Publications	(USA)	£1.7bn	Aviation Trade	⎬ £41m	
				Publications	(USA) ⎭	
1989	William Collins	(UK)	£400m[3]	*Elle Magazine*	(USA)	£110m
				Travel Trade		
				Publications	(USA)	£480m
1990				*Star*	(USA)	£243m
				Medical journals	(USA)	£140m
				South China Morning		
				Post (49%)	(Hong Kong)	£160m
1991				Magazine interests	(USA/UK)	£520m
1992				Magazine and printing		
				interests (55%)	(Australia)	£208m
1993	Star Television (63.6%)	(Hong Kong)	£323m	San Antonio Express		
				News	(USA)	£114m
	Delphi Internet Services					
1994				*South China Morning*		
				Post (51%)	(Hong Kong)	£323m
1995	Star Television (36.4%)	(Hong Kong)	£194m			

[1] Disposed of in compliance of the USA Federal Communication Commission's general rule that joint ownership of a newspaper and television station in the same market is not permissible.
[2] Disposed of to comply with Australian Trade Practices Law.
[3] Acquisition of the outstanding 58% not already owned. Subsequently merged with Harper & Row to create HarperCollins.

Source: Annual reports, 1984–1995.

Nokia: the consumer electronics business

MARTIN LINDELL and LEIF MELIN

Introduction

Nokia, the large Finnish industrial group, was founded in 1966 through a merger of three companies. The main business units at that time were pulp and paper, tyres and cables, with paper manufacturing as the oldest business, established 130 years ago. During the 1970s Nokia started to diversify through expansion in different electronic product areas. In 1995, after twenty years of acquisitions, divestments, internationalisation and rapid growth, 99 per cent of the turnover (36,810 million FIM)[1] was represented by three business units in electronics: mobile phones, telecommunications and consumer electronics. The three original businesses had been divested and 91 per cent of the turnover was derived from exports. Nokia had become one of the leading global producers of mobile phones and telecommunication systems, and the third biggest in Europe in consumer electronics, with 34,000 employees, 14,000 of them working outside Finland in 45 different countries.

The Nokia case is a remarkable corporate transformation, achieved through focusing the company's strategic activities in the consumer electronics industry, where Nokia attained its position after a series of rapid acquisitions of five different European companies between 1983 and 1992 (Table 1). Colour TV was the dominant product group in the consumer

[1] The exchange rate in June 1996:

1 British pound (£)	= 7.27 FIM
1 Swedish krona (SEK)	= 0.70 FIM
1 German mark (DM)	= 3.07 FIM
1 US dollar ($)	= 4.70 FIM

Table 1   The acquisitions made by Nokia in consumer electronics

1983	Salora (Finland), Luxor (Sweden)
1987	Oceanic (France)
1988	Standard Electric Lorenz (Germany)
	Main plants: Bochum (Germany) and Ibervisao (Portugal), with six other plants
	supporting the manufacturing of TV sets
1992	Finlux (Finland)

electronics business, with audio systems and satellite receivers as other product groups.

The radical changes in Nokia can be seen from the division of the turnover into various business areas for four fiscal years (Table 2). The main products in these different business areas have been as follows:

- *Paper industry* — soft tissues, consumer products, power.
- *Tyres fabric* — tyres, industrial rubber, footwear.
- *Telecommunications* — telecommunication systems used in mobile and fixed networks.
- *Mobile phones* — products for all major digital and analogue systems.
- *Consumer electronics* — colour TV sets, satellite receivers, VCRs and audio equipment.
- *Cable* — cables, accessories and systems for use in the construction industry, and the telecommunications and power-transmission sectors.

Furthermore, for more than a decade from the mid-1970s, computers/information systems also formed a business area within electronics.

Entering the consumer electronics industry was quite a dramatic process involving a number of difficulties, not least in integrating the different units in consumer electronics after several acquisitions. The case focuses on three questions: Why and how did Nokia enter the consumer electronics industry? Why was the post-acquisition integration so difficult? Finally, why did

Table 2   Division of Nokia's turnover into different business groups (%)

	1972	1983	1988	1995
Paper industry	19.9	22.7	10.0	0
Tyres fabric	24.5	11.1	6.0	0
Electronics	8.0	19.1	60.0	99
Telecommunications				27
Mobile phones				43
Consumer electronics				29
Cable fabric	47.6	22.0	9.0	—
Others	—	25.1	15.0	1

Nokia, after a decade of investments, finally divest its consumer electronics business in 1996?

Formulation of a new long-term vision for Nokia

During the mid-1970s, after the oil crisis in 1973, Nokia experienced strategic problems. The original core businesses, representing the main part of the corporation, were expected to have limited growth in the future. Top management felt that the company could get into serious trouble if no strategic changes were initiated. The change process began with the formulation of a growth vision, which implied new strategic directions for Nokia. The ambition was to enter industrial sectors with growth potential, so as to increase the share of products with growth potential in Nokia's product portfolio. The top management set out the following strategic goals for future development:

- Internationalisation.
- Increased share of high-tech products.
- Maintain the competitiveness of the original businesses (paper, tyres and cables).

The chief executive officer of Nokia at that time, Kari Kairamo, was the strategist behind the vision. His belief was that growth could not be achieved by remaining in Finland. Nokia had been too dependent on its domestic market. He also made a strong point of the need for strategic flexibility and a readiness to take opportunities.

In order to increase the share of high-tech products, Nokia soon started to diversify. Entering the consumer electronics market was one of the main moves towards the vision of diversification and internationalisation. All in all, five major acquisitions created the bridge into consumer electronics. The manufacture of televisions was to prove an important element in this.

At the beginning of the 1980s, the total annual sales of TV sets in Europe were almost 20 million, about the same as in both the USA and Japan. However, the European market was much more fragmented, with several technical standards and local protectionism. The consequence was more local producers in Europe, each with a rather small production volume. The two biggest European competitors were Philips and Thompson (France), but even these firms had fairly local strategies. Large production volume was at this time not regarded as a major critical factor for success. Instead, the flexibility to change production rapidly from one type of TV set to another brand, model or size was a critical factor for competitiveness. Eventually, the non-European competition from the Japanese and other Far East companies led to an increased focus on price competition in

Europe. With more focus on price, the small-scale orientation created vulnerability for several European companies.

The acquisitions of Salora and Luxor: Nokia enters the consumer electronics industry

In the mid-1970s Nokia moved into computers, with the importation and distribution of Honeywell Bull computers, following which the then small electronic business area was divided into professional electronics and computers. At the same time, another opportunity to expand in electronics appeared when the Finnish army wanted a new type of portable radio telephone. It invited most domestic firms in the electronics industry to develop them, and nearly all Finnish electronics firms started to construct mobile radio telephones. The military order was eventually placed with three different companies, Salora, Televa and Nokia. The top management in Nokia thought that three domestic companies in this area were too many. As Salora was regarded as slightly ahead in its R&D activities, Nokia made an initial contact with that company. A co-operation agreement was soon signed between Nokia and Salora regarding their radio telephone businesses, and in 1980 the co-operation was extended. A joint venture on a fifty-fifty basis was formed — Mobira, a mobile telephone business unit.

Salora was also the biggest manufacturer of TV sets in Finland. But in the late 1970s Salora had problems with its TV business because of a decline in the Scandinavian market. At the same time, the company's owners were accused of selling on the black market and were forced to relinquish their ownership. The Union bank looked for new owners and Nokia was invited to acquire Salora. But the head of Nokia's electronics division, Kurt Wikstedt, was only interested in Salora's mobile telephone business and not at all in consumer electronics, which were not seen as high-tech products. He saw no competitive advantages for Nokia in the consumer electronics sector:

> In Finland we cannot produce on such a scale in this product area that we could be successful. The production scale of Salora is too small. We should concentrate on products where the production costs are high, as in professional electronics.

Nokia's group chief executive officer and his corporate planner were in favour of an acquisition, as they regarded consumer electronics as a growth industry. But Wikstedt's arguments were stronger, and instead Salora was taken over by the shipbuilding company Hollming.

The difficulties in Salora continued and the company made huge losses: 18 million FIM in 1980 and 25 million FIM in 1981. The president of Salora was forced to resign after only a few years in office and Salora was put up for sale again. But Nokia did not show any interest in the consumer electronics part of Salora. It just wanted Mobira. In this situation the owners of Salora, the Hollming Group, linked the possible sale of their share of Mobira to the sale of the rest of Salora. The result was a compromise — Nokia acquired 18 per cent of the shares in Salora in order to be allowed to acquire the remaining 50 per cent of Mobira from Salora. In 1982 Mobira became a subsidiary of Nokia, and Nokia became represented in the Salora board. Nokia later acquired Televa as well and eventually became a global leader in mobile phones.

The new president of Salora, Antti Lagerroos, succeeded in improving the company's performance in consumer electronics. 1982 was a good year and 1983 was expected to be even more successful. Markets were growing rapidly. Salora obtained two big orders for colour TV sets which gave rise to capacity problems. Lagerroos looked for more production capacity and became interested in Luxor, a Swedish competitor, which itself had survival problems in the late 1970s (Table 3). In 1979 the Swedish state saved Luxor from bankruptcy, acquiring it from the family owners for the symbolic sum of one Swedish krona, and put fresh capital into the company in an attempt to improve its fortunes. In 1983 the Swedish Minister of Industry wanted a new solution for Luxor, after having subsidised a financial reconstruction of the company. The minister looked for a large corporation as a partner, but held the opinion that Salora was not large or strong enough. Other firms showed an interest in acquiring Luxor, but none found favour with the Swedish governmental officials.

In this situation, Antti Lagerroos introduced a new idea to Nokia's top managers. Although Nokia's previous interest in Salora was lukewarm, a Salor–Luxor combination put the matter in a quite different light. As pointed out earlier, internationalisation was an important ingredient in the Nokia corporate vision, and Finnish firms have traditionally made their initial foreign expansion in the Swedish market. Nokia had also become more interested in know-how in mass production and marketing. The production knowledge in consumer electronics was quite different from that in the production of computers, for instance. At the beginning of the 1980s, computers were still mostly tailor-made. Marketing too was

Table 3   Turnover and profit of Luxor, 1975–82 (in millions of SEK)

Year	1975/6	1976/7	1977/8	1978/9	1979/80	1980/1 (16 months)	1982
Turnover	484	523	611	700	745	1,010	730
Profit/loss	12	15	−104	−69	−50	−117	−45

Source: *Affärsvärlden*, 1983, no. 48, p. 33.

different. Brands and distribution channels were important success factors in consumer electronics, where a good product was not enough in order to obtain a large market share. An acquisition of both Salora and Luxor could give Nokia the possibility of supplementing the competences in R&D and small-scale production with mass production and market orientation.

Relations between the group chief executive officer of Nokia, Kari Kairamo, and ministers in the Swedish government were good, and Sweden was motivated to accept the successful Nokia Group as the acquiring company. The production capacity of a combined Salora and Luxor was expected to make it a strong unit. The acquisition took place in January 1984 and Kari Kairamo stated:

> Nokia's acquisition of Salora and Luxor means that the company's position in Sweden is now much stronger. The Luxor, Salora and Nokia venture means that Scandinavian co-operation in this important area has improved.

Kairamo saw Luxor as a first step in further international co-operation, and expected that the clear boundary between consumer electronics and professional electronics would disappear in the future. Kurt Wikstedt strongly stressed the international side of the acquisition:

> Now we enter Europe. We begin with Scandinavia. We try with Luxor to see if we can be successful in this business, and then continue with Europe. That is the strategy.

After many twists and turns, Nokia had entered the consumer electronics business and taken a serious step into the international market. The initial result of the acquisitions was that Nokia got 58 per cent of the shares in Salora and 51 per cent of the shares in Luxor. Later in 1984, Nokia increased its share to 70 per cent of the capital stock in Luxor. In 1983 the turnover for Luxor was 590 million FIM and for Salora 737 million FIM. The staff of Luxor was 1,500 and of Salora 1,700. All in all, Nokia now had 8,000 employees in its electronics businesses. Nokia's acquired market share in the TV sector was 36 per cent in the Finnish market and over 20 per cent in the Swedish market.

The integration of Salora and Luxor

The new consumer electronics business was organised as a separate division in Nokia, partly because of the doubt over consumer electronics expressed by the head of the electronics division, Kurt Wikstedt. The president of Salora, Antti Lagerroos, was selected as the new president for consumer electronics (Salora–Luxor), and Kurt Wikstedt stayed as president for the remaining businesses in electronics, relabelled 'industrial electronics'.

The integration of Luxor and Salora was arduous, and made no real

Table 4   Production of TV sets in Luxor

1983	120,000
1984	184,000
1985	240,000
1987	380,000

progress until the Swedish president of Luxor was forced to leave the company in May 1985. Besides the declining consumer electronics business, Luxor also had a successful personal computer division. Nokia closed this computer division, which of course aroused a lot of criticism. Several managers in Nokia were of the opinion that the co-ordination of activities in Salora and Luxor was not sufficient and that the potential synergy advantages had not been fully realised. In 1985 Salora–Luxor got a new president, Heikki Koskinen, when Antti Lagerroos was appointed director in charge of consumer electronics in the top management team of the Nokia Group. Koskinen was a spokesman for decentralisation and local autonomy. Salora and Luxor kept their own sales subsidiaries; only logistics and R&D were integrated. Still, the development of Salora–Luxor was very favourable and quite profitable in the mid-1980s. The production of TV sets in Luxor increased rapidly, although small (14-inch) TV sets represented almost 50 per cent of all production (see Table 4).

In 1987, the Salora–Luxor TV brands had a market share of 35 per cent in the Nordic markets. In Finland the market share was about 45 per cent. According to Heikki Koskinen, Salora–Luxor was the only profitable significant consumer electronics producer in Europe in 1987. Gradually, Nokia increased its ownership share in both Luxor and Salora to 100 per cent. The aim of the continued integration was to arrange production in a more optimal way, and to utilise more effectively all the possibilities of synergy, including integrating production plants in a total product planning and production system, in order to decide more efficiently which products should be produced where and in what quantities.

Nokia enters major European markets

In 1986, when the Luxor–Salora integration was considered to be under control, Nokia began to think of the future. Market share was already about 40 per cent in the Nordic markets, which implied that further expansion for Salora–Luxor in Scandinavia was not possible. An alternative growth and product brand strategy, to turn to western Europe, was decided during the strategic planning process in spring 1986. Heikki Koskinen explained the plans:

We had plans to acquire two major brands in Europe, of which we intended to build a local net of brands. One of the brands was going to be more extensive to be sold in all European countries where Nokia was active in consumer electronics.

There were several reasons for entering the western European markets:

1. It was important to be in the home markets of major competitors, in order to prevent them from dumping their products on Nokia's domestic markets.

2. European co-operation might prevent the Japanese and American firms taking over the European TV markets. The major European competitors Philips and Thompson started to co-operate within the Eureka framework (European Research Co-ordinating Agency)[2] in order to develop the European HDTV (high-definition TV) concept. This joint development was a threat to smaller European producers, which were afraid of not getting the key technology when needed. In order to become a partner in the development process of the HDTV concept, the common opinion was that Nokia had to grow bigger.

3. At this time the situation in consumer electronics in Europe changed dramatically. The competition became more intensive. Philips, the biggest TV manufacturer in Europe, with a market share of 25 per cent, acquired an American firm and began to think more globally. Thompson, the second biggest TV manufacturer in Europe, with a market share of 20 per cent, acquired two main competitors in the USA and England. Economies of scale through mass production were now considered as very important. The Salora and Luxor factories had a capacity of only 400,000 TV sets each. Nokia was number three in Europe, but still had only 5 per cent market share. The opinion within Nokia was that a volume of 2 million TV sets per year was needed to be competitive with both Philips and Thompson, and the Japanese and Korean competitors. In the late 1980s, the price competition became tougher in the European consumer electronics markets because of a more aggressive penetration from Far Eastern competitors. It was also expected that the fixed R&D costs would rise, which implied that there was going to be a volume advantage regarding R&D too.

The acquisition of Oceanic

Nokia's profitability in consumer electronics was good, especially in 1987,

---

[2] Originally, the Eureka programme was launched to serve as a European complement to the Strategic Defense Initiative launched by the Reagan administration in the United States. Another reason was that previously launched European technology development programmes were considered too bureaucratic, too slow or too narrowly defined.

and it had passed Philips in market shares in all Nordic markets. In April 1987 the Nokia board of directors approved the strategic plan to acquire European TV brands. The plan was to acquire a French and a German brand, and a factory in either of these two countries. There were negotiations with different sellers, including the French company Oceanic which was for sale. Personal relationships between Nokia top management and the owner of Oceanic, the Swedish Electrolux Group, resulted in a rapid acquisition of Oceanic. Electrolux wanted to divest this business, which had no synergy with its core know-how. Through the acquisition of Oceanic, Nokia got inside the EC with the production of TV sets. Furthermore, Nokia acquired a significant market share in the French market, which was rather closed and difficult for an outsider to penetrate.

The pre-acquisition phase took less than three months and only four meetings were needed. Immediately after the acquisition, the integration process between Salora, Luxor and Oceanic was started. Oceanic had a turnover of 600 million FIM, mainly in colour TVs, and 800 employees. Oceanic's market share of consumer electronics in France was just below 10 per cent, with the Oceanic and Sonolor brands. The strategy was to keep the French production unit apart from the other factories because of differences in standards, while accounting systems, logistics and marketing should be integrated. The French local managers were trusted by the Finnish management and retained.

The next step in the conquest of European markets was to look for other brands. Nokia was interested in Thompson's German brands Saba, Nordwede and Telefunken. According to Heikki Koskinen, who headed the negotiations, an agreement was close for one of the brands, when the Standard Electric Lorenz possibility emerged.

Nokia doubles its TV production: the acquisition of Standard Electric Lorenz

At this time, an internal struggle for power was going on between future candidates for the top position in the Nokia corporation. Top managers were traditionally recruited internally, and in 1985 a new manager for industrial electronics was appointed, Timo Koski, after close internal competition. He was seen as the probable next chief executive officer of Nokia. However, the earlier successful president of Salora, Antti Lagerroos, now heading the consumer electronics businesses in Nokia, had strong personal ambitions to advance to the very top of Nokia. This thirst for power became a driving force behind the next acquisition.

Parallel to Heikki Koskinen's negotiations with Thompson, Antti Lagerroos made the initial analysis that resulted in his suggestion to acquire a very big competitor, Standard Electric Lorenz (SEL) in the former

West Germany. Lagerroos then used the freedom of action given to him by Kari Kairamo, and started to negotiate with SEL and its owners on his own, partly assisted by the director of technology in Nokia. Almost at the same time, Timo Koski acquired the whole personal computer and information systems business of the Ericsson Group in Sweden — an acquisition of the same size as SEL. Nokia became the largest information technology company in Scandinavia. Ericsson's large-scale production of terminal systems and established position in systems for commercial, industrial and banking sectors, together with Nokia's intelligent workstations and retail systems, were expected to enhance the Nokia Group's competitiveness in the information technology sector. The significantly enlarged division led by Timo Koski was named Nokia Data. Both Antti Lagerroos and Timo Koski had now extended their internal domains significantly in the struggle for further power in Nokia. However, in 1987 Timo Koski suddenly died of a heart attack.

The acquisition of SEL from the US conglomerate ITT was made early in 1988, just a couple of months after the Oceanic acquisition. The production capacity increased from 1 million TV sets annually to almost 2.5 million. The chief executive officer, Kari Kairamo, attached great importance to this acquisition. The opinion was that SEL completed Nokia's consumer electronics business both technically and regionally. SEL was ahead of Nokia in digital TV technology. And regionally Nokia now became strong not only in France, but also in German-speaking Europe (15 per cent market share) and even in southern Europe as SEL exported to Italy, France, Spain and Portugal. The net sales of SEL were 4.9 billion FIM in 1988, with an annual production of 1.2 million colour TVs, 1.7 million picture tubes and 350,000 video recorders. The main production facilities for SEL's colour TV sets and video recorders were located near Bochum in the Ruhr region. The picture tube factory was located near Stuttgart, and the loudspeaker factory was in Bavaria. SEL also had four other smaller production facilities in West Germany. The SEL acquisition included assembly plants in Spain and Portugal as well, and shares in joint ventures in Hungary, Malaysia and Italy.

With the incorporation of SEL, Nokia's position as Europe's third largest colour TV manufacturer was strengthened. Nokia was now the ninth largest colour TV manufacturer in the world, and the market share in Europe was estimated to be about 15 per cent, with the new brand names ITT, Schaub–Lorenz and Graetz.

In 1992 Nokia acquired the only remaining Finnish competitor, Finlux, which was in good shape and profitable. The production capacity of Finlux was just over 200,000 TV sets. The turnover was about 600 million FIM and the personnel 770.

The post-acquisition integration becomes problematic

In January 1988, Simo Vuorilehto, the chief operations officer of Nokia, was of the opinion that all Nokia's consumer electronics units should be consolidated within a wholly new division with its headquarters in continental Europe. Significant investments in upgrading and modernisation of production technology and logistics were needed in the new division that was formed, which was named Nokia Consumer Electronics. The integration and co-ordination of Salora–Luxor, Oceanic and SEL started in February 1988 with the appointment of an integration group led by Antti Lagerroos. The group was working hard during spring 1988 with the aim of integrating administration and production in all four acquired consumer electronic units, a total of ten factories, within six months. The purpose was to be able to present an integrated structure for the new division in the summer of 1988. But the timetable could not be met entirely.

The chief executive officer, Kari Kairamo, was worried that Nokia did not have enough internationally experienced personnel, and believed that many new managers were needed, especially in the consumer electronics business. This opinion was further strengthened by some managerial tests carried out by external consultants, in early 1988. Furthermore, Antti Lagerroos could not implement the necessary changes fast enough and lost Kari Kairamo's confidence to lead Nokia Consumer Electronics into Europe. Instead, he was appointed president of Nokia's Mobile Phones (previously Mobira). He soon wanted to merge Nokia Consumer Electronics and Nokia Mobile Phones, but did not get any support for that. Antti Lagerroos eventually left the Nokia Group in February 1990.

In June 1988 a new president, Jacques Noels, was appointed for Nokia Consumer Electronics. Head hunters found him in France at Thompson — one of Nokia's large competitors in consumer electronics. Before that he had been working for many years in European units of large US companies in the electronics industry. Jacques Noels had to start to organise the consumer electronics division from scratch, and at least half a year of integration was totally lost. Furthermore, ten senior managers in SEL had left the company. Initially, Noels rented an office in Paris for three months and brought his secretary with him from Thompson. The first task was to build a new management team with the right mixture of competence. A new head office for Nokia Consumer Electronics was established in Geneva (regarded as 'neutral ground') in order to facilitate further recruitment and the establishment of a truly international division.

In 1989, Jacques Noels presented a new organisation structure for Nokia Consumer Electronics, more than one year after the latest acquisition. During that time Nokia's market share of TV sets had declined from 14 to 11 per cent in the European markets. Not only the consumer electronics business but the whole group showed weak results. The relations between the chairman of the Nokia board and the chief executive officer, Kari Kairamo, became more and more strained. The external directors were expected to suggest some changes in the top management structure of Nokia. In this situation, Kari Kairamo suddenly died (suicide, according to the media) in December 1989.

After Kari Kairamo's tragic death, Simo Vuorilehto became the new chief executive officer. According to him, the key factors in the consumer electronics strategy were marketing, design and production:

> We are not at all the kind of company that could develop semiconductors or picture tubes in the future. But we can be competitive and ahead of other competitors in marketing, design and production. In production we perhaps cannot be superior to our competitors, but we can at least be at the same level. We cannot develop everything ourselves, which was a mistake in the first integration plans.

Heikki Koskinen, responsible for strategic planning in Jacques Noels' new management team, emphasised similar competitive advantages of Nokia Consumer Electronics:

> Our strength is in rapid application of new technology. When technologies shift you have to forecast the trends and minimise the investment costs. Our competitive advantage is in the brain of the engineers. That is especially true in application issues.

He had never fully understood the volume thinking behind the acquisition of SEL:

> The only advantage you reach by large-scale production is that you can control the material costs. On the other hand, you have less flexibility and you have to be global. In 1987 we manufactured 900,000 TV sets in Salora–Luxor, and we were very profitable. In Europe there are other profitable but small companies. It is a question of the overall strategy. A small company making half a million TV sets can be profitable. That firm has to co-operate with manufacturers of components and in that way reduce the cost for necessary R&D activities. With small R&D costs, a clear market focus and a strong product range there are good possibilities to be successful.

The manager in charge of export sales also held the opinion that too much emphasis had been put on production costs:

> I cannot understand that acquisitions are made based on production advantages. In our acquisitions there were no synergies between the brands. When you combine factories and brands you take away a large part of the turnover. I am astonished that Nokia had not made clear the future brand policy before the acquisitions. That was the greatest problem.

Jacques Noels' strategy was to become big in some niches, not in the whole market. Nokia should concentrate in high-quality and high-technology TV sets, with good profit margins. According to him, the market share of the

Table 5 Turnover in the production units of Nokia Consumer Electronics, 1988

Production unit	Turnover (in millions of FIM)
Germany	3,000
Finland, Salora	1,500
Sweden, Luxor	900
France, Oceanic	500
Portugal, Ibervisao	100

total market was therefore not as important. Still, the most profitable markets were the Nordic ones, with a total demand of 1.5 million TV sets, and in these markets Nokia was strong.

Jacques Noels saw Nokia's portfolio of different electronics businesses as a future strength. The group had telecommunication, mobile phones, information systems, computers and consumer electronics, and more and more synergies were expected to emerge between these different business areas. The border between professional and consumer electronics was expected to disappear. According to Jacques Noels, Nokia already had a strong technological capacity and good management resources. But he saw some disadvantages compared with the main competitors:

> I think they have a different position, because they have very strong brands. Telefunken is a much stronger brand than, for example, Graetz [an SEL brand]. They have also much stronger corporate brands, e.g. Philips compared to Nokia. Their strategy can be very different; they can let almost every brand have its own life. Grundig can have its own strategy, nobody has to know that it is owned by Philips. But at the same time Philips is not putting the same efforts in Grundig as in the Philips brand. Their positioning is very different from ours.

The magnitude of the integration task is illustrated by Table 5, which shows the turnover of the acquired Nokia Consumer Electronics units in five European countries. A 6,000 million FIM division had to be integrated. In order to integrate the acquisitions, Jacques Noels had two possibilities. The first was to continue as before and integrate the different units over a long period. The second was to try to merge the different units into one organisation more rapidly. The latter alternative was chosen despite the fact that the president thought that, in the short run, this approach would lead to bigger difficulties because the units were used to working on their own. In the long term, after a few hard years of integration, the profits were expected to be considerable.

A new organisation structure and culture

Jacques Noels wanted strong functional centralisation and stressed the importance of a competent and powerful management team. This was the first priority because the management team was seen as the motor of the organisation. But it took time to put together the new team. Both old and new managers were tested by external consultants. Eventually, about 35 people were working at the head office in Geneva. All decisions concerning production, R&D and marketing were made there. Finance and strategic planning were centralised as well. All acquired companies became pure production plants, separated from the sales and marketing activities, but with some R&D activities decentralised to these plants.

Jacques Noels especially emphasised the connection and co-operation between R&D and marketing:

> We have regrouped the marketing and R&D centres so that the head of marketing and the head of R&D work side by side in Geneva, because we believe that they have to work closely together on new models. Production is only how to manufacture as cheap as possible, when the products have been developed.

He highlighted the cultural difficulties in integrating the different units and nationalities. A new integrated culture for Nokia Consumer Electronics needed to be built on new management principles, but it had to emerge over several years. The tools for cultural integration were an international management group, circulation of leaders between countries, and a 'Euro-manager' programme. Young and recently employed graduates from all countries involved were taken into this Euro-manager programme, developed in 1989–90. The creation of this new pan-European culture was planned to continue after 1990 for another three to five years. But Jacques Noels did not have an easy task in seeking to create a 'Europeanised' business unit out of Nokia Consumer Electronics:

> If you make two major acquisitions in three months, you get many problems regarding product strategy; sales channels; general management, etc. There is nothing that works by itself. You have to struggle and that is what we did. First we worked out a product strategy in order to concentrate our R&D efforts. Then, from the middle of 1989, we put a lot of efforts in new brand, sales and marketing policies.

Marketing and production strategies within Nokia Consumer Electronics

In 1989 Nokia Consumer Electronics launched a universal brand, ITT–Nokia, that would be positioned as a middle-range product. The ITT–Nokia brand would then be combined with one or two other and more local Nokia brands in each local market, including a 'high-end' brand representing higher quality and/or more exclusive design. For the integration of product development and manufacturing, a 'Euro-line-concept' was launched. Nokia Consumer Electronics reduced the number of chassis from 25 to 10, and the goal was to come down to three or four product chassis. All R&D centres were supporting this product concept, but it was modified in accordance with the country and the brand characteristics. The different centres were concentrated on different levels in the product range, from low-end to high-end chassis.

The marketing strategy was to be achieved through an integrated sales, product and distribution strategy. Marketing of the brands was the most important part. All acquired brands were local brands, and Nokia as a brand was unknown within the distribution channels. The problem after the acquisition of SEL was to convince the distribution channels that the brand ITT–Nokia had a future. The solution was to combine the innovation image of ITT and resource image of Nokia[3] in this new brand ITT–Nokia, with the intention of later dropping ITT. There were many discussions and different opinions about the wisdom of using the Nokia name. Many managers were sceptical about the possibilities of transferring the ITT image to the Nokia name. However, ITT–Nokia was introduced as the pan-European brand in the medium range; a modern brand with modern technology, which was going to compete with Philips. Salora was marketed as high-range brand, while the other brands were used as local brands. Jacques Noels stated:

> Our strategy is to have three brands per country. The major brand, in the beginning, has to be the established local brand. But this is short term. Gradually we are introducing Nokia as the major European brand. But we want to do that gradually, not brutally. In all countries we are also supporting the original brand. That is why we support Luxor in Sweden, Salora in Finland, ITT–Nokia in Germany and Oceanic in France, and then gradually introduce Nokia as a complementary brand.
>
> A brand strategy with three brands means three different channels. The specialised independent retailers are very important. They want to have their local brands. Then we have the large specialised channels that are only selling electronics. Finally we have the supermarkets, big stores, they want to have one brand, one styling, easy to recognise.

Some managers were critical of using acquisition as a means of growth and also sceptical of the possibility of transferring the image of one brand to another. The brand Salora had a quite good image. Investigations by Nokia showed that Salora had some recognition in England, Italy, France, Netherlands, Belgium, Austria and Switzerland, and much more recognition than the new brand Nokia.

Finally, Jacques Noels distinguished between three different production strategies:

> Today we have two or three complementary strategies. One is volume; it is clear that the volume in TV assembling is important. We are working with that in Germany, where our Bochum plant is one of the largest in Europe; one million TV

---

[3] The Nokia Group had a very strong financial position in 1987. The use of Nokia as a brand name indicated that the top management of the group was serious about the business and also acted as a signal to the distribution channels.

sets. The second strategy is to specialise, when a plant only produces one product and we can extend that product line. We are doing that in Salo where we are producing our high-end chassis. In Luxor we are producing all our decoders and satellites, and there we also have the technical expertise for these products. In those products the technical expertise is what makes the cost, not so much the production volume, but also how well and quickly we can introduce our products. We have a factory in Portugal, where labour cost is an important factor. We are trying to rationalise our production by stage of the product life, labour cost, volume and engineering. Those are the four criteria and they give different answers for different products.

The divestment of consumer electronics

However, the integration of the units in Nokia Consumer Electronics proved to be much more difficult than expected and the profitability much lower than predicted. The development of Nokia Consumer Electronics was problematic after the acquisition of SEL. In 1990, the director of corporate finance, Jorma Ollila, described the German acquisition as a big disappointment. The chief executive officer, Simo Vuorilehto, stressed the importance of a new strategy so that the company could take control of the situation. The first step in this turnaround of Nokia Consumer Electronics was to close down both the Oceanic plant in France and the plant in Portugal.

A new chief executive officer with radical changes

Simo Vuorilehto (chief executive officer) and Kalle Isokallio (chief operations officer) did not agree on many issues and did not work well together. Competing proposals were often brought to the board. Early in 1992 the board of the Nokia Group made the radical decision to replace both men. Simo Vuorilehto retired earlier than originally planned and Kalle Isokallio was asked to look for a new job externally.

Jorma Ollila became the new chief executive officer for Nokia in 1992, after two very successful years as the president of Nokia Mobile Phones. He started to reconstruct the group immediately. Only two weeks after Ollila's arrival, Jacques Noels had to leave Nokia Consumer Electronics. The group controller of Nokia, Hannu Bergholm, was appointed the new president for Consumer Electronics and Heikki Koskinen re-entered the top management team of Consumer Electronics after having left the Noels team in 1990. Later in 1992, production of TV sets in Sweden at the Luxor plant was ceased. All production of TV sets was concentrated on Bochum in Germany and Turku in Finland (at the recently acquired Finlux plant).

The aim was to decrease the costs of logistics and to make production more efficient in the remaining two plants.

The basic goals for the Nokia Group in 1992 were still the same as two decades previously: that is, growth through products with growth potential and internationalisation. But there were additions. Central values were formulated in a slogan, 'the Nokia way'. The values common to all businesses were customer satisfaction, respect for the individual, achievement and continuous learning. New key words were telecommunications, global, focus and value added. It was decided that telecommunications (including mobile phones) should be the future core business area. Jorma Ollila stated in the annual report of 1992 that the fastest growth, the most productive investments and the best results were in Nokia's telecommunication sector. Europe remained Nokia's largest market, but growth was concentrated outside Europe: in North America and the Far East. The strategic focus on telecommunications was confirmed in a statement by the board of directors:

> Nokia's strategy is to invest in telecommunications and closely associated business operations. It focuses on industry segments and geographic regions that have good opportunities for growth and profitability.

But what was to be done with the still unprofitable Nokia Consumer Electronics? One internally discussed possibility was to develop an alliance with another company in the industry. A corporate analyser at Morgan Stanley in London was of the same opinion: 'Nokia has to co-operate with another European or a Japanese firm in order to be competitive.' However, the Nokia Group acted more radically. A decision was made to concentrate more and more on telecommunications. Digital signal processing became the key concept in most of Nokia's operations and in the group's future strategy. This direction was further strengthened in 1993 when part of the cables and machinery businesses was divested. Telecommunications increased its share of net sales to 52 per cent. By this time Nokia had become a global leader in the manufacture and supply of telecommunication systems and mobile phones.

The divestments continued. In 1995 Nokia divested all its remaining tyres and cable businesses. Finally, in February 1996 Nokia announced its total withdrawal from the consumer electronics business and its main product, colour TV sets. In April 1996 Nokia made a provision of 2,000 million FIM in order to close the consumer electronics plants in Germany. The only TV plant left after that was the Finnish Finlux. But in June 1996 Nokia announced that the Hong Kong-based group Semi-Tech Ltd had acquired the remaining TV business. After these moves Nokia has almost 100 per cent of its operations in the telecommunications and mobile phones industry. Jorma Ollila stressed in the annual report:

This is an important milestone since we shall now have the structure in place to concentrate on the growth segments of the telecommunications industry, thereby improving our shareholder return. This strategy has already helped us to grow faster than the overall market during the past few years. With operations in 120 countries, manufacturing on four continents and with improved brand-recognition worldwide, we are now a truly global player.

The internally much debated journey of Nokia into consumer electronics had come to an end.

Appendix 1

Turnover and personnel of the Nokia Group, 1990–5

	Turnover (in millions of FIM)	Personnel
1990	22,130	37,336
1991	15,500	29,100
1992	18,168	26,700
1993	23,697	25,800
1994	30,177	28,000
1995	36,810	31,900

Net sales as a percentage of total sales and number of personnel in each business group, 1991–5

	1991		1992		1993		1994		1995	
	%	No.	%	No.	%	No.	%	No.	%	No.
CE	33	10,854	31	9,386	29	8,268	22	6,611 ⎱	29	9,937
CM	20	7,766	25	6,307	20	5,070	16	4,560 ⎰		
MP	12	3,545	20	3,164	26	4,223	35	7,554	44	11,821
NT	16	4,474	17	5,219	19	6,365	22	8,082	28	11,297
OO	9	1,874	7	1,606	6	1,597	5	1,786	1	729

CE = Nokia Consumer Electronics
MP = Nokia Mobile Phones
NT = Nokia Telecommunications
CM = Cables and Machinery
OO = Other Operations

Net sales by market area of the Nokia Group (%)

		1990	1991	1992	1993
1.	Scandinavia	45	38	32	25
2.	Other western European countries	39	44	44	47
3.	Other countries	16	18	24	28

		1994	1995
1.	Finland	11	9
2.	Other EU countries	50	48
3.	Other European countries	9	8
4.	Other countries	30	35

Appendix 2

Nokia 1992–5 according to International Accounting Standards (IAS)

	1992	1993	1994	1995
Profit and loss account				
(in millions of FIM)				
Net sales	18,168	23,697	30,177	36,810
Cost of sales	(17,880)	(22,232)	(20,808)	(25,518)
Operating profits	288	1,465	3,596	5,012
Share of results of associated companies	(5)	28	22	85
Net interest and other financial expenses	(441)	(347)	384	(164)
Profit before tax and minority interests	(158)	1,146	4,933	4,002
Tax	(167)	(299)	(932)	(769)
Minority interests	(88)	(80)	(75)	(77)
Profit before extraordinary items	(413)	767	2,995	2,232
Extraordinary items	(310)	(1,917)	944	–
Net profit	(723)	(1,159)	3,939	2,232
Balance sheet items				
(in millions of FIM)				
Fixed assets and other non-current assets	7,630	7,930	7,943	9,047
Current assets	13,608	14,653	19,906	23,714
Inventories and work in progress	3,840	5,129	6,803	9,982
Accounts receivable and				
pre-paid expenses	6,650	6,227	7,835	9,518
Liquid funds	3,118	3,297	5,268	4,214
Current liabilities	10,111	11,520	11,319	15,955
Accounts payable and accrued liabilities	4,314	5,976	8,086	9,388
Restructuring provision	342	1,436	–	1,652
Advance payments	399	534	502	396
Current portion of long-term loans	1,221	139	278	187
Bank overdrafts and short-term loans	3,835	3,435	2,453	4,332
Net current assets	3,497	3,133	19,906	23,714
Shareholders' funds	6,727	6,511	12,418	13,806
Minority shareholders' interests	695	536	555	422
Long-term liabilities	3,705	4,080	3,557	2,578
Long-term loans	3,124	3,397	3,071	2,121
Other long-term liabilities	581	683	486	457
Total assets	21,238	22,647	27,849	32,761
Key ratios				
Earnings per share (FIM)	neg.	13.7	10.97	14.36
Dividend per share (FIM)	2.00	3.2	2.50	3.00
Shareholders' fund per share	113		43.65	48.55
Return on capital employed (%)	5.9	12.5	25.4	29.1
Return on shareholders' funds (%)	neg.	12.4	31.6	31.2

Appendix 3 Key managers: approximate periods at top positions

Kari Kairamo	Chief executive officer	1976–88
Simo Vuorilehto	Chief operations officer	1986–8
	Chief executive officer	1989–91
Kalle Isokallio	President of Cable Machinery	1983–5
	Head of Nokia Information Systems	1986–7
	President of Nokia Data	1988–9
	Chief operations officer	1990–1
Jorma Ollila	Corporate finance	1986–9
	President of Mobile Phones	1990–1
	Chief executive officer	1992–
Kurt Wikstedt	Head of professional electronics (industrial electronics)	–1986
Antti Lagerroos	President of Salora	1982–3
	President of Salora–Luxor	1984
	Executive board member (in charge of consumer electronics)	1985–8
	President of Mobile Phones	1989
Heikki Koskinen	President of Salora–Luxor	1985–7
	Nokia Consumer Electronics, strategic planning	1988–9
	Technology manager in Nokia	1990–1
	General manager, Nokia Consumer Electronics	1992
	Head Office positions	1993–6
Timo Koski	President of Nokia Data	1985–7
Jacques Noels	President of Nokia Consumer Electronics	1988–91
Hannu Bergholm	Controller of Nokia	1987–91
	President of Nokia Consumer Electronics	1992–5

International Service System A/S (ISS)

SUMANTRA GHOSHAL and MARY ACKENHUSEN

With a turnover of DKK 14 billion (Danish kroner), equivalent to more than US$2 billion, and employing over 120,000 people in 32 countries spread around four continents, ISS is an anomaly in the world of megacorporations. The company counts advanced technology, high levels of professional skills and a global brand image among its key sources of competitive advantage. It is not in the business of computers or pharmaceuticals, however, nor in packaged foods or luxury cosmetics. ISS, as described by Poul Andreassen, the company's chief executive officer between 1962 and 1995, 'is the world's largest and best cleaning service company'. In a highly fragmented industry in which the three key success factors are believed to be 'cost, cost and cost', ISS is rarely the low-cost vendor. Yet in 1994, nearly 80 per cent of its worldwide revenues came from the 'mom and pop' business of daily office cleaning.

Poul Andreassen also believed that opportunities for further development were practically unlimited for ISS:

> The business is ours to lose. Where ISS will be in the future all depends on ourselves because the market is out there. There is not a serious threat unless we are not doing what we're saying, what we believe in.

ISS' ambition was to continue improving its service levels so that 'Some day, ISS and the word service will be synonymous, just like Xerox and photocopying once were.' To achieve this vision, however, Andreassen believed that two key hurdles had first to be overcome.

This case study has been revised and updated by Tony Jacobs, Cranfield School of Management, based on the original case study prepared by Mary Ackenhusen, Research Associate, under the supervision of Sumantra Ghoshal, Professor at INSEAD. It is intended to be used as a basis for class discussion rather than to illustrate either effective or ineffective handling of an administrative situation. Partial support for this case was provided by International Financial Services. Reprinted with thepermission of INSEAD. © 1996 INSEAD, Fontainebleau, France.

In the second half of the 1980s, ISS achieved spectacular growth in both sales and profits: 17 and 25 per cent, respectively, per annum (see Exhibit 1 for financial information). Yet its relative profitability, at 3 per cent of sales, remained several percentage points lower than that of either ServiceMaster or BET,[1] its two key competitors. Improving profitability was therefore the first priority.

> I have seen too many 'wheeler-dealer' companies grow rapidly only to go under for not taking quality seriously. They did not try to compile resources for product development, to build personnel development systems, or invest to create a modern way of managing their enterprises. To improve service quality, we must continue to make these investments. But for that, we must achieve 5 per cent profit before tax, at the least.

Second, ISS' admirable pace of growth had thus far come primarily from acquisitions. This strategy of acquisitive growth had reached its limit and the company's target of 15 per cent annual growth through the 1990s had now to come from in-house developments. Given the size of the company,

Exhibit 1   Financial history for ISS, 1992–4 (millions of DKK)

	1994	1993	1992
Turnover by division			
Scandinavia	4,246	4,707	5,079
Europe and Brazil	3,634	3,192	2,943
North America	6,180	5,048	3,001
Clorius*	167	356	323
Others	6	4	10
Total turnover	14,232.5	13,307	11,356
Operating profit by division			
Scandinavia	218	228	288
Europe and Brazil	211	226	159
North America	269	221	127
Clorius*	4	21	21
Others	(69)	(63)	(58)
Total operating profit	633.2	632.9	537
Consolidated net profit	288.4	461.7	265.9
Total assets	5,420.6	5,877.6	4,669

*The Clorius division was sold in 1994.

Source: Company annual reports.

[1] BET was acquired by Rentokil in 1996.

continued growth through acquisitions would require either too many small acquisitions or acquisitions of very large companies, both of which would entail unacceptable levels of risk. Importantly, there was a large amount of goodwill on the corporate balance sheet. Thus, the new strategy of organic growth needed to achieve a consistent improvement in earnings per share in order to protect and enhance the value of ISS' stock.

While ample opportunities for organic growth remained available, the company needed to reassess its organisational approach and replenish its management skills to reorient itself to this new growth process. Many managers felt that the comany was too conservative, financially, and did not provide the funding necessary to build new businesses from scratch. However, this is where Andreassen saw growth and profitability improvement as two inseparably intertwined objectives:

> We've invested a lot of money over the years in management training and now is the time to show for it. We have got to come up and make the 5 per cent before tax. Then we will have a very important cash flow and can make available those funds the businesses need to grow.

ISS spreads its wings

ISS was created in 1901 by a Danish lawyer to provide security services for office buildings in Copenhagen. The company grew in the security business, and in 1934 it expanded its activities to include commercial cleaning. By the time Andreassen took over the management of the company in 1962, it had grown to 2,000 employees and 50 million DKK in sales.

At this time, office cleaning was considered to be neither an attractive nor a sophisticated business. The margins were very low and the companies which served the market were almost entirely small businesses. Andreassen liked to emphasise how negatively people viewed their positions as cleaners by recalling experiences of employees who left their houses at 5 a.m. in full tennis garb, drove to their places of work and then changed into their cleaning clothes. They did not ever want the neighbours to know what they really did between 5 and 8 in the morning. Andreassen spent the next 30 years of his life working to mould ISS into a professionally managed service company which would combat the low-class image of the industry.

The 1960s: professional management

The market for commercial cleaning and security services was changing at the time Andreassen took over the management of ISS in the early 1960s. Companies were beginning to focus on their main lines of business and contracting out secondary activities such as cleaning, security and food service. This 'structural rationalisation' trend supported Andreassen's personal philosophy that cleaning was a professional business and must be managed as such.

Prior to ISS, Andreassen had earned a degree in industrial engineering and then worked in positions ranging from time-study engineer to plant manager in several multinational companies, including Remington Rand and SAS. In his new job, he immediately began applying some of the basic management techniques he had learned in a manufacturing environment to the cleaning business.

In his first days as chief executive, Andreassen was somewhat surprised to find that the only information collected to measure the work of the cleaners was how much material (cleaning products) had been used. Since this comprised only 3 per cent of the cost of a contract and wages accounted for 65–70 per cent, Andreassen began his task of professionalising ISS' operations by developing a system to plan the work better. The new planning system ensured the job would be performed efficiently and to a given standard by specifying the work methods, the frequency of each task and how the various jobs were to be distributed among the workers. With this innovation, a cleaner now had a personalised job sheet of the tasks to be performed by him or her each day. The planning system also allowed ISS to bid accurately for new business.

The system remained a key tool at ISS, although it was now more sophisticated and computerised. When a tender offer was being prepared for a new site, a group of planners estimated the labour, equipment and material content by entering the building parameters, including the size of the area to be cleaned, types of floor, number of toilets, frequency of cleaning tasks, etc., into a special computer program developed by ISS. The program then calculated the estimated cost of the job using the pre-established standards for cleaning.

To address the efficiency of his workers, Andreassen implemented a combination of improvements to substantially increase the cleaning rate, which stood at 40 square metres per hour. Often the rate could be increased by improved tools, such as better cleaning products, specially designed mops and dust rags, and new or additional machinery. Likewise, the growing popularity of carpets in office buildings helped boost the productivity of the cleaning operators. By 1992, average cleaning rates had been improved to 250–350 square metres per hour.

At the same time, Andreassen hired a chemical engineer to take responsibility for the technical function of developing and producing new cleaning products. Referring to the bad image of the cleaning business, Andreassen remembers that in 1962, when he placed an advertisement for this position in a Copenhagen paper, he had no responses because 'Who wants to be in the cleaning business?' In the end, he pressured a friend into taking the position. The result of this drive for state-of-the-art cleaning tools was the establishment in 1963 of a separate company, Darenas, under the ISS banner.

His next action was to break the company up into profit centres, units with full operational and financial responsibility. This change supported his philosophy that the most motivated managers were those who thought of the business as their own. To monitor these relatively autonomous business units, he adopted a financial reporting system, the Management Reporting System (MRS), which provided a detailed profit and loss statement, called the after-calculation, for each business unit. This information was compiled monthly and the report was distributed to all senior managers of the company.

The basis of the report was a cost accounting system, starting at the contract level, which deducted all direct costs such as material, equipment and wage costs for every cleaning contract against the contract's turnover, to find the 'contract contribution'. Enabling management to understand their overhead costs, the expenses of each successive layer of management (i.e. branch, district and country) were subtracted to calculate CBI (contribution I), CBII and CBIII. CBIII was the operating profit earned by the business unit after all costs were deducted. Monthly, the budgeted direct costs were compared with the actual results using the after-calculation report, giving the unit manager immediate insight into the profitability of each job under his or her control.

The MRS had two major benefits. First, it focused on the smallest and most basic unit of performance, the cleaning contract and team, and provided the transparency necessary for corrective actions at that level. Second, this financial system became the basis for measuring a manager's success and identifying areas which needed improvement. Andreassen explained the value of the system:

> One of the most important ingredients of management is that all levels of management know exactly on which criteria to measure whether or not a manager is successful. This takes care of half of the management process as ... one does not have to kick everybody around. [With MRS] people were well aware when they were successful, and they knew how to take corrective actions if they had bad results.

When ISS acquired a company, the implementation of this system was the priority management action in order immediately to improve profitability.

With the realisation that people were his largest cost on a contract, Andreassen was convinced that he must focus his attention on the individuals doing the cleaning, the cleaners. Beyond his drive to improve the efficiency and standards of cleaning, Andreassen wanted to improve his employees' satisfaction with their work. Andreassen's mother had been a shop steward in a tobacco company, and this gave him an appreciation for the feelings of workers who performed manual labour and a desire to improve their status.

Andreassen began improving his workforce's self-image by giving ISS employees an identity of which they could be proud. All ISS employees were given attractive uniforms with the ISS logo. All supervisors were given company cars to drive with the ISS blue letters emblazoned on the side. Andreassen explained:

> We all need a certain degree of recognition. We want to identify with something … I want a cleaner to be able to point out to her children the smart white car in the street with its blue stripes driving past and say to them, 'This is my company.'

Likewise, Andreassen extended the existing training programmes for the cleaners and added new training programmes for his management to help them carry out the work in a professional manner. He recalled:

> At the time, there was a growing understanding of the importance of this type of work, that it had to be carried out in a professional manner and that the persons doing the work were entitled to wages on a level with the industrial workers. The work had to be done professionally in order for us to be able to develop the systems and methods … and this called for resources for both training and professional management.

This era was one of expansion within Scandinavia and the rest of Europe. ISS is believed to be the first cleaning company to have worked outside of its home country when it entered Sweden in the 1940s and Norway in the 1950s. In the 1960s, ISS increased its international presence by entering Germany, Switzerland, Holland and the UK through local acquisitions.

The 1970s: service management

By the early 1970s, ISS had a strong system of procedures and standards which ensured high-quality, efficient cleaning, but management realised that the market was beginning to demand more. As Sven Ipsen, one-time head of ISS' Scandinavian division, remembered:

> Earlier we thought that if we gave the customer the quality he wanted, shiny floors, clean lavatories, then he should be satisfied because that was what he paid for. Then we realised that we needed to not only focus on what we delivered as service, but how we delivered it.

ISS' new service philosophy was based on 'The Magic Formula' (see Exhibit 2). The thrust of the formula was that every market segment, such as hospitals, schools or office buildings, had unique characteristics. Thus, the service package, including methods and product offerings, should reflect the needs of each segment. A unique delivery system for each segment was the most effective way of handling the different needs of the segment, yet the

Exhibit 2 The ISS Magic Formula

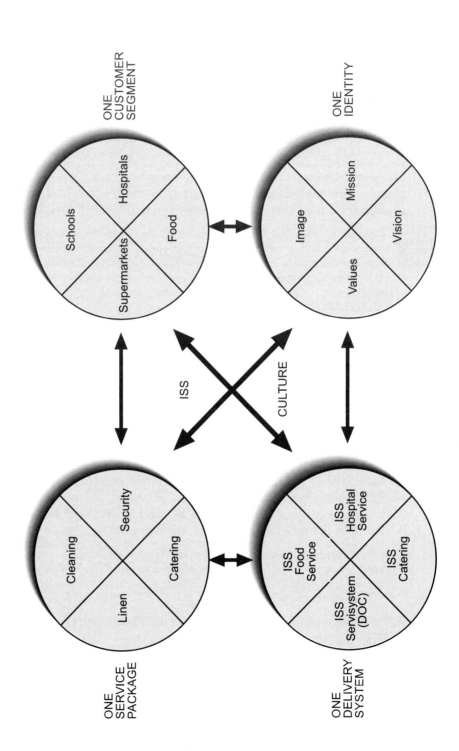

company could still be tied together by one identity, such as a common logo. Additionally, the company should carry the same culture for a high level of service throughout all aspects of the operation.

Thus, instead of the same workers cleaning hospitals, schools and other buildings using the same methods and equipment, there was a recognition of the difference in customer needs. This drove ISS to set up separate organisations to serve each of its markets. While before the only separate groups were security, food service and cleaning, now cleaning was broken into groups to meet the special, different needs of offices, schools, hospitals and food (mainly slaughterhouses, known as abattoirs). The cleaners and managers received special training on the specific needs of these areas and remained dedicated to a market segment in order to build the experience and expertise needed to serve customers effectively in these segments.

Focused attention on specific market segments allowed ISS to leverage its knowledge of a customer's business with its on-site presence to offer special cleaning and other services. For example, in a supermarket, ISS would gain entrance to the customer through a contract to do traditional cleaning of the shop area and offices. Over time, after ISS had proven its professionalism in cleaning, it expanded its service offering to include special cleaning of the meat section, freezers, shopping trolleys or even air filters, as well as non-cleaning tasks such as labelling, coffee making, uniform cleaning, lighting and repair of shopping trolleys.

A key element of 'The Magic Formula' was to nurture the 'front line', the primary contact with the customer: the supervisors and workers. Close attention was paid to the hiring, training and retention of these employees. For example, in Denmark, all managers including the managing director spent up to two days per month interviewing candidates for the cleaning operator position. Then a video presentation of what a cleaner can expect from his or her job was shown to each candidate and a formal job bank used to try to match cleaners to jobs, primarily based on location of the job relative to the cleaner's home.

The high turnover which is usually found in low-paying jobs such as cleaning (cleaners earn close to the bottom of the wage scale) has always been a concern to ISS. The actual turnover rate of ISS varied greatly between countries, from 50 to 100 per cent annually, depending somewhat on the tightness of the labour market in that country. As Andreassen explained:

> Many, perhaps 60 per cent of them, will stay many years, a lot for 25 years . . . but the last 40 per cent is turning around two or three times. Some of that you cannot avoid because they are coming in to earn money for a wedding or other special event, so they only stay a couple of months. Also, we hire quite a few students.

ISS believes that a good supervisor can reduce the turnover. Though the supervisors are responsible for training, quality control and scheduling of their work team, the most important part of their job is letting the cleaners know that they care. As described by one of the supervisors:

> The ISS advantage is that the supervisor is there for the people ... that they can come to us for time, for a coffee. It's not always possible to help them, but they need someone to listen. If they know this, they'll work for a supervisor on Saturdays and Sundays.

The supervisor also served as the primary customer contact, interacting with the customer daily to ensure that he or she is satisfied with the service, as well as to suggest added services which might be performed either regularly, such as more frequent waxing of the floors, or on a one-time basis, such as cleaning the telephones.

The company used a whole array of formal reports and surveys to measure customer satisfaction, in addition to regular customer contact by the branch and district management, yet it was the supervisors who helped most in differentiating ISS from the other cleaning companies. As one of the supervisors explained:

> Other cleaning companies are cheaper, but they have less supervision. We supervisors are a very good internal control system. Also, we are there for the customer, an on-site answer for all the customer's problems.

Service management layered on top of professional methods and quality standards proved to be a successful formula, which helped ISS to grow to be a 3 billion DKK business by the end of the 1970s. Contributing to this geographic and market growth were the additional acquisitions of cleaning services in Europe, the purchase of Clorius, an energy control company, and its first expansion into North America through the purchase of a majority share in Prudential Building Maintenance Corporation of New York.

The 1980s: strategic planning

By the beginning of the 1980s, ISS was operating in three continents and had ventured into a dozen specialised cleaning and related businesses. With the good fortune to have too many growth opportunities, both geographically and market-wise, Andreassen decided it was time to guide the further development of ISS formally through the adoption of a strategic planning system.

The ISS 'team planning process' is a top-down, bottom-up participative system to develop detailed and integrated plans to support defined corporate objectives. The key elements of the plan answer the questions 'Where are we?', 'Where do we want to go?', 'How do we get there?' and 'Who does what and how?': that is, status, goals, strategies and action plans. The process involves many team members at each level, necessitating that it begin in April each year in order to finish by the end of October.

The team planning process begins with training for all participants new to the process to ensure that everyone 'speaks the same language'. Starting from the top at the corporate level, a planning team is formed which will develop both qualitative and quantitative goals and objectives to be passed down to the next level, the divisions, as input to their plans. The divisions will also each have a team which will develop its mission, goals and objectives. This continues in the same manner down each of the levels of management and stops at the level of branch management within each country. Then the plans with the detailed proposals on how the various units expect to meet the corporate guidelines flow upward by management level, with the lower-level management plan becoming input for the next higher level. Therefore, each planning team at each level has two major planning sessions per year as the plans flow downward and then climb back up. To ensure smooth communication of plans between levels, planning teams include members from the management level directly above and below.

The process is designed to complement the autonomy granted to the local operating managers, with each level of management giving the level below it a framework of strategic guidelines. Andreassen and his management team placed a high value on the process:

> The process holds our organisation together and is the basis for our development and success . . . It is the national leaders of ISS, with their teams, who contribute to the corporate strategy, the strategy for the development of each national unit, adapted not only to each country's particular personnel, social and legal conditions, but also the cultural and behavioural conditions. This complex task cannot be dealt with from behind a desk in Copenhagen.

The tool was credited for helping to build and maintain the ISS culture through extensive communication of mission, guidelines, rules and expectations.

Guided by this formal strategic planning process, ISS continued its growth throughout the 1980s by expanding the US cleaning business nationwide through acquisition: acquiring additional cleaning companies in Denmark, Sweden and Germany, sponsoring further acquisitions of energy companies under the Clorius umbrella and acquiring a hospital service company, Mediclean, in the UK.

The 1990s: total quality management

Andreassen was not concerned about other service companies copying the ISS formula because he drove ISS to develop new initiatives continuously. He liked to say: 'Walking in the footsteps of somebody else will not put you in front.' To this end, ISS initiated a programme in 1991 to implement total quality management as the next step for achieving service excellence. The TQM mission, as stated by the company, was to:

> Target the Group's functions and resources throughout the entire supply chain towards the creation of a perceived service quality which, as a minimum, fulfils the customers' demands and expectations, with the specific objectives of increasing customer satisfaction, reducing the loss of contracts, increasing sales to existing customers and reducing the staff turnover.

The two primary tools of TQM were extensive measurement systems in important areas, such as employee and customer satisfaction, and work analysis. The objective of the work analysis is to improve the operational processes used in ISS by identifying every step of the current process backwards from the customer to the beginning of the ISS supply chain, and then looking for ways to rationalise the process (process mapping). This extensive analysis will eventually be done for every activity within the company.

To support this massive effort, a special subsidiary, ISS Quality Institute A/S, was established in 1992 near Copenhagen with its own managing director. One reason for the separate operating company was that a programme which was perceived to be a 'corporate programme' would not be easily accepted.

As the concept grew to address other ISS needs beyond its stated objectives, its internal acceptance increased. TQM is now envisioned to be a marketing tool to other multinational corporations which are also embracing the concept in their own businesses; it is a means of enabling cleaners to involve themselves more easily in initiating and implementing new ideas; and it is an integration tool to help transfer best practices between business units.

Flemming Schandorff, the managing director for the cleaning business in Denmark, was enthusiastic about TQM and felt that it could make a real difference in the bottom line of his business:

> Every year we lose 140 million Danish kroner in turnover through loss of contracts to our competitors. We believe that after we have educated our people in TQM, and begin monitoring the customer satisfaction index and the employee satisfaction index, we will be able to reduce that.

By the end of 1992, only the Scandinavian division had started the TQM training process. The other countries outside of Scandinavia, and some within Scandinavia, had taken a first step towards TQM by starting the process of achieving ISO 9000 certification, an international quality standard which ensures documentation and consistency of process.

Although the European division did not expect to begin the TQM process for several years, one of the first tangible results of the TQM thrust occurred in this division in 1992 when the UK operation brought in the head of the ISS Quality Institute to convince the Heathrow Airport management of the value of the ISS TQM programme. Primarily due to that competitive difference, ISS subsequently won a cleaning contract for Terminal 1 at the airport. The TQM training for the employees involved in this contract began in 1993, ahead of the rest of the European division.

Within the Chinese Walls: the business unit

The ISS organisational structure was based on the philosophy that the most efficient, profitable way to provide services is through small stand-alone companies led by a local manager who was encouraged to think of the business as his or her own. Andreassen had intentionally erected a barrier around the operating units, which he called the 'Chinese Wall', to keep out top management.

Each national subsidiary of ISS is a legally separate company, with the country manager carrying the title of managing director with his or her own board of directors. This board is normally staffed by key members of the country's management team, the head of the divisional management team, one or two outsiders who provide professional services to the country organisation (i.e. the lawyer) and often another ISS country manager. The board meets three times per year to review budgets, potential acquisitions and any non-urgent policy decisions that need to be made.

The managing director's direct reports are, typically, several regional directors for the cleaning business and one or more directors of a special service such as hospitals or food. There are three usual levels of management under the regional director, starting with the district manager who has overall responsibility for a specified geographical area within the country, the branch manager with responsibility for the profitability and quality of coverage for an even smaller geographical area, and the supervisor who has responsibility for the daily execution of one or a few specific contracts. See Exhibit 3 for a typical country organisation.

The title of managing director is considered to be a valuable tool for attracting and keeping good country managers. Not only do the title and the legal structure reinforce the philosophy that the country organisation is his or her own company, but it also enables the country manager more easily to call on the managing directors of potential customers. The title gives both professional and social prestige to the country manager in what many would consider to be an unprestigious industry. The compensation package for each managing director is renegotiated each year and varies by country.

This arrangement enabled ISS to hire successful managers who might otherwise not have been interested in the company. Theo Buitendijk joined ISS as managing director in Holland in 1990 after working in a multinational oil company for 25 years. He remarked that: 'Here it's more

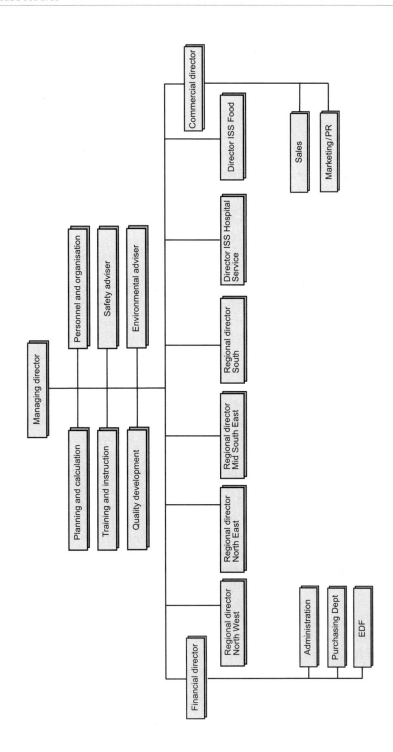

Exhibit 3 ISS country organisation: the Netherlands

fun because I'm in charge of the whole thing. You can keep your independence as long as you meet your budget.'

Similarly, David Openshaw used to work for ISS' largest competitors in Europe, BET, in a position with responsibility for £35 million turnover. Upon joining ISS, Openshaw became the managing director of a new ISS company whose mission was to build from scratch a cleaning operation in London: 'The one thing that attracted me was the promise that I would have my own business, that I could run the business the way I wanted to run it.' In two years, he was proud to note that his turnover had reached £6 million.

In the early 1990s, the country-level managing directors were encouraged to create independent companies with their own managing directors within the country structure to focus specifically on food or on hospitals. Taking the philosophy even further, Germany was in the process of establishing five additional independent companies under the country managing director to focus on daily office cleaning in the various regions of Germany. The key reason for breaking up the country units in this manner was to motivate and focus the managers of these segments.

This organisational philosophy imposed some additional costs in terms of additional management, audit and legal fees. For this reason, some country managers resisted the push from the corporate centre to develop the special service businesses as separate legal entities as they were too small to support the additional overheads. On the other hand, focused activities seemed to create more profit.

The head of the cleaning business in Denmark was not pleased when the decision was made to relieve him of his responsibility for hospital cleaning in Denmark in order to combine all the hospital business in Scandinavia under one company. Yet after this happened, as related by his then boss, Sven Ipsen: 'His PBT is up by half a percent and his growth in turnover is better than before. He admits it's because of his new focus just on cleaning.'

The new chief executive, Waldemar Schmidt, former head of the European group, is a long-time ISS manager who originally developed the Brazilian operation. From this experience and seeing how the European countries which he once managed have benefited from the 'own your company' approach, he comments: 'One can easily quantify the cost of creating smaller companies … the value added is something you must believe in.'

The success or failure of a country manager is viewed by the ISS corporate centre almost exclusively in terms of financial results: his or her performance against profitability and growth targets. The profitability target is a minimum of 5 per cent profit before tax and the growth target generally ranges from 10 to 15 per cent, varying by country. The country manager's bonus is a reflection of these parameters.

The ISS requirement that its unit managers provide consistent financial returns often takes priority over any strategic objectives. In the early 1990s,

Gerhard Marischka, the managing director of Austria, was one of ISS' 'stars' because he averaged 16 per cent organic sales growth annually over three years and earned a profitability (before tax) above all other ISS countries, approaching 8 per cent in 1991 and 1992. Strategically, however, he had to chart a path that was not always consistent with the overall ISS priorities. He retained his profitable security business, for example, despite the divisional decision to exit that activity. He has also not developed any significant business in either of the targeted areas of special service, hospitals or food, which tend to be less profitable, at least initially.

Theo Buitendijk, the managing director of Holland who came to ISS in 1990 from Exxon, tried to balance the financial and strategic objectives laid out by ISS' divisional and corporate managements. By doubling his sales by acquisition between 1990 and 1991 without increasing overheads, he doubled his financial returns, which allowed him to invest in building a new service area, food. Though he suffered a short-term drop in profitability before tax at the country level as he built up the food business, be believes it was the more profitable long-term strategy. As a measure of his market success, in 1992 he was servicing 50 food contracts and was the market leader in that segment in Holland. By 1994, Holland reported a profit of 5 per cent. Speaking from experience, Buitendijk commented:

> We as entrepreneurs are paid on results — that makes us risk avoiders, not risk takers. The system as it stands now doesn't stimulate focused attention to new areas . . . change is costly. Corporate says they accept the costs if you try new things . . . but I really don't know.

Within the challenging objective of meeting the financial plan, the managing directors have almost complete freedom to manage their business as they like. For example, Rolf Witt, the German managing director, used his freedom quickly to exploit the need for a service to dispose of building rubble when the former East Germany was first opened to the West. Using 'petty cash', he acquired a small concern in East Germany to perform this type of work. After a period, he made a tidy profit by selling off pieces of the company, such as the vehicles which were bought by a concern in Poland. There are limits, however, to such freedom. When the former head of the Brazilian operation signed an agreement for a major acquisition committing ISS corporate resources without corporate approval, he was later asked to resign.

This local freedom also served as a breeding ground for new ideas when the investment can be justified at the operating unit level. Andreassen explained:

> With only 43 people at headquarters, it's clear that it is not from there that development springs. Our development is based on what goes on around us . . . But we put a good deal of money into education and committee work. So you see, what we have here are companies working together, developing something new, under

the leadership of corporate management, a process involving all companies, a process which does not start at the top.

One of the most important innovations springing from an operating unit was the five-star training programme. It originated in Brazil, but then was shared with Belgium and Austria, which greatly enhanced the programme. This key programme for supervisors and managers became a part of the corporate human resources strategy. The five stars refer to the five levels of training, which cover the ISS philosophy, cleaning techniques, labour law, contract management, quality control, customer relations, employee relations and other key areas.

Building bridges: divisional management

The corporate management team at ISS had always been small because Andreassen 'dreads bureaucracy'. He felt that the primary role of the headquarters staff should be to:

> Procure the financial opportunities, check and control the company's development, and create resources for strategic development, training, R&D and marketing on an international basis ... The number should be small at the headquarters office, but they must be extremely qualified.

Thus, until 1989, Andreassen and his corporate staff of 50 people managed the ISS operations, employing 100,000 people scattered across sixteen countries. In 1989, the divisional level of management was added to reduce the span of control sufficiently so that the leadership of the company could work with the managing directors more closely. In 1992, the European division totalled 8 people, the Scandinavian division management numbered 22 people and the North American division, which also served as the country management team for the United States, totalled 40 people.

The majority of the staff are oriented towards the financial function, although there are also experts to provide advice on marketing, human resource management, quality, strategy and acquisitions. To support the management above the country level, each country paid a royalty of 1.5 per cent of turnover to the ISS corporate centre, of which 0.5 per cent was forwarded to the division management organisation. The performance improvement in Europe in just two years proved the value of the divisional management: the PBT for the countries within the division more than doubled from 2 per cent in 1989 to almost 5 per cent in 1991.

Strategy

The heads of the European and Scandinavian divisions spend much of their time developing the strategy for their areas of the world and working individually with the country managers to develop their respective business plans. They also give a lot of thought to optimising the organisational structure, such as creating or spinning off a new operating company at the right time. Though the divisional management team is very respectful of the autonomy of the local management, their mandate is to make the division greater than the sum of its parts, the countries. The corporate and divisional management can persuade and negotiate but, for the most part, the quest for entrepreneurial freedom seems to take priority over upper management directives. The Chinese Wall works.

One example of this is the freedom which the operating companies have when they choose a supplier for their cleaning products. The ISS operating company, Darenas, provides a full line of cleaning products, but the operating units are not required to buy them, though some formerly reluctant country managers have yielded to pressure to do so. In a similar vein, corporate or divisional-level strategic priorities are not normally pushed onto a country manager who does not 'buy in'. That is why there were several countries in Europe which had little or no activity in hospitals or food in the early 1990s, in spite of the corporate strategy to target these areas.

The country management can be a barrier to strategic plans from above, but there are also instances when the local managers find the corporate strategy to be a barrier to their own initiative. The managing director of Mediclean, the UK hospital service company, saw an attractive opportunity to purchase an interest in a prepared food company which sells its product to the UK National Health Service. He felt that it would be a strong complement to the hospital catering business he provided. The investment was not approved by divisional management because: 'Our strategy is not to invest in food manufacturing.' The managing director feels that if he had been the true owner of Mediclean, he would have risked his capital on the new venture. In the end, informal ties were made with the company that allow Mediclean to enjoy most of the sought-after benefits without any risk of capital.

The divisional manager took the lead in developing the strategy and infrastructure to meet the emerging demand by customers for single-point facilities management. The European division became a partner in 1992 in a marketing company called Service Interface, which co-ordinates a number of service companies to provide an all-inclusive facility management contract. Beyond the cleaning service offered by ISS, the companies in the partnership provide catering, technical maintenance, waste management, textile services and security services. The idea was well received in the UK market, and Schmidt hoped to sell the idea across to other countries in Europe. He commented: 'It's an interesting alternative to acquiring companies.'

The overall demand for such one-stop shopping was uncertain, however. The Scandinavian division provided a similar type of 'multiservice' to clients in the early 1990s by offering a complete ISS contract covering the range of available services: cleaning, security, catering, landscaping and textiles, with one contract manager and integrated billing. The programme was discontinued when it became evident that the majority of customers actually preferred dealing with multiple vendors so that they could leverage one against another to gain a better overall price. Additionally, customer decision making often occurred in different parts of the organisation for the various services that ISS was providing, making smooth co-ordination very difficult.

Measurement

The divisional management team is responsible for setting the targets for the MRS budget for each unit manager based on the corporate guidelines for the year as articulated during the planning process. These targets, such as sales growth, contribution margin and profit before tax, vary slightly by country and are always an improvement over the previous year's performance. This emphasis on the financials prompted one manager to exclaim: 'The only vision we get from above are numbers!'

Retained earnings which are accumulated by each operating company are not its own to keep. For historical reasons, ISS Scandinavia is an exception and enjoys the right to keep the balance of the earnings of its operating companies not paid out as dividends and to reinvest the funds as it chooses. The European division was not set up with this autonomy and therefore, in principle, its earnings are returned to the corporate centre to be redistributed throughout ISS as headquarters sees fit.

There is some dissatisfaction with the policy which allows one division to keep its retained earnings. Its opponents believe that investment funds should be applied to the best opportunity within the entire corporation. As one manager remarked:

> When ISS Scandinavia bought the rest of the Finnish cleaning company in 1992, it was probably the best opportunity they had to grow their turnover ... but I think there were better investment opportunities in the European division where ISS has a very small presence.

The drive for continually improving financial returns combined with an extremely conservative approach to reinvesting in the local business is a source of frustration for some business unit managers. As one remarked:

> There is no extra money to develop a business on your own. I could expand more rapidly if I got some funding from corporate. It's easier to acquire a company [than grow internally] because corporate will provide that money.

Transferring knowledge

ISS has several formal platforms which attempt to transfer best practices among operations and geographies. Until 1991, a group of all the senior management and managing directors (the Top Management Conference, or TMC) within ISS met annually to discuss relevant issues. As the company grew, the group exceeded 100 people, making it hard to create a participative environment for sharing. Therefore, the divisions began holding a similar meeting several times a year with the appropriate participants within their division, which limited the group to a more workable number.

In the last European division TMC, attended by 30 managers, the group spent the first day discussing how to improve their business development capabilities by using Belgium's process as an example of one successful strategy. The second day was spent discussing methods to improve customer retention by learning from the progress that Holland had made in this area.

At the corporate level, and within the European and Scandinavian divisions, there were a number of committees which shared information and made decisions on common systems. At the corporate level, the committees met two to four times each year on the subjects of quality, strategy, human resources, finance and marketing to develop general policies in these areas. The membership of these committees was drawn primarily from the divisional and corporate management. Similar committees existed in many of the same functions at the divisional level to provide a forum for sharing ideas among countries. While some within ISS saw the committee structure to be one of the few available mechanisms to share expertise within the company, others were less supportive of the system. One manager commented: 'The committees are not very well liked. They're too expensive with no value.'

There was no formal mechanism for sharing ideas and practices between line managers below the country management level. While contact with other ISS managers outside their own country structure was limited for managers in staff functions (i.e. finance and sales), it was practically non-existent for line management. Thus, a district manager for office cleaning in Austria had no contact with his or her counterpart in the UK, for example. Explaining the difficulty of sharing new methods, one manager remarked: 'A new idea which appears in one country has to go all the way up through the division or even corporate and back down to another country to be shared.'

ISS had a matrix organisation in the early 1980s of corporate-level product managers for each service segment, such as food and hospitals, whose mission was to transfer best practices across the operating units in different countries. Most of these product managers were young and inexperienced in the cleaning business; thus, they spent much of their time 'publishing manuals'. The limitations of this approach to sharing best practices was revealed when the hospital service manual for Denmark was given to ISS in New York to assist them in their entry into the business. The New York management was disappointed to find that the education level of their workforce was not high enough to read the manuals and execute the complicated calculations used in the procedures. Results such as this one made it difficult to justify the value added and, after a short time, the product manager positions were eliminated. In 1992, corporate management again proposed a matrix structure which would assign a product manager at the corporate level for two service areas. In part due to the last experience with this type of position, the division management opposed the proposal and it was dropped.

Communication within ISS seemed to work best on an informal basis, with the business unit managers reaping the most benefit when sharing their experiences in new service areas. Denmark has supported a significant amount of training of managers from other countries in the food business, both in Denmark and in their home countries. An idea for a new vacuum cleaner which could be carried on the operator's back for cleaning trains travelled from Denmark back to the UK through a chance visit by a British manager. Yet informal sharing has its limits. As the German country manager explained:

> I would like to be aggressive on food, but I don't have enough knowledge. I can't ask Denmark to lend me a person for four weeks. The royalty [paid to the corporate centre] doesn't cover that.

Nevertheless, he did not support the idea of paying for this service because: 'These things must work informally, colleague to colleague.'

The most successful example of transferring learning within ISS occurred when a very experienced and multilingual planner from Denmark spent several years travelling between offices in Europe, giving advice to the operations and sharing his experiences. Also, helping to share ideas on a regular basis, the ISS corporate centre publishes a quarterly newsletter, 'ISS News', which gives an in-depth review of one country's business in each issue, as well as the key events happening throughout the rest of the ISS world. Within the countries, other newsletters update the employees on the latest happenings.

Beyond the organisational difficulties, the lack of a common language inhibited the sharing between countries, and discouraged common training and teamwork across countries. One manager, with the experience to compare ISS' ability in this area with other multinational companies in other industries, felt that ISS managers have a lower level of multilingual ability than most multinational companies of its size.

Expertise

The division management provides mainly financial and marketing expertise to the countries. In the financial domain, the divisional financial director spends several days a year with each country, performing an in-depth audit of its financial records and systems. During this visit, and as needed throughout the year, he gave advice on such matters as cash management, insurance, reduction of debtor days, and other similar concerns. The divisional-level finance committee was also active in sharing financial tools between countries.

The marketing expertise at the divisional level was added in the late 1980s to assist the countries in meeting the challenge of organic growth. Several years later, all managing directors were not yet comfortable with the new emphasis in this area. As one managing director expressed it:

> When I'm thinking of marketing, I'm saying ooh, it costs. I'm much more operations-oriented. All the problems my people are having today, I was through years ago. I have a much more open eye and ear for operations problems than marketing issues.

In recognition of the fact that most of the country managers had grown up with ISS, building their organisations through their expertise in operations, the two most recent country manager recruits in Holland and Belgium came from marketing and sales backgrounds in non-service industries.

The ISS sales and marketing function varied in strength and sophistication from country to country. In most country organisations, the two were combined into one function, with the sales function being the stronger of the two. To target customers, an ISS salesperson would typically drive through a neighbourhood noting all large buildings which were not ISS clients and any new office buildings under construction. These potential customers would then be contacted by mail or telephone to try to set up a meeting to discuss the client's needs. In some countries, ISS was the only cleaning company to have a professional sales and marketing department.

The European divisional efforts to assist in the country marketing plans have been met with mixed feelings. Though the market data which the division provides were welcomed by the countries, the feeling was that marketing was a line function, not a staff position. One country manager commented: 'How can someone from the division help us write a marketing plan when they don't even know the market?'

In 1992, the European marketing director sponsored a study of the cleaning opportunities in the food-processing segment within Europe. When the study showed a very attractive opportunity for ISS in this area, the European division proposed to its member countries that they aggressively go after the market with a pan-European salesperson who could support and leverage the countries' individual efforts by selling to customers which have multiple food-processing operations across Europe. This thrust met with strong resistance from the country management for a variety of reasons, but primarily because 'it was too much, too fast'.

Although Theo Buitendijk of Holland had the leading food business in the European division, he opposed the plan. He argued that everyone in Europe must first get some experience in the industry so that they could properly support it: 'We must not sell hot air.' He remembered very well a contract he lost with a multinational in the Netherlands due to problems in the service provided by the Spanish ISS subsidiary with the same multinational client in Spain. In explanation, he said: 'In professional services we sell confidence. My customer must believe in my blue eyes. We don't sell on our name in Europe, we're too small.'

Buitendijk felt that, as long as the ISS corporate centre promotes the virtues of high strategic autonomy at the country level, it would be a long time before ISS Europe could provide the consistent, high-quality service in food that he believed was needed to support a pan-European strategy. He suggested that, if ISS wanted to speed the implementation of these types of multiple-country strategy, 'They should direct or force us . . . rather than leaving it up to each country manager.' In the end, the pan-European proposal was 'shelved', awaiting further market analysis and discussions. In spite of the lack of progress in food, the European division was still working to market office-cleaning services to multinationals across Europe.

The divisional management teams also provided other services which an individual country would not normally be able to support on its own. For example, the European division did a study for its countries to help them understand the impact of the 1992 single market in terms of labour law, health and safety, public sector policies and other areas relevant to the ISS operating companies.

When head of the European division, Schmidt felt that, beyond his strategic, control and support roles, the biggest help he could provide to his country managers was by showing that he cared:

> It's very difficult with 25 companies to spend a lot of time with each. The most important thing is to show an interest, show that you care about them and their performance. When I receive the monthly management report, I often call people who do not even report to me and say 'well done'. When David Openshaw was struggling to build a business from scratch, I would send him a bottle of champagne every time his turnover increased by a million pounds . . . I also try to notice when things aren't going so well and give a call to say 'what happened?'.

Additionally, several managing directors have profited from the one-on-one assistance that divisional management has been able to provide during some rough times. When the managing director in Belgium was hired in 1989 from the pharmaceuticals industry, Ken Pepper, the European chief operations officer worked very closely with him for a year to turn the business around.

Pepper was able to add value due to his many years in line management in the UK cleaning industry. He remembers that a big part of this help was in the role of a sounding board for his colleague as he tried to apply some of his marketing ideas from the pharmaceuticals industry to ISS' cleaning business.

Poul Andreassen's legacy

Poul Andreassen stood down from his post as chief executive of ISS in October 1995. He left a company deeply imprinted with his management ideals and felt satisfied with the role he played in more than 30 years of leadership because, during that period, he laid down a network of values which have served ISS well. He explains: 'I was the right man at the right time ... with the entrepreneurial personality and qualifications. I believe I had the right approach, maybe because of my [working-class] background.'

Establishing values

ISS had been built upon a few guiding principles laid down by Andreassen from his early days: financial conservatism, respect for workers and the professionalism of the industry. Though ISS had always functioned as an extremely decentralised organisation, he had used 'centralised training and information functions to, more or less, instil in the people the same attitude to handling various situations'.

Andreassen characterised ISS as a conservative company and pointed to the monthly MRS reports as an example of a tool to keep the business on track. ISS exited a number of businesses over the years, including restaurants in Scandinavia, and cleaning operations in Australia and France, because of negative returns. The message to the rest of ISS concerning how failures are handled is very clear because of the transparency of the MRS reports, which are widely available within the company. Andreassen commented:

> We never cut a failure before everyone expected it. I mean everyone can see the MRS, month by month, year by year. I would say it's more the other reaction ... if I had too much patience with a company, then the other people said, hey, wait a minute. We're not going to pay a lot of money for that other business to blow it.

Andreassen allowed a large margin for failure, but if someone failed too often, action was taken.

> A manager shouldn't be afraid in a given situation to make his decisions, even if he doesn't know all the prerequisites. But then again, he has to accept the fact that

there is a professional hazard involved if he wants to be a leader, that if he doesn't succeed he won't have the glory. He risks losing his stars.

The financial conservatism of ISS was one reason why large amounts of funding were not made available to develop businesses from scratch. Andreassen was not against new investments of this type, but he was very cautious; they had to be backed by a budget and a plan. ISS' bad experience in France taught the company a strong lesson. He described what ISS learned:

> You can't just say I want to go into this business — let me hire ten salesmen. I saw that in Security in France. Fifty salesmen with all their allowances ... He got the fifty people, but certainly did not live up to the expectations for sales performance and revenue. So we had big losses and then he didn't want to stop. So it depends on how realistic the plans and profits are.

Andreassen points to the example of when David Openshaw started an ISS business from scratch in London to show that even a conservative financial policy can support the right investment:

> He came with a plan and a budget. We looked at the plan and said OK, go ahead. It's the third year now. If they come up with a plan and a budget, very few people have negative answers.

Andreassen held his workforce in high respect and strongly believed in training as a lever for building professionalism in the firm and the industry:

> These people are trained, which gives us an image, a profile in public that this is a modern company that is doing an important job. We try to build this image all the time. Not so much with lots of advertising, but by doing what we're doing. Training is also a demonstration of caring because it costs someone. People need to know that they're number 1, well trained and to be told that 'You're important and this is your company'.

The professional reputation that Andreassen built was recognised by the multinational clients that ISS seeks. In 1992, the company won a contract with Eastman Kodak for its whole industrial complex in Rochester, New York. The work had previously been performed by in-house employees. ISS was asked to make an offer for the job in an unusual situation where the job was not opened up for bidding. Andreassen attributed its 'win' with Kodak to be due to the ISS professional image and the fact that it is subscribing to the same TQM principles that Kodak espouses to its employees.

Challenge and stretch

Andreassen saw his personal role as that of innovator and challenger, not administrator. His managers had complained in the past that he moved too fast, changing direction before they had implemented the first plan.

Understanding that it takes a large company more time to move, his philosophy remained that: 'If you stop struggling for it, then nothing will happen.' Expanding on his personal management style, he continued:

> I like new ideas, I like to stir up new things, new concepts ... One of my best days is when they [the divisions or business units] ask me to come out and sit down and discuss for one or two days with them, where I challenge them ... But I say to them, 'This is what I am criticising and this is what I recommend, but in the end it is your choice.'

He saw no one management style which was essential for ISS' continued development, although he believed that there needed to be a good balance between entrepreneurship and management controls:

> As an innovator, I chose to have good planning administrators among the top executives around me. But another man could come in and be a planner or an economist, for instance, and run this company on a more bookkeeping approach. Then he would need to have some aggressive people underneath him to spark the innovation, as well as someone to judge what they're doing.

Although within ISS the managing directors are commonly called entrepreneurs, Andreassen characterised them differently:

> Those people are intrapreneurs, not entrepreneurs. The people that are willing to stay at ISS have more or less the same values as I ... that they like to grow and they have talents for making this happen, but not for their own money. From the start they like to be in a company where they have some control, where they're not on their own, they like to work for other people.

Poul Andreassen saw no change in the ISS mission as the company continued its geographic and service expansion:

> ISS' mission is to be the international market leader, within our business areas, not only regarding our product areas, but also how we manage a service company, how we treat and work with our employees, how we organise, how our customer service works, how we are conceived as an investment object.

He worked with his management team to create a shared Vision 2000 for ISS to help drive its service and personnel development into the future. It included services for the elderly, service in the private home market and increased partnering with the public sector.

Andreassen considered the TQM strategy to be critical to ISS' future, not only as a marketing tool but, more importantly, to help integrate the ISS units through the communication needed to pursue quality.

> Training people, bringing them together, creates new ideas for new services. I think this is one of the most important benefits of TQM. The Quality Institute will be the driving wheel. The people in the special service companies will be in a group under the Quality Institute. No product management, but they themselves will have to say how we can improve our business, customer satisfaction, our value-added service.

Carrying the benefits of communication through training even further, Andreassen created an on-going training programme which began in 1994 for ISS top management at the Quality Institute to help establish a stronger network at the very top of the company.

> They have to sit together for fourteen days and get to know each other. And when they have a problem in San Francisco, they can call someone in Amsterdam and say 'Hey John, can't you send me some. . . .'

ISS in the mid-1990s

ISS was by far the largest cleaning company in Scandinavia, with an estimated 28 per cent of the contracted-out cleaning market in 1994. It also had about 3 per cent of the market in the rest of Europe and just under 5 per cent of the much larger US market. Traditional cleaning and maintenance contributed 78 per cent of total revenues in 1994. (See Exhibit 4 for a list of ISS' principal activities.)

The importance of America to its continued growth led ISS to obtain a listing on the New York Stock Exchange in 1994. This complemented its existing presence on the Copenhagen and London stock markets, and gave the company further access to capital.

In October 1995, Waldemar Schmidt, previously in charge of the ISS Europe and Brazil division, became chief executive of the company, succeeding Andreassen who had held the post for over 30 years. Schmidt stated that his appointment would not change the values of the organisation, and that it was ISS' ambition to raise the level of cleaning personnel from unskilled to semi-skilled, thus increasing wage levels and improving service quality. Their commitment to this ideal was shown by their refusal to bid for contracts which would push wages too low.

Significantly, ISS' British operation introduced works councils — which gave workers a voice in their company's management process — despite Britain's opt-out from the Social Chapter, European legislation which required their introduction. ISS stated that they were part of the group's philosophy of paying people well and competing on productivity.

Extending the company's caring philosophy, ISS introduced a range of environmentally friendly cleaning products — the Green Line products — a move which was complemented by bidding for environmental contracts, such as ISS Belgium's bid to handle the sorting and recycling of waste paper for Begacom, a telecommunications company.

Demographic changes in Europe also created further opportunities which complemented ISS' values. Against a background of an ageing population and increased out-sourcing of social services to the private sector, ISS developed a care services concept based on security, integrity and a sense

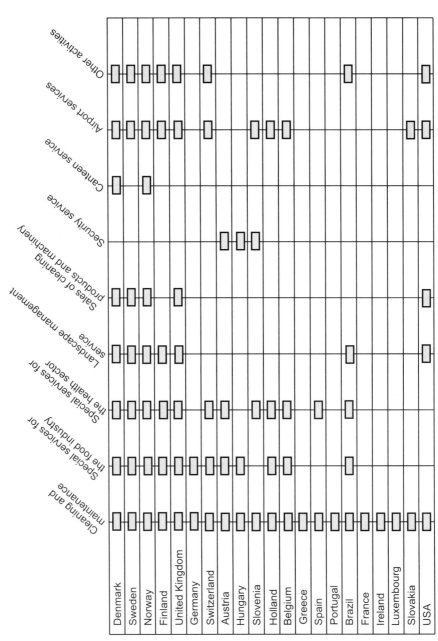

Exhibit 4   Principal ISS activities

Source: Adapted from data within the ISS annual report and accounts, 1994.

of community. In 1995, ISS acquired VardBo, a private care services provider in Sweden, seeing this as an ideal basis for developing the concept.

Under Schmidt, ISS strived for an annual growth rate of about 10–12 per cent through both acquisition and internal means. One of Schmidt's first jobs as chief executive was to integrate the ESGO Group, which employed over 10,000 people within east Asia, into ISS. This acquisition gave the company a presence in over 30 countries on four continents around the world. Expansion continued with a 60 per cent stakeholding being purchased in Harvilla Sro, based in the Czech Republic, in 1995.

Schmidt made the improvement of ISS' profitability his major goal: indeed, he registered his Jaguar car 'PBT 9' (profit before tax 9%). He believed margins could be improved in the future by concentrating on contracts within specialist areas such as hospitals, airports and catering services, and on big customer key account businesses.

Competition continued from three groups: in-house cleaning, a market estimated to be twice that of the contract market; small/medium-sized firms, which had minimal management and training costs, and competed on price; and the other multinational companies such as BET and ServiceMaster.

Further opportunities arose during the 1990s through the development of multiservice contracts. Many companies out-sourced all their basic services, such as cleaning, security and heating, to one service provider. ISS believed that large multinationals like itself were well placed to provide this type of facilities management package and that the international nature of its operations could lead to worldwide contracts.

Andreassen was a hard act to follow, but in 1995 ISS seemed well placed to meet the challenges of business into the next century.

Doman Synthetic Fibres plc

PETER H. JONES

> Over the past few years, as the results of major companies continue to show,
> textiles — and fibres in particular — have continued to be a difficult market and,
> although last year's results were up on the previous year, they were still very poor
> compared to other industries.
>
> From an article in the textile trade press, July 1995

It was against this gloomy scene that Doman Synthetic Fibres (DSF) had
been trading. Appendices 1 and 2 give details of its financial results for
1993–5. DSF was a small but technically successful company by the
standards of the man-made fibre industry. Founded in 1936 by Wilfred
Doman, grandfather of the present managing director, Wendy Doman, the
company was heavily dependent on the sales of Britlene, which accounted
in 1995 for some 95 per cent of total sales. This heavy dependence on a single
product had been a familiar characteristic of the company for nearly twenty
years, first with Decalene and then since the late 1980s with Britlene. It was
only the patent protection on Britlene which had enabled DSF to survive the
turbulent and difficult situation of recent years.

Synthetic fibres as a whole represented some 40 per cent of the total UK
textile production, but within that, Teklatite fibres, of which Britlene was
the leading commercial type, accounted for only 3 per cent of total synthetic
fibre production. Britlene was used mainly in the manufacture of heavy-duty
clothing, although small quantities were used to produce industrial goods
such as tyre cord and industrial belting.

In 1994, however, the R&D department had developed a new product,
Britlon, which like Britlene was a Teklatite fibre. Britlon had all the
properties of Britlene but was superior in its heat-resistant qualities. It
was hoped that this additional property would open up new clothing uses

---

(e.g. a substitute for asbestos clothing, adding to night wear to improve its flame resistance), and new industrial uses in thermal and electrical insulation.

Wendy Doman expressed her attitude to Britlon:

> For too long we've relied on Britlene as our only product. It's been a faithful friend to us, but with patent protection running out in 1997, we must expand into something else and Britlon is the obvious candidate. We've got the technical experience in this area; it'll use our existing sales outlets; we could even convert some Britlene capacity to cut down on our capital costs and our agent has drawn up a watertight patent.

By late 1995, the major technical and engineering problems associated with bulk production of Britlon seemed to have been solved, but two years of the patent had already expired. Wendy Doman had set up a Capital Investment Working Party to put forward proposals on how the new product should be phased into the company's activities.

Production

The basic production method of Britlene and Britlon is similar to that of most man-made fibres. To make a man-made fibre, an oil-based organic chemical is polymerised (a process of joining several molecules into a long chain) in conditions of intense pressure and heat, often by the addition of a suitable catalyst. This polymerisation takes place in large autoclaves (an industrial pressure-cooker). The polymer is then extruded (similar to being forced through the rose of a garden watering can), rapidly cooled and then either spun on to cones and bobbins or collected in bales. The spun material is known as filament yarn; the bales are called staple fibre.

For Britlene, DSF had bought the polymer Polymutastine 15 as its raw material, which it chemically processed before the extrusion stage. However, for Britlon, it would be buying Hexatitanone and polymerising this organic chemical itself. The raw materials for Britlene and Britlon were produced at Teesside by ICI. For both raw materials, DSF took a low percentage of ICI's production and ICI was not a direct competitor of DSF in the fibre market.

Britlene facilities

Britlene was produced at three factories: Teesside, Bradford and Dumfries. The largest site was Teesside with three plants. There was one plant at each of the other two sites. The Teesside plant was next door to the raw material supplier and was not too far from the main markets in Lancashire and

Yorkshire. Bradford was close to the main customers, and as such proved a help for sorting out customer liaison on matters such as quality and rush orders. The factory at Dumfries dated back to the Second World War.

All five production plants, purchased over the last eight years, had a design capacity of 5.5 million lbs per annum of Britlene, independent of whether filament or staple was produced. However, after allowing for maintenance and an annual shutdown, expected output was 5 million lbs pa. Each plant was still in excellent order. Production was done on a 5 days per week, 24 hours per day (3 shifts) basis. There was no weekend production, although Saturday had been worked occasionally in times of high demand and the trade unions had agreed to allow members to work one Saturday per month at overtime rates.

Each plant employed about 72 people on production and 11 on maintenance. There was no difference in plant labour levels for the three shifts, but maintenance workers were mainly attached to the day shift.

Proposed Britlon facilities

The distinctive features of Britlon were created in the new polymerisation process. When asked to explain the differences between the two products, the research director, Roger Tillotson, used to draw the diagram shown in Figure 1.

> The key to Britlon is in the dotted boxes. What we'll need is a new polymerisation-cum-autoclave unit to replace the old autoclave-only unit. The extrusion unit for Britlon is basically the same as we are using for Britlene. By the time we've reached the molten polymer state, we've done the chemistry. Extrusion is just to get a storable and saleable product.

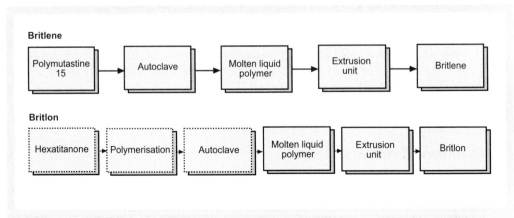

Figure 1   Production processes for Britlene and Britlon

Together with a major construction company, DSF had produced an acceptable plant design. A pilot plant was working very satisfactorily. This had provided valuable cost information. Jim Lewis explained:

> Our self-produced Britlon polymer should be about 10 per cent cheaper than Polymutastine 15, despite the extra costs of about 15 men on the new polymer plant and its extra depreciation. Of course, these are only estimated from our pilot plant experience.

Acquiring Britlon capacity

There were two ways of acquiring Britlon capacity. DSF could convert a Britlene plant, or it could construct an entirely new plant.

For a *conversion*, a new polymer unit would need to be constructed first; when complete it would be connected to the extrusion unit, which would require minor conversion taking three months. Instrumentation and start-up checks would then be performed for a further three months, during which time there could be roughly half capacity. This meant that from the completion of the new polymer unit, the whole plant would not be at full capacity for about six months. At least six months' planning and technical work was required by Alpens before construction could start.

Figure 2 sets out Alpens' estimated time scale for conversion of a Britlene unit to make Britlon.

A *newly constructed* plant would mean building both a polymerisation and an extrusion unit. Although no conversion was involved, such a plant could only operate at roughly half capacity for three months after start-up, while testing took place. Alpens' estimated time scale for a newly constructed unit is shown in Figure 3.

Preliminary market estimates for the new product made in 1995 indicated that an increase in the total number of plants might well be needed, especially if the predicted new industrial uses materialised. Wendy Doman, however, had gone on record saying:

Figure 2 Time scale for conversion of a Britlene unit

Figure 3   Time scale for a newly constructed unit

The creation of an entirely new site for operations would increase the complexities of multisite operation to an unacceptable level. Conversely, the complete closure of one of the three existing sites is, I consider, a waste of the human and physical resources that we have invested in that location. I believe expansion could take place at one, two or all of the existing sites.

Estimated Britlon capital costs

The estimated costs and stage payments required by Alpens for Britlon polymer plant and extrusion unit construction were as follows:

For a Britlon polymer plant	£3,000,000
For a new Britlon extrusion unit	£1,800,000
For conversion of a Britlene extrusion unit to Britlon	£600,000

Thus, the total cost of a new Britlon plant would be £4.8m and that of a conversion £3.6m.

The cost of the polymer plant was payable in three 6-monthly instalments of £1,000,000, the first being due one year after ordering. The cost of new extrusion units or conversions was due on completion.

Land for two more plants was already available at Teesside and for one more at Bradford, but any other developments would require an additional purchase.

Marketing

Since the mid-1970s, DSF had been a one-product company. Prior to the introduction of Britlene in 1987, the company had relied on the patent-protected product Decalene before moving into Teklatite fibres with Britlene. Experience with Decalene suggested that the new monopoly position held by Britlene could be eroded fairly rapidly once patent rights were removed at the end of 1997. One other UK manufacturer was producing Teklatite fibres and was thought to have plans to produce Britlene after that date.

Supply and demand — Britlene

Britlene had carved out a secure niche in the man-made fibre market. Sluggish world trade in textiles and fibres had curtailed growth since 1992, but DSF had been able to produce and sell at virtually full capacity during 1992–5. They had not needed, nor had they tried, to penetrate foreign markets, with the exception of a small effort in 1990.

Peter Moore, DSF's marketing director, was confident that Britlon would enable DSF to regain a 90 per cent share in the UK of Teklatite fibres within three years of its introduction. He felt confident in the future of Britlon:

> With the right kind of effort, I believe we can also generate sales of 5–10 million lbs of Britlon for use in thermal and electrical insulation. This is a mere flea-bite in comparison to sales of asbestos, glass and mica for this purpose.

Pricing

Since 1993, prices for Britlene had moved only marginally. DSF had not really tried to pass on cost increases, as in the depressed textile market Peter Moore felt that this would have been resisted by customers. DSF had opted to keep running at full capacity with lower sales margins rather than risk a drop in sales at higher prices. In 1995, the list price for Britlene was 98 pence/lb.

There was considerable uncertainty about the price which could be obtained for Britlon. For textile uses it might command a premium (estimated at 10–20 per cent) over Britlene due to its improved qualities, but Peter Moore felt that this premium could well be used up in trying to shift customers on to the new product. Additionally, the increased competition anticipated once Britlene patents expired was expected to depress Teklatite prices.

The industrial market was a great unknown. Rough-and-ready calculations suggested that a price between 100p and 120p/lb ought to put it on a competitive basis with existing materials. However, the conservative nature of manufacturers which would be taking a totally new material threw doubt on these estimates.

Selling and promotion

In 1995, promotion expenditure was £50,000, spent on sales literature (£13,000) and limited advertising in newspapers and trade journals (£37,000). This expenditure level was typical of the previous few years. For the launch of Britlene in 1987–9, the company had 'gone to town' by industry standards, spending £250,000, on press advertising (£80,000) and a joint promotion with selected customers (£170,000). This was equivalent to £550,000 at 1995 prices. This had enabled the rapid acceptance of Britlene by the textile industry.

Peter Moore felt that, once Britlon was established in the textile market, its promotional needs would be similar to those for Britlene, but to break into the new industrial markets would require a much greater promotional effort.

Personnel

In December 1995, DSF employed 556 people. Of these, weekly payroll employees, concerned mainly with production and maintenance, numbered 415. There were approximately 83 payroll employees at each of the five plants. The remaining 141 employees were monthly paid staff. Apart from supervisory production staff and commercial staff at the sales offices, all staff worked at the Teesside headquarters. Nearly all payroll employees in DSF were unionised. John Williams described the company's relationship with the union as 'good', although there was unease about possible plant closures. He was also concerned about poor labour relations in the construction industry, which he feared could delay building programmes and increase costs.

Unemployment

At all locations there was higher than average general unemployment, but the unemployment rate for skilled workers was lower at all sites. Supply of the particular skills DSF wanted was low, and only at Teesside would extra demand for skilled labour be readily met.

Finance

Financial performance

The financial performance of the company during 1993–5 had been a cause of real concern (see Appendix 1). Up to the early 1990s, the profit figures had been steady and a return on capital employed before tax of over 25 per cent was considered to be most satisfactory. As Mr Greenhaugh put it:

> In the late 1980s this company was considered a good investment by most analysts. We have always been financed solely by the share capital and retained earnings, and this, coupled with our patent protection, made us a safe bet. In the last two or

three years, however, things haven't looked so good. Our share price has dropped to a disturbing level, despite our continuing policy of maintaining the level of dividends. Our P/E ratio is now 7 and this is very disappointing. Investors are not sure where we are going as a company, but I hope the introduction of Britlon, if it comes through in time, will restore some of that confidence.

Raising finance

Mr Greenhaugh compared the 1995 situation to the similar position in 1987 when Britlene had been introduced to the market. Then, the initial development costs had been financed internally out of previous profits, as had about half the capital investment. Another £2.5m had been required from external sources. This was a substantial quantity for a company the size of DSF, but confidence had been high and a 1 for 1 rights issue at 62.5p had been fully subscribed. (The share price at the time had been standing at 68p.) Mr Greenhaugh wished that confidence in DSF was as buoyant in 1995 and the share price as strong.

Investment grants were part of the measures taken by successive governments to increase the level of investment undertaken in the economy, and also to direct this investment to areas of particular concern. As far as DSF was concerned, the latest measures might enable grants of up to about 20 per cent of the capital cost to be obtained at Teesside and Dumfries. The Bradford site was unlikely to attract a grant.

The first working party meeting

In setting up the working party to consider the Britlon case, Wendy Doman had picked one up-and-coming manager from each major function. It was clear that she considered this exercise as part of their development, and success could easily mean rapid advancement on the back of Britlon expansion. As they sat down for their first meeting, the members of the working party realised that they all had a personal as well as a professional interest in how the study progressed. They did, however, differ in their initial views on the pace of expansion into Britlon and on whether a price premium could be commanded for Britlon.

Les Hill, the most cautious of the team, was not convinced that there was a need to replace Britlene with Britlon at all. He argued that they ought to be able to ward off major potential inroads into their market share by reducing prices slightly, given that all their capital plant would be fully depreciated and any new entrants' capital would have to bear a depreciation cost.

Chris Henson disagreed, arguing that the new product would give benefits to most customers and that they knew about it anyway from samples available from the pilot plant built in 1994. She did, however, agree with Les's view that not all customers would transfer to Britlon, so she wanted to retain some Britlene capacity. She believed that it would be appropriate to enter the industrial market with Britlon in a small way.

Trevor Bryant's initial views were considerably more optimistic about Britlon. He could see no point in 'hanging on to a dying product', as he put it. He felt that nearly all customers would be forced to move to Britlon once the majority had. He also wanted to tackle the industrial market vigorously.

A computer simulation model had been commissioned to help the team forecast the future, given varying assumptions about future price levels, demand, etc. Key assumptions and corresponding results for the main protagonists' views are given in Appendix 3. In these results, it was assumed that a government grant of 20 per cent towards capital purchase would be available.

Appendix 1   Profit and loss summary, 1993–5 (£000s)

	1993		1994		1995
Sales					
Products	23,602		23,840		24,042
Licences	951		976		1,050
		24,553		24,816	25,092
Cost of goods sold					
Raw materials	6,086		6,592		7,230
Direct labour	6,391		6,940		7,521
Prod. overheads	2,177		2,602		2,869
Depreciation	700		700		700
		15,354		16,834	18,320
Gross profit		9,199		7,982	6,772
Other overheads					
Promotion and sales		374		395	402
Distribution		905		986	1,030
General admin.		2,738		3,009	3,320
R&D		890		1,250	950
		4,907		5,640	5,702
Operating profit		4,292		2,342	1,070
Interest payable		(189)		(231)	(240)
Net profit before tax		4,481		2,573	1,310
Corporation tax		1,814		1,146	704
Net profit after tax		2,667		1,427	606
Dividend declared		750		750	750
Retained earnings		1,917		677	(144)

Source: Company annual reports.

Appendix 2   Balance sheet at 31 December 1995 (£000s)

	Cost	Depreciation	Net
Fixed assets			
Freehold land and buildings	8,010	(150)	7,860
Teesside 5,210			
Bradford 1,605			
Dumfries 1,195			
Plant and machinery	8,790	(7,000)	1,790
Teesside 4,780			
Bradford 2,050			
Dumfries 1,960			
			9,650
Trade investments at cost			4,152
Working capital			
Current assets			
Work in progress and stock	2,720		
Debtors	2,980		
Cash	868		
		6,568	
Less current liabilities			
Creditors	2,307		
Taxation	436		
Dividend	510		
		3,253	
Net working capital			3,315
			17,117
Financed by:			
Share capital			5,000
Capital reserves			
Share premium		500	
Revaluation reserve		4,500	
			5,000
Retained earnings			
Balance at 31.12.94		7,261	
Retained profit 1995		(144)	
			7,117
			17,117

Source: Company annual report.

Appendix 3   Alternative strategies

Table A   Les Hill — consolidation strategy

	1996	1997	1998	1999	2000	2001
Assumptions						
Volume of Britlene (m lb)	25	25	24	22	22	22
Price of Britlene (£/lb)	1.00	1.00	0.95	0.95	0.95	0.95
Key results						
Net profit before tax (£m)	2.0	2.3	1.6	0.6	0.5	0.5
Annual trading cash flow (£m)	1.6	1.6	0.3	−0.3	0.1	0.2
Investment capital (£m)	−	−	−	−	−	−
Net cash flow (£m)	1.6	1.6	0.3	−0.3	0.1	0.2
Cumulative cash flow (£m, inc. trade investments)	6.6	8.2	8.5	8.2	8.3	8.5

Table B1   Chris Henson — 'two-horse strategy' — no price premium

	1996	1997	1998	1999	2000	2001
Assumptions						
Volume of Britlene (m lb)	25	25	20	15	10	10
Volume of Britlon (m lb)	−	−	5	11	17	20
Price of Britlene (£/lb)	1.00	1.00	0.95	0.95	0.95	0.95
Price of Britlon (£/lb)	−	−	0.95	0.95	1.00	1.00
Key results						
Net profit before tax (£m)	2.0	2.3	−1.3	−1.8	−0.4	1.9
Annual trading cash flow (£m)	1.6	0.6	−2.0	−0.9	0.6	3.2
Investment capital (£m)	−	1.6	4.5	5.1	1.3	−
Net cash flow (£m)	1.6	−1.0	−6.5	−6.5	−0.7	3.2
Cumulative cash flow (£m, inc. trade investments)*	6.6	5.5	−1.0	−7.0	−7.7	−4.5

*The lowest negative figure indicates the maximum cash injection needed by DSF to fund the strategy, in addition to selling its trade investments of £4.2m.

Table B2   Chris Henson — 'two-horse strategy' — with price premium

	1996	1997	1998	1999	2000	2001
Assumptions						
Volume of Britlene (m lb)	25	25	20	15	10	10
Volume of Britlon (m lb)	−	−	3	11	17	20
Price of Britlene (£/lb)	1.10	1.10	0.95	0.95	0.95	0.95
Price of Britlon (£/lb)	−	−	1.15	1.15	1.20	1.25
Key results						
Net profit before tax (£m)	4.5	5.0	−0.5	0.6	3.4	7.5
Annual trading cash flow (£m)	3.8	2.6	−2.7	1.3	4.0	6.9
Investment capital (£m)	−	1.6	4.5	5.1	1.3	−
Net cash flow (£m)	3.8	1.0	−7.2	−3.8	2.7	6.9
Cumulative cash flow (£m, inc. trade investments)*	8.8	9.8	2.6	−1.2	1.5	8.4

*The lowest negative figure indicates the maximum cash injection needed by DSF to fund the strategy, in addition to selling its trade investments of £4.2m.

Table C1   Trevor Bryant — 'go for it' — no price premium

	1996	1997	1998	1999	2000	2001
Assumptions						
Volume of Britlene (m lb)	25	25	16	5	—	—
Volume of Britlon (m lb)	—	—	9	22	33	40
Price of Britlene (£/lb)	1.00	1.00	0.95	0.95	0.90	0.90
Price of Britlon (£/lb)	—	—	0.95	0.95	1.00	1.00
Key results						
Net profit before tax (£m)	2.0	1.7	−3.8	−5.3	−1.8	1.7
Annual trading cash flow (£m)	1.6	1.0	−1.9	−2.9	−1.1	4.4
Investment capital (£m)	—	4.8	9.6	8.0	3.5	—
Net cash flow (£m)	1.6	−3.8	−11.5	−10.9	−4.6	4.4
Cumulative cash flow (£m, inc. trade investments)*	6.6	2.8	−8.7	−19.6	−24.3	−19.9

*The lowest negative figure indicates the maximum cash injection needed by DSF to fund the strategy, in addition to selling its trade investments of £4.2m.

Table C2   Trevor Bryant — 'go for it' — with price premium

	1996	1997	1998	1999	2000	2001
Assumptions						
Volume of Britlene (m lb)	25	25	16	5	—	—
Volume of Britlon (m lb)	—	—	9	22	33	40
Price of Britlene (£/lb)	1.1	1.1	0.95	0.95	0.9	0.9
Price of Britlon (£/lb)	—	—	1.15	1.15	1.2	1.25
Key results						
Net profit before tax (£m)	4.4	4.4	−1.8	−0.6	5.5	12.9
Annual trading cash flow (£m)	3.8	2.0	−1.5	1.5	5.8	12.5
Investment capital (£m)	—	4.8	9.6	8.0	3.5	—
Net cash flow (£m)	3.8	−2.8	−11.1	−6.5	2.3	12.5
Cumulative cash flow (£m, inc. trade investments)*	8.8	6.0	−5.1	−11.6	−9.3	3.2

*The lowest negative figure indicates the maximum cash injection needed by DSF to fund the strategy, in addition to selling its trade investments of £4.2m.

The Royal Alexandra Hospital

SANDRA HILL

Background

The Royal Alexandra Hospital (RAH), a district general hospital in Paisley, opened to the first patients in October 1986 and after a period of six months, 880 of the 950 bed capacity was opened. In line with the Griffiths Inquiry into the management and organisation of the National Health Service (NHS) in 1983, the concept of general management was introduced to the hospital and, as a result, Martin Hill was appointed as the first general manager of the General Acute and Maternity Services Unit at the hospital in 1987. This post was accountable to the Health Board and, unlike previous administrators' posts, was responsible for the management of all of the service, including doctors and other professional and clinical staff.

The concept of the district general hospital had been largely born out of a National Health Service which gave priority to hospital provision accessible to local people. The RAH came on stream towards the end of a 25-year period of development of such hospitals throughout Britain. Long before its opening, however, concerns were being raised throughout the UK about the cost of the public sector, and from its beginning, the RAH had to fight hard for resources to operate in competition with the more established and politically stronger institutions in the west of Scotland. It did, however, benefit from being a new institution less burdened with restrictive trade practices, which allowed industrial relations within the hospital to be conducted with fewer problems than might otherwise have been the case.

This case study was prepared by Sandra Hill, Glasgow Caledonian University, with the assistance of Martin Hill, chief executive of the Royal Alexandra Hospital. It is intended as a basis for class discussion and not as an illustration of either good or bad management practice. © Sandra Hill, 1996.

In order to address concerns over the organisation of the health service, the government focused attention initially on the management of the service in the form of the Griffiths Inquiry of 1983. The most fundamental impact of government policy affecting the hospital came in the wake of the Thatcher government's reforms, heralded in its White Paper, *Working For Patients*, published in January 1989.

The reforms brought about three major changes for the RAH:

- The creation of an internal market and the distancing of the Health Board through the separation of the purchaser and provider functions.
- The contracting process, resulting in hospitals no longer receiving budgets based on what was spent, but contract income in return for the delivery of specified patient services.
- The opportunity for the RAH to become a self-governing Trust.

Recent years have seen public services come under closer and closer scrutiny to ensure value for money, and this has led to significant differentiation in the resourcing of different parts of the NHS. As community and primary care services were seen to be in need of development, the general acute hospital sector came under increasing pressure to shift resources to facilitate the process. As demand for hospital care continued to grow and the resources available began to reduce in real terms, the policy of 'more for less' provided a new challenge for the RAH. Coping successfully with the pressures which arose out of the inexorable drive for efficiency year after year highlighted the need for particularly effective management and a different form of partnership between clinicians and managers. The involvement of the local community was also seen as essential to bring about the culture changes.

Decision to move to Trust status

As the implications of the reforms became clearer, the Secretary of State for Health asked Health Boards to discuss the issue of Trust status with hospital doctors in order to elicit any interest, but with very little success. It was not until after the general election in April 1992, which returned the Conservative government for a further term, that the matter was debated by the Corporate Management Team (CMT) of the RAH and serious consideration was for the first time given to the RAH applying for Trust status.

Two important factors influenced the outcome and produced unanimous support among the CMT in favour of the RAH preparing an application for Trust status.

- The hospital was still expanding the volume of its patient treatment well above the national average and, if the reforms' promise of 'money following patients' was to happen, then a Trust might be in a stronger negotiating position to secure the funds.

- The three closest competitors (other large acute hospitals within a 20 mile radius) were applying for Trust status and, if a competitive market was allowed to develop, the RAH needed to be able to respond appropriately, unfettered by a Health Board's management agenda, driven by different priorities.

Although the CMT was unanimous in its view that Trust status was the right step to take to secure the future of the hospital in the longer term, it was also well known that there was not the same support among the community and even among many of the hospital staff. Unlike England and Wales, Scotland (and particularly the west of Scotland) was predominantly represented by Labour MPs and Labour-dominated local government. The Trust movement was therefore slower in gathering momentum in that part of the country and the RAH encountered considerable opposition when the hospitals' Corporate Management Team decided to apply to the Scottish Office for self-governing status. Trust status was granted in shadow form from 1 January 1993 and with full effect from 1 April 1993.

Fears about the move mainly centred around privatisation and the reduction of local accountability. The staff's main fear was that they would lose the protection of nationally negotiated terms and conditions of service, since the Trust would have the power to determine pay and conditions locally.

A campaign was launched by the unit general manager and two of his supporting managers to educate staff and the public through staff magazines, newspaper articles and a large number of meetings both within and outside the hospital.

The Trust Board

The Royal Alexandra Hospital NHS Trust came into being in shadow form with the appointment of a part-time non-executive chairman, closely followed by the appointment of five non-executive directors. These appointments were made by the Secretary of State for Scotland following a nomination process which included widespread public advertisement. Nevertheless, the process was to engender fierce political opposition a few years later in the war against quangos.[1]

The first task of the new shadow board was to appoint a chief executive. They had the options of interviewing and appointing the incumbent unit general manager or to marketing the post publicly. In this case Martin Hill,

---

[1] Quango stands for 'quasi-autonomous non-governmental organisation'.

the unit general manager, was appointed without the post being advertised. The next task was for the chief executive and shadow Trust Board to appoint the other four executive directors. In the event, the existing director of nursing was confirmed, both the directors of finance and human resources were external appointments from industry in England, and the medical director was 'headhunted' from the post of director of health promotion at a neighbouring Health Board. Also in attendance at Trust Board meetings (although not a voting member) was the board secretary/director of services. The board secretary, the director of nursing and the chief executive were the only members of an eleven-strong board with any experience or knowledge of the RAH (Appendix 1).

The cost of the Trust Board was a new cost, representing an expensive overhead which clearly had to demonstrate its value in order to justify itself in the face of mounting attacks by the government on public spending.

While the non-executive directors, including the chairman, were additional to the previous management structure, the executive directors replaced previous senior managers. It was clear that the new director posts would require to function at a higher strategic level than the posts which they replaced, and the significant change at the top of the management structure was thereby justified.

Roles and responsibilities

For the first time, the RAH was to be directly responsible to the Secretary of State and accountable for its own future, albeit within a framework of powers for Trusts which subsequently reduced, and constraints which increased, as time went by.

The new Trust Board had three distinct areas of responsibility:

▪ Shaping the strategic direction of the organisation and overseeing its management.
▪ Developing relationships with professionals while challenging their advice.
▪ Building a partnership with the community.

Although the chief executive and the director of nursing had, to a limited extent, the advantage of development specifically geared towards preparation for Trust status, training for the other directors was superficial and occurred after the event. The preparation of chairmen and non-executive directors was particularly poor, representing little more than single-day induction programmes arranged by the Management Executive (ME) of the National Health Service In Scotland (NHSIS). The RAH had the added challenge of having two directors from industries (brewing and confectionery) unrelated to hospitals or the health service, but felt confident that the experience of these individuals in commercial accounting and industrial relations would be highly beneficial to the Trust in its formative years. Appendix 1 shows the management structure in 1996.

The new strategic context within which Trusts were now operating had been described superficially in the ME of NHSIS guidance and tailored to individual Trusts in their applications for Trust status. However, questions such as whether a market in health would develop and how free Trusts would really be to determine their own futures remained largely unanswered. The new role for a Trust Board to shape the strategic direction for the organisation required insight, robust information and a not inconsiderable amount of crystal ball gazing. It also required a reinvention of local priorities and aims in keeping with the new Trust Board and emerging national policy considerations. In the early stages, between 1993 and 1994, the Trust Board tended to approach strategic issues individually and to determine direction on the basis of a relatively short time frame, but it soon realised that a much longer-term vision had to be created to give cohesive form to its actions and confidence to its stakeholders. All of this was happening as many of the reforms increasingly came under political attack from all sides.

Another new and, to some, disconcerting aspect of the board was the existence of non-executive members who were expected to challenge the views, advice and pressure which came from both health care professionals and professional managers. Their role was to ensure common sense and decisions which could justifiably be represented as being in the best interests of the community, not merely in pursuit of professional or managerial aggrandisement. The chairman and chief executive were keen to develop the Trust Board in its new role and went to some lengths to encourage necessary challenge by, and involvement of, the non-executive directors. Martin Hill commented:

> It is very important for building public confidence that these new players are seen to involve themselves in the running of the hospital and that they can represent the interests in the local community.

By 1993 the RAH had existed in the life of its community for seven years, but the RAH NHS Trust was new and threatening, born out of reforms opposed by the majority of local people. Its challenge was to establish an identity which would be understood and trusted. This was not easy given the lack of understanding from within the Trust, the political 'shifting sands' and the increasingly tough policy constraints imposed from the centre. Considerable effort had gone into staff and public education in the lead-up to Trust status: the chief executive, director of nursing and director of services had addressed countless staff and public meetings, and the application for Trust status had been published and circulated widely.

Changes for staff

On 1 April 1993, all staff employed within the RAH, together with certain other staff employed in central services, were transferred to the new Trust. TUPE[2] rules applied in the shift. Staff concerns at the time were mainly related to changes in their terms and conditions of service, since one of the much vaunted freedoms of the new Trusts was the ability to employ staff on different terms and conditions. Since TUPE requirements afforded protection upon transfer for the existing staff, and given the lack of experience of Trusts in formulating local pay strategies, this freedom was always going to take time to be fully exercised. Attempts to move away from national pay bargaining began in 1995, but they were not helped by central intervention in England, which acted in response to vociferous union opposition to local pay bargaining and made impossible any substantial moves away from national bargaining. The result by the end of 1995 was that local pay bargaining at Trust level was arguably more symbolic than real.

Innovations in training and in the involvement of staff in new styles of management began to emerge, and were generally welcomed by staff given the pace of change across the NHS. Management roles of clinical directors were extended, and Trusts were seen to invest more heavily in training and development than had been the case by Health Boards. New training initiatives included customer awareness training for all front-line staff, training in new technology, objective setting and performance appraisal, and the development of problem-solving skills required under the Continuous Improvement Programme.

On the down side, tighter money and an increasing pace of change were seen to be the fault of these new NHS Trusts, which increased the concerns and affected the morale of staff, many of whom were used to an NHS which had expanded consistently and existed without serious disruption for 45 years.

Purchasers

Health Boards

As soon as the Trust was established, the RAH ceased to be managerially or organisationally part of the Argyll and Clyde Health Board. The relationship between the two bodies became a contractual one of purchaser and supplier. Some 5 per cent of the patients treated at the RAH were residents of two other Health Boards (Greater Glasgow, and

---

[2] Transfer of Undertakings (Protection of Employment) regulations.

Ayrshire and Arran) and contracts had also to be struck with them to ensure continuity of income to the Trust (Appendix 2). The purchasing base has widened slightly since 1993 with the emergence of GP fundholders, although in income terms they still represent less than 1 per cent of the Trust's total business. It was clear, therefore, that the Argyll and Clyde Health Board was strategically essential to the survival of the Trust, as indeed the RAH was an essential provider to Argyll and Clyde. Nevertheless, misunderstandings and macho management, together with a particularly tight financial regime in the Trust's first year, made the daunting task of establishing a new 'business' and mutually dependent positive relationships an even harder one.

Health Boards had enjoyed a very clear line management relationship with hospitals ever since their establishment in 1974, and had seen their primary task as that of provider of hospital and other health services. A number of Health Boards were comfortable with the command and control style of management, and since the majority of senior people at Health Boards remained unchanged post-reforms, it was, and in some instances still is, difficult for them to adjust to a new type of relationship with the Trusts, while developing their new roles as commissioner (not provider) of health services and assessor of the population's needs.

General Practitioner (GP) fundholders

The concept of GP fundholding is to involve GPs more in the planning of services provided to their patients, and to give them responsibility for their referral decisions. Like hospital Trusts, this has been slow to take off in many parts of Scotland, and even now (early 1996) there are no GP fundholders practising within the RAH's local catchment district.

Experience elsewhere was showing that GPs had great influence over purchasing arrangements in hospitals, by fundholders switching contracts for patient services away from poor-performing hospitals to those offering easier or quicker access. Prices also began to play a part in influencing fundholders' referral patterns.

In the case of the RAH, GP fundholders from Argyll and Dumbarton have referred small but increasing numbers of patients to the RAH rather than to the traditional referral hospitals in Glasgow. To date, GP fundholders have not created major changes in the Argyll and Clyde area, partly because they are few in number and they are limited in what the fundholding scheme allows them to purchase. Nevertheless, there are significant transaction costs involved in fundholding contract negotiation, patient tracking and billing, which add yet another strain on hospital information and financial management systems.

Increasing financial pressures

Until the 1980s, hospital budgets had generally been determined on the basis of what had been spent the previous year, what would be required in addition to cover pay and price inflation, and the funding requirements of anticipated developments. This had created financial demands on a public purse which became less and less sustainable. Although the proportion of GDP devoted to health in the UK was relatively well contained compared with other developed countries, the government of the day decided that tighter control was necessary. This was one of the first justifications for the purchaser/provider split, and contracts were seen as the vehicle for delivering tighter control on expenditure. Trusts were now required to deliver agreed levels of service in return for an income which is negotiated each year with Health Boards. The latter have the objective of reducing hospital expenditure at the same time as driving up productivity.

Health Boards were also set efficiency savings targets by the ME which they generally imposed upon Trusts without discrimination or regard to relative efficiency. Savings targets for the RAH between 1993 and 1996 are shown in Table 1.

This meant that, in the case of the RAH, which was already a lower-cost hospital than its neighbours (see Appendix 3), it suffered the imposition of efficiency targets which were more difficult to achieve. This scenario also demonstrated the absence of any kind of true market for hospital services, and it was not until later in 1995 that strategic shifts in the purchasing pattern for services were seen.

Alongside the changes in the organisation, several strategic decisions were made to secure, and in some cases develop, the RAH's position as the major provider of acute care in the locality.

Increasing activity

With the RAH still being a relatively new hospital, the number of patients being treated had grown at a rate greater than the national average. This, allied to changes in technology and medical techniques, led to total in-patient numbers growing by 50 per cent in the hospital's first eight years. While some of this additional activity was at the expense of Glasgow

Table 1   RAH savings targets

1993/4	1%	£430,000
1994/5	1.5%	£700,000
1995/6	2.75%	£1,250,000

hospitals, much was natural growth in demand, for which funding did not exist within the totality of NHS resources. Funding or income did not, therefore, grow at the same rate.

Even more spectacular growth was seen in day surgery and day case attendance, which increased fivefold during the same period (see Appendix 4).

It was believed that the share of patient hospitalisation across the local population was steadily increasing at the RAH compared with the Glasgow hospitals. By 1995 market share had stabilised and, in one speciality in particular, urology, it had begun to decline because of the hospital's inability to meet the demand of local GPs. It was clear by then that the principle of money following patients applied only within the available resources and within the contract boundaries, but did not cater for the latent demand that increased access to local service produced. The strategy of the RAH striving to increase market share was therefore beginning to be questioned as a viable strategy, given the immaturity of the market and the pressure on Health Boards to reduce acute hospital investment. Very limited spare capacity and generally lower costs meant that the RAH had to recognise its limitations within a system which was becoming increasingly distant from that of a free market.

Expanding the range of services

By 1992 specialist services had expanded to include urology, cardiology, endocrinology, clinical haematology and infertility services. Demand for these services had largely come from local GPs, although certain ones had developed as particular interests of new consultants. The availability of these new services also brought about problems for the hospital in meeting latent demand, such as in the case of urology where management by contract created particular difficulties for the speciality early in the life of the Trust. A new specialist urology service had been established at RAH at a pre-planned and agreed level. However, the number of patients referred by their GPs for this service very quickly outstripped the capacity of the service and huge waiting lists began to develop. The Health Board was neither convinced nor equipped to support additional services and it took eighteen months from when the problem first appeared for the board to identify additional contract income. During that time, waiting lists had grown and GPs, impatient with the local service, had begun referring back to the traditional hospitals in Glasgow. This was a good example of the Trust failing to convince its major purchaser of the need to act quickly and a major purchaser being slow to respond to the very obvious demands of its population.

Increasing the geographic market

The original intention of the RAH was to serve the local population of Renfrew local government district (pop. 201,000). However, the reforms are changing the nature of district general hospitals, and local markets are increasingly being served by hospitals able to offer shorter waiting times. The RAH saw an opportunity to compete for work in neighbouring districts and began to focus on Argyll and Dumbarton, which were part of the same Health Board area, but did not have the same range or as well-developed local services. A number of general hospital services were provided to Argyll and Dumbarton by teaching hospitals in Glasgow, which now found themselves competing with the RAH to provide the services. In 1993, a large and well-respected teaching hospital in Glasgow lost the contract for hospital ophthalmology services in Argyll and Dumbarton to the RAH. A similar but more extensive competitive tendering situation applied to orthopaedic services for Argyll and Dumbarton in 1995, which the RAH won against fierce competition from two larger Glasgow hospitals. The total cost of the development to Argyll and Clyde Health Board was around £1.6m, of which more than half was awarded to the RAH as the base hospital.

Relationship with the Management Executive

Around 1990, central government responsibility for the NHS in Scotland was devolved to the ME, consisting largely of civil servants, but over the years featuring managers from industry and the NHS itself. Health Boards are managerially responsible to the ME in Edinburgh and there is a clear line of accountability for delivering NHS reforms. NHS Trusts were new organisations, ostensibly autonomous, but with very strict financial accountability to the ME. This was exercised through detailed financial monitoring returns submitted by Trusts every month, and through Trust Boards being required to achieve government-dictated financial objectives; that is:

- 6 per cent return on assets.
- External financing limits.
- Break even.

In fact, the ME monitored and managed Trusts at arm's length, becoming involved only to ensure that business plans and capital investment proposals were in line with national strategy or when Trusts got into financial difficulties. Nonetheless, the ME's responsibility for servicing and protecting ministers ensured close interest in Trust affairs when featured in parliamentary questions or other public controversy. Such is the network of meetings and working groups that the ME is also effective at influencing and enforcing national policies designed to support the NHS reforms.

Managing the changes

Accountability review

The chief executive developed the process which became known as 'accountability review' to monitor and review the progress and achievements of clinical directorates. Standard review documentation contains all of the business plan objectives, including activity targets, financial budgets and other performance indicators. These are formally reviewed once a quarter in meetings which end with both the clinical director and the chief executive commenting on the progress achieved, and highlighting both the positive and negative features of the preceding three months. This is an essential monitoring and management tool which reinforces the responsibility of the clinical directorate to achieve previously agreed objectives and the importance of appropriate support from top management.

Business planning

Early attempts at business planning tended to resemble the production of 'wish lists', with little understanding of the economic implications of what was being sought or whose responsibility it was to pay for them. They also tended to be set in very short time frames, lacking in strategic direction. In recent years, business plans from Trusts have improved and, in the case of the RAH, an increasing number of longer-term strategic aims have appeared.

The process of business planning within the Trust involves directorates and departments fully, and can therefore be described as 'bottom up'. At the same time, the Trust Board has found increasing appetite to identify strategic direction, a difficult task given the radically changing nature of health care provision in today's NHS.

Relationships with clinical directors and executive directors

Clinical directors had been appointed in 1991, well before the emergence of the Trust, and were directly accountable to the unit general manager. After April 1993, they found themselves answering to the new executive director post of medical director, who in turn was responsible to the chief executive. Since the roles of the chief executive and medical director were new and not well understood, there was initially some resentment by clinical directors, who felt that their role had been devalued. This resentment was fuelled by the fact that, in the first year of the Trust, Martin Hill as chief executive was less visible within directorates than had been Martin Hill as unit general manager. It was not until the Trust's second year that the executive director team began to operate effectively at a strategic level and were able to support clinical directors, enabling greater devolution of responsibility: for example, the full Corporate Management Team, including all clinical directors, developed the budget allocation process which was to shape directorates' finances in the following year.

Objective setting and review

In 1993 the NHS performance appraisal system covered a relatively small number of managers and was seen as a paper-heavy, bureaucratic system which was not wholly relevant to the tasks required of hospital managers. This was reinvented over the following three years, and is to be relaunched with a much clearer understanding and linkage between individual objectives and corporate goals. Although directorate objectives flowed from the business plan, there was not the same relationship between individuals' objectives and the requirements of their department. Nonetheless, some such process was regarded as essential to make explicit and clarify the organisation's expectations of the individual, and to form the basis of targeted developments. As Martin Hill said: 'There is nothing better than having a discipline to ensure that staff and their managers communicate, and that managers acknowledge people doing things right.'

Continuous Improvement Programme (CIP)

The concept of continuous improvement is not new to many successful service-orientated organisations. In many senses, however, it was quite alien to the NHS, which is essentially a centralist bureaucratic organisation that had done little until recently to encourage local responsibility and differentiation.

The CIP model developed by the RAH was based on a tried and tested method adopted by other sectors, and adapted to meet the specific needs of the hospital. Initially, consultancy support was used for some of the training awareness and support but, after the first year (1993–4), there was sufficient momentum driven by the chief executive to ensure over a dozen projects by the end of 1994. These projects included:

- Out-of-hours treatment for patients admitted with fractured neck or femur.
- Waiting lists review.
- Marketing the Trust for future staff recruitment.
- Appropriateness of uniform design.
- Formal support structure for junior doctors.

By the end of 1995, over 40 projects were either completed or under way. The main feature of this programme stressed by the chief executive was that the project teams were to be populated and driven by staff themselves, working in multidisciplinary groups across the organisation to solve problems and improve processes which the traditional management system was failing to address. It is believed that this has had a positive effect on staff morale. Martin Hill believes that 'It is a great way of getting staff involved and of teaching them problem-solving skills that will be useful to them back in their departments.'

Management styles

Martin Hill decided that he wanted an organisation which was sharing the responsibility for success as well as failure, and wanted to move away from tight command and control styles of management. However, hindsight showed that the tribal culture of the NHS was not ready for the level of participative management which he aimed for. A number of departments refused to accept the rigours of budgetary control, and the reins had to be pulled in to ensure that the Trust met its financial objectives by the end of the first year.

This strengthened his resolve to develop the CIP as a vehicle for involving staff in the management of their own areas and of spreading the understanding of resource management as a concept. It has taken two years to see any real 'buy in' of doctors into the process. On a personal level, Martin Hill realised that he had become too distant from the wards and departments, and set about increasing his visibility and awareness by setting aside a regular half-day each week away from his office to renew his contact with staff other than managers and consultants.

January 1996

By the beginning of 1996, the pressures and challenges of tight money and ever-increasing demand were being joined by increasingly political considerations as parties vied for support in the run-up to the next general election. The Trust Board had embarked on yet another strategic review, this time at least informed by a more communicative purchaser. Some of the clouds which previously obscured the horizon were beginning to clear, but the hard decisions were being taken. Martin Hill said:

> Life in the NHS has not been easy in recent years, but the challenges are being recognised by more and more professional groups. Patients are benefiting from faster treatment and better services, and the community as a whole is enjoying better value for money. However, the culture change happening within the service is yet to be recognised outside. As a political football the NHS will never be portrayed accurately, nor its difficulties dispassionately considered.

Appendix 1 Royal Alexandra Hospital management structure (1996)

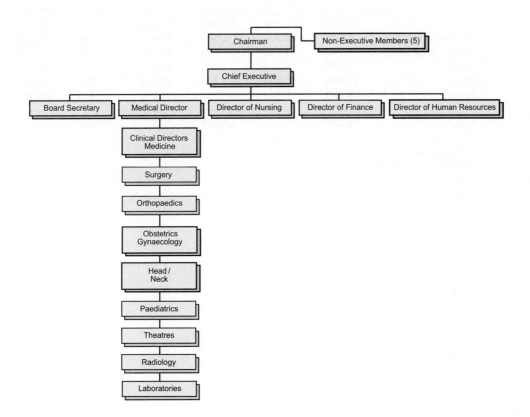

Appendix 2   Royal Alexandra Hospital Trust income, 1993–6

	1993/4 (£000s)		1994/5 (£000s)		1995/6 — projected (£000s)	
Argyll and Clyde	37,743	(77.3%)	38,290	(75.6%)	38,531	(76.2%)
Greater Glasgow	636	(1.3%)	642	(1.3%)	674	(1.3%)
Ayrshire and Arran	778	(1.6%)	813	(1.6%)	754	(1.5%)
GPFH[1]	97	(0.2%)	118	(0.2%)	125	(0.2%)
ECR[2]	131	(0.3%)	170	(0.3%)	180	(0.4%)
Other	9,442	(19.3%)	10,620	(21.0%)	10,324	(20.4%)
Total	48,827		50,653		50,588	

[1] GP fundholders.
[2] Extra-contractual referral.

Appendix 3   Royal Alexandra Hospital published in-patient costs per case for selected specialities and whole hospital (£)

	1990/1[1]		1991/2		1992/3		1993/4		1994/5	
	RAH	SA	RAH	SA	RAH	SA	RAH	SA	RAH	SA
General medicine	471	541	775	1,170	779	1,246	898	1,238	946	1,202
General surgery	891	549	1,222	1,158	1,206	1,231	1,381	1,242	2,098	1,822
Orthopaedics	728	669	1,883	1,615	1,786	1,672	1,786	1,766	2,098	1,822
Ophthalmology	584	617	960	1,058	861	1,047	950	1,125	958	1,137
All specialities[2]	968	1,008	1,256	1,336	1,275	1,466	899	1,451	1,013	1,333

SA = Scottish average.

[1] 1990/1 specialities are direct patient care and staff costs only. All other costs are total costs, including indirect (allocated) costs.

[2] RAH total costs are compared against all similar (Group 02) hospitals, except for 1994/5, which compares RAH with all Scottish Acute Trusts.

Appendix 4   Royal Alexandra Hospital in-patients and day cases for selected specialities and whole hospital (discharges, deaths and transfers out)

	1990/1		1991/2		1992/3		1993/4		1994/5	
	IP	DC	IP	DC	IP	DC	IP	DC	IP	DC
General medicine	5,451	n/a	7,170	n/a	7,976	1,011	7,566	1,626	7,595	2,010
General surgery	4,326	n/a	4,493	n/a	5,115	1,831	5,208	2,073	5,271	2,596
Orthopaedics	1,784	n/a	1,821	n/a	1,877	240	1,837	284	1,757	313
Ophthalmology	938	n/a	1,099	n/a	1,096	247	1,153	374	1,056	553
All acute specialties	23,832	4,212	25,259	7,365	26,730	8,971	28,387	10,088	28,050	13,362

IP = In-patients.
DC = Day cases.
n/a = Not available.

Source: Scottish Health Service Costs Books and RAH Annual Report.

The United Nations Development Programme

LYNN WALLIS and GERRY JOHNSON

Introduction

Global changes in the past 10–15 years have, more than ever, made it apparent that no country can live in isolation from the rest of the world. Exciting changes in technology, such as fax machines, electronic mail and the Internet, have reinforced the possibilities for individuals to understand issues independent of their governments, resulting in increased pressure for greater democracy throughout the world. Changes in climate patterns have led to the realisation by governments and individuals alike that the actions of people in countries other than their own can dramatically impact on the economies and daily lives of their countries. The example of the progress made by the East Asian 'tigers' in modernising their economies has brought home to the world at large the challenges of a global economy. There is also recognition that the pressure of populations growing too rapidly leads to economic and social unrest, and ultimately results in more illegal immigrants and refugees, and the need for greater levels of humanitarian and emergency relief.

These global changes have significantly affected the role of the United Nations (UN), and led to much speculation and many public pronouncements throughout the 50th anniversary celebrations which took place in 1995. The member states are clear in their stated belief that the UN is an essential element in the process of ensuring world peace and development. They are equally clear that this must be achieved through a more cost-effective and better-managed organisation. This led to significant cutbacks in funding and the need to implement more modern management practices to ensure efficiency, effectiveness and improved accountability.

What is the United Nations Development Programme (UNDP)?

Within the UN system, UNDP, which was created during the 1960s, has been the largest funding agency for technical assistance to the developing world. This funding takes the form of grants, not loans, and relates to developing the capacity of people, and not the provision of infrastructure such as dams, roads, bridges and buildings. By 1996, UNDP was working in 175 developing countries, spending upwards of US$1.8 billion annually.

UNDP aims to help countries achieve sustainable human development with an overriding focus on poverty elimination. Programmes include the following activities:

- In China, UNDP was supporting a project to generate income-earning opportunities for rural villagers, and to bolster health and education services.
- In Namibia, UNDP was assisting in a national housing project that enables the poor to build their own home or improve existing ones.
- In El Salvador, about 7,000 people in rural areas were benefiting from a UNDP-supported project to teach environmentally sustainable agricultural techniques to small-scale farmers and to give a boost to rural entrepreneurs.

How are projects initiated?

Projects are initiated by UNDP in conjunction with the recipient country's government on the basis of an overall Country Co-operation Framework, which outlines the areas of focus for UNDP-supported activities. UNDP approves, monitors and reviews all projects, which are increasingly nationally executed, i.e. a national institution assumes responsibility for the management of each project. In the cases where national execution is not possible, projects are executed by UN specialised agencies such as the Food and Agriculture Organisation (FAO), the UN Office for Project Services (UNOPS) and the World Health Organisation (WHO).

How is UNDP funded?

Funding for UNDP activities is provided by countries on a voluntary basis. Slightly more than 50 per cent of annual spending is for core activities, i.e.

those activities that fall within a general set of criteria established to address issues such as poverty eradication, job creation and social development; public sector reform and assistance in establishing democratic systems and processes; the advancement of women as a means of ensuring more effective development; and working to sustain the environment. Pledges are made annually for core funds towards a three-year rolling plan, and allocations to each country are established on the basis of an agreed formula which takes account of economic and social factors. In 1995, the allocation process was modified to include, for the first time, performance criteria in the allocation formula.

The balance of annual spending addresses similar issues, but is provided by donors through trust funds with more specific guidelines as to its use and cost sharing, i.e. where UNDP manages funds for governments and/or organisations such as the World Bank.

All recipient countries are required, depending on their economic status, to partially or fully fund the local costs within their countries. They are also encouraged to contribute to the annual funding of UNDP activities as a reflection of their commitment to the organisation. In addition, many countries, particularly in Latin and Central America, Eastern Europe and the Arab States, are undertaking projects on a cost-sharing basis with UNDP.

How is UNDP structured?

UNDP is based in New York and has a network of 131 offices working with 175 developing countries. The organisation is headed by the administrator, appointed by the UN secretary-general and responsible to a 36-member executive board comprising representatives of both donor and recipient countries. James Gustave Speth, an American, was appointed to the position in mid-1993. The executive committee, which is chaired by the administrator and consists of the associate administrator and all heads of bureaux, is the most senior body for co-ordination, control and decision making in the management of UNDP.

In 1996, headquarters' operations were organised into five geographic bureaux (Africa; Asia and Pacific; Arab States; Eastern Europe and the former Soviet Union; and Latin America and the Caribbean) and three service bureaux (Policy and Programme Support; Resources and External Affairs; and Finance and Administration). Each country office was headed by a UNDP resident representative. Primarily, they reported to the heads of the geographic bureaux, but they were considered to be the representatives of the administrator. In addition, the UNDP resident representative was in most cases the UN resident co-ordinator for technical assistance, an appointment made by the UN secretary-general. In this capacity, he or she had overall responsibility for ensuring that, wherever possible, there was co-ordination between the UN-funded activities within the country.

UNDP is a multicultured organisation with staff from all donor and recipient countries. The administrator had always come from a donor country and the associate administrator from a recipient country. The heads of the geographic bureaux were appointed from within their region; considerable effort was made to ensure that UNDP staffing reflected a reasonable geographic balance. UNDP is, above all, a country-based organisation with 85 per cent of its staff living and working in programme countries.

Staffing and the assignment of staff within UNDP was made more difficult by the complexities of the compensation and benefits system, and the need to ensure that each UNDP office could operate effectively in a fashion reflecting the neutrality of the UN system. Staff hired into the UN system are granted either an international or a local contract. UNDP staff on an international contract rotated between countries every four or five years, and the head of each country office was always selected from the international staff group as a means of ensuring neutrality. Locally hired staff did not rotate between countries, thus ensuring continuity within each country office. In addition, they provided a pool of qualified resources for recruitment of international staff.

The challenges facing UNDP

When James Speth took the helm as UNDP administrator in 1993, he found an organisation that was facing many challenges. While financial pressures, due to cuts in core funding, were a key issue compelling the organisation to make changes, he found that the organisation was also looking at a number of other substantive issues:

- Donor attention and funding were being diverted from development to emergency, humanitarian and peace-keeping activities. Peace-keeping operations spent nearly four times as much in the period 1990–5 as they had in the previous 45 years. Spending on refugees and internally displaced persons tripled in the period 1990–3, from US$500 million annually to US$1.5 billion.
- Development activities, with their longer-term objectives, were finding it significantly more difficult to get the attention of the world media, which increasingly placed emphasis on reporting daily crises and disasters.
- Questions were being raised by most donor countries as to the effectiveness of multilateral development assistance.

- Significant changes were taking place in the funding provided to UNDP. Core funding for general activities, which had traditionally provided the organisation with the ability to plan on a five-year basis, was being replaced by earmarked funding provided on a shorter-term basis. Earmarked funding increased from 10 per cent of core funding in 1980 to an estimated 50 per cent in 1995.
- A competitive technical assistance market was emerging, with UNDP no longer enjoying a unique position. Many other multilateral organisations, in particular the World Bank, had expanded their provision of technical assistance and more countries had qualified local talent, thus reducing their need for expatriate involvement.
- There was a strong sense that UNDP, after nearly 30 years in the business of development assistance, lacked a clear mission and focus, and was being pulled in too many ways by too many forces.
- The co-ordination role for technical assistance, which had been assigned to UNDP by the UN secretary-general and was considered important for the effective use of limited funds, was not fully accepted within the recipient countries and/or by other organisations within the UN system. This problem had been exacerbated by growing competition between organisations and within governments for decreasing funds.

UNDP was at a watershed in its existence, and action was necessary if the organisation was to move forward positively while living in a world of uncertainty. The administrator, therefore, initiated a major programme for establishing the strategic and organisational changes necessary to achieve this goal.

The response to the challenge

Considerable effort was made to involve a broad cross-section of staff and external advisers in the process of defining change. In addition to the extensive travel undertaken by the administrators to countries in Africa, Asia, Europe and the Americas, consultations were intensified with UNDP's development partners (governments, other UN agencies and the World Bank), and two groups were set up to define a programme of change. These comprised the following:

- An external high-level panel established to solicit the views of non-governmental stakeholders, to add outside perspectives and to build outside support.
- An internal Transition Team, composed of staff drawn from all parts of the organisation and at all levels. This was formed to examine key issues of the organisation and to frame proposals for repositioning UNDP within its market place.

When viewing the issues facing UNDP, it was readily apparent that the organisation could not afford to assume that those competences which had been strengths in the past would continue to be strengths in the coming decade. For this reason, it was necessary to define clearly UNDP's 'competitive advantage': why would donors fund activities through UNDP rather than other organisations, and why would recipient countries prefer to work with UNDP? After careful review, it was concluded that its competences and strengths were seen as follows:

- *Leverage due to neutrality.* As part of the UN system, with its universal coverage, UNDP has leverage for addressing political, legal and institutional issues from a neutral perspective. This neutrality is a vital element in the acceptance of assistance by recipient countries, and has proved an essential factor in the co-ordination and brokering of many issues throughout the developing world.
- *Extensive coverage.* UNDP's worldwide network of country offices provides a significant base for influencing development activities through the provision of accumulated knowledge. No other multilateral or bilateral development organisation has as extensive a network of offices with as broad a perspective on what is happening in each country. This is partially a function of the international and national staffing, but also a reflection of the relationships which can develop due to the neutrality of the UN.
- *Development philosophy.* UNDP's multisectoral and integrated view of development, combined with the emphasis that UNDP has placed on promoting people-centred sustainable development as opposed to purely economic growth, is considered particularly important by recipient governments.
- *Development experience.* Over the years UNDP has developed, in conjunction with the specialised agencies such as the World Health Organisation, access to a wealth of expertise and technology on a universal basis.

UNDP in the future

In February 1994, as a result of this process, UNDP established an overall focus for the future known as *sustainable human development* (SHD), and in May 1994 the administrator announced a programme of change designed to allow the organisation to achieve the revised direction within the constraints of current funding.

Sustainable human development, defined as people-centred development activities, was not a new direction for UNDP, but rather a strengthening of the organisation's focus to ensure that not only UNDP-funded development activities, but also those funded by other donor groups, were focused on the achievement of the following objectives:

- Development activities that not only generate growth, but also distribute the benefits of this growth equitably.
- Development that focuses on regenerating the environment, not destroying it.
- Development activities that empower people through the enlargement of choices and opportunities, and by providing for their participation in decisions affecting them.

From an organisational perspective, there were a number of major challenges:

- In the past, the UNDP country representatives' role was primarily one of managing programmes throughout their life cycle. In the future the representative must not only be able to manage a programme effectively, but must also have the capacity to ensure full funding for the programme. This is a significant challenge for staff who have not previously seen their role as including marketing and sales-type activities.
- With fund raising becoming a more integral part of the country office role, it was expected that some tensions will occur, with governments wanting UNDP to manage programmes which did not meet the criteria for sustainable human development. UNDP representatives would need to hone their skills in balancing the needs of the government with the objectives of SHD.
- The programme of change was taking place at a time of significant downsizing (staff had been cut back by 25 per cent during 1990–1995), where staff, who joined the organisation with the expectation of a 'job for life', were beginning to realise that this may not continue. Not surprisingly, this created considerable unease. In addition, UNDP had committed itself to a competence-based human resource strategy with the need for all staff to maintain and develop skills which ensure mobility. Again, this created a sense of unease among long-serving staff as to whether their generalist development skills and experience would be adequate to meet future needs.
- The climate in which UNDP was operating in the 1990s was very much affected by growing demands for accountability. In particular, donor countries, which are themselves facing growing cynicism from their taxpayers in regard to the efficiency and effectiveness of the public sector, have been very concerned that the international public sector be held to the same standards of accountability as they are. Within UNDP there was no general aversion to this, but there was concern that it would result in a search for scapegoats rather than dealing with the real issues.

This did not help in establishing a working environment that encouraged creativity and risk taking at a time when these characteristics were much needed.

The change management process

Recognising that the overall goal of helping the developing world to achieve sustainable human development could not be achieved without the full commitment of UNDP staff, the administrator held a three-day retreat with all senior managers in February 1996 to decide on how best to address the challenges. This meeting was facilitated by a management adviser in the process of change.

As a result of this meeting, it was decided that UNDP needed to make a stronger commitment to the change process, by establishing a separate organisation to manage the change activities considered vital for achieving the objectives that had been established in 1994. In general, it was agreed that UNDP had made good progress in establishing a clearer vision for the organisation, but it had not been as successful in making the organisational changes necessary to implement the vision. The UNDP 2001 Change Management Programme, which was launched in May 1996, involved the establishment of a core team to co-ordinate the activities of key projects targeted to be completed within an eighteen-month period. These key projects, which would be managed separately from the 'business as usual' activities, included the following:

- *Funding strategies and partnerships:* focusing on alternative scenarios for UNDP funding, including possible relationships with the private sector and non-governmental organisations; and efforts related to building constituencies of varied donors.
- *Strategic competence areas:* focusing on UNDP's comparative advantages in thematic and functional areas; and defining and promoting special competency areas.
- *Management and organisational structure:* focusing on the corporate and country office roles; the strengthening of leadership and management skills; decision-making processes; and those activities necessary to achieve excellence.
- *Accountability and results orientation:* focusing on strengthening the linkages between the corporate plan and the budget process; more effectively linking performance and results; and strengthening processes for evaluation, audit and management review.
- *Human resource development:* focusing on implementing the newly approved human resource strategy, which committed the organisation to competence-based hiring with effective staff development to ensure

that UNDP attracted and kept the staff necessary to achieve the objectives of the future.

■ *Information management and technology:* focusing on ensuring that UNDP makes efficient and creative use of technology, and becomes considerably more effective in its use of management information as a basis for planning and decision making.

■ *Communications and public affairs:* focusing on evolving a comprehensive and systemic approach to communications and public affairs. UNDP had to be easily recognised and understood as an organisation promoting sustainable human development, with a strong focus on poverty eradication.

It was envisaged that these projects would provide the basis for addressing the challenges facing the UNDP.

A strategy for change at KPMG

GERRY JOHNSON

Background to KPMG

KPMG is a large international firm of accountants and consultants. By 1996, the fee income of KPMG International was over US$7.5 billion, about half of which was accounted for by its European operations. Within that European total, the UK accounted for over £588 million, about 15 per cent of the worldwide total, most from the south-east region. Table 1 shows the relative size of the main competitors worldwide, in terms of market share. In the UK, KPMG was perceived by clients to be in the lead in several of its market sectors and, where not in the lead, was generally placed second or third by external surveys (see Table 2). The fee split between the various activities for several leading firms is shown in Table 3. Within the UK, KPMG employed around 8,500 staff and partners, over half of those in the south-east region and the rest spread over five other regions.

Table 1   Worldwide fees and competitive ranking of KPMG and its competitors, 1995

	Rank	Fees ($m)
Arthur Andersen	1	8,100
KPMG	2	7,500
Ernst Young	3	6,870
Coopers & Lybrand	4	6,200
Deloitte Touche Tohmatsu International	5	5,950
Price Waterhouse	6	4,455

Source: *International Accounting Bulletin*, 21 December 1995.

Table 2   Ranking of activities of leading accountancy firms (as perceived by UK clients)

	Audit	UK tax	International tax	Management consultancy	Corporate finance	Corporate recovery
KPMG	1	2	3	4	1	2
Coopers & Lybrand	3	2	4	2	2	1
Price Waterhouse	1	1	2	3	2	4
Ernst & Young	4	5	5	5	5	3
Arthur Andersen	5	4	1	1	4	6
Touche Ross	6	6	6	6	6	5

Source: MORI survey, October 1995.

Table 3   The fee split for leading accounting firms (%)

Firm	Audit and accounting	Tax	Consulting	Other
KPMG	42	12	20	26*
Arthur Andersen	36	15	49	—
Ernst & Young	48	21	22	9
Coopers & Lybrand	55	18	16	11
Price Waterhouse	49	23	22	6

* Includes 7 per cent corporate recovery fees.

Sources: *International Accounting Bulletin*, 21 December 1995; KPMG annual report.

Colin Sharman, KPMG's UK senior partner, explained the competitive position of the firm in 1995:

> The accountancy profession is in a period of turbulence and change. It is threatened by litigation, subject to 'low-balling', increasingly governed by rules and regulations, and lacking a recognised market leader. The market is dominated by six large firms who have clearly distinguished themselves from smaller players and have built up barriers to entry. These barriers to entry are substantially due to the range of services and skills the major firms now have.
>
> In the 1980s, the leading firms underwent a series of international mergers and diversified into a range of professional services — corporate finance, consulting, investigations and forensic accounting.
>
> There are portfolio differences — for example, KPMG is clearly a leader in corporate finance and the only player in career consulting, but the similarities are far greater than the differences.
>
> The players are broadly similar in size and in their range of resources. Consequently, there is no natural leader to direct and structure the market. Even where the professional offerings are similar, effective relationships can provide a competitive edge through understanding the business and client needs.

The ability to co-ordinate and integrate people to create a real benefit for the client can also be a distinguishing factor, since this is the area that accountancy firms have been notoriously bad at. The result is that teamwork, relationship management and integration are the competences that may distinguish one firm from the pack given their equivalence in many technical aspects. One of the fascinating aspects of this struggle of the giants is that success lies not necessarily in the originality of the idea or strategy, but in the ability to implement the idea effectively.

In developing strategy to achieve such competitive advantage, he believed it was important to understand KPMG's past culture.

KPMG is a partnership, which makes its structure, and the way it operates, quite different in many respects from that of a company. For example, in the south-east region of KPMG there are around 300 partners, each of whom is an owner/manager. As a matter of law, all partners have to agree to certain things: for example, the taking of leases on new premises. This reinforces the feeling that partners are involved in major decision making. In practice, of course, we have moved a long way from the Victorian notion of partnership and we run ourselves increasingly on corporate lines. The senior partner is, in effect, chief executive, with a management team who make many of the operational decisions of an executive board. But those 300 partners have to be consulted and have to agree — or at least not disagree — with any change. And that is not just an issue of communicating well through the organisation, but also of winning the hearts and minds of partners.

We had a matrix structure like many other professional service organisations. We had a delivery structure for services along discipline lines, and different practice units for audit, tax, management consultants and corporate recovery [see Figure 1]. Separately, we focused on our market sectors through firm-wide multidisciplinary groups that were industry based, focusing on banking, insurance, manufacturing and so on. But the dominant axis remained the discipline-based practice units, and that was the primary interface to the market.

Our mission involved providing the highest quality of services to our individual clients, but our practice units were discipline based. The only way that we focused across disciplines was through our market sector groups, but they merely co-ordinated and did not run the business. Hence there was a conflict between our stated goals and our structure.

If we look at our market place, the 1980s were terrific. The demand for our services seemed to be infinite. Our top line fee growth was frequently 30 or 40 per cent per annum. In 1992 the market became far tougher. The recession hit our clients and hence our market. Either clients were not buying or we found ourselves in highly competitive situations where differentiating ourselves was a major issue.

In addition to the recession, KPMG faced changed market circumstances in the 1990s. The expectations of clients were changing: they expected their advisers to understand the problems they faced and to be able to provide a range of services to meet their needs. The issue for KPMG was therefore to ensure that partners were seen as, and performed the role of, business advisers.

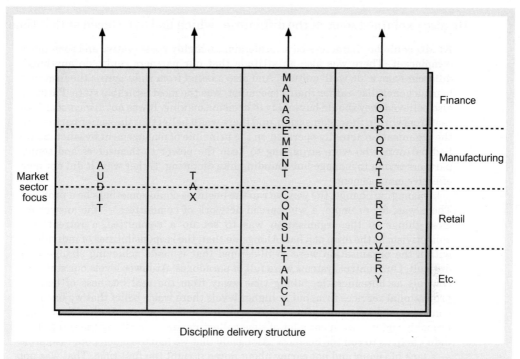

Figure 1   Delivery structure for services

The need for change at KPMG

In 1992 Colin Sharman, at that time in charge of the south-east region, spoke at a Strategic Planning Society meeting in London about the need for strategic change in KPMG:

> The key was to get client focus into our organisation. Initially I thought that I could operate successfully by changing only the behaviour and skill sets of our people, in particular our partners. But I came to the conclusion that was not going to work. If I changed the behaviour of partners and staff to become more client focused, more market sector focused, more knowledgeable about the market place, that would rapidly fall apart. We would need to reinforce it by measurement systems to ensure that our people were measured by these new ways of doing things; and by a structure which aligned with what people were being asked to do. If people, accountable in one direction, were told to focus their efforts in another, it was likely that one or other would lose out, probably the new focus. And if our measurement systems and reward systems measure something other than the new behaviour we are asking for, it is fairly clear what would happen. So I concluded that we needed what I call a virtuous circle of change consisting of three interlinking elements — structure, measurement and behaviour, all needing to operate on each other. But of course, changing all three elements was a much bigger task taking much more time.

He also explained some of the difficulties which had to be faced at that time:

KPMG could be characterised as professional, highly conservative and sometimes complacent. There was also an attitude that our partners could 'do anything'; different from a 'do well' culture. And also a belief from right across the firm that being a generalist, rather than a specialist, was the most desirable state. Partners also believed they should have a say in decision making. It was not always seen like that from within the organisation, and there was a belief that the senior partners in the organisation actually operated on the principle of management by edict. So we had partners who were struggling to keep the power to themselves and senior partners trying to manage but sounding like dictating. Either way, it did not help effective management.

In managing change, the way we ran the business could sometimes be a problem. There was, for example, a widespread network of committees — the answer for most things in the organisation was to set up a committee, a retreat into collectivism at the drop of a hat. Alongside that, the responsibilities of individuals within the organisation were so ill-defined that it made achieving change very difficult. Our control systems were full of paradoxes. At lower levels our staff saw controls as bureaucratic, taking time away from the real business of being a professional services firm, but at higher levels there was a belief that we had poor controls and poor management information to run the business. Both of those were probably right — we spent a lot of time collecting and controlling the things that didn't help us to run the business. Alongside that we had too much poor discipline — a lack of rigour and not caring about doing it right the first time. That was not surprising if we were asking people to spend of lot of their time on data that were never used to manage the business. There was too little value placed on managing carefully to time scales. It was regarded as much better to whirl around in frenzied activity at the last minute. That applied whether we were serving clients or whether we were trying to do something that contributes towards managing the business.

The 'mystique of partnership' didn't always help. Promotion to partner was seen as the summit of a KPMG person's career, with virtually no second prizes for those who did not make it — we had a culture of 'up or out'. Partners, once created, were quite distinct and elevated people within the organisation. There were also problems with the discipline structure of audit, tax, consultancy and so on being dominant: problems illustrated, for example, by the tales people told about how awful one of the other disciplines was. Nor was the 'cult of the individual' always helpful. The kind of people who were lionised were mavericks — people out of the mould; people who had broken the mould; people who didn't conform, who were entirely individuals. You can imagine the way some of this expressed itself; especially when it came to 'them and us' — partners and the rest or, at lower levels, senior managers and the rest. For example, in our London office we had three levels of dining room.

However, KPMG was a very successful organisation, which of course reinforced the aversion to change. Change is always all right provided someone else has to change. And if we were successful — winning new clients, making a reasonable amount of money — why on earth should partners change? But change was necessary.

The impetus for change at KPMG

Colin Sharman explained what was done to promote change:

> We organised a series of eight strategy workshops for the region's partners; around one-third went through them. Quite deliberately, those who attended the workshops, particularly the early ones, were partners with a desire for change and views about what those changes might be; and they were not necessarily my views. What those workshops did was to work through the strategic position of the firm, what the competitive strategy should be, what the blockages to change were, what the critical success factors were and crucially what actions needed to be put in place.
>
> I personally attended a debriefing session at the end of each of the workshops. The messages that came out of them were remarkably consistent. They confirmed the need for increased client focus. Major issues of specialism and integrating our service delivery also emerged. Importantly, partners on the workshops recognised the need for major strategic change.
>
> At the end of the series of workshops, I arranged for some more detailed feedback sessions for all of the partners. I held ten evening sessions with all but a small handful of partners coming to one of the sessions. There we took the main messages from the workshops, discussed the main directions of the firm and tried to surface any real concerns. Those proved a very useful way of building the consensus that we need and also reinforcing the fact that change was definitely coming.
>
> But I did not just work with partners. I used the senior management conference, which was an annual ritual for our senior managers to complain about the firm, as a way of getting them into strategic issues. The managers worked through much the same process as the partners had done on the workshops. At the end of that, the senior managers produced a serious analysis of the issues facing the firm and the kind of actions that were needed.
>
> I tried to capture that enthusiasm, that commitment, that sense of change by holding a series of briefing sessions for partners and senior managers together to spread some of the messages. The messages I wanted to get across were that we were serious about change; that we needed to become a much more open organisation; that we needed to involve people at all levels in the development in the organisation and that we needed to communicate very much better than we had done in the past. All of those are fairly abstract messages, but to make them have a real impact I had the sessions designed to reinforce the underlying message, which was that we are going to do things very differently in future. For example, you might think that the visuals [see Figure 2] we used were pretty ordinary, but my KPMG audience was accustomed to nothing more exciting than slides with a KPMG-blue background and logo. So if nothing else my pop art images made an impact. People started talking openly about wanting to change, wanting to try new things and wanting to succeed.

By early 1992 the main elements of the strategy had been identified:

> The major feature is that we needed to be a client-focused organisation. That meant that we needed to work on the three elements of the virtuous circle that I described earlier to achieve client focus. We needed to change the *structure* of the firm to put clients first and discipline second. We needed to change the *behaviour* and *skills* of

Figure 2 Visuals for the presentations

our partners to be client-focused professionals, specialised and dedicated to client service. And we needed to have *measurement systems* that line up with our new structure and reinforce the new behaviours and skills.

The most important change to achieve was in the behaviour and skills of our people. This needed to be reinforced by ensuring that symbols of the old way of doing things, including committees, go. Stories of excellent client service across disciplines needed to replace ones about how part of the firm has failed. We also had to have a proper identification of accountabilities and responsibilities for individuals.

I was also clear that our communication systems — which were primitive — had to be very much better. Communications needed to be used in a positive way to ensure that partners and staff understood and were committed to the new direction.

The launch of 20:20 Vision

Following the strategy workshops in February 1992, the partners within KPMG had become impatient for action. Colin Sharman was rather more cautious: 'what some of the partners did not understand was that to get from strategic concepts to implementation you had to do some work'. He believed it might take 3–4 years to put proposed changes into effect. However, a plan which set out structural changes had been put together by the end of April 1992. This plan was central to the guiding vision of the future and became known as '20:20 Vision'.

In an innovative move for KPMG, a special partners' conference was called in which 20:20 Vision was presented, together with details of the key players. Colin Sharman recognised that 'the culture at the time meant that partners were frightened to ask questions', so in an attempt to overcome this, Jonathan Dimbleby, the well-known British TV current affairs commentator, was invited to field questions from the floor to the panel. Two similar events were then held to inform senior managers and junior managers of the plan, and it was cascaded throughout the whole organisation 'down to the chauffeurs, tea ladies and telephonists' through in-company press releases.

The underlying strategic thrust of 20:20 Vision was to move to an industry-based focus for service delivery to clients; to develop teams of auditors, consultants, tax specialists and so on, who were experts by industry sector, not just by discipline. To do this, a new structure for the firm was introduced made up of four industry-based business units and four skills-based business units, headed by senior partners reporting to two partners in charge of operations, Mike Rake (industry units) and Alan Reid (skills units). These were directly accountable to Colin Sharman (see Figure 3).

Over time, personnel would move more and more to become based in the industry-based units. Colin Sharman's initial aim was to start with 60 per

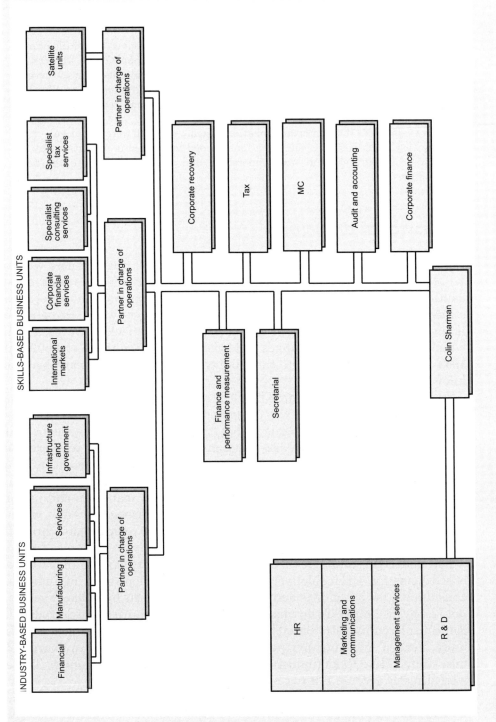

Figure 3 The new structure

cent of staff in industry-based units and move over time towards 80 per cent. The timetable of events prepared in April 1992 envisaged that this structure would begin with one business unit in October 1992, with the others being introduced a year later. Colin Sharman initially considered this cautious approach appropriate because he 'was desperately worried about maintaining control of the business, with the existing steam-cranked information systems not capable of being changed quickly enough'. However, by mid-June the initial time scale had been dismissed as being too cautious. Colin Sharman changed his view and argued that 'if we make a decision now, we can roll out the new structure across the whole organisation on 1 October, get it into place and make it work'. Three weeks later that decision was taken and, on 1 October, the south-east region of KPMG undertook the most significant restructuring in the firm's history, involving physically moving 2,500 people to achieve co-location of partners and managers in the new industry units.

A mixed response

There was a mixed response to these moves initially. Some parts of the firm were enthusiastic; others were not. As Alan Reid explained:

> It was audit that went hell for leather into it, led by Michael Fowle; it was a way of getting the audit practice managed. If you talked to them at the time, they thought that this was something for the audit practice. I don't think they recognised that 20:20 Vision was for the whole firm. It was thought to be long overdue. However, on the tax side, 49 out of 50 partners did not want it because they had been going through three years of change themselves, had only just come to the end of it and felt well poised to drive forward. What they thought they could do was to co-locate rather than merge. They accepted they had to work together, but there was a question of whether they were managed by tax people. They had come out of subservience to the audit practice and they thought that this was a magnificent ruse to get them back into that position. Consultancy never really debated it.

Alan Reid admitted that, initially, he too did not welcome the changes:

> I was the guy who had put the change through the tax practice. I had sweated and lost a lot of blood doing it, and to see it removed a week after it had finished was annoying. I thought we could achieve it with co-location, and not with the dramatic steps that were being proposed. Within six months I was convinced otherwise.

He then took a lead in selling it to the tax partners:

> I knew the tax partners were against it, but I was willing to explain to them it was worth giving it a try; and I was able to sell it very effectively to the staff because there were features that enabled me to say it was the rest of the firm building on what the tax practice had already done. We had introduced industry specialisation a year before. We would also work closer to the auditors in the future, therefore we could get closer to clients.

In the initial stages, the staff were probably the most supportive and that's perhaps worth learning from. We were much more concerned with partners' reactions and developing it than with staff. The staff saw the reality of the vision quicker than partners. Partners saw their own personal positions.

We put three or four tax departments into the industry units. We then said, as the right moment comes to change the client relationship, we will move more work across and more staff across. In fact, as staff became more excited, the whole thing accelerated, but quite a few partners lingered behind. The ratio of staff to partners was much greater in the industry business units. I think some partners thought that all this might cancel itself out in due course.

By 1993 the structure was in place and co-location had occurred. However, the extent to which the new strategy had become accepted and put into effect was mixed. In some industry units, it was being pursued energetically. One of the heads of the industry-based units established a co-located multidisciplinary team, with team briefings, and tailored training in the strategic analysis of clients for all partners and managers, whether consultants, auditors or tax specialists; and was able to demonstrate the effective working of the unit in half the time initially planned. In others, it was little more than co-location at that time. As one audit manager put it: 'I had moved my office, but nothing else had changed. As far as I was concerned, I was dealing with the same clients in the same way.'

Although the new structure had set up a management team for running the region, its early contributions were sometimes indecisive, especially in sorting out inevitable 'turf disputes' which arose, for example, between industry-based and skills-based units. Changes to established control procedures were also slow. For example, it was unclear who would be allocated fee income for an assignment between business units and skills-based units, where joint teams were operating. This lack of clarity was exacerbated by the concentration of some of the senior partners on the traditional monitoring of chargeable hours on client business.

In 1993, Colin Sharman was appointed to UK senior partner and Mike Fowle, previously a senior audit partner, was appointed as senior partner of the south-east region. Colin Sharman readily admitted that Mike Fowle was seen to be 'driven by technical excellence' and that 'the chat in the office was that Mike would undo it all'. However, 'that has not happened. He has been committed and has driven "20:20" harder than I would have done.' He added:

My appointment and the process of confirmation happened so quickly because the London partners were so keen to get me out. Certainly, in Tax it was seen as 'Oh, Michael will stop all this nonsense', but in fact he hasn't and the Tax people have had a much harder time under Michael than they would under me.

The Leadership Project

At the time Colin Sharman became UK senior partner, there were other developments taking place. At an international level in KPMG there were the beginnings of an international strategy to position KPMG as the leading 'advisory firm' rather than an audit firm. This eventually took shape in the UK in what became known as the 'Leadership Project'.

In his address to the UK partners' meeting in October 1994, Colin Sharman announced KPMG's aims 'to become the leading accountancy firm in the UK'.

> The very fact that KPMG has more long-standing and enduring client relationships than any other firm gives us a superb opportunity to build our business. If we can develop these relationships and win more business from our clients, then we have the potential to achieve clear leadership across the whole range of our client services ... Our research shows that clients are saying: 'know me, know my business. Give me advice, help me to compete. I want frequent contact, robust and independent opinions, proactive advice and fast reactions to changes in my business. I want value for money.' ... They want a trusted and valued relationship ... In many respects, clients have told us we are doing quite well. But they also have told us we lack innovation; we don't do enough to offer advice ... If KPMG can succeed in genuinely making the transition from audit firm to business adviser, it can pull ahead of its competitors rather than being just one among the leaders ... I want us to be indispensable to our clients because we give robust opinions, offer advice and provide business solutions that they simply could not get for themselves. I want us to attract the best people and to be the best firm to work for. The best firm because we have the most interesting clients, and the most attractive careers, the most demanding assignments. I want us to employ people who will make a real difference to their clients' business. I want us to be the firm that other leading advisers want to work with. We want the merchant banks, the lawyers, the specialist consultants to be alongside us. I want us to be the leading firm in the new markets — business transformation, forensic accounting — right at the cutting edge. I want us to foster a culture that sees opportunities and not problems, strengths not weaknesses, teamwork and not just individuals.

He later explained how this would be put into effect:

> The concept of having a leader on a client account — the lead partner — is not new. However, in KPMG, the role historically adopted has been that of a senior audit partner with the key relationship at the finance director level. It is now much more than this. The role is defined as an account management role that carries the ultimate responsibility for management of the client relationship, particularly at the chairman/chief executive level. The aim is to allow a single individual to be the integrator of all the firm's services to a client and of the people supplying those services. There is also a leadership aspect to the role, as it includes responsibility for effective teamwork and managing internal relationships.
>
> A lead partner is identified for every client and potential client of the firm. Selection is based on client needs, personal chemistry and relationships, ability to perform the role and industry knowledge. It is not related to the original skill

set or technical background of the partner. It is widely recognised within the firm that this is not the role that all the partners should aspire to, since specialist partners and engagement partners are essential to ensuring that the service delivery and advice is first class, and this is the 'must have' of any professional service firm. It would not be commercially sensible to use the time of leading edge specialists in what is essentially a generalist role.

Each project or piece of work performed for the client will be led by an engagement partner whose role is to deliver that specific piece of work. Take an audit, for example: the audit engagement partner retains responsibility for the independent opinion. However, all services and relationships are co-ordinated through the lead partner. While the lead partner will not necessarily be involved in each project or service delivery, he or she has responsibility for selection and appraisal of engagement partners and overall control of fees.

The Leadership Project also provided a vehicle to roll out some of the changes already made in the south-east to the rest of the UK, and develop human resource practices and policies in line with the changing strategy.

Competences

It was acknowledged that the new strategic focus would not be achieved successfully by structural means alone; other changes would be needed to reinforce it. The idea of a competency framework was established and developed early in 1993. David Westcott (HR partner) explained that:

> The starting point for this framework was the question — what are the characteristics we need in our future partners? External consultants conducted a whole series of interviews which asked partners in key positions together with younger partners what they thought the behavioural characteristics should be for the future success of the company.

From this, six categories of competences emerged (see Figure 4). David Westcott went on to explain:

> Later a project team under Roger Dickens, the senior managing partner of the Midlands region, revisited the competences and asked, if we wished to become the leading firm of accountants, what sort of behaviour we would require. What we did differently was to involve client groups within the firm and we also went to external clients.

Rewards

Reward systems were also revised, beginning in mid-1993. David Westcott:

> Pay had been largely a matter of how long anyone had been in a particular grade . . . We set out to introduce a pay structure and review system which sought to reward improvement and achievement rather than time in grade.

The leadership competences are set out under the following six categories. Examples of specific competences within these categories are provided.

Client responsiveness
- Relationship building — establishes rapport and builds long-term relationships with key decision-makers.
- Professional judgement — knows who the 'real' client is at all times and uses this knowledge to operate effectively for KPMG.

Business skills
- Commerciality — relates all aspects of KPMG's service to client's business perspective and commercial drivers.
- Business development — is seen by existing clients to market effectively and appropriately.

Management
- Task management skills — controls the process of delivery to the client.
- Team skills — encourages openness and co-operative working.
- People development — gives staff responsibility and autonomy appropriate to their level of competence.

Personal effectiveness
- Drive and commitment to results — goes beyond client's expressed requirement and meets its real need.
- Resilience — recovers crisis situations; is resourceful at times of pressure and stress.

Social skills
- Communication skills — speaks clearly, and with impact.
- Social confidence — is perceived to enjoy the company of a wide range of people.

Thinking skills
- Analytical thinking — analyses large amounts of complex data, extracts essentials.
- Proactive thinking — comes forward with ideas unprompted by clients.

Figure 4   The competency framework

Colin Sharman explained the basis of the system:

> We changed all our systems to move everybody into just five bands so that instead of having everybody promoted every year, which was the old system, we had a situation where promotion meant something ... Promotion would only be between the bands, on the basis of performance in terms of the competences. Eventually, we completely restructured the reward system for partners, right the way across the UK.

There were problems with these changes, as David Westcott explained:

> A language problem existed because we were talking about performance, which had never really featured before. Time was no longer an issue, people wouldn't be promoted after a year or eighteen months. Disquiet around this was driven by the uncertainty many people were feeling — they knew where they were under the old system and so did their managers, and senior managers and partners, because it

had been going on for years. Suddenly the whole thing was turned upside down. As far as many people were concerned, there were inadequate answers on what would happen in the future.

Another issue was the introduction of discretionary bonuses:

> The principle had been decided that we would have a discretionary bonus for those at the senior manager level. It would be for good performance over and above that which was expected and it would be a one-off — not recurring. This produced a tremendous amount of heat and no light. There was a lot of concern expressed and rumours were around before the thing was even debated. The alternative would have been to spend two years sorting this out, the normal KPMG practice, and we probably would never have achieved it.

Development centres and assessment centres

Development centres were also established, to which newly promoted senior managers were sent to identify personal development plans to prepare them for the role of partner. David Westcott explained the purpose of these senior management development centres:

> There had been some concern within the practice that the role of the senior manager, which is a very important one within KPMG, but is largely a production and operational job, did not prepare people for partnership, which is more about relationships and social skills. So we ran a development centre as people were promoted to senior manager. It was initially seen as being to do with judgement, assessment and appraisal rather than development; but they have now been accepted, are now used and people find them very valuable.

In the past, appointment to partner was considered by many in the firm as dependent on a senior manager being seen by existing partners as 'the right sort of chap'. However, in 1994, partner assessment centres were introduced:

> Before anyone is admitted to partnership in any of the regions of the firm, they have to have the approval of the UK board. The UK board had for some time expressed concern that their job had become one of a rubber stamp. Another concern was that a number of partners around the UK had been asked to leave the partnership within five years of their becoming a partner. The combination of those two concerns led to the conclusion that we needed something more rigorous in the way partners were admitted into the firm. We needed to ensure that the competences we had defined for future partners were those in evidence or they had the potential to be. So in 1994 the board agreed to establish nationally two processes for partner admission. One was an assessment centre and the other was an interview panel which represented the board.
>
> It's much clearer now what it takes to become a senior manager and to become a partner because there is a greater openness in terms of the sort of behaviour expected of people. There are those who are upset that the patronage system has gone ... but by and large there is a general belief that it is a better way of doing things.

Colin Sharman commented:

> It was the most unfair thing we've done really. What we were saying was the old system finishes here. Very justifiably, a lot of the guys said, 'until today I knew how to become a partner: you attach yourself to a powerful guy, keep your head down and you don't make mistakes; and he will see you all right'. That was the problem, there was enormous patronage in the system and at a stroke we took that away. In fact, we probably put too many through that initial assessment centre, but we learnt from it. In 1994 we had about ten that were rejected by the panel. Of the ten, seven were withdrawn by their senior regional partners. Three of these were put forward to the board for admission even though they did not have the support of the panel, and those three were rejected by the board. For the first time, the board was not going to accept someone bullying through his boy — and that had never happened before. In 1995 we had a large number, but of the people rejected by the panel, 100 per cent were withdrawn by their senior partners. Down the line people are saying, 'OK, the rules have changed, but I know what I have to do and I can still make it even if I don't have a patron.' It is one of the key things helping us get behavioural changes.

Assessment centres were also adopted for recruitment. David Westcott:

> We asked if we were happy about the quality of the graduates that we were getting. So we introduced a new selection process, which incorporated a mini assessment centre, whereas previously we, like all other firms of accountants, had relied exclusively on interviews. By introducing a new and very much more rigorous selection process for the 600 graduates that we take on, we are getting a much higher acceptance rate of people we offered positions to. Our feedback from them is (a) we seem to know what we want from a new recruit, and (b) we have made it difficult to join — and that has an attraction.

Communications and feedback

Colin Sharman believed that one of the most significant mechanisms for change was communication:

> For example, internally we now do a report on the partners' conference. In the past it would have been a paragraph in the house magazine saying we had a partners' conference. What we now do is take a video of it, interview the partners as to what they think and then we roll that right out immediately after the partners' conference to tell everyone about it. I exercise very little editorial control over that.
>
> Then there is the UK-wide staff opinion survey. Some people say, 'we shouldn't ask because they will tell us we are not very good'. Interestingly enough, the survey work I have seen shows that an awful lot of them identify with what we are trying to do, but that they think some of the partners need to change their behaviour. One of the things we are doing for this year's partners' conference is to give some feedback from the staff to the partners about partner behaviour and about what the partners are doing. The other thing that is being developed is upward appraisal. That's becoming accepted throughout the organisation.

In addition to internal communication, Colin Sharman became very visible in the national press explaining KPMG's new strategy and the changes in the firm. As one manager put it, 'You can hardly pick up a paper these days without seeing Colin in it. It's good for the firm and of course we all read it in here.'

Integration into industry-based units

Colin Sharman believed that:

> Where we have been able to integrate things into the industry-based business units, we have had unparalleled success. Consulting volumes delivered through the industry groups are growing like topsy. Where we have failed is in those bits we left in the skills groups.

There were certainly problems in integrating the consultancy practice. Alan Reid explained:

> There were very few consultants put into the industry business units originally. Two consultants headed up industry units because it was important that not all the business units were headed by auditors. But I would say maybe 70–80 consultants went into industry business units and 600 were left in the skills unit. So there was a very strong force of consultants left.
>
> I don't think that they wanted to be submerged below auditors. It's still a big issue around here. Our auditors are very suspicious of our consultants. If you actually assess them as separate business units, some of our most talented people are in our consultancy, but audit has performed better than consultancy. The audit practice puts that down to lack of hard work, poor management, general slothfulness, when in fact it is a lot to do with their market place and the nature of their work. We have to win £2 million of new work every week for our consultancy — our audit practice has a more recurring base of work. There is a lot of concern that they just don't understand each other. Also, we had a recession, and the consultancy business unit managing partner at the time spotted it three or four months too late and we had to make some redundancies. We had also grown consultancy by just adding on services; little cottage industries and boutiques here and there. They went in and sold the service they had to a client, worked hard in doing it, then came away again and left it, instead of nurturing the relationship and trying to sell other services. They acted as 35 cottage industries.

Eventually, more of the consultancy operations were integrated within industry units:

> We ended up with three business units, one in business transformation, with about 50 people in it and 7 partners, an IT business unit with 350 people in it, and a third unit which is international markets. There are a further 300 consultants in the industry units ... We've got consultants in regions as well; we do actually have 13 different business units doing consultancy.

Progress on the Leadership Project

An internal KPMG attitude survey on the progress of the overall Leadership Project showed that staff and partners saw KPMG as above average compared with the rest of the big six, as a firm with a successful future, and that job satisfaction was above average for a professional firm. However, it confirmed some concerns. KPMG was not seen as a people-orientated firm, and development and career opportunities were still not clear. The Leadership Project had not yet impacted in practical terms on the way most staff worked day to day. Teamwork was not yet fully effective. And while relationships between partners and staff were seen as good locally, barriers still existed: there was still a sense of 'us and them'. This was borne out in a survey of the consultancy operation reported in *Accountancy Age* in February 1995:

> Over half of the 74 staff questioned said they would not recommend KPMG 'as a good place to work', nor did they 'expect to be with this organisation two years from now' ... And well over 60% said they only knew what was expected of them to a 'slight' or 'moderate' extent ... A huge 82% of staff named 'avoidance' as a key feature, involving 'shifting responsibility, procrastinating and avoiding issues'. Power was another dominant characteristic, with 'empire-building' at the fore. And while 90% said that 'winning is valued and staff feel they have to outperform each other', just 20% believed there was any 'value placed on constructive interpersonal relationships, friendliness and openness' within the KPMG culture. Similarly, just 16% felt that any regard was given to 'coaching and developing people, being supportive and constructive'.

Talking about the strengths and weaknesses of the change programme so far, Colin Sharman commented:

> Everyone has heard the key messages about leadership and change, and there is strong support for the concepts. What we have to achieve next is to translate the concepts into everyday actions everywhere in the business. Two contrasting recent examples: we've just retained a high-profile client, and pre-empted a tendering process through proactive contact and management of the relationship. This isn't startling — it's just what I expect from client lead partners. But we've also just lost a major client simply because for the past two years no one had asked them if they were happy with our services.
>
> I'd say we're where I thought we'd be at this stage of the change process. The next stage will be even more challenging because it's not just about changing systems and structures — which we've done — it's about really changing people's everyday actions and decisions at every level in the business.

Contrasting responses were also received when staff were asked in an informal poll what the Leadership Project means to them. For example:

> 'I have it in the back of my consciousness when I'm doing business development. I ask myself, "Can we be a leader in this?".'

'It hasn't been brought down to the individual level . . . so how do you know what to do differently?'

Learning from experience

Looking back on the developments since 1992, David Westcott reflected:

> Perhaps we did too much in too much of a hurry, but it is now actually working, so there will be others that say that we did it at the right speed. There were too many threads left untied in retrospect. It has had the required impact, but there were a lot of negative reactions which could have been reduced had we given ourselves a year, rather than six months, in which to do things. In the past there would have been great debate; it would have been decided by committees of partners and then dropped on an unsuspecting world. Suddenly, Colin opened it all up, said we were going to do this, here are the principles, here is what we are going to achieve, asked people for their views and then the infrastructure followed on.
>
> We have got some superb HR practices and procedures, but we have variable quality in the nature of our people management. No amount of procedures or policies can necessarily affect this. There are those people around who will say, 'we've seen all this before, if we keep our heads down it will go away and we will carry on as usual'; so it's business as usual. And there are those who capture the vision and say, 'yes, we see the need for change and we will pursue it energetically'. All that HR were able to do was to provide the framework to support and effect that change. But change can only come about when the management of the units want it to happen, and visibly demonstrate that.

Colin Sharman believed that, although 'there was still some of the old politics lurking around', overall the changes had been a success:

> Individuals very clearly identify with the new units. And we've been able to capture the imagination of the troops with what we are doing with a lot of the newer initiatives. They will now say, 'well, we don't care what you middle-ranking partners say — you don't matter'. Our managers are now more confident. In the old days it was 'keep your mouth shut, keep your head down and patronage will take care of you'. Now it is 'we don't care, we have been told what is going to happen and you guys had better change, because if you don't you're going to get squeezed from the top'.
>
> Clients love it. We asked them what they wanted and then we were able to sell it to them and they bought more of it. We've gone back and said, 'do you like what you're getting?' and, by and large, our clients are very positive about what we have done.
>
> All the evidence that we can see from the market place is that we are number 1 or number 1 equal with Coopers. In terms of quality of service, we usually come out very high, usually ahead of Coopers. The question is whether we can continue to sustain that because others will respond. We are not making progress in the areas of innovation — we are seen as the premier prestige accounting firm that leads the market place. We are not being seen any more favourably in the areas of innovation, we have always been seen as a bit dusty, a bit conservative. However, we have put six points on our market share in the last four years.

The future

In 1995, KPMG announced that it planned to incorporate that part of its audit practice dealing with companies listed on the UK Stock Exchange or in the regulated financial services industry. One reason for this was the need to protect the personal assets of partners from increasing threats of litigation affecting the profession as a whole, especially in the USA. However, as the *Financial Times* reported on 25 January 1996, KPMG believed that the move would provide competitive advantages:

> KPMG felt that a stronger corporate management structure would give it an edge in competing with the looser partnerships of the other Big Six firms. With incorporation comes disclosure. Accounts will have to be published for the audit company, but KPMG has pledged that it will go further — it will produce full financial results for the whole firm. This has wrong-footed the competition, most of which are still pondering a response ... KPMG's focus on auditing is a strategy which sets it apart from many of the other big firms. While some firms have boosted volumes by entering markets such as out-sourcing and information technology — and the implementation of services — KPMG is seeking to preserve the pre-eminence of auditing.

The *FT* reported the publishing of 50,000 copies of KPMG's annual report for the UK — the first major accountancy firm to do so:

> Why has KPMG become the first to disclose so much about what it still, legally, a private business? Whatever the truth, the firm's chutzpah is admired by most — albeit privately. The firm admits that it would have had to publish full results for the audit plc, but that its decision to open all the books was prompted by a desire to present a transparent business to clients and the general public. It feels the public has a legitimate interest in an organisation which audits 400 listed companies.

By 1996, Colin Sharman could reflect on four years of managing change in an increasingly competitive environment. However, his term as UK senior partner was due to end in 1998, and he also needed to consider what would happen to the Leadership Project and change programme without him.

> We have to get away from the idea of change as a project, with a beginning, a middle and an end. Change is continuous, and my prime objective is to turn KPMG into an organisation which continually renews itself. That's the only way we will be able to maintain our leadership position. Right now, I'm just providing the 'push' which gets that process going. Once the momentum gets going, change will be independent of me, and unstoppable by anyone else: it will simply become part of the way we do things in KPMG.

Burmah Castrol Chemicals Group

GERRY JOHNSON

Background

With its head office in the UK, Burmah Castrol is a manufacturer of specialised lubricants and chemicals, marketing to consumers and industrial customers in over 150 countries. In 1995 its worldwide turnover exceeded £3 billion with profit before tax of £253 million. The lubricants business is centred on the Castrol brand automotive, industrial and marine products.

The Chemicals Group had been formed by Burmah Castrol in 1981 by bringing together two of its businesses, Dussek Campbell (waxes) and Expandite (operating in the construction market); and this was followed by a series of acquisitions including Foseco plc in 1990 (see Table 1), with the

Table 1   Chemicals Group acquisitions (chronological order of significant acquisitions)

Year	Acquisition	SBU
1982	Industrial Adhesives Ltd, UK	Adhesives
1983	Sericol, UK	Printing Inks
1985	Yates Manufacturing, USA	Coatings
1986	National Wax, USA	Coatings
1986	Columbia Cement, USA	Adhesives
1987	Midwest Coatings, USA	Printing Inks
1990	Fragival, Spain	Printing Inks
1990	Foseco plc, UK	Metallurgical, Construction and Timber Treatment
1991	Dysons, UK	Metallurgical
1992	Tri-Union, Hong Kong	Printing Inks
1993	Kerax, UK	Coatings

intention of bringing together chemicals businesses of a speciality, rather than commodity nature, based on formulatory skills. By 1995 its turnover was £810 million with profits of £62.4 million. On taking over as chief executive in 1995, Mike Dearden was determined to develop a clear strategy for the group, and by the end of that year this process had begun.

The divisions and the businesses

Figure 1 shows the structure of Burmah Castrol in 1995, and in particular the businesses in the Chemicals Group. The group included five divisions, Metallurgical Chemicals (Foseco), Construction and Mining Chemicals (Fosroc), Printing Inks (Sericol), Coatings (Dussek Campbell and Protim Solignum) and Adhesives (IAL, Columbia). These in turn included fourteen business units (SBUs), brief summaries of which are provided in Appendix 1. An indication of the 1995 performance of these business units is shown in Table 2.

The main business activities of the divisions of the Chemicals Group were described by the divisional chief executives as follows. John Briggs of the Printing Inks division:

> Sericol sells printing inks to screen printers around the world. It is market leader in many of its markets and shares are growing. Success comes from the strong customer orientation of the whole company and the value that the customer has then placed on our product offering. We offer reliability and a commitment to outstanding product availability and speed of delivery. In effect, we encourage customers to expect more than competitors can achieve. This offering has particular value to our market — one which is highly fragmented with a large number of small players. One of our main advantages is our knowledge of where the customers are and we have achieved this through a very sophisticated IT system. Given that we keep innovating in the areas of reliability, consistency, delivery, IT and so on, competitors are always trying to catch up, but they are one or two steps behind. We do all this by working as a team, not individuals. Really, it's getting a lot of things right in detail in relatively small markets. You can see why it's not that attractive to competitors. For many of them, screen printing inks is a small part of their portfolio; and they have to try and compete with us in very small markets. It's not very attractive for them.

Warren Galloway, chief executive of the Metallurgical Chemicals division, summarised the differences between the Foundry, Steelmills and Aluminium businesses:

> The Foundry business addresses a very large, fragmented and international customer base. The ability to offer solutions based on an intimate understanding of all areas of the customer's process and product application skills is key to differential advantage and success. Whilst still dependent to a large extent on the experience and knowledge of its technical sales and product management people,

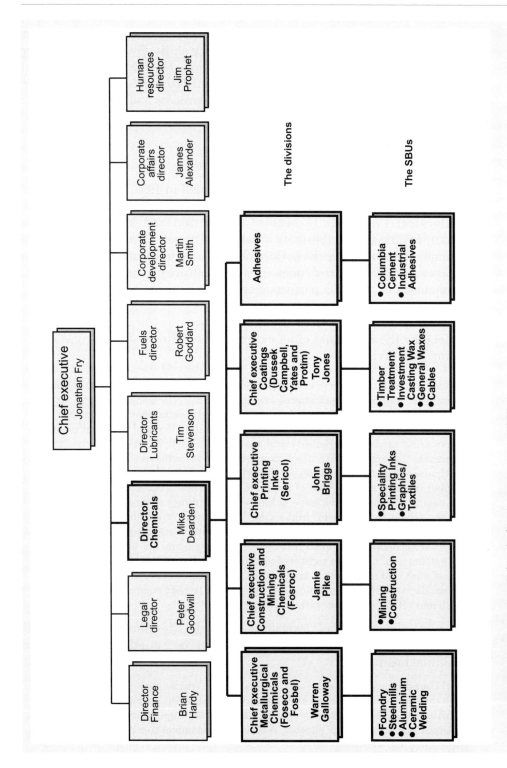

Figure 1   Burmah Castrol and Chemicals Group structure, 1995

Table 2   Financial performance of SBUs, 1995

	Sales (£m)	Gross margin (%)
Foundry		M
Construction		H
Printing Inks	100+	H
Graphics/Textiles		
Speciality		
Steelmills		M
General Waxes		L
Adhesives		L
Aluminium	30–100	M
Mining		M
Ceramic Welding (Fosbel)		H
Timber Treatment		H
Cable Products	Below 30	L
Casting Waxes		L

Note: Gross margin key: H, 40%; M, 30–40%; L, below 30%.

Foseco has enhanced its skills in this area through the development of computer simulation software. Customer needs and buyer behaviour varies from complex multinational automotive foundries such as Fiat, Ford and General Motors at one end of the scale to relatively small, local jobbing operations at the other, where, in effect, Foseco also act as technical consultants.

The Steelmills business sells its products and services to a small number (300+) of large but mainly nationally-based customers spread around the world. The main target market is the slab and bloom steel producers, and these clients have many common characteristics and Foseco has been good at spotting niche opportunities within the operations of these large customers.

The main Foseco products are consumed in the continuous caster area, which is at the heart of the steel plant and critically important to its successful operation. The products are all used in, or close to, the tundish,[1] and Foseco steelmills engineers are specialists in controlling steel flow through the tundish and mould. This operation is extremely complex and Foseco offers to take responsibility, through its Tundish Management Services, for lining the tundishes with refractory. Though critical, this is peripheral to the process of making steel.

In this way Foseco Steelmills become partners with their clients in jointly controlling the successful management of the steel casting process.

As for Fosbel, he saw this as rather different from the other businesses within the division: 'There are differences with Fosbel. This is a business heavily reliant still on patent technology across the world.'

[1] Tundishes are 5–10 metre refractory troughs that feed molten metal to continuous casters. As well as lining tundishes, Foseco provides comprehensive on-site monitoring in the Steelmills and Aluminium businesses.

Jamie Pike, chief executive of the Construction and Mining Chemicals division, reviewed the Fosroc businesses:

> Construction in particular is an applications business; applications in complex and difficult circumstances. The applications are very often customer specific and the key issue is how teams of sales people and technical people working together in different parts of the world can work effectively. To do this they have to do things differently in different markets sometimes with very localised needs. It's difficult to put your finger on why we are successful where we are, but in some markets we have 80 per cent share and competitors are less than 5 per cent. There are many reasons, primarily about teams of people interfacing very closely with local customer needs.
>
> I suppose Mining is more structured in the way we operate. The provision of powders to the mining industry requires, again, a close understanding of customer needs and high-quality teams to do it; but the market is more concentrated than in construction. We are successful in our resin capsules — indeed, probably the largest in the world — and if I have to explain why, I suppose it is because we are good at bringing new products to market in ways which reduce cost to customers.

Tony Jones, chief executive of the Coatings division:

> As far as Cables is concerned you need type approvals to get into the market, so there are not that many competitors. There are also usually large, often global, buyers and they regard as important long-term relationships and a proven track record in those relationships. When you have got in, the key to success is therefore customer relations and, again, between teams rather than individuals and the customers. You then have to offer good reliable supply with a global back-up in product development. The Yates Investment Casting business serves a highly fragmented and geographically widespread market, but one in which technical service is important.
>
> The market for general waxes is fairly concentrated in packaging and very fragmented in candles, but in both cases success comes down to intimate knowledge of customer applications again, and tailoring products to their needs. The same success factors apply to the Protim Solignum treatment business, where, due to the complications of handling environmentally sensitive products, a thorough knowledge of customers' processes is vital.

Finally, the Adhesives division:

> The market for Adhesives is very fragmented. Products are becoming more commodity-oriented, with increasing competitor consolidation in the industry. A large part of our business is in pressure-sensitive adhesives, where tailoring products to customer needs is important. But here again, cost is a key driver, with raw material supplies starting to move downstream to supplying customers directly.

The need for a group strategy

Mike Dearden held the view that the key questions to be asked by the Group

Executive were how, and to what extent, the group or the divisional levels within the group could be of benefit to the business units; and to what extent the businesses gained by being part of the same portfolio.

> If the centre doesn't or can't add value, then we are just a cost and may destroy value. The businesses would be better off on their own, or with someone else. If we can add value, how: and how should we be organised to do it?

Burmah Castrol had made clear it was seeking to develop a chemicals business with global dimensions and investment potential for growth. However, Mike Dearden believed that, in order to be clear about the role of the group centre, it was necessary to begin by considering the bases of strategy at the business level; and then ask how the centre could or should help the businesses. This process began with workshops for representatives of most of the business units so that they could contribute to the debate in two ways:

- To consider and identify bases of SBU competitive strategy in terms of competitive position and the core competences of the SBUs.
- On these bases, to consider how, if at all, they thought structures above SBU level — for example, the Chemicals Group itself — could add value to the SBUs.

These workshops were completed by January 1996. Each was attended by David Hughes and Mark Rowley, who worked with Mike Dearden on strategy development.

In January 1996 the Chemical Group executive met to consider the outcome of the workshops and asked David and Mark to produce a report drawing together the findings from the workshops and summarising the key issues which arose. The report is summarised in Appendix 2.

The executive debate

The executive of the Chemicals Group met to consider the report from the workshop at a two-day meeting in March 1996. After dinner the night before the meeting, Mike Dearden outlined the issues:

> The Chemicals Group has been through a number of phases in its development. There was the creation of the portfolio in the 1980s; this was followed by the acquisition of Foseco plc; and our emphasis has been on improving performance in each of the businesses in the last few years. The question now is: what next? I think we have got two or three years more of improvement — efficiency growth, if you wish — but where do we go from there? It seems to me in answering that we have to take into consideration three very important issues. The first is that the investment community is not yet convinced of what Burmah Castrol really brings to running a chemicals business. We have to be much clearer about that. The

second is that we ourselves have to be clear what we add to the businesses. If we as a Chemicals Group bring no benefits to them, then presumably we are just a cost. They would be better off on their own or with someone else. The third issue is just what the synergy is between the businesses. It seems to me the workshops didn't show much 'hard' synergy. We have to ask if there is anything else and what this says about how we, as a group, can help the businesses.

Within all this I think it is clear that Burmah Castrol is looking for investment opportunities and they are as likely, perhaps more likely, to be in our area than in Lubricants. However, we cannot expect that sort of investment unless we are very clear as to where we are going. They also expect us to be developing, if not a truly global, then a clear international strategy.

Adding value to the businesses

The executive meeting discussed the views of the SBUs on how the centre had and could add value. They began by considering what the centre's role had been traditionally. Using the same checklist as the workshops had used, they concluded that in their view the main skills had been in managing people, internationalisation, strategic planning, intervention and central financial services, although there was some discussion of whether the way they were delivered was in line with SBU needs.

> I think the central personnel function has been good when it comes to recruitment, management succession, training and the provision of central services. Certainly, historically we have been active in acquisitions and disposals; and in the last few years businesses have seen us intervening quite a lot to get better efficiencies; but the emphasis has been on cost efficiency. I think our strategic planning is rather formalised and that the businesses see it as much more to do with us or Burmah Castrol than to do with them. I am also not sure that they would be very clear about what the corporate strategy is — but then that is what we are meeting about.

There was a good deal of debate about skills and needs in internationalisation. One view was:

> It surprises me that the report says we are not so good at internationalisation. I cannot think of many firms that would give as much encouragement to local management to set up local manufacturing plants or invest locally. In some companies the suggestion to invest in somewhere like Thailand might raise all sorts of difficulties. We tend to regard that sort of thing as relatively normal. I would have thought we are very encouraging in the internationalisation process.

Another:

> But I think we are less good when it comes to proactive internationalisation. Everyone ends up 'inventing the wheel'. One business does something and a year later someone else is doing the same sort of thing without any knowledge of what the other business has done. We make difficulties for ourselves rather than helping businesses on internationalisation. We don't build on our experience.

Many of the businesses had been established either as UK firms which had developed international divisions or export businesses, or as widely scattered and largely independent subsidiaries. Over the past few years, some of these had developed more coherent global strategies, but the extent to which this was happening was variable. To get a picture of this, they used a matrix of global co-ordination versus local independence and responsiveness (see Figures 2–5) to map the historic position and the future direction of the businesses in terms of international structures. The figures below show these for each of the main businesses.

It seems to me that many of our businesses are developing clearer global strategies; but many of them need to retain a great deal of local flexibility. How we deal with that is problematic. How we do that within the businesses and what role the centre plays in that needs to be thought about very carefully. From what we have been discussing so far, it seems we have some different views about that.

Figure 2   Foseco

Figure 3   Fosroc

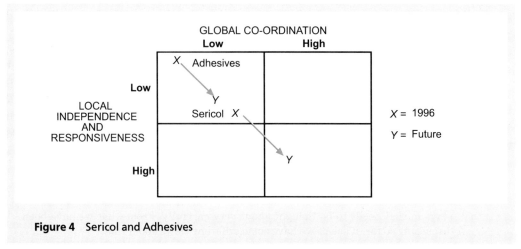

Figure 4   Sericol and Adhesives

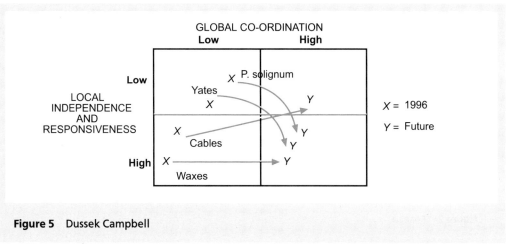

Figure 5   Dussek Campbell

The role of the centre

The meeting also discussed what the role of the group centre should be in the future. The first view was this:

> Whatever the criteria for the acquisitions of the businesses in the group, the fact of the matter is there are very few linkages between them. It is not enough to say that they are all chemicals businesses. They use chemicals as raw materials, but that is all. There are really no linkages technologically between many of the businesses. There are not many market linkages either. To the outsider, a steel mill and foundry may sound very similar, but they are very different indeed; and what relationship they have to screen printers is very difficult to see. I tried drawing out what linkages I could see and couldn't find many [see Figures 6 and 7]. There are rather more on technology than markets, but not so many you could build a group rationale around them.

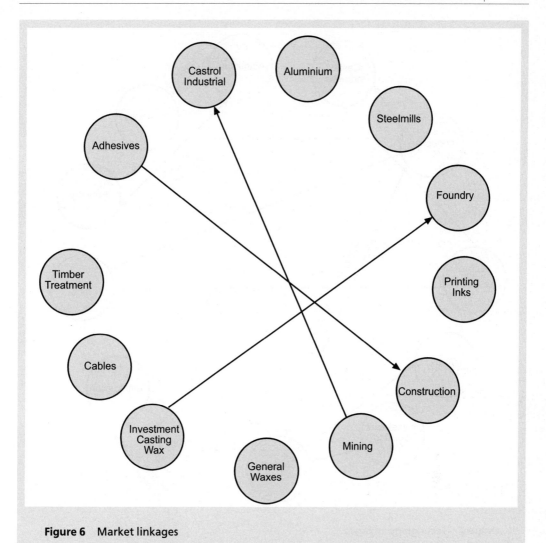

Figure 6   Market linkages

My recommendation is that we should regard the businesses as a set of discrete units, each with their own technology and their own markets, and each perfectly capable of making good returns for the group. But they should be left alone to get on with it. We should recognise that the group really cannot add value to these businesses because there are not substantial linkages between them. The centre should recognise that it is at real risk of simply adding costs without value, and should therefore seek to reduce cost to a minimum and simply exercise financial control. It should set clear targets about what returns are expected, provide investment if returns are being met, change the management if they are not or, at the extreme, dispose of the business. If we follow this route, we can manage the portfolio we have more efficiently and cost effectively than we are doing currently. We could probably also get rid of some of the intermediate divisional structures because we would not require the degree of co-ordination that we currently try to achieve.

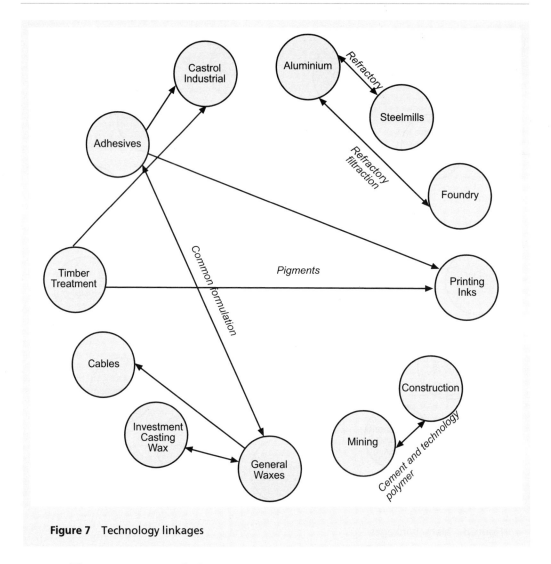

Figure 7   Technology linkages

There was a second view:

> Burmah Castrol has chosen to set up a chemicals business and has acquired or developed business units in chemicals over two decades. I think we should start by asking what Burmah Castrol wants of these businesses, not just what these businesses happen to be doing now. The fact is that a main aspiration of Burmah Castrol is to become a much more global organisation than currently; in particular, to grow in the developing economies of the East. We should therefore be aiming to create a chemicals business which is much more global than it is now. I do not necessarily mean we should be in all parts of the world, but at least multidomestic with a very real presence in the Far East. We already have some businesses that do this, but we do not have a co-ordinated strategy to achieve it.
>
> The role of the centre should be to develop a global strategy for chemicals. First,

we should identify which businesses are, or can be, more global. They are the businesses in which we should invest, and the centre should take a proactive line in developing them. If businesses cannot be developed in this way, then we should review whether they should be part of the portfolio.

Second, we cannot leave it to the individual businesses to develop global strategies in a haphazard way. The centre has to be much more proactive in the strategic development of these businesses. The centre should be identifying the market opportunities, the product requirements and the market entry strategies.

The centre also has a role to play in implementing this strategy. Suppose we see China as a major opportunity — and we do. We should have a co-ordinated, planned entry into China across the group. If we do not, we will have any number of businesses entering markets in all sorts of different ways.

If we truly intend to be a global firm, then the centre has a role in planning it and developing it. Of course, this might mean we need a slimmer portfolio than we have currently; but then not all of our businesses might meet the global criteria that we set.

A third view was as follows:

I agree that, unless we believe that the centre can add something to enhance the value of the business, then we should simply try to cut the costs at the centre and reduce the burden on the businesses. The question is: just what can and should we be doing? The interesting conclusion the workshop report comes to is the businesses themselves think they need help. They may not always think we do it that well; but they do think they need help.

One of our problems is the very title of Chemicals Group. We are not a chemicals business in the sense ICI is. We don't make profits out of selling chemicals. We make profits out of mixing and blending basic materials in ways which are useful to customers. We are particularly successful where those formulated products account for a low percentage of cost to customers, but are really important to them. Many of our products may not cost much; but if they go wrong or fail in their purpose, the risk is high. If you are filling a crack in a dam, the actual cost is low, but the risk is enormous if it goes wrong. If we get that right, then we can sell at premium prices.

There is another way we are different from basic chemicals. We make our money out of knowing our customers well enough to spot the sorts of opportunities that solve their problems and make us money. It's knowing our customers intimately that matters; not being good as chemists. It tends to point us to niche markets; sometimes quite small niche markets. It is not technologies as such, but application skills which give us real advantages. It isn't a question of market or technology linkages; it's about know-how, teamwork and applying that to the benefit of customers by knowing their businesses intimately.

We should also recognise that we are most successful at managing certain sorts of businesses. They are businesses which have relatively low capital intensity; they are not based on rocket science R&D; and they are where service requirements are high, so people matter.

What we should be doing is focusing on such businesses; businesses where marketing expertise can be leveraged and where we can add value to customers' processes. In particular, businesses where the cost of our products to the customer is low, but where there is high potential risk for the customers.

Virtually all of our businesses are like this or ought to be. I suppose Steelmills and Aluminium are more dependent on basic technology; and Cables relies heavily on type approvals and large global buyers. I am not sure we really capitalise on all this in the Aluminium and Construction and Waxes businesses, but I think we ought to be able to. Of course, Fosbel is different. The role of the centre is therefore to build a portfolio of such businesses and make sure they learn from one another.

Mike Dearden summed up the discussions:

I did not expect us to reach clear and absolute conclusions today. We started off the workshops some months ago with ideas of the questions we needed to ask. I think we have added a lot of information and discussion about those questions. What we need to do between now and at the next meeting is think about this, pull our thoughts together and start moving to some decisions. I think the questions we posed at the beginning of the workshops should form the agenda for the next meeting. What is the fit of businesses within the group; do they all fit equally well? Whatever the fit, is the current structure within the group sensible? And just how should we manage all this from the centre? I think we have thought a good deal about all this over the last day or so, but we need to move forward to some decisions.

Appendix 1   Chemicals Group divisions and SBUs in 1996

Metallurgical division — Foseco

Foseco Metallurgical is the leading supplier of metallurgical chemicals to the world's metals industries, serving the vehicle manufacturing, construction, engineering and aerospace sectors. A truly international company, with operations in some 34 countries, Foseco has a particularly strong position in the important markets of Germany, Japan, the USA and the UK.

Foundry

The Foundry business unit comprises sales to ferrous and non-ferrous foundries. Ferrous foundry products include a complete range of feeding systems, fluxes, filters, molten metal transfer materials, binders and coatings that offer significant benefits in the production of high-quality castings.

The non-ferrous business supplies filters, direct pouring units, degassing systems and granulated fluxes. Ceramic foam filters and direct pour filtration systems raise yield and productivity, and remove inclusions through purpose-built engineering equipment, such as the degassing systems.

Foseco understands the requirements of Foundries and is committed to proactive research and development to further increase customers' productivity and competitiveness.

Steelmills

Foseco products allow steelmills to produce steels capable of meeting the most demanding specifications, quickly and cost effectively. Foseco supplies tundish lining systems, where a tundish can be lined in around one hour using either Tuncast (a spray system) or Garnex (insulating refractory boards).

As well as tundish lining systems, Foseco also offers an extensive range of products for the tundish area, including black refractories (ladle shrouds, stopper rods, submerged entry shrouds and nozzles), pre-cast and castable refractories, and continuous casting mould fluxes. Foseco offers extensive technical advice and support, including on-site assistance.

Foseco's strategy is to focus resources globally on the tundish and near tundish area in the key market segments of slab and bloom continuous casting.

Aluminium

Foseco products and services are used in the production of light metals and their alloys, principally aluminium.

Products offered include degassing equipment, special ceramic and refractory materials, filters and filtration systems, grain refiners, modifying and alloy additions, and refractory coatings.

The products represent a comprehensive range for the cast house and are supported by a proactive technical service.

Foseco is in the process of separating the Aluminium and Steelmills businesses from the Foundry business to form distinct global business units.

Fosbel

Ceramic Welding

Fosbel provides customers in the glass, coke and iron/steel industries with a specialised furnace lining repair service, based on advanced ceramic welding technology.

Construction and Mining division — Fosroc

Mining

Fosroc's products to the mining industry include resin and cement-based anchors, which ensure reliable roof anchoring and side wall strata control; and high-yield grouts for roof supports and tunnel stoppings.

Fosroc's chemical-based products and services for strata control are recognised as being leaders in the international mining field. Customers are served across five continents, ranging from global conglomerates and state-owned organisations to small public and private companies.

The Fosroc name is established in each of the world's mining markets, most notably in the UK, the USA, Australia, India, South Africa and eastern Europe.

Construction

Fosroc is a leading world supplier of construction chemicals, focusing on the civil engineering and repair and protection sectors. It has close working relationships with international contractors, specifiers and operators, with a strong emphasis on after-sales service.

For the civil engineering sector, Fosroc provides concrete admixtures, surface treatments, precision grouts, chemical anchors, sealants and ancillary products. Products are used extensively in brick and concrete structures, including reservoirs, dams and tunnels, as well as commercial and residential developments.

In concrete repair and protection, Fosroc has built an international reputation for protecting new concrete and extending the life of old structures. It provides a wide variety of repair mortars, fluid micro-concretes and modified liquid polymers, together with protective coatings and sealants.

Fosroc recently acquired Norwegian Concrete Technologies (NCT), an Oslo-based company offering electrochemical methods for concrete repair.

Printing Inks division — Sericol

Speciality

Sericol is the world leader in screen printing inks, a specialised niche in the printing industry. To retain its market focus on screen printing applications, Sericol does not supply printing inks for other printing processes, such as gravure and lithography.

Sericol's major market sectors are graphic printing (traditional posters and point-of-sale displays), textiles (leisure and sports wear) and packaging (labelling, bottle printing and box cartons).

The major markets are the graphic and textile markets, where customers are generally independent screen printers. Speciality markets have been earmarked for strategic growth, principally by acquisition. Speciality customers are those where screen printing is part of the process (e.g. compact discs and rub removable applications).

Sericol has operations in the UK, the USA, France, Germany, Hong Kong, Spain, Switzerland and India. Sericol products are supplied worldwide to over 80 countries through a network of distributors and licensees.

Graphics/Textiles

Sericol is the world leader in screen printing inks and chemicals. Sericol's major markets are in graphics and textile printing, with its market position in graphics being particularly strong.

Graphic printing includes traditional posters and point-of-sale displays. Textile printing covers leisure and sports wear, but excludes the commodity reel-to-reel textile market for printing curtain materials, furnishings, etc.

Sericol supplies water-based, solvent-based and ultraviolet (UV) curable inks. Both water-based and UV curable inks have substantial environmental benefits.

Strong service support is a particular feature of Sericol's marketing approach. Its customer service centre networks provide rapid delivery, backed by technical support and colour-matching service. Sericol also has an International Training Facility for customers, distributors, licensees and staff.

Coatings division

Timber Treatment

Protim Solignum (PS) is a leading UK supplier of wood treatment chemicals, with companies in the UK, Eire, New Zealand and Australia. A range of decorative stains is also supplied under the Solignum brand.

PS supplies mainly solvent-based wood preservatives, where it has a dominant market share. However, the worldwide wood preservative market is predominantly water based, in which PS has a minor market position. Environmental pressures are being placed on the use of solvent-based preservatives. Decorative stains are supplied principally to timber and builders merchants, so avoiding direct competition in the retail 'shed' with Cuprinol, Saddolins and Sikkens.

Investment Casting Wax

Dussek Campbell-Yates supplies investment casting wax from operations in the USA and the UK. Recently, the two businesses were restructured into a single entity managed from the USA, with a European manager based in the UK.

Investment casting wax is supplied to the aerospace/defence and commercial markets for the precision engineering of high-performance alloys.

General Waxes

Dussek Campbell supplies waxes for a wide range of applications, including packaging, construction, rubber tyres, candles, pharmaceuticals and cosmetics, histology, paint and ink additives, PVC lubricants, additives for plastic processing, anti-corrosives, cheese coatings and adhesives.

The largest market for wax application is in paper and board lamination. In construction, wax emulsions are used in board sizing. Candles is a substantial market, with the more specialised segments being craft and pressed candles. In packaging, Dussek Campbell has developed water-based barrier coatings, with the environmental bonus of being recyclable.

Following the acquisition of the UK-based Kerax company in 1993, Dussek Campbell's European wax business and Kerax were integrated into a single European wax business. In North America, waxes are supplied by National Wax.

Cables

Dussek Campbell is the world leader in the supply of cable compounds and application machinery. It supplies two market segments in the cable industry — power cables and telephone cable compounds, with the latter further divided into copper and fibre optic cable compounds.

In the power cable market, Dussek Campbell has a long-established presence in the supply of resin-based insulants. It markets a range of void-filling gels for copper and fibre optic telephone cables, backed by a comprehensive engineering service, which designs and installs the equipment with which the products are applied.

In 1995 cable compounds were organised into a global business unit within the Coatings division.

Adhesives division

The Adhesives division comprises two companies, Columbia Cement in the USA and Industrial Adhesives Limited (IAL) in the UK.

Columbia Cement is the leading supplier of contact adhesives for decorative laminates in the USA. The product range is primarily solvent based, although water-based adhesives have been developed to meet the technical demands of the high-pressure decorative laminate market and the environmental regulations in the USA.

IAL is the leading UK supplier of pressure-sensitive adhesives. The company offers a wide range of adhesive technologies, including solvent based, water based, hot melt and reactives. Markets served include converting, which covers packaging and pressure sensitives, and industrial. The industrial markets include construction, insulation, fire protection and laminating.

IAL exports to Europe, the Middle East and Asia, principally with pressure-sensitive adhesives and insulation products.

Appendix 2   Summary of the report on strategy workshops to the Chemicals Group executive

As a means of considering:

1.   The fit of the different SBUs within the Chemicals Group.
2.   The role of the parent (or centre) in managing the businesses.

Each SBU in the group undertook the following exercise:

- A consideration of its competitive strategy and the competences underpinning that strategy.
- The parenting skills required of the centre by the business units.

Competitive strategies

All the SBUs saw the need to develop competitive strategies on the basis of differentiation or focused differentiation. Whilst there was an acknowledgement of the need to reduce costs or keep costs low, it was recognised that this was not a basis for achieving competitive advantage.

Competences

Exhibit A summarises the competences identified by each SBU (together with competences they identified as likely to be needed to pursue the strategies they wished to follow). There is a considerable degree of commonalty of competences between the businesses which can, in generic terms, be summarised as:

> Close customer relationships, intimate understanding of customers' processes, ability to 'package' the businesses' product/service in innovative ways on the basis of customer need, focus on particular types of businesses, ability to work internationally and teamwork between business functions based on the delivery of customer need.

There were, however, some qualifications to this: in particular, the Adhesives division recognised that a difficulty they face is that they buy in processed materials, whereas their competitors are raw material processors with adhesives as a by-product.

Parenting skills

Each business unit considered parenting skills against a common list of such skills (see Exhibit B). Exhibit C summarises the parenting opportunities/skills identified by the SBUs. In aggregate, these are summarised in Exhibit D, which also shows how required parenting skills differ from that which the SBUs currently perceive being provided by the group.

The most important parenting skills, as seen by the businesses, are to do with the development of people required for strategy development, the facilitation of international development, group intervention to sort out problems, and the questioning and challenging of SBU strategy through 'coaching' and shared learning.

Questions raised

There are questions which arise from the workshops which the executive should consider.

- Managing international businesses is seen as a key parenting characteristic. However, SBUs vary in the degree to which they are, or have the potential to be, internationalised. Should the SBU potential and quality, over the next ten years, for international growth — and the likely ease of implementation — be determined and taken as a measure of fit within the Chemicals Group?
- Traditionally, SBUs have been grouped principally by technology linkage. Recently, the divisions have created distinct SBUs to improve market focus. However, few major market linkages seem to exist between SBUs.
- What are the linkages — if any — between SBUs?
- Should SBUs be separately managed by the group, without the divisional layer, and with technology linkages facilitated by some other means?
- Should SBUs be grouped by market linkage, rather than technology linkage, whenever appropriate, e.g. Investment Casting Wax and Foundry?
- Should SBUs with similar multinational styles, particularly global businesses, be grouped together due to common parenting skills being required to manage those businesses?
- SBUs consider the parent (or centre) to be anything above SBU level. There is duplication at the divisional, Chemicals Group and overall Burmah Castrol centres in providing parenting skills, e.g. financial and strategic planning. Where should the central (or parental) services be located — at divisional, group or SBU level?
- Certain key parenting skills are not provided sufficiently well to the SBUs, particularly skills to internationalise SBUs in emerging markets. How can key parenting skills, particularly internationalisation skills, be better provided to the SBUs?

Exhibit A   SBU competences — core/missing

SBU	Perceived competences	Perceived missing competences
Foundry	• Customer relationships — understanding customers' processes and costs	• Professional marketing • Manufacturing/engineering — lowest-cost producer experience • Purchasing — international leverage/partnership • Internal communications/teamwork • Product costing systems
Construction	• Customer responsiveness — but not good in UK, Australia	• Operational effectiveness • Supply chain management • Creative/innovative approach
Printing Inks	*Graphics/Textiles* • Reputation/relationships — customers/suppliers • Application skills • Supply chain management *Speciality* • Package of services • International skills • R&D expertise/innovation • Market focus	• Digital printing expertise • Environmental solutions • Brand/name • Industry alliances — with machinery manufacturers • Independent assessments — of product performance
Steelmills	• Customer relationships — knowledge of customer needs/processes • Full system application engineering • Team culture — local/global • Strategic global marketing	• Strategic marketing and teamwork introduced by Burmah Castrol to overcome missing competences
General Waxes	• Purchasing relationships • Customer relationships • Blending, formulating, engineering skills • Innovative development	• Attitude to quality

SBU	Perceived competences	Perceived missing competences
Adhesives	• Supplier relationship • Customer relationship — marketing assistance partnership • Market focus • Supply chain management	• Geographic spread — increasing internationalisation of customer base • Being basic in raw materials • Synergy between IAL and Columbia Cement • Lack of critical mass
Aluminium	• Customer knowledge/ relationships Ceramic/metallurgy/ engineering know-how • International organisation plus local presence • Guru culture	• Management/team culture • Marketing skills • Customer-driven R&D
Mining	• Technical leadership • Material-linked technology — backfill, anchoring, coatings • Complete system engineering — with a focus on strata control • Personal customer relationships	• Supply chain management • Geographic covering in emerging markets — India, China, Indonesia, Vietnam, Russia
Timber Treatment	• Collective industry experience • Reputation • Quality of advice/support (consultancy) • Engineering/environmental service	
Cables	• Complete product/service package — including bespoke service • International business • Image/reputation • Attitude — 'can do, will do'	• Product innovation
Investment Casting Waxes	• Global international network — through BC/Foseco Foundry • Executive experience — dependence on a few individuals • Innovative capability	• International market development resources • Lack of critical mass • Lack of central product development

Exhibit B Parenting opportunities/skills

INTERVENTION
- Acquisition and disposal
- Turnaround
- Change agency

COACHING
- Questioning and challenging
- Transferring knowledge

FINANCIAL
- Banking
- 'Insurance'
- Alternative revenue stream
- Treasury

SPECIALIST EXPERTISE FOR SBUs
- Research and development
- Legal

EXTERNAL RELATIONS
- With governments
- With financial institutions

LINKAGES (within portfolio)
- Vertically   } formal or
- Horizontally } through networks

BROKERING (outside portfolio)
- Encouraging alliances
- Facilitating networks

SHARING
- Capabilities and competences
- Resources (plant, office, etc.)

LEVERAGING
- Buying power
- Marketing power

PEOPLE
- Management succession
- Skill injection
- Management development

STRATEGIC PLANNING
- Support to SBU
- Making 'corp' strategy clear

INTERNATIONALISATION
- Geographic expansion
- Cultural understanding
- International structuring

Exhibit C   Comments on parenting opportunities/skills by SBUs

These are comments made by SBUs about parenting opportunities and skills required by each SBU, but which could be better provided by parent.

Intervention

Timber Treatment. Assistance required in acquisition for internationalisation.

Adhesives. The adhesive business in its key sectors does not have critical mass or sufficient multinational presence to meet future key objectives. Acquisitions are an important area for intervention.

Construction. Need assistance with acquisitions to support strategic objectives. Group needs greater turnaround skills.

Coaching

Foundry. General transfer of knowledge, both technical and marketing.

Aluminium. Marketing practice, brand management, best practice transfer. More best practice/benchmarking identification and transfer is needed.

Construction. Transfer of knowledge is possibly where group can add greatest value.

General Waxes. Transferring knowledge is not effective, but centre dictatorial in coaching approach.

Adhesives. The SBU requires some intellectual 'beefing up' — no change since takeover. The main players are industry specialists rather than general managers with associated problems of succession and envisaging a move from a small to large business culture.

Specialist expertise

Timber Treatment. Legal requirements are often urgent, but due to SBU size, we do not always get acceptable response from the corporate legal department.

Aluminium. Legal services should be bought in as needed; present set-up cannot provide an effective service across the businesses. An IT strategy is also needed.

Linkages

Cables. Transferring best practice, i.e. supply/purchasing information.

General Waxes. There is a lack of focus on integrating the international units. To ensure complete flow of information, this has to be addressed within the centre and the units in a coordinated way. The centre is not structured to transfer experience.

Brokering (outside portfolio)

Timber Treatment. No specific mechanisms exist (for encouraging alliances/facilitating networks) other than the Chemicals Industry Association.

Adhesives. As the SBU has no (significant) multinational position, assistance in alliances, networks, joint venturing is crucial.

Sharing

Aluminium. Financial management/administrating sharing. Resource sharing to develop economies. More sharing of basic business services and functions.

Leveraging
Foundry. Marketing power in the automotive industry with Castrol Industrial.
Adhesives. The centre makes very little use of its corporate clout in areas of purchasing, best business practice, marketing skills.

People
Aluminium. Setting standards, training, appraisal, rewards, organisation development.
Construction. A key potential area to add value, with added benefit of spreading BC culture.
General Waxes. Essential to provide people with career path and training of people. Even short-term 'Expert' transfer of value.
Mining. Culture is the greatest asset. Invested in relatively few people, therefore needs protection.
Steelmills. Clearly, divisional interchange is good for all staff. A better understanding of each other's business is key. This will create opportunities for everybody. Cross-divisional management succession is crucial to the strength of Chemicals in the future.

Strategic planning
Construction. Need a Burmah Castrol process for strategic planning. A joint exercise would be valuable. Burmah Castrol need to share strategy more openly.
Aluminium. Provide more leadership. Train/coach to improve quality of strategy.
Foundry. Clear strategic objectives/definition.
Steelmills. A clear SBU strategy needs to be defined and discussed with the parent. This is key now and differs from financial targets. Unaware of Chemicals strategy and hence how SBU fits into the overall plan.
General Waxes. Facilitating corporate strategy to allow SBUs to 'dovetail' into it.
Adhesives. There is a lack of clear corporate strategy.

Internationalisation
Timber Treatment. Support level is limited.
Printing Inks. Assisting geographic expansion and future international structuring.
Aluminium. Pooling group resources to develop economies and reduce cost/risk, particularly in emerging markets such as China, eastern Europe, etc.
Cables. New start-ups may require looking after by local group company. Important to use overseas offices when and where required.
General Waxes. Co-ordination around the world is vital to take advantage of the wealth of knowledge.
Adhesives. Chemicals Group needs to take a view on decentralisation versus corporate. Setting up of corporate facilities (as opposed to SBU facilities) in strategic markets would be a start.
Mining. Assistance required in Russia, China and South America.
Steelmills. We are a small voice that may gain strength from cross-divisional support, i.e. Chemicals China. The use of corporate offices may allow us to grow into areas that each SBU cannot afford.

Exhibit D SBU provision rating of parenting skills: summary table

Ranking of rating importance by SBUs	Parenting skill		Rating of current parenting skills of parent*
1	People		−1
2	Internationalisation		−3
3	Strategic planning	Seen as particularly important	−1
4	Intervention		+1
5	Financial		+2
6	Coaching		A
7	Sharing		+1
8	Brokering		A
9	Specialist expertise		+1
10	Leveraging		+1
11	Linkages		+1
12	External relations		+3

*This rating indicates SBU perceptions of how valuable the centre has been to SBUs in terms of specific parenting skills. The ratings indicate:

+3	Much more than needed
+2 +1	More than needed
A	Appropriate
−1 −2	Less than needed
−3	Much less than needed

Index of companies and organisations

General Index